Medical Informatics
An Executive Primer

Third Edition

Edited by

Ken Ong, MD, MPH, FACP, FIDSA, CPHIMS, FHIMSS

HIMSS

HIMSS Mission

To globally lead endeavors optimizing health engagements and care outcomes through information technology.

Printed in the U.S.A. 5 4 3 2 1

Requests for permission to reproduce any part of this work should be sent to:

Permissions Editor
HIMSS
33. W. Monroe St., Ste. 1700
Chicago, IL 60603
nancy.vitucci@himssmedia.com

ISBN: 978-1-938904-76-9

For more information about HIMSS, please visit www.himss.org.

About the Editor

Ken Ong, MD, MPH, FACP, FIDSA, CPHIMS, FHIMSS, Clinical Informatics Board Certified, is the Chief Medical Informatics Officer of New York Hospital Queens, an urban teaching hospital serving the most diverse county in the nation and an affiliate of the New York-Presbyterian Health System. Dr. Ong serves as chief of the hospital's Clinical Informatics Department and chair of the Clinical Decision Support Committee. His past projects include developing and implementing the acute care electronic health record (EHR) with computerized provider order entry (CPOE); clinical decision support for the acute care and ambulatory EHR; a hospital pharmacy system; web-based results review; medication reconciliation; a patient portal; and mobile physician charge capture. Dr. Ong is a former Deputy Commissioner in the New York City Department of Health and Mental Hygiene.

Active in a number of professional groups, Dr. Ong is a member of the board of directors of the Healthcare Information and Management Systems Society (HIMSS), Healthcare Association of New York State's Health Information Strategy Group, Greater New York Hospital Association Health IT Steering Committee, and also has served as president of the New York State chapter of HIMSS and as president and current board member of Medical Informatics New York.

Dr. Ong served as editor of the first and second editions of *Medical Informatics: An Executive Primer*, which received the 2007 HIMSS Book of the Year Award. *ExecSense* selected Dr. Ong's Consumer-Patient Engagement presentation as one of the Top Talks of 2013. *Modern Healthcare* chose Dr. Ong as one of the top 25 clinical informaticists in 2012. He is also a previous recipient of the AMDIS Award in Applied Medical Informatics and the Centers for Disease Control Charles C. Shepard Science Award.

Residency-trained and board certified in family practice, internal medicine, and infectious diseases, Dr. Ong is a Fellow of the American College of Physicians, the Infectious Disease Society of America, HIMSS, and the New York Academy of Medicine. He received his MPH at Columbia University in New York, his MD at Wayne State University in Detroit, Michigan, and his BS at the University of Michigan in Ann Arbor.

About the Authors

Erika Abramson, MD, MS, is an assistant professor in the Departments of Healthcare Research and Policy and Pediatrics at Weill Cornell Medical College. She is also the associate program director for Pediatric Graduate Medical Education and the co-director of the Fellowship Program in Health Care Quality and Medical Informatics. Dr. Abramson completed her undergraduate work at Yale University in 1999. She received her medical degree at New York University School of Medicine in 2003, achieving membership into the Alpha Omega Alpha Medical Honors Society. She completed her residency in Pediatrics at New York-Presbyterian Hospital in 2006, serving as chief resident from 2006 to 2007. She received her Masters of Science in Clinical Investigation from Weill Cornell Medical College in 2009. Dr. Abramson's research portfolio includes a mixture of quantitative and qualitative evaluations. It is novel for its application of rigorous methodologies to evaluate the implementation and effectiveness of health IT both in academic and community-based settings. Her primary focus has been studying the effects of health IT on safety. She has more than 40 peer-reviewed publications.

Dana Alexander, RN, MSN, MBA, FHIMSS, FAAN, brings more than 30 years of healthcare system, executive management and clinical experience. Her past and current experiences include roles in academic, integrated delivery network (IDN), and community health systems settings, with responsibilities that span the care continuum to include long-term care, post-acute care, home health, hospice and other specialty services. For the past 10+ years, she has been employed in the healthcare IT arena and currently serves as vice president of Integrated Care and chief nursing officer at Caradigm, a health analytics and population health management company. She actively participates and represents leadership roles in a number of professional and industry organizations, including HIMSS Board of Directors, where she serves as chair-elect; NQF Population Health Committee; Measure Application Partnership Hospital Workgroup; Joint Commission International Standards Committee; CMS Technical Expert Panel for Post-Acute Care; AONE; ANA; American Academy of Nursing Fellow; and other national initiatives. She has contributed to healthcare, nursing, and the nursing informatics field through support of research and numerous presentations and publications.

Janey Barnes, PhD, is a principal and human factors specialist at User-View, Inc. Dr. Barnes leads client programs that encompass every aspect of human factors and usability from design research, testing and evaluation, and user interface design to hardware and workspace design. Throughout her career, Dr. Barnes has worked with clients in the healthcare, medical device, automotive, consumer product, and financial industries and has educated others about the field of human factors. She has developed and taught human factors and psychology courses at a number of universities and for professional organizations. Dr. Barnes is affiliated with several professional organizations and participates in these organizations by making presentations and teaching workshops. Dr. Barnes serves in the Office of the National Coordinator's Implementation, Usability and Safety Workgroup. She is active in the HIMSS User Experience Community and served as chair of the HIMSS Usability Task for 2012–2013. In addition, Dr. Barnes serves on the TriangleUXPA Advisory Board. She holds a PhD in cognitive psychology from the University of Massachusetts, Amherst.

Adam D. Cheriff, MD, is chief medical information officer and associate professor of Clinical Medicine and Health Policy and Research for the Weill Cornell Physician Organization. Dr. Cheriff is a graduate of Harvard College. After receiving his medical degree from Johns Hopkins School of Medicine, he completed a residency in Internal Medicine at New York Presbyterian (Weill Cornell Campus). Dr. Cheriff joined the faculty within the Department of Medicine at Weill Cornell in 2001. In 2009, he was appointed chief medical information officer for the Weill Cornell Physician Organization. He has maintained an active internal medicine practice while overseeing clinical IT operations for the Weill Cornell Physician Organization. In addition to managing the implementation and support of Weill Cornell's shared ambulatory EHR and practice management system, Dr. Cheriff is responsible for Weill Cornell's data warehouse, data dictionary, online physician directory, and patient portal.

Curtis L. Cole, MD, FACP, is chief information officer for Weill Cornell Medical College where he is also an associate professor of Clinical Medicine and Healthcare Policy and Research. He practices internal medicine at Weill Cornell Internal Medicine Associates at New York Presbyterian Hospital. After medical school at Cornell and residency at New York Hospital, he was a clinical investigator in medical informatics. He has led the implementation of several EMR systems. Dr. Cole is also responsible for the other core information systems that support research, education, and administration at the college. He is particularly interested in the secondary use of clinical data, integration of research data with clinical data, terminology systems, and measuring the value of information systems.

Sarah Collins, RN, PhD, is a nurse informatician in Clinical Informatics Partners eCare at Partners Healthcare Systems and an instructor in medicine at Harvard Medical School and Brigham and Women's Hospital Division of Internal Medicine and Primary Care. She holds a PhD in nursing informatics from Columbia University School of Nursing and was a National Library of Medicine Post-doctoral Research Fellow at Columbia University's Department of Biomedical Informatics. She received her Bachelor of Science in Nursing from the University of Pennsylvania, where she minored in Health Care Management. Dr. Collins is an experienced critical care nurse. Her research as well as her applied clinical informatics work is focused on modeling, developing, and evaluating standards-based, patient-centered collaborative informatics tools to further patient safety, knowledge development, clinical decision support, and coordinated patient-centered care. In 2012, Dr. Collins was selected as one of two national Emerging Leaders by the Alliance for Nursing Informatics and investigated models of nursing informatics governance within healthcare organizations as part of that program. Her research has been recognized and awarded by the American Medical Informatics Association (AMIA) and the 11th International Congress on Nursing Informatics.

Anuj Desai is currently vice president of Market Development for the New York eHealth Collaborative (NYeC). In this role, he is responsible for developing and managing strategic relationships and alliances with the various vendors and partners that interact with NYeC. He also leads the New York Digital Health Accelerator, the multistate/multi-vendor EHR/HIE Interoperability Workgroup, work related to development of an application programming interface (API), and the incubation of new capabilities within the statewide network. Desai has more than 14 years of experience in business development and healthcare strategy. He received his MBA from University of Maryland's Robert H. Smith School of Business and his undergraduate degree in biotechnology from Rutgers University. He was a member of *Crain's* New York Business 2013 Class of "40 Under 40" and *Modern Healthcare's* Up and Comers 2013.

J. Travis Gossey, MD, serves many roles at Weill Cornell Medical College. In the summer of 2010, Dr. Gossey became the medical director of Information Services for the Physician Organization. A large part of his duties revolve around the electronic medical record (EMR) system and the research systems that interact with the EMR. Dr. Gossey also serves as an internist specializing in primary care. In addition, he serves as an assistant professor of Medicine. Dr. Gossey completed his undergraduate work at Washington University in 1997. He received his medical degree from Northwestern University Medical School in 2002. He received his MS degree from the University of Texas at Houston Graduate School of Biomedical Sciences in 2010, followed one year later by his MPH degree from the University of Texas School of Public Health.

Ray Hess, FHIMSS, RRT, MSA is the vice president for information management at Penn Medicine Chester County Hospital in West Chester, Pennsylvania. His information management and process improvement experience includes having overseen business intelligence for 18 years, health information management for 6 years, and workflow automation/clinical decision support efforts for 10 years. He is a Six Sigma Green Belt. His clinical experience includes 10 years in patient care and rehabilitation, and he has administrative experience from managing cardiology services for 4 years. He holds a master's degree in healthcare administration from West Chester University. Hess has addressed audiences throughout the United States and internationally and has published multiple articles and book chapters. Hess is a Fellow of HIMSS and is involved in multiple HIMSS' communities and projects.

David Jacobowitz is the managing director of The Health Innovators, a strategy and business development firm dedicated to accelerating the success of start-up and growth companies in the dynamic digital health market. Jacobowitz has over 30 years of experience in health IT/digital health/HIE strategic planning, business development, marketing, sales, product management, and implementation. He has held leadership positions on diverse sides of healthcare, including hospital, payer, vendor, medical provider, pharmaceutical, and consulting organizations. Jacobowitz has specialized in business development and partnering, mobile and e-health, strategic marketing, and product development and has deep experience identifying, evaluating, marketing and deploying digital solutions that offer compelling value propositions. Companies where he has held leadership positions include the New York eHealth Collaborative, Bergen Regional Medical Center, Mt. Sinai Medical Center, Memorial Sloan Kettering Cancer Center,

MEDecision, Siemens Medical Solutions, Novartis, Philips, Empire Blue Cross, and Booz and Company.

Rainu Kaushal, MD, MPH, is the Frances and John L. Loeb Professor of Medical Informatics, chairman of the Department of Healthcare Policy and Research at Weill Cornell Medical College, and Chief of Healthcare Policy and Research at New York-Presbyterian Hospital/Weill Cornell Medical Center. Dr. Kaushal is an international leader in the clinical effectiveness, cost effectiveness, and comparative effectiveness of novel healthcare delivery interventions and models, particularly those based on health IT. A Fellow of the American College of Medical Informatics, she currently leads a large Patient-Centered Outcomes Research Institute-funded Clinical Data Research Network, which connects the major academic institutions in New York City for the purposes of patient-centered research and improvements in healthcare delivery systems.

Paul Kleeberg, MD, FAAFP, FHIMSS, is Chief Medical Informatics Officer for Stratis Health, a non-profit quality improvement organization based in Bloomington Minnesota, and Clinical Director for the Regional Extension Assistance Center for HIT (REACH) funded by the American Recovery and Reinvestment Act to assist small hospitals and primary care providers in Minnesota and North Dakota to adopt and become meaningful users of EHRs. Dr. Kleeberg has over 20 years of experience working in health IT, implementing EHR systems and improving processes for electronic workflow to enhance care delivery. Before coming to Stratis Health, he was Medical Director for CDS for HealthEast Care System in St. Paul, Minnesota, and Allina Health in Minneapolis, the organization that won the Davies Award of Excellence for its EHR implementation in 2007. Dr. Kleeberg received his medical degree from Stanford University and completed his residency in Family Medicine at the University of Minnesota. He is board certified in Family Medicine and is a fellow in the American Academy of Family Physicians (AAFP). He is also a Fellow of HIMSS, where he currently serves as chair of the Board of Directors and also serves on the Board of Trustees for the Certification Commission for Health Information Technology (CCHIT).

Gilad J. Kuperman, MD, PhD, is Director for Interoperability Informatics at New York-Presbyterian Hospital. In this capacity, he assists the hospital in realizing the benefits of interoperability internally, with its business partners, and through participating in regional data interchange efforts. From 2005 to 2011, Dr. Kuperman was Board Chair and Executive Director of NYCLIX, Inc., a nonprofit corporation creating HIE services in New York City. Dr. Kuperman has an extensive research record measuring the impact of health IT information technology on the quality and efficiency of medical care. He is Adjunct Professor of Biomedical Informatics at Columbia University Medical School. He has been an author on ninety articles related to medical informatics and lead author on sixteen of those. He was Board Chair of the American Medical Informatics Association (AMIA) in 2012–2013.

Naomi Levinthal is a senior consultant with The Advisory Board Company's Health Care IT Advisor and Meaningful Use Navigator. She specializes in medical informatics, electronic health record (EHR) systems, the CMS EHR Incentive Program, and the Office of the National Coordinator for Health Information Technology (ONC) certification programs. Levinthal's research interests include topics related to meaningful use, population health management, and telehealth. Naomi joined the Advisory Board in 2012. Previously, Naomi served as certification manager for the Certification Commission for Health Information Technology (CCHIT), guiding EHR vendors and hospitals with self-developed systems through testing and certification processes. Prior to her tenure at CCHIT, she was the medical informatics specialist at the American Academy of Dermatology. Naomi received an MS from Northwestern University in Medical Informatics, an MA from Loyola University Chicago, and is a Certified Professional in Healthcare Information & Management Systems (CPHIMS).

Virginia Lorenzi has more than 24 years of experience in the field with vendor, consultant, and provider experience. As IT manager and subject matter expert at New York-Presbyterian Hospital, Lorenzi specializes in interoperability, health IT standards, and health IT–related regulations including meaningful use. She is also on faculty at Columbia University where she teaches segments of several courses and directs a graduate certification program in health IT. Lorenzi has participated in health IT standards efforts, including co-chairing the Healthcare Information Technology Standards (HITSP) ECO Webinar workgroup, and in long-term service to HL7, where she has been honored as an HL7 Volunteer of the Year and as an HL7 Fellow. She has been called to Washington to testify on topics related to health IT standards and meaningful use. She is CPHIMS-certified and active in HIMSS. She authored numerous posters for the AMIA annual conference and serves on the Mid-Atlantic AMIA Education Board.

Sameer Malhotra, MD, MA, is the associate medical director of Informatics at the Physician Organization of Weill Cornell Medical College and is working on several projects in the realm of medical informatics pertaining to improvement of healthcare delivery and patient safety. Dr. Malhotra is the director for development and analytics of clinical decision support systems (CDSS) of the institution's outpatient EHR. Dr. Malhotra has an academic faculty appointment as clinical instructor in the Department of Public Health in the Division of Quality and Medical Informatics. His research focuses on CDS, medication safety, adoption of interoperable health IT, and impact of HIE on patient care. His research and publications have focused on healthcare technology and quality of care. Dr. Malhotra cares for adult patients in the inpatient setting as an Internal Medicine Hospitalist. In his current role at the POIS of Weill Cornell Medical College, Dr. Malhotra is closely involved with the ongoing deployment and optimization of the institution's ambulatory medical record. Dr. Malhotra attended medical school at the All India Institute of Medical Sciences (AIIMS) in New Delhi, India and received his MB, BS degree in 2003. He then pursued a Masters in Biomedical Informatics at Columbia University, New York.

Geeta Nayyar, MD, MBA, is a nationally recognized leader in health IT and a board-certified practicing physician. She brings an integrated perspective to physicians, hospitals, pharmaceutical companies, and accountable care organizations that are facing the challenges of the nation's changing healthcare system. Dr. Nayyar was most recently Chief Medical Information Officer at AT&T, where she provided a clinical perspective to the AT&T ForHealth℠ strategy and portfolio. She also served as CMIO at Patient Point, principal medical officer at Vangent, Inc., and as the Chief Medical Officer of

APCO Worldwide, a public affairs and strategic communications firm. A specialist in rheumatology, she maintains an active practice while serving on the medical school faculty at Florida International University and George Washington University. Dr. Nayyar received her MD and BS degrees from the University of Miami. She earned her MBA from George Washington University. Dr. Nayyar holds memberships and committee appointments in several professional organizations including the American College of Rheumatology and the Association of Medical Directors of Information Systems. She is a member of the HIMSS Advisory Board.

Jan Oldenburg is a senior manager in Ernst & Young's Advisory Health Care Practice focusing on advising clients how to create engaging consumer health solutions. She is the former vice president of physician and patient engagement at Aetna Accountable Care Solutions, working with physician groups in accountable care organizations to create and implement population health and patient engagement programs. Prior to Aetna, Oldenburg was a senior leader in Kaiser Permanente's Digital Services Group. She is a past president of the Northern California HIMSS Board, a HIMSS fellow and vice chair of the National HIMSS Connected Patient Committee. She frequently speaks and writes about patient and physician engagement. Oldenburg served as the primary editor of *Engage! Transforming Healthcare through Digital Patient Engagement*, published by HIMSS in March 2013. She is the author of the Patient Engagement chapter in this 3rd edition of *Medical Informatics*, as well as numerous articles.

Anantachai (Tony) Panjamapirom, PhD, serves as a senior consultant and a subject matter expert in the Meaningful Use Navigator practice at the Advisory Board Company. He provides policy analysis, strategic and operational guidance, and meaningful use best practices. His other research focuses on the benefits of EMRs, IT performance management, and IT implications in the accountable care environment. Panjamapirom earned a PhD in Health Services Administration, an MBA from the University of Alabama at Birmingham, and an MS in Information and Communication Sciences from Ball State University. He is a Certified Professional in Healthcare Information & Management Systems (CPHIMS).

Ryan Sandefer, MA, CPHIT, is assistant professor and chair at the College of St. Scholastica in the Department of Health Informatics and Information Management. Previously, he was research coordinator for the Center for Healthcare Innovation at the College of St. Scholastica. Sandefer has a master's degree in political science and is completing a PhD in Health Informatics with a focus on consumer engagement in the use of health information technology. He is on the editorial advisory board and review panel for Perspectives in Health Information Management with AHIMA. He is an elected Board member and the Chair-elect of the American Health Information Management Association (AHIMA) Council for Excellence in Education, and is the Chair of its Research and Periodicals Workgroup. He teaches research methods and healthcare data analytics and participates in the Minnesota eHealth Advisory Workgroups.

Robert M. Schumacher, PhD, is the Executive Vice President of GfK User Experience. Dr. Schumacher has more than 25 years of experience applying usability within corporate and academic environments. He is active in the HIMSS Usability Community and served as its Chair in 2013–2014. He was a lead author on NIST's guidance on EHR usability—NIST IRs 7804 and 7742. Dr. Schumacher has written standards for graphical user interfaces, invented a patent for a web browser, and published dozens of technical and industry articles. He has held leadership positions in several professional organizations and is a frequent speaker on user research and user interface design. He holds a PhD in Cognitive and Experimental Psychology from the University of Illinois, Urbana-Champaign.

Susan Severson is the vice president of Health Information Technology Services for Stratis Health and the program director for the Regional Extension Assistance Center for Health Information Technology (REACH). Severson is devoted to and responsible for Stratis Health's growing portfolio of health IT service offerings, especially as health IT supports care delivery and payment transformation. She has more than 15 years of experience in healthcare, with special focus on clinical process improvement in the ambulatory and hospital settings. Severson has worked with hundreds of healthcare entities and is proficient in all aspects of EHR adoption and more recently health reform. In June 2014, she received the Leadership and Impact Award for contributions to the MN e-Health Initiative. Severson is an Affiliate Faculty member at the University of Minnesota Institute for Health Informatics and a member of the MN e-Health Advisory Committee. She has completed two years of post-graduate studies in Healthcare Administration at the University of Minnesota-Carlson School of Management and a Bachelor of Applied Sciences, Community Health and Wellness Education at the University of Wisconsin-Superior, as well as earning Certified Professional Health Information Technology Professional (CPHIT) and Electronic Medical Records Professional (CPEHR) certification.

Jason Shapiro, MD, is an associate professor in the Department of Emergency Medicine at the Icahn School of Medicine at Mount Sinai and an informatics researcher focusing on HIE, emergency medicine, and health services research. Dr. Shapiro is PI on a grant from the Agency for Heathcare Research and Quality to create an HIE–enabled frequent ED user notification system and 72-hour returns report and is a co-investigator on several other studies, including GEDI WISE, a geriatric ED care coordination intervention utilizing HIE–generated notifications, funded through a CMS innovations award.

Pete Shelkin, MSHA, CISSP, PMP, FHIMSS, has 25 years of experience serving in senior IT leadership roles for healthcare organizations. His experience includes providing IT leadership for health plans, hospital systems, academic medical and research centers, as well as clinic groups in CIO, CTO, and consulting roles. Shelkin is currently a Managing Consultant for Encore Health Resources, headquartered in Houston, TX. Before joining Encore, Shelkin served as President of The Osuna Group where he provided interim management, strategic planning, and other health IT–related consulting services to healthcare organizations nationwide. He has served HIMSS in leadership roles since 2000 when he became President-Elect of the Washington State chapter. When he moved to Ohio in 2004, he joined the board of the Central and Southern Ohio chapter where he served for 5 years. At the national level, Shelkin currently serves as Vice Chair of the HIMSS Board of Directors. In addition, he has served on numerous HIMSS committees and workgroups, including as Chair of the HIMSS11 Annual Conference Education Committee. A strong believer in providing support for future leaders, Shelkin has served as a mentor and provider of career guidance for managers and staff. His most recent contribution along these lines was working to found the HIMSS eMentoring Program.

Daniel M. Stein, MD, PhD, is a physician and clinical informatician. He is Associate Medical Director of Informatics at the Weill Cornell Physician Organization, where he helps manage the ambulatory EHR. He is also Assistant Professor of Healthcare Policy and Research at Weill Cornell Medical College where he is involved in teaching and conducting informatics research. Dr. Stein's research interests in clinical communication, collaboration, and care coordination have motivated his studies of how EHRs can be used to support patient handoff and the cooperative management of clinical tasks across care transitions. Complimentary interests in the "quantified self," mobile, social, and other emergent technologies have motivated his work in pioneering methods to measure and positively impact communication, decision-making, and behavior of both clinicians and patients.

Salvatore Volpe, MD, FAAP, FACP, CHCQM, has 25 years of a primary care experience. He has achieved board certification in Pediatrics, Internal Medicine, Geriatrics, and Quality Assurance. He serves as Chairman of the MSSNY HIT Committee and as consultant to NYC PCIP and NYCREACH. Dr. Volpe is recipient of the 2007 IPRO Quality Award. In 2009, Dr. Volpe's medical practice became the first solo practice in the state of New York to achieve Level 3 2008 NCQA PCMH Recognition. In 2010, HIMSS recognized Dr. Volpe as the Chapter Leader of the Year. In 2011, SUNY Downstate Medical School presented Dr. Volpe with the Geriatrics Medicine Award. In 2012, his medical practice became the first solo practice in the United States to achieve Level 3 2011 NCQA PCMH Recognition. In 2012, Dr. Volpe became the Chief Medical Officer for PDR Network, aka the Physicians' Desk Reference company. He has used an EHR and patient portal in his practice for nearly 10 years.

Keith Richard Weiner, RN, MSc, is the Information Systems Security Officer at New York Hospital Queens serving on a several multidisciplinary committees. Weiner has an eclectic education and work experience in both healthcare and IT. He has worked as a Registered Nurse in Canada and the Unities States, managed a security software company division, and has been a senior clinical systems analyst for an electronic medical record company. He is currently pursuing a PhD in Nursing at Molloy College and has co-authored academic presentations for research conferences. As an active member of HIMSS, he has presented at the New York State Conference, co-authored a poster presentation at the national conference, and chaired the mHIMSS Mobile FAQ Committee.

Patricia B. Wise, RN, MS, MA, FHIMSS, Colonel (USA ret'd), joined the staff of HIMSS in August 2002 as the Director of HIMSS EHR Initiatives following the merger of HIMSS and CPRI-HOST. Currently she is Vice President for Health Information Systems overseeing various HIMSS Committees and Initiatives including the Davies Award Program. During her tenure at HIMSS, Wise has specialized in the adoption and implementation of EHR systems and their application via mobile platforms. She is a national subject matter expert on the implications of ARRA and the HITECH Act, with a particular focus on meaningful use and certification. Wise is a former military officer who served in a variety of positions worldwide, retiring in 1998 with the rank of Colonel. She obtained her BSN from Villanova University, an MS from the University of Maryland at Baltimore, and is a graduate of the U.S. Army War College in Carlisle, Pennsylvania.

Mary Ann Zelazny, MBA, has been CEO of Finger Lakes Community Health since 2006, responsible for leading a federally qualified health center (FQHC) organization that provides quality healthcare services to many rural, underserved communities in Upstate New York. As CEO, Zelazny has led a major expansion effort to provide access to healthcare services throughout the Finger Lakes region of New York State. During her tenure, Finger Lakes Community Health has opened seven additional health center sites that provide a wide range of services to their patients. Zelazny has focused much of her work on integrating health IT into the organization, including the creation and operation of the Finger Lakes Telehealth Network, connecting many healthcare providers to each other including primary care offices, specialty care providers, hospitals, and social service agencies. As the leader of an organization with PCMH Level III recognition, she has promoted the incorporation of technology into primary care that has created new collaborative relationships, resulting in expanded patient access and long-distance learning opportunities, as well as nationally recognized best practice programs. Additionally, Zelazny is CEO of the National Farmworker Telehealth Network, created to link community and migrant health centers across the United States to provide healthcare for a mobile population.

Dedication

"EHR4ALL," THE LEGACY OF ROBIN RAIFORD

From her beginnings as an obstetrics nurse to the Senior Research Director she became, Robin believed in health information technology (health IT). She saw the power in the data we could harness to identify trends and improve outcomes for patients. Robin "sang the gospel" of the meaningful use program and was a tireless advocate of its aims. She always had a keen eye to take large amounts of information and reduce it down to more digestible pieces. One of her crowning achievements was the White Board Story, which told the story of all the meaningful use-related regulations in one huge poster. Many members found this poster an invaluable resource. And for those members, Robin was known to drop everything to help with a complex question. She was recently recognized by her peers for going over and above expectations in this regard.

Robin was the 2012 recipient of the Healthcare Information and Management Systems Society (HIMSS) Nursing Informatics Leadership Award. Robin volunteered countless hours to HIMSS and developed many lasting friendships with HIMSS colleagues. She presented at conferences nearly every year including a well-attended meaningful use symposium.

As we reel from her passing in 2014, we remember Robin's devotion to her work. To say Robin commanded a room when she spoke about health IT is an understatement. Her dedication to this industry and its hope for transformative change exuded from her every cell. She spoke to healthcare providers encouraging them to adopt health IT, and in true form, chose a relevant slogan for her license plate, "EHR4ALL." We carry on Robin's vision for that future where everyone uses the systems she believed would change the way we provide healthcare, and for the better.

Acknowledgments

Thanks to Donna, my wife, for her unending encouragement for not only this project but also in my pursuing medical informatics when it was less well appreciated than it is today. My special thanks to all chapter authors who so generously took time out of their busy schedules to share their expertise and knowledge. Thanks to Nancy Vitucci, Senior Manager of Publications at HIMSS Media—our publisher, whose enduring patience and commitment made this project a reality.

Contents

Foreword

The journey to high-value healthcare enabled by health IT is well underway. In the United States, the Health Information Technology for Economic and Clinical Transformation (HITECH) Act of 2009 set in motion incentives and accountability to accelerate adoption and "meaningful use" of certified electronic health record technology (CEHRT) to drive gains in healthcare quality and value. The Meaningful Use Incentive Program was structured to ensure that participating providers and hospitals have the information technology, data and reporting capabilities to support new payment models as they shift from predominantly fee-for-service to value-based payment and shared savings.

The Meaningful Use Incentive Program stimulated remarkable increases in CEHRT adoption. Most participants successfully attested for Stage 1 Meaningful Use, passing such early mile markers as capturing data, using CPOE and electronic prescribing, testing electronic information exchange, implementing clinical decision support (CDS), reporting clinical quality measures, and giving patients online access to their health information. The front-loading of Meaningful Use incentive payments and the strenuous but manageable Stage 1 measures inspired willingness to complete this first leg of the health IT-enabled care transformation journey, even when CEHRT functionality seemed "bolted on" without improving workflows or quality.

Stage 2 Meaningful Use has been much more difficult. If program participation falls significantly, the Stage 2 goals of advanced clinical processes, interoperability and patient engagement may be at risk.

Medical Informatics: An Executive Primer, Third Edition is an excellent resource for healthcare executives seeking to ensure effective use of health IT to improve value while also addressing physician concerns about health IT usability, interoperability, safety and security. Ken Ong, MD, MPH, FACP, FIDSA, CPHIMS, FHIMSS, the book's editor and a nationally recognized clinical informatics leader, engaged select experts and thought leaders to share their insights on a wide range of topics including health IT software selection and implementation, project and change management, usability, meaningful use, CDS, electronic quality measure reporting, clinical and business intelligence, health information exchange, and mobile health. These and other important and timely topics are followed by case studies illuminating the principles from the earlier chapters, with specific stories of success.

Regardless of the direction or fate of current regulatory programs, our patients and colleagues need our help to guide them on the IT-enabled journey to high-value healthcare. To maximize health IT value, we need to ensure our systems "talk" to each other and our clinicians see the technology as usable, useful and satisfying. Patients need relevant data to manage their health and "shop" for the best healthcare value. Executives need clinicians, clinical informaticists, IT analysts, and data scientists working together to combine people, processes, and technologies in support of team-based care; engaging patients; tracking costs; identifying high-risk populations; and supporting clinical decisions. They need data visualizations that help improve performance, decrease unwarranted variation, enhance safety, improve efficiency, minimize complications, and anticipate the road beyond the visible horizon. *Medical Informatics: An Executive Primer, Third Edition* will help executives and their organizations successfully navigate this exciting and essential journey to quality and value.

Michael Zaroukian, MD, PhD, MACP, FHIMSS
Vice President & Chief Medical Information Officer
Sparrow Health System
Lansing, Michigan
Professor, Department of Medicine
College of Human Medicine, Michigan State University
East Lansing, Michigan

Introduction

Ken Ong, MD, MPH, FACP, FIDSA, CPHIMS, FHIMSS

In today's world of Meaningful Use and Accountable Care, healthcare managers must know more about information technology and information technology professionals have to know more about healthcare.

More than two decades have passed since the Institute of Medicine released *The Computer-Based Patient Record: An Essential Technology for Health Care* in 1991.[1]

Since the start of the CMS Meaningful Use EHR Incentive Programs, the nation has made significant strides in adopting this essential technology.

In 2001, 18.2 percent of office-based physicians reported using any type of EHR system. In 2012, the number had grown to 71.8 percent (see Figure 1).[2]

The earliest available data for hospitals reported that 5 to 9.6 percent of hospitals had computerized provider order entry (CPOE) in 2002–2003.[3,4] From HIMSS Analytics, the latest data available at the time of this writing is 15.7 percent of the nation's hospitals now have CPOE (see Table 1).[5]

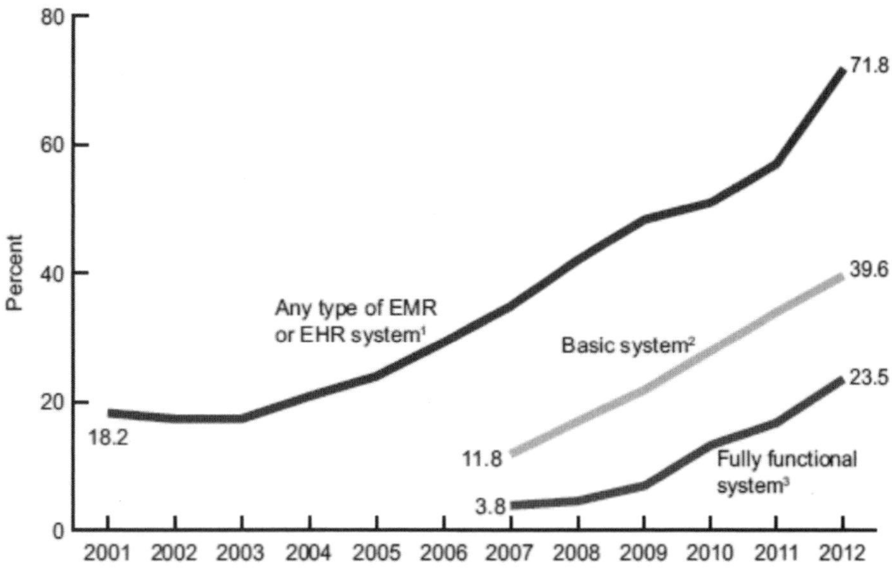

[1]Either all or partially electronic and excludes systems used solely for billing.
[2]Includes a minimal list of necessary EHR features.
[3]Includes a more complete list of necessary EHR features.
NOTES: EMR is electronic medical record and EHR is electronic health record. See Table B in this report for definitions of basic and fully functional systems. Data include nonfederal office-based physicians and exclude radiologists, anesthesiologists, and pathologists.
SOURCE: CDC/NCHS, National Ambulatory Medical Care Survey, 2001–2012.

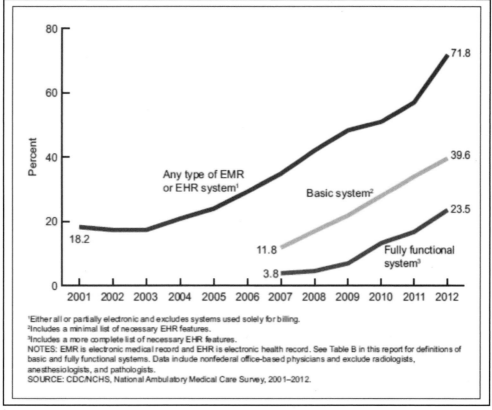

Figure 1: Office-based Physicians with an Electronic Medical Record or Electronic Health Record System: United States, 2001–2012.

Table 1: Data from HIMSS Analytics® Database

United States EMR Adoption Model SM			
Stage	Cumulative Capabilities	2013 Q4	2014 Q1
Stage 7	Complete EMR; CCD transactions to share data; Data warehousing; Data continuity with ED, ambulatory, OP	2.9%	3.1%
Stage 6	Physician documentation (structured templates), full CDSS (variance & compliance), full R-PACS	12.5%	13.3%
Stage 5	Closed loop medication administration	22.0%	24.2%
Stage 4	CPOE, Clinical Decision Support (clinical protocols)	15.5%	15.7%
Stage 3	Nursing/clinical documentation (flow sheets), CDSS (error checking), PACS available outside Radiology	30.3%	27.7%
Stage 2	CDR, Controlled Medical Vocabulary, CDS, may have Document Imaging; HIE capable	7.6%	7.2%
Stage 1	Ancillaries - Lab, Rad, Pharmacy - All Installed	3.3%	3.2%
Stage 0	All Three Ancillaries Not Installed	5.8%	5.6%
Data from HIMSS Analytics® Database ©2012		N = 5458	N = 5449

Looking beyond CPOE, 44 percent of the nation's hospitals now have what is defined as a basic EHR system.[6]

While the nation has not yet completed its journey in fully adopting EHR technologies in a meaningful manner, it is clear that the journey must succeed if we are to meet the triple aim of better care, better health, and lower costs.[7]

This book is a guidebook for this journey.

Each chapter speaks to a waypoint on the journey and is authored by recognized subject matter experts:

- Value of Health IT: HIMSS Health Information Technology Value Model by Patricia B. Wise, RN, MS, MA, FHIMSS, Colonel (USA ret'd)
- Personal Health Engagement by Jan Oldenburg
- Fostering Innovation in Health IT by Anuj Desai and David Jacobowitz
- mHealth: Transforming the Delivery of Healthcare by Geeta Nayyar, MD, MBA
- Patient-Centered Medical Home by Salvatore Volpe, MD
- Meaningful Use: Increasing EHR Adoption and Paving the Path Toward Healthcare Transformation by Anantachai (Tony) Panjamapirom, PhD, MBA, CPHIMS, and Naomi Levinthal, MA, MS, CPHIMS
- Regional Extension Centers by Paul Kleeberg, MD, FAAFP, FHIMSS, and Ryan Sandefer, MA, CPHIT

- Ambulatory Systems by Curtis L. Cole, MD; Adam D. Cheriff, MD; J. Travis Gossey, MD; Sameer Malhotra, MD; and Daniel M. Stein, MD
- Hospital Systems: History and Rationale for Hospital Health IT by Virginia Lorenzi
- Improving Usability through the User-Centered Design Process by Janey Barnes, PhD, and Robert Schumacher, PhD
- Clinical Decision Support by Ken Ong, MD, MPH, FACP, FIDSA, CPHIMS, FHIMSS
- E-Measures by Erika Abramson, MD, MS, and Rainu Kaushal, MD, MPH
- Clinical and Business Intelligence by Ray Hess, MSA, RRT, FHIMSS
- Nursing Informatics Today and Future Perspectives for Healthcare by Dana Alexander, RN, MSN, MBA, and Sarah Collins, RN, PhD
- Health Information Exchange by Gilad J. Kuperman, MD, PhD, and Jason Shapiro, MD, MA
- Privacy & Security by Keith Weiner, RN, MSc
- Software Selection by Ken Ong, MD, MPH, FACP, FIDSA, CPHIMS, FHIMSS
- Project Management and Health IT by Pete Shelkin, MSHA, CISSP, PMP, FHIMSS
- Why Do Projects Fail? by Ken Ong, MD, MPH, FACP, FIDSA, CPHIMS, FHIMSS
- Case Study: Reaching Out with Technology—Telehealth in Rural America by Mary Ann Zelazny, MBA
- Case Study: Children's Medical Center Dallas—Patient Engagement
- Case Study: White River Family Practice—Population Management
- Case Study: Texas Health Resources—Clinical and Business Intelligence
- Case Study: UC Davis Health System—Health Information Exchange
- Case Study: Mount Sinai Medical Center—How the Preventable Admission Care Team (PACT) Used IT to Expand Program

REFERENCES

1. Institute of Medicine. *The Computer-Based Patient Record: An Essential Technology for Health Care*, 1st ed. Dick RS, Steen EB, eds. Washington, DC: The National Academies Press, 1991.
2. Trends in electronic health record system use among office-based physicians: United States, 2007–2012. Hsiao C, Hing E, Ashman J. National Health Statistics Report, no. 75. May 20, 2014.
3. Cutler DM, Feldman NE, Horwitz JR. U.S. adoption of computerized physician order entry systems. *Health Aff.* 2005;24(6):1654-1663.
4. Ash JS, Gorman PN, Seshadri V, et al. Computerized physician order entry in U.S. hospitals: results of a 2002 survey. *J Am Inform Assoc* 2004;11(2):95-99.
5. HIMSS Analytics. United States EMR Adoption Model. http://www.himssanalytics.org/emram/emram.aspx. Accessed June 16, 2014.
6. DesRoches CM, Charles D, Furukawa MF, et al. Adoption of electronic health records grows rapidly, but fewer than half of U.S. hospitals had at least a basic system in 2012. *Health Aff.* 2013;32(8):1478-1485.

7. Berwick DM, Nolan TW, Whittington J. The Triple Aim: care, health, and cost. *Health Aff.* 2008; 27(3): 759-769. doi: 10.1377/hlthaff.27.3.759.

CHAPTER 1

Value of Health IT: HIMSS Health Information Technology Value Model

Patricia B. Wise, RN, MS, MA, FHIMSS, Colonel (USA ret'd)

INTRODUCTION

The value of health IT is demonstrated in many ways.

Some may be unique to an organization, while others may be highly adoptable and scalable. The Healthcare Information and Management Systems Society (HIMSS) created the Health IT Value Model to organize and create a common vocabulary to identify, classify, and discuss the many known examples of health IT value. The HIMSS Health IT Value Model organizes a growing collection of known examples of value attributable to health IT into five broad categories (STEPS™), with additional subtypes within each of the STEPS™ (see Table 1-1). HIMSS currently has documented thousands of examples of value.

In an attempt to capture the benefits organizations gain from implementation of health IT, HIMSS developed a database that captures organizational characteristics, as well as the benefits reported in published case studies and peer reviewed research. A group of graduate research assistants were tasked with searching and summarizing case

Table 1-1: The HIMSS Health IT Value Model

	Value Category (STEPS™) and Subtypes	Documented Examples
S	Satisfaction: Patient; Provider; Staff; Other	Improved communication with patients; improved patient satisfaction scores; improved internal communication
T	Treatment / Clinical: Safety; Quality of Care; Efficiency	Improved patient safety; reduction in medical errors; reduced readmissions; improved scheduling
E	Electronic information / Data: Evidence Based Medicine; Data Sharing and Reporting	Increased use of evidence-based guidelines; increased population health reporting; improved quality measures reporting
P	Prevention and Patient Education: Prevention; Patient Education	Improved disease surveillance; increased immunizations; longitudinal patient analysis; improved patient compliance
S	Savings: Financial / Business; Efficiency Savings; Operational Savings	Increased volume; reduction in days in accounts receivable; reduced patient wait times; reduced emergency dept. admissions; improved inventory control

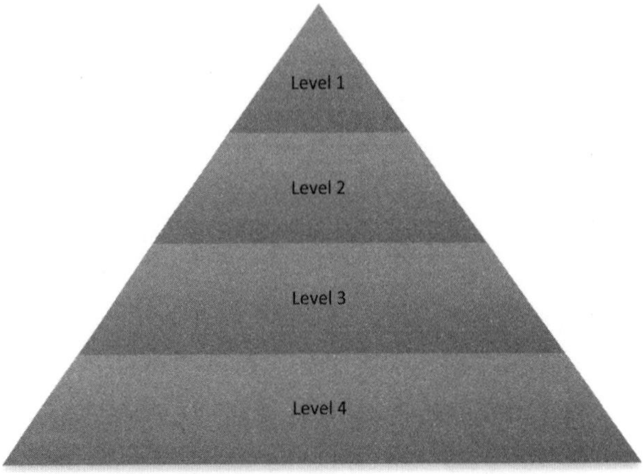

Figure 1-1: The HIMSS Health IT Value Model Level of Evidence

studies found across the Internet. An assortment of search terms were entered into a variety of search engines including, but not limited to, Google, Bing, and Yahoo. Once a case is identified, these research assistants enter the pertinent information into the database including demographics, technologies used, and relevant designations such as patient-centered medical home (PCMH) or accountable care organization (ACO). Values identified in the case are also entered into the database in free text form, ensuring that as much detail is captured as possible.

A key aspect of the collection of data is identification of the rigor under which the case was reviewed prior to publication. This component is called the level of evidence and falls in one of four categories, as shown in Figure 1-1.

The levels of evidence for the Health IT Value Suite reflect the objectivity and level of peer review of the cases in the database. These levels are determined based on the source in which each case was reported, e.g., peer-reviewed reports, various websites, vendors, etc. It should be understood that the benefits identified in each of the cases were identified after implementation of the electronic health record (EHR). However, those benefits may not be due solely to the EHR, but to a combination of factors that were supported and made possible by the EHR. For example, workflows that lead to greater efficiency can be achieved only with an electronic system for recording and sharing of data, but they also rely on changes in processes and adoption/use of the technology by the end users.

Peer-reviewed Cases (highest level of evidence)

These cases were prepared and reported following initial submission of the cases and the subsequent review by a team of experts who visited the provider organization to verify that the EHR systems and functions described in the case and the values received by the organization from those systems and organizations were accurate. The sources of these cases are:

- HIMSS Nicholas E. Davies Award
- HIMSS Analytics Electronic Medical Record Adoption Model (EMRAM)[SM]-recognized providers

Cases Reviewed by an Outside Party

These cases were reviewed by an unrelated party with expertise in health IT. For example, some regional extension centers (RECs) have submitted cases that have been published by the Office of the National Coordinator for Health Information Technology (ONC) on their website. These cases may have been prepared with minor bias in that it is the role of the RECs, and their financing was dependent on the implementation of EHRs in physician practices and critical access hospitals. The sources of the cases at this level are:

- Government websites (ONC, Agency for Healthcare Research and Quality [AHRQ], Health Resources and Services Administration [HRSA], Centers for Disease Control and Prevention [CDC], and others)
- International government websites
- Websites of international associations or health IT publishers
- Association websites (non-HIMSS, e.g., American Academy of Family Physicians [AAFP], Association of Medical Directors of Information Systems [AMDIS], etc.)
- The Commonwealth Fund and other healthcare "think tanks"

Cases That Do Not Indicate an Objective, Outside Health IT Expert Review

These cases were reported but there is no evidence that they have been reviewed by anyone other than a copy editor or other related publishing professional who is not a health IT expert. The sources of the cases at this level include:

- Public search engines
- Newsletters (regional, state and local)
- Consumer sources

Cases with Perceived Bias

Some cases in the database were published by a source that may be perceived as biased. While they provide valuable information, some users of the data from these sources may want to understand the source and work with the data accordingly. The sources of the cases at this level include:

- Vendor-prepared cases that have not been reviewed by an objective health IT expert
- Self-reported cases that have not been peer reviewed by an objective health IT expert

Cases undergo a rigorous review process in which senior level researchers review the cases to ensure no documented values are missing and that all demographic information, including the levels of evidence, is correct. The value statements are then reviewed by another senior level researcher who assigns one of the standard value statements or subcategories to the free text comment. Currently 85 different types of realized value have been identified. Only after this final review are cases finalized and included in data analysis.

SATISFACTION

Satisfaction embodies the fulfillment of one's need, wishes, or expectations.[1] In the healthcare field, many stakeholders are involved, and each are satisfied in their own way. In this first category of the STEPS Model, health IT is analyzed to determine how health IT affects the satisfaction of three major stakeholders in healthcare: patients, providers, and staff.

Patient Satisfaction

To meet the needs of patients, focusing solely on healthcare outcomes is no longer enough. Today, the bar is set higher and patients are satisfied only when their expectation for the total healthcare experience has been met. According to Fottler, Ford, and Heaton,[2] the total healthcare experience is all encompassing and includes the customer service received from the staff and physicians, the appeal and cleanliness of the environment, the ambience, the food, and cultural responsiveness. Furthermore, the Health Information Technology for Economic and Clinical Health Act (HITECH) of 2009 provides incentives for hospitals and physician offices to adopt health IT and to use it meaningfully.[3] Even though hospitals and medical offices were already using technology to support their medical care of patients, the HITECH law requires health IT to be an integral component of a patient's care and treatment plan. Hospitals, medical offices, and physicians all have to adopt health IT and meet meaningful use (MU) requirements.

So what is known about the impact health IT has on patient satisfaction? In a 2011 study by Buntin, Burke, Hoaglin, et al.,[4] a review of literature from July 2007 to February 2010 on health IT was performed to determine the effects of the adoption of technology on patient and provider satisfaction. A total of 154 studies were analyzed for outcome measures; approximately 92 percent of the recent articles on health IT concluded that the outcomes of health IT were positive.

Health IT can also engage patients in their own healthcare with the use of electronic patient portals. Patient portals serve a couple of purposes: they give patients secure access to health information, and they allow for secure information sharing and communication between the provider and the patient.[5] The types of information that are accessible vary with the types of patient portals available to patients. However, patient portals do share commonalities, including access to test results, summary of care notes, the ability to refill medication, appointment setting, access to educational resources, and the ability to send secure messages to providers.[5]

A recent study in which researchers looked at patients' experience with the My HealtheVet Personal Health Record Pilot Program at the U.S. Department of Veterans Affairs[6] showed similar positive results with the use of patient portals. Through their study, patient's experiences with the HealtheVet Personal Health Record were categorized into four broad themes. Of the four themes, three were perceived benefits, while one was centered on their concerns. Perceived benefits included improved communication between visits and during visits, a sense of empowerment because of the access to educational materials, and engagement with their health. The only theme focused on the concern with the use of patient portals was the possibility of induced stress on the patient as a result of seeing a doctor's notes and the inconsistencies of what was verbally communicated to patients versus what was actually documented in their medical records.[6] The perceived benefits of health IT and its impact on patient satisfaction as evidenced in the literature and in case studies suggest the importance of health IT in the healthcare setting.

Provider Satisfaction

Similar to patient satisfaction, provider satisfaction comprises multiple elements that measure this level of satisfaction. Using the American Medical Group Association Provider Satisfaction Survey, provider satisfaction is measured based on the following items: leadership and communication, quality of care, time spent working, patient interaction, administrators, compensation, relationship with staff, resources, acceptance by colleagues, paperwork, computers and preauthorization hassle.[7] According to the HIMSS STEPS Model resources, a high level of provider satisfaction is predicated on several factors, including improved communication with patients, staff, and other providers, and improved quality of life.[8]

Four years have passed since adoption of the HITECH Act in 2009. There is a large body of research focused on studying the perceived benefits and drawbacks of the implementation of health IT. Much attention has been given to providers and their opinion. Physicians are the end-users of such systems, as well as the primary decision makers on patients' course of treatment in a healthcare setting. Thus, physicians are an integral component to determine the success or failure of the health IT investment.

Improvement of communication channels between providers and patients, providers and staff, and providers with other providers has been known to increase provider satisfaction. The use of patient portals has fostered the ability for physicians and patients to communicate outside of visiting hours.[6] Additionally, use of an EHR has decreased the amount of time required to share information from provider to staff and referrals to other providers. As Amit Gupta, DO, solo practitioner and owner of AG Pain Management states, "With the EMR's incoming and outgoing fax system, when any of my notes are done they are usually sent out in less than 24 hours to the referring physician."[9] On a similar note, Anne Rose Eapen, MD, an internal medicine physician practicing in Virginia, vetted many EHR systems and found one that was the perfect fit for her solo practice in 2008. Three years later, in 2011, Dr. Eapen attests that she "will never practice medicine without an EHR…it improved the quality of life both inside and outside of the office, and truly impacted the care we provide to patients."[10]

In a recent study, 146 primary care physicians (PCPs) in Texas affiliated with one of the following health systems: University of Texas Southwestern Medical Center (UTSW), Dallas; Parkland Health & Hospital System, Dallas; and University of Texas Health Science Center, San Antonio (UTHSCA) were surveyed to determine the perceived capabilities of a commonly used EHR system.[11] Results from the study found that the EHR improved communication between providers and allowed for timely access to patients' medical records and usefulness with medication refills. Moreover, PCPs also liked the ability to communicate information electronically to patients through a patient portal system. Nonetheless, drawbacks with use of an EHR exist, and the PCPs in this study cited difficulty in maintaining eye contact with their patients, and, further,

40 percent of PCPs citied that the EHR interfered with "provider-patient communication during visits."[11]

Staff Satisfaction

Satisfaction among staff members depends on an organization's ability to motivate, empower, fulfill, and reward them.[2] Not only has health IT benefited providers and nurses, but staff members have experienced an increase in efficiency and job satisfaction as well. The integration and adoption of health IT has led to improved productivity, morale, and a heightened sense of happiness in one's workplace and has also led to improvements in communications. It is no surprise that when employees and staff enjoy a high level of satisfaction, that positive response is then translated to better patient care, which ultimately leads to higher patient satisfaction.[2]

Other Satisfaction

As mentioned previously, patient satisfaction is based on the total healthcare experience. As such, family members of patients are an integral component in the healing process of patients. Health IT can assist in care coordination and facilitate the transition of care from a healthcare setting into a patient's home environment through the use of mobile and telemedicine technology. Telemedicine technology such as telehealth, including remote patient monitoring and video visits, allows for the provision of care at a distance.[12] Lastly, the use of patient portals can disseminate educational materials not only to patients, but to family members as well.

Findings

Of the 4,597 instances of value derived from the EHR in the database, approximately 12 percent are related to the satisfaction of patients, providers, staff, or other forms of satisfaction (see Figure 1-2). Of those cases focusing on satisfaction, the majority (50%) related to provider satisfaction including improved quality of life and other satisfiers. Patient satisfaction, including an overall increase in patient satisfaction and/or

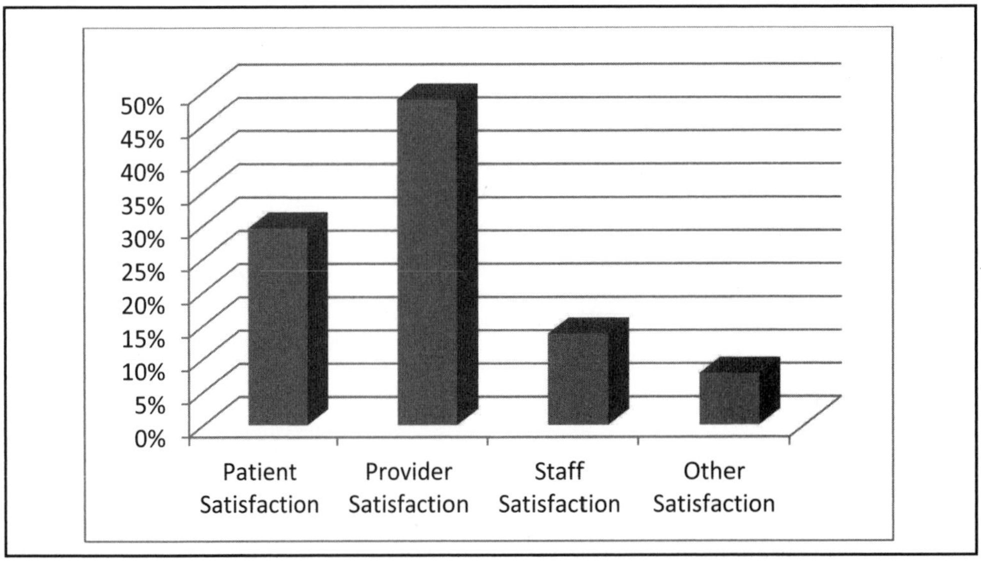

Figure 1-2: Satisfaction

survey score and increased use of the patient portal, was indicated in 30 percent of the cases. Staff satisfaction was indicated in 14 percent of the cases, including increased staff morale and job satisfaction. Other satisfaction benefits were indicated in approximately eight percent of cases.

Communication is a recurring theme in this STEPS value category. Forty percent of cases reporting satisfaction benefits indicated they believed that the implementation of health IT had improved communication with patients, staff, other providers, and internal communication. This subgroup of benefits demonstrates the importance of health IT in improving the way a healthcare organization functions.

TREATMENT/CLINICAL

The treatment/clinical category is designed to capture the clinical benefits and quality improvements that patients and providers may encounter as a result of health IT. This classification encompasses the subcategories of safety, quality of care, and efficiencies and captures the clinical quality improvements that can be experienced by a fully integrated health IT infrastructure.

There are many forms of health IT that support clinical care, and they fall into three general categories: clinical information systems, administrative information systems, and clinical decision support systems (CDSSs).[13] Clinical information systems, including CPOE, are usually coupled with a CDSS and utilize alert systems, such as drug-to-drug interaction alerts, to notify clinicians of potential dangers. CPOE as a standalone "refers to any system in which clinicians directly enter medication orders (and, increasingly tests and procedures) into a computer system, which then transmits the order directly to the pharmacy."[14] Medical errors resulting from illegible handwriting are also minimized. EHRs, which also fall under clinical information systems, are used to capture patients' medical information. EHRs make electronically stored medical records easily accessible and searchable.[15]

Safety

Safeguarding patients from harm in a healthcare setting is of utmost importance. Our healthcare system is becoming more and more immersed in health IT and its use can assist in mitigating medical errors and harm to patients. Nevertheless, health IT alone cannot reduce medical errors and improve patient safety. It requires the knowledge of people and proper clinical implementation of health IT, as much as the technology to adequately leverage the use of health IT in improving patient safety in a healthcare setting.[16] Some literature has suggested that health IT has made significant strides in improving patient safety, while other studies have shown that health IT has little to no effect on patient safety.

According to AHRQ (2003), health IT such as CPOE, if implemented and used properly, can reduce errors and improve safety. In addition to CPOE, other types of health IT include bar coding, electronic medication administration records (EMARs), clinical documentation, electronic medical records (EMRs), and e-prescribing.[17] These health IT applications can increase patient safety by reducing medical errors, improving clinical documentation and use of clinical alerts, and reducing medical-related errors. Sentara Norfolk General Hospital, part of the Sentara health system, reported that it "avoided 117,400 potential medication errors due to medical bar coding." Furthermore, EHRs and their alert systems have enabled hospitals to reduce hospital-acquired infections such as catheter-associated urinary tract infections (CAUTIs).[18]

The use of health IT and its impact on patient safety differs in the types of healthcare settings that adopt health IT. For instance, in emergency department care, the success of health IT in improving patient safety is largely based on the design and implementation of the health IT. When implemented properly, health IT, such as CPOE and CDS, has been cited to enhance legibility, which leads to a reduction in transcription errors, promotes the standardization of naming conventions, conducts automatic calculations, generates alerts, and screens at-risk populations.[15] Nevertheless, without proper implementation, health IT leads to workarounds, which may adversely impact patients.

Improvements to patient safety were also found in a study surveying 16,352 nurses in 316 hospitals operating in four different states (California, Florida, New Jersey, and Pennsylvania). Kutney-Lee and Kelly[19] reported that hospitals that fully implemented a basic EHR system promoted patient safety. Utilizing logistic regression, they found a higher percentage of nurses (22.5%) in hospitals without a fully implemented basic EHR reported their hospital management did not place patient safety as a high priority compared with nurses (16.8%) in hospitals with a fully implemented basic EHR. Additionally, hospitals with a fully implemented EHR had fewer reports of medication errors. A limitation of their study was the small number of hospitals (21) that had fully implemented basic EHRs. Nonetheless, the authors found statistically significant associations.

Children are the top priority at Children's National Medical Center in Washington, DC; thanks to their EHR system, Children's is able to provide a much higher level of care to their patients. The order sets of their EHR enable the medical center to "promote evidence-based, safe, effective and consistent care," while forcing physicians to "think through processes with a fresh perspective and create new sets of orders."[20]

Quality of Care

Quality, as defined by the Institute of Medicine, is the "degree to which health services for individuals and populations increase the likelihood of desired health outcomes and are consistent with current professional knowledge."[21] The use of health IT enhances quality of care through the implementation of DSSs, point-of-care systems, and EMRs.

The implementation of health IT has been associated with improvements to the quality of care in healthcare settings. These improvements include a reduction in hospital-acquired infections (HAIs), decreased response time to patient requests, reduction in readmissions, improved continuity of care, reduction in hospital-acquired pneumonia, improved management of diabetes, and improved management of congestive heart failure.

In 2013, Texas Health Resources, located in Arlington, Texas, was the recipient of the 2013 HIMSS Davies Enterprise Award. The Davies Award recognizes "excellence in the use of health information technology, specifically EHRs, to improve healthcare delivery, processes, and patient safety."[22] Texas Health Resources, through the implementation of a CDSS and advanced clinical analytics, saw improved "outcomes for their cardiac patients, reduced cases of venous thromboembolism, and significantly reduced hospital-acquired infections."[22]

HAIs threaten patient safety and quality of care. In 2011, there were an estimated 722,000 HAIs reported in U.S. acute care hospitals and approximately "75,000 hospital patients with HAIs died during their hospitalizations."[23] The most commonly reported HAIs include pneumonia, gastrointestinal illness, urinary tract infections, surgical site infections from any inpatient surgery, and other types of infections. The literature on the benefits of CPOE is mixed, but the use of CPOE has shown to reduce hospital-wide mortality and "improvement in Hospital Quality Alliance measures for acute myocardial infarction, chronic failure, and pneumonia."[24] For hospital-acquired antibiotic-associated *Clostridium difficile* colitis, the use of a CDSS was effective in reducing *C difficile* colitis because the CDS helped to guide the prescribing of antibiotics.[25]

The most common nosocomial infections are CAUTIs. Research has shown that the length of time the catheter is in place greatly increases the risk of contracting a CAUTI.[26] The 2014 update to "Strategies to Prevent Catheter-Associated Urinary Tract Infections in Acute Care Hospitals"[27] provided recommendations on strategies to detect and prevent CAUTIs. In their recommendation, the authors suggested the use of electronic documentation. Since one of the attributable causes of CAUTIs is the length of time a catheter is in place, documentation of when the catheter was inserted is extremely important in the prevention of CAUTIs.

In a case study featuring University of California Davis (UC Davis) Health System, clinicians identified several goals of priority to be addressed, and the deployment of the EHR has been transformative in this process. The goals identified included the reduction of CAUTIs, central line bloodstream infection, ventilator-associated pneumonia, narcotic overdoses, and hypoglycemic episodes. Health IT at the UC Davis Health System was instrumental in meeting their goals, with utilization of CPOE, EHR clinical order sets, clinical templates, EHR-based chemotherapy protocols and voice recognition to generate documentation in the EHR. Reported outcomes as a result of the implementation of their EHR system included a 44.4 percent decrease in central line bloodstream infections, a 8.6 percent reduction in CAUTIs, and a 65.9 percent reduction in surgical site infection.[28]

Efficiency

Efficiency in the world of healthcare is defined as the ability to maximize results, while using resources in an optimal manner. Time and resources are not unlimited in healthcare. Therefore, the use of health IT allows hospitals, doctors' offices, clinicians, and staff to increase efficiencies in the areas of patient interaction, scheduling, and improved communication channels between clinicians, as well as between clinicians and patients.

A study of nine hospitals, including Carillion Roanoke Hospital, Gundersen Lutheran Medical Center, Metro Health Hospital, New York-Presbyterian Hospital, Sentara Norfolk General Hospital, VA Central Iowa Health Care System, and Yale-New Haven Hospital, reported that "the EHR contributes to faster, more accurate communication between providers within the hospital and between ambulatory and hospital settings."[18] The EHR also enhances the ease of access to patient medical records. For the discharge process, the EHR allows for customizable discharge plans "which has made discharge faster, improved the process of instructing patients, and strengthened communication among providers and families." For example, Geisinger Health System built into their EHR a "discharge button" to alert the discharge team of tasks that are required to be completed prior to discharging a patient.[18] As evidenced by the Silow-Carroll, Edwards and Rodin study, the EHR has allowed for processes to be streamlined to reduce the time required to complete certain processes in a hospital setting.

The reduction in the redundancy of ordering labs and x-rays has also been cited as a benefit following the adoption of EHRs. In a case study of Kaiser Permanente in California, after implementation of their EHR system, they were able to reduce use of their outpatient lab by 12 percent just from eliminating duplicate tests.[29]

As evidenced in the literature and case studies, health IT has an instrumental impact on the treatment of patients in healthcare settings. Increased patient safety, quality of care, and efficiency in the delivery of care have all been cited as important contributions of health ITs.

Findings

Treatment/clinical benefits are by far the most commonly reported value in the database. As shown in Figure 1-3, more than 43 percent (n=2,027) of cases report a benefit related to improved treatment as a result of health IT. This includes increased safety, quality of care, efficiencies, and other treatment/clinical benefits. Of the cases indicating improved treatment/clinical care, approximately 43 percent cited increased clinical efficiencies as benefits derived from health IT implementations. Some of these values include real time or remote access to health records, decreased redundancies in testing, and improved access to lab or x-ray reports. Improved quality of care is also highly represented in these cases; these values were reported in 28 percent of cases reporting a treatment/clinical benefit. Some of the values captured in quality of care are improved

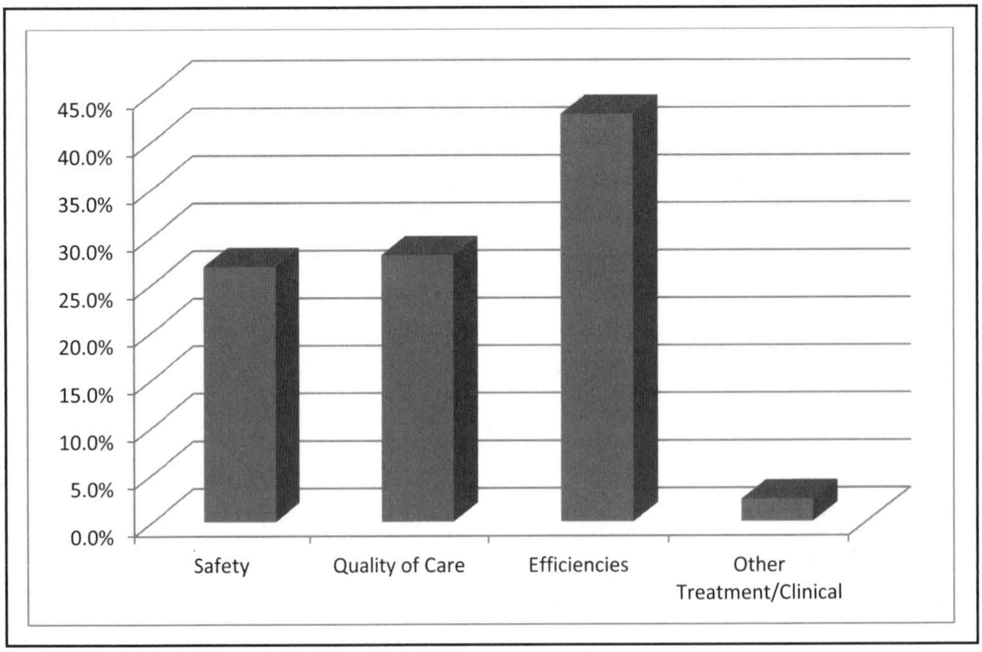

Figure 1-3: Treatment/Clinical

continuity of care, reduction in HAIs, and reduction in readmissions. Improved safety is also a common theme (27 percent) in those cases reporting treatment or clinical improvements. These improvements include reduction in medical and medication-related errors, improved clinical documentation, and improved use of clinical alerts.

ELECTRONIC INFORMATION/DATA

The sharing of electronic information is the cornerstone of true data integration and one of the ultimate goals of the HITECH Act. This category in the STEPS Model captures the degree to which this sharing is occurring in practice. Benefit subtypes of evidence-based medicine and data sharing/reporting capture improved population health reporting, increased use of evidence-based medicine guidelines, and other data-sharing and reporting trends.

Evidence-based Medicine

Evidence-based medicine uses clinical research data and information to determine the most effective care for patients. "The practice of evidence-based medicine means integrating individual clinical expertise with the best available external clinical evidence from systematic research."[30] The explosion of health IT has given us the ability to capture large amounts of data and to analyze these data to make it useful knowledge to the organization. Health IT also has the ability to support clinical decisions made by clinicians and inform different stakeholders such as patients, doctors, and third-party payers.[31]

CDSS comprise one of the key functionalities of health IT used in the clinical care of patients. CDSS is defined as a "computer software that presents users with a knowledge base, patient-specific data, and related information at the point of care to enhance healthcare provision and management."[31] CDSS also offers tools, including computerized alerts, clinical guidelines, order sets, data reports and summaries, diagnostic support, and other important functions.[32]

In a study evaluating the success of a CAUTI-preventative, quality improvement (QI) project in a 505-bed hospital, the hospital demonstrated the effectiveness of their EHR in preventing and reducing the rate of CAUTIs. This success was largely attributed to their integration of evidence-based practices in preventing and lowering rates of CAUTIs. By incorporating evidence-based criteria for catheter insertion and indwelling urinary catheters from the CDC in their CDSS, the hospital instilled and sustained evidence-based CAUTI practices and minimized variability of CAUTI practices.[33]

Data Sharing and Reporting

With the implementation of health IT, data sharing and reporting is seamless and can occur without geographic boundaries. Electronically stored data can be analyzed, and trends can be determined with regard to clinical processes and patient outcomes. Additionally, it also makes data reporting to the Centers for Medicare & Medicaid Services (CMS) and other agencies much easier. Some positive benefits attributable to health IT related to data sharing and reporting include improved quality measure reporting, improved claims management, increased data sharing and recording, increased clinical tracking, increased population health reporting, and improved security of patient records.

Using nationally recognized standards, the health information exchange (HIE) is a "framework that enables the movement of patient health data and information across organizations."[31] HIE is a federal initiative to share information between disparate information systems. Interoperability among different information systems is key to HIE. According to HIMSS, interoperability is defined as the ability of information systems to exchange, interpret, and understand the data that is shared amongst different information systems.[34]

Electronic HIE also supports public health reporting and is a powerful tool for disease surveillance, identification of health risks, and the overall promotion of a healthy population.[35] In a study evaluating implementation of an electronic HIE for public reporting, success was contingent on a need to understand the HIE using IT and a requirement for consistent champions and communication among leadership during the duration of the implementation of HIE for public health reporting.[35]

HIE also makes data sharing possible within a regional health information organization network (RHIO). RHIOs are a network of regional hospitals and clinics that use interoperable health IT systems.[31] The Keystone Health Information Exchange (KeyHIE) is connecting hospitals, physician practices, and other healthcare organizations. This network of healthcare organizations can coordinate a continuum of care as they can share discharge notes, hospital admittance records, tracking of medications, and view results of lab work and diagnostic testing.[36]

Findings

More than 500 cases tout the benefits of health IT on their ability to use electronic information/data. As shown in Figure 1-4, of these cases, an overwhelming 76.4 percent

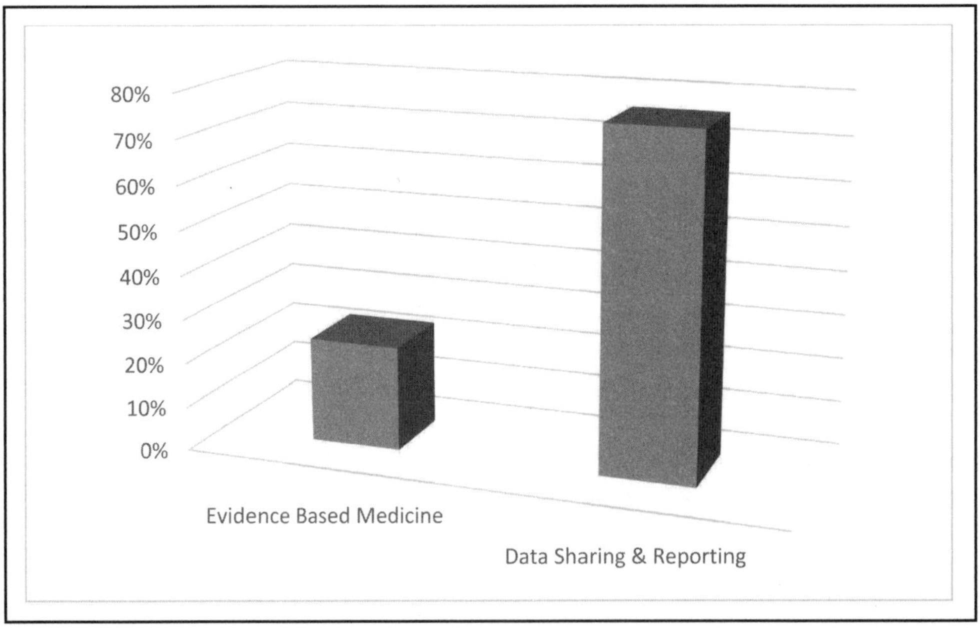

Figure 1-4: Electronic Information/Data

demonstrate improvement in data sharing and reporting, including improving quality measures reporting, with 23.6 percent of the cases showing a benefit in improved evidence-based medicine. Within this category is also a subset of values related directly to improving reporting. These include increased number of patients tracked, increased clinical trends tracking, improved quality measures reporting, and increased population health. These essential reporting benefits account for 28 percent of the benefits in this area.

PREVENTION & PATIENT EDUCATION

Central to the success of both the HITECH and the Patient Protection and Affordable Care Act (PPACA) is the idea that disease prevention and patient education are crucial to reducing preventable diseases, while engaging patients in their own healthcare. The Prevention and Patient Education category in the STEPS Model captures the degree to which health IT is helping to achieve these goals. Subcategories such as prevention and patient education, for example, measure the extent to which cancer screenings are increasing, patient compliance and diabetes test results are improving, and improvements in educating patients about their health are increasing.

While our system once approached healthcare in a reactive manner, now emphasis is centered on preventative healthcare. We are much more proactive in preventing diseases from developing rather than having to treat the disease. Such preventative measures include promoting health and disease screenings, educating patients, and engaging patients in their healthcare.[37]

Prevention

A 2012 article titled "From Sick Care to Health Care – Reengineering Prevention into the U.S. System" indicated the need to forestall "the development of disease before symptoms or life-threatening events occur."[38] The PPACA also strongly advocates for preventative healthcare. With this in mind, health IT such as mobile apps, personal health records (PHRs), and interactive, patient-oriented technology can contribute to prevention through the tracking of a patient's vitals.

An example of this is using health IT for diabetes care. Diabetes affects approximately 25 million people in the United States.[39] Although there are mixed opinions on the ability of health IT to improve diabetes care quality, health IT has shown some promising results in improving diabetes care. For example, there is evidence that shows the effectiveness of CDSSs relating to modest gains in care recommendations such as reminders and monitoring of blood pressure, low-density lipoprotein-cholesterol (LDL-C), and hemoglobin A1c control.[39] At Bangor Beacon Community,[40] a network of partners including hospitals, health systems, long-term care, behavioral health facilities, and home care strongly advocated for the interoperability of EHRs to promote care management and collaboration among their network of partners. As a result, in just over a two-year period, they saw improved LDL-C control and depression screenings among their diabetes patients.[40]

Health IT has also increased preventative measures such as screenings and immunizations rates. At Mount Sinai Medical Center (MSMC) located in New York City, documentation of vaccination records was occurring in both outpatient and inpatient settings but without a centralized searchable database for both types of settings.[41] Having to rely on patients' memory for their immunization history was problematic. Therefore, after implementation of the EHR, clinicians were able to record and search a centralized database for a patient's vaccine history. The EHR also generated reminders for administration of vaccines. A patient's discharge process could not be finalized until the vaccine was given. Consequently, the EHR workflow increased MSMC's vaccination compliance for pneumonia and influenza vaccinations to almost 100 percent compliance. This example highlights the effectiveness of EHRs in increasing vaccination compliance, an important and simple preventative measure in decreasing the potential for the development of preventable diseases.

Patient Education

Patient education is an important component to preventative medicine. For patients to be active participants in their healthcare, they need to be educated in their own health. The use of IT can aid in this process as health IT can be used to engage patients in disease awareness through the distribution of patient educational materials and help to increase patient compliance.

While EHRs have built-in educational materials and resources for patients, it is important to teach patients to understand and learn how to properly use health IT functions, such as a PHR. An essential provision of the HITECH Act is using health IT in a meaningful way—not only used meaningfully by hospitals and clinicians, but patients, too. Patients are a critical component to the success of the MU requirement.[42] Therefore, it is important to teach patients how to utilize EHRs to reap the full potential of these systems to aid in their own healthcare. According to Galbraith,[42] MU is only meaningful when both clinicians and patients overcome barriers inherent with technological advancement. These problems relate to patients "who are unable to access the Internet, for those who have very limited understanding of the information provided, or for those who, for other reasons, are unable to act on that information."[42] Nevertheless, when these barriers are broken down, that is when health IT can truly be used in a meaningful manner.

One such example is a case study on the Central Ottawa Family Medicine Associates. This practice truly embraced their EMR to improve patient care. Patients are involved in their own care through the use of a patient portal. They have the opportunity to log certain health information such as their blood pressure. The physician will then go over that information with them during an appointment. The EMR also offers other disease management tools to give patients more control of their own health.[43] Meeting MU requirements requires the efforts of both the clinicians and patients to meet the goals set by both the PPACA and HITECH Act.

Findings

Prevention and patient education benefits were documented in 337 of the cases currently in the EHR Value database. As shown in Figure 1-5, of those cases, 46 percent indicated a benefit related to prevention, and 54 percent found that their patient education was improved by implementation of a health IT system. Of particular interest as it relates to recent legislation is the 62 percent of cases that described how health

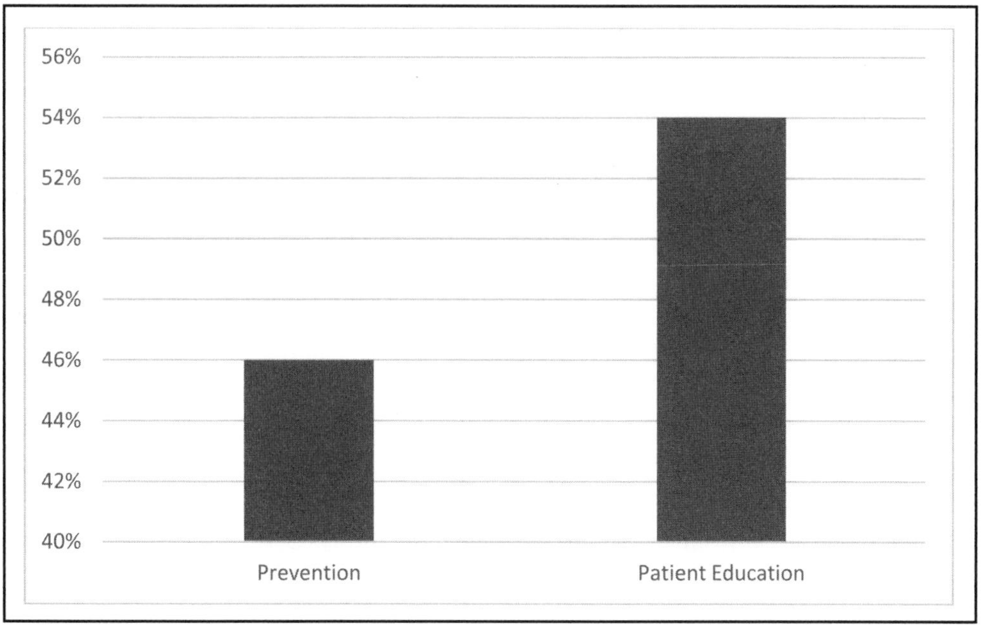

Figure 1-5: Prevention and Patient Education

IT improved their patient engagement. This includes patient compliance, engagement, smoking cessation, and awareness of disease symptoms.

SAVINGS

The final category of the STEPS Model is savings. This category seeks to identify financial, efficiency, and operational savings realized by healthcare organizations as a result of a health IT implementation. These savings are reported in the form of increased patient revenue or volume, improved workflow, improved use of space, and reduced FTEs or other benefit statements.

Financial/Business Savings

Through the use of health IT, financial savings have been realized in many healthcare organizations. The use of administrative information systems, such as revenue cycle management systems, supports practice and hospital administrators in financial operations. These include billing, materials management, budgeting, cost control, and predictive modeling. Predictive modeling uses "claims data to identify patients who are likely to generate significant healthcare costs."[13] Systems such as revenue cycle management solutions assist practices and hospitals in managing their revenue cycle. This is extremely helpful because the healthcare system is experiencing massive changes to the payment landscape.[44]

Hawaii Pacific Health (HPH) is a prime example of how the implementation of an EHR can achieve a significant return on investment (ROI). Experiencing a significant operating loss totaling $3.8 million in 2003, HPH knew something had to be done to mitigate continual financial loss. A large reason why HPH was operating with a negative operating margin was because payments for medical care were not enough to cover the actual cost of care. A solution HPH knew would generate an ROI was the integration of their EMR with a revenue cycle system. Using a single EMR paired with a revenue cycle system allowed HPH to streamline administrative functions to achieve an ROI of nine percent per year over a 10-year period. Savings were realized from reducing write-offs such as those resulting from the denial of payments by insurance plans because of a failure to receive preauthorization from the payer. HPH attributed their success to their integration of all revenue cycle functions, while maintaining transparency, collaboration, and accountability.[45]

As this one example showcases, ROI can be realized in healthcare organizations adopting health IT. Nonetheless, barriers still exist in the adoption of health IT. These barriers include the initial cost of the health IT systems, the unknown ROI, and the decrease in productivity.[46] The study by Fleming et al. reported on the productivity, staffing, and financial measures of 26 primary care practices that implemented an EHR system. Their study concluded that although expenses increased along with a decrease in productivity as a result of the EHR implementation, these impacts were mostly minor and not long lasting.

Efficiency Savings

Efficiency savings as a result of the implementation of health IT affects multiple stakeholders including patients and administrators. For instance, patients experience a reduction in wait times, while hospital administrators and clinicians experience improvements to their organizations' workflow.

A case study highlighting the experiences at All Island Gastroenterology, following their EHR implementation in 2009, described how they increased their efficiency and, therefore, could see 25 more patients per week.[47] Similarly, at Aquidneck Medical Associates, by adapting their EHR to their physician's workflow, they were able to do more with less time, while reducing the need to search through paper medical records.[48] However, increased efficiency by a healthcare organization after implementation is not always achieved.

In a study conducted on community health centers (CHCs) located in an urban area, the researchers looked at perceived efficiency impacts following implementation of an EHR. Data were collected using semi-structured interviews with a sample size of 39 participants across four different sites. CHCs present unique systems challenges because they are a one-stop shop for the indigent population. They provide a full range of healthcare services including primary care, dental, behavioral health, public health, and support services. Their results suggest efficiencies were gained as a result of the EHR implementation. However, the study also discussed inefficiencies that were introduced. Two main efficiencies with regards to the utilization of an EHR include workflow efficiencies gained and laboratory turnaround efficiencies gained. Inefficiencies that were introduced include "new work resulting from the introduction of the EHR, work to address EHR-related errors, and creation of workarounds to address limitations of the EHR."[49] Consequently, tailoring an EHR to organizational needs is key to reducing inefficiencies generated by the implementation of the EHR.

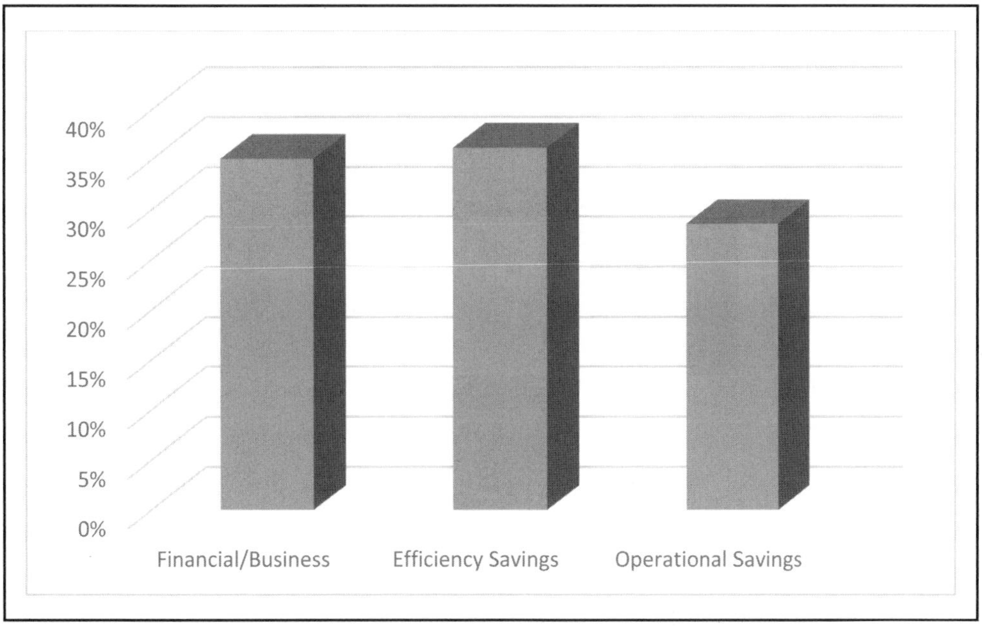

Figure 1-6: Savings

Operational Savings

Health IT contributes to operational savings in the form of improved inventory control, space utilization, a reduction in overtime, and an improved business recovery plan (i.e., disaster planning). In the previously cited case study, All Island Gastroenterology realized operational savings after the implementation of their EHR system. By storing medical records electronically, the amount of physical space needed to store paper medical records was reduced.[47]

Three Links Care Centre, a Canadian long-term care facility located in Vancouver, British Columbia, was able to improve their inventory control of medication after adoption of their EHR system. Since migrating to an EHR for medication delivery, a surplus is no longer necessary. Prescription orders are requested at the point of care and the pharmacy is then notified when an order is placed.[50]

Findings

Savings were highlighted as a benefit of health IT 1,175 times in the database. As shown in Figure 1-6, the benefits were evenly spread across the value subcategories: Financial/Business Savings (35%), Efficiency Savings (36%), and Operational Savings (29%). Improved workflow and practice efficiency was the most often cited value, making up 41 percent of the efficiency savings benefits.

DISCUSSION

Importance of Findings

This database serves as the beginning stages of quantifying the values derived from health IT implementation. These results can be used to justify spending on new and emerging technologies that can assist healthcare organizations in reaching their goals of satisfaction, improved treatment and clinical outcomes, efficiencies, prevention and patient education, and savings. The next edition of the Health IT Value Model will drill down into the details of how an organization can maximize the value derived from their technology.

Limitations

As with any research project, this attempt to value health IT has limitations. While a large number of cases are captured in the database, the focus to this point has been to capture only positive reviews and related outcomes. In addition, not all positive values reaped by the organization may be captured. For example, if the case is written for a financial publication, it is likely that the financial savings associated with the health IT implementation would be highlighted and other benefits, e.g., clinical, may be missed.

REFERENCES

1. Satisfaction. (2014). Oxford Dictionary Online. http://www.oxforddictionaries.com/us/definition/american_english/satisfaction. Accessed November 23, 2014.
2. Fottler MD, Ford RC, Heaton CP. *Achieving Service Excellence: Strategies for Healthcare*. Chicago, IL: Health Administration Press, 2010.
3. Health Information Privacy. (n.d.) U.S. Department of Health & Human Services. http://www.hhs.gov/ocr/privacy/hipaa/administrative/enforcementrule/hitechenforcementifr.html. Accessed November 23, 2014.
4. Buntin MB, Burke MF, Hoaglin MC, et al. The benefits of health information technology: A review of the recent literature shows predominantly positive results. *Health Aff.* 2011;30(3):464-471.
5. Goldzweig CL, Orshansky G, Paige NM, et al. Electronic patient portals: Evidence on health outcomes, satisfaction, efficiency, and attitudes. *Ann Int Med.* 2013;159:677-687.
6. Woods SS, Schwartz E, Tuepker A, et al. Patient experiences with full electronic access to health records and clinical notes through the My HealtheVet personal health record pilot: Qualitative study. *J Med Internet Res.* 2013;15(3).
7. Scammon DL, Tabler J, Brunisbolz K, et al. Organizational cultural associated with provider satisfaction. *J Am Board Fam Med.* 2014;27(2):219-228.
8. HIMSS Value Step. (2014). Healthcare Information and Management Systems Society [HIMSS]. http://www.himss.org/ResourceLibrary/ValueSuite.aspx#/steps-app. Accessed November 23, 2014.
9. Waiting Room Solutions. (2012). Going Solo: Getting bang for your buck. https://www.waitingroomsolutions.com/sites/default/files/testimonials/pdfs/pain-management-ehr-testimonial-gupta.pdf. Accessed July 20, 2013.
10. Virginia Health IT Regional Extension Center. EHR enables organizational transformation for internal medicine physician. Accessed October 4, 2011.
11. Makam AN, Lanham HJ, Batchelor K, et al. Use and satisfaction with key functions of a common commercial electronic health record: A survey of primary care providers. *BMC Medical Inform Decis Mak.* 2013;13(86).
12. Adler-Milstein J, Kvedar J, Bates DW. Telehealth among U.S. hospitals: Several factors, including state reimbursement and licensure policies, influence adoption. *Health Aff.* 2014;33(2):207-215.
13. Shi L, Singh DA. *Delivering Health Care In America*. Sudbury, MA: Jones & Bartlett Learning; 2013.
14. Computerized Provider Order Entry. (2012). Agency for Healthcare Research and Quality [AHRQ]. http://psnet.ahrq.gov/primer.aspx?primerID=6. Accessed November 23, 2014.

15. Handel DA, Wears RL, Nathanson LA. Using information technology to improve the quality and safety of emergency care. *Academy Emergency Medicine*. 2011;18:45-51.

16. Institute of Medicine [IOM]. *Health IT and Patient Safety*. Washington, DC: The National Academies Press, 2012.

17. Harrison JP, Daly MA. Leveraging health information technology to improve patient safety. *Public Administration & Management*. 2009;13(3):218-237.

18. Silow-Carroll S, Edwards JN, Rodin D. Using electronic health records to improve quality and efficiency: The experiences of leading hospitals. Issue Brief (Commonwealth Fund). 2012;17:1-40.

19. Kutney-Lee A, Kelly D. The effect of hospital electronic health record adoption on nurse-assessed quality of care and patient safety. *J Nurs Adm*. 2011;41(11):466-472.

20. Children's National Medical Center. (n.d.). Utilizing the EHR to achieve excellence. http://www.cerner.com/uploadedFiles/Content/Solutions/Customer_Stories/Childrens_national_medcenter_casestudy.pdf. Accessed November 23, 2014.

21. Institute of Medicine [IOM]. Crossing the Quality Chasm: A New Health System for the 21st century. Washington, DC: The National Academies Press, 2001.

22. Healthcare Information and Management Systems Society [HIMSS]. (2013). Texas Health Resources Selected as 2013 Enterprise HIMSS Davies Award Winner. http://www.himss.org/News/NewsDetail.aspx?ItemNumber=23066. Accessed November 23, 2014.

23. Healthcare-associated Infections. (n.d.) Center for Disease Control and Prevention. http://www.cdc.gov/HAI/surveillance/. Accessed November 23, 2014.

24. Pham JC, Aswani MS, Rosen M, et al. Reducing medical errors and adverse events. *The Annu Rev Med*. 2012;63:447-463.

25. Abramson EL, Kern LM, Brenner S, et al. Expert panel evaluation of health information technology effects on adverse events. *J Eval Clin Pract*. 2014;20(4):375-382. doi: 10.1111/jep.12139.

26. Agency for Healthcare Research and Quality [AHRQ]. (2009). Reduction in hospital-acquired complications and infections. http://healthit.ahrq.gov/sites/default/files/docs/page/09-0097.pdf. Accessed November 24, 2014.

27. Lo E, Nicolle LE, Coffin SE, et al. Strategies to prevent catheter-associated urinary tract infections in acute care hospitals: 2014 update. *Infect Control Hosp Epidemiol*. 2014;35(5):464-479.

28. Nguyen H, Siefkin A. (2013). University of California, Davis health system – Davies Enterprise Award submission. http://himss.cmsplus.com/files/FileDownloads/2013%20Enterprise%20Award_UC%20Davis%20Medical%20Center%20CLINICAL%20VALUE.pdf. Accessed November 24, 2014.

29. Kaiser Permanente. (2014). HIMSS Analytics. http://www.himssanalytics.org/emram/stage7caseStudyKP.aspx. Accessed November 24, 2014.

30. LaTour KM, Maki SE, Oachs PK. *Health Information Management: Concepts, Principles, and Practice*. Chicago, IL: American Health Information Management Association, 2013.

31. Brown GD, Patrick TB, Pasupathy KS. *Health Informatics: A Systems Perspective*. Chicago, IL: Health Administration Press, 2013.

32. Clinical decision support. (2013). HealthIT.gov. http://www.healthit.gov/policy-researchers-implementers/clinical-decision-support-cds. Accessed November 23, 2014.

33. Welden L. Electronic health record: Driving evidence-based catheter-associated urinary tract infections (CAUTI) care practices. *The Online Journal of Issues in Nursing*. 2013;18(3).

34. What is interoperability. (2013). HIMSS. http://www.himss.org/library/interoperability-standards/what-is. Accessed November 23, 2014.

35. Merrill JA, Deegan M, Wilson RV, et al. A system dynamics evaluation model: Implementation of health information exchange for public health reporting. *J Am Med Inform Assoc*. 2013;20(e1):e131-e138.

36. Keystone Beacon Community. (2012). HealthIT.gov. http://www.healthit.gov/sites/default/files/beacon-factsheet-keystone.pdf. Accessed November 23, 2014.

37. Dolan. (2012). New technology coming to boost preventive care. Amednews.com. http://www.amednews.com/article/20120730/business/307309966/5/. Accessed November 23, 2014.

38. Marvasti FF, Stafford RS. From sick care to health care – Reengineering prevention into the U.S. system. *New Engl J Med.* 2012;367(10):889-891.

39. Ahmad FS, Tsang T. Diabetes prevention, health information technology, and meaningful use: Challenges and opportunities. *Am J Prev Med.* 2013;44(4S4):S357-S363.

40. Bangor Beacon Community. (2012). HealthIT.gov. http://www.healthit.gov/sites/default/files/beacon-factsheet-bangor.pdf. Accessed November 23, 2014.

41. HIMSS 2012 Enterprise Davies Award. http://himss.cms-plus.com/files/FileDownloads/2012%20Enterprise%20Award_Mount%20Sinai%20Medical%20Center%20CLINICAL%20VALUE.pdf. Accessed November 23, 2014.

42. Galbraith KL. What's so meaningful about meaningful use? *Hastings Cent Rep.* 2013;43(2):15-17.

43. Leonard K, Mitchell S, Shaw N, et al. (2009). Central Ottawa family medicine associates. EMR Case Studies Research Project Case Study Report. https://www.cma.ca/multimedia/CMA/Content_Images/Inside_cma/Future_Practice/May2009/ottawa-full-e.pdf. Availity. (2014). Accessed November 23, 2014.

44. Availity achieves outstanding first quarter growth; broad network expansion. http://www.availity.com/availity-achieves-outstanding-first-quarter-growth/. Accessed November 23, 2014.

45. Robertson S. (2012). HIMSS Davies Enterprise application. http://himss.cms-plus.com/files/FileDownloads/2012%20Enterprise%20Award_Hawai'i%20Pacific%20Health%20ROI.pdf). Accessed November 23, 2014.

46. Fleming NS, Becker ER, Culler SD, et al. The impact of electronic health records on workflow and financial measures in primary care practices. *Health Serv Res.* 2014;49(1):405-420.

47. All Island Gastroenterology. (2013). HealthIT.gov. http://www.healthit.gov/providers-professionals/group-practice/all-island-gastroenterology. Accessed November 23, 2014.

48. Rhode Island Quality Institute. (n.d.). Rhode Island Quality Institute. http://www.docehrtalk.org/case-study/ehr-implementation/guide-successful-ehr-implementation. Accessed November 23, 2014.

49. McAlearney AS, Robbins J, Hirsch A, et al. Perceived efficiency impacts following electronic health record implementation: An exploratory study of an urban community health center network. *Int J Med Inform.* 2010;79(12):807-816.

50. Leading Age Case. (2012). A Leading Age CAST Report. http://www.leadingage.org/uploadedFiles/Content/About/CAST/Resources/CAST_EHR_Case_Studies-2012.pdf. Accessed November 23, 2014.

CHAPTER 2

Personal Health Engagement

Jan Oldenburg

INTRODUCTION

Patient engagement is acknowledged to be a critical issue in heathcare transformation. It has moved beyond the boundaries of the hospital, clinic, and insurer—as Regina Benjamin, MD, former U.S. Surgeon General, noted in March 2011, "It's not just in the doctor's office. It's got to be where we live, we work, we play, we pray."[1]

Part of the evolution in thinking about patient engagement is the recognition that health is intensely personal, a critical dimension of people's whole lives, not limited to their role as patients within the healthcare system. This allows us to look more broadly at what it means to be engaged with your own health, as well as the health of your family, friends, and community—and how digital tools can support you in all these dimensions. Much of the available research, however, is still focused on patient engagement—the way people interact within the healthcare system. As a consequence, this chapter will talk both about personal health engagement and patient engagement.

Many forces are converging today to force changes in the healthcare system, but four have special impact on consumers' attitudes and perspectives about health and healthcare:

- The rise of consumerism and personal empowerment in our society as a whole means that individuals are coming to their healthcare experiences expecting to be treated and cared for as individuals and partners.
- The rise of digital tools and ubiquitous access to technology and information globally creates expectations that the same capabilities people use in their everyday lives will be available to them to manage their health.
- In the United States, consumers are paying a much more significant part of their healthcare costs, which means that individuals expect to be able to research prices; understand ahead of time what treatments will cost; receive timely, clear and straightforward bills; and pay in convenient ways.
- The quantified self movement involves a small percentage of consumers who use digital tools to track their health and life extensively. The concepts of the quantified self movement are becoming mainstream, with nearly 21 percent of

the U.S. population using applications or devices to track their health and wellness.[2] All of these factors together are driving change that promises to be a key lever in health system transformation.

In healthcare, we have tended to assess a person's level of engagement based primarily on whether he/she is compliant with the plan of care that we've created. In short, we have assumed that patient engagement is synonymous with compliance. We have taught people to believe that in relation to the healthcare system, their role is to be passive and obedient. We have only recently begun to see that the ideal of "compliant" patients needs to shift if we are going to see patients who take responsibility for their health. Today many consumers expect to be in control even when they are patients in the healthcare system. They expect to be treated as partners who have a say in what happens. They expect digital tools that will make interacting with the healthcare system easier. They may even choose self-service, telehealth, or other do-it-yourself (DIY) services rather than consulting a traditional doctor in a traditional healthcare system.

The healthcare system is gradually responding to these changes. In 2011, the Center for Advancing Health (CFAH) published a new definition of patient engagement as part of their "Engaging Behavior Framework." They defined patient engagement as follows:

> Actions individuals must take to obtain the greatest benefit from the health care services available to them. This definition focuses on behaviors of individuals relative to their health care that are critical and proximal to health outcomes, rather than the actions of professionals or policies of institutions.[3]

Engagement is not synonymous with compliance. As described by CFAH,

> Compliance means an individual obeys a directive from a healthcare provider. Engagement signifies that a person is involved in a process through which he or she harmonizes robust information and professional advice with his or her own needs, preferences, and abilities in order to prevent, manage, and cure disease.[3]

To extend this thinking to incorporate personal health engagement, as well as patient engagement, we would modify CFAH's definition as follows: "Personal health engagement signifies that a person is involved in a process through which he or she harmonizes robust information, professional advice, and tools available to him/her with his or her own needs, preferences, and abilities in order to live healthily and prevent, manage and cure disease as an individual, caregiver, patient, and community member."

Personal health and patient engagement are significant because when individuals take responsibility for their care, all dimensions of the Triple Aim are affected in positive ways:

- Improving the individual experience of care (including quality and satisfaction);
- Improving the health of populations; and
- Reducing the per capita costs of care for populations.[4]

In this chapter, we will show the impact that personal health tools are having on improving engagement in all of these dimensions of care.

CURRENT STATUS OF PERSONAL HEALTH IT

For more than 10 years, consumers and patients have said they are interested in having access to their own healthcare data and the ability to email their doctors, as well. Only recently is this becoming a reality for many Americans.

The increased level of access is directly related to the increase in implementations of electronic health record (EHR) systems in physician offices and in hospitals. This increase is supported in the United States by the Meaningful Use (MU) provisions of the American Recovery and Reinvestment Act of 2009 (ARRA), which first encouraged doctors to begin using EHR systems in the MU Stage 1 goals. When health data are digitized in EHR systems, it becomes liquid and easier to access, move around, and share. The Stage 2 regulations particularly encourage physicians and hospitals to share data with patients and families and develop secure methods to communicate with patients. Specifically, organizations seeking to achieve Meaningful Use 2 certification must be able to attest to the Meaningful Use Stage 2 Core Measures (see Table 2-1).[5]

These core MU components make it a priority for physicians and hospitals to provide consumers with direct access to their personal health records (PHRs) and the ability to send a secure message to members of their care team. If knowledge is power, the unequal distribution of knowledge in healthcare has been one of the things that has kept patients at a disadvantage when interacting with their doctors. Providing direct access to clinical records is a key step in equalizing the balance of power between patients and their doctors.

Other recent actions on the part of the U.S. Department of Health and Human Services (HHS) have given additional support to the movement to provide patients with access to their clinical information. A 2013 letter from Leon Rodriguez, Director of the Office of Civil Rights, highlighted consumers' rights to their health information and the advantages of access to digital health records in helping consumers to be true partners in their own health and healthcare.[6] In addition, in early 2014, HHS announced an amendment to the Clinical Laboratory Improvement Amendments of 1988 (CLIA) rules "to allow laboratories to give a patient, or a person designated by the patient, his or her 'personal representative,' access to the patient's completed test reports on the

Table 2-1: Meaningful Use Stage 2 Core Measures

Core Measure	Objective	Measure(s)
7-**Patient Electronic Access** (EP and EH)	Provide patients the ability to view online, download and transmit their health information within four business days of the information being available to the EP or EH.	**Measure 1:** More than 50 percent of all unique patients seen by the EP during the EHR reporting period are provided timely (available to the patient within 4 business days after the information is available to the EP) online access to their health information. **Measure 2:** More than 5 percent of all unique patients seen by the EP during the EHR reporting period (or their authorized representatives) view, download, or transmit to a third party their health information.
17-**Secure Electronic Messaging** (EP only)	Use secure electronic messaging to communicate with patients on relevant health information.	**Measure:** A secure message was sent using the electronic messaging function of CEHRT by more than 5 percent of unique patients (or their authorized representatives) seen by the EP during the EHR reporting period.

Note: EH: eligible hospital; EP: eligible provider

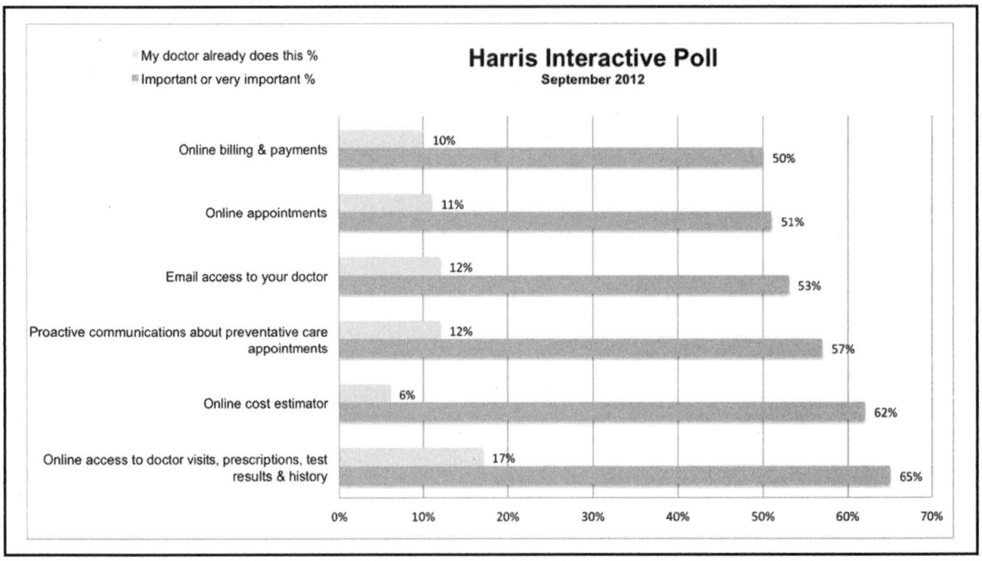

Figure 2-1: Patient Choice an Increasingly Important Factor in the Age of the "Healthcare Consumer"[8]

patient's or patient's personal representative's request."[7] While patients can still obtain laboratory results from their physicians, this amendment provides them a wider range of options.

In fall 2012, a Harris Interactive poll showed a wide disparity between the number of Americans who wanted access to digital information and capabilities from their providers and the number who actually had such access. Excerpted results from this poll are shown in Figure 2-1.

These statistics seem to be changing rapidly, partly due to the MU provisions and other factors noted earlier. A year after the Harris Interactive survey, in fall 2013, an Accenture survey found that more than a third of the U.S. consumers surveyed now said they had online access to their records,[9] in contrast to the 17 percent who had such access in the Harris Interactive poll. The same two polls also suggest that while the levels of access to care are rising, the percentage of consumers who want such access is also rising. For example, in the Harris Interactive survey, 53 percent said they wanted email access to their doctor; the Accenture study a year later showed that 77 percent wanted email access to their doctors.

While some of the statistics previously noted may be explained by different survey methodologies and different ways of framing questions, it is not surprising that consumers are looking for convenient services from the healthcare system, as they use similar technologies in managing the rest of their lives. Approximately 87 percent of consumers worldwide book travel online.[10] A similar study from Pew Research in January 2014 showed that 81 percent of those who managed household finances banked online at least once in the past 12 months.[11] Shopping online has been growing in favor, and for the first time, in fall 2013, consumers told Deloitte that online would be their favorite shopping destination for the holidays.[12] Many of these activities are now being conducted from smartphones while consumers are mobile. It is no wonder that consumers, patients, caregivers, and family members expect the same level of 24/7 capabilities to be available from their healthcare providers and insurers as well.

That expectation translates into action. The Accenture survey previously quoted shows that 41 percent of surveyed patients who rank access to their records online as important or very important would consider shifting doctors to have that access. Separate studies have shown slightly higher statistics: In 2011, Intuit found that nearly 50 percent of consumers surveyed would switch doctors to gain access to digital tools,[13] and in a 2011 survey, Deloitte found that 66 percent would consider such a change.[14] As a corollary, a Kaiser Permanente study published in the *Journal of Managed Care* in June 2012 found that patients with access to the EHR's patient portal, My Health Manager, were 2.6 times more likely than nonusers to remain Kaiser Permanente members if given an option to switch plans.[15] In healthcare, as in other industries, convenience translates to loyalty.

In addition, people are increasingly using wearable devices, smartphone applications, and social media to engage with and about their health outside of the constraints of the healthcare system. In its January 2013 report on tracking for health, Pew Internet found that 69 percent of adults track a health indicator for themselves or others. Of that 69 percent, 34 percent use non-technological methods such as notebooks or journals and 21 percent of individuals who track use at least one form of technology such as apps or devices.[16]

LINK BETWEEN USE OF DIGITAL TOOLS AND ENGAGEMENT

There is no single perfect study showing how use of digital tools directly raises consumer and patient activation and engagement regarding their health. Nonetheless, emerging research highlights strong correlations between use of digital tools and engagement rates.

Judith Hibbard, PhD, developed the Patient Activation Measure (PAM) as a way to measure differences in individual level of activation about health. Since its inception, the measure has been used in a variety of studies that show more highly activated patients, as assessed by the PAM score, correlate to better healthcare outcomes, lower costs, and higher satisfaction with the healthcare system. Qualitative research suggests that patients who are highly activated view themselves as working in partnership with professionals, whereas patients who are at low levels of activation view their role as one of compliance. Dr. Hibbard's research has also shown that higher activation levels are correlated to likelihood of using digital tools. Her research indicates that providers were 30 percent more likely to recommend use of a patient portal to highly activated patients compared with patients at low levels of activation. Among patients whose providers recommended use of the patient portal, highly activated patients were 20 percent more likely to take them up on the offer than less activated patients.[17]

New research indicates that digital tools not only support already-activated patients, but also help individuals increase their activation levels. A 2012 study published in the *Journal of Medical Internet Research* randomly assigned patients with chronic diseases either to 12 weeks of access to Internet-based education or to a full online portal with access to their clinical record, My Health Record. After 12 weeks, the group assigned access to My Health Record had statistically significant improvements in their activation levels over the control group. The study also noted that the effects were more significant for people who started with lower activation levels.[18]

Another study was part of an IT Challenge Grant awarded by ONC to Indiana Health Information Technology in 2011. The project focused on a small group of 200 patients who either had a cardiac stent implanted or had undergone bypass surgery. Each individual was set up and trained on the NoMoreClipboard PHR application, and their Patient Activation Measure scores were assessed both before and after they had used the PHR. Michael Mirro, MD, a cardiac electrophysiologist at Parkview Physicians Group and medical director at Parkview Research Center, noted that based on the Patient Activation Measure, "We found that those patients, if they used a PHR, were definitely more engaged than a control group. Even better," says Mirro, "we could demonstrate in that study that patients were more engaged in their care, but also that some of their intermediate outcomes were improved, such as their LDL-[low-density lipoprotein] cholesterol, and hemoglobin A1c."[19] The same organization is now sharing defibrillator information directly to cardiac patients, which has additional promise as a way to engage and educate patients about their conditions.

In February 2013, the *Journal of Internet Research* published a study that reviewed existing literature to examine the effect of Web-based interventions on self-efficacy and self-management.[20] The study authors concluded: "Our review suggests that Web-based, interactive interventions have a beneficial effect on patient empowerment and/or physical activity in people with various chronic conditions. Program elements that were frequently observed included education, self-monitoring, feedback/tailored information, self-management training, personal exercise program, and communication (with either healthcare providers or fellow patients). Although the results of these studies did not necessarily differ from those of traditional interventions, it is likely that the elements increased patient centeredness and efficiency of the interventions."

Similarly, a recent Veterans Administration (VA) study with Sue Woods, MD, as the lead author reported on a series of focus groups with VA participants who had access both to their clinical record and to physician notes. The study authors found that access to digital health records including notes increased self-management and a sense of self-efficacy. They summarized their findings as follows:

> Our findings support prior qualitative research that shows full health record access is empowering for patients and caregivers. Patients' perspectives provide insight into how shared notes can foster active patient participation in their care. In all focus groups, participants put knowledge from their records to use by learning more about their health issues, gaining more knowledge about their providers' views, and advocating for themselves in discussions about their care… Records were also a starting place for online research. As a result, patients felt more prepared for clinic visits but sometimes were also less likely to call the clinic or request an appointment. Of particular interest were stories of patients serving as their own "clinical reminders," making an effort to improve the quality of their care by ensuring follow-up care was provided.[21]

This is a fast-growing area of study, and we expect that further research will continue to support the link between use of Internet and mobile tools and corresponding increases in patient activation, feelings of empowerment and self-efficacy regarding their health, and improved health outcomes.

HEALTH INFORMATION SEEKING

The most common digital activity that people do for their health is search for health information on the Internet. By any measure, this should be considered engagement, as it speaks to individuals looking for information about their own or someone else's health status. There is a deep connection between people's health literacy—the ability to understand and make decisions about care and treatment—and engagement with their health. The extent of searches for health information can be read as an indicator of a deep hunger to understand health, wellness, and illnesses.

While always having been aware that people are used to getting information and referrals about medical issues from friends and neighbors "over the back fence," they are now demonstrating that propensity online. Susannah Fox noted in January 2014 that the latest Pew Internet Survey findings show, "Seven in ten (72%) adult Internet users say they have searched online for information about a range of health issues, the most popular being specific diseases and treatments. One in four (26%) adult Internet users say they have read or watched someone else's health experience about health or medical issues in the past 12 months. And 16 percent of adult Internet users in the U.S. have gone online in the past 12 months to find others who share the same health concerns."[22] Fox goes on to say that one of the enduring findings of the Pew Research Center is that health search is social—more than half of all health searches online are performed on behalf of someone else, even by people with multiple chronic conditions.

In addition, PatientsLikeMe offers a model of engagement that highlights peer-to-peer sharing of information about treatments, medications, and conditions. Patients agree to participate and must agree that their anonymous data will be shared openly. They highlight their "Openness Philosophy" rather than their privacy policy, and state, "Because when patients share real-world data, collaboration on a global scale becomes possible. New treatments become possible. Most importantly, change becomes possible. At PatientsLikeMe, we are passionate about bringing people together for a greater purpose: speeding up the pace of research and fixing a broken healthcare system."[23]

The site not only allows patients and caregivers to find support and information about their conditions and medications, it is emerging as a significant resource to researchers. PatientsLikeMe is experimenting with crowdsourcing research to incorporate patients in both design and funding of studies. This innovative model is shifting the ways that patients, researchers, and the healthcare system overall think about research.[23]

There is reason to be concerned that people may find inappropriate, false, or misleading health information online, or be unduly influenced by ads offered in conjunction with health information. There is also a need to create reliable health information in multiple languages so that non-English speakers can engage appropriately around their health. In general, however, the behavior of health information seekers online should give us hope about the desire people have for reliable and curated information to support their health journeys. New models of learning and research such as Patients-

LikeMe, as well as a wide variety of applications focused on delivering personalized and targeted education, offer hope that the journey to health literacy can be enhanced as a critical first step in patient engagement.

Patient and Consumer Engagement Impacts All Dimensions of the Triple Aim

As noted earlier, activation and engagement matter because they affect all dimensions of the Triple Aim. With digital tools we can effect changes to the healthcare system that increase convenience for patients and their families while improving the quality of care, the cost of care, and the experience of care.

DIGITAL HEALTH ENGAGEMENT IMPACT ON QUALITY

As more people gain access to their records via digital means, evidence is emerging that is having a positive impact on quality and outcomes. We discussed earlier the way that access to digital records has been shown to increase self-efficacy and self-management. In addition, there are specific indications that digital patient engagement increases quality of care. The VA noted in a study of Open Notes that patients with access to their health record, including clinical notes, feel more in control of their health.[24] Geisinger, as well as other participants in the Open Notes study, reported that patients with access to open notes are more likely to find and report errors in their record along with a wide variety of other positive impacts that included feeling more in control of their care, being more cooperative with their medication regimen, and increasing efforts in self-care.[25]

A 2012 study funded by the Agency for Healthcare Research and Quality (AHRQ) found that patients who used interactive health records were almost twice as likely to be up to date on recommended preventive care, including screening tests for breast, colon, and cervical cancers, and immunizations like the yearly flu shot. After 16 months, a quarter of patients who used the online records were up-to-date on their preventive care—double the rate of non-users.[26]

Several Kaiser Permanente studies also indicate correlations between portal use and improved outcomes. A study published in 2014, funded by the National Institutes of Health, concluded that diabetic Kaiser Permanente members who used only online tools to refill their medications were more likely to be cooperative with their medication regimen and get positive associated outcomes. Compared with portal users who did not refill medications online, adherence to statin medications and LDL levels improved among diabetic patients who initiated and exclusively used the patient portal for refills, suggesting that wider adoption of online refills may improve adherence.[27]

Another retrospective Kaiser Permanente study noted that children whose parents used Kaiser's online portal were 2.5 times more likely to attend all well-child visits.[28] A third Kaiser Permanente study published in *Health Affairs* indicated that diabetic patients who used the portal to securely message their physicians had higher HEDIS [Healthcare Effectiveness Data and Information Set] scores than non-users.[29]

Finally, transparent access to health records, as well as secure messaging with the care team seems to increase components of a healing relationship between patients and providers. A number of studies in the early 2000s indicated that there are correlations between the level of trust patients have in physicians and their medical outcomes. Specific components associated with a healing relationship include trust, hope, and the feeling of being known. These factors are enabled by the way physicians interact with their patients. Those who are good at engendering trust do the following things: show patients they value them by being present and making clear their empathy; mitigate the power relationship by treating the patient as a partner, educating, and sometimes pushing them; and abide with the patient by being present across time and through major events, by not giving up, and demonstrating caring through actions.[30]

These behaviors can translate into digital relationships as well. The ability to reach out to one's provider online, as well as the potential to receive reminders, information, and encouragement between visits may positively impact a person's sense of being known and can provide a sense of the caring and abiding presence of the physician. The TeleVox Healthy World study, "Technology Beyond the Exam Room," reported that, "Of the 66 percent of patients who have received a voicemail, text, or email from a healthcare provider, many reported a variety of positive outcomes. Fifty-one percent reported feeling more valued as a patient, 35 percent said digital communication improved their opinion of their provider, and 34 percent reported feeling more certain about visiting that healthcare provider again."[31]

All of these factors highlight the impact that patient engagement can have on the quality of care and the development of healing relationships between patients and providers.

DIGITAL HEALTH ENGAGEMENT IMPACT ON COST

The holy grail of healthcare has been the hope that engaged and activated patients will take better care of themselves, reducing the progression of disease and impacting the cost of care in positive ways. There are strong indications that digital tools can support these outcomes. As previously noted, evidence indicates that patients who use digital services or whose caregivers use them are more likely to be up to date on preventive care services and take their medications as planned. Judith Hibbard has also demonstrated that more highly activated patients actually make better health decisions.[32]

In addition to the advantages from a clinical standpoint, self-service features such as appointment scheduling, online prescription refill requests, pre-visit registration capabilities, and online bill-payment programs can save health systems money while increasing satisfaction with the system. As noted earlier, other industries have introduced a variety of self-service tools over the past two decades, often finding that the shift from full service to self-service reduces costs by a factor of 10:1. When consumers can complete activities such as these online—at a time that is convenient for them, their satisfaction levels rise.

Health economists and health plans have been working on benefit designs that support and nudge consumers to make wise, as well as cost-conscious, decisions regarding medical care by taking into account the principles of behavioral economics. They are using a potent combination of incentives, transparent cost and quality data, and responsibility for a growing share of cost to help consumers take more responsibility for healthcare costs. In part as a consequence of this work, the last 10 years have seen a significant rise in the amount consumers pay for their healthcare. A study by the Kaiser

Family Foundation found these increases to be significant: the employee contribution to premium fees increased by 89 percent between 2003 and 2013 while the percentage of employees in plans with deductibles of $1,000 or more went from 16 percent in 2006 to 58 percent in 2013.[33]

Although consumers bear a higher percentage of healthcare costs and are interested in spending their money wisely, it is difficult to make cost-conscious health decisions today. One reason is the lack of easily available (and comparable) information about cost. Another reason is that they tend to use the cost of medical services as a proxy for their quality.[34] This equation, which works effectively in the rest of their purchasing decisions, does not work particularly well in healthcare, where there are wide variations in the cost and quality of specific procedures, where appropriate care may mean less rather than more intervention, and a consumer's experience may not fully translate to the best clinical care. Until we provide consumers with a straightforward way to understand the intersection of cost and quality, along with cost estimation and cost transparency—tools that fully reflect the effect of both variations in plan design and variations in treatment effectiveness—we may not see the full benefits of creating a consumer marketplace in healthcare.

The picture of shifting costs also means that consumers are looking for more convenient ways to pay healthcare bills. This is no easy feat in a situation where provider and hospital bills come on monthly cycles while claims are resolved as they are submitted. It is confusing to try to reconcile the Explanation of Benefits (EOBs) coming from your insurer with the bills coming from your provider to determine what is actually due and appropriate to pay, especially in the middle of a healthcare crisis or its aftermath. Tools that help consumers understand and reconcile bills with claims or—better yet—back-end innovations that eliminate this discrepancy would significantly reduce the stress of handling healthcare financials for many consumers. United Health Group has taken an innovative approach to this problem, allowing consumers to pay providers what is owed after insurance processing directly from the myuhc.com website, eliminating confusion about what is owed to whom.

With more of their revenue coming from consumers rather than payers, healthcare systems need to increase payment convenience—both to increase consumer satisfaction and to reduce the cost of collection. Many consumers, faced with bearing more cost for healthcare, may need payment plans to allow them to pay high deductibles over time. A Harvard Study from 2009 estimated that approximately 62 percent of U.S. bankruptcies are due to healthcare costs.[35] Nerd Wallet updated that study in 2013 and found similar numbers. Even with more people in health insurance plans due to the Affordable Care Act (ACA), a high deductible can overwhelm a family hovering on the edge of financial disaster.[36] Healthcare systems that offer convenient, online ways to predict costs, pay bills, apply for payment plans, or otherwise finance the cost of care are likely to find positive impacts in consumer satisfaction, as well as rise in payments collected.

DIGITAL HEALTH ENGAGEMENT LINKED TO SATISFACTION AND LOYALTY

Access to digital tools is only one dimension of the overall patient experience, albeit an emerging and important one. Organizations that understand the importance of focusing on providing seamless care centered on helping and supporting patients and families are well positioned to build both trust and loyalty. Existence of the Medicare Stars program, as well as increasing attention to JD Powers health rankings and Net Promoter Scores, means health plans are paying more attention to consumer satisfaction. At the same time, patient satisfaction is a factor in the payment infrastructure for new Centers for Medicare & Medicaid Services (CMS) programs, which means providers are also focusing attention on consumer and patient satisfaction and loyalty.

Convenience and digital access build loyalty and "stickiness" by increasing the perceived cost of switching providers or plans.[37] The impact of these loyalty features is multidimensional. Patients who feel loyal and value convenience are more likely to stay inside the system for care, enabling better care coordination and reducing duplicative tests and procedures. New models of care put providers at risk for the care of their population of patients, wherever the patients get care, and building loyalty via convenience is one of the ways to support this requirement. "'If we're not able to limit [leakage], it makes it harder to...manage the entire population to the best of our capabilities," says Reinhold Llerena, MD, medical director of Arlington Heights, Illinois-based Alexian Brothers Accountable Care Organization, a Medicare Shared Savings ACO (accountable care organization).'"[38]

There are many opportunities for health systems to benefit from these correlations. Expanding the use of self-scheduling, online bill payment, and electronic prescription refill are some of the early wins for healthcare, but their use could be expanded still further. Some of the most promising of these opportunities focus on pre-check-in, by allowing patients or caregivers to confirm health and coverage information ahead of time rather than while sitting in the waiting room. Susan Kressly, MD, (@kiddrsue) reported in a conference panel and on Twitter that her clinic gives preferential treatment to those who complete forms online by taking them directly back to the exam room; one result is that the visit can begin with the patient's, rather than the doctor's, questions.

MOBILE AND SOCIAL CAPABILITIES

Mobile applications, especially when combined with tracking or monitoring devices, offer great promise for improving consumers' engagement with their health. In 2014, at least 60 percent of U.S. adults had a smartphone and 90 percent had a cell phone. There are indications from several Pew Internet studies that many individuals in underserved populations are likely to use a smartphone as their main source of Internet access.[39] With this widespread availability comes the opportunity to extend healthcare capabilities into daily lives and daily routines.

Part of the promise of mobile technologies for healthcare is that people carry their mobiles with them almost all the time—including 44 percent who sleep with their phone near their bed so as not to miss updates during the night.[40] As Predrag Klasnja and Wanda Prat note in "Healthcare in the Pocket: Mapping the Space of Mobile-phone Health Interventions,"[41] there are four reasons that smartphones offer such promise as behavior change tools:

1. Increasingly, everyone has a mobile phone; at least 60 percent of the U.S. population now has a smartphone.
2. People carry phones on their person or near them almost all of the time, which makes them useful for health-related reminders and interventions at many points in a person's day.
3. They are very personal devices, which may reduce barriers to acceptance of interventions delivered through their devices.
4. The built-in technology and increasing sophistication of the devices mean that they have information about a person's context, which can make them particularly able to deliver targeted messages that are relevant in real time and contextually appropriate.

Consumers, application developers, health plans, and providers alike are exploring ways to use mobile devices in health contexts to exploit these opportunities to help individuals monitor and manage their health, as well as to perform tasks in conjunction with their healthcare system. One of the simplest usages is text-based alerts and reminders. For example, a consumer might sign up for access to texts about when it is time to refill prescriptions, to remind him/her of scheduled appointments, or to receive positive messages about meeting health goals. Studies show these have merit for keeping people up to date on their preventive health services, medicines, and prescription refills. Geisinger, for example, implemented a six-week program with motivational messages for weight loss delivered by text messages. They found that patients participating in the pilot program averaged a 0.5 greater body mass index (BMI) loss than nonparticipants and participated in their care plans to a greater degree than nonparticipants. The program was so successful that Geisinger has rolled it out systemwide and is working on additional text-based programs to support other care management initiatives.[42]

Many health systems venture into the mobile space by offering capabilities similar to those available through their web portal. These may include access to one's health data, the ability to make or view appointments, the ability to securely message one's doctor, and the ability to find a clinical location. Having these capabilities while mobile seems to improve access to capabilities overall, though data on adoption levels of specific applications is sparse. It is suggestive, however, that Kaiser Permanente surpassed 1 million downloads of its mobile software in June 2014.[43] Another Kaiser Permanente presentation referenced the fact that 25 percent of registered kp.org users now access their data via mobile tools.[44]

Health systems and start-ups alike are exploring ways to use mobile devices to stay connected with people about their health, especially during the 90 percent of time when individuals are not interacting directly with the health system, including sending encouragement and timely information, as well as gathering key data that can help keep people out of the hospital or help them achieve health goals.

People are also downloading fitness and weight/diet tracking apps. They are using mobile devices that interact with their phones and computers, such as Fitbit and Jaw-Bone. All of this indicates an interest in being involved with health. Nielsen's 2014 Connected Life Report found that "Nearly one-third of U.S. smartphone owners—about 46 million unique users—accessed apps in the fitness and health category in January 2014, an 18 percent increase in users compared with the same month a year earlier."[45]

The bad news, however, is that most of these capabilities fail to have sustained engagement. Endeavour Partners' research reveals that more than half of U.S. consumers who have owned a modern activity tracker no longer use it. A third of U.S. consumers who have owned one stopped using the device within six months of receiving it.[46] A retrospective study looked at users of The Eatery app, a free app designed to help people eat more healthily. The study found that dropout rates were high and sustained usage low. Only 2.58 percent actively used the application. Another study from 2010 to 2011 found that across all applications launched on smartphones, health apps represented only 26 percent of all launches compared with the nearly 50 percent of all launches that focus on communication applications.[47]

There is some good news. In the past, Flurry, which tracks mobile usage, observed that apps in the health and fitness category grew more slowly than the general growth of apps. In the first half of 2014, health and fitness app usage exploded, growing 62 percent compared with the general market at 33 percent, perhaps indicating that health and fitness apps reached a tipping point.[48]

Social media is an important part of the engagement picture as well. It serves as a channel consumers can use for everything from obtaining information about their health to critiquing the care they get to managing both acute and chronic illness. We have known that health is social. In fact, analysis of data from the Framingham study demonstrated that obesity is contagious, as are other bad health habits.[49]

Several recent studies have shown that healthy habits can be contagious as well—and that online social networks can support those behaviors.[50] A meta-analysis published in February 2014 concluded, "This review offers preliminary evidence that social networking-based health interventions may be effective in changing behavior."[51]

Increasingly, it is clear that the potential for digital tools to support behavior change lies not in the channel (web, mobile, or social) as much as the way media are combined to create rich, engaging, in-the-moment experiences. This is the process of engineering teachable moments that are personal, relevant, convenient, and contextual. In the future, we are likely to see less focus on the channel and more interesting combinations that involve social capabilities seamlessly delivered on multiple platforms, so that users can interact with whatever channel is most convenient for them at any given time. We are also likely to see capabilities that incorporate tracking, social support, direct access to personal clinical information and provider support, personalized education, and competition. Applications with these intertwined elements are already emerging, especially in some of the apps that incorporate game-playing technologies.

Gamification is defined by Merriam-Webster as "the process of adding games or game-like elements to something (as a task) so as to encourage participation."[52] While the concept has been around for some time, the word is a product of the digital age, with the first known use in 2010. When applied in healthcare, it represents the process of using appealing (and potentially addicting) techniques from the world of games to help people get engaged with their health. Not everyone is motivated in the same way, but engaging game-like applications can have any number of desirable effects when applied to health: motivation, participation, a sense of mastery, and a sense of community.

The field is so promising that a number of major healthcare companies have been making significant investments in gamification strategies. Optum, a subsidiary of UnitedHealth Group, for example, recently purchased a majority interest in Audax, which it will operate as a freestanding subsidiary. Audax told *MobiHealth News* that the strategy would not change its existing customer relationships, even with UHG competitors like Cigna, whose CIO sits on the Audax board and which has a 5-year strategic alliance with Audax "to develop a customized digital engagement platform designed to help our customers improve their health through fun and engaging health-related activities and information."[53]

Blue Shield of California launched Wellvolution in 2009, which incorporated a well-being score that can be measured over time, a daily challenge, and the ability to ask friends and family for support. The program aims to be rewarding, easy, social, and fun, and incorporates products like Walkadoo, Healthrageous, and Shape Up Shield as initiatives employers can choose to keep people healthy.[54] Wellvolution participants pay $3 million less in insurance premiums than those who choose to not participate and have reduced their rates of smoking by 50 percent and the prevalence of hypertension by 66 percent.[55]

Keas provides a social platform with incentives and games built in that employers can easily roll out to their employees. Keas clients report benefits that include both statistically significant improvements in health and positive increases in teamwork and attitude.[56]

Humana has also experimented with a range of health-focused games. They include several apps that encourage exercise, Goldwalker and Colorfall; the Humana Horsepower Challenge, a game for school teams that challenges sedentary kids; and an Xbox Kinnect video game with partner Ubisoft that offers players a variety of fitness activities, from cardio boxing to yoga.[57]

The Wall Street Journal, reporting on the gamification trend in April 2014, noted that "UnitedHealth Group offers a free app, called OptumizeMe, for iPhones, Android phones, and Microsoft Windows Phone 7. The app, available to the general public, allows people to earn digital badges as virtual rewards for health efforts, working individually or as a group."[58] Kaiser Permanente has experimented with games to encourage exercise, teach children food choices, and help patients manage chronic diseases. Aetna has introduced "Mindbloom" as a life improvement resource.

In addition, a number of start-ups—some already partnering with payers—are creating games focused on various aspects of health, ranging from managing conditions like asthma and diabetes (CoHero Health, Ayogo) to staying fit, meeting health goals (Utilifit, Gympact), providing education (Syandus, GameMetrix), and encouraging employee wellness (Audax, Welltok, Hubbub).

As previously noted, one of the most promising elements of the introduction of game-playing tools is the way that they combine numerous strategies that are known to positively impact behavior change, engagement, and stickiness; these include social support, competition, the ability to track achievements over time, and, importantly, fun.

THE FUTURE OF PERSONAL HEALTH ENGAGEMENT

The future is bright for personal health engagement. Fueled by the changes in society and technological capabilities, it is here to stay as a focus for health transformation. Although we have made great progress using digital tools to support and encourage personal health engagement, we also have a considerable distance to travel—partly to make these tools accessible to everyone and partly to improve our ability to help people make and sustain behavior changes.

Looking forward, we make the following predictions about personal health engagement:

- **Healthcare value.** Consumer share of cost will drive increasing attention to cost transparency in healthcare, with a variety of tools designed to help consumers understand the appropriate price for a service and compare prices. If we are lucky, the conversation will not just be about cost, but about value. Fueled with data, new tools will emerge to help consumers understand quality, efficacy, and cost tradeoffs to become informed consumers.
- **Personal health analytics.** Big data analytic tools that enable a deeper understanding of patterns of disease and causality, combined with gene sequencing and quantified self-tracking, will enable individuals to obtain in-the-moment personalized analysis of the state of their health. When combined with emerging tools that enable accurate measurement of the calories in food and drink, as well as more accurate wearables to track and measure caloric expenditure and location, there is the potential for moment-by-moment predictive analytics at a deeply personal level. When provided in sensitive ways that recognize who the person is and what motivates him/her, new tools may turn the tide on helping people make and sustain changes. With these capabilities will come far more attention to consumers' rights to choose what data are shared with whom—as well as more opportunities to trade privacy for increased privileges, such as lower costs or better access.
- **Interconnected care.** Changes in healthcare incentives and financing are already leading to more seamless care for patients at all of their healthcare interactions. This trend will accelerate, fueled by the rise in consolidated community data and quality measures that reward systems that get it right. These changes will give people more choices about where and when they get care and more opportunity to understand the full picture of their health. Consumers will also benefit from changes that allow them to receive more care at home, supported by remote monitoring and better community support. The same motivators will also enable more seamless, multi-channel, and interconnected care management programs where information is available to and shared between patients, caregivers, physicians, nurses, health coaches, and insurers—all focused on supporting individuals most appropriately in managing health and disease.
- **Convenience.** Payers and providers alike will find themselves competing as to who offers the most convenient experience. This will affect the channels available to consumers to complete healthcare interactions, the quality and quantity of do-it-yourself applications, and drive innovation around virtual medicine

capabilities. These changes will benefit consumers while reducing the cost of many healthcare services.

- **Attitude and culture change.** Individuals, health systems, providers, employers, and insurers are going through a gradual but inevitable change in perspective from viewing individuals as passive recipients of instructions and knowledge to viewing them as partners in wellness, treatment, and care. This shift from paternalism to independence will have long term positive impacts on helping people take responsibility for their health and healthcare. In addition, the bright line we have drawn between wellness and illness will fade, making it easier to understand the continuum between health and disease.

CONCLUSION

Although it is clear that people have good intentions about their health—perennial favorite New Year's resolutions are to lose weight, exercise more, eat healthier, stop smoking, and better manage stress—most of us fail to sustain those resolutions over time.[59] Many people wear tracking devices only for a short period of time or sporadically engage with health games and activities, programs designed to improve their health.

Rather than seeing the short-term nature of these engagements as a sign that people have little desire to engage around their health, we should still take hope from them. They indicate a hunger on the part of consumers to be more aware of their health and a belief that changes could make a significant difference in helping them live happier and healthier lives. What they also indicate is that we have not completely "cracked the code" on what helps people make and sustain behavior change to live happier and healthier lives.

New research is helping us better understand the science of motivation and change and how to create applications and digital tools that help us make such changes while eliciting support (and participation) from friends and family. Digital tools that help us understand our health, track health activities, and engage with the health system are increasingly available and are improving in providing interactions that raise people's knowledge and sense of empowerment. Interconnected data and interconnected systems raise the potential for understanding one's health over time and providing everyone—family, friends, care team members, health plans, and life sciences companies—with more complete information to support each individual's personal health goals.

Personal health engagement continues to emerge as an agent of transformation both for individuals and for the healthcare system as a whole.

REFERENCES

1. Brown E. Surgeon general discusses health and community. March 2011. http://articles.latimes.com/2011/mar/13/health/la-he-surgeon-general-20110313. Accessed March 2014.

2. Fox S, Duggan M. Tracking for health. January 2013. http://www.pewinternet.org/2013/01/28/tracking-for-health/. Accessed March 2014.

3. Grumman J, Holmes-Rovner M, French ME, et al. Patient engagement behavior framework: What is "patient engagement"? March 2010. http://www.cfah.org/pdfs/CFAH_Engagement_Behavior_Framework_current.pdf. Accessed April 2014.

4. Berwick D, Nolan T, Whittington J. The triple aim: care, health, and cost. May 2008. http://content.healthaffairs.org/content/27/3/759.full. Accessed May 2014.

5. Medicare and Medicaid Programs; Electronic health record incentive program—Stage 2. September 2012. Available from: http://www.gpo.gov/fdsys/pkg/FR-2012-09-04/pdf/2012-21050.pdf. Accessed April 2014.

6. http://www.hhs.gov/ocr/privacy/hipaa/understanding/consumers/righttoaccessmemo.pdf. Accessed August 2014.

7. http://www.hhs.gov/news/press/2014pres/02/20140203a.html. Accessed August 2014.

8. Harris Interactive; Patient choice; an increasingly important factor in the age of the healthcare consumer; September 2012. http://www.harrisinteractive.com/NewsRoom/HarrisPolls/tabid/447/ctl/ReadCustom%20Default/mid/1508/ArticleId/1074/Default.aspx. Accessed April 2014.

9. Accenture Consumer Survey on patient engagement: US Research Recap. September 2013; http://www.accenture.com/SiteCollectionDocuments/PDF/Accenture-Consumer-Patient-Engagement-Survey-US-Report.pdf. Accessed April 2014.

10. The New Online Travel Consumer. January 2014. http://blog.euromonitor.com/2014/01/webinar-the-new-online-travel-consumer.html. Accessed March 2014.

11. Fox S. 51% of U.S. adults bank online. August 2013. http://www.pewinternet.org/2013/08/07/51-of-u-s-adults-bank-online/. Accessed March 2014.

12. Deloitte Annual Holiday Survey: More consumers shopping mobile and local. November 2013. http://www.deloitte.com/view/en_US/us/press/Press-Releases/f916362e99d22410VgnVCM1000003256f70aRCRD.htm. Accessed March 2014.

13. Health Care Check-Up Survey: Intuit Health Survey: Americans worried about costs; want greater access to physicians. March 2011.www.intuit.com. Accessed March 2014.

14. Deloitte Center for Health Solutions. 2011 Survey of Health Care Consumers in the United States: Key findings, strategic implications. www.deloitte.com. Accessed March 2014.

15. Turley M, Garrido T, Lowenthal A, et al. Association between personal health record enrollment and patient loyalty. 2012. http://www.ajmc.com/publications/issue/2012/2012-7-vol18-n7. Accessed March 2014.

16. Fox S, Duggan M. Tracking for health. January 2013. http://www.pewinternet.org/2013/01/28/tracking-for-health/. Accessed March 2014.

17. Hibbard J, Sacks R, Overton V. When seeing the same physician, highly activated patients have better care experiences than less activated patients. December, 2013. http://heller.brandeis.edu/executive-education/pdfs/Jan2014MassMedDocs/DeborahGarnick/601CGreenJHealthAff2013Greene1299305.pdf . Accessed April 2014.

18. Solomon M, Wagner S, Goes J. Effects of a web-based intervention for adults with chronic conditions on patient activation: Online randomized controlled trial. February 2012. http://www.jmir.org/2012/1/e32/. Accessed May 2014.

19. Donnell J. Case Study: An HIE-populated personal health record for cardiac revascularization patients. May, 2014. https://www.nomoreclipboard.com/wiki/images/9/95/NMC_Case_Study_COPE.pdf. Accessed June 2014.

20. Eysenbach G. A Systematic review of web-based interventions for patient empowerment and physical activity in chronic diseases: Relevance for cancer survivors. February 2013. http://www.jmir.org/article/viewFile/jmir_v15i2e37/2. Accessed April 2014.

21. Woods S, Schwartz E, Tuepker A, et al. *Patient experiences with full electronic access to health records and clinical notes through the My HealtheVet Personal Health Record Pilot: Qualitative study.* March 2013. http://www.jmir.org/2013/3/e65/. Accessed April 2014.

22. Fox S. The social life of health information. January 2014. http://www.pewresearch.org/fact-tank/2014/01/15/the-social-life-of-health-information/. Accessed May 2014.

23. Patients Like Me Blog; *Patients like Me Research Outcomes*; 2014. www.patientslikeme.com. Accessed July 2014.

24. Woods S, Schwartz E, Tuepker A, et al. Patient experiences with full electronic access to health records and clinical notes through the My HealtheVet Personal Health Record Pilot: Qualitative study. March 2013. www.jmir.org. Accessed April 2014.

25. Delbanco T, Walker J, Bell S, et al. Inviting patients to read their doctors' notes: a quasi-experimental study and a loot ahead. *Ann Intern Med.* 2012;157(7):461-470.

26. Krist AH, Woolf SH, Rothemich SF, et al. Interactive preventive health record to enhance delivery of recommended care: A randomized trial. *Ann Fam Med.* 2012;10(4):312-319.

27. Sarkar U, Lyles C, Parker M. Use of the refill function through an online patient portal is associated with improved adherence to statins in an integrated health system. May 2014. http://journals.lww.com/lww-medicalcare/Fulltext/2014/05000/Use_of_the_Refill_Function_Through_an_Online.12.aspx. Accessed May 2014.

28. Tom J, Chen C, Zhou Y. Personal health record use and association with immunizations and well-child care visits recommendations. January 2014. http://download.journals.elsevierhealth.com/pdfs/journals/0022-3476/PIIS0022347613010743.pdf. Accessed May 2014.

29. Zhou Y, Kanter M, Wang J, et al. Improved quality at Kaiser Permanente through e-mail between physicians and patients. *Health Aff (Millwood).* 2010; 29(7):1370-1375.

30. Scott J, Cohen D, DiCicco-Bloom B, et al. Understanding healing relationships in primary care. *Ann Fam Med.*, 2008;6,4; July/August 2008 315. www.annfammed.org. Accessed May 2014.

31. Zimmerman, S. Technology beyond the exam room. April 2013. www.televox.com. Accessed June 2014.

32. Hibbard J, Greene J, Overton V. Patients with lower activation associated with higher costs; Delivery systems should know their patients' 'scores'. *Health Aff.* 2013;32:216-222; doi:10.1377/hlthaff.2012.1064.

33. The Kaiser Family Foundation and Health Research & Educational Trust; Employer Health Benefits 2013 Annual Survey. 2013. http://kaiserfamilyfoundation.files.wordpress.com/2013/08/8465-employer-health-benefits-20132.pdf . Accessed June 2014.

34. American Institutes for Research. Lessons learned: Consumer beliefs and use of information about health care cost, resource use, and value. October 2012. http://www.rwjf.org. Accessed May 2014.

35. Himmelstein D, Thorne D, Warren E. Medical bankruptcy in the United States, 2007: Results of a national study. 2009. http://www.pnhp.org/new_bankruptcy_study/Bankruptcy-2009.pdf. Accessed April 2014.

36. LaMontagne C. NerdWallet Health finds medical bankruptcy accounts for majority of personal bankruptcies. March 2014. http://www.nerdwallet.com/. Accessed April 2014.

37. Buell R, Campbell D, Frei F. Are self-service customers satisfied or stuck? May 2009. http://www.pomsmeetings.org. Accessed May 2014.

38. Punke H. Reducing ACO patient leakage begins with education. September 2013. www.beckershospitalreview.com. Accessed May 2014.

39. Zickhuhr K, Smith A. Digital differences. April 2012. www.pewinternet.org. Accessed May 2014.

40. Smith A. The best (and worst) of mobile connectivity. November 2012. www.pewinternet.org. Accessed May 2014.

41. Klasnja P, Pratt W. Healthcare in the pocket: Mapping the space of mobile-phone health interventions. February 2012. http://www.j-biomed-inform.com. Accessed June 2014.

42. Geisinger Health System. Weight Management Text Program. February 2014. www.himss.org/mobilehealthit. Accessed May 2014.

43. Kaiser Permanente Press Release. Kaiser Permanente Flagship app surpasses 1 million downloads. June 2014. www.kp.org/Share. Accessed June 2014.

44. Durham M. Integrating prevention measures in a healthcare system. 2014. www.uppsalahealthsummit.se. Accessed June 2014.

45. Hacking Health: How consumers use smartphones and wearable tech to track their health. April 2014. http://www.nielsen.com/us/en/insights/news/2014/hacking-health-how-consumers-use-smartphones-and-wearable-tech-to-track-their-health.html. Accessed June 2014.

46. Ledger D. Inside wearables: How the science of human behavior change offers the secret to long-term engagement. January 2014. http://endeavourpartners.net. Accessed April 2014.

47. Helander E, Kaipainen K, Korhonen I, et al. Factors related to sustained use of a free mobile app for dietary self-monitoring with photography and peer feedback: Retrospective cohort study. April 2014. http://www.jmir.org/2014/4/e109/. Accessed April 2014.

48. Khalaf S. Health and fitness apps finally take off, fueled by fitness fanatics. June 2014. http://www.flurry.com. Accessed June 2014.

49. Christakis N, Fowler J. The spread of obesity in a large social network over 32 years. July 2007. http://www.nejm.org/doi/full/10.1056/NEJMsa066082. Accessed April 2014.

50. Ball K, Jeffery R, Abbott G, et al. Is healthy behavior contagious: associations of social norms with physical activity and healthy eating. July 2010. http://www.ijbnpa.org/content/7/1/86. Accessed April 2014.

51. Maher C, Lewis L, Ferrar K. Are health behavior change interventions that use online social networks effective? A systematic review. February 2014. http://www.jmir.org/2014/2/e40/. Accessed April 2014.

52. Gamification. Merriam Webster. www.merriam-webster.com. Accessed January 2015.

53. O'Donnell A. Cigna Partners with Audax Health on digital engagement platform. January 2013. http://www.insurancetech.com. Accessed April 2014.

54. Pai A. *Two Blues discuss healthy behavior change, rewards, loss aversion, and regret theory*. July 2013. http://mobihealthnews.com. Accessed April 2014.

55. Cheung K. Consumer engagement in the post-reform era: Payer strategies for engaging members. July 2012. http://servicecenter.fiercemarkets.com. Accessed April 2014.

56. Keas. Keas rolls out turnkey solution for Incapital to raise health awareness while lowering stress and healthcare costs. January 2013. http://www.keas.com. Accessed April 2014.

57. Schlaikjer E. Health insurer Humana gamifies fitness. October 2012. http://www.triplepundit.com. Accessed April 2014.

58. Mathews A. Playing for wellness. April 2012. http://online.wsj.com. Accessed April 2014.

59. Norcross J. New Year's resolutions for 2013. January 2013. http://degreesearch.org/blog/wp-content/uploads/2013/01/Poll-Results-Changeology.pdf. Accessed April 2014.

CHAPTER 3

Fostering Innovation in Health IT

Anuj Desai and David Jacobowitz

INTRODUCTION

Unlike banking, travel, and consumer goods, the health IT market historically has not been a fertile area for dynamic innovation. Until the advent of the personal computer and the Internet, disparate market players displayed a marked reluctance to embrace innovative health IT solutions.

Through most of the latter part of the 20th century, health IT innovation was limited to major medical centers or commercial enterprises that targeted the healthcare industry. Both entities had to fight an uphill battle against the prevalent healthcare market culture that shunned workflow innovation. This culture results, to a large extent, from doctors' medical training experience, which resembles an apprenticeship leading to entry in the medical guild. After being subjected to years of rigorous and often rigid medical training, many healthcare practitioners emerge determined to do things their own way, rather than being directed by any authority.

One of the most pervasive elements of the healthcare culture—and one which continues to stymie innovation—has been the plethora of often conflicting interests that converge in the market. As expressed by Harvard's Regina Herzlinger, "The healthcare sector has many stakeholders, each with an agenda. Often, these players have substantial resources and the power to influence public policy and opinion by attacking or helping an innovator. Hospitals and doctors, for instance, sometimes blame technology-driven product innovators for the healthcare system's high costs. Medical specialists wage turf warfare for control of patient services, and insurers battle medical service and technology providers over which treatments and payments are acceptable. Unless innovators recognize and try to work with the complex interests of the different players, they will see their efforts stymied."[1]

At hospitals fortunate enough to possess advanced IT resources, chief information officers (CIOs), historically, were compelled to give highest priority to customized systems that reflected the desires of administrative and physician leadership. These needs were driven by the ever-changing healthcare regulatory/reimbursement environment, as well as the dynamic advances in clinical care. IT management tried to be responsive, often creating multidisciplinary information systems committees with membership drawn from the administrative, financial, and clinical ranks to set priorities and deadlines. Often, however, the demands were so numerous and the IT resources so thin that the most frequently heard response from IT was "We can't do that" or "We will eventually get to that."

Meanwhile, commercial corporates, recognizing the opportunity to capitalize on the lucrative healthcare market, created and marketed centralized shared systems based on time-sharing technologies and, later, standalone systems running on minicomputers installed at hospital sites. Initially focused on revenue cycle management, the systems eventually began to address clinical workflow challenges like order entry/reporting and ancillary department management. Enterprising companies had to contend with the notoriously long sales cycles and significant regulatory burdens indigenous to the healthcare market, both of which exerted a drag on rapid innovation.

As the first decade of the 21st century came to a close, the need for health IT innovation intensified. With the passage of the American Recovery and Reinvestment Act of 2009 (ARRA), Congress authorized funding for providers adopting EHR systems. The next year, Congress passed the Patient Protection and Affordable Care Act (PPACA), which created new programs like accountable care organizations (ACOs), charged to align various healthcare market stakeholders and provide them with incentives for quality care. These congressional actions spurred the development of new IT solutions. Even though EHR vendors invested heavily in newer technology, they could not keep up with the high market demand. Customers and investors wanted new, innovative solutions that would best meet government requirements.

Luckily, the advent of personal computers and the unprecedented adoption of the Internet have utterly altered the landscape. No longer will innovation be held hostage to the business plans and sales cycles of "big iron" health IT companies. No longer will hospital administrators or doctors need to queue up outside the IT department's front door, only to be told to "come back when I have finished my other priorities." Today, healthcare apps of real value can be created by entrepreneurs possessing a disruptive idea, access to some funding, and an understanding of healthcare workflow.

Even the most useful, clever, and innovative app will not see the light of day unless adopted by providers in the rendering of healthcare. Healthcare culture has not yet changed all that much. "The entrenched channels, long sales cycles, and significant regulatory burden in health care are at odds with the volume-driven model of rapid start-up development…the risk-averse culture of health care and a lack of proven revenue models…can make pilots and early revenue difficult to obtain."[2]

All of this highlights the need for healthcare technology innovators to carefully balance the competing interests of varying stakeholders and seek opportunities to establish relationships with key providers who control much of the funding being sought by innovators. Innovators need to understand the necessary steps and stages in growing a successful health IT business that is dynamic, sustainable, and responsive to its market.

THREE STAGES OF HEALTH IT INNOVATION

Any successful health IT innovation solution goes through three distinct stages of development: concept, seed funding/start-up, and scale (see Figure 3-1).

	Concept/Idea	Startup	Scale
Characteristics	• Business idea developed • Business plan created • Prototype developed	• Product complete • Initial customers in pilot or sales • Initial Funding raised from investors	• Well positioned product(s) in market • Many paying customers • Series B and later funding raised from investors.
Innovation Programs	• Hackathons • Challenges • University-led programs	• Accelerators • Public & Private Sector growth initiatives	• Partnerships with entrenched players and new markets

Figure 3-1: Stages of Innovation

(Reprinted with permission: TechColumbus, http://www.techcolumbus.org/startups/startup-lifecycle/)

Concept Stage

At this stage, an individual or small group of entrepreneurs develops a business idea addressing a significant issue in healthcare. The founder begins to conduct research to assess product features, likely demand, benefit to stakeholders, cost to develop/deploy, and potential customers.

Seed Funding/Start-up Stage

At this stage, the entrepreneurs raise funds from friends and family, as well as angel and venture capitalist (VC) investors, enabling them to build an innovative product in preparation for market introduction. By running pilot programs with carefully selected beta customers, innovators can gain valuable insights that yield product improvements, enabling an optimal fit to market needs. This enables their products to be provided to early adopters for initial market introduction. At minimum, innovators must put into place all of the basic accounting, operations, client services, marketing and sales processes, channel strategies, and resources needed for a successful market introduction, along with identifying first adopters, size of market, pricing, anticipated revenue, sales approaches, and profitability.

Scale Stage

Here, the entrepreneur drives toward profitability, focusing on the milestones to reach breakeven before investing to achieve a dominant position in their market. The innovator develops solid sales strategies, with paying clients generating revenue. In addition, the innovator may engage with VCs for Series B and later funding to further grow their business capabilities. The focus is on building out robust businesses, enabling market development and the addition of new customers. The companies have developed marketing/sales/support/distribution strategies and are focusing on strategic partners who can help them scale at a rapid pace.

INNOVATION TARGETED AT CONCEPT STAGE COMPANIES

At the first stage, innovators can avail themselves of hackathons and challenges. A hackathon or code-a-thon is an event in which developers and designers collaborate intensively on software projects. Hackathons typically last one or several days. Some hackathons are intended simply for educational or social purposes, although in many cases, the goal is to create usable software that could be spun out into a product.

Examples of hackathons include:

- **NYC BigApps:**[3] NYC BigApps is an annual competition sponsored by the New York City Economic Development Corporation providing programmers, developers, designers, and entrepreneurs with access to municipal data sets to build technologic products that address civic issues affecting New York City (NYC). Programming teams compete for up to $100,000 in cash prizes. Through the NYC Open Data portal and other private and nonprofit data sources, contestants have access to more than 1,000 data sets and application programming interfaces (APIs). Examples of available data include healthy living, weekly traffic updates, schedules of citywide events, property sales records, catalogs of restaurant inspections, and geographic data about the location of school and voting districts. The contest is part of a broader NYC effort to increase government transparency and encourage entrepreneurship.
- **Cajun Code Fest:**[4] The Cajun Code Fest is a healthcare coding competition seeking to identify the next innovative idea (app, software, device, etc.) related to a particular issue in healthcare (e.g., aging in place). Winners receive a cash prize to help move their idea to reality and they earn the opportunity to pitch the idea to investors.
- **Clinton Foundation Code-Down:**[5] The Clinton Foundation's Health Matters Initiative, along with Tumblr, Jawbone, and the Ace Hotel, has partnered to put together a series of code-a-thons to challenge developers and designers to build a health-based application prototype over three days.
- **InnovateNYP:**[6] New York Presbyterian (NYP) Hospital held a hackathon to develop prototypes of innovative ways to use their online patient portal to track health records and coordinate doctor's appointments. The winning team received a cash prize and an opportunity to develop their solution into a product to be rolled out to patients within the large NYP hospital system.

A healthcare challenge is a project in which multidisciplinary teams are tasked with building technology solutions that address issues identified by a sponsoring organization, such as a nonprofit, foundation, or for-profit company. Often, these are held as part of conferences or standalone events geared to digital health app development. Prizes are typically awarded to the team with the best app.

Health 2.0 is the largest facilitator for healthcare challenges through their Developer Challenge program. As of July 2014, Health 2.0 had facilitated over 75 challenges with prizes totaling close to $7 million. Sponsors of their challenges include healthcare foundations, the government, corporate partners such as pharma companies and tech companies, and provider networks.[7]

INNOVATION TARGETED AT THE SEED FUNDING AND START-UP STAGE

As companies move into the next stage of innovation (seed funding and start-up), they are eligible to participate in incubator or accelerator programs. Whereas incubators usually provide space, work resources, management, and mentoring to assist companies to create prototype products that can qualify for seed money, accelerators generally look for companies that can benefit from a blend of mentoring, funding, and market relationships that will prepare them to go to market.[8]

The California Healthcare Foundation report aptly summarizes the genesis of the healthcare accelerator innovation phenomenon:

> The origin of the accelerator model can be attributed back to 2005 with the launch of the first Accelerator called "Y Combinator" (YC). The former cofounder and CEO of Viaweb, Paul Graham, founded YC with the strategy that making small investments in large number of start-ups, typically less than $20,000 in exchange for between 2% and 10% equity, would result in more successes than investing in only a few. The start-ups in the program move to Silicon Valley for 3 months to get access to a co-working space, mentors from the business community, and work intensively on their pitches for investors. The conclusion of the program is a demo day in which they pitch their business plans to a group of outside investors with the hope that the pitch will turn into subsequent venture capital investment. Since 2005, YC has invested in over 630 start-ups including highly successful companies such as Reddit, DropBox, Airbnb, Codeacademy, and Stripe, among others. Following the success of YC, other notable tech accelerators emerged as well.[9]

There are four models of health accelerators: commercial seed accelerators, market-led programs, virtual networks, and university-affiliated accelerators.

1. **Commercial seed accelerators:** These accelerators leverage the successful YC model and offer capital, guidance, access to mentors, and a demo day for investors. These accelerators are typically aimed at very early-stage companies who may be at the idea stage or may have a beta product. The program length is typically 3–4 months and provides from $20,000 to $100,000 in return for an average of 6 percent equity. Successful commercial seed accelerators include Rock Health, HealthBox, BluePrint Health, Dreamit Health, and Tech Wildcatters.
2. **Market-led programs:** The newly-emerging model of market-led programs is being created by customers and economic development organizations looking for particular types of innovation in specific focus areas. The New York Digital Health Accelerator is an example. This program was created with a focus on healthcare providers who are looking to adapt new technologies. Market-led programs typically are longer than commercial seed accelerators, offer more investment capital, and take less equity stake (~2%). The focus of these programs is often on economic development in addition to commercial success of the companies.
3. **Virtual networks:** StartUp Health is an example of a virtual network model. This program provides its network members with access to business connections, vir-

Table 3-1: Types of Accelerator Models

	Commercial Seed	Market-led	Virtual Networks	University-affiliated
Structure	3–5 months, demo day, 2 classes per year, up to 10 companies per class	5–9 months, demo day, 2 classes per year, up to 10 companies per class; location-specific job creation requirements	36-month program; up to 100 start-ups per year	6-month program; demo day, 2 classes per year, 10 companies per class
Capital	$20,000; 6% equity	$100,000–$300,000; 2.5% equity; funding for pilots	No direct funding; program receives 2–10% equity over 3 years	$5,000 stipend per founder, no equity stake
Focus	Concept to early-stage health tech companies	Late-seed to growth-stage health tech companies focused on needs of particular customers	Seed to Series B health tech companies	Concept to Series B health tech companies and biotech
Market Ties	Academic institutions, pharma, health plans, corporate sponsors	Healthcare providers, pharma, health plans strategic investors, corporate sponsors, economic development, government	Corporate sponsorships, health plans, government	University-affiliated, corporate sponsors
Examples	Rock Health, HealthBox, BluePrint Health, Dreamit Health, Tech Wildcatters, Microsoft Ventures	New York Digital Health Accelerator	StartUp Health	StartX Med, Georgia Tech Health @ei2, StartupUCLA, U of Miami Project LIFT

tual collaboration, and quarterly CEO summits. The program does not provide any direct capital to companies, but takes a small equity stake in each company over a three-year period. StartUp Health focuses on CEOs, whom they term "Healthcare Transformers." The vision of StartUp Health is to invest in 1,000 companies over 10 years. The organization has also formed strategic partnerships with a number of corporate sponsors.

4. **University-affiliated accelerators:** The structure of university-led accelerators is similar to commercial seed accelerators, but often they do not take as much equity from the entrepreneurs involved. The most notable university-affiliated accelerator is StartXMed, which is affiliated with Stanford University. However, some commercial seed accelerators have also formed strategic relationships with universities. For example, Dreamit Health has formed a strategic relationship with Drexel University and Johns Hopkins, while Rock Health has formed a strategic partnership with the University of California San Francisco (UCSF). Thus, the categories have become somewhat blurred (see Table 3-1).

PUBLIC-PRIVATE SECTOR INITIATIVES

There are several public-private sector initiatives focusing on helping start-ups find ways to fix healthcare problems faced by government entities. These initiatives typically provide seed funding, office space, and mentorships to civic start-ups. Examples include:

Code for America (San Francisco). Code for America,[10] the technology world's equivalent of the Peace Corps, provides seed funding, office space, and mentorship to civic start-ups. It aims at helping early-stage start-up companies focused on civic issues get the financial, strategic, and operational support they need to succeed. Start-ups receive 200+ hours of mentorship from industry leaders, pitch to numerous government officials, and gain access to civic tech investors and sales leads. There is a 4-month residency and a demo day.

- Capital: $25k per company
- Focus: Start-ups targeting issues that matter to cities and communities

In addition to running an accelerator-type model, Code for America runs challenges and programs with cities and local governments to solve issues using public data.

Health Data Consortium (District of Columbia). Health Data Consortium[11] is a public-private partnership working to foster the availability and innovative use of open health data to improve healthcare. The mission is to liberate health data to ignite innovation and foster collaboration among health data users and stakeholders for the benefit of everyone. Its website houses Health Data All-Stars, a directory of 50 prominent domestic resources for health data at the federal, state, and local levels. It runs the Health Data Challenge Series, which helps private, nonprofit, and government organizations apply the best practices of the leading tech incubators and accelerators to identify the most innovative uses of data to improve health or healthcare. Health Data Consortium also runs the Health Datapalooza conference, one of the largest health tech conferences in the United States, as well as the Health Data Affiliates program made up of regional participants who promote the use of open healthcare data.

INTERNATIONAL SPONSORED PROGRAMS DRIVING INNOVATION IN HEALTH IT

Health IT innovation is not just a focus within the United States; internationally sponsored programs have been developed that seek to drive the same types of goals, such as fostering entrepreneurship and job creation, and driving the open use of health data. These programs work with batches of start-ups to prepare them for marketing their digital health products in the local and international market. Examples include:

Ignition Labs (Australia). Ignition Labs,[12] an accelerator program, provides up to five founders with the business tools and processes necessary to validate their ideas and refine their technologies in a condensed time frame. It provides mentoring by a mix of serial entrepreneurs and healthcare professionals. The program's duration is three to six months, and it culminates in an investor road show attracting Australian and international investors. The funding for successful, early-stage applicants will total $25,000.

European Connected Health Alliance (ECH) (Europe): The European Connected Health Alliance[13] is a nonprofit organization focused primarily on the European Union countries to support and promote the wider adoption of healthcare products, services, applications, and innovation. The Alliance has membership that includes corporates, foundations, academia, and government members and is seen as the primary convener of these disparate organizations within the region.

INNOVATION TARGETED AT THE SCALE STAGE

Once it reaches the scale stage, a company has proved the value of its portfolio of products, has a strong management team and sustainable funding, and has achieved successful adoption. It must continue to innovate to stay ahead of the market, and it must pull together a mix of resource talent, strategic and tactical plans, and effective marketing and sales so as to achieve a market leading position. Two examples of successful companies in this stage are ZocDoc and Medidata Solutions.

ZocDoc[14]

ZocDoc is an online medical care scheduling service, providing a medical care search facility for end users by integrating information about medical practices and doctors' individual schedules in a central location. ZocDoc provides a scheduling system on a paid subscription basis for medical personnel. The scheduling system can be accessed by subscribers, both as an online service and via the deployed office calendar software, or integrated with their websites. The subscribers' schedules are available to the end users—patients—free of charge.

The service was launched in 2007. Initially limited to Manhattan, the service is currently used by more than 5 million people per month and has further expanded to cover 40 percent of the U.S. population across 2,000+ cities (www.zocdoc.com accessed on January 26, 2015). ZocDoc is available in Android, iOS, or web applications, as well as a Spanish-language version with the launch of ZocDoc en Español. In October 2012, the company launched its first new product since inception—ZocDoc Check-in. This feature allows patients to fill out their paperwork online in advance of their visit. As of June 2013, the company had raised over $95 million in venture capital from investors including Khosla Ventures, Goldman Sachs, and DST Global.[14]

Medidata Solutions

Medidata Solutions is an American-based multinational computer technology corporation that specializes in developing and marketing cloud-based solutions to address functions throughout the clinical development process. The Medidata platform is designed to improve study design, protocol development, trial planning and management, site collaboration and management, patient-centric data capture and management, randomization and trial supply management, monitoring, safety event capture, clinical data capture and management, advanced reporting, and business analytics. Headquartered in New York City, Medidata employed 900+ people worldwide by the end of 2012.[15]

Medidata Solutions has a total of nine offices with locations in the United States, U.K., Japan, and China. Customers include pharmaceutical, biotechnology, medical device and diagnostic companies, academic and government institutions, contract research organizations, and other organizations around the world that are engaged in clinical trials that bring medical products to market and explore new indications for existing products.

SUSTAINING INNOVATION

To sustain the innovation initiated by entrepreneurs, many companies need access to additional capital. The venture capital industry is oftentimes the source of this funding. VC investment is money given to an entrepreneur or start-up business by a venture capital firm at an early stage in the company's development, with the hopes that the firm will receive a large return on its investment. Some of the world's largest companies, including Starbucks, Home Depot, Whole Foods, Apple, Microsoft, and others were originally backed by VC investors. While the 2009 Health Information Technology for Economic and Clinical Health (HITECH) Act helped launch the sector through its $17 billion allocation toward the adoption of meaningful use of health IT, private investments into the sector have continued to rise with increasing EHR adoption.[16]

According to Rock Health, 258 companies were funded in 2014 by investors. The year 2014 had $4.1B invested, more than the previous three years combined, representing a 125% growth compared to 2013.[17] According to Rock Health, six major themes comprised almost 50 percent of all funding in health tech in 2013:[18]

- **EHR and clinical workflow:** EHRs and surrounding applications including clinical workflow support ($245M)
- **Analytics and big data:** Data aggregation and analysis to support healthcare use cases ($161M)
- **Digital medical devices:** Hardware/software designed to treat a specific disease or condition ($146M)
- **Wearables and biosensing:** Wearable consumer devices that measure specific biometrics ($136M)
- **Population health management:** Comprehensive platforms designed to manage the health of populations under the shift to risk-based payment models ($126M)
- **Healthcare consumer management:** Consumer tools for the purchasing of healthcare services or health insurance ($119M)

FUNDING INNOVATION

As a company graduates from the concept stage into the start-up phase and beyond, it is important to seek the counsel of an expert financial advisor to identify the appropriate means of gaining access to capital. Some funding sources that are the most prevalent for start-ups include:

- **Friends and family:** Many very early-stage start-ups gather some initial seed funding from friends and family to survive on until the business raises additional capital.
- **Small Business Innovation Research[19] (SBIR) grants or SBA loans:** The U.S. government has created grant programs and loans for small businesses to succeed. The Small Business Association[20] (SBA) has taken a keen look at health technology and is actively looking to fund high-potential businesses that will create jobs and solve big healthcare issues. For more information, see www.sbir.gov and www.sba.gov.

- **Angel investors:** Angel investors[21] are individuals or groups that invest their own money in early-stage companies. Oftentimes, these are high net worth individuals who are looking to take a small part of an emerging business. More information is available at http://www.angelcapitalassociation.org/.
- **VC investors and strategic investors:** By far, the most active group of investors is traditional VC firms. Many new entrants who previously focused on biotech deals are now entering the health technology space. Corporate venture capital groups typically led by pharma and tech firms have created funds that often offer better terms than traditional VCs.
- **Organic growth:** This funding comes from growth of the business based on sales alone, thus obviating the need to raise external funds. Organic growth can be a viable option if a business has enough dollars from the founders or backers to succeed. However, the pace of growth may not be satisfying enough, and the company may need additional capital in order to scale.

THE ROLE OF THE MENTOR

At the concept and start-up stages, a strategy for success for a start-up is to work with multiple mentors. Mentors can assist an early-stage start-up in several different ways, including validating product concepts, identifying unmet needs, advising on leadership decisions, and assisting with business development and identification of customers, investors, and partners, to name just a few. For a mentor, access to cutting-edge innovation, an opportunity to share their insights and learning, and networking with other industry partners are often motivations for getting involved. Mentors may seek compensation in the form of payment or equity share in the company, although often mentors work with start-ups gratis, as they see it as a way of giving back to the community.

It is important for an early-stage company to recognize that it can't solve every problem on its own and, instead, should work with many different types of mentors, as each provides a different set of capabilities. Some different types of mentors include:

- **Entrepreneur mentors:** These mentors are successful CEOs of businesses that may be in the same industry as the start-up or in different industries. These leaders can provide valuable insights into what has worked and what has not, guidance on scaling a business and raising capital, and strategic insights into product strategy. These relationships can often lead to new business development partnership opportunities. Seed and later stage accelerators work with this mentor group as a core part of their program.
- **Corporate mentors:** Large companies are often interested in working with early-stage companies to identify new innovations and to seek potential pilot opportunities that can lead to investments. Often, corporate development executives at large companies including tech firms, pharma, insurance companies, and consulting firms are very well connected and are able to assist start-ups in identifying strategic partners. Also, these firms may be interested in funding pilots for start-ups.
- **Customer mentors:** One of the most important types of mentors are customer mentors. For an early-stage start-up, it is critical to identify a potential cus-

tomer who is willing to provide candid feedback on product development and validate the market need the start-up is trying to fulfill. Often, start-ups focus on sales and not on the important mentorship aspect of this relationship. By collaboratively working with a customer, especially for business-to-business (B2B) companies, start-ups can maximize the benefits received and may even gain a reference client that will vouch for the company and its credibility. In return for their time, customers may seek advisory board representation, discounts on product fees, or equity stakes.

CASE STUDY: THE NEW YORK DIGITAL HEALTH ACCELERATOR

A prime example of a successful digital health accelerator that promotes innovation is the New York Digital Health Accelerator, a program run by the New York eHealth Collaborative (NYeC) in conjunction with the Partnership Fund of New York.

New York State is a national leader in healthcare. The third most populous state in the United States, New York's healthcare community comprises more than 230 hospitals, 60,000 physicians, and 19.5 million consumers of health services.[22] New York has pioneered numerous innovations in healthcare delivery, including insurance market reforms and regulatory approaches that long predated the country's recent adoption of comparable strategies under comprehensive healthcare reform.

In recent years, New York has taken unprecedented steps to improve both the quality and efficiency of healthcare delivery, making substantial investments in health IT and undertaking a broad range of other regional/local and private sector initiatives to improve health services through IT.

Since 2006, the New York State (NYS) Department of Health has invested over $840 million toward the adoption of health IT in the state.[23] This funding has led to significant adoption of EHRs across the state and the formation of 11 regional health information organizations (RHIOs), which, with appropriate patient consent, have the capacity to share medical information between healthcare providers in their region. Connecting all these RHIOs or regional health information exchange (HIE) is the Statewide Health Information Network of New York (SHIN-NY), which contains statewide clinical data from EHRs, labs, radiology reports, and more.

The NYeC[24] was founded by New York healthcare leaders, with leadership and financial support from the New York State Department of Health, to serve as the focal point for health IT in the state. NYeC, a not-for-profit, public-private partnership, is the state-designated entity to coordinate policy and governance for health IT and is also responsible for overseeing and managing the SHIN-NY. NYeC is currently the technical service provider for six of the NYS RHIOs and is establishing connections with the remaining RHIOs. The goal of NYeC is that no patient, wherever they may need treatment within the state, should ever lack fast, secure, accurate, and accessible health history information. NYeC is governed by a board of directors comprising 20 individuals across different sectors of the healthcare industry, including hospital systems, health policy think tanks, and health plans, representing the interests of many different types of stakeholders across the state.

New York is a National Center of Tech Innovation

New York has a strong technology community with access to many resources that can be leveraged by early-stage companies to thrive. New York is already the hub of the financial technology, digital media, and VC industries. Beginning with Google's move to NYC in 2003, the strong growth of tech start-ups has made NYC the host to many of the most important Silicon Valley companies, including Facebook and Yahoo. From 2007 to 2012, more than 11,000 new IT jobs were created in NYC, up 28.7 percent, from 41,100 to 52,900. Former Mayor Michael Bloomberg recently expanded the "We Are Made in NY" initiative to include IT companies, with more than 900 tech start-ups currently hiring for over 3,000 jobs.[25] NYC is also unrivaled in the density of major healthcare organizations and hospitals. More than 80 percent of its hospitals use EHR systems, up 200 percent since 2008. More than half of doctors and other eligible providers also use EHRs, leading to more healthcare data available to developers than ever before.[26]

All of this has created a tremendous opportunity for NYeC to work with the emerging health technology industry to establish New York as the hub of health IT innovation. Health IT entrepreneurs highlight as key impediments such issues as a lack of access to potential customers, misunderstanding of health policy issues, and lack of a support network to engage with other entrepreneurs and healthcare leaders facing similar challenges. Healthcare providers have cited the lack of awareness of new applications and the lack of time and staff to engage with the healthcare entrepreneurial community. This is where NYeC can and does play a crucial role as a catalyst for entrepreneurship and as the trusted intermediary between healthcare providers, using the SHIN-NY network and emerging health technology companies.

Partnering to Create the NY Digital Health Accelerator

The New York Digital Health Accelerator[27] (NYDHA) was developed by NYeC with the Partnership Fund for New York City in 2012 to stimulate a new marketplace and create the next generation of healthcare tools, while positioning New York as a hub of health IT innovation. The nine-month program, modeled after the Partnership Fund's successful Fintech Innovation Lab for emerging financial start-ups, provides companies with mentorship and feedback from senior executives as their potential customers. Geared toward early- and growth-stage digital health companies, the Accelerator Program supports the development of cutting-edge technology products focused on care coordination, patient engagement, analytics, and workflow improvement for healthcare providers. With its initial investment of $4.2 million, the NYDHA program has already created more than 100 jobs and is expected to create hundreds more over the next five years. In addition, it is expected that the companies participating in the Accelerator will attract upwards of $150 million to $200 million in investment from the VC community over the next five years.[28]

NYeC's partner in the program, The Partnership Fund for New York City, is the vision of Henry R. Kravis, founding partner of Kohlberg Kravis Roberts & Co., who serves as its Founding Chairman. The Partnership Fund has raised over $110 million to mobilize the city's financial and business leaders to help build a stronger and more diversified local economy.[29] It has formed a network of top experts from the investment and corporate communities who help identify and raise VC for NYC's most promising entrepreneurs in the for-profit and not-for-profit sectors. The Partnership Fund is an affiliate of the Partnership for New York City,[30] an organization of the leaders of New York City's top corporate, investment, and entrepreneurial firms. The Partnership Fund has identified and focused on healthcare as an area where New York City has a rich source of assets that can be used to diversify the economy.

Innovation Objectives of the Accelerator Program

With the advent of the PPACA and healthcare reform activities, innovative solutions are critical to support the complex needs of patients and providers, as well as the changing healthcare market. The Accelerator Program is well positioned to facilitate and support the development of technology solutions to champion new payment and service delivery models, including ACOs, Shared Savings, and Bundled Payment programs spearheaded by CMS and the New York State Department of Health.

With the strong shift in incentives and payment models, providers in New York and across the country are being forced to review their workflow, seeking new tools to better coordinate care. Typically, providers ask their EHR vendors to provide these tools. While an EHR system can help physicians manage their patients within a practice, hospital, or system, providers currently need to share data across systems to support entirely new models of care.

Providers are demanding innovative tools, particularly in the areas of care coordination and patient engagement. Care coordination refers to collaborative care solutions that reflect the continuum of information regarding a patient. Patient engagement refers to personal health management solutions that facilitate better healthcare decisions and help improve care management communications between the provider and/or family members.

Through partnerships between the providers and the technology companies, the Accelerator Program fosters the creation of products that meet the needs of the providers by facilitating timely communication and providing coordinated and integrated care to improve the lives of patients. The Accelerator is unique in that it provides tech companies accepted into the program direct access to customers and product development feedback from senior-level executives of leading healthcare provider organizations in New York. It is through this partnership between the tech companies and providers that the Accelerator is able to successfully stimulate growth of an ecosystem in which new IT tools and new jobs are created. The Accelerator is at the heart of NYeC's approach toward growing a vital digital health ecosystem in the state.

Accelerator Selection and Evaluation Process

The 2012 inaugural class was chosen based on a rigorous and competitive selection process. When the program was launched, NYeC received applications from 250 companies from 27 states and 10 countries. The selection committee comprised participating provider leadership, VC participants, clinicians, and technology experts. Based on review criteria—which included product innovation, management's track record, and company maturity—the Selection Committee chose eight companies to participate in the program.

The inaugural class enjoyed participation from a broad network of 23 leading provider organizations in New York, including hospitals such as New York-Presbyterian, North Shore-LIJ Health System, Montefiore, Mount Sinai, long-term care providers, community health centers, and primary care physicians. Each company was paired with two to four providers over the course of the program. The Accelerator provided $300,000 of funding per company structured as a convertible note from a syndicate of leading VC and strategic investors.[31]

Investors included a combination of strategic investors and VC investors including Aetna, UnitedHealthcare, Janssen, New Leaf Venture Partners, Milestone Venture Partners, Safeguard Scientifics, and Quaker Partners. NYeC received no equity share in the Accelerator companies, but provided the operations of the program and maintained the relationships with each of the program participants. VCs and strategic investors provided private investments totaling $3.7 million that were awarded to the Accelerator companies.[32]

During the nine-month program, each of the companies was provided with high-caliber mentorship; senior-level executives from 23 of New York State's leading healthcare organizations provided product development feedback. The companies also benefited from mentorship by world class investors and executives from the health insurance, pharma, and health IT entrepreneurial sectors.

The companies that were part of the inaugural class of the NYDHA included:[33]

- **ActualMeds:** ActualMeds provides cloud-based, interoperable software solutions to support team-based medication management and reconciliation for high-risk patients at the point of care.
- **Aidin:** Aidin is a web-based referral platform for hospitals discharging patients to post-acute care. Aidin collects hard data about how well post-acute providers perform and makes it easy for hospital staff to present that information to patients when they are choosing their post-acute provider—helping patients choose better providers for better outcomes.
- **Avado:** Avado allows clinicians and patients to securely communicate, track, and manage health information. Avado centralizes data from many EHRs and makes them usable for all stakeholders. Avado was acquired by WebMD in October 2013.
- **CipherHealth:** CipherHealth follows up with patients over mobile technologies to make sure they are following discharge instructions, which helps hospitals reduce preventable readmissions and avoid government penalties.
- **Cureatr:** Cureatr provides a messaging system that integrates with existing directory, scheduling, and paging systems to improve communication and coordination of care among doctors and other care providers within a hospital.
- **MedCPU:** MedCPU delivers accurate real-time clinical care advice through its Advisor Button technology. It captures the complete clinical picture from clinicians' free-text notes, dictations, and structured documentation entered into any electronic medical record (EMR) and analyzes it against a growing library of best-practice content, generating real-time precise prompts for best care consideration.

- **Remedy Systems:** Remedy Systems leverages the power of mobile to lower the cost and improve the quality of healthcare via a flexible care coordination platform that enables physicians and nurses to concentrate on delivering the highest quality of care possible while fostering engagement from patients and family/friends.
- **SpectraMedix:** SpectraMedix's analytics platform offers real-time data integration, analytics, and reporting solutions for healthcare organizations to track key performance indicators in financial, operational, clinical, utilization, and satisfaction domains, with focus on reducing readmissions for heart failure, heart attack, and pneumonia.

Results

The Accelerator delivered solid results. Key highlights include:

- **Launch of pilot programs:** Twenty-three of New York State's leading healthcare organizations provided product feedback and facilitated 33 pilots at their organizations.
- **Creation of new jobs:** Each of the participating companies has grown rapidly and created a total of 120 high-tech jobs in New York.
- **Growth of new tech companies:** As of July 2014, the companies raised $23 million in funding and two companies were acquired.[34]

The program received significant accolades from many leading experts in the health IT industry. The California Healthcare Foundation called the Accelerator one of the most successful accelerator models in the country, in light of the financial and strategic ties that have already been forged. The Rotman School of Management in Canada ranked the Accelerator number one in the world among 21 similar programs. Their ranking was based on 10 different criteria including access to customers, investors, government, and support for innovation. Todd Park, former chief technology officer (CTO) of the United States, has said that this program is the one that other states should seek to emulate.[35]

OTHER INNOVATION INITIATIVES

Blue Button

The Blue Button program enables patients to view and download their personal health records (PHRs). The initiative began in 2010 as a cooperative program among several federal agencies, including the Departments of Defense, Health and Human Services, and Veterans Affairs, which implemented this capability for their beneficiaries. Data from Blue Button–enabled sites can be used to create portable medical histories that facilitate dialog among healthcare providers, caregivers, and other trusted individuals or entities.

Currently, Blue Button usage has become widespread, and many innovators are availing themselves of the capability to download human-readable health history data. The next phase of the program, Blue Button Plus, will enhance the ways consumers get and share their health information in human-readable and machine-readable formats and will further enable the use of this information in third-party applications.

In September 2011, the Robert Wood Johnson Foundation launched a website to advocate cross-industry use of the Blue Button; its website collects the pledges of industry adopters of the technology, including United Health Care, Humana, PatientsLikeMe, and Walgreens.

One of those pledging support, Aetna, announced in September 2011 that it had added the Blue Button function to its patient portal, and, in addition, offered its beneficiaries the ability to share their Blue Button downloads with Aetna providers. Other private sector organizations that have contributed to the growth of Blue Button include:

- Iatric Systems, Inc., a hospital-focused EHR vendor, includes the Blue Button on the patient portals of its products.
- Humetrix, Inc. offers a mobile Blue Button application through which patients can send their Blue Button data directly to their physicians.
- Microsoft HealthVault and Dossia, which are patient-controlled repositories of personal health information, each accept Blue Button data.
- Napersoft, Inc., a consumer communications management software company, uses Blue Button in its Talk2Health product to transmit data between patients, payers, and providers.

In 2012, ONC held the Blue Button Mash-up Challenge to encourage the development of third-party applications that increase the usefulness of data downloaded via Blue Button. The first-prize winner, iBlueButton, is a smartphone app that takes data from Medicare's online portal and organizes it into an easier-to-read, easier-to-navigate format. The second-prize winner, ID BlueButton, is a tablet-based application that parses health information downloaded through Blue Button and presents it in a form that more clearly shows changes in health indicators and medication use over time. The third-prize winner, InstantPHR, is a web app that uses data downloaded through Blue Button to automatically populate PHRs in Microsoft HealthVault.

Health APIs

One conversation topic that is constantly discussed at digital health industry events is the idea of data silos. The real potential for health data, many people believe, will come when it can be combined with other data and integrated into other apps and platforms, rather than being locked away wherever it was originally collected.

This is increasingly being done through application programming interfaces, or APIs, which are offered by consumer devices such as Fitbit, Withings, and Jawbone, but also EHRs such as drchrono, Allscripts, and Practice Fusion. APIs are also being used in high-profile platforms looking to create an integrated user experience for the variety of digital health apps available—services such as Aetna CarePass, Kaiser Permanente's Interchange, or RunKeeper's Health Graph.

The now-defunct patient health information hub, Google Health, and its surviving competitor Microsoft HealthVault, both made APIs an important part of their strategy as early as 2008. But back then, they were arguably too early for the space and were not able to find many API-ready partners with which to integrate. In 2011, RunKeeper launched Health Graph, an attempt to use APIs to create a health and fitness-focused social experience that would resemble Facebook's social graph.

"Imagine a system that can identify correlations between a user's eating habits, workout schedule, social interactions and more, to deliver an ecosystem of health and fitness apps, websites, and sensor devices that really work, based on a user's own historical health and fitness data," RunKeeper CEO Jason Jacobs wrote in a 2011 blog post that is no longer online.[36]

The next year, 2012, saw two big API moves: Aetna opened its CarePass API to developers and Nike+ started offering its API via hackathons and its own accelerator, specifically for companies building technology that would integrate with Nike+.

Aetna's CarePass began as a data-sharing initiative but evolved to be more of a consumer health dashboard that brings different apps together. It gradually added a range of health and fitness apps and, just recently, medication adherence and stress apps.

"When we launched the developer portal I think we had a hypothesis that the data we were opening up—things like aggregated claims data that had not been opened up before or aggregated cost of claims information—would catch on in the developer community like wildfire," Jesse Givens, head of CarePass product at Aetna, told MobiHealthNews last year. "When we put that out there, we found that people were interested in it, but conversations we had were far more focused around how to get their app in front of our members and in front of a large user community."[37]

Nike+ Fuelband has always put a lot of stock and store in its brand and its own invented fitness metric of Nike Fuel. The accelerator had the goal of getting more currency for Nike Fuel by coaxing developers to create different ways for consumers to use it. Nike listed a handful of examples for the types of start-ups it is searching for: training or coaching programs that help athletes reach their goals; games that use NikeFuel to remind people that movement is supposed to be fun; tools to motivate millions of Nike+ runners to perform better or train smarter; programs built around achievement and rewards for activity; wellness solutions that promote active, healthy lifestyles; social challenges that deliver motivation and challenges with friends; and master dashboards for the ultimate "quantified self geeks."

CONCLUSION

The time is ripe for innovation across the health IT space. Government initiatives, commercial interests, and consumer needs are aligning and are all pointing to an era of explosive opportunity for digital health entrepreneurship. Mobile devices and Internet access are ubiquitous and are being universally adopted. Fitness, wellness, care collaboration, telemedicine, patient engagement, "the Internet of Everything," big data, small data, predictive analytics—each of these areas is attracting innovators and investors in unprecedented numbers. And there is no end in sight.

Innovators who wish to succeed in the digital health market should be mindful of these points:

- One doesn't have to be a healthcare expert to build an app that will be useful in the market space. If you have an idea that works well in another market and have reason to believe it is applicable to healthcare, validate it with healthcare experts and make it happen.
- The best start-ups are built around a team of founders possessing the requisite business, marketing, and tech development skills necessary for early success.

- Take advantage of the plethora of incubators, code-a-thons, hackathons, accelerators, and other programs that are rapidly spreading across the globe. They can provide you with the funds, space, and market exposure so immeasurably valuable to a start-up enterprise.
- Look for funding beyond the familiar friends-and-family sources. Angel investors and VCs are actively seeking "the next big thing" in healthcare. Attend conferences where they congregate and network, network, network.
- Actively seek mentors, both healthcare subject matter experts and leaders of companies that stand out as successful in the market. Their advice and counsel will be invaluable and save you the trouble of learning through your own (inevitable) mistakes.
- Read everything you can get your hands on about digital health and stay on top of the latest developments in this most dynamic industry. Clients want to deal with innovators who understand their market and can teach them something they do not already know.
- Above all, enjoy yourself and allow yourself the satisfaction that derives from doing something that tangibly improves the health of your fellow humans.

REFERENCES

1. Regina Herzlinger. Why innovation in health care is so hard. *Harv Bus Rev.* 2006; May.
2. Greenhouse effect: How accelerators are seeding digital health innovation. California Healthcare Foundation. 2013. http://www.chcf.org/~/media/MEDIA%20LIBRARY%20Files/PDF/G/PDF%20GreenhouseSeedingDigitalHealth.pdf. Accessed January 26, 2015.
3. www.nycbigapps.com. Accessed January 26, 2015.
4. http://www.health2con.com/devchallenge/cajun-code-fest-2012-the-louisiana-code-a-thon/. Accessed January 27, 2015.
5. http://blog.acehotel.com/post/88281788733/ace-clinton-codeathon?utm_campaign=Code-athon+Blog+Post&utm_medium=shortlink&utm_source=https%3A%2F%2Fwww.google.com%2F&utm_content=www.acehotel.com%2Fclinton-codeathon
6. http://innovatenyp.challengepost.com
7. http://www.health2con.com/devchallenge/. Accessed January 26, 2015.
8. Accelerator vs. incubator: What's the difference? *Christina Desmarais, Inc. Magazine*, 2012; February.
9. Accelerator vs. incubator: What's the difference? *Christina Desmarais, Inc. Magazine*, 2012; February.
10. http://codeforamerica.org/. Accessed January 26, 2015
11. http://www.healthdataconsortium.org/. Accessed January 26, 2015
12. http://atp-innovations.com.au/medtech/ Accessed January 26, 2015.
13. http://www.echalliance.com/. Accessed January 26, 2015.
14. www.zocdoc.com. Accessed January 26, 2015
15. www.medidata.com. Accessed January 26, 2015.
16. http://www.hhs.gov/ocr/privacy/hipaa/administrative/enforcementrule/hitechenforcementifr.html. Accessed January 26, 2015
17. Digital Health Funding Year in Review, 2014 Edition. http://rockhealth.com, Accessed January 26, 2015.

18. Digital Health Funding Year in Review, 2013 Edition. Accessed online at http://rockhealth.com, January 27, 2015.

19. www.sbir.gov. Accessed January 26, 2015.

20. www.sba.gov. Accessed January 26, 2015.

21. http://www.angelcapitalassociation.org/. Accessed January 26, 2015.

22. https://www.health.ny.gov/statistics/sparcs/. Accessed January 26, 2015

23. https://www.health.ny.gov/technology/. Accessed January 26, 2015.

24. www.nyehealth.org. Accessed January 26, 2015.

25. New Tech City. Center for an Urban Future. May 2012. https://nycfuture.org/pdf/New_Tech_City.pdf. Accessed January 26, 2015.

26. www.nyehealth.org. Accessed January 26, 2015.

27. http://digitalhealthaccelerator.com/. Accessed January 26, 2015.

28. http://digitalhealthaccelerator.com/. Accessed January 26, 2015.

29. http://pfnyc.org/our-investments/. Accessed January 26. 2015.

30. http://pfnyc.org. Accessed January 26, 2015.

31. http://digitalhealthaccelerator.com. Accessed January 26, 2015.

32. http://digitalhealthaccelerator.com. Accessed January 26, 2015.

33. http://digitalhealthaccelerator.com. Accessed January 26, 2015.

34. http://digitalhealthaccelerator.com. Accessed January 26, 2015.

35. http://digitalhealthaccelerator.com. Accessed January 26, 2015.

36. https://gigaom.com/2011/06/07/runkeeper-builds-a-fitness-network-with-health-graph-api/. Accessed January 26, 2015.

37. http://mobihealthnews.com/23103/aetna-carepass-is-no-longer-just-for-developers/. Accessed January 26, 2015.

CHAPTER 4

mHealth: Transforming the Delivery of Healthcare

Geeta Nayyar, MD, MBA

INTRODUCTION

Martha is a 59-year-old woman being seen by her primary care physician, Dr. Sue, for shoulder pain. She made her appointment online, including completing a comprehensive intake form regarding the reason for her visit and details about her pain. She was also instructed to update her medical record with insurance information, current medications, and new medical issues since her last visit. Her responses prompted a suggestion to take a couple of web-based screening tests, including one about her health-related quality of life and one assessing her risk of depression. At the same time, she received a referral for the routine blood tests she requires with instructions to complete them before her visit.

The day of the visit, the office staff texts Martha an hour before her appointment to tell her the doctor is on time. When Martha arrives, she signs in at the patient kiosk, which is similar to the boarding pass kiosks at the airport; swipes her credit card to pay her copayment; and uses the automatic blood pressure cuff, pulse oximeter, and thermometer to take her vital signs (the results are automatically uploaded into her medical chart).

At the same time, Martha uploads information from the fitness app she's been using to track her diet, exercise, and sleep patterns, as well as her blood glucose results from the past three months. Her blood test results are already in her chart.

An algorithm embedded into the medical record flags any issues Dr. Sue needs to follow up on, in addition to the shoulder pain. Before Dr. Sue even opens the examining room door, she has a single-page checklist of issues to discuss with Martha, thanks to the automated medical record.

Dr. Sue suspects Martha has a rotator cuff injury, so she electronically sends her a referral for physical therapy; a copy goes to the physical therapy center. She also emails Martha an information sheet about rotator cuff injuries and the recommended conservative treatment. Martha makes the appointment with the physical therapist via her electronic medical record (EMR) before she leaves the office.

Turns out Martha's blood pressure is also trending high, based on the results of the past two months, so Dr. Sue prescribes a diuretic, wirelessly sending the prescription directly to Martha's pharmacy (with a copy to her medical record, of course). At the same time, she reviews Martha's food diary and highlights a few areas for improvement, uploading some sample menus into Martha's record. She reminds Martha to continue using her home blood pressure cuff, which wirelessly beams the results into her medical record, and flags the record to evaluate the results in real time. Then she recommends a pain-tracking app so Martha can evaluate the pain levels in her shoulder in real time.

Martha checks out at the kiosk in the reception area, booking her next appointment at the same time.

Fantasy? Not quite. This is how the medical office of the near future will and should operate.

Healthcare may be one of the last industries in the country to go digital, but now that it has started, the transformation is occurring at warp speed. Just consider the recent rollout of Apple's iPhone 6 and iWatch, which are built on a suite of healthcare apps designed in conjunction with the Mayo Clinic. "We believe Apple's HealthKit will revolutionize how the health industry interacts with people," Mayo Clinic CEO John Noseworthy, MD, said in an interview with *Forbes* magazine.[1] The national media reports that Apple's movement into the healthcare industry will "revolutionize" it. Apple isn't the only tech company making big moves into healthcare, however; Google and Microsoft are also on the cutting edge.

Why are technology companies entering the healthcare space? Because healthcare in the United States is undergoing a sea change as it moves from a volume-based, provider-centric, uncoordinated, acute-care focused system to one based on quality and value that is facing an aging population, most of whom have multiple chronic conditions. The goal is to meet the Triple Aim to improve the patient experience of care, improve the health of the population, and reduce the per-capita cost of healthcare.

The Triple Aim builds a heavy reliance on mobile technology and big data. At the same time, increasingly empowered patients are demanding the same experience accessing healthcare they have when they access their bank accounts: across multiple platforms on their own time with seamless, simple processes.

For a clearer picture of where healthcare is heading, consider how the real estate industry has changed over the past two decades. Realtors and brokers used to have far more information on homes for sale than buyers and sellers because of their access to local multiple listing services.

Today, consumers can access as much or more information about homes, neighborhoods, and communities from their laptops, tablets, and smartphones. As a result, realtors have had to redefine their value proposition and treat buyers and sellers as partners rather than simply customers.

Now this transformative change from other industries is coming to healthcare.

THE GROWTH OF MOBILE TECHNOLOGY DRIVING MOBILE HEALTH

The growth of smartphones and tablets is driving the mHealth revolution. According to the Pew Research Internet Project, 90 percent of American adults today have a cell phone, and 58 percent of them have smartphones. A third own an e-reader, and 42 percent have a tablet.[2] Consulting firm Pricewaterhouse Coopers (PwC) estimates global mHealth revenue will reach $23 billion in 2017.[3]

"Mobile is rapidly growing as the most important channel throughout the customer journey," according to KBM Group's "Top 10 Healthcare Trends: 2014 Report." Almost a quarter of Facebook's 1 billion users are mobile, and the number is almost three times that for Twitter. "For Millennials, who send an average 88 texts per day, mobile isn't an activity, it's a lifestyle—it's their way of connecting."[4]

Americans are using their mobile devices for so many things related to everyday life that they are threatening the personal computer market, as well as traditional entertainment such as television and movies. And, increasingly, they are using them for health and medical needs. Why wouldn't they?

A recent report from Juniper Research indicates that 44 million mobile health applications were downloaded in 2013, a number projected to rise to about 142 million in 2016.[5]

In just five years, a March 2014 study by Research and Markets predicts there will be more than 3.4 billion smartphone and tablet users, half of whom will have downloaded mHealth applications.[6]

The KBM report found that approximately one third of consumers use their mobile devices or tablets on a daily basis for health research and/or to book medical appointments,[4] while a 2013 *Harris Interactive/HealthDay* survey found that one third of respondents who are online are "very" or "extremely" interested in using smartphones or tablets to make medical appointments, obtain test results, or ask their physicians questions. The survey also found that 16 percent of smartphone and tablet users regularly access health apps. In addition, 13 million wearable connected devices, like the Fitbit, will be integrated into patient treatment and management plans.[7] "Communication between patient and provider is no longer a one-way monologue, but rather a data-driven, personalized interactive dialog that's portable," say authors of the KBM report.[4]

The following statistics from the 2013 IMS Institute for Healthcare Informatics' report "Patient Apps for Improved Healthcare" highlight the challenges and opportunities facing providers in the mHealth sector:

- There were 43,000+ mobile health and wellness or medical apps available for download in Apple's iTunes store.
- Apps were categorized by seven capabilities, including "inform" (10,840), "instruct" (5,823), and record/capture data (5,095).
- Five apps accounted for 15 percent of all downloads.
- Smartphone use was lowest (18%) in the 65+ demographic.[8]

PATIENT ENGAGEMENT AND EMPOWERMENT

A child gets sick at school and the nurse pulls out her laptop for a quick consultation with a pediatrician 25 miles away. A woman with cancer brings her tablet to the examination room and shows her oncologist several clinical trials she found online. A retiree with diabetes checks his blood sugar levels each day with a small device attached to his smartphone. These are just a few of the ways in which mHealth devices and applications are empowering patients to take a more active role in their own care and partner with their physicians.

"We are moving away from physician- and hospital-centered care to a more patient-centric model where patients are more likely to share in the decision making if they can do so via their smartphones and tablets," says Bill Bria, MD, Chairman of the Board of the Association of Medical Directors of Information Systems.

The Veterans Administration (VA) is a leader in this effort. It created the Blue Button Initiative, an app designed to consolidate and integrate all medical information about the veteran in one place. But it is more than just a personal health record; it allows patients to enter their own data about diet and exercise; feeds information about vital signs such as weight and blood sugar directly into the app and, thus, medical record; automatically receives information on all tests; and even allows patients to read their doctor's progress notes. The VA has now rolled out the Blue Button initiative to providers in the private sector, including large employers and insurance companies.

When properly implemented—and embraced by both the provider and the patient—these types of mHealth solutions offer a team approach that not only increases patient satisfaction and loyalty, but also leads to better clinical outcomes.

Other patient engagement solutions include:

- Using secure messaging to communicate with patients on relevant health information
- Implementing certified EHR technology to identify patient-specific education resources and provide those resources to the patient
- Providing patients with the ability to wirelessly view, download, and transmit (VDT) their health information
- Using clinically relevant information to identify patients who should receive reminders for preventative/follow-up care
- Providing clinical summaries to patients after an office visit
- Recording whether patients have advance directives

Managing Patient Populations

A key component of healthcare reform and the Triple Aim is to improve the health of populations by providing quality, cost-effective care. Indeed, many of the new delivery and payment models are based on this approach. This is another area where mHealth is critical: by making it easier for patients and physicians to communicate, for patients to provide real-time health data to clinicians, and for healthcare providers to deliver customizable, interactive health information, mHealth has the potential to revolutionize population health management.[9] Indeed, population health management companies are attracting hundreds of millions in venture capital funding today.[10]

One example of the power of mHealth to change population behavior comes from Geisinger Health System where clinicians used a text-based weight management program to engage patients and improve care. Participants using the app reduced their body mass index 0.5 more than nonparticipants while demonstrating greater engagement in their own health.[11] Geisinger is now developing similar programs for post-discharge follow-up, medication reminders, and hepatitis C treatment.

Centura Health gave patients who had been hospitalized with a chronic health condition a mobile tool that collected vital sign data. Participants reported the results of their weight, blood pressure, pulse, and temperature to a nurse who could spot early signs of any problems and intervene. The system helped Centura reduce its 30-day readmission rate for this population from 19 percent to 4 percent.[12] Other providers are also deploying mHealth to reach remote patients in their service area, improving the quality of care for the underserved.

Meanwhile, developers are creating apps and devices to further empower patients, such as inhaler sensors for asthma medication that wirelessly connect with a patient's smartphone to track adherence and send reminders when they miss a dose.[13]

mHEALTH AND HEALTHCARE PROVIDERS

Physicians, hospitals, and other providers are also helping unlock the potential of mobile technology. A December 2012 survey by the Healthcare Information and Management Systems Society (HIMSS) found that 80 percent of physicians were already using mobile technology to provide patient care.[14]

In the 2014 HIMSS survey, respondents said that the top benefit of mobile technologies was increased access to patient information and the ability to view data from a remote location, while medication management, including medication reminders or medication reconciliation, topped lists as the most likely use of mobile technologies. Funding limitations was cited as the leading barrier.

However, many providers are also still early in their adoption and implementation of mobile technology. For example, only one third (36% percent) use mobile technologies to collect data at the bedside.

"The mobile health market is one of the fastest growing areas in the health IT space," says David Collins, senior director of mHIMSS. "We recognize the growing importance of mobile technologies and its impact to transform the delivery of patient care." The HIMSS survey, he said, "is a great example of how providers are integrating mHealth into today's healthcare workflows." However, he added, "There is still work to be done by formally embracing mobile implementation strategies and measuring [return on investment]."

Other key findings from respondents to the 2014 HIMSS report include:

- Third-party vendors develop the majority of apps.
- More than half of respondents planned to expand their use of apps in the future.
- One third of respondents offer apps for patient/consumer use, up from 14 percent a year ago.

- Sixty-two percent of respondents said they offered patients access to at least one of the mobile tools identified in the research, including patient portals, telehealth services, and remote monitoring devices.
- Fifty-nine percent have a mobile technology plan governing the use of mobile technology in their practices and institutions.
- Twenty-nine percent are developing a mobile technology plan.
- HIPAA requirements are most likely to impact the organizational mHealth environment.
- Ninety-five percent use at least one security tool to secure data on mobile devices.
- Passwords are the most widespread security device in place.
- Only 22 percent indicated that three quarters of the data captured by mobile devices was integrated into the organization's electronic medical record (EMR).
- Most respondents can access data from clinical systems via mobile devices, with most Internet access using a virtual private network.
- More than half of respondents received alerts/notifications from remote monitoring devices delivered via an EMR/clinical system alert.

(The survey reflects the responses of 170 healthcare IT and clinical personnel and can be downloaded by visiting http://bit.ly/1jRhGXa.)

Deploying mHealth Tools in the Provider Setting
Increasingly, healthcare providers are relying on mHealth to deliver better quality, patient-centered care that, not coincidentally, can also increase revenues.
This ranges from the simple—Vanderbilt University used a mobile app to track hand hygiene compliance—to the complex, such as remotely monitoring heart failure patients after discharge to prevent avoidable readmissions.[15]
Other hospital systems are using mHealth to improve care coordination between departments and providers; reduce patient no-shows; and streamline registration, discharge, and accounting functions.

DELIVERING REMOTE CARE

Across the country, providers are investing in telemedicine and telehealth programs that leverage mHealth platforms to expand their service footprint and provide patients with convenient access to care. For example, Miami Children's Hospital (MCH) recently launched, "MCH Anywhere," a telemedicine program built around a mobile platform designed to deliver specialized pediatric care to medically underserved communities in South Florida and Latin America. It allows MCH's specialists to examine, diagnose, and treat patients; consult with primary care physicians; write e-prescriptions; and assist paramedics preparing a child for air ambulance transport. It also incorporates mobile apps and mobile devices purpose-fit for specific telehealth uses, such as mobile robots with interactive video capabilities, diagnostic medical carts for physician offices, and medical kiosks within retail stores.

In the Midwest, Mercy Health, a four-state system, has deployed mobile vans and telemedicine programs that bring clinic services into rural communities. "We offer tele-psychology sessions, and our patient families reported they drove 55,000 fewer miles last year for their kids—a big savings in time and money for them," said Lynn Britton, president and CEO, at a 2014 University of Miami conference, "The Business of Health Care: Bending the Cost Curve."[16]

Because of the potential of telemedicine programs to promote wellness, reduce costs, and improve patient care in rural areas, the U.S. Department of Health and Human Services (HHS) is offering grants and incentives to promote these mHealth initiatives. "Teleheath refers to any remote telecommunications healthcare providers use to interact with and manage patients," notes the department. "It can range from teleconferencing between patient and provider to high-quality online voice and video interactions. Properly implemented, telehealth can expand access and reduce costs of healthcare, and save time and money for both the patient and the provider.[17]

Opening Retail Clinics

Major pharmacy chains and shopping centers are taking advantage of mHealth platforms to open limited-service clinics in retail locations. Consumers can access care for themselves and their families as part of a regular shopping trip. Staffed by nurses, nurse practitioners, or other physician extenders, these clinics may use tablets for check-in and patient education services, and incorporate telemedicine capabilities in case a physician needs to be contacted about a patient.

"Retail outlets providing clinical care have moved into mobile health from their established footholds," a 2012 Deloitte report "mHealth in an mWorld" states. Most retail centers, notes the report, already have a strong online presence and mobile functionality in terms of store locators, customer relationship management, and online/mobile shopping. The report continues, "As urgent care centers and retail clinics expand, they are using mobile for appointment scheduling, prescription management, and patient record access. Other convenience-related applications include mobile wallets, text message reminders, and tie-ins with in-store promotions."[18]

Retail outlets may also become associated with ACOs and integrated networks, creating the need for networked health records, kiosk-based consultations, transmission of biometric data, and virtual consultations.[19]

Helping Stroke Patients

By establishing a telemedicine link using videoconferencing and image-sharing technology, stroke specialists from Brigham and Women's and Massachusetts General Hospitals can examine patients at remote hospitals miles away to help diagnose patients' ailments and recommend a plan of care.

One form of treatment is to administer tissue plasminogen activator (tPA), a clot-busting drug that can greatly reduce disability resulting from a stroke. However, tPA must be administered within 4.5 hours of symptom onset.

"Patients are arriving at smaller community hospitals who are candidates for this clot-buster therapy and in some cases may not be getting it," said Lee Schwamm, MD, Massachusetts General Hospital. This may occur because some hospitals lack the resources to make this determination and cannot physically transfer the patient quickly enough to enable him or her to receive this therapy when warranted. Hospitals can now, however, subscribe to the hospital's TeleStroke system and receive acute stroke care for a patient without physically transferring the patient for an exam.

"I can examine someone very interactively with the help of a physician or a nurse on the other end and I can make a determination of the stroke severity and the type of stroke by looking at the patient and at the brain image," said Schwamm. "It's almost like being in the room."[20]

Monitoring Patients from Home

In addition to smartphones equipped with diagnostic devices and mobile apps, a growing number of patients with serious conditions are wearing sensors that allow providers to monitor their well-being from home. In fact, the remote monitoring services segment of the mHealth market accounted for about 63 percent of the sector's revenue in 2012, according to a report from market research firm Transparency Market Research.[21] Looking ahead, ABI Research has projected that by 2016, wearable wireless medical device sales will reach more than 100 million devices annually.[22]

Remote sensors are particularly appropriate for patients with high-risk cardiac conditions, such as congestive heart failure or arrhythmias. If the sensor detects a problem with a patient's heartbeat, an alert can immediately be sent to the patient along with instructions such as taking a medication dose. The provider is also alerted and can contact the patient and summon an emergency rescue team if there is no response. Devices using Bluetooth technology also allow caregivers to track elderly patients' movements and monitor their health.

"There is increasing clinical evidence of the value of continuous physiological data in managing chronic diseases and monitoring patients' post-hospitalization," said Theo Ahadome, senior analyst at IMS Research, in a recent interview. "As a result, a growing number of medical devices are becoming wearable, including glucose monitors, ECG monitors, pulse oximeters, and blood pressure monitors."[23]

In addition to saving lives, remote monitoring of patients can help reduce provider costs by shortening the amount of time the patient spends in the hospital and by lowering the frequency of follow-up visits to the physician, according to Pawan Kumar, head of ICT and Semiconductor Practices at Transparency Market Research. "The introduction of newer and improved mobile health applications in the market is helping the healthcare providers to cater (to a higher) number of patients in less time with significant cost saving," he added.[24]

Wearable Fitness Devices

Another aspect of the mHealth revolution is the growing consumer demand for wearable devices for tracking physical activity and managing their own health. These devices range from headsets that measure brainwaves to smart watches with fitness monitoring capabilities, clothes with built-in sensing devices, and Internet-connected eyeglass displays that allow consumers to receive hands-free notifications. For example, fitness monitors can track an individual's heart rate, calories burned, and distance covered while running, walking, bicycling, or taking part in sports.

"In the past year, wearable technologies have emerged as the next big consumer electronics market category, particularly for health and wellness," said Mattias Lewren, global managing director of Accenture's Electronics and High-Tech industry group, which conducted the Accenture Digital Consumer Tech Survey 2014. The survey of more than 6,000 people in six countries—Australia, Canada, India, South Africa, the United Kingdom, and the United States—showed that more than half of respondents were interested in buying fitness monitors, smart watches with mHealth features, and Internet-enabled eyeglasses. "Every consumer is a digital consumer, and the keen interest in wearable technology provides further evidence of that," added Lewren.[25]

mHEALTH AND THE GOVERNMENT

Because of the potential for mHealth solutions to increase access to care, improve outcomes, and manage costs, the federal government is supporting mobile technology initiatives. The Affordable Care Act (ACA) provides financial incentives for providers to implement innovative health IT programs, including mHealth solutions.

In addition, the U.S. Food and Drug Administration (FDA) encourages the development of mobile medical apps that improve healthcare and provide consumers and healthcare professionals with valuable health information. The agency notes, "Mobile applications (apps) can help people manage their own health and wellness, promote healthy living, and gain access to useful information when and where they need it. These tools are being adopted almost as quickly as they can be developed."[26]

While many mobile apps carry minimal risk, those that can pose a greater risk to patients will require FDA review, said the agency, noting it has a public health responsibility to oversee the safety and effectiveness of medical devices and apps.

According to the FDA, mobile apps are considered to be medical when they meet the definition of a medical device, are an accessory to a regulated medical device, or transform a mobile platform into a regulated medical device. Mobile medical apps currently on the market can, for example, diagnose abnormal heart rhythms, transform smartphones into mobile ultrasound devices, or function as the "central command" for a glucose meter used by a person with insulin-dependent diabetes.

"Some mobile apps carry minimal risks to consumers or patients, but others can carry significant risks if they do not operate correctly. The FDA's tailored policy protects patients while encouraging innovation," said Jeffrey Shuren, MD, JD, director of the FDA's Center for Devices and Radiological Health.[27]

In September 2013, the FDA issued the "Mobile Medical Applications Guidance," which explains the agency's oversight of mobile medical apps as devices. The FDA's focus is on apps that present a greater risk to patients if they fail to work as intended and on apps that cause smartphones or other mobile platforms to affect the performance of traditional medical devices. The FDA states it will apply the same risk-based approach it uses to assure safety and effectiveness for other medical devices.[28]

Providers should understand the difference between mobile medical apps and mobile apps (medical mobile apps fall within the overview of the FDA while non-medical apps do not) because consumers will use both types of mHealth tools to manage their health and wellness. For example, the National Institutes of Health's LactMed app provides nursing mothers with information about the effects of medicines on breast milk and nursing infants.

Other apps aim to help healthcare professionals improve and facilitate patient care. The Radiation Emergency Medical Management (REMM) app gives healthcare providers guidance on diagnosing and treating radiation injuries. Some mobile medical apps can diagnose cancer, in addition to monitoring heart rhythm abnormalities or diabetic patients' glucose readings.

Providers who plan to develop their own mobile apps should be aware of the difference already mentioned: medical mobile apps fall within the overview of the FDA while nonmedical apps do not.

CHALLENGES FACING mHEALTH

While mHealth has a bright future, there are a number of challenges that need to be addressed before providers can take advantage of the power of these mobile tools. In general, those challenges fall into two categories: technology and provider culture. In both cases, they require healthcare professionals to change their habits, attitudes, and procedures—a difficult shift for both individuals and organizations.

On the financial side, mHealth solutions may require providers to invest in new platforms and applications, such as developing mobile apps or deploying electronic patient check-in/check-out tablets. This typically means a change in using internal financial and human resources and necessitates training staff on the systems and procedures.

For providers to make those investments, they must consider the potential return on their investments (ROI) in terms of clinical outcomes, operating costs, and overall revenue. Because many mHealth solutions are relatively new, some providers may decide to delay their purchases until there is more evidence of a solid ROI on these investments.

"Evidence of clinical efficacy needs to be both outcomes- and cost-based for payers and providers to support and endorse patient use," notes the IMS Institute study.[8]

Security and Privacy Concerns

One type of technology challenge involves data security and patient privacy requirements. The Deloitte report noted earlier states, "The extent to which stakeholders create user confidence through adequate privacy and security protections will play a key role in accelerating or retarding the adoption of mHealth and the realization of benefits."[18]

The ability to access patient data and applications from remote locations through mobile devices raises a number of security concerns:

- If the device is lost or stolen, can a former spouse, ex-boyfriend, employer, or criminal access that confidential medical information?
- Will users follow strong password requirements and change them regularly—a best practice in terms of security?
- How can providers secure their EMRs and patient databases from unauthorized intruders?

One solution is a secure web-based messaging system that allows patients and healthcare team to communicate nonurgent, health-related information in a private and safe computer environment. It is built around existing communication tools such as the patient portal, secure email, and the EMR.[29]

Mobile devices can be equipped with autolock, disabling or tracking applications that allow a consumer to "brick" a mobile device so that no data can be extracted. However, not all smartphones and tablets have these applications, and some consumers may be reluctant to use them in hopes that their device might be recovered intact.

In general terms, IT security issues may require providers to build partnerships with mHealth companies for strategic advice, implementation, and ongoing support. After all, IT is not a core competency for most healthcare providers.

Interoperability

As healthcare providers increasingly form collaborative partnerships, such as ACOs, their databases, networks, and mHealth platforms need seamless connections. This is essential for data to flow from a check-in kiosk to a physician's tablet to a hospital's admitting office, a pharmacy issuing e-prescriptions, or a patient's smartphone with a mobile app.

Health IT professionals know it is a daunting challenge simply to move patient records from a paper-based system to an EMR. The technology issues multiply when trying to connect multiple providers with different networks and database formats. Then, once various systems have been integrated, there is a further interoperability challenge: being able to access those data on various mobile devices and platforms.

Without getting into the technical details, it is clear that the ability to transmit patient and provider data quickly and easily across networks and mobile devices will remain a significant challenge in the years ahead.

Provider Culture

In addition to the technology challenges, providers considering mHealth initiatives must be willing to change their attitudes and behaviors concerning patients, engaging and educating them about their care. They must also look at changes to their office systems, policies, and procedures and be willing to tolerate short-term disruption in order to receive long-term benefits.

For instance, employees may be reluctant to adopt new technology, especially if it means reducing staffing levels. Physicians may find it difficult to take time out of their busy patient schedules to learn how to use these new tools effectively. And in many cases, providers will also have to place a greater emphasis on patient education, such as downloading a tethered mobile app and demonstrating how to use it effectively.

CONCLUSION—THE OPPORTUNITY AHEAD

Regardless of the challenges, mHealth tools offer a wealth of opportunities for providers to deliver better care, more efficiently and at a lower cost. They offer creative approaches to improving patient care and for reaching out and engaging patients more effectively.

Mobile applications and devices are well suited to address the needs of the nation's demographic groups, as well. For instance, aging Baby Boomers will increasingly require care for chronic diseases, which may be monitored by remote applications. They may find it difficult to drive to a physician's office or clinic and may prefer telehealth services from the comfort of their homes.

At the other end of the spectrum, the young adult Millennials already rely on mobile devices and apps for information and entertainment. Many already incorporate mHealth medical, wellness, and health apps into their daily lives and prefer to use these tools to schedule appointments and contact their physicians.

Today, mobile devices and applications enable patients and families to have 24/7 access to physicians, hospitals, and other providers. A large primary group practice might find it worthwhile to have a doctor on call at all times, as an alternative to visiting an urgent care clinic or emergency department. Of course, a way of generating revenue from those voice, text, or video consultations would be needed.

Social media is another mHealth tool with untapped potential for the healthcare sector. Even though many providers are venturing into this space with their own Facebook pages or YouTube videos, far more could be done to engage patients and families. A hospital or physician practice could set up a support group for patients which chronic diseases or schedule daily check-ins with homebound patients who are elderly or have disabling conditions.

Gaming systems provide another opportunity to engage patients through tablets and smartphones. Health educators and even insurance companies have already started to use gaming technology to more effectively engage patients. Additional advancements and adoption could lead to real-life discounts or rewards for "winning" games with positive health outcomes.

In addition to its impact on clinical care, mHealth is likely to have an even bigger role in healthcare organizations in the next few years. The changeover to EMRs is creating new opportunities for faster and better coordinated clinical care, and far-sighted providers are applying IT across the continuum of care—such as patient scheduling, tracking, engagement, pharmacy and follow-up appointments—with impressive results.

As mHealth plays a bigger role in the delivery of services, providers will need to invest more resources into this sector, whether using an in-house or outsourcing strategy. It will not be enough to purchase systems and solutions on a project-by-project basis. The key for providers will be developing a clear technology strategy to capitalize on the many mHealth opportunities as healthcare moves into the future.

REFERENCES

1. http://www.forbes.com/sites/dandiamond/2014/09/09/iphone-6-apple-and-mayo-clinic-partnership-could-be-smart-medicine-2/. Accessed November 14, 2014.
2. http://www.pewinternet.org/fact-sheets/mobile-technology-fact-sheet/. Accessed November 14, 2014.
3. PWC Report: Touching Lives through Mobile Health http://www.pwc.in/assets/pdfs/telecom/gsma-pwc_mhealth_report.pdf. Accessed January 28, 2015.
4. http://content.kbmg.com/downloads/TOP_10_Healthcare_Trends_2014_Whitepaper.pdf. Accessed January 28, 2015.
5. https://www.juniperresearch.com/reports/mobile_healthcare_opportunities. Accessed January 28, 2015.
6. http://www.researchandmarkets.com/reports/2497392/mobile_health_app_market_report_20132017_the. Accessed January 28, 2015.
7. http://www.harrisinteractive.com/NewsRoom/PressReleases/tabid/446/mid/1506/articleId/1215/ctl/ReadCustom%20Default/Default.aspx. Accessed January 28, 2015.

8. http://www.imshealth.com/deployedfiles/imshealth/Global/Content/Corporate/IMS%20Health%20 Institute/Reports/Patient_Apps/IIHI_Patient_Apps_Report.pdf. Accessed January 28, 2015.

9. http://www.mhealthnews.com/news/using-mhealth-enhance-population-health-management? single-page=true. Accessed November 14, 2014.

10. http://ehrintelligence.com/2014/07/22/population-health-analytics-mhealth-vendors-raise-1-8b-in-q2/. Accessed November 14, 2014.

11. http://himss.files.cms-plus.com/FileDownloads/Use%20Case%20Study%20Geisinger%20Health%20 System%20Weight%20Management%20Text%20Program.pdf. Accessed November 14, 2014.

12. http://www.commonwealthfund.org/publications/case-studies/2013/jan/telehealth-centura. Accessed November 14, 2014.

13. http://www.himss.org/ResourceLibrary/genResourceDetailPDF.aspx?ItemNumber=20223. Accessed November 14, 2014.

14. http://www.himss.org/files/himssorg/content/files/FINALwithCOVER.pdf. Accessed January 28, 2015.

15. http://www.himss.org/resourcelibrary/TopicList.aspx?MetaDataID=2935. Accessed November 14, 2014.

16. "The Business of Health Care: Bending the Cost Curve." Lynn Britton. University of Miami Conference Presentation. January 17, 2014; University of Miami, Coral Gables, FL.

17. http://www.healthcareitnews.com/directory/telehealth. Accessed November 14, 2014.

18. http://www2.deloitte.com/us/en/pages/life-sciences-and-health-care/articles/center-for-health-solutions-mhealth-in-an-mworld.html. Accessed January 28, 2015.

19. http://www.deloitte.com/view/en_US/us/Industries/life-sciences/2545b66b8dc4b310VgnVCM-2000003356f70aRCRD.htm. Accessed November 14, 2014.

20. http://telestroke.massgeneral.org/telestroke.aspx. Accessed November 14, 2014.

21. http://www.healthcareitnews.com/news/mhealth-market-hit-102b-2018. Accessed January 28, 2015.

22. http://www.informationweek.com/mobile/10-wearable-health-tech-devices-to-watch/d/d-id/1107148. Accessed January 28, 2015.

23. http://www.informationweek.com/mobile/10-wearable-health-tech-devices-to-watch/d/d-id/1107148. Accessed January 28, 2015.

24. http://www.informationweek.com/mobile/10-wearable-health-tech-devices-to-watch/d/d-id/1107148. Accessed January 28, 2015.

25. http://www.healthcareitnews.com/news/mhealth-market-hit-102b-2018. Accessed January 28, 2015.

26. http://www.fda.gov/medicaldevices/productsandmedicalprocedures/connectedhealth/mobilemedicalapplications/default.htm. Accessed January 28, 2015.

27. http://www.fda.gov/NewsEvents/Newsroom/PressAnnouncements/ucm369431.htm. Accessed November 14, 2014.

28. http://www.fda.gov/medicaldevices/productsandmedicalprocedures/connectedhealth/mobilemedicalapplications/default.htm. Accessed November 14, 2014.

29. http://www.himss.org/library/patient-engagement/secure-messaging?navItemNumber=17848. Accessed November 14, 2014.

CHAPTER 5

Patient-Centered Medical Home

Salvatore Volpe, MD

INTRODUCTION

Much has transpired since the previous edition's chapter on the Patient-Centered Medical Home (PCMH) was written.

- First, most experts would agree that we have moved from pilot stage to actual working models.
- Second, more payers and employers have accepted the need to modify reimbursement systems from the Acute Care Model to one that helps cover the cost of managing populations and rewarding for positive outcomes and improved patient satisfaction.
- Third, most studies now support that PCMHs have a positive impact on quality, though the degree of the impact varies widely.
- Fourth, there is a greater alignment between government programs such as meaningful use (MU) and PCMH.
- Fifth, PCMH recognition programs are being offered to specialists.
- Sixth, PCMH recognition programs are also being offered by The Joint Commission (where PCMH refers to Primary Care Medical Home) and by the Utilization Review Accreditation Commission.

In this updated chapter, we will review the origins and philosophy of PCMH and also touch on some of the new literature and the new 2014 standards.

ORIGIN OF THE PATIENT-CENTERED MEDICAL HOME MODEL

In French, there is a phrase, "Plus ca change, plus ca ne change pas." (The more things change, the more they stay the same.) I am sure that there are few primary care providers (PCPs) who have not heard of the term *medical home*. Compare that with awareness of the concept 10 years ago, as American medicine was reaching its peak in dividing care into the maximal number of silos possible. The drive to sub-subspecialization, the inadequate reimbursement for anything other than acute procedure-driven healthcare, and rising medical liability led to many PCPs being little more than gatekeepers.

Forty-six years ago, the Council of Pediatric Practice (COPP) had a prescient opinion regarding healthcare. At that time, they were trying to address children with special healthcare needs (CSHCN). The federal Maternal and Child Health Bureau defines CSHCN as: "Those who have or are at increased risk for a chronic physical, developmental, behavioral, or emotional condition and who also require health and related services of a type or amount beyond that required by children generally."[1]

"For children with chronic diseases or disabling conditions, the lack of a complete record and a 'medical home' is a major deterrent to adequate health supervision. Wherever the child is cared for, the question should be asked, 'Where is the child's medical home?' and any pertinent information should be transmitted to that place."[2]

Back in 1967, there were no fax machines, no secure email, no GUI (graphical user interface) EHRs. There was, however, the realization that without the coordination of care by all providers, the families of these children would suffer from gaps in care, redundant "care," and skyrocketing expenses. Sound familiar?

The COPP made three recommendations:

> The first requirement is the teaching of all medical students that a medical home and a complete central record of a child's medical care are the sine qua non of proper pediatric supervision. Second, the concept must spread from physicians to all agencies and people caring for children—schools, child guidance clinics, well-infant stations, surgical specialists, emergency departments, and so forth. The third step is the indoctrination of parents.[3]

While the goals were laudatory, it was not until Calvin Sia, MD, took up the gauntlet that the concept gained the exposure and funding needed to be implemented. Between 1978 and 1979, Dr. Sia succeeded in having the term *medical home* incorporated in legislation passed in Hawaii. "This was the birth of the medical home concept as we know it today. It stated that a medical home would be family centered; be community-based (geographically and financially accessible and available); offer continuity, comprehensive, and coordinated care; and, use the resources of related services in the neighborhood."[4]

In 1998, Edward H. Wagner, MD, proposed the following model for chronic disease management based on his work at Group Health Cooperative (see Figure 5-1). Communities depend on healthcare delivery systems to have four key features:

- **Self-management Support:** Patients and their families are given tools and resources to participate in management of their health.
- **Delivery System Design:** The system to deliver healthcare has to take into account the multiple agents and facilitate communication.
- **Decision Support:** Evidence-based clinical support tools need to be available at the point of care.
- **Information Systems:** Information technology needs to be developed to facilitate communication between providers, patients, and the community.[5]

In 2002, the American Academy of Pediatrics (AAP) issued the following description of the medical home:

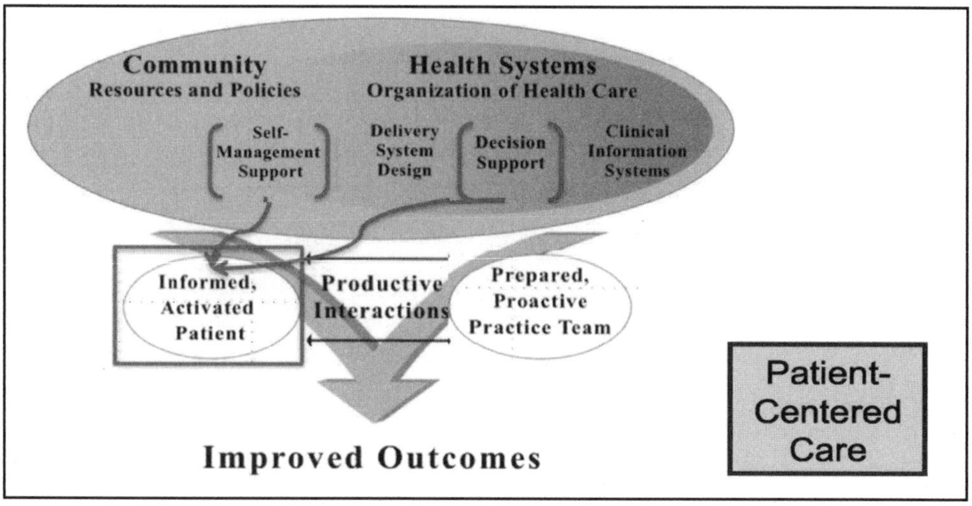

Figure 5-1: Model for Chronic Disease Management.[5]

1. Provision of family-centered care through developing a trusting partnership with families, respecting their diversity, and recognizing that they are the constant in a child's life.
2. Sharing clear and unbiased information with the family about the child's medical care and management and about the specialty and community services and organizations they can access.
3. Provision of primary care, including, but not restricted to, acute and chronic care and preventive services, including breastfeeding promotion and management, immunizations, growth and developmental assessments, appropriate screenings, healthcare supervision, and patient and parent counseling about health, nutrition, safety, parenting, and psychosocial issues.
4. Assurance that ambulatory and inpatient care for acute illnesses will be continuously available (24 hours a day, 7 days a week, 52 weeks a year).
5. Provision of care over an extended period of time to ensure continuity. Transitions, including those to other pediatric providers or into the adult healthcare system, should be planned and organized with the child and family.
6. Identification of the need for consultation and appropriate referral to pediatric medical subspecialists and surgical specialists. (In instances in which the child enters the medical system through a specialty clinic, identification of the need for primary pediatric consultation and referral is appropriate.) Primary, pediatric medical subspecialty, and surgical specialty care providers should collaborate to establish shared management plans in partnership with the child and family and to formulate a clear articulation of each other's role.
7. Interaction with early intervention programs, schools, early childhood education and child care programs, and other public and private community agencies to be certain that the special needs of the child and family are addressed.
8. Provision of care coordination services in which the family, the physician, and other service providers work to implement a specific care plan as an organized team.

9. Maintenance of an accessible, comprehensive, central record that contains all pertinent information about the child, preserving confidentiality.[6]

In 2007, AAP, the American Academy of Family Practice, American College of Physicians, and American Osteopathic Association, representing approximately 333,000 physicians, developed the following joint principles to describe the characteristics of the PCMH.

- **Personal physician.** Each patient has an ongoing relationship with a personal physician trained to provide first contact, continuous and comprehensive care.
- **Physician-directed medical practice.** The personal physician leads a team of individuals at the practice level who collectively take responsibility for the ongoing care of patients.
- **Whole-person orientation.** The personal physician is responsible for providing for all the patient's healthcare needs or taking responsibility for appropriately arranging care with other qualified professionals. This includes care for all stages of life: acute care, chronic care, preventive services, and end-of-life care.
- **Care is coordinated and/or integrated** across all elements of the complex healthcare system (e.g., subspecialty care, hospitals, home health agencies, nursing homes) and the patient's community (e.g., family, public and private community-based services). Care is facilitated by registries, IT, health information exchange (HIE), and other means to assure that patients get the indicated care when and where they need and want it in a culturally and linguistically appropriate manner.
- **Quality and safety** are hallmarks of the medical home:
  - Practices advocate for their patients to support the attainment of optimal, patient-centered outcomes that are defined by a care planning process driven by a compassionate, robust partnership between physicians, patients, and the patient's family.
  - Evidence-based medicine and clinical decision-support tools guide decision making.
  - Physicians in the practice accept accountability for continuous quality improvement through voluntary engagement in performance measurement and improvement.
  - Patients actively participate in decision making, and feedback is sought to ensure patients' expectations are being met.
  - IT is utilized appropriately to support optimal patient care, performance measurement, patient education, and enhanced communication.
  - Practices go through a voluntary recognition process by an appropriate non-governmental entity to demonstrate that they have the capabilities to provide patient-centered services consistent with the medical home model.
  - Patients and families participate in quality improvement activities at the practice level.
- **Enhanced access** to care is available through systems such as open scheduling, expanded hours, and new options for communication between patients, their personal physician, and practice staff.

- **Payment** appropriately recognizes the added value provided to patients who have a PCMH. The payment structure should be based on the following framework:
  - It should reflect the value of physician and non-physician staff patient-centered care management work that falls outside of the face-to-face visit.
  - It should pay for services associated with coordination of care both within a given practice and between consultants, ancillary providers, and community resources.
  - It should support adoption and use of health IT for quality improvement.
  - It should support provision of enhanced communication access such as secure email and telephone consultation.
  - It should recognize the value of physician work associated with remote monitoring of clinical data using technology.
  - It should allow for separate fee-for-service payments for face-to-face visits. (Payments for care management services that fall outside of the face-to-face visit, as previously described, should not result in a reduction in the payments for face-to-face visits.)
  - It should recognize case mix differences in the patient population being treated within the practice.
  - It should allow physicians to share in savings from reduced hospitalizations associated with physician-guided care management in the office setting.
  - It should allow for additional payments for achieving measurable and continuous quality improvements.[7]

PCMH Recognition

The National Committee for Quality Assurance (NCQA) produced a set of standards by which a practice can be recognized as having patient-centered medical status. Based on a point system, a practice may be rated as having achieved Level 1, 2, or 3 Recognition.[8]

In 2008, there were nine Physician Practice Connections (PPC®) standards, including 10 "must pass elements," which can result in one of three levels of recognition (see Figure 5-2). Practices seeking PPC®-PCMH™ complete a web-based data collection tool and provide documentation that validates responses. Level 1 only requires passage of five of the ten elements.

Since 2008, there have been several revisions, first in 2011 and again in 2014, as noted in Table 5-1.

In 2014, the NCQA PCMH recognition program was consolidated to six standards:

1. PCMH 1: Patient-Centered Access
2. PCMH 2: Team-Based Care
3. PCMH 3: Population Health Management
4. PCMH 4: Care Management and Support
5. PCMH 5: Care Coordination and Care Transitions
6. PCMH 6: Performance Measurement and Quality Improvement[9]

PPC-PCMH Content and Scoring

Standard 1: Access and Communication	Pts
A. **Has written standards for patient access and patient communication****	**4**
B. **Uses data to show it meets its standards for patient access and communication****	**5**
	9
Standard 2: Patient Tracking and Registry Functions	Pts
A. Uses data system for basic patient information (mostly non-clinical data)	2
B. Has clinical data system with clinical data in searchable data fields	3
C. Uses the clinical data system	3
D. **Uses paper or electronic-based charting tools to organize clinical information****	**6**
E. **Uses data to identify important diagnoses and conditions in practice****	**4**
F. Generates lists of patients and reminds patients and clinicians of services needed (population management)	3
	21
Standard 3: Care Management	Pts
A. **Adopts and implements evidence-based guidelines for three conditions ****	**3**
B. Generates reminders about preventive services for clinicians	4
C. Uses non-physician staff to manage patient care	3
D. Conducts care management, including care plans, assessing progress, addressing barriers	5
E. Coordinates care//follow-up for patients who receive care in inpatient and outpatient facilities	5
	20
Standard 4: Patient Self-Management Support	Pts
A. Assesses language preference and other communication barriers	2
B. **Actively supports patient self-management****	**4**
	6

Standard 5: Electronic Prescribing	Pts
A. Uses electronic system to write prescriptions	3
B. Has electronic prescription writer with safety checks	3
C. Has electronic prescription writer with cost checks	2
	8
Standard 6: Test Tracking	Pts
A. **Tracks tests and identifies abnormal results systematically****	**7**
B. Uses electronic systems to order and retrieve tests and flag duplicate tests	6
	13
Standard 7: Referral Tracking	PT
A. **Tracks referrals using paper-based or electronic system****	**4**
	4
Standard 8: Performance Reporting and Improvement	Pts
A. **Measures clinical and/or service performance by physician or across the practice****	**3**
B. Survey of patients' care experience	3
C. **Reports performance across the practice or by physician ****	**3**
D. Sets goals and takes action to improve performance	3
E. Produces reports using standardized measures	2
F. Transmits reports with standardized measures electronically to external entities	1
	15
Standard 9: Advanced Electronic Communications	Pts
A. Availability of Interactive Website	1
B. Electronic Patient Identification	2
C. Electronic Care Management Support	1
	4

Figure 5-2: PPC-PCMH Content and Scoring

Table 5-1: PCMH Revisions

2011	PCMH 2011	• Explicitly incorporated health IT MU criteria. • Added content and examples for pediatric practices on parental decision making, age-appropriate immunizations, teen privacy, and other issues. • Added voluntary distinction for practices that participate in the CAHPS PCMH survey of patient experience and submit data to NCQA. • Added content and examples for behavioral healthcare.
2014	PCMH 2014	• More integration of behavioral healthcare. • Additional emphasis on team-based care. • Focus care management for high-need populations. • Encourage involvement of patients and families in QI activities. • Alignment of QI activities with the Triple Aim: Improved quality, cost, and experience of care. • Alignment with health IT MU Stage 2.

Note: CAHPS: Consumer Assessment of Healthcare Providers and Systems

Just as in 2008, there are "must pass" elements. The provider must achieve a score of 50 percent or greater on each.

1. PCMH 1, Element A: Patient-Centered Appointment Access
2. PCMH 2, Element D: The Practice Team
3. PCMH 3, Element D: Use Data for Population Management
4. PCMH 4, Element B: Care Planning and Self-Care Support

5. PCMH 5, Element B: Referral Tracking and Follow-up
6. PCMH 6, Element D: Implement Continuous Quality Improvement[10]

As you can see, the six standards reflect the agreed on Joint Principles of PCMH. All six standards depend on the practice performing regular self-reviews to identify gaps or areas for improvement. We will now review some highlights of the standards.

PCMH 1: Patient-Centered Access. Practices need to provide patients with a physician who will have responsibility for their care. As practices attempt to fulfill this seemingly simple measure, they also need to put into place policies that will ensure that this will occur. As a physician in solo practice for over 15 years prior to making my first application, this was a given. That notwithstanding, it was valuable to create the policies to ensure that patients had adequate and timely access for communication, as well as office visits.

Some changes do not rely on technology, but just a possible change in policy. Some time should be allocated each day for patients who need same-day visits.

Just as smartphones and tablets have evolved, so must practices and reimbursement models. A growing number of health plans and soon CMS as well, will provide payment for telemedicine services. Asynchronous secure email may be a consideration for some, as well as group visits.

Providing patients access to their medical information 24/7 is becoming the norm. Until posting the office visit on the web becomes the norm, I recommend that practices consider following the model we have used since we began using the EHR. We give out a copy of the office visit to each patient. While PCMH and MU require electronic posting of the Visit Summary and other health information, giving out a hard copy of the visit has many benefits, including recruiting patients and their caregivers as proofreaders.[11,12]

If any errors are identified, they are quickly addressed. Family members at home are encouraged to review the notes as well. These family reviewers become members of my healthcare team. In a solo practice like ours, it is a major benefit to have others identify gaps in the patient's medical history and to encourage the patient to follow through with our recommendations. Our patient portal permits the patient and designated significant others to access most of their medical record short of the chief complaint and physical exam. We thus have family members living hundreds of miles away assisting us in fulfilling our mission.

We also provide patients with access to vetted medical information. Our website includes links to the Centers for Disease Control and Prevention (CDC) Medline (http://www.ncbi.nlm.nih.gov/pubmed/), and other sites that provide information at the appropriate reading level and in a multitude of languages.[13,14]

The third step is to provide patient access to communication. This can be as simple as giving them a few extra moments to collect their thoughts to giving them access to a secure email system via the patient portal and EHR.

A patient portal with or without a static website will assist the practice in many ways. The sample website described next provides several benefits for patients.

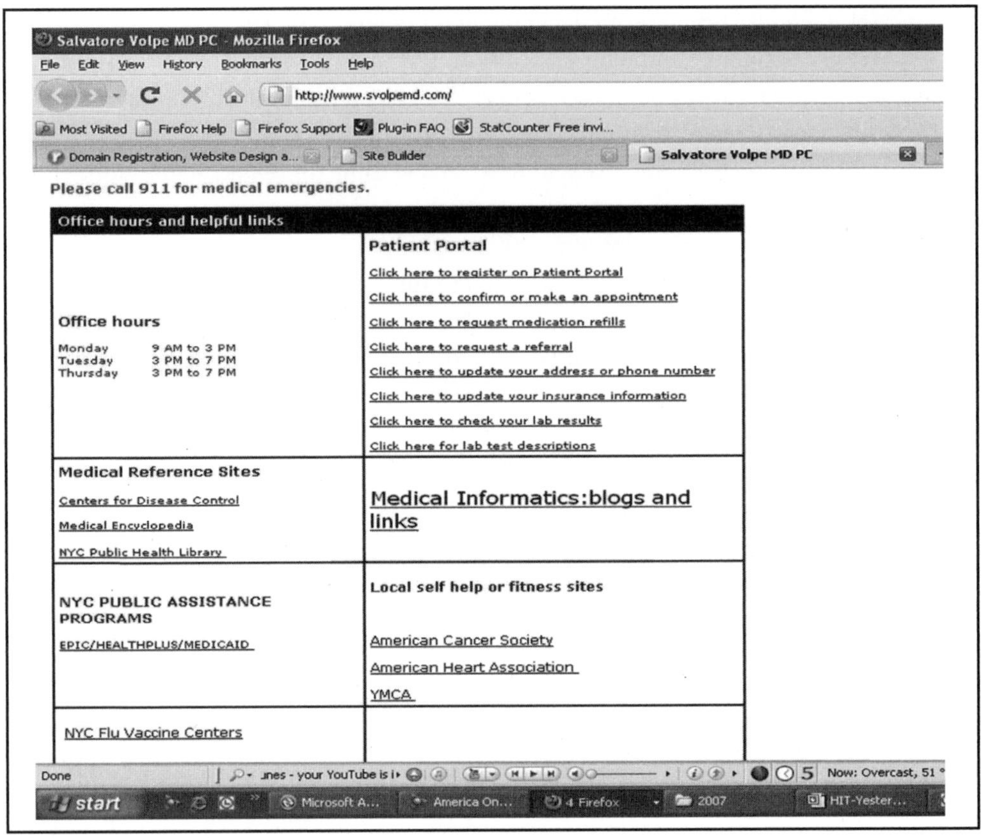

Figure 5-3: Sample Physician Practice Website[15]

1. A listing of the office hours
2. A listing of the services available via the patient portal: appointment requests, referral requests, medication refill requests, demographic updates, personal health information
3. A list of vetted web-based reference sites such as the CDC and Medline
4. A list of public assistance sites, including coverage information for the uninsured
5. A list of self-help sites
6. Potential to forward personalized health information to each patient's account
7. Online billing
8. Secure health messaging

PCMH 2: Team-Based Care. The goal here is to provide culturally and linguistically team-based care.

Patients need to be made to feel welcome when they join the practice. Just as one would introduce a guest to the family, a patient should be introduced to the team members of the practice who will be responsible for their care. This can be done face to face or by reviewing the roster and providing the recommended means of contacting the different members as needs arise. As PCMH is still a relatively new concept in many communities, the practice needs to review how the staff will help the patient transition into the practice, work with caregivers, and coordinate care with others.

A practice will need to access the linguistic needs of its patients and provide, when necessary, translation services and educational materials in the preferred language of its patients.

A team huddle prior to seeing the day's patients provides many benefits. By reviewing the reason for the day's visit, previously ordered diagnostic tests, pending preventative services, and potential barriers the patients have expressed for achieving their goals, the day actually runs more efficiently. Each member of the staff is to be encouraged to work to the highest level of his or her training or license. By having the staff more engaged in the care of each patient, there is a greater likelihood of improved staff satisfaction as each person now has a tangible role in helping another human being.

Either by completing surveys or by participating in an advisory council, patients and their caregivers can provide valuable information and advice to further improve the practice's operations.

PCMH 3: Population Health Management. The United States does not compare favorably with many other nations in the management of many chronic diseases. Studies of care within the United States show large disparities along geographic, as well as socioeconomic lines. For example, the disparities in hemoglobin A1C testing is well illustrated in the *Dartmouth Atlas of Healthcare.*[16]

These disparities can account for 80 percent of health outcomes. Minnesota-based HealthPartners adopted a Community Business Model which depended on an alliance of school systems, community-based organizations, foundations, state and local governments, as well as other organizations to help address these disparities. Clinical practices can impact the remaining 20 percent. This requires collecting adequate demographic and clinical information and applying evidence-based decision support to guide care.[17]

Most EHRs will provide evidence-based guidelines, which can be linked to diagnoses, procedures, diagnostic tests, or medications chosen during an encounter. If an EHR is not being used, consider many of the e-books and online references that are available and run on smartphones and computers. Use of an EHR is an opportunity to retrain staff from paper-chart–based activities to those that can provide greater benefit to the practice. These include performing outreach to patients based on registry reports. Sample registry reports include patients who have not had mammograms, colonoscopies, or labs based on evidence-based criteria. Most EHRs have predefined reports that can be run with little training. Many EHRs now have relatively simple registry report tools for custom reports, which can be saved and used in the future.[16,18,19]

PCMH 4: Care Management and Support. There is a growing body of research in personalized pharmacology based on pharmacogenomics. The goal with this standard is to provide a similar targeted approach to identify addressing the unique needs of those patients who need more intensive intervention and coordinating their care with other providers. Medication management of prescription and over-the-counter medication would include e-prescribing, medication reconciliation, medication education, and discussing barriers to compliance.

While pharmacies provide medication information as a medication is dispensed, EHRs and patient portals are also providing means for educating patients.

Patient self-management is also addressed. According to the Institute of Medicine, self-management support is defined as "the systematic provision of education and supportive interventions by health care staff to increase patients' skills and confidence in managing their health problems, including regular assessment of progress and problems, goal setting, and problem-solving support."[18,20,21]

PCMH 5: Care Coordination and Care Transitions. No man is an island and a PCMH really is not limited to one medical practice.

While it is possible to track referrals for consultations, diagnostic tests, and procedures by paper, the EHR makes this somewhat daunting task more manageable and quite frankly would be the only way to comply with the PCMH and MU elements that require electronic transmission of data. Staff that normally would have been responsible for pulling and filing paper charts can be employed to contact patients about pending items and help coordinate care. The patient portal permits posting of lab results with commentary by the provider. Most patients find this feature very useful for the follow-up visit.

Whether they reviewed the results on their home computer, tablet, smartphone, or exam room kiosk, the resulting discussion is more fruitful for both patient and provider.

Coordination with other providers is benefited by submitting medical summaries, as well as the reason for the requested evaluation. Whether using the NHIN DIRECT messaging, Provider-to-Provider Portals, or regional health information exchanges, the ability to provide useful information to collaborating providers has gone beyond the simple writing on a prescription pad and phone call.

Managing transitions in care is an important aspect of this standard. The practice needs to have protocols in place to be notified of admissions to and discharges from hospitals, emergency departments, and other facilities. Assisting patients in arranging timely follow-up after discharge helps close the loop.

One of the EHR features to have enabled is a bidirectional lab interface. This will permit you to submit your lab orders directly from the EHR and to receive the results directly into the EHR as structured data. Confirm that the EHR will store all lab results locally as LOINC (Logical Observation Identification Names and Codes) values. This will help ensure that results from different labs can be consolidated and queried together. Otherwise, the office will have to run separate queries for each lab company, i.e., Bioreference, LabCorp, Quest, etc. The abnormal lab results will automatically be flagged and normal values will be provided for reference.[22]

PCMH 6: Performance Measurement and Quality Improvement. As previously stated, all six standards depend on the practice performing regular self-reviews to identify gaps or areas for improvement. This standard includes specific elements related to immunizations, clinical care measures, preventative care measures, disparities in care, and feedback from the practice's patients.

As practices strive to meet the PCMH and MU measures, it will be important to quickly and easily assess the gaps in achieving a high level of fulfillment of various quality measures. Solo practices can benefit just as well as group practices. A simple survey of one's practice can identify easily rectifiable barriers to care such as telephone waits on hold, time spent in the waiting room, time spent in the exam room awaiting the healthcare provider, the ease of making an appointment, quality of the communication with the provider, quality of the coordination of care, and lastly, an impression of the overall care provided. One commonly used tool is the PCMH version of the CAHPS Clinician & Group Survey Tool.[23]

A useful guide for implementing a Quality Improvement program is the Plan-Do-Study-Act (PDSA) available at the Agency for Healthcare Quality and Research. These measure reports can then be transmitted to entities such as Bridges to Excellence, ACOs, CMS, or local health departments to coordinate enhanced reimbursement.[24,25,26]

CONCLUSION

In conclusion, we can see that team-based, evidence-supported healthcare is here to stay.

To be sustainable we will need at least three events to occur:

1. A revision of the healthcare educational system that encourages multidisciplinary training
2. Raising public awareness as early as grammar school of the role of patients in their own healthcare maintenance
3. Fair and equitable payment models that encourage the delivery of the best care possible

NCQA Patient-Centered Specialty Practice Recognition

As previously stated, NCQA now offers recognition for specialty practices, even for those practices that see patients infrequently. There are six requirements:

1. Track and coordinate referrals
2. Provide access and communication
3. Identify and coordinate patient populations
4. Plan and manage care
5. Track and coordinate care
6. Measure and improve performance[22]

REFERENCES

1. McPherson M, Arago P, Fox H, et al. A new definition of children with special health care needs. *Pediatrics.* 1998:102:137-140.

2. American Academy of Pediatrics. Council on Pediatric Practice. Pediatric Records and medical home. In: *Standards of Child Care.* Evanston, IL: American Academy of Pediatrics; 1967:77-79.

3. American Academy of Pediatrics. Council on Pediatric Practice. Fragmentation of Health Care Services for Children. *News and Comment.* Supplement, April 1977.

4. History of the medical home concept. *Pediatrics.* 2004:113(5 Suppl):1473-1478.

5. Wagner EH. Chronic disease management: What will it take to improve care for chronic illness? *Eff Clin Pract.* 1998:1(1):2-4.

6. The Medical Home. Pediatrics. 2002;110(1 Pt 1):184-186

7. http://www.aafp.org/dam/AAFP/documents/practice_management/pcmh/initiatives/PCMHJoint.pdf. Accessed November 25, 2014.

8. http://www.ncqa.org/Portals/0/Programs/Recognition/PCMH_Overview_Apr01.pdf. Accessed November 24, 2014.

9. http://www.ncqa.org/Programs/Recognition/Practices/PatientCenteredSpecialtyPracticePCSP.aspx. November 24, 2014.

10. http://www.ncqa.org/Portals/0/Programs/Recognition/PPC-PCMH%202008%20vs%20PCMH%202011Crosswalk%20FINAL.pdf. November 24, 2014.

11. Shenikin BN, Warner DC. Sounding board. Giving the patient his medical record: A proposal to improve the system. *N Engl J Med.* 1973;289:688-692

12. www.tedeytan.com/2010/07/25/5864. Accessed November 24, 2014.

13. www.cdc.gov. Accessed November 24, 2014.

14. www.nlm.nih.gov/medlineplus/. Accessed November 24, 2014.

15. www.salvolpemd.com. Accessed November 24, 2014.

16. Dartmouth Atlas of Health Care. http://www.dartmouthatlas.org. November 24, 2014.

17. http://content.healthaffairs.org/content/32/8/1446.abstract. Accessed January 28, 2015.

18. One size does not fit all. *JAMA*. 2014;311(108):802-803.

19. The patient-centered medical home, electronic health records, and quality of care. *Ann Int Med.* 2014:160:741-749.

20. Personalized medicine: Challenging pharmaceutical and diagnostic company business models. *J Med.* Jan 2007:10(1):59-61.

21. AHRQ. (2013). Health Information Technology. Ambulatory Safety and Quality Program: Findings and lessons from enabling Patient-Centered care through Health IT.

22. https://loinc.org/. November 24, 2014.

23. https://cahpsdatabase.ahrq.gov/CGSurveyGuidance.aspx. November 24, 2014.

24. http://www.innovations.ahrq.gov/content.aspx?id=2398. November 24, 2014.

25. www.bridgestoexcellence.org. Accessed November 24, 2014.

26. www.pcpcc.net/pcpcc-pilot-projects. Accessed November 24, 2014.

Chapter 6

Meaningful Use: Increasing EHR Adoption and Paving the Path toward Healthcare Transformation

Anantachai (Tony) Panjamapirom, PhD, MBA, CPHIMS, and Naomi Levinthal, MA, MS, CPHIMS

INTRODUCTION

From 2009 to 2012, national EHR adoption rates nearly tripled.[1] Many industry experts believe this dramatic increase is due in part to the Centers for Medicare & Medicaid Services (CMS) Electronic Health Record (EHR) Incentive Programs—also known as meaningful use (MU). These programs allow hospital systems and physician practices (herein referred to jointly as *providers*) to earn cash incentives for EHR adoption and use. To do so, a provider must "attest" to its use of a certified EHR system over a defined period of time (i.e., a reporting period). MU participation has been very popular; total incentives paid as of June 2014 have reached $24.6 billion.[2] The last year to collect an incentive for Medicare participation is 2016; for Medicaid it is 2021, depending on the year the provider began.

MU was born from HITECH, which mandated Medicare and Medicaid incentive payments for "meaningful use" of "certified EHR technology (CEHRT)." CMS later defined MU eligibility and program requirements, and ONC developed CEHRT criteria in separate rulemaking.

There are three defined MU stages, each with a specific focus. Stage 1 encourages CEHRT adoption and structured data capture. Stage 2 focuses on advanced clinical processes in three main areas: information exchange, care coordination, and patient engagement. The exact objectives and measures have not yet been proposed for Stage 3; however, improving outcomes will be the focus.

Each stage of MU builds on the previous as stage-specific objectives and measures mirror the National Health Priority Goals:

1. Improve quality, safety, and efficiency, and reduce health disparities.
2. Engage patients and families in their healthcare.

3. Improve care coordination.
4. Improve population and public health.
5. Make care affordable.
6. Ensure adequate privacy and security protections for patient health information.[3]

As reflected in these goals, the overarching purpose of the MU programs and CEHRT adoption is to support healthcare transformation.

Not every hospital or physician in the country is eligible to participate in MU. There are specific MU requirements depending on the eligibility status of the provider's participation in Medicare and/or Medicaid. Hospitals eligible to participate in the Medicare MU program include Subsection (d) hospitals[4] paid under the Inpatient Prospective Payment Systems (IPPS), critical access hospitals (CAH), and Medicare Advantage hospitals. Eligible hospitals (EHs) may receive incentives from Medicare for a maximum of four years. Payments to EHs are determined by several factors: discharge volume; Medicare charges; and a transition factor, which phases down the incentive payments over the four-year period. If an EH chooses not to participate in MU at all or is unable to continue participation each year after it began, the EH will be subject to a payment adjustment. Adjustments are assessed two years after the EH misses the deadline to file its MU attestation and applies a reduction in the annual market basket update. There are no payment adjustments for the Medicaid Incentive Program. Medicaid EHs are acute care hospitals or CAHs with average length of stays of less than 25 days and at least 10 percent Medicaid volumes. Children's hospitals are also eligible for Medicaid incentives and require no minimum Medicaid patient volumes. Medicaid incentive payments are determined by volumes and Medicaid charges, and each state determines disbursement policies, which can range from three to six years in length.

While EHs that meet all the eligibility criteria can participate in both Medicaid and Medicare, a physician participating in MU must choose which version of the Incentive Program the EH will participate in. A Medicare eligible professional (EP) is non-hospital based, with at least 50 percent of all patient encounters in a location using CEHRT, and is a doctor of medicine or osteopathy, a doctor of dental surgery or dental medicine, a doctor of podiatric medicine, a doctor of optometry, or a chiropractor. Medicare EPs can receive up to five incentive payments totaling more than $43,000 if they participated as soon as the program began (in 2011). Medicare EPs beginning in 2013 or 2014 receive substantially fewer incentives than those "early adopters." Akin to their EH counterparts, if Medicare EPs do not continue to demonstrate MU, they are subject to payment adjustments, a percentage reduction in the Medicare physician fee schedule (PFS) amount for covered professional services. Medicaid does not impose payment adjustments for EPs, and physicians can still earn the maximum incentive available if they begin in calendar year (CY) 2016.

Original MU eligibility criteria established within HITECH exclude behavioral health and long-term post-acute care (LTPAC) providers from MU. Legislative efforts to expand the eligibility criteria for benefit of other provider types have not been successful. Yet ONC has continued to engage stakeholders from both behavioral health and LTPAC, so that they could influence EHR adoption and certification outside MU purposes alone. In their Voluntary 2015 CEHRT Certification Criteria Proposed Rule,

ONC sought comment on a certification program for EHR systems designed for use in settings in which providers are not eligible for MU.[5]

BECOMING A MEANINGFUL USER—PROGRAM REQUIREMENTS

To meet the definition of MU, both EPs and EHs must satisfy three key tenets of the EHR Incentive Programs:

1. Use CEHRT.
2. Demonstrate all core and selected menu objectives/measures.
3. Report clinical quality measures (CQMs).

Providers must attest to these requirements in each stage and year of participation and comply with the specified reporting period and attestation deadline.

CEHRT

In addition to CMS MU stage-specific regulations, ONC issues an accompanying regulation that identifies the set of standards, implementation specifications, and certification criteria to which EHRs used for MU must be certified.

CEHRT is available to providers as an EHR module or as a Complete EHR, the former for technologies certified to less than all certification criteria, and the latter to all. The original ONC 2011 Edition Final Rule required providers to possess CEHRT for every available certification criteria. This stipulation oftentimes meant that providers had to license a particular functionality that they did not ultimately report on for MU. ONC later acknowledged that this policy imposed a regulatory burden on providers to license software they did not need to use. To resolve this, ONC created a new framework in the 2014 Edition Final Rule that requires providers to possess CEHRT for a more limited set of functionality, called the Base EHR. Providers then must determine what CEHRT functionality is necessary to demonstrate core objectives specific to their stage and those measures they choose to report on from the menu set. For example, while the 2011 Edition CEHRT specifies the certification criteria for all functionality needed to meet all Stage 1 objectives, the 2014 Edition CEHRT contains all certification criteria required for both Stages 1 and 2. This policy is expected to continue when ONC introduces the 2017 Edition certification criteria that adds the EHR capabilities necessary for Stage 3.

ONC released a proposed rule in early 2014 to develop a voluntary 2015 Edition certification program and update its previous rules. This rule provides vendors and providers greater visibility into its regulatory aims, which will help the industry anticipate future functionality in subsequent rulemaking. Furthermore, when the proposal is finalized, the rule allows ONC to adopt newer versions of industry standards that can enhance interoperability. However, providers are not required to adopt the voluntary 2015 Edition CEHRT. ONC has defined a three-year roadmap[6] for its later rulemaking cycles.

Core and Menu Objectives

CMS develops the core and menu objectives/measures based on recommendations from the Health IT Policy Committee (HITPC), a federal advisory committee of industry stakeholders. These objectives are stage-specific and vary in complexity; some are performance-based with a set threshold providers must achieve, whereas others require providers to enable a certified functionality for the entire reporting period or conduct a test.

Providers must meet the requirements of all core objectives and some selected from menu objectives. This approach allows providers to meet the fundamental elements of MU requirements and at the same time affords the latitude to providers to enhance maturity in their technical capability and improve workflows to fully meet the more advanced criteria. Each stage of MU builds on the previous and introduces higher performance thresholds and more advanced functionalities. CMS transitioned the majority of Stage 1 menu objectives into the core set of Stage 2.

Stage 1 objectives include electronic data capture in a structured, coded format, use of the information to track key clinical conditions, and implementation of a clinical decision support (CDS) intervention to facilitate management of a high-priority condition. Stage 2 objectives take a huge leap forward and move providers into advanced clinical processes: information exchange, care coordination, and patient engagement. In Stage 3, it is expected that CMS will develop objectives and measures that aim to increase implementation of CDS tools for national high-priority conditions, measure patient and family engagement and their access to self-management tools, encourage care coordination through access to comprehensive patient data including patient-generated data, and use public health data to better manage population health.

Although the final rules of each MU stage determines the number of core and menu objectives providers must achieve, CMS can revise and modify the requirements in subsequent rulemaking based on feedback from the industry and attestation data analysis. For example, CMS modified Stage 1 requirements when it finalized Stage 2, thus creating two versions of Stage 1 objectives/measures: 2013 definition and 2014 definition. Table 6-1 illustrates the number of core and menu objectives finalized by CMS for each stage and provider type, as well as the modified versions. The detailed requirements of stage-specific core and menu objectives can be found in CMS's specification sheets noted on the additional resources list at the end of this chapter.

CQMs

In addition to the core and menu objectives, providers are required to report clinical quality measures (CQMs). CMS finalized a list of CQMs providers must report for each stage, but no performance thresholds are required. CQM data must be reported exactly as generated by their CEHRT. Table 6-1 includes the number of CQMs that providers must report for each stage to meet the number the MU program requires.

Beginning in 2013, CMS instituted a significant change to CQM reporting requirements. Originally, CQM reporting was one of the core objectives, but CMS removed it from that set and incorporated it into the definition of a meaningful user. In other words, providers must report CQMs to fully demonstrate MU, but this does not count toward one of the core objectives. CQM reporting became a mandatory requirement of demonstrating MU.

Another important aspect to CQM reporting is that as MU progresses, CMS will align clinical quality reporting among its various programs. This alignment is needed to reduce the reporting burdens providers experience when they participate in multiple CMS programs. As a result, starting in 2014, providers may report CQMs in a man-

Table 6-1: The Number of Meaningful Use Core and Menu Objectives and CQMs by Stage and Provider Type

Stage/Year	Eligible Professionals						Eligible Hospitals					
	Finalized			Must Meet			Finalized			Must Meet		
	Core	Menu	CQM	Core	Menu	CQM	Core	Menu	CQM	Core	Menu	CQM
Stage 1												
2011/2012	15	10	Total of 44 3 - core 3 - alternative core 38 - menu set CQMs	15	5	Total of 6 3 - core OR alternative core 3 out of 38 menu set CQMs	14	10	15	14	5	15
2013	13[a]	10	Total of 44 3 - core 3 - alternative core 38 - menu set CQMs	13	5	Total of 6 3 - core OR alternative core 3 out of 38 menu set CQMs	12[a]	10	15	12	5	15
2014 and subsequent years	13[b]	9[c]	64	13	5	9[e]	11[d]	10	29	11	5	16[e]
Stage 2												
2014 and subsequent years	17	6	64	17	3	9[e]	16	6	29	16	3	16[e]

[a] Starting 2013, Exchange of Key Clinical Information was eliminated. Reporting on CQMs was removed from the core objectives and is incorporated into the definition of "meaningful use." Providers must still report on CQMs, but it does not count toward the total number of required meaningful use measures.

[b] Starting in 2014, Electronic Copy of Health Information is replaced by the first measure of View, Download, and Transmit (VDT).

[c] Starting in 2014, Timely Electronic Access is replaced by the first measure of VDT.

[d] Starting 2014, Electronic Copy of Health Information and Electronic Copy of Discharge Instructions are replaced by the first measure of VDT.

[e] CQMs must cover at least three of the six National Quality Strategy Domains.

ner that can qualify to meet the requirements of other quality reporting programs. In general, both EPs and EHs have two options to report CQM data: attestation via the CMS's EHR Incentive Programs Registration and Attestation System[7] or electronic submission. The attestation option allows providers to only meet the MU CQM reporting requirements, but not the quality reporting requirements of other CMS programs.

Providers who choose to report CQMs electronically using their CEHRT are able to receive credit for both the MU and other programs. EPs that choose to electronically submit CQM data using CEHRT may satisfy the requirements of both MU and the Physician Quality Reporting System (PQRS) requirements. To receive the full credit for both programs, EPs must ensure they follow all program-specific requirements. EPs may also choose to report CQMs as a group and satisfy the requirements for both the MU program and one of the following: PQRS group reporting, the Medicare Shared Savings Program, or Pioneer Accountable Care Organization model (see Table 6-1). Those EPs in their first year of MU are not eligible for group reporting, as it does not allow them to meet the attestation deadline to avoid payment adjustment in a subsequent year.

Along the same lines, EHs may choose to electronically report CQM data and satisfy the CQM reporting requirements of the MU program and receive partial credit in the hospital inpatient quality reporting (IQR) program. Per the 2015 IPPS final rule, electronic CQM reporting remains voluntary for EHs, but CMS indicated that it may become a mandate in future years. EHs may find electronic CQM reporting requirements cumbersome, as CMS requires providers to use only the latest update of electronic specifications, which may differ from those available in the EH's CEHRT. See the list at the end of this chapter for more resources on CQM reporting. EPs and EHs interested in electronic CQM data submission must monitor an annual update of these requirements through other related final rules, which are the Medicare PFS final rule and the Medicare IPPS final rule, respectively.

Reporting Periods and Attestation Deadlines

To demonstrate MU, providers must attest to the requirements previously discussed within a specified timeframe and deadline. The reporting period refers to the specified time frame during which a provider must demonstrate MU and achieve the requirements for all core objectives, selected menu objectives, and CQM reporting. The attestation deadline is the last day providers can report their data in the registration and attestation system. The reporting period and attestation deadline vary by the provider's year of participation.

In the first year of participation, providers must meet the requirements and report data on a continuous 90-day reporting period during a CY or federal fiscal year (FFY) (i.e., for EPs, any 90 days from January 1 to December 31; and for EHs, any 90 days from October 1 to September 30). For the subsequent years, the reporting period becomes an entire CY or FFY. There was an exception applicable in only CY/FFY 2014, in which CMS allowed EPs and EHs beyond their first year to attest using one of the calendar or fiscal quarters as a reporting period.

In addition to the reporting period, providers must successfully attest by a deadline in order to be eligible for an incentive payment, and avoid payment adjustment. In general, the attestation deadline is two months after the end of the CY or FFY. For example, in 2013, EPs had until February 28, 2014 to submit attestation data for their CY 2013 participation year. The same attestation deadlines apply to all providers regardless of stage, except those in their first year.

For those first-year providers in 2014 or subsequent years, the attestation deadline is three months shorter than the regular deadline previously described. The reason for this shortened deadline is because starting in 2015, those eligible physicians and hospitals that do not demonstrate MU are subject to payment adjustment, and CMS will make such determination based on the attestation data in 2013 or 2014. For instance, EHs and EPs that are first-time attesters in 2014 must complete attestation by July 1 and October 1, 2014, respectively, so that CMS can identify those providers who are subject to payment adjustment in FFY/CY 2015.

First-time EH and EP participants that miss the July 1 or October 1, 2014 deadline may attest by the regular deadline (i.e., November 30, 2014 or February 28, 2015) to be eligible for an incentive payment, but these providers will be subject to payment adjustment in FFY/CY 2015. This policy applies in the subsequent years for providers that have never participated in the programs until at least 2021 (the last year the program is slated for according to CMS's Stage 2 Final Rule).[8] These specific attestation dates apply to the Medicare EHR Incentive Program. Each Medicaid state agency may set a different attestation deadline. EPs that participate in the Medicaid program and EHs that are dually eligible for both Medicare and Medicaid programs should contact their state agencies to determine whether the attestation deadline differs. Table 6-2 summarizes the reporting period and attestation deadline by provider type and participation year.

Table 6-2: The Meaningful Use Reporting Period and Attestation Deadline by Provider Type

Provider Type and Participation Year	Reporting Period	Attestation Deadline
Eligible Professionals		
Year 1	– Any continuous 90 days from January 1 to September 30: to avoid payment adjustment – Any continuous 90 days from January 1 to December 31: to be eligible for an incentive payment, when applicable	– October 1: to avoid payment adjustment – February 28: to be eligible for an incentive payment, when applicable
Year 2+	One full calendar year (i.e., January 1 - December 31)*	February 28: to be eligible for an incentive payment when applicable and to avoid payment adjustments two years later
Eligible Hospitals		
Year 1	– Any continuous 90 days from October 1 to June 30: to avoid payment adjustment – Any continuous 90 days from October 1 to September 30: to be eligible for an incentive payment, when applicable	– July 1: to avoid payment adjustment – November 30: to be eligible for an incentive payment, when applicable
Year 2+	One full federal fiscal year (i.e., October 1 - September 30)*	November 30: to be eligible for an incentive payment when applicable and to avoid payment adjustments two years later

Asterisk (*) denotes that in FFY/CY 2014, all providers in Year 2 or beyond need only report on a three-month quarter.

MEANINGFUL USE ATTESTATION DATA TRENDS

As of June 2014,[9] CMS paid nearly $25 billion in incentive payments to both EPs and EHs that have participated in the program. About $15 billion or 60 percent of the incentive payments are distributed to EHs/CAHs, whereas EPs have banked approximately $10 billion in the incentives.

More than 90 percent of the hospital incentives are allocated to EHs that participate in both the Medicare and Medicaid programs. In contrast, of the total incentive payouts to EPs, almost $7 billion were paid through the Medicare program, whereas $3.1 billion incentives were paid to EPs who participate in the Medicaid program. Due to the sequestration executive order on March 1, 2013, Medicare incentive payments that have been paid on or after April 1, 2013 are reduced by 2 percent. The sequestration resulted in a reduction of about $51 million and $80 million from the incentive payments to EPs and EHs, respectively.

Latest payment data show that 4,588 hospitals and 403,471 EPs across the country have received at least one incentive payment. Only 8 percent of these incentivized hospitals are eligible for either the Medicare or Medicaid program, whereas 92 percent of them are dually eligible and have received incentives from both programs. Of the 403,471 EPs, about 69 percent have received incentive payments from Medicare and about 31 percent from Medicaid. The high volume of successful attestations suggests that most providers around the country have made an investment in an EHR system and committed to meaningfully use health IT to improve efficiency in care delivery processes and enhance patient safety and the overall quality of care. This trend continues to grow as 4,714 hospitals (95% of the total EHs) and 479,840 EPs (90% of the total EPs) have registered to participate in the programs.

According to the first two years of attestation data, CMS found that most providers that attested to Stage 1 requirements greatly exceeded the required threshold of most percentage-based objectives, but some providers' performance stayed close to the margin. The most challenging and least popular Stage 1 menu set objective is Transition of Care. The data may suggest that most providers have little experience in information exchange with other providers, implying a low level of care coordination. When comparing the performance between EPs and EHs, CMS found insignificant differences.

In terms of continuity in participation and ability to attest year over year,[10] ONC conducted a detailed analysis among Medicare EPs and found that 84 percent of about 58,000 EPs who attested in 2011 continued to attest in 2012, while 16 percent skipped year 2. However, 43 percent of those who skipped 2012 returned to the program in 2013, but 9 percent of those who had attested in 2011 and 2012 consecutively skipped attestation in 2013. Some of the reasons EPs skipped MU years were retirement, death of the provider, and change in eligibility. Our experience with EPs suggests that some likely skipped a year "accidentally," as they did not realize MU attestation is an annual requirement.

At the Health Information Technology (HIT) Policy Committee meeting in May 2014, CMS reported for the first time the number of Stage 2 attestations, and it was surprisingly low: 4 EHs and 50 EPs by May 1, 2014.[11] While the numbers swelled to 78 EHs and 1,898 EPs by August 1, 2014,[12] they remain low compared with those providers that achieved Stage 1 in 2011 and 2012. Along with the number of attesters, ONC also provided the attestation data of early Stage 2 attestations.[13] Even though a statistically significant result cannot be drawn from such a limited amount of data, their report showed that VDT and Transitions of Care proved to be the two most challenging Stage 2 objectives to achieve, as most providers attested with only marginal performance. CMS and ONC update all attestation data on a monthly basis at the Health IT Policy Committee (HITPC) meetings[14] and plan further analyses of Stage 2 data. See the additional resources list at the end of this chapter for more information on attestation trends.

CHALLENGES IN THE MEANINGFUL USE PROGRAMS

Both EPs and EHs face challenges to prepare for and meet MU requirements and survive audits. To meet minimum MU requirements, all providers must select, implement, and achieve sufficient adoption of an EHR system that has been certified for use in a particular year. It is critical that providers identify the exact "Edition" of certification necessary for each Stage and year of MU. This also means that providers are prevented from using any EHR system not certified for use in MU. From 2011 to 2013, all providers were required to possess an EHR certified to the "2011 Edition" of CEHRT. Beginning in 2014, all providers who participate in MU, regardless of year or stage, had to make a mandatory system upgrade to a new certified system designated as "2014 Edition." Oftentimes, providers and vendors are challenged to meet the aggressive time lines expected by CMS and ONC. For example, the 2014 Edition CEHRT included new vocabulary standards that required mapping tools, and many vendors were unable to deliver those conversions in a timely manner because of delays in certifying the product. CMS and ONC recognized this challenge, and in September 2014 finalized a rule to make it possible for providers to utilize either 2011 or 2014 Edition software or a combination of both for 2014 attestation. However, the flexibility is short-lived, as the 2014 Edition upgrade became mandatory the following year in 2015, and the reporting period for providers beyond the first year in 2015 is a full year (i.e., October 1, 2014–September 30, 2015 for EHs and January 1–December 31, 2015 for EPs).[15]

Providers in MU experience the same growing pains common in EHR implementations today: staff resistance and long-term training, process and/or workflow redesign, cost overruns, lack of interoperability, inefficient data transfer from paper-based records, and system performance and downtime. The pressure to achieve sufficient EHR adoption is magnified for providers when the system must be used to meet a performance metric during a defined period of time. For example, if computerized provider order entry (CPOE) is a newly installed functionality, the Stage 2 CPOE measures are a true test of adoption, as they measure usage by a defined set of end users (those licensed to enter orders per the state or local laws).

In addition, there is a constant flow of clarifications, modifications, and new policies from CMS and ONC. The monitoring providers must do to keep abreast of these changes is quite labor-intensive. New clarifications are released to providers on a near-weekly basis on a "Frequently Asked Questions" website hosted by CMS. These FAQs serve to explain regulatory intent or provide further guidance, and providers must ensure their plans reflect the latest guidance. New policies CMS and ONC issue via rulemaking can have major impacts on a provider's MU plan. For example, annual updates in the IPPS and PFS final rules determine the CQM reporting options to meet MU requirements.

These new policies and clarifications speak to the confusion many providers experience when they determine how they will meet a given measure. Because CMS regulations typically do not define all acceptable workflows, providers must strike a balance between organizational capability and regulatory intent. For example, the Stage 2 VDT objective's second measure requires providers to track the number of patients who login to the patient portal or personal health record (PHR) to VDT their health information. Hospitals are permitted to take credit for patients who login to the portal or PHR prior to their discharge date as long as health information is available for the patient to access at that time. Many hospitals are unable to validate whether such a requirement was met given their available reporting methods and face a dilemma: take undue credit or lose out on any predischarge credit where it may be due.

Providers must ensure they follow all MU rules because their attestations are subject to audit, up to six years post-attestation. Audits can occur pre-payment or post-payment. According to CMS estimates, it plans to audit 1 in 20 attestations.[16] A hospital that receives incentives from both Medicare and Medicaid may receive audit requests from both programs. If an auditor determines a provider did not meet even one MU requirement, that provider is asked to return the entire incentive earned for the year in question plus interest. In addition, if providers failed an audit, they would not have met the definition of MU, and thus would also be subject to payment adjustment. Therefore, an audit failure equates to "double jeopardy:" CMS is due full incentive recoupment (plus interest) and the provider incurs an adjustment. CMS indicates that one of the main reasons providers fail audits is because they did not collect and retain sufficient support documentation. The documentation an auditor requests can be detailed or cursory, and providers are challenged to ensure they collect sufficient documentation.

ALIGNMENT OPPORTUNITY OF MEANINGFUL USE WITH OTHER STRATEGIC INITIATIVES

Where there are challenges, new opportunities exist. Seeking a sustainable solution to high healthcare costs and unparalleled quality of care, the federal government and the healthcare industry have begun to transform payment structures, which in turn drives health systems to develop more responsive care delivery models. Embedded in healthcare reform is the paradigm shift from a volume-based, fee-for-service standard to a value-driven delivery environment in which providers are held accountable to their services, and patients can be selective and make informed decisions about their own health. In response to the new demand, providers must be able to demonstrate to all types of payers, including individual patients, that they can render high-quality care at an attainable cost.

To achieve such a future state, providers must rethink their care delivery process to enhance efficiency and improve outcomes. As previously mentioned, MU is built on the six National Health Priority Goals: (1) Improve quality, safety, and efficiency, and reduce health disparities; (2) Engage patients and families in their healthcare; (3) Improve care coordination; (4) Improve population and public health; (5) Make care affordable; and (6) Ensure adequate privacy and security protections for patient health information. These goals are well aligned with the strategic direction providers are working toward in the accountable care environment.

Leading organizations view their progress in MU as a means to achieve an end. They create an organizational synergy by leveraging the resources and efforts spent in MU and align them with the other strategic initiatives. For example, health systems can map each of the MU objectives to their population health management framework. Structured data collected as part of the MU requirements can serve as a basis to identify patient populations by different levels of risk. Subsequently, health systems can use other MU objectives—such as creating a patient list, public health objectives, and CQM reporting to map and track care for each patient population. In addition, CDS, CPOE, and e-prescribing enables evidence-based capabilities to ensure the right care is rendered accurately at the point of care. Transitions of Care also serves as a stepping-stone for information exchange geared toward care coordination across settings. Lastly, health systems have a great opportunity to engage patients and empower them in their own health through patient electronic access. These examples illustrate just one way that health systems can align MU with other strategic goals such as population health management. The possibilities are nearly endless, but it all depends on whether health systems will commit to carry out such change.

Providers' participation in MU fosters organizational capabilities that support and enable other goals. As providers advance through higher stages of MU, they collectively build both human and technology assets that are necessary for health systems to thrive in the new care delivery models emerging today.

REFERENCES

1. ONC Health IT Dashboard. http://dashboard.healthit.gov/.
2. CMS EHR Incentive Programs, Data and Reports. http://www.cms.gov/Regulations-and-Guidance/Legislation/EHRIncentivePrograms/DataAndReports.html.
3. ONC Federal Health Information Technology Strategic Plan. http://www.healthit.gov/sites/default/files/utility/final-federal-health-it-strategic-plan-0911.pdf.
4. Social Security Act, Payment to Hospitals for Inpatient Hospital Services. http://www.ssa.gov/OP_Home/ssact/title18/1886.htm#act-1886-d-1-b.
5. ONC Fact Sheet: Voluntary 2015 Edition EHR Certification Criteria. 2015 Ed. Proposed Rule. http://healthit.gov/sites/default/files/final2015certedfactsheet.022114.pdf.
6. Three-Year ONC Rulemaking Roadmap. http://www.healthit.gov/sites/default/files/rulemakingtimeline_2014thru2016.pdf.
7. Medicare & Medicaid EHR Incentive Program, Registration and Attestation System. https://ehrincentives.cms.gov/hitech/login.action.
8. Table 3, Page 53974, Medicare and Medicaid Programs; Electronic Health Record Incentive Program—Stage 2; Federal Register / Vol. 77, No. 171 / Tuesday, September 4, 2012 / Rules and Regulations.
9. June 2014 EHR Incentive Program. http://www.cms.gov/Regulations-and-Guidance/Legislation/EHRIncentivePrograms/Downloads/June2014_SummaryReport.pdf.
10. ONC Health IT dashboard, attestation patterns among Medicare professionals who first attested to Meaningful Use in 2011. http://dashboard.healthit.gov/quickstats/pages/FIG-Medicare-Professionals-Stage-One-Meaningful-Use-Attestation-Cohort-2011.html.

11. CMS Medicare & Medicaid EHR Incentives Programs Report to HITPC. May 6, 2014. http://www.healthit.gov/FACAS/sites/faca/files/HITPC_CMS_Update_2014-05-06.pdf.

12. CMS Medicare & Medicaid EHR Incentives Programs Report to HITPC. August 6, 2014. http://www.healthit.gov/FACAS/sites/faca/files/HITPC_August2014_HITPC.pdf.

13. ONC Data Analytics Update to HITPC on July 8, 2014. http://www.healthit.gov/FACAS/sites/faca/files/HITPC_Data_Analytics_Update_2014-07-08.pdf.

14. HITPC. http://www.healthit.gov/facas/health-it-policy-committee.

15. Medicare and Medicaid Programs; Modifications to the Medicare and Medicaid EHR Incentive Program for 2014 and Other Changes to the EHR Incentive Program; and Health Information Technology: Revisions to the CEHRT Definition and EHR Certification Changes Related to Standards; 42 CFR Part 495, RINs 0938-AR71 and 0938-AS30. September 4, 2014.

16. Irving FI. Meaningful use audits 'inevitable.' *Healthcare IT News*. February 19, 2014. http://www.healthcareitnews.com/news/meaningful-use-audits-inevitable.

Additional Meaningful Use Educational Resources

1. CMS's specification sheets detailing core and menu objectives, their measures and reporting requirements by stage and type of providers:
   Eligible Professionals
   - Stage 1 – 2013 Definition
     http://www.cms.gov/Regulations-and-Guidance/Legislation/EHRIncentivePrograms/Downloads/EP-MU-TOC.pdf
   - Stage 1 – 2014 Definition
     http://www.cms.gov/Regulations-and-Guidance/Legislation/EHRIncentivePrograms/Downloads/EP_MU_TableOfContents.pdf
   - Stage 2
     http://www.cms.gov/Regulations-and-Guidance/Legislation/EHRIncentivePrograms/Downloads/Stage2_MeaningfulUseSpecSheet_TableContents_EPs.pdf

   Eligible Hospitals and CAHs
   - Stage 1 – 2013 Definition
     http://www.cms.gov/Regulations-and-Guidance/Legislation/EHRIncentivePrograms/Downloads/Hosp_CAH_MU-toc.pdf
   - Stage 1 – 2014 Definition
     http://www.cms.gov/Regulations-and-Guidance/Legislation/EHRIncentivePrograms/Downloads/EH_CAH_MU_TableOfContents.pdf
   - Stage 2
     http://www.cms.gov/Regulations-and-Guidance/Legislation/EHRIncentivePrograms/Downloads/Stage2_MeaningfulUseSpecSheet_TableContents_EligibleHospitals_CAHs.pdf
2. CQM reporting:
   a. General CQM reporting information for the meaningful use program
   http://www.cms.gov/Regulations-and-Guidance/Legislation/EHRIncentivePrograms/ClinicalQualityMeasures.html
   b. CQM reporting options for EPs and EHs
   http://www.cms.gov/Regulations-and-Guidance/Legislation/EHRIncentivePrograms/2014_ClinicalQualityMeasures.html
   c. CMS eCQM library
   http://cms.gov/Regulations-and-Guidance/Legislation/EHRIncentivePrograms/eCQM_Library.html
   d. CMS PQRS Website
   http://www.cms.gov/Medicare/Quality-Initiatives-Patient-Assessment-Instruments/PQRS/
   e. Medicare Shared Savings Program
   http://cms.gov/Medicare/Medicare-Fee-for-Service-Payment/sharedsavingsprogram/Quality_Measures_Standards.html
   f. Hospital Inpatient Quality Reporting Program
   https://www.cms.gov/Medicare/Quality-Initiatives-Patient-Assessment-Instruments/HospitalQualityInits/HospitalRHQDAPU.html

3. Meaningful use data and program reports:
   a. CMS's data and meaningful use program reports
      http://cms.gov/Regulations-and-Guidance/Legislation/EHRIncentivePrograms/DataAndReports.html
   b. ONC's health IT dashboards
      http://dashboard.healthit.gov/index.php
4. Meaningful use payment adjustments and hardship exception:
   a. CMS's payment adjustment tipsheet for EHs
      http://www.cms.gov/Regulations-and-Guidance/Legislation/EHRIncentivePrograms/Downloads/PaymentAdj_HardshipExcepTipsheetfor-Hospitals.pdf
   b. CMS's payment adjustment tipsheet for EPs
      http://www.cms.gov/Regulations-and-Guidance/Legislation/EHRIncentivePrograms/Downloads/PaymentAdj_HardshipExcepTipSheet-forEP.pdf

CHAPTER 7

Regional Extension Centers

Paul Kleeberg, MD, FAAFP, FHIMSS, and Ryan Sandefer, MA, CPHIT

INTRODUCTION

Early in 2010, in order to assist providers in underserved and rural areas to adopt electronic health records (EHRs), the American Recovery and Reinvestment Act (ARRA) funded 62 regional extension centers (RECs) to assist small primary care practices and hospitals in adopting EHRs. The idea behind RECs was based on previous experience the United States had with the agricultural extension centers created to assist farmers in developing more efficient farming practices. The agricultural extension centers were very successful in reaching out to farmers throughout the country.[1] Much like their predecessors, these health IT RECs have been successful in their task and are now moving into the next stage of development, practice transformation.

HISTORY

On January 20, 2004, in his State of the Union address, then President George W. Bush declared that "by computerizing health records, we can avoid dangerous medical mistakes, reduce costs, and improve care."[2] This was the first sign that the federal government was eager to move healthcare into the 21st century and adopt the types of information technologies that were common in other industries. Three months later, he created the Office of the National Coordinator for Health Information Technology (ONC) by Executive Order to provide leadership for the development and nationwide implementation of an interoperable health IT infrastructure.[3] In the five years that followed, adoption remained slow. In a 2008 study, only 8 percent of hospitals[4] and 13 percent of physician practices in ambulatory settings had adopted at least a basic EHR (see Figure 7-1).[5]

Then on February 13, 2009, in direct response to the economic crisis, the U.S. Congress passed the ARRA of 2009 known as the stimulus package. Built into the legislation was the Health Information Technology for Economic and Clinical Health Act (HITECH), which authorized the U.S. Department of Health and Human Services (HHS) to spend $25.9 billion to promote and expand the adoption of health IT.[6] To achieve this goal, the law embedded ONC in statute and greatly expanded its resources.

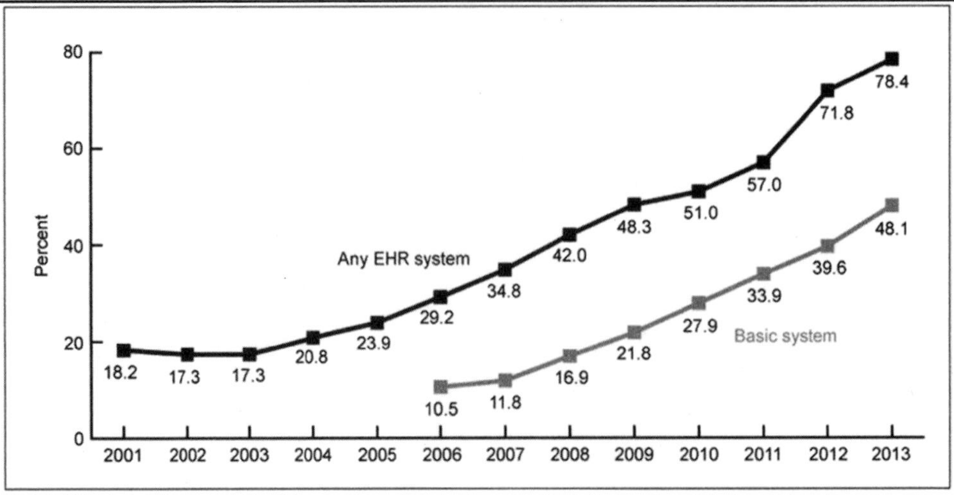

NOTES: EHR is electronic health record. "Any EHR system" is a medical or health record system that is either all or partially electronic (excluding systems solely for billing). Data for 2001–2007 are from in-person National Ambulatory Medical Care Survey (NAMCS) interviews. Data for 2008–2010 are from combined files (in-person NAMCS and mail survey). Estimates for 2011–2013 data are based on the mail survey only. Estimates for a basic system prior to 2006 could not be computed because some items were not collected in the survey. Data include nonfederal, office-based physicians and exclude radiologists, anesthesiologists, and pathologists.
SOURCE: CDC/NCHS, National Ambulatory Medical Care Survey and National Ambulatory Medical Care Survey, Electronic Health Records Survey.

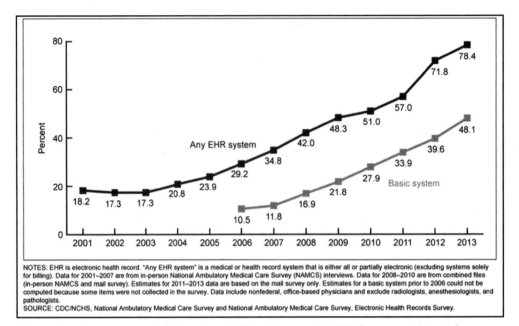

Figure 7-1: Percentage of Office-based Physicians with EHR Systems: United States, 2001–2013.

One of the first responsibilities of the national coordinator was to create a strategic plan for a nationwide interoperable health information system. In 2009, David Blumenthal, MD, revealed that plan in which he created a multifaceted approach for providers and hospitals to adopt EHRs and achieve meaningful use (MU).[7] The overall impact of the EHR Incentive Program is undeniable. According to the most recent estimates by ONC, adoption of EHRs by hospitals have increased five-fold since 2008 (from 9% to 59%)[8] and adoption of EHRs by office-based physicians has increased four-fold (from 18% to 78%).[9]

Part of ONC's strategic plan was the creation of local RECs to help small primary care practices, those serving underserved populations, and hospitals with fewer than 50 beds in adopting and meaningfully using health IT. The intent of the RECs was to ease the financial cost and organizational effort of adopting and implementing health IT within these types of organizations, which have historically been less likely to adopt technology, by providing education, resources, and technical assistance. The services RECs provide include selecting an EHR system, negotiating price, training and implementation, achieving and reporting MU, achieving a return on investment (ROI), and addressing privacy and security concerns.[10]

By late 2010, 62 RECs were established by a cooperative agreement across the United States and its territories. Each extension center had its own service area, and there was no overlap between extension centers.

To motivate RECs to meet the goals of reaching 100,000 primary care providers and the greatest number of small hospitals, their funding was broken into three milestones:

1. Milestone one occurred when an eligible provider (EP) or eligible hospital (EH) signed with the extension center.

2. Milestone two occurred when an EP or EH had adopted an EHR and were able to use it to run a report and use it to electronically order medications.
3. Milestone three occurred when the EP or EH achieved MU.

WHAT RECS HAVE ACCOMPLISHED

Because RECs and the related programs of the HITECH Act were set up rapidly, there were challenges in the initial months. The RECs adapted quickly. As of February 2012, less than 2 years into the program, 120,783 (39.9%) of the total office-based primary care providers (PCPs) in the United States were participating in a REC. That included 37.9 percent of providers from metropolitan areas, 47.3 percent from micropolitan areas, and 56.1 percent from non–core based statistical areas (CBSA) (rural areas).[11] By June 2013, that number had climbed to 134,000 (44% of the nation's PCPs and 83% of the nation's federally qualified health care centers) with 86 percent of those using EHRs with advanced functionality and 48 percent with demonstrated meaningful use. In addition, 78 percent of the nation's critical access hospitals were also participating with an REC.[12] That number has continued to climb. According to the 2014 ONC report to Congress, "As of June 2014, RECs assist over 150,000 providers, of which over 136,000 are now live on an EHR, and over 100,000 have achieved meaningful use through the EHR Incentive Programs. RECs are partnered with over 46 percent of all primary care providers in the nation, 54 percent of all rural providers, 83 percent of all community health centers, and 80 percent of all critical access hospitals."[13]

By April 2014, RECs had signed up more than 150,000 PCPs into the program (see Figure 7-2).[14] In short, RECs exceeded the number of providers enrolled by 38 percent, the number of providers live on an EHR by 27 percent, and are 94 percent to goal on the number of providers demonstrating MU.[15]

Research has shown that REC clients were disproportionately located in rural areas and communities of high poverty and low employment. In fact, rural providers signed up for REC services at twice the micropolitan and metropolitan rates, and RECs were successful overall at assisting underserved populations regarding health IT.

While rural providers are significantly less likely to achieve MU and receive incentive payments than their micropolitan and metropolitan counterparts, research has also shown that providers who worked with RECs were 2.6 times as likely to receive incentive dollars[16] and twice as likely to achieve MU than those who did not (see Figure 7-3).[17,18]

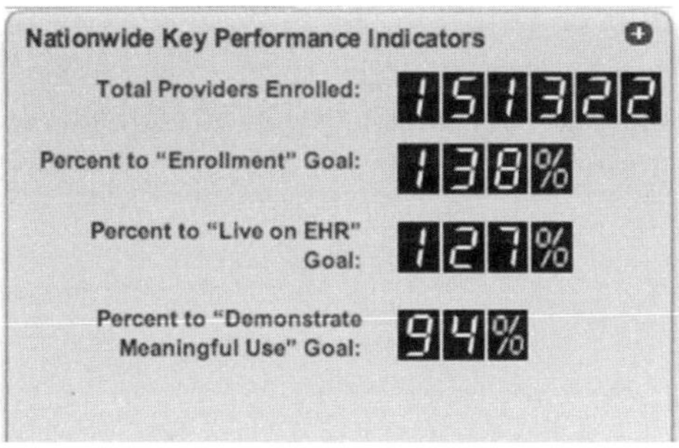

Figure 7-2: Nationwide Key Performance Indicators

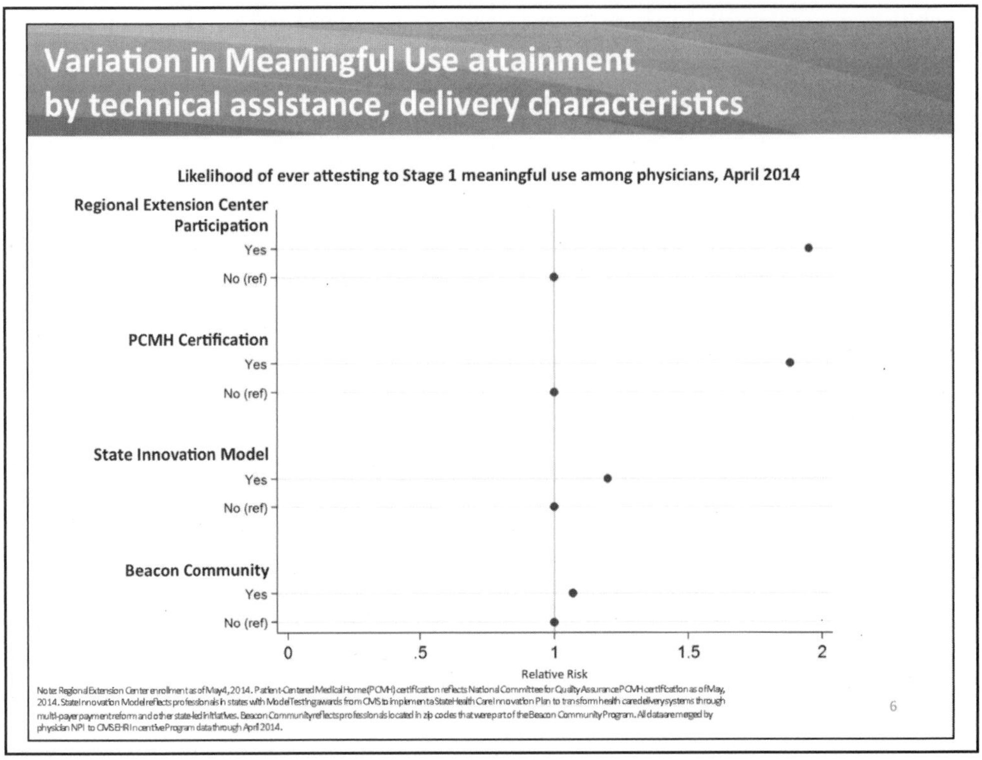

Figure 7-3: Variation in Meaningful Use Attainment by Technical Assistance, Delivery Characteristics

RECs provided many services to their clients. From our perspective, one of the most important services RECs provided was interpretation of the EHR Incentive Program's Final Rule and its associated objectives and measures related to MU. RECs were able to provide education, technical assistance, and guidance on all aspects of the EHR Incentive Program, but were also able to document challenges and barriers to achieving MU and work with ONC to identify solutions to known problems. Research has demonstrated the major barriers of office-based physicians to EHR adoption. The top five barriers are cost of purchasing the system, loss of productivity, annual maintenance cost, adequacy of training, and finding an EHR to meet practice needs.[13] According to analysis by ONC, RECs documented 19,209 issues and challenges in their customer relationship management tool. The top five challenges related to clinical summaries, security risk analyses, medication reconciliation, summary of care record, and patient reminders. "RECs collectively organized and addressed these [issues and challenges] by building tools and processes that were proactively shared with providers, ultimately leading to more timely attestation and payment."[19]

TYPES OF RECS

There are essentially three types of organizations that came forward to establish RECs: quality improvement organizations, health IT firms, and academic institutions. Based on experience with agricultural extension centers, these RECs had a lot of freedom in how they were to approach the challenge of helping providers and hospitals adopt and meaningfully use health IT. Approximately one third of all RECs were quality improvement organizations (QIOs) that had contracts with CMS to work with hospitals and clinics. These types of RECs philosophically viewed health IT as a tool to improve quality and had used these tools to improve patient care. Many of these QIOs had gained skills in this area eight years earlier through a CMS-QIO sponsored program called Doctors Office Quality Information Technology (DOQ-IT). The mission of the DOQ-IT program was similar to the REC program. As a result of this previous experience, these QIO RECs have a heavy emphasis on workflow redesign, cultural adoption, and coaching. Other RECs have a health IT consulting orientation. In these organizations, the adoption and use of health IT has been more focused on installing and optimizing the technical side of health IT. These RECs typically provide staff augmentation and ensure that the technical infrastructure is running optimally.

The third group of RECs arose from academic institutions rich in understanding and applying best practices. Some of these academic institutions have Area Health Education Councils (AHECs), which puts them in a unique position as they are tasked with meeting the state's health and health workforce needs by providing educational programs in partnership with healthcare agencies and other local organizations committed to improving the health of the population. The North Carolina REC is an AHEC and has taken this broader role and applied a more holistic approach. As a strategy, they form a relationship with provider organizations and more systematically move them along the continuum, matching funding streams to support a continuous and progressive intervention path. This would include EHR adoption, MU, patient-centered medical homes (PCMHs) and quality improvement.

Though each of these RECs worked its own defined geographic region, they did not work in isolation. ONC created the Health Information Technology Resource Center (HITRC) where RECs shared their knowledge, tools, and resources to help each other in accomplishing their task, as well as a National Learning Consortium (NLC) to assist in creating tools, disseminating best practices, facilitating discussions about optimizing health IT, and understanding the requirements of the incentive program.

CHALLENGES RECS ENCOUNTERED

Surprisingly, one of the most difficult tasks for extension centers was recruiting clinics to participate. Many of the small practices and providers in underserved communities were reluctant to sign on to the program. Even though the service was offered virtually free of charge, it took many calls to and contacts with these organizations to convince them that working with RECs would be valuable. This was also the case when EHRs and implementation services were offered to ambulatory practices.[20] These practices and providers were very busy and reluctant to try anything new. In addition, there was a lot of uncertainty in the press about RECs in the early stages.

Another challenge for RECs was the funding structure. As mentioned earlier, RECs were paid on a milestone basis (three payments for EHs and three payments for each EP). Because recruitment was so challenging and because a large number of organizations recruited into RECs were at a low rate of EHR adoption, the amount of time between initial contact, sign up, and go-live was extremely long in many cases. This forced RECs to operate on thin margins for a large portion of the project.

Milestone payments for hospitals versus clinics also posed a major challenge. The REC program made available up to $18,000 for EHs (i.e., three payments of $6,000). On the other hand, the REC program made close to $5,000 per EP up to a maximum of ten professionals per practice location (i.e., $52,500 per clinic). This disparity between the levels of funding available for hospitals versus clinics made it difficult to provide support to hospitals at the levels needed.

One of the other major challenges encountered by RECs was the eligibility of professionals for services. The RECs were surprised to learn of the ineligibility of their providers who worked in rural health clinics to earn incentives. These professionals used different billing methodology than the Medicare part B reimbursement schedule and, therefore, were ineligible for the MU incentives. Sadly, these providers were in the more economically disadvantaged communities, affiliated with under-resourced critical access hospitals and, consequently, had difficulty finding the funds to cover the cost of implementing an EHR. Though MU was intended to assist them in the adoption of EHRs, the wording in the statute excluded them from eligibility. It was not until October 2013 that CMS released a fix that allowed for some providers at these facilities to become eligible to attest to MU. Since that rule was released in October 2013, these providers were unable to attain the full incentive under the Medicare Program. It also took several months to conduct MU education and training at these rural facilities. Consequently, with reduced funds, complex rules, and long waits for 2014 certified software, adoption by these facilities has been slow to occur.

Finally, one of the major obstacles facing RECs was the diverse types of organizations, providers, geographies, and EHR systems participants were using. Every organization faced different challenges and had different needs, which forced RECs to develop creative solutions and efficient means of delivering technical assistance with limited resources.

ONE REC'S APPROACH

Our REC, the Regional Extension Assistance Center for HIT (REACH), is an extension center that is part of a QIO and is partnered with the College of Saint Scholastica and the National Rural Health Resource Center. It covers the states of Minnesota and North Dakota. Our philosophy is to teach our clients how to be self-sufficient on completion of the project and the end of technical assistance. REACH's motto has been to teach clients "how to fish" rather than fishing for them. Our REC uses a process that was adopted by the Minnesota e-Health Initiative Advisory Group prior to the passage of the HITECH Act; it is designed to assist providers in the state of Minnesota to adopt EHRs. It broke the process into three stages: adopt, implement, and exchange. As was true with other QIO–affiliated RECs, our focus was having our clients understand their readiness, assess their needs, aid in EHR selection, assist in implementation and training, and, finally, optimize their workflow.

As with many other RECs, we serve an extremely diverse territory. Within our region, there are large, densely populated urban areas, suburbs, small towns, and sparsely populated rural counties. Serving this variety of settings required us to develop diverse service delivery mechanisms.

Mechanisms for Serving Clients

Depending on client needs, REACH developed three broad service delivery mechanisms:

- MU Advisement
- Collaborative Consulting
- Individualized Consulting

Several clients received services under more than one mechanism. The collaborative consulting mechanism varied widely, based on the types of clients that participated.

MU Advisement: A key to REACH's success, as with other RECs, is that we became the *trusted advisor* for MU in Minnesota and North Dakota. Because both providers and hospitals could receive incentives for "meaningfully" using their EHR and risk penalties if they attested incorrectly, both providers and hospitals required assistance in understanding and operationalizing the requirements. MU advisement services consisted of explaining and interpreting MU requirements to EPs and critical access hospitals. It meant explaining the physics of meaningful use, while also helping them understand the vision.

During the first two years of the program, MU *Boot Camps* were a powerful way to help clients understand the complex MU rules. Day-long workshops featured presentations by REC staff who walked the attendees through the details of the program: registering, finding a certified EHR, the detailed requirements for usage, understanding quality measures, and attestation. Group exercises allowed attendees to problem-solve and share experiences, which allowed for a deeper understanding of the information and a sharing of novel ways to address challenges.

Clients also took advantage of REACH's "Burning Issues Radio" program, which was a lunch-hour webinar/phone conference where a hot topic was discussed in a casual, chatty way. Some of the most popular topics were related to audits, provider engagement, health information exchange, and the states' Medicaid program. This format allowed for rapid delivery of relevant and breaking news topics. Like the Boot Camps, Burning Issues Radio encouraged open discussion and information sharing.

Clients would frequently ask REC consultants for advice on interpretation of specific MU requirements. Many of these were questions that RECs could answer directly. For more challenging questions, extension center staff could turn to other RECs by using HITRC. Questions that remained unanswered were escalated to CMS and ONC staff who were able to give definitive answers. This ability of extension centers to directly ask their questions to experts at CMS and ONC played a significant role in allowing them to be seen by their clients as trusted advisors.

Collaborative Consulting: Many RECs realized that groups of their clients were very similar and that a collaborative approach would be the most efficient and effective way to serve them. An example of one collaborative effort was the Teen and Reproductive Clinic Collaborative, a group of eight small clinics that provided services to teens and patients with reproductive health needs. None of these clinics had implemented an EHR; furthermore, they were fairly even in the amount of progress they had made in their journey to adoption of EHRs (see Table 7-1). Note that only two had looked at vendors, but all had identified the need and that seven of the eight had formed project teams.

Table 7-1: Similarities in Stage of EHR Adoption Process

Step in Process	Clinic							
	A (Teen Clinic)	B (Repro Health Clinic)	C (Teen Clinic)	D (Repro Health Clinic)	E (Repro Health Clinic)	F (Teen Clinic)	G (Repro Health Clinic)	H (Teen Clinic)
Identification need	X	X	X	X	X	X	X	X
Form project team	X	X	X	X		X	X	X
Document processes	X	X	X			X		X
Document Requirements			X	X		X		X
Looked at vendors		X				X		
Have funding								
Chose vendor								

The clinics discussed the concept of collaborating on the process of selecting and implementing an EHR and developed a list of benefits and concerns related to such an arrangement. While the project would allow for some efficiencies, such as sharing training, developing best practices and learning from each other in real time, and potentially reducing cost by sharing support, the project would also have to consider multiple organizations' schedules, determine resourcing arrangements for group purchasing, and the limitations of transitioning to one system and losing previous IT investments.

In this particular instance, the benefits of collaboration outweighed the concerns, so the collaborative was formed. During the three-year period from 2010 to 2013, this team worked collaboratively to create requirements, select an EHR vendor, implement EHR software, and achieve the requirements of MU. In the words of one of the members:

> [REACH] is why we have been able to select and implement an electronic health record. Their idea to pull similar reproductive teen clinics together was very smart; it helped us pool resources and we continue to work very closely on things today that would've been very difficult or not possible for each organization alone. We are just beginning to really use our EHR data for program improvement....and again this wouldn't be possible if we did not get REACH expertise.

Based on the success of the Teen and Reproductive Collaborative, our REC formed other collaborative groups. Among them, a Healthland Collaborative of rural health centers that used Healthland EHR software. This collaborative shared best practices in Healthland workflows, training, and reporting, and in the support of 17 critical access hospitals (CAHs)/rural health centers.

The collaborative methodology was also effective for the large integrated delivery networks as well. Project managers from these facilities started meeting to address concerns associated with managing the reporting requirements of EPs who work in more than one clinic. The integrated delivery networks (IDNs) in this group are the largest providers of care in Minnesota and North Dakota, including Health Partners, Mayo Health System, and Essentia Health. These organizations serve over 75 percent of the population across the two states. Despite the fact that these organizations compete with one another, the REACH collaborative provided a neutral space for them to discuss MU issues and to share best practices. Breakthroughs enabled by this collaborative, named Shared EP Collaborative, include:

- A procedure to identify EPs who work in more than one organization and a standard for deciding which organization would get the incentive payments.
- Working together to draw attention to issues associated with failure of CMS registration and attestation systems to keep up with user traffic.
- Developing a shared directory of direct addresses to enable effective exchange of transition-of-care documentation.

In summary, the use of collaboratives served clients well. By sharing expertise, collaborative members were able to achieve much more than they would have if they worked as individual clients.

Individualized Consulting: There were many instances in which clients were best served with a traditional one-to-one consulting engagement. Under this model, an REC consultant would meet with the clients, understand their needs, and develop a work plan to ensure the client would achieve MU (see Figure 7-4).

These types of engagements were most effective with organizations that were experiencing specific issues associated with their EHR technology, for example, clients that had difficulty running the MU reports. These engagements also worked well with clients who started late in the EHR selection and implementation process. Enabling these clients to meet the MU deadlines required intensive intervention in which the consultant served as a part-time project manager. Though this was not a role we would normally take, given our teach-them-to-fish analogy, it was sometimes necessary to assist them in meeting deadlines. Extension center involvement was beneficial to isolated clients in that it gave them more leverage with their EHR vendor. The REC could also translate some of the issues into a format that the vendor was able to understand and help the vendor to troubleshoot difficult problems.

This individualized consulting also led to several other specialized programs developed to address the particular needs of our clients. One area was an attestation and audit readiness plan. This was a checklist that clients could use to assess their readiness to attest and provide guidance on the appropriate documentation needed to demonstrate their attainment of MU in the event of an audit. Because of the complexity of some of the audit requirements, this proved to be very popular with our clients.

Another service, which was acutely needed and discovered as a result of the readiness assessment, was a security and privacy risk assessment. Many of these small hospitals and practices were not skilled in this area and required substantial guidance to understand the process. We developed a risk assessment checklist for them to work through and then walked them through the results. We also assisted them in developing a mitigation plan.

These are examples of three types of service delivery mechanisms that served our clients well and some of the specialized programs that were developed in response to specific needs.

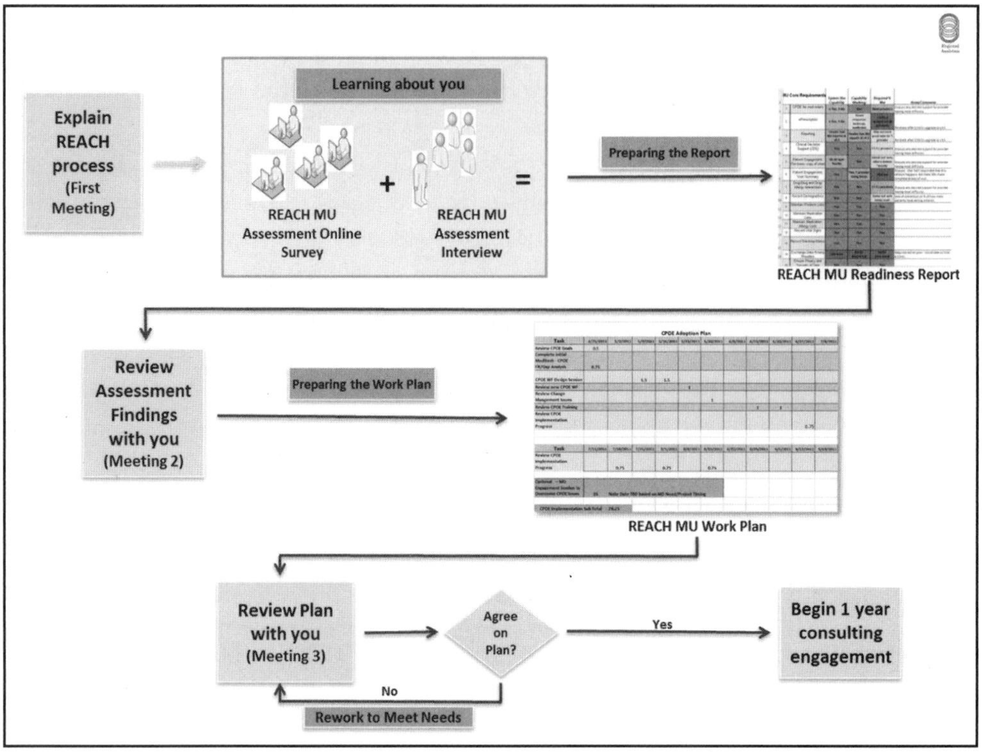

Figure 7-4: Process for Individualized Consulting Engagement

Note: Using the process illustrated in Figure 7-4, REACH consultants would determine the level of a client's MU readiness. Based on the assessment, the consultant would develop a work plan, gain client consensus and begin work.

RECs as Advocates

As a result of their broad experience of working with clients in the field, RECs have been able to provide feedback to policymakers and lawmakers as to the complexities and difficulties encountered by small hospitals and rural providers in meeting the Stage 1 MU requirements. Through the HITRC, we were able to aggregate all the challenges encountered by providers across the country. Provider engagement and administrative issues were among the more common issues. The most challenging MU Stage 1 measure was the clinical summaries measure, but measure challenges varied by practice setting.[21] Feedback from the RECs was valuable input to the policy committee as it began to craft requirements for future stages of MU.

CHALLENGES GOING FORWARD

While there have been major successes by RECs in assisting underserved healthcare organizations to adopt technology (measured by the number of EPs and EHs achieving MU), MU Stages 2 and 3 increase in difficulty by adding functional requirements (such as secure messaging between patients and providers) and increased measurements for existing functional requirements (such as additional clinical decision support rules). For organizations to avoid CMS reimbursement penalties in 2015, they will need to successfully implement systems with advanced capabilities. This poses a major challenge for underserved healthcare organizations, as research has demonstrated that organizations in rural areas, areas of lower socioeconomic status, and areas with high unemployment are demonstrating MU at lower rates.[22]

As of this writing, the future of REC programs is uncertain. As a result, organizations in underserved areas are at greater risk of financial penalties in 2015 and beyond because it will be difficult, if not impossible, for them to get affordable implementation assistance and rule interpretation as the MU requirements progress. RECs are needed more than ever as healthcare facilities progress into advanced stages of MU—particularly those who are underserved, small, and rural. The REC program has proven to be an exceptional resource that would be a mistake to discard. The relationships these local agencies have developed with smaller practices and hospitals would go a long way in helping lead healthcare transformation in the smaller facilities. Though their initial contract goal was to bring a provider just to the point of attesting to 90 days of MU, many have continued providing services to these facilities to help them optimize the use of EHRs and achieve more advanced use of health IT through care coordination, patient engagement, health information exchange, and workflow optimization.

OPPORTUNITIES

A major challenge facing EHR implementation, MU, and practice transformation is ensuring that the gap between urban and rural healthcare does not widen. The President's Council of Advisors on Science and Technology recently released a report[23] that advocates leveraging the RECs to assist clinicians in small, rural, and underserved areas in incorporating system engineering approaches to their care processes. Due to their developed infrastructure and established relationships with organizations in these settings, RECs are well positioned to expand the type and level of technical assistance to rural and underserved healthcare organizations as they adopt and optimize their technology to improve care processes.

As health reform gains steam, many of the RECs have firmly set their strategic plans toward supporting this enormous transition for the United States. The New Jersey REC has moved steadily forward with a plan to assist with data aggregation services for organizations taking on shared risk contracts. The North Carolina REC continues to advance the practice transformation knowledge base through their continued programming efforts. In states that received State Innovation Model implementation grants, RECs are heavily involved in helping their state move toward Medicaid ACO support. The rate of readiness for practice transformation varies heavily state by state, but with policy and payment changes taking place in the near term, RECs are in a good position to play a key role in supporting better care at a lower price.

Many extension centers are also continuing to provide privacy and security risk assessments, mitigation plans, assistance with Stage 2 of MU, effective use of EHRs, and assisting providers in the Million Hearts programs. Regarding leveraging EHRs to improve quality, CMS in its 11th scope of work for the QIOs provide funding to quality improvement networks to work with RECs to leverage health IT to improve care.

Finally, in October 2014, the CMS Center for Medicare and Medicaid Innovation (CMMI) announced the Transforming Clinical Practice Initiative, a funding opportunity designed to support 150,000 clinicians in sharing, adapting, and further developing comprehensive quality improvement strategies. RECs are expected to be central in this push to transform healthcare.

As federal funding ends for the majority of the RECs in February 2015, many RECs have found other opportunities to continue this important work. Through their work with small and frequently ignored providers, they have built an incredible support system for these communities around topics that support healthcare reform. This support system is key in helping us transform all corners of this nation to a more advanced pay-for-value system and help us achieve the Triple Aim of healthcare by improving the quality and experience of care and improving the health of all populations, including the underserved, while reducing the cost of care.

REFERENCES

1. Birkhaeuser D, Evenson RE, Feder G. The economic impact of agricultural extension: A review. *Economic Development and Cultural Change*. Yale University. 1991:607-650. Accessed November 21, 2014.
2. http://georgewbush-whitehouse.archives.gov/infocus/technology/economic_policy200404/chap3.html. Accessed November 21, 2014.
3. http://georgewbush-whitehouse.archives.gov/news/releases/2004/04/20040427-4.html. Accessed November 21, 2014.
4. Jha AK. Meaningful use of electronic health records: The road ahead. *JAMA*. 2010;304,15:1709-1710.
5. DesRoches CM, Campbell EG, Rao SR, et al. Electronic health records in ambulatory care—a national survey of physicians. *N Engl J Med*. 2008;359,1:50-60.
6. http://www.hhs.gov/ocr/privacy/hipaa/understanding/coveredentities/hitechact.pdf Accessed November 21, 2014.
7. Blumenthal D. Stimulating the adoption of health information technology. *New Engl J Med*. 2009; 360,15:1477-1479.
8. http://www.healthit.gov/FACAS/sites/faca/files/HITPC_DataAnalyticsUpdate_2014-05-06.pdf. Accessed November 21, 2014.
9. http://www.healthit.gov/FACAS/sites/faca/files/HITPCdata_analytics_update020414.pdf. Accessed November 21, 2014.
10. Maxson E, Jain S, Kendall, M, et al. The regional extension center program: Helping physicians meaningfully use health information technology. *Ann Int Med*. 2010;153(10):666-670.
11. Samuel CA, King J, Adetosoye F, et al. Engaging providers in underserved areas to adopt electronic health records. *Am J Manag Care*. 2012;19(3):229-234.
12. Lynch K, Kendall M, Shanks K, et al. The Health IT Regional Extension Center Program: Evolution and lessons for health care transformation. *Health Serv Res*. 2014;49.1pt2:421-437.
13. Office of the National Coordinator. Report to Congress: Update on the adoption of health information technology and related efforts to facilitate the electronic use and exchange of health. October 2014. http://www.healthit.gov/sites/default/files/rtc_adoption_and_exchange9302014.pdf. Accessed November 21, 2014.
14. http://dashboard.healthit.gov/rec/. Accessed November 13, 2014.
15. http://dashboard.healthit.gov/rec/. Accessed November 13, 2014.
16. http://gao.gov/assets/600/593078.pdf. Accessed November 21, 2014.
17. http://www.healthit.gov/FACAS/sites/faca/files/HITPC_DataAnalyticsUpdate_2014-06-10.pptx. Accessed November 21, 2014.

18. Casey MM, Moscovice I, McCullough J. Rural primary care practices and meaningful use of electronic health records: The role of regional extension centers. *J Rural Health*. 2014;30(3):244-251.

19. Heisey-Grove D, Danehy LN, Consolazio M, et al. A national study of challenges to electronic health record adoption and meaningful use. *Med Care*. 2014;52(2):144-148.

20. Goroll AH, Simon SR, Tripathi M, et al. Community-wide implementation of health information technology: the Massachusetts eHealth collaborative experience. *J Am Med Inform Assoc*. 2009;16(1):132-139.

21. http://journals.lww.com/lww-medicalcare/Abstract/2014/02000/A_National_Study_of_Challenges_to_Electronic.9.aspx. Accessed November 21, 2012.

22. Casey MM, Moscovice I, Klingner J, et al. Rural relevant quality measures for critical access hospitals. *J Rural Health*. 2013;29(2):159-171.

23. http://www.whitehouse.gov/sites/default/files/microsites/ostp/PCAST/pcast_systems_engineering_in_healthcare_-_may_2014.pdf. Accessed November 21, 2014.

Chapter 8

Ambulatory Systems

Curtis L. Cole, MD; Adam D. Cheriff, MD; J. Travis Gossey, MD; Sameer Malhotra, MD; and Daniel M. Stein, MD

INTRODUCTION

When considered from the patient's perspective, the ambulatory electronic health record (AEHR) is probably the closest approximation of the patient's archetype of MyChart, a cradle-to-grave record of a patient's healthy growth, sickness, recovery, and aging. Over the past several decades various specialty systems, acute care systems, ancillary systems, and ambulatory systems have advanced individually and have converged as well. Increasingly a representation of this vernacular chart is emerging either through large multi-functioned EHRs or the aggregation of data from disparate systems through sophisticated interfaces and information exchange. This reflects technological advancement, organizational changes within healthcare, and evolving reimbursement methods. It also creates new problems of how to sort and organize so much information to prevent data overload, alert fatigue, and a very different kind of provider inefficiency than was the challenge of AEHR pioneers decades ago.

In this chapter, we will review the key features of the AEHR as they have evolved and discuss some of the remaining challenges facing the designers of future AEHRs. We begin with practice management because, other than the nature of technology itself, healthcare reimbursement methods remain the core driver of how AEHRs are structured. We discuss the fundamental clinical features such as order entry, documentation, results review, messaging, and decision support. We then move to reporting and analytics where the increasing quantity and quality of data captured in the AEHR can be used to improve care delivery, outcomes, and the AEHR itself. To achieve an integrated view of the patient and a longitudinal time perspective, data integration is required. We review this in the context of the AEHR and the role of niche systems. We will touch on patient engagement as an increasingly important aspect of the AEHR, though this is also addressed in other chapters. We end with a discussion of the cost and value of the AEHR, an argument that has evolved from a defensive justification to a more mature analysis of clinical and business value.

PRACTICE MANAGEMENT SYSTEMS

It is widely accepted that administrative complexity is an important driver of healthcare costs.[1,2] Ambulatory practice management systems (PMSs) supply the increasingly important tools to manage patient flow and the revenue cycle. These are the operational and financial sides of the same coin. They are the outpatient cousins to ADT (admit, discharge, transfer) and patient accounting systems. While many providers have implemented some form of a PMS in the absence of an EHR, tight integration between the administrative and clinical functions is becoming increasingly necessary to insure maximum productivity and revenue cycle efficiency.

While the key functions of a mature PMS are patient registration, scheduling, and billing, full-featured PMSs provide many more features and functions. Some provide scanning and document management capabilities. Some manage paper charts in ways analogous to a hospital health information management system. Many have sophisticated materials management capabilities, which are particularly important in specialties where expensive medications or equipment are used.

Registration

Whether you view the PMS with an operations lens or a financial lens, the business begins with patient identification. It is from this starting point that the divergence with inpatient systems begins. The concept of *registration* is very different between the inpatient and outpatient worlds. The conceptual difference is permanence. The ambulatory world treats registration as a persistent beginning of a lifetime record. Patients see their doctors over and over, but they only register once; they reasonably expect their doctor to remember them. In the inpatient world, registration is the beginning of a finite stay and is repeated with each admission. Inpatient electronic medical records (EMRs) may share demographics across stays, but the patient's chart, in many systems, is broken up by hospital admission rather than remaining a continuous record.

From a systems perspective, the difference is the combination of three related functions: identification, registration, and scheduling. Patient identification is increasingly the realm of specialized systems specific to this task known as the electronic master patient index (EMPI). These systems contain a database with a very small amount of identity and demographic data about every patient in their dominion. The job of the EMPI is to make sure that each patient has only one set of data, even across multiple systems, specialties, locations, and institutions.

Almost all PMSs have some EMPI functionality built in. Large PMSs tend to have more sophisticated functionality. For example, advanced EMPI systems can make use of complex algorithms to transactionally evaluate and weight dozens of patient characteristics to determine possible identity matches. A caveat for PMS selection is to make sure this functionality is sophisticated enough to meet organizational needs or that the system is capable of integration with an external EMPI, which is increasingly the preference of large organizations.

The details of patient identification can be mind numbing, particularly to those who fail to grasp their importance—but ignore them at your own peril. The ambulatory world can be deceptively simple in this regard. If you view each practice independently, it may be easy to keep a few thousand patients straight without a large number of duplicates, but when you combine practices or try to combine data from patients across practices or locations, you quickly realize that the ambulatory world is very large indeed. The lack of a single universal patient identifier makes matching logic more critical. and the well-documented failures and risks of using Social Security numbers (SSNs) make the task ahead look even more challenging.[3,4] Inadequate or improperly implemented EMPIs can lead to duplicate records or inappropriately merged patient records within clinical and administrative systems. These identity problems are not rare and can impede productivity, compromise revenue cycle efficiency, and introduce significant patient safety risks.[5]

The U.S. Congress has banned the government from creating a national patient identifier, leaving it to each provider to calculate unique identities across shared patients.[6,7,8] One particularly disturbing aspect of this decision is that the negative impact of this inefficiency is not equally distributed across society because of the different frequency of names among various ethnic groups (see Table 8-1).

Once the patient is identified, the formal registration can begin. This is the collection of more detailed patient demographics including insurance coverage information, emergency contacts, customer service information such as contact preferences, and similar nonclinical information. In the most sophisticated PMSs, insurance eligibility verification may occur at this step in an electronic data interchange (EDI) transaction analogous to a retailer validating a credit card. PMSs are often connected to large clearinghouses for these eligibility queries.

Failure to completely and accurately collect all necessary registration information can have profound consequences in the subsequent workflows. A failure to standard-

Table 8-1: EMPI Data Noting Frequency of Names Among Various Ethnic Groups

Same First and Last Name	Same First and Last Name and Same Date of Birth
Jose Rodriguez	Yan Chen
Jose Rivera	Mei Chen
Jeffrey Xu	Xiu Chen
Joel De La Cruz	Kevin Chen
Maria Rivera	Jose Rodriguez
Maria Perez	Xiu Lin
Jose Gonzalez	Yan Lin
Ana Rodriguez	Yu Chen
Jose Martinez	Jin Chen
Juan Rodriguez	Jason Chen
Maria Lopez	Li Chen
Carmen Rivera	Xiao Chen
Jose Garcia	Hui Chen
Taylor Li	Kevin Lin
Jose Hernandez	Ying Lin
Jose Rodriguez	Yan Chen

Note: Taken from our institutional EMPI in 2014 with more than 11 million patients, these are the most frequent names in which the first name and the last name are the same or the first and last name plus the date of birth are the same.

ize data storage conventions can lead to patient misidentification. Incomplete or inaccurate contact information can delay clinical communications between providers and patients. Perhaps most commonly, registrations fail to accurately record patient insurance coverage attributes. This can lead to claim denials, time-consuming follow-up by both providers and patients, and ultimately, lost revenue for rendered services.

Scheduling

In the inpatient world, the next step in the workflow is bed management. In the ambulatory environment, the critical next step is the scheduling of clinical services. Because patients are admitted to the hospital at a particular time and date, scheduling is inherent in the admission process. For the ambulatory patient, all future encounters will key off the original registration (generally with registration data confirmation and/or necessary updates), and the schedule is the focus of subsequent patient interactions.

Because the process of scheduling is so tightly linked to registration, it is not surprising that many clinical scheduling systems are integrated with registration systems within the PMS. There are a few key qualities of ambulatory scheduling that differentiate the various systems available on the market. Perhaps the most important is how they differ from nonclinical scheduling systems such as Microsoft Outlook™ or Google Calendar,™ which for clarity are referred to here as *calendaring systems*.

Calendaring systems have been (and continue to be) used to schedule patient visits/services in the ambulatory context, though this is increasingly less common with the adoption of the EHR. The main distinction between a scheduling system and a calendaring system is the linkage to the patient record. In a typical business calendaring system, the user cannot quickly locate a whole history of a given patient's appointments or sort them by type. The appointment is usually free text, whereas in a clinical scheduling system the appointment is with a specific patient already registered in the database.

Clinical schedules are also linked to billing transactions. This is critical from the financial perspective, as most medical service charges are linked to specific encounters. One of the first interventions in a typical revenue cycle enhancement program is to match charges against the schedule. This is possible manually with a calendaring system but can be made into an automated missing charge report in a clinical scheduling product.

Clinical scheduling systems typically support complex templates and rules to maximize patient flow and appointment availability. Concepts such as appointment type, bump lists, freeze and thaw, recurring visits, previsit instructions, and team care will have variable importance in different practices and specialties. For example, patients on specific chemotherapy protocols or physical therapy routines can be extremely complicated to schedule. Sophisticated clinical scheduling systems can offer appropriate searching algorithms and decision support that can span visits or include resource availability.

Resource linking is particularly critical in procedural areas. For example, in specialties with endoscopes, the availability of the scope itself and the time needed for sterilization must be accounted for by the scheduling system to maximize throughput. A decision support rule may alert a radiology scheduler regarding total radiation dose. Similar issues exist for many other procedures such as oncology infusions, dialysis, and physical therapy. Linkage to materials management systems may also be important for inventory and cost controls.

In academic environments, there are complex regulatory rules affecting scheduling that must be accounted for to allow compliant billing. For example, the 1969 CMS IL372 supervision regulations require that primary care supervisors oversee no more than four residents at a given time.[9] Without that ratio, the supervisor cannot bill for their supervision. Similarly, patients may be part of a clinical trial protocol and, therefore, communication regarding a research visit with a clinical trials management system may be important.

Increasingly, the most sophisticated ambulatory practices are providing online access to self-directed scheduling. Online scheduling is frequently offered via patient health portals that are tightly integrated with the EHR or PMS. Recently, some standalone consumer services such as ZocDoc™ (zocdoc.com) have gained popularity by offering patients the ability to directly schedule appointments with participating providers. Though offering online access for self-directed scheduling is not extremely complex technically, there are workflow challenges to its implementation. Particularly for highly subspecialized medical service, patients cannot be made aware of complex business rules that might factor into the assignment of the correct resources, appointment duration, or even service provider. Further, the need to properly address managed care precertifications and medical necessity rules also can impede the delivery of this popular convenience.

Some form of a patient tracking system is often implemented in conjunction with PMSs to track all aspects of clinical workflow and patient throughput. Some systems can parse a variety of wait times such as time-to-room, time-in-room, time-with-RN, and time-with-MD. Some systems use radio-frequency identification (RFID) or other technologies to automate patient tracking, though that is hardly mainstream. When used well, these tools provide practice administrators and clinicians the necessary data to optimize patient flow, maximize resource utilization, and improve patient satisfaction.

Billing and Collections

The core of most PMSs is the financial component. The tools needed to manage billing and accounts receivable are enormously varied due to the wide variety of reimbursement rules and methods throughout the country. Most PMSs are optimized for the predominant reimbursement model within the United States—fee-for-service. Generally speaking, providers are paid a negotiated or (in the case of government payer) determined fee for specific procedures or services on the basis of justifying diagnoses. The PMS must allow for efficient charge capture, generation of medical service claims to payers, and mechanisms for follow-up and resolution of accounts receivable.

Within ambulatory systems, the focus is generally on professional fee billing rather than facilities fee billing. While facility and professional fee billing are increasingly happening concurrently within single enterprise billing systems, historically distinct systems were used to manage facility and professional fee billing. One important and possibly counterintuitive feature this may imply is the need for the *ambulatory* PMS to support *inpatient* professional billing. Physicians who see inpatients and do not bill globally or through the hospital send their bills from their office. Therefore, certain types of integration with the inpatient system, such as an ADT interface, may be desirable.

Virtually all PMSs have the ability to transact with partner entities via EDI standards. The Health Insurance Portability and Accountability Act of 1996 (HIPAA) EDI transaction set governs system communication format for electronic eligibility queries, claims submission, statusing, and remittance.[10] Ambiguity in operating rules and implementation standards have made system integration complicated and expensive. Many PMS vendors partner with EDI clearinghouse vendors to simplify their own EDI communication. The concept is that providers only need to communicate with one company, which communicates with all the payers on their behalf. Conversely, the payers only need to communicate with a few clearinghouses rather than thousands of providers. In theory, maturation of Internet standards, further refinement of operating rules, and regulatory pressure may simplify system integration and facilitate some degree of disintermediation.

Charge Capture. Today's financial systems put increasing emphasis on capturing data as early in the encounter as possible. Before widespread adoption of EHRs, charge capture was often done as a separate step from clinical documentation. Procedure (current procedural terminology, CPT) and diagnosis (International Classification of Diseases, ICD) codes were often captured via specialty-specific *superbills* and then manually transcribed into the billing system. Gradually, the process of charge capture moved into the electronic realm. In the past decade, some practices began using portable devices like smartphones to capture charges. These systems may be standalone or integrated with a PMS or clinical system. Regardless of the platform, these systems offer another way to eliminate paper encounter forms and capture data more accurately and directly into the billing system.

With more widespread adoption of the EHR, charge capture has become more integrated into clinical workflow at the point of care. Procedure (CPT) and diagnosis (ICD) codes are now captured as part of routine clinical documentation within the EHR. This information can then be interfaced to a separate PMS or the content can be provided directly to the billing functions for those EHR platforms that have integrated practice management capabilities. A major step that has facilitated clinician charge capture is the trend toward embedding clinician-friendly terminology to document procedures and diagnoses. Because these clinician-friendly interface terms are mapped to reference terminologies such as CPT or ICD-9/10, providers can easily capture clinical intent while still supplying the necessary administrative billing codes.

The shift from back-office to point-of-care charge capture can provide significant opportunities to decrease costs and enhance revenue. The potential elimination of charge-entry clerks and certified professional coders is an obvious opportunity to decrease labor costs. Further return on investment (ROI) from these systems stems from a possible reduction in lost charges and reduced service to posting lag. Charge capture within the EHR also affords the opportunity to deploy financial decision support such as medical necessity rules or level of service calculations. Responsibly deployed, these interventions can have very beneficial effects on revenue cycle efficiency. Recently, though, EHRs have come under fire for potentially facilitating systematic up-coding for non–medically-necessary services.[11] While there is certainly potential for abuse, many argue that EHRs have simply allowed providers to more efficiently document and bill for medically necessary services.

Executives attuned to the current regulatory environment will note the need to synchronize the facility and the professional fee bills in terms of procedure and diagnosis. Given that two staffs with two different managers, following two sets of rules, using two different systems are responsible for documentation and billing suggests this will be fraught with peril. Adding further complexity, multiple specialists may be billing for the same case (e.g., surgery and anesthesia) and different coding systems may be required (e.g., Healthcare Common Procedure Coding System [HCPCS] and CPT. At this point, few systems on the market today are facile at this kind of cross-provider billing reconciliation. If pressure increases toward global billing, hospitals and doctors will be forced to coordinate to unify their bills and determine how to split the fees. This will create new challenges for sites without integrated billing systems.

Another nuance executives need to beware of is the definition of the encounter itself. As with registration, terminology here is imprecise and can be confusing. Some prefer *encounter* to refer to the billable event and visit for the face-to-face meeting with the patient. But the increasing prevalence of phone, web, and other virtual visits makes this topic inherently fluid. Regardless of how you refer to the event, the system must know the rules for the definitions, which are generally determined by the payer and may or may not make sense to the clinician. For example, a nine-month pregnancy may be a single encounter with multiple visits. Similarly, a visit to a doctor's office that results in referral to the emergency department may be combined as a single encounter (the 72-hour rule). A visit to multiple different doctors on a single day may be considered a single encounter. The billing system needs to understand these rules. Again, cross-institutional reconciliation may be necessary to ensure complete accuracy in some scenarios.

Managed Care, Coding Rules, and Claims Submission. The most fundamental distinction among practice management systems is support for the various forms of managed care and the associated coding and reimbursement rules. While traditional fee-for-service still exists in some form in most markets, some permutation of managed care is the norm in most areas. The critical functionality within modern PMSs is the ability to embed rules engines and workflows to enforce the often astoundingly complex business rules that govern reimbursement. Practices that take on capitation require use of a PMS that is fully capable of tracking expenses and supporting risk. Because of the diversity of payer rules, the frequency of changes to the rules, and the frequency with which patients change payers, the proper setup and maintenance of a PMS are critical for revenue cycle efficiency.

The first fundamental aspect of a highly functional PMS is disciplined master file management. All information systems use a variety of tables and dictionaries to drive the lists and other user interface elements for relevant discrete data capture. In the case of billing systems, there are dozens of relevant master files, such as providers, locations, specialties, payer/plans, procedures, and diagnoses. Some of these dictionaries can be standardized, but some will always be local and the ability to customize and control these tables is a key vendor differentiator. For large and/or decentralized ambulatory practices, master-file management can be an extremely labor intensive management effort.

The complexities inherent in managing a provider master file are instructive. IT managers are vexed by the need to provide users with accurate data without good sources for the data. This issue is relevant to claims adjudication because of the many nuances of billing that require accurate lookup tables. For example, specialists may need to indicate the license number of a referring physician on the claim or it will be rejected. In the world of managed care, keeping track of who is "in plan" and "out of plan" is a major problem. Many providers who have dropped out of plan will tell you that it may take months or even years for their name to disappear from the payer's list, particularly if they are in a shortage specialty.

Another critical aspect of the sophisticated PMS is a rules engine (and associated task management tools) for evaluating the accuracy and/or validity of billing transactions. Charges must be analyzed for exceptions, discounts, consistency with other claims, the addition of modifiers, or other necessary interventions. The goal of the editing functions is to ensure that every claim that is sent to the payer is a clean claim. Sophisticated PMSs provide native tools (or support for third-party rules engine integration) that mimic the adjudication rules used by payers. Coding decision support can sometimes be deployed real time at the time of charge-entry. In addition, claims are often batched and analyzed in bulk, generating exceptions that must then be reviewed and edited. Clean claims mean no rejections, faster payment, and reduced reprocessing costs. Not surprisingly, claim editing is another frequent focus of revenue enhancement efforts.

Once through the edit process, a claim is ready to be sent. Most claims are sent electronically to payers or claims clearinghouses as the intermediary. The ability to print a paper claim remains a requirement of any PMS—if for no other reason than downtime at an intermediary. In either event, logs of the transactions are essential to avoid disputes over lost claims. On receipt, a payer adjudicates the claims and, if a flaw is found, the claim for reimbursement may be denied. Here again, there is an opportunity for efficiency if the payer communicates the denial electronically, using standardized rejection codes. Well-managed practices are continually analyzing denial codes so that practice administrators can track the reasons for rejection over time and correct any systematic problems.

Some proportion of the cost of medical services is often the direct responsibility of the patient. This may be due to co-pays, co-insurance, deductibles, or non-covered services. The PMS must have the capability to generate itemized statements for patients to bill for these self-pay balances. Often, this information is extracted from the PMS to specialized statement vendors. Increasingly, progressive ambulatory practices are offering online financial statements and bill-pay functions via patient portals. This not only reduces the costs of statement generation and mailing but can help automate the process of recording the payment against the outstanding balance within the PMS.

Payment Posting and Contract Management

Payments made by payers or patients all must be reconciled or posted within the PMS. Payment posting has historically been complex and labor intensive due to a lack of electronic automation. There may be manual effort involved with interpreting paper EOBs (explanation of benefits) and assigning the correct amount of money (via paper checks) to each claim. The procedure can also be error prone, making this whole process a ripe target for automation. Bar coding, optical character recognition, and a variety of other technologies have been applied with varying degrees of success in an attempt to clean up payment posting.

The use of the HIPAA transaction standard for electronic remittance advice (HIPAA X12N 835 standard) has simplified payment posting by providing an electronic version of the EOB. For ambulatory practices that transact with large, established payers, manual payment posting has largely been replaced by automated processing of electronic remittance advice (ERA). The ACA of 2010 mandated the creation of more specific operating rules for electronic funds transfer (EFT). This eliminates the effort of depositing paper checks and simplifies the process of reconciling large payer payments with individual patient balances.

Once posted, there are two more problems the PMS must contend with: overpayment and underpayment. Overpayment most commonly occurs when both the patient and the payer send the provider a payment. This necessitates a method for refunding which, in many practices, requires a link to a separate accounts payable system. In today's world of managed care conglomerates, underpayment is the more serious problem. Even within one company, claims may be processed by multiple systems that may not have the current contract and payment policies loaded. Therefore, inappropriate rejections and underpayments are common and often appear to be idiosyncratic. Further, in many states, there is little accountability by regulators. In a study performed at Weill Cornell and Emory, between three and eight percent of all reimbursements from managed care companies were underpaid compared with contract. While this represents tens of millions of dollars to providers annually, payers are only fined a small fraction of this amount by regulators, leaving enforcement of the contract up to the prowess of the providers' management and IT.[12]

Contract management systems, integrated or added on to the PMS are the provider's defense against these errors. If the PMS knows how much the payer is supposed to reimburse for a given procedure, it can alert the provider to underpayments, individually or systematically. Underpayments of a few dollars are the most insidious, as the cost of reprocessing the claim will exceed the difference collected. This is why tracking underpayments over time is essential so that underpayments can be addressed in bulk.

Analytics and Business Intelligence

One final critical feature to any PMS is reporting. The biggest payoff to any information system comes from the ability to extract and manipulate data that have been captured during the routine course of business. Cheaper systems come with preconfigured reports and few tools to manipulate them. More sophisticated systems provide myriad options for extracting data and configuring reports. Increasingly, operational reports are embedded directly within the PMS to assist with task management by providing visibility on data quality and staff productivity. Rather than generating a report for a manager to review, the most sophisticated systems create a live task list within the application that staff may use to manage their workflow. More complex analytic reports are often executed outside of the PMS to allow for long-term trending of patient access and revenue cycle metrics. These tools are imperative for driving ongoing process improvement efforts.

AMBULATORY CLINICAL SYSTEMS

Clinical Systems and Biomedical Devices

There are many types of ambulatory clinical systems. The focus within this chapter will be the core EHR, but the AEHR can be just one piece of a generally complex system architecture to manage clinical workflow and information storage. The AEHR is often integrated with niche diagnostic and/or procedural systems, such as a lab information system, a radiology information system, and potentially dozens of smaller specialty-based systems. Other highly specialized workflows such as clinical trials management, materials management, and image capture/storage are often addressed via standalone systems. Much of the data generated in the context of routine patient care are from a wide array of biomedical devices.

The distinction between clinical systems and biomedical devices is becoming both difficult to make and less important. Traditionally the line between them was apparent. Devices were typically electromechanical, diagnostic, and procedure oriented. From an IT perspective, they were data sources. Perhaps the most important distinction was that biomedical devices were regulated by the U.S. Food and Drug Administration (FDA). Any changes to their function required recertification. Conversely, information systems were electronic, transaction and documentation oriented, and unregulated in their plasticity.

While some of these distinctions still hold today, their importance is increasingly moot. Clinically, it is completely natural that the systems cardiologists or radiologists use to make a diagnosis should be fully integrated with the systems they use to report their findings. Similarly, from the patients' perspectives, the test report is no less part of their medical chart than the note of the physician who ordered the test or procedure. It is not surprising, therefore, that the marketplace for these once separate entities is now merging. The leading manufacturers of biomedical devices such as GE and Siemens are now also leading vendors of EMRs.

That said, this chapter will not examine further traditional biomedical devices like EKG and x-ray machines, regardless of how proximal they may have become to clinical systems. One reason for this is that they are still purchased and managed differently in most institutions. But more important, biomedical devices do not fit as cleanly into the major thesis of this section. That is, clinical systems are the essential workflow managers of ambulatory medicine—or, at least, they should be.

The reason to emphasize workflow is that it is the key to success when purchasing, implementing, and managing these systems. A brief history of clinical systems shows that this was not always the case. In fact, many if not most clinical systems on the market today reveal a modular orientation that reflects how their development was funded, as much as any well-thought-out technical architecture.

The Ambulatory Electronic Health Record

A Brief History. The first attempts to build EMRs were largely in the outpatient arena. Barnett's landmark work in the 1960 with COSTAR[13] emphasized the increasing availability and organization of medical records. Separate modules for registration, scheduling, and the actual clinical encounter form were implemented.

In the 1970s, McDonald at Regenstrief and Stead and Hammond at Duke also developed outpatient medical record systems.[14,15] The Regenstrief system also used encounter form data input similar to COSTAR, but pioneered the emphasis on automated reminders. Stead and Hammond's TMR system actually attempted to go paperless using clerks to enter data.

Throughout the 1970s and 1980s technology became more affordable and adequate to the task of building medical records. Computers moved from mainframes to minicomputers in the 1970s and from minicomputers to microcomputers in the 1980s. Recall that at this time, most medical centers were organized in a very decentralized manner. Outside the institutions, independent practitioners and small groups were still the norm. Therefore, it is not surprising that the medical record systems that were developed reflected this departmental and practice-oriented organization. In the 1990s, when graphical programming and database management tools became ubiquitous, the forces working against integration were even more profound. Commercial systems were specialty focused, procedure oriented, and doctor-centric.

Large institutions were installing more centralized systems in hospitals but, even there, the industry was moving toward decentralized client-server designs. The sales teams advocated best-of-breed—as much a justification for the way things were as for any nobler architectural reason.

What resulted is a situation many institutions and practices are still in today. Every business unit or clinically distinct entity has (or wants) its own information system that meets its needs. There are significant merits to this approach. Many niche systems do, in fact, meet the workflow requirements of any given specialty much better than general purpose systems that are customized for the environment. The needs of a cardiology practice offering echocardiography and cardiac graphics are quite distinct from gastroenterologists offering in-office endoscopy, though both are subspecialties of internal medicine. Venture into radiation oncology, physiatry, ophthalmology, or almost any other common outpatient medical specialty and you will find radically different functional requirements, workflows, and expectations.

This challenge of subspecialization exemplifies perhaps the most fundamental strategic IT choice facing an executive managing clinical systems: the choice between an aggregation of interfaced best-of-breed systems versus a monolithic system. If each subspecialty can have a better system for itself if they purchase items separately, is the total greater or less than the sum of the parts? Does a unified platform offer economies of scale and degrees of interoperability not feasible with multiple interfaced systems?

This struggle is illustrated in the history of results reporting and order entry systems discussed in the next section. Just 15 to 25 years ago, many order entry and results reporting systems were separate. Integration allows loop closure; an order is closed when the result comes back. But in ambulatory practices that order from many different (often external) labs, that integration is more complex and costly and might lock such practices in to one laboratory provider.

Recently the sophistication of large, unified systems and interfacing technology has improved significantly, so technology itself has not resolved this debate. Big integrated EHRs are better than ever, and it is also easier to integrate data from subspecialty systems if they follow the latest standards for data exchange.

Order Entry and Results Reporting. The earliest and most basic clinical systems were results reporting systems that allowed viewing of the output of laboratory and other biomedical devices. Lab data are typically numeric and relatively easy to categorize and display. Textual results, such as pathology, microbiology, and radiology results were also fairly analogous to other data routinely managed by early business computers. Graphical results and images arrived later with the more powerful hardware and software required to support these modalities. Radiology results, in particular, bring in additional complexity, as the non-textual part of the result (the image) is stored and viewed on a picture archiving and communications system (PACS) typically separate from the EHR, requiring additional interface and patient context synchronization needs.

Typically absent from simple result reporting systems is any facility for data *entry*. The user interface characteristics required for data entry and data display are radically different, the former being far more challenging. Early monolithic systems had a relatively modest goal of unifying all the entered data into a single repository, while specialized data entry systems were permitted in departmental silos.[16]

Starting in the 1990s, due to the economics of unrestricted physician orders, many hospitals focused on order entry systems as the centerpiece of their clinical systems efforts.[17,18] In the ambulatory world, order entry can be a small component of the workflow in some specialties. Further, the economic imperatives are very different in the outpatient world (especially with fee for service) and the ROI from an order entry system may be harder to realize than at a hospital (with prospective payment). That said, ambulatory order entry is still a big business.

Many laboratories and radiology practices will give physicians a results reporting system if they will use the lab's online order entry system. The laboratory gains efficiencies, but they still have to give the physician an incentive to use a potentially less convenient system than paper, especially given the high likelihood that more than one such proprietary system may need to be used. Administrative tasks such as preauthorization and eligibility checks for ordered procedures further complicate the use of such systems. In large institutions and practices, order entry systems can be very helpful in controlling the flow of referrals. These are achieved through real-time decision support or through enabling of more sophisticated analytics to determine leakage and referral patterns. Order entry systems are all but essential in ambulatory practices under capitation in order to control utilization.

Evidence suggests that ambulatory CPOE can be time neutral to physicians, but not all order entry systems are created equal.[19] Minimal systems, some of which are now free, just write prescriptions. For specialists who prescribe a lot of medications, comprehensive support for refills, including aging and reminders, can be a major time saver and are frequently the first clinical systems installed. Prescriptions are different from inpatient orders in several respects. The ability to print prescriptions in locally mandated formats is not to be assumed. Inpatient systems also generally have limited formularies, whereas outpatient systems generally need all available drugs. Worse still, in managed care environments, ambulatory systems often have to maintain multiple formularies and distinguish between drugs that are on- and off-plan. Medicare Part D has made this function almost essential and yet support within EHRs remains awkward at best.

Inpatient systems tend to be more focused on drips and compound preparations. These exist in the outpatient world, as well such as in oncology infusion centers. Such sites need the full medication administration record (MAR) functionality common to inpatient systems. But they are certainly less common and typically less complex than in the inpatient setting. Conversely, ambulatory centers that do dispense drugs often do so without a pharmacist as intermediary. This means that the system must support the functions pharmacists provide. For example, when a sample is given, the system must produce a label with instructions for the patient and log the lot number of the drug dispensed.

E-prescribing, the electronic transmission of prescriptions, has been expanding rapidly due to recent incentives from the federal government and certain payers. As of this writing, such systems still have a lot of rough edges, particularly surrounding narcotic prescriptions and refill management. The standards were pushed through without fully bidirectional communication, which requires reconciliation of currently incompatible drug vocabularies between pharmacy and physician systems. Therefore, acknowledgement, cancellation, and some safety features are lacking. Some pharmacies still cannot accept electronic prescriptions; therefore, systems may resort to faxing behind the scenes, which is fraught with security and privacy problems. Still, even without the meaningful use (MU) incentives, the efficiencies from e-prescribing are so overwhelming that failure to implement this technology would require a rather exceptional justification.

Similarly, prescription fill information is becoming available electronically from payers. The availability of this information has the potential to alter physicians' ability to monitor patient compliance. Policies around viewing fill history before ordering of narcotic medication have been implemented to prevent abuse;[20] however, there is great variability in their execution from state to state. Lack of a national patient identifier and limited sharing of such fill histories between states limits the utility of such efforts. Because ambulatory patients administer their own individual doses and may not submit claims for every prescription filled, the reconciliation of fill data with the original prescription is still imperfect. Further, the mismatch between AEHR and pharmacy master files generates a lot of noise when originating systems cannot match a returning filled prescription. The potential of this capability to improve care is large,[21] but too little has been done to contemplate the workflow impact these data will have on routine visits. Physicians may object to another uncompensated demand on their time.

For laboratory orders, key features in an ambulatory environment differ from the inpatient world. Most hospitals send all their lab specimens to one laboratory. In the outpatient world, this may be desirable, but managed care contracts often mandate the use of a particular lab. The ability to control default routing rules based on contracts is a vital revenue control point for sites that maintain their own laboratory. Routing to the most affordable laboratory for a particular payer is also a key determinant of patient satisfaction.

True integration with multiple laboratories is technically very challenging, but it is also very desirable for many reasons. If the outbound order and the incoming result are linked, known as *loop closure*, there is more potential for sophisticated features like alerts and reports. For example, a common cause of malpractice claims is the failure to note an abnormal Pap result. Systems with loop closure can alert a physician both to the arrival of an abnormal result and the failure of any result to return after a specified time, thereby diminishing the risk of lost data.

The most difficult aspect of linking to multiple labs is reconciling the coding systems for the orders and the results. As of this writing, there is no satisfactory coding system for either orders or results, and those that do exist are poorly cross-mapped. CPT® is often used when placing orders, but it is too imprecise and incomplete to be used exclusively. Similarly, Logical Observation Identifiers Names and Codes (LOINC®) is the dominant standard for coding results, but it is also very incomplete and idiosyncratically applied. Certain areas, such as microbiology and transfusion medicine, remain particularly problematic. The National Library of Medicine funded an effort to map CPT and LOINC.[22] While this helped, the fact remains that operations managers faced with multiple laboratories need to commit considerable resources to map procedures and result components. Failure to accurately map the clinical tests can severely compromise the usability of the EHR.

The ability to configure order sets in ambulatory systems is not dissimilar to inpatient order entry systems. Likewise, clinical decision support rules have similar value in both settings. In the outpatient world, there is the additional uncertainty of knowing all medications a patient is taking. This is a topic of considerable conflict in organizations with shared charts. Some specialists object to seeing the full list of medications in their chart fearing responsibility for drugs they do not prescribe. Of course, this is an issue of legal liability, not medical care. But it can require system managers to jump configuration hurdles before specialists will buy in to a common EHR.

The Joint Commission made medication reconciliation one of its national patient safety goals in 2005,[23] requiring that at transitions of care providers exchange a complete list of the patient's medications. This explicitly includes discharge to ambulatory settings. A shared EMR should make this process easier, if not automatic, with the record itself. But a seamless pass-off between EHRs requires a substantial improvement in the state-of-the-art interfacing technologies. The Joint Commission based its recommendation on staffing and process models from the inpatient world,[24] and implementing their ideas outside of hospitals has proven difficult.

Analogous to diagnosis-related group (DRG) reimbursement in inpatient settings, one of the more complex features in ambulatory order entry is "medical necessity" checking. The quotation marks here are to emphasize that the definition of medical necessity is an insurance construct and not a clinical assessment per se. The primary impetus for this requirement comes from Medicare. Through a process called National and Local Coverage Determinations (NCD/LCD – previously called Local Medical Review Policies [LMRP]), Medicare will only reimburse for tests that it deems medically necessary.[25] Since these rules frequently do not meet the needs of individual patients, physicians need to be alerted when they are ordering a test that is not covered. For example, a patient with cancer might need heart tests prior to taking a cardiotoxic drug. It would be clinical malpractice not to perform the test, but it may still not be considered financially "medically necessary."

There are two major reasons to generate NCD/LCD alerts. The first is the intended effect of the regulation—to draw attention to the physician that the test or drug may not be clinically indicated and an alternative should be sought. The second reason is to alert both patient and provider that charges will go unpaid by the carrier. For providers, particularly laboratory and radiology facilities, this can be a key source of uncollected debt. The ordering provider should give the patient an Advance Beneficiary Notice (ABN) that alerts the patient how much they are likely to be charged for what the payer may deem unnecessary.

The process for documenting medical necessity is fairly crude. The diagnostic code (typically ICD-9, soon perhaps ICD-10) the physician associates with the order (typically coded by CPT) either matches an approved list designed by the NCD/LCD or it does not. Practices that are very focused on downstream revenue may seek even more sophisticated alerts to question providers who order tests with codes that they may incorrectly be using as "rule outs" rather than using symptom codes. This is presently at the boundary of commercial system functionality.

The last major category of order entry functionality is referrals. These are similar to inpatient consult orders, but are a great deal more complex due to third-party reimbursement rules and geographic variation inherent to outpatient care. In many managed care plans, the ordering provider is supposed to solicit an eligibility and preapproval code before sending a patient to another specialist. Some systems automate this process to some extent, but the rules and documentation requirements are quite variable making full automation very difficult. If providers find themselves or their staff spending hours soliciting these approvals, executives would be wise to spend as much time renegotiating contracts to simplify and standardize these procedures as they might trying to get the IT staff to automate an unnecessarily chaotic process.

In an ideal patient experience, the referrals can be linked to the scheduling process. This is quite plausible if the order entry system is integrated with the scheduling system and the payer rules allow for such simplification. In reality, this kind of service is most likely to be found only in highly integrated care delivery systems, regardless of their IT infrastructure.

Documentation. While results reporting and order entry remain the core of many electronic medical records, the key to the ambulatory medical record is documentation, particularly physician documentation. This is also the most technically difficult challenge for any medical record system for several reasons. The major challenges in medical informatics generally come together in physician documentation. User interface design, workflow management, structured vocabulary, database performance, and hardware limitations are all major limiting factors to what we can practically deliver to support the most elemental component of medical care: doctor-patient interaction.

A very fine balance exists between entering information in EHRs via structured documentation versus unstructured documentation. Structured documentation allows the clinician to discretely capture his or her observations about patients. The most common forms use check boxes and other tools that limit the clinician's choices to only that which has been previously programmed. This method provides rich reporting and affords the system greater capabilities to know what is contained in a note. Unstructured documentation in an EHR allows for more free-form narrative while still providing legibility, practice standardization, and ubiquitous access. Even though unstructured documentation may involve fewer clicks, it still potentially requires more time for the clinician to enter it into the system than pen and paper. Many notes are a hybrid between structured and unstructured data. For example, the physical exam may be documented in a structured manner, while the assessment and plan are entered via free text. The speed at which clinicians can document in the system has become a great concern. To reduce the amount of time required, EHR vendors and health systems have developed methods that offload some of the data entry tasks to others besides the clinician. Patient-entered information can aid clinicians in documenting visits. Some patients log into web portals, while others may use tablets to interact with EHRs to provide both patient-specific and visit-specific information. For example, a patient may fill out both their past medical history and their review of systems using these tools. The clinician can then review the patient's responses with the patient and choose to accept or reject their inclusion in the visit's documentation.

Dictation can be used to enter nonstructured data into EMR systems. Voice recognition software and trained professional transcriptionists are widely used in practices utilizing EMR systems. As the accuracy of voice recognition software has increased, so has its usage. To assist clinicians in entering structured data, some systems use similar software to read a provider's documentation and then suggest possible discrete data for the clinician to approve and include in a patient's chart.

Another method to speed up documentation is to hire scribes to perform most, if not all, of the documentation tasks in the EHR. The scribe must be present while the provider interacts with a patient, and he or she records the information exactly as the clinician tells them. The clinician can then review the documentation and attest that it is an accurate reflection of what occurred during the visit. Scribes can reduce the amount of time that clinicians spend documenting in the EHR, and there is some evidence that the increase in productivity can offset the cost of the services.[26]

Copy-and-paste presents a quandary for many who manage EMR systems. While the use of copy-and-paste can dramatically reduce the amount of data entry that a clinician has to do, if the content is not edited properly to reflect what occurred during the patient's visit, it can often prove to be confusing to those who want to know what actually occurred in the visit. In addition to copy-and-paste, many EHRs have functionality that allows clinicians to import large amounts of data into their notes. This phenomenon, often referred to as *note bloat*, creates lengthy notes that can be very difficult to comprehend.[27]

In addition to these issues, the manner in which a clinician documents visits varies depending on his or her specialty. Drawing is a basic element of some physician documentation, such as ophthalmology, that is completely absent in some specialties. Similarly, photography is essential in plastic surgery, but optional in most general internal medicine practices. Flow sheets are the primary method of documenting in some specialties, particularly those with repeated visits over a finite period of time such as obstetrics or in practices focused on a particular disease or procedure such as diabetes or dialysis. Many disease management systems focus on this kind of documentation. Some practices have extensive forms-completion requirements, such as general pediatrics or practices with heavy managed care oversight such as cognitive psychology. Similarly, specialists who do procedures have very different documentation requirements than those doing evaluation and management. In academia, the ability to extract data generated at the point of care into research databases is critical to the research mission over and above immediate clinical needs. Consultation-heavy practices require robust correspondence support. Any practice with a wide referral base outside the EHR user base will require a scanning system to handle paper brought into the office, while practices that are completely self-contained will have little need for this feature. Practices using physician extenders or supervising residents and students will have complex co-signature and/or attestation requirements.

Most practices will use a combination of these tools. The challenge for the executive is to differentiate the essential business functions from optional features that may slow down implementation and run up costs. The key to understanding which features provide value and which do not is to examine workflow. This is where systems that deliver functionality in modules reach their limits. All the features in the world can be present in a system, but if they do not hang together for the users in a manner that flows logically within real-world use, then the system may cause more harm than good. The unwritten requirement is that all these function without compromising productivity or provider sanity.

EMR enthusiasts try to sell these inherently inefficient modular systems by emphasizing the myriad benefits that occur downstream once the initial penalty is paid. These downstream benefits are real and profound. They start with simple legibility, simplified filing and access, and the ability to use one data entry point for multiple purposes, such as a progress note and a consultation letter.

These benefits are the essential foundation on which most present office automation efforts are currently justified. But executives looking for ambulatory solutions today need not stop there. The greatest potential of these systems comes when they can predict where the user will go next and lead the provider through the visit. This is exactly the opposite of a modular system in which the provider may have to disrupt the workflow to search for different functions.

This is beyond the current state of the art in commercial clinical systems. Still, it is where today's executive should be looking when deciding what is needed.[28] Workflow analysis quickly leads to the recognition that system integration is required to make sure data flow in a coordinated manner to the work.

Through examination of workflow, four additional key functions of clinical systems that go beyond any individual module are revealed as essential to the system architecture: messaging, interfaces, decision support, and patient data entry.

Decision Support. Most modern clinical systems have some form of rules and alerts engine to improve quality, revenue, and compliance. These tools improve safety and help narrow the gap between knowledge and practice.[29] Contemporary descriptions of clinical decision support (CDS) have been more liberal and include tools for providers, patients, and administrators that facilitate decision making by means of alerts, reminders, flow charts, guidelines, condition specific order sets, defaults, and care plans.[30] We confine our discussion to knowledge-based systems integral to an AEHR, which have the following cardinal components: (a) Data or trigger, (b) Knowledge base, (c) Rules/ Inference engine, and (d) User interface/action.

Patient safety alerts such as drug-allergy and drug-drug interaction alerts are examples of simple point-of-care warnings and have great potential for avoiding adverse events. Unsurprisingly, these were included as part of MU Stage 1 core measures.[31] The construct is fairly simple—an ordered medication (trigger), if known to interact with another medication on the patient's record (knowledge-base–defining pairs of interacting drugs), will generate (rules engine) an alert (action) to warn the ordering provider. However, the complexity lies in how the knowledge base defines the severity or level of evidence behind the interactions and how well the rules engine can make use of it. Alert fatigue may result from misconfiguration of these rules and can be potentially dangerous and counterproductive by overwhelming physicians with excessive alerts.[32,33,34,35]

Modern systems also allow for real-time alerts that can actively modify how care is delivered. Adoption of best practice tenets such as Choosing Wisely and prevailing societal guidelines on disease management or screening are archetypal use cases of decision support with demonstrated efficacy in literature.[36,37,38,39] Besides bringing the latest evidence toward patient care, they serve as a means to meet various pay-for-performance measures and quality metrics. Having a structured construct for acting on and recording these metrics greatly facilitates documentation and reporting. This can have a significant financial impact and can possibly affect physician or hospital reputation or ranking.[40] For example, metrics such as patients older than age 65 receiving a pneumococcal vaccine would be meaningless if the vaccine was given at an outside facility and recorded as free text in the clinician's documentation. But an alert triggered by virtue of its absence in the immunization section offers the clinician an opportunity to record this fact in a discrete, structured format.

From an implementation standpoint, the use of decision support tools requires a great deal of discretion and unremitting evaluation. For ambulatory systems managers, a good starting point is whatever alerts can be purchased in a subscription form so that the knowledge base is easy to maintain. Drug interactions, medical necessity rules, and formulary lists are some examples of commercially available rule sets. Still, these would need to be configured to suit the purposes of one's practice and providers. A sensible strategy is to first introduce alerts of high value (e.g., high-severity drug interaction alerts) and high specificity, and then gradually dial up the potential alert sensitivity. Establishment of committees with technical and clinical representation to review parameters such as alert volume, alert acceptance, and clinical impact on an ongoing basis can help achieve the ideal configuration.[41,42] Human and workflow factors also need to be part of this ongoing evaluation as described in the following examples:

a. Where should alerts be triggered in the workflow? For example, does a research study for migraines recruitment alert really need to show up when the provider has just entered the chief complaint of headache and just started seeing the patient?

b. Is this the right person? Does the ophthalmologist really need to see an alert recommending an ACE (angiotensin-converting enzyme) inhibitor for the patient's heart failure diagnosis?
c. Is this the right presentation channel/mode? Does a "drug adverse effect of altered taste" need to be a pop-up alert requiring active dismissal? Noninterruptive alerts may have limited efficacy[43] in changing behavior but, in this case, would an FYI appearing next to the drug have served better than a pop-up?

In summary, the two quintessential challenges for ambulatory managers implementing decision support are knowledge maintenance and improved relevancy of alerts. For knowledge maintenance, subscribing to third-party CDS content wherever possible and having a distributed ownership for reviews and updates of guideline content by specialty or department are recommended. To improve relevancy of alerts, constant evaluation and adjustment of AEHR rule configurations is necessary. Rules engines are becoming more sophisticated in their utilization of discrete data elements to improve alert specificity. Non–knowledge-based systems using machine learning techniques to recognize clinical data patterns also hold great potential in making alerts more relevant. Such systems can potentially adapt to alert override patterns and determine which ones hold more relevance for particular specialties, disease states, or patient populations. However, we need to wait until such systems become pragmatic for EHR integration and have proven efficacy and safety.[44]

Messaging and Communication. Messaging could, perhaps, be viewed as a module itself. Indeed, if a practice had limited funding, the cheapest and easiest system to implement to increase efficiency would probably be an instant messaging system. But within a full-featured EHR, clinical messaging can become the central task management tool of a practice. The key difference is the ability to route a message within the context of a patient's chart. This context extends the physician's capacity to utilize support staff, freeing the physician for more productive work. Leading products categorize messages into multiple queues such as new results, orders awaiting co-signature, messages from colleagues, and even personal notes about tee times. Messages can go to multiple staff at once to work down a queue and can be rerouted during vacations or for on-call coverage.

Some systems clearly separate messaging from task management. In larger practices this is probably wise. As the physician workflow progresses along the patient encounter, a variety of tasks queue for the ancillary staff such as rooming and taking vitals, drawing blood, and processing referrals. How elegantly these processes are integrated with the system will dictate the success of managing the entire practice workflow rather than just isolated pieces of it.

Secure messaging is generally inherent within a given EHR. MU provided the incentive to increase the use of secure messages both between EHRs and to/from patients themselves. Secure messaging between patient and physician most commonly occurs using a patient portal that is tethered to the EHR. Patients can send messages to their providers seeking medical advice or requesting appointments, refills, and referrals. Providers can actively engage patients regarding diagnostic testing results, health maintenance needs, and patient-specific education. When the patient has a new communication from the practice, he or she receives a tickler message in their designated email address. He/she then logs into the portal for the actual message. While this does create an extra step, it provides the assurance that the message was delivered in a secure manner.

Secure messaging between EHRs is rapidly becoming an industry standard function. For physician-to-physician communication, the Consolidated-Clinical Document Architecture (C-CDA)[45] format was chosen by CMS as part of the MU requirements for Stage 2. The format allows EHRs to exchange discrete data in a manner that foreign systems can digest. Medications, problem lists, and lab results can be shared between systems, in addition to narrative messages between providers.

As payers increase the demands to increase patient involvement in his or her own care, new communication methods between patient and practice will be established. This includes the use of text messaging technologies to remind patients about important health-related tasks. The further extension of this will be the delivery of data taken in the patient's home back to the practice's EHR. Glucometers, blood pressure cuffs, and activity monitors are but some of the devices that will securely communicate information back to practices.

System Integration and Intraoperability

Interfaces are the glue between modules of nonintegrated systems and the mechanism for sharing data across entirely dissimilar systems. The rich complexity of interfaces is more than enough of a topic for a whole book in itself. Some of the key points to understand about interfaces in ambulatory systems relate to what interfaces can and cannot accomplish and the buzzwords to look out for.

A purely standalone system requires no interfaces. Such systems are not uncommon in a small ambulatory setting, though they are quite limited in functionality. We have already reviewed the key administrative interfaces required for practice management. Electronic linkages to insurance companies are mandated by HIPAA, and federal MU guidelines have required increasing levels of interoperability. The era of standalone systems is clearly coming to a close.

Early efforts at interfaces were so-called point-to-point custom interfaces that required coding far too extensive for all but the largest ambulatory providers. In 1979, the American National Standards Institute (ANSI) chartered the Accredited Standards Committee (ASC) X12 "to develop uniform standards for inter-industry electronic interchange of business transactions—electronic data interface (EDI)." In the past 35 years, that body has developed more than 300 business-to-business transaction sets.[46] In the late 1980s healthcare joined the EDI standardization process with the creation of Health Level 7 (HL7), a set of semantic standards for exchanging data between healthcare information systems. HL7 was accredited by ANSI in 1994.[47]

The HL7 standards define many of the key transactions that are necessary to implement clinical and practice management systems. Anyone attending to practice workflow quickly realizes that more and better interfaces are critical to physician efficiency.[48] Besides the basic insurance transactions, ambulatory systems generally rely on ADT/registration and scheduling interfaces. HL7 supports a wide array of transactions that support clinical processes, including transmission of orders, results, and documents. These HL7 interfaces support very common EHR integration with laboratories, radiology systems, transcription providers, pharmacy systems, and a host of specialty niche diagnostic and procedural systems.

Another HL7 standard, called clinical context object workgroup (CCOW), has shown promise for ambulatory centers in that it can help avoid other costly interfaces altogether. CCOW is a standard for changing between different applications without requiring a new logon and even maintaining the existing patient context.[49] Therefore, a user can move from a laboratory results reporting system to a documentation or order entry system with a few clicks. The actual data stay in each system and cannot flow between them without building more specific interfaces. For sites that lack the resources to deal with all of the complexity of transactional interfacing, CCOW may offer enough pseudo integration to allow providers to work effectively in disparate systems.

While HL7 interfaces continue to be the mainstay of local transactional integration, there are obvious deficiencies and inadequacies. The first problem is the need for multiple interfaces itself. Interfaces are rarely *plug and play* and, even once implemented, they generate error queues and exceptions that require policies, procedures, and staff resources to handle. In a large healthcare system, an interface group may be dedicated to these issues. In a small ambulatory practice, this is often impossible and the errors may go uncorrected or the interface might need to be eliminated.

Ambulatory practices within larger institutions face a related problem of scale. While large IT shops may have the staff to handle implementation and error queues, the priorities of integrating a single obscure medical device may be quite low compared with a new laboratory feed for the whole hospital. But without that device, the single physician or practice cannot do his/her job. For example, it may be easier for a whole hospital to do without an interface to a spirometer than it is for an allergist or pulmonologist in their private office.

A second problem rests in the interfaces themselves. As HL7 is primarily a *semantic* standard, it dictates what the message means, not how it is said. There are two problems left unsolved. First, the semantic standards are quite limited. HL7 covers the basics only, and even there, enormous flexibility remains such that two vendor systems can be compliant yet unable to understand one another. Second, HL7 does not standardize how messages are sent. This is called *syntax*. HL7 has integrated a widespread syntactic standard called XML into its new standards, which should help ease this problem, though adoption is far from complete.[50]

Though HL7 interfaces have remained an efficient mechanism for transacting between clinical systems, there has been a persistent push for more complete yet simplified intraoperability. This initially manifested itself as a debate about the best way to combine semantic and syntactic standards. Those who had wide-ranging systems with rich feature sets favored comprehensive standards to move and reconcile data between systems. Those who had fewer resources or more modest ambitions about data normalization have been willing to settle for far simpler standards.

Competing standards emerged for transmitting electronic patient snapshots at transitions of care. HL7 created its clinical document architecture (CDA) to support clinical document exchange.[51] The CDA standard matured to a 2.0 version in 2005.[52] In 2006, a competing standards-making body proposed a much simpler standard than HL7, ASTM CCR[53] (Continuity of Care Record), which was embraced by the American

Academy of Family Physicians. The CCR takes a snapshot of patients at transitions of care in an XML document standard that includes content such as patient demographics, problems, medications, allergies, and results. Semantic details are optional, allowing for the basic transmission of information, which advocates called "good enough," but critics viewed as the lowest common denominator. HL7 ultimately proposed the Continuity of Care Document (CCD), which was a revision of the CDA standard that represented a harmonization with the CCR.[54] CCD has become the favored standard for transmission of structured patient data between systems.

Improving intraoperability between clinical systems has been a focus of the federal government via certification standards, as well as MU incentives. Certified EHRs must have the capability to exchange CCDs,[55] and a core objective of Stage 2 MU is to electronically transmit summary CCDs for more than 10 percent of transitions of patient care.[56] Due in large part to these certification criteria and incentives, data exchange between disparate systems is becoming more commonplace. These electronic patient data transmissions are happening via local and national exchanges and have the benefit of being vendor platform agnostic.

Though the use of CCD is increasing, true intraoperability in terms of consumption and reconciliation of discrete data is still a work in progress. Some of the features that lay people desire or even expect from clinical systems require extremely advanced interfacing techniques. Consider the perfectly reasonable expectation that a patient's laboratory results or medication list should be able to move from provider to provider. To do this without any loss of information would require the consistent use of sophisticated semantic standards that include reference vocabularies for diagnoses, lab tests, and medications. As reference vocabularies and corresponding mappings to SNOMED CT (Systemized Nomenclature of Medicine – Clinical Terms), LOINC®, and RxNorm are becoming more comprehensive and more widely implemented, true data intraoperability is slowly becoming a reality.

Patient Engagement Tools

Evidence suggests that engaging with patients to increase health literacy and to conduct shared decision making can lead to higher patient satisfaction, increased positive behavioral change, and even improved health outcomes.[57] Personal health records (PHRs) are seen by many as a key technology to assist with patient engagement. PHRs contain an individual patient's health information, including medical history, lab test results or imaging studies, medication and problem lists, etc. They are accessible via the Web (sometimes referred to as a patient portal), and they are controlled and accessed by patients or their proxies. When a PHR is connected to an EHR, it is sometimes referred to as a tethered patient portal. Adoption of standalone (non-tethered) PHRs has not been very widespread, but EHR-connected portals are increasing in use, especially given the critical role they play in the MU incentive programs. Functionalities required to meet several of the core objectives of MU Stage 2 are either dependent on or benefit from implementation and use of a patient portal. Examples include online access to health information, the ability to download health information or transmit it to a third party, secure messaging between patients and their providers, and the provision of tailored educational resources to patients based on their data in the EHR.[58]

While expectations are high for the potential for patient portals to enhance the healthcare process and there are incentives in place to increase implementation and adoption, the evidence of their impact on clinical outcomes has yet to be firmly established. Possible mechanisms for positive impact include enhanced patient-physician communication, improved patient adherence, increased patient empowerment, reduced health resource consumption, and others; however, few if any studies have actually shown measureable impact in these areas.[59]

One workflow-optimizing role that the patient portal can play is to facilitate patient data entry (PDE). Through these services, patients can be given questionnaires, consents and authorizations, or even clinical interviews. As vendors begin to integrate these technologies into the full EHR, the power to radically alter physician workflow becomes apparent. If patients can fill out their complaints, family, social and past medical history, and review of systems online before meeting with the physician, several positive consequences will result. Computerized interviews provide more data; allow for asking more sensitive questions; give patients more time; can be adapted for language, hearing impairments, and education level; and when fed into the AEHR can lower the amount of time physicians spend documenting.[60] Further, by obtaining structured data before the patient is seen, these systems provide clues the computer needs to present physicians with the most appropriate content and structure for their own workflow.

Some vendors are even starting to support PDE for more quantitative types of data such as weight and blood pressure measurements, as well as blood glucose measurements for patients with diabetes. Support is also trickling in for device integration to help automate the data entry process for patients. For example, some vendors provide interfaces that will allow data uptake from an array of devices such as glucometers and even fitness trackers such as the increasingly popular smart pedometers and scales with wireless data transmission capabilities. More and more consumer devices and smartphone apps are debuting that collect health-related data, and it is reasonable to assume that EHR vendors will continue to expand their capabilities to interface with and digest this patient-generated data. Although these systems are still at the cutting edge of clinical computing today, the very first computer applications for medicine, a half-century ago, were patient interviewing tools.[61,62] The goals of those systems remain compelling today. With the adoption of patient portals rapidly accelerating, these kinds of techniques should become easier.

Clinical Reporting and Analytics

As described earlier in this chapter, reporting and analytics are key functionalities of PMSs, but such tools are also becoming a critical functionality in the clinical and clinician-facing parts of ambulatory EHRs. Traditionally, EHR-based reporting functions were (and still are) used for operational/financial purposes, or to extract clinical data for secondary research use. In the setting of shifting models of care and reimbursement, there is increased appetite for clinically meaningful and actionable analytics based on the data in EHRs. The accountable care organization (ACO) and patient-centered medical home (PCMH) delivery models both depend heavily on EHR implementation and analytic capabilities.[63]

At the organizational level, reporting and analytics that are based on clinical data are utilized by a variety of stakeholders, from quality officers and clinic/department heads to care management teams. The transition from paper charts to electronic records with structured data entry enables analytics at the population level to help ensure appropriate preventive screening and chronic disease care. Reporting and business intelligence tools can identify gaps in care, in order to focus their efforts in areas that will yield the most benefit for the organization's patient population. Beyond finding patients with known care gaps, there is much buzz surrounding big data analytic methods and the potential to use data mining techniques to identify at-risk patients and to develop predictive models that reveal opportunities for clinical interventions that have not previously been possible.[64]

At the provider level, clinical analytics will likely play an increasing role as well. One consequence of our work to provide a comprehensive, exchangeable EHR that spans time (birth to death) and space (different care settings) is that it becomes challenging for a clinician to thoroughly review even one patient's aggregated data. As difficult as it is to digest all of this individual patient data, an even greater challenge for the clinician arises as we move from a fee-for-service model to incentivizing physicians based on outcomes of the entire patient panel. In that context, clinicians must be concerned with monitoring their panel as a whole, staying vigilant for patients who are outliers in terms of management or outcomes.

The concept of a data-driven dashboard is making its way from the business and financial sectors into the healthcare setting as one method to address such information overload challenges. Dashboards generally leverage visualization techniques to summarize complex data in a real time or near–real time fashion, and they are most effective when linked to workflow tools to enable users to quickly take action. It is common to see dashboards in the acute care setting as a means of quickly summarizing patient data and helping to triage hospital resources (e.g., in obstetrics, ICU, or emergency departments).[65,66] In the ambulatory setting, clinical dashboards can help summarize all of the longitudinal data the EHR contains about an individual patient, and they can also give a bird's-eye view of a provider's entire patient panel.[67] When integrated directly into the EHR, dashboards are even more useful, as they are directly actionable within the clinician's primary workflow system.

Infrastructure Considerations

The infrastructure issues for ambulatory systems are also similar to inpatient systems but different in emphasis. The scale of ambulatory systems varies from single physician offices to large multistate groups with thousands of providers. Obviously, very different technologies are needed to serve these different constituencies. Regardless of size, one of the most fundamental questions that needs to be answered early on is the degree to which integration is desired in technology and content. Some vendors provide a centralized platform from which huge numbers of users can share a common chart over large geographical distances. Others distribute the systems, often replicating the chart in multiple locations if content needs to be shared. Smart, well-intentioned people can argue the pros and cons of this and a thousand other architectural differences. The key to getting the right solution for your organization is, once again, workflow.

If you know how your organization works (or should work) you can find the right system. If you share a medical record number across disparate sites, then chances are you need some kind of centralized system for keeping them in sync. If not, then you do not need to solve this problem unless you want to share other data. If you have a lot of remote rural sites with variable networking infrastructures, then a system that relies on high bandwidth connectivity is off the table. Conversely, if you are in an urban environment with immense radio interference issues, a system that relies on a crowded wireless network band may not be advisable. If workstation management presents challenges, then a thin-client architecture may be appealing. In settings without the necessary IT staff, this may add complexity rather than reduce it.

Cloud-based systems are a new variant on these old themes. While primarily just a buzzword, the main concept behind a cloud solution is that the software is hosted offsite, typically by someone else, and accessed as a shared service by many providers. While very reminiscent of old mainframe solutions, many cloud solutions in theory are more redundant, more easily updated, and provide significant economies of scale. Almost by definition they require flawless Internet access, which is a challenge in many practices. The cloud is just one more option, but the key questions regarding appropriateness remain the same.

Supportability and reliability are other key issues that differ in the ambulatory world. Think about the impact of the loss of a single computer to a busy outpatient center without technical support for 24 or 48 hours. Is that acceptable? Can you afford a shorter timeframe? Downtime happens, by accident or design. Does your system provide you with the backup tools to get by for an hour? A day? A week?

Conversely, diffuse geography may put you at the mercy of an unreliable Internet provider or application service provider (ASP). In that case, your workflow may be forced to accommodate the idiosyncratic infrastructure rather than vice versa.

Interoperability with inpatient records varies in importance by practice and specialty. Security and privacy issues similarly may differ according to the interoperability of the workflow both locally (e.g., nurse and doctor charting on the same patient in the same room) and regionally (e.g., subspecialty referrals across a multi-entity organization).

Earlier the monolithic versus best of breed decision was referenced, as well as repository-based architectures. A related dimension to consider is the segregation of transactional and reporting systems. The system that supports day-to-day operations needs to be oriented toward high-speed, single-patient transactions. Reporting systems generally look across patients and do not require sub-second response times. Therefore, these jobs are often separated into separate systems.

A more detailed discussion of infrastructure is beyond the scope of this chapter. One rule of thumb to keep in mind is that while it may seem expensive, infrastructure is rarely a good place to skimp. Hardware is often the cheapest way to hide the inadequacies of software. But this is only true if you focus on the real bottlenecks, as opposed to technical fashion or fads. When selecting infrastructure components, it is important to plan for the future but also to be realistic about the pace of institutional change. Otherwise, one risks wasting money on capacity that will not be used before it becomes obsolete.

Costs and Return on Investment and Meaningful Use

Thanks in part to the federal MU incentive payments, most physician practices now have an AEHR.[68] Not surprisingly, practice management systems have far greater market penetration than purely clinical systems. As previously discussed, PMSs provide a direct impact on revenue and cost control. The value of purely clinical ambulatory systems is often more abstract or delayed. Chismar et al. have presented an economic model of EHR adoption that illustrates how larger entities like payers and hospitals gain more quickly from EHRs than small providers.[69] Scrutiny of other models that show benefit from EHRs also reveals the system benefits are greater than those to the individual physician.[70,71] That doesn't mean the value is not present, but given the large start-up costs, there is little incentive for physicians to adopt systems that benefit others more than themselves—especially if system adoption costs them more than the prime beneficiaries.

At a very high level, the value of the EHR to society is potentially huge.[72] Enhanced quality, better outcomes, an improved patient experience, and lower total costs are all great. But should the individual doctor or practice foot the bill? There are plenty of other barriers to adoption of EHRs, including physician resistance to change, concerns about productivity, the complexity of installation, and conversion of existing paper medical records.[73,74,75]

The value equation was altered considerably by federal incentive payments built into ARRA of 2009 and HITECH. HITECH designated billions of federal dollars to incentivize the adoption of health IT via grants for education projects that integrated EHR technology into the clinical education of health professionals, funding for strategic health IT projects, and bonus payments for providers and hospitals to adopt certified health IT.

To promote the adoption of the EHR, the federal government designed a CMS bonus payment program (via both Medicare and Medicaid) for both eligible providers and hospitals. The program was initially designed to make incentives available for five years, with early qualification leading to maximum potential monetary bonus. The program's incentives taper and then transition to penalties via withholding of escalating percentages of Medicare/Medicaid reimbursement. In May 2014, CMS proposed revised deadlines.[76]

The EHR incentive program mandates that hospitals and providers use certified EHR technologies to qualify for bonuses. EHR certification standards and bodies are described in detail in the Meaningful Use chapter of this book (Chapter 6) but continue to evolve via ongoing national committee work and legislation. In addition to installing a certified EHR system, providers and hospitals must demonstrate that they are using the technology in a meaningful fashion. The now ubiquitous term meaningful use refers to these sets of important behaviors. Conceptually, MU objectives are those behaviors or functions that promote a core set of health outcome priorities delineated by the federal government. Those key priorities include:

- Improve quality, safety, efficiency, and reduce health disparities
- Engage patients and families
- Improve care coordination
- Improve population and public health

- Ensure adequate privacy and security protections for personal health information

The detailed mechanics of the incentive programs are subject to change and are beyond the scope of this summary. In general terms, the HITECH Act mandated that the MU objectives would be defined in stages, with escalating sophistication of objectives and behavioral thresholds. The Stage 1 MU criteria assume the capture of clinical information in coded format, use of coded information to track key clinical conditions and coordinate care, implementation of basic CDS tools, and the ability to report clinical quality measures and public health information.

As of July 2010, CMS published a final legislative rule that incorporated the comments and feedback of industry experts and stakeholders. This rule defines, in detail, the Stage 1 MU requirements. The Stage 1 requirements are nicely summarized by Blumenthal and Tavenner in an editorial published in the *New England Journal of Medicine* that coincided with the publication of the final rule (see a summary in Table 8-2).[77] This legislative rule defines 15 mandatory core objectives and their associated measures. Of the remaining 10 "menu" objectives, a provider or hospital can choose to implement a minimum of five and still achieve Stage 1 MU.

In September 2012, CMS published the final rule for Stage 2.[78] Stage 2 focuses on advanced clinical procedures, including:

- Measures focused on more rigorous health information exchange (HIE)
- Additional requirements for e-prescribing and incorporating lab results
- Electronic transmission of patient care summaries across multiple settings
- Increased patient and family engagement[79]

The key objectives are summarized in Table 8-2. Stage 3 MU criteria will be defined in the future. It is also likely that the mechanics of the incentive program and the EHR certification process and standards will continue to evolve.

While the federal incentive program dramatically altered the economics of EHR adoption, it is only temporary. Further, money is only one barrier in a properly considered ROI equation. Doctors also care about quality, time, convenience, regulatory compliance, and a host of other issues that must all be taken into account to truly calculate ROI. This is, of course, not feasible and the inadequacy of the literature to date reflects that reality.

For example, some studies show ROI by reducing duplicate orders. Under capitation that is valid, but under fee-for-service, one's revenue might fall. At our center, we recovered millions of dollars of revenue that was going to outside providers that our EHR very gently pointed back inside. The cost was borne by our doctors and the benefit accrued by our hospital. From a business perspective, this is a big win for the medical center, but it will not show up in academic studies of ROI. From society's perspective, this was just a cost shift and not a real reduction in the total cost of healthcare.

Other studies have shown return from up-coding and the converse is also touted as a benefit by improving regulatory compliance.[80] Other financial benefits include reduced transcription costs, reduced chart pulls, decreased charge posting costs, pay-for-performance incentives, and various other efficiencies.

Critics of these studies abound.[81] Accounting for costs of implementation is difficult. Once live, there are hidden costs rarely accounted for in any analysis. Dealing

Table 8-2: Summary of Key Stage 2 Meaningful Use Objectives.
From CMS Stage 2 Overview Tipsheet - Last Updated: August 2012.

Report on all 17 Core Objectives:

1. Use computerized provider order entry (CPOE) for medication, laboratory, and radiology orders
2. Generate and transmit permissible prescriptions electronically (eRx)
3. Record demographic information
4. Record and chart changes in vital signs
5. Record smoking status for patients 13-years-old or older
6. Use clinical decision support to improve performance on high-priority health conditions
7. Provide patients the ability to view online, download, and transmit their health information
8. Provide clinical summaries for patients for each office visit
9. Protect electronic health information created or maintained by the Certified EHR Technology
10. Incorporate clinical lab-test results into Certified EHR Technology
11. Generate lists of patients by specific conditions to use for quality improvement, reduction of disparities, research, or outreach
12. Use clinically relevant information to identify patients who should receive reminders for preventive/follow-up care
13. Use certified EHR technology to identify patient-specific education resources
14. Perform medication reconciliation
15. Provide summary of care record for each transition of care or referral
16. Submit electronic data to immunization registries
17. Use secure electronic messaging to communicate with patients on relevant health information

Report on 3 of 6 Menu Objectives:

1. Submit electronic syndromic surveillance data to public health agencies
2. Record electronic notes in patient records
3. Imaging results accessible through CEHRT
4. Record patient family health history
5. Identify and report cancer cases to a state cancer registry
6. Identify and report specific cases to a specialized registry (other than a cancer registry)

Available at: http://www.cms.gov/Regulations-and-Guidance/Legislation/EHRIncentivePrograms/Downloads/Stage2Overview_Tipsheet.pdf

with temporary employees is far more complex in an automated environment where training is more complex and less intuitive than in the paper world. Conversely, benefits like integrated access to reference materials or sophisticated reporting capabilities are extremely difficult to assign value to in a finite period of time. Even the cost of the software itself is hard to standardize and is almost always overemphasized as a cost relative to the much higher intangible costs such as disruption, morale effects, and functional losses from system deficiencies.

For our faculty practice at Weill Cornell, we attempted to address some of these issues by looking at bottom line measures of productivity. We implemented a commercial EHR between 2001 and 2007. We compared monthly visit volume, charges, and work relative value units (wRVUs) before and after each provider's EHR implementation go-live date. We also compared these data with a group of physicians who did not implement, though they had too many confounds to be considered formal controls.

Our data matched the anecdotal impression in the industry showing that those practitioners who adopted the EHR had a statistically significant increase in average monthly patient visit volume (nine visits per provider per month) while the nonadopter cohort's visit volume was statistically unchanged. Likewise, while both groups had significant increases in average monthly charges, only the adopters showed a statistically significant increase in wRVUs (12 per provider per month).[82]

HIMSS (the publisher of this book) publishes an online tool[83] that highlights scores of individual benefits and provides anecdotes about providers who achieved them. It is primarily inpatient focused, but it is relatively easy to adapt many of the constructs to the ambulatory world. The plural of anecdote is not data.

While these and other data[84] suggest that EHRs do not harm productivity and probably help it, we believe the value of the EHR ultimately needs to be judged similarly to an elevator in a skyscraper. It has become an essential tool of the trade.[85,86] Too few ROI analyses ask what the ROI is of the analysis itself. Like the word processor and the typewriter, email and the fax machine, or cars and the horse, the EHR will come and will transform ambulatory care. Today's executives need to manage the change, not attempt to justify it.

That said, predicting the future direction of the ambulatory EHR industry is relevant. Vendors still rapidly come and go. The technology is evolving quickly. What you buy today will be obsolete soon. Expect it and plan accordingly. Assume your vendor will change by protecting your data and your investment in the knowledge it took to automate your practice. As a rule of thumb, only 20 percent of the costs of an implementation are vendor fees. Not all of the remaining 80 percent is lost if you will need to change vendors. Wise process redesign will deliver value now and in the future, independent of the specific technical platform. The delayed returns from automation will also translate from one system to the next, as they come from the EHR technology itself, not necessarily from any given brand.

Large vendors with full inpatient and outpatient suites offer the hope of increased interoperability. Sixteen vendors account for 75 percent of the market.[87] While pure software companies like Epic and Cerner are currently on top, bigger conglomerates like GE and Siemens offer both biomedical devices and EHRs in their suites—and yet, interoperability remains elusive. Will these vendors oversimplify and cut the wrong costs? Will their size and oligopoly power destroy innovation? Consider the conflicting incentives facing just one vendor with multiple product lines and seemingly competing interests. Will a vendor that sells MRIs (magnetic resonance imaging) and EHRs support an EHR to help reduce the overutilization of expensive MRIs—a business with far more profit potential than software? Large health IT software vendors are also employers who need to control medical insurance costs. Interoperability with competitors would reduce healthcare expenditures but might cause loss of market share. How large health IT vendors balance their own internal conflicts could have as much impact on the future of the industry as technology itself.

The technology is also hard to predict. The big problems facing informatics for the past 40 years have not fundamentally changed. The nature of the human-machine interface, the physical limits of hardware, and the complexity of medical vocabulary are still problems today. The expansion of the EHR outside academia only adds new problems of scale, configurability, flexibility, complexity, control, and ever-lower fault tolerance.

The next generation EHR, evolving today, is focused on integration, standards, ubiquity, mobility, reliability, quality, outcomes, and, of course, workflow. Dangers to look out for include oversimplification, information overload, alert fatigue, overdependence, and depersonalization. The next generation of ambulatory care is also emerging today—full of potential opportunities and dangers. And as a key part of that future, the ambulatory EHR is surely both an opportunity and a danger.

REFERENCES

1. Berwick DM, Hackbarth AD. Eliminating waste in U.S. health care. *JAMA*. 2012;307(14):1513-1516.
2. Cutler D, Wikler E, Basch P. Reducing administrative costs and improving the health care system. *New Eng J Med*. 2012;367(20):1875-1878.
3. Carpenter PC, Chute CG. The universal patient identifier: a discussion and proposal. Presented at the Annual Symposium on Computer Applications in Medical Care, 1993:49-53. Washington, DC.
4. Social Security numbers. Electonic Privacy Information Center. September 2004. www.epic.org/privacy/ssn. Accessed March 19, 2006.
5. Bittle MJ, Charache P, Wassilchalk DM. Registration-associated patient misidentification in an academic medical center: causes and corrections. *Jt Comm J Qual Patient Saf*. 2007;33:25-33.
6. Ritz D. It's time for a national patient identifier. July 11, 2013 http://www.himss.org/News/NewsDetail.aspx?ItemNumber=21464. Accessed June 29, 2014.
7. Dooling JA, Durkin S, Fernandes L, et al. Managing the integrity of patient identity in health information exchange (updated). *J AHIMA*. 2014;85(5):60-65. http://www.ncbi.nlm.nih.gov/pubmed/24938040. Accessed November 10, 2014.
8. Shattuck J. In the shadow of 1984: National identification systems, computer-matching, and privacy in the United States. Hast LJ. 1983. http://heinonlinebackup.com/hol-cgi-bin/get_pdf.cgi?handle=hein.journals/hastlj35&section=46. Accessed November 10, 2014.
9. Physicians at teaching hospitals audits. www.aamc.org /advocacy/library/ teachingphys/phys0040.htm. Accessed March 12, 2006.
10. CMS. Transaction and code sets standards. http://www.cms.gov/Regulations-and-Guidance/HIPAA-Administrative-Simplification/TransactionCodeSetsStands/index.html?redirect=/TransactionCodeSetsStands/. Accessed November 10, 2014.
11. Abelson R, Creswell J. U.S. warning to hospitals on Medicare Bill abuses. http://www.nytimes.com/2012/09/25/business/us-warns-hospitals-on-medicare-billing.html?_r=0. Accessed November 10, 2014.
12. Zall RJ. The truth about managed care: the silent provider discount. *Manag Care Q*. 2004 Winter;12(1):11-15.
13. Grossman JH, Barnett GO, Koespell TD. An automated medical record system. *JAMA*. 1973;263:1114-1120.
14. McDonald CJ, Overhage JM, Tierney WM, et al. The Regenstrief Medical Record System: a quarter century experience. *Int J Med Inf*. 1999; 54:225-253.
15. Stead WW, Brame RG, Hammond WE, et al. A computerized obstetric medical record. *Obstet Gynecol*. 1977 Apr;49(4):502-509.
16. Clayton PD, Sideli RV, Sengupta S. Open architecture and integrated information at Columbia-Presbyterian Medical Center. *MD Computing*. Sept-Oct 1992; 9(5):297-303.

17. Ash JS, Gorman PN, Seshardri V, et al. Computerized physician order entry in U.S. hospitals: results of a 2002 survey. *J Am Med Inform Assoc.* 2004;11:95-99.

18. Cutler DM, Feldman NE, Horwitz JR. U.S. adoption of computerized physician order entry systems. *Health Aff.* Nov/Dec 2005;24(6):1654-1663.

19. Marc Overhage M, Perkins S, William M, et al. Controlled trial of direct physician order entry: Effects on physicians' time utilization in ambulatory primary care internal medicine practices. *J Am Med Inform Assoc.* 2001;8(4):361-371.

20. NYS Department of Health. I-STOP/PMP - Internet System for Tracking Over Prescribing - Prescription Monitoring Program. https://www.health.ny.gov/professionals/narcotic/prescription_monitoring/. Accessed June 29, 2014.

21. Baehren DF, Marco CA, Droz DE, et al. A statewide prescription monitoring program affects emergency department prescribing behaviors. *Ann Emerg Med.* 2010;56(1):19–23.

22. National Institutes of Health. UMLS: LOINC To CT Mapping. http://www.nlm.nih.gov/research/umls/mapping_projects/loinc_to_cpt_map.html. Accessed June 29, 2014.

23. The Joint Commission. 2005 National Patient Safety Goals. http://www.jointcommission.org/PatientSafety/NationalPatientSafetyGoals. Accessed November 10, 2014.

24. Rozich JD. Standardization as a mechanism to improve safety in health care. *Jt Comm J Qual Saf.* January 2004;30(1):5-14.

25. Centers for Medicare & Medicaid Services. Medicare Coverage Center. http://www.cms.hhs.gov/center/coverage.asp. Accessed November 10, 2014.

26. Bank AJ, Obetz C, Konrardy A, et al. Impact of scribes on patient interaction, productivity, and revenue in a cardiology clinic: a prospective study. *Clinicoecon Outcomes Res.* 2013;5:399-406.

27. Hirschtick RE. A piece of my mind. Copy-and-paste. *JAMA.* 2006;295:2335-2336.

28. East TD. The EHR pParadox. *Front Health Serv Manage.* 2005; 22(2):33-35.

29. Bates DW, Kuperman GJ, Wang S, et al. Ten commandments for effective clinical decision support: making the practice of evidence-based medicine a reality. *J Am Med Inform Assoc.* 2003;10(6):523–530.

30. Berlin A, Sorani M, Sim I. A taxonomic description of computer-based clinical decision support systems. *J Biomed Inform.* 2006;39(6):656–667.

31. Meaningful_Use. 2014. http://www.cms.gov/Regulations-and-Guidance/Legislation/EHRIncentivePrograms/Meaningful_Use.html. Accessed June 27, 2014.

32. Koppel R, Metlay JP, Cohen A, et al. Role of computerized physician order entry systems in facilitating medication errors. *JAMA.* 2005;293(10):1197–1203.

33. Phansalkar S, Van Der Sijs H, Tucker AD, et al. Drug–drug interactions that should be non-interruptive in order to reduce alert fatigue in electronic health records. *J Am Med Informatics Assoc.* 2012;1–5.

34. Van Der Sijs H, Aarts J, Vulto A, et al. Overriding of Drug Safety Alerts in Computerized Physician Order Entry. *J Am Med Informatics Assoc.* 2006;13(2):138–147.

35. Isaac T, Weissman JS, Davis RB, et al. Overrides of medication alerts in ambulatory care. Arch Intern Med. 2009;169(3):1337; author reply 1338. http://www.ncbi.nlm.nih.gov/pubmed/19786683. Accessed November 10, 2014.

36. McDonald CJ, Hui SL, Tierney WM. Effects of computer reminders for influenza vaccination on morbidity during influenza epidemics. *MD Comput.* 9(5):304–312. http://www.ncbi.nlm.nih.gov/pubmed/1522792. Accessed June 27, 2014.

37. Shea S, DuMouchel W, Bahamonde L. A meta-analysis of 16 randomized controlled trials to evaluate computer-based clinical reminder systems for preventive care in the ambulatory setting. *J Am Med Inform Assoc.* 3(6):399–409. http://www.pubmedcentral.nih.gov/articlerender.fcgi?artid=116324&tool=pmcentrez&rendertype=abstract. Accessed June 27, 2014.

38. Rao VM, Levin DC. The overuse of diagnostic imaging and the Choosing Wisely initiative. *Ann Intern Med.* 2012;157(8):574–576.

39. Johnston ME. Effects of Computer-based clinical decision support systems on clinician performance and patient outcome: A critical appraisal of research. *Ann Intern Med.* 1994;120(2):135.

40. Mukamel DB, Mushlin AI. The impact of quality report cards on choice of physicians, hospitals, and HMOs: A midcourse evaluation. http://www.ingentaconnect.com/content/jcaho/jcjqs/2001/00000027/00000001/art00002. Accessed June 29, 2014.

41. Long A-J, Chang P, Li Y-C, et al. The use of a CPOE log for the analysis of physicians' behavior when responding to drug-duplication reminders. *Int J Med Inform.* 2008;77(8):499–506.

42. Turning off frequently overridden drug alerts: Limited opportunities for doing it safely. 2008;15(4):439-448. doi:10.1197/jamia.M2311.Introduction.

43. Lo HG, Matheny ME, Seger DL, et al. Impact of Non-interruptive medication laboratory monitoring alerts in ambulatory care. *J Am Med Informatics Assoc.* 2009;16(1):66–71.

44. Abbasi M, Kashiyarndi S. Clinical decision support systems: A discussion on different methodologies used in health care. 2006. http://www.idt.mdh.se/kurser/ct3340/ht10/FinalPapers/15-Abbasi_Kashiyarndi.pdf. Accessed June 29, 2014.

45. HL7 Implementation Guide for CDA® Release 2: IHE Health Story Consolidation, Release 1.1 - US Realm. http://www.hl7.org/implement/standards/product_brief.cfm?product_id=258. Accessed June 8, 2014.

46. Schrotter FE. ASC X12 25th birthday celebration: 25 years of business to business Accomplishments keynote Address. June 7, 2004; Chicago, IL. http://public.ansi.org/ANSIOnline/Documents/News%20and%20Publications/Speeches/. Accessed March 19, 2006.

47. Health Level Seven International. www.HL7.org. Accessed November 10, 2014.

48. Walker J, Pan E, Johnston D, et al. The value of health care information exchange and interoperability. *Health Aff.* Web Exclusive, January 19, 2005. http://content.healthaffairs.org/cgi/content/abstract/hlthaff.w5.10. Accessed March 18, 2006.

49. Health Level Seven International. Context Management Specifications (CCOW) V1.1 https://www.hl7.org/implement/standards/product_brief.cfm?product_id=126. Accessed November 10, 2014.

50. Interchange standards in healthcare IT –Computable Semantic interoperability: Now possible but still difficult. Do we really need a better mousetrap? *J Healthcare Information Management.* Winter 2006;20(1):71-78.

51. Dolin RH, et al. HL7 Clinical document architecture, Release 2. *J Am Med Inform Assoc.* 2006:13(1):30–39.

52. Health Level Seven International. CDA Release 2 https://www.hl7.org/implement/standards/product_brief.cfm?product_id=7. Accessed November 10, 2014.

53. ASTM Committee E31 on Healthcare Informatics http://www.astm.org/cgi-bin/SoftCart.exe/COMMIT/COMMITTEE/E31.htm?L+mystore+kprv3048. Accessed March 19, 2006.

54. Health Level Seven International. HL7/ASTM Implementation Guide for CDA® R2 -Continuity of Care Document (CCD®) Release 1 https://www.hl7.org/implement/standards/product_brief.cfm?product_id=6. Accessed November 10, 2014.

55. Information technology: Standards, implementation, specifications, and certification criteria for electronic health record technology, 2014 Edition; Revisions to the Permanent Certification Program for Health Information Technology. *Fed Regist.* September 4, 2012;77:171.

56. Centers for Medicare & Medicaid Programs; Electronic Health Record Incentive Program—Stage 2. *Federal Regist.* September 4, 2012;77:171.

57. Coulter A. Patient engagement—what works? *The J Ambul Care Manage.* 2012(35)80–89.

58. CMS Meaningful Use EHR Incentive Programs. (n.d.). June 12, 2014. http://www.cms.gov/Regulations-and Guidance/Legislation/EHRIncentivePrograms/Meaningful_Use.html. Accessed November 10, 2014.

59. Ammenwerth E, Schnell-Inderst P, Hoerbst A. The impact of electronic patient portals on patient care: a systematic review of controlled trials. *Journal of Medical Internet Research*. 2012;14(6), e162.

60. Bachman JW. The patient-computer interview: a neglected tool that can aid the clinician. *Mayo Clin Proc*. 2003 Jan;78(1):67-78.

61. Brodman K, van Woerkom AK, Erdmann AJ, et al. Interpretation of symptoms with a data-processing machine. A.M.A. *Arch Intern Med*. 1959;103:776-782.

62. Brodman K, Erdmann AJ, Lorge I, et al. The Cornell Medical Index; an adjunct to medical interview. *JAMA*.1949; 140:530-534.

63. Britton A, Flier LA, Jha AK. Health information technology in the era of care delivery reform. *JAMA*: The Journal of the American Medical Association. 2012; 307(24),2593–2594.

64. Groves P, Kayyali B, Knott, D, et al. The "big data"revolution in healthcare. *McKinsey Q*. 2013.

65. Stone-Griffith S, Englebright JD, Cheung D, et al. Data-driven process and operational improvement in the emergency department: the ED Dashboard and Reporting Application. *J Healthc Manag / American College of Healthcare Executives*. 2012;57(3):167–180.

66. Egan M. Clinical dashboards: impact on workflow, care quality, and patient safety. *Crit Care Nurs Q*. 2006; 29(4):354–361.

67. Koopman R.J, Kochendorfer KM, Moore JL, et al. A diabetes dashboard and physician efficiency and accuracy in accessing data needed for high-quality diabetes care. *Ann Fam Med*. 2011;9(5):398-405.

68. Hsiao C. Office-based physicians are responding to incentives and assistance by adopting and using electronic health records. *Health Aff*. 2013;32(8):1470-1477.

69. Chismar WG. Thomas SM. The economics of integrated electronic medical record systems. *Medinfo*. 2004;11(Pt 1):592-596.

70. Wang SJ, Middleton B, Prosser LA, et al. A cost-benefit analysis of electronic medical records in primary care. *Am J Med*. 2003;114:397-403.

71. Miller RH, West C, Brown TM, et al. The value of electronic health records in solo or small group practices. *Health Aff*. Sept/Oct 2005;24(5):1127-1137.

72. Hillestad R, Bigelow J, Bower A, et al. Can electronic medical record systems transform health care? Potential health benefits, savings, and costs. *Health Aff*. Sept /Oct 2005;24(5):1103-1117.

73. Kaushal R, Bates DW, Mills SA, et al. Imminent adopters of electronic health records in ambulatory care. *Inform Prim Care*. 2009;17:7-15.

74. Gans D, Kralewski J, Hammons T, et al. Medical groups' adoption of electronic health records and information systems. *Health Aff*. Sept/Oct 2005;24(5):1323-1333.

75. Miller RH, Sim I. Physicians' use of electronic medical records: Barriers and solutions. *Health Affs*. Mar/Apr 2004,23(2):116-126.

76. Press release: CMS rule to help providers make use of Certified EHR Technology.http://www.cms.gov/Newsroom/MediaReleaseDatabase/Press-releases/2014-Press-releases-items/2014-05-20.html. Accessed June 8, 2014.

77. Blumenthal D, Tavenner, M. The "meaningful use" regulation for electronic health records. *N Engl J Med*. www.nejm.org. July 13, 2010 (10.1056/NEJMp1006114). *Perspective*.

78. Medicare and Medicaid Programs; Electronic Health Record Incentive Program—Stage 2 53968. *Fed Regist*. September 4, 2012;77:171. Rules and Regulations 42 CFR Parts 412, 413, and 495 [CMS–0044–F] RIN 0938–AQ84.

79. Centers for Medicare & Medicaid Services. Eligible Professional's Guide to STAGE 2 of the EHR Incentive Programs. http://www.cms.gov/Regulations-and-Guidance/Legislation/EHRIncentivePrograms/Downloads/Stage2_Guide_EPs_9_23_13.pdf. Accessed November 10, 2014.

80. Barlow S, Johnson J, Steck J. The economic effect of implementing an EMR in an outpatient clinical setting. *JHIM*. Winter 2004;18(1):5-8.

81. Walker JM. Electronic medical records and health care transformation: EMR supported health care transformation is too immature for credible estimates of its costs or benefits. *Health Aff*. Sept/Oct 2005;24(5):1118-1120.

82. Cheriff AD, Kapur AG, Qiu M, et al. Physician productivity and the ambulatory EHR in a large academic multi-specialty physician group. *Int J Med Inform*. 2010;79:492–500.

83. HIMSS Realizing the Value of Health IT Value Steps Interactive Tool. http://www.himss.org/ResourceLibrary/ValueSuite.aspx#/steps-app. Accessed June 9, 2014.

84. Buntin MB, Burke MF, Hoaglin MC, et al. The benefits of health information technology: A review of the recent literature shows predominantly positive results. *Health Aff*. March 2011;30:464-471.

85. Goodman C. Savings in electronic medical record systems? Do it for the quality. *Health Aff*. Sept/Oct 2005; 24(5):1124-1126.

86. King J, Patel V, Jamoom EW, et al. Clinical benefits of electronic health record use: National findings. *Health Serv Res*. February 2014;49,1(II):392-404.

87. Gold M, Hossain M, Charles DR, et al. Evolving vendor market for HITECH-Certified Ambulatory EHR products. *Am J Manag Care*. http://www.ajmc.com/publications/issue/2013/2013-11-vol19-sp/evolving-vendor-market-for-hitech-certified-ambulatory-ehr-products/1. Accessed June 9, 2014.

CHAPTER 9

Hospital Systems: History and Rationale for Hospital Health IT

Virginia Lorenzi

INTRODUCTION

The typical modern-day hospital relies heavily on computer systems to support many of its functions, both clinical and administrative. This was not always the case. Only recently have hospitals exchanged paper processes for computer-reliant processes, especially in regard to the medical record.

Technology has changed significantly over the years, enabling EHRs and other health IT within the daily workflow of hospitals today. However, back in the 1960s, hospitals with computers had a monolithic mainframe system referred to as the hospital information system (HIS).[1]

Over time, some of these systems were expanded to include functionality to support ancillary departments, and some even supported clinical functions such as order entry (orders were typically entered by clerks). In the 1970s, the availability of minicomputers made it possible for departments of large hospitals to have their own systems.[2] For example, the laboratory would have its own laboratory information system (LIS), and the radiology department would have its own radiology information system (RIS). And smaller hospitals could also have an HIS on a minicomputer.

Microprocessors become available in 1975, and IBM introduced the IBM Personal Computer (PC) in 1981. Personal computers presented many more opportunities because of their affordability for niche systems and distributed architectures. Around the same time, local area networks (LANs), and the Internet were beginning to gain traction. Now connectivity between systems was possible, allowing for a more distributed approach to health IT versus the single HIS approach of the 1960s.[2]

Some tech-savvy hospitals built their own clinical systems. Vendor clinical systems started to appear, especially for nurse charting and results review. In 1991, the Institute of Medicine published a report, "The Computer-Based Patient Record: An Essential Technology for Health Care." Forward-thinking clinicians dreamed of electronic charting: "We envision the day when the physician's computer workstation is an integral part of the normal practice environment" so physicians can "obtain patient information when they need it, where they need it."[3]

However, electronic order entry was still primarily done by clerks, and the patient record—or at least many parts of it—remained on paper at many hospitals.

Financial pressure has been a primary driver of IT in hospitals. Prior to the 1970s, hospitals charged the costs they incurred in care delivery. In the late 1960s, after the creation of Medicare and Medicaid, U.S. healthcare spending was increasing at an exponential rate.[4] A change was needed. CMS adopted the Diagnostic Related Group model for provider reimbursement:

> "Inexorably rising medical inflation and deep economic deterioration forced policymakers in the late 1970s to pursue radical reform of Medicare to keep the program from insolvency. Congress and the Reagan administration eventually turned to the one alternative reimbursement system that analysts and academics had studied more than any other and had even tested with apparent success in New Jersey: prospective payment with diagnosis-related groups (DRGs). Rather than simply reimbursing hospitals whatever costs they charged to treat Medicare patients, the new model paid hospitals a predetermined, set rate based on the patient's diagnosis."[5]

The idea of limiting payment to only what seemed fair for a diagnosis meant that hospitals had to develop tighter controls on operations to ensure they were able to provide efficient care. This concept, otherwise known as capitation, became more developed over time with the advent of managed care and the concept of pay-for-performance, not pay-for-service. Computer systems to manage financial, as well as clinical and operational, aspects of the hospital were helpful in meeting these new requirements.

Hospitals were not always able to remain viable, and it was a common occurrence to read news about hospitals going out of business or merging. In the 1990s, a trend of hospital consolidation began. Hospitals merged or developed affiliations with each other and with other delivery organizations across the continuum. This was reflected in the architecture of health IT in these organizations. In these networks, health IT services commonly became centralized and standardized so that the same health IT was deployed at multiple sites in the network.

In addition, there has been a longstanding program with hospital staffing, especially nurse-patient ratios. Computers could potentially help reduce the problems with staffing by providing automated support of workflows of key hospital workers.[6]

Probably the most important catalyst to the modern day EHR was the "To Err is Human" report published in 1999 by the Institute of Medicine. This report noted that:

> "Health care in the United States is not as safe as it should be—and can be. At least 44,000 people, and perhaps as many as 98,000 people, die in hospitals each year as a result of medical errors that could have been prevented."[7]

and that:

> "Among the problems that commonly occur during the course of providing health care are adverse drug events and improper transfusions, surgical injuries and wrong-site surgery, suicides, restraint-related injuries or death, falls, burns, pressure ulcers, and mistaken patient identities. High error rates with serious consequences are most likely to occur in intensive care units, operating rooms, and emergency departments."[7]

The report goes on to explain that these errors are not usually the cause of any one person but instead are a systemic problem that included many missed communication opportunities. A hospital, a place of healing, was now considered downright dangerous. A handbook was even published entitled *You, the Patient*, which described how to take charge of your health and included a chapter on surviving a hospital stay. It opens with the quote:

> "Only $2,900 a Night and Free Sponge Baths – What a Deal!
>
> Just Make Sure You Check Out."[8]

It was becoming clear that computer applications could play an important role in enabling safer and more efficient patient care in hospitals.

A landmark event in U.S. health IT history was the 2004 creation of the Office of the National Coordinator of Health Information Technology. This creation marked the beginning of a concerted effort to encourage vendors to voluntarily adopt certified EHR technology. HL7 was tasked with creating a standard functional model of an EHR system that could help inform the certification process and another organization, the Certification Commission for Healthcare Information Technology (CCHIT) took on the task of certification of EHRs. Another landmark event was ARRA of 2009, which included the HITECH section and its subsequent MU and certified health IT regulations that followed. With the MU incentive program, a dramatic update in EHRs began to occur. Now hospitals were incentivized to buy and use certified EHRs, and vendors were encouraged to build and certify applications that provided more robust functionality.

> "In 2013, nearly six in ten (59%) non-federal acute care hospitals had adopted at least a Basic EHR system with clinician notes. This represents a 34% increase from the previous year and a more than five-fold increase in EHR adoption since 2008."[9]
>
> "In addition to growth in EHR adoption overall, hospital adoption of advanced functionality has increased significantly. Hospital adoption of comprehensive EHR systems has increased more than eight-fold in the last four years."[9]

SUMMARY OF HEALTH INFORMATION TECHNOLOGY IN THE HOSPITAL

Health IT in the hospital consists of systems in these broad categories:

1. Technology related to patient care provision (EHR)
2. Systems supporting the administration of the hospital
3. Departmental systems supporting care provision
4. Integration technology
5. Analytics systems
6. Information services support and infrastructure

Care Provision Systems—EHR Technology

The EHR in the Inpatient Setting. Inpatient and outpatient settings have similarities, but a key difference is that the inpatient EHR is encounter specific, concerned about a single acute encounter for the patient and not as much about his or her record over the continuum of care. This differs from ambulatory primary care, the focus of which is care across the continuum. A hospital stay is a major event requiring an acute level of care. *Acute care* is defined as "the health system components, or care delivery platforms, used to treat sudden, often unexpected, urgent or emergent episodes of injury and illness that can lead to death or disability without rapid intervention."[10] That care requires a specialized 24x7 environment; a wide range of clinical and support staff; and a lot of clinical interventions, testing, and technology in a short time period. The amount of data collected related to patients during their stay will be substantial—medication administrations, x-rays, lab tests, cardiology interventions, therapy and specialty consults, nursing interventions, etc.

The MU program encourages adoption of basic EHR functionality with Stage 1 and then additional functionality in each subsequent phase. For example, an important function in Stage 1 was to ensure that hospitals could meet a low threshold showing that a percentage of medication orders were entered into the EHR electronically—computerized provider order entry (CPOE). In Stage 2, this threshold was increased, and laboratory and radiology orders were included. Stage 2 also introduced the concept of electronically assisted medical administration (EMAR). Both CPOE and EMAR can help with patient safety, because the computer assists in safe medication ordering including checking for drug/drug interactions and allergies, as well as safe medication administration—assuring that the right patient is getting the right medication.[11] CPOE, when integrated with ancillary systems, can also improve efficiency, because the ancillary receives and responds to an order electronically instead of paper communication and double entry. It is important to note that the EHR functionality required for MU is obtained by hospitals from Certified EHR Technology (CEHRT); however, that technology does not have to be provided using a single comprehensive EHR. Instead multiple CEHRTs could be used that each provide some of the needed functions, which allows the provider to mix and match to reach 100 percent functionality. One example would be for a provider to use a different patient portal than the portal its main EHR vendor provides. The requirements for certification of EHRs are well documented at www.healthit.gov and in other parts of this text. However, it is important to note that the functionality required for MU does not represent all functionality that has been recommended for EHRs; it is a prioritized subset.

A hospital could have a variety of architectures for its EHR. Sometimes the EHR is comprehensive with all functions in a single system; other times, it is made of two or more components. For example, a hospital might have an EHR with a separate patient portal and a separate system for public health reporting. Alternatively, the hospital might have a single system with two or more functions within one system, such as patient administration and EHR functionality or EHR, laboratory, radiology, and pharmacy system functionality. This is especially true for smaller hospitals. Some smaller hospitals still have a model similar to the HIS model of the 1960s, but one that uses modern technology and functionality. Sometimes the EHR is shared across multiple hospitals in a network. Alternatively, a single hospital might have multiple EHRs based on site or on specialty (ED, ICU, behavioral health, etc.).

The HL7 Functional Model[11] attempts to cover EHR functionality in a more comprehensive manner than the MU program. It describes function points that an EHR *shall, should*, or *may* have in the categories of Care Provision, Care Provision Support, Administration Support, and Population Health Support. Central to patient care are the Care Provision functions, which are as follows:

1. Manage Clinical History
2. Render Externally-sourced Information
3. Manage Clinical Documentation
4. Manage Orders
5. Manage Results
6. Manage Medication, Immunization, and Treatment Administration
7. Manage Future Care
8. Manage Patient Education & Communication
9. Manage Care Coordination & Reporting

HIMSS takes another approach to defining EHR functionality and adoption in its EMR adoption surveys using the HIMSS Analytics EMR Adoption Model SM (EMRAM). The model has eight stages starting with Stage 0, with each stage building on the one before. Figure 9-1 shows the EMR Adoption Model and the rate of U.S. EMR adoption as of 2006. Figure 9-2 is the 2014 version of the model. A comparison of these models shows how much HITECH has served as a catalyst for EHR adoption and robustness.[12]

EHR Counterparts: Patient Care Devices. The EHR itself can have many appendages. There are numerous small devices and technologies that interact with the EHR in a patient's care. Vital signs equipment measure pulse, oxygen level, and blood pressure. Other equipment includes spirometers, fetal monitors, ventilators, and infusion pumps. There are point-of-care (POC) testing devices such as glucometers, portable x-rays, and portable EKG machines. Identification technology such as RTLS (real-time locating system) and RFID (radio frequency ID), barcodes, and biometrics as well as signature pads can be used to identify patients, clinicians, and equipment. Data input technology such as tablets, kiosks, and dictation systems are also sometimes used. Workstations on wheels (WOW), high-resolution viewing stations, and mobile devices like wireless tablets allow clinicians to interact more efficiently with the EHR in the workplace. In

EMR Adoption Model

Stage	Cumulative Capabilities	% of Hospitals
Stage 7	Medical record fully electronic; CDO able to contribute to ICEHR as byproduct of SEHR	0.0%
Stage 6	Physician documentation (structured templates), full CDSS (variance & compliance), full PACS	0.1%
Stage 5	Closed loop medication administration	0.5%
Stage 4	CPOE, CDSS (clinical protocols)	3.0%
Stage 3	Clinical documentation (flow sheets), CDSS (error checking), PACS available outside Radiology	18.0%
Stage 2	CDR, CMV, CDSS inference engine, may have Document Imaging	38.8%
Stage 1	Ancillaries – Lab, Rad, Pharmacy	18.9%
Stage 0	All three Ancillaries not installed	20.7%

December 31, 2006

Figure 9-1: EMR Adoption Model, 2006[12]

rural areas, telemedicine technology might be employed to provide remote healthcare services.

Administration

One of the oldest areas of automation in the hospital is administration. Patient administration is the identification of patients and the management of their hospital encounters including scheduling, census management, admissions, transfers, and discharges. Insurance information is collected and is automatically checked for authorization with insurance companies. Medical records systems ensure that all of the documentation for the patient is complete and that encounters are coded accurately. Patient accounts and revenue cycle management are closely integrated with patient administration as well. A quality system can support the reporting of quality measures to regulatory bodies. There are also general hospital management functions that are supported by computer systems—human resources, nurse scheduling, time tracking, general accounting, and materials management are all examples.

Departmental Systems

Larger hospitals often have one or more systems in their department. The next three sections cover three of the main ancillaries at a hospital: laboratory, pharmacy, and radiology. The fourth section lists other kinds of departments that potentially have automation.

US EMR Adoption Model℠

Stage	Cumulative Capabilities	2014 Q1	2014 Q2
Stage 7	Complete EMR; CCD transactions to share data; Data warehousing; Data continuity with ED, ambulatory, OP	3.1%	3.2%
Stage 6	Physician documentation (structured templates), full CDSS (variance & compliance), full R-PACS	13.3%	15.0%
Stage 5	Closed loop medication administration	24.2%	27.5%
Stage 4	CPOE, Clinical Decision Support (clinical protocols)	15.7%	15.3%
Stage 3	Nursing/clinical documentation (flow sheets), CDSS (error checking), PACS available outside Radiology	27.7%	25.4%
Stage 2	CDR, Controlled Medical Vocabulary, CDS, may have Document Imaging; HIE capable	7.2%	5.9%
Stage 1	Ancillaries - Lab, Rad, Pharmacy - All Installed	3.2%	2.8%
Stage 0	All Three Ancillaries Not Installed	5.6%	4.9%
Data from HIMSS Analytics™ Database © 2014		N = 5,449	N = 5,447

Figure 9-2: EMR Adoption Model, 2014[12]

Health IT in the Laboratory. In a highly automated laboratory, there might be a laboratory information system, a specimen tracking system, a robotics system controlling specimen flow, a dashboard showing the current state of high-priority tests, and many different automated laboratory devices. The most common tasks relate to testing blood specimens. With a CPOE lab order interface, the LIS learns about a new lab order via an inbound HL7 interface. In a highly automated environment, phlebotomists and nurses use mobile devices to identify patients by barcode and print specimen labels with patient and order identification via wireless mobile printers. The labels are placed on the blood collection test tubes. Drawn specimens arrive at the lab in tubes and then are placed in robotics equipment, which divides the sample into smaller samples for specific tests (aliquoting). Each sample is automatically routed to the appropriate testing device. The testing is done and the result is uploaded to the LIS and validated against past results. Verified results are sent back to the EHR via an HL7 results interface.

Hospital laboratories may also interact with other EHRs and LISs since they may process tests sent to them from ambulatory clinics or outside doctors or labs and may send out some of their testing work to outside labs.

There are also specialized lab systems or functions such as pathology and blood bank. Pathology workflow is different, often involving specialized specimen preparation and review by a clinical pathologist. Blood bank systems might support blood typing, as well as the management of blood products. There are also automated refrigerated storage cabinets for blood products in some operating rooms.

Health IT in the Pharmacy. In a hospital, medications are ordered by clinicians, dispensed by the pharmacy, and administered by nursing. In a fully automated environment, the clinician enters the order in the EHR and drug-drug and drug-allergy checking is performed, as well as other clinical decision support. The order is sent to the pharmacy information system (PHIS) via an HL7 interface. The received order is verified by a pharmacist who may then specify compounding, mixing, and dispensing information. Complex medications such as multi-ingredient IVs (intravenous) must be mixed. There is specialized robotic equipment in hospital pharmacies that can help with the counting and filling of pills, as well as the mixing of IVs. When the medication is ready to be dispensed, it might be placed in an automatic dispensing system. Automated dispensing systems are located near where medications are dispensed (such as on the nursing unit) and allow for careful control of medication inventory and appropriate dose dispensing. MU Stage 2 requires the use of electronically assigned medication administration technology. This technology allows the nurse to scan the barcode on the medication and on the patient's wristband to be sure that the medication and the patient are correct before administration.

Health IT in Radiology. The process of radiology begins with the ordering of an imaging exam by the clinician. In an automated environment, the order would be entered into the EHR and then sent to the RIS via an HL7 interface. An important function of the RIS is scheduling the patient for the procedure. There are many kinds of exams—examples include x-rays, computed tomography (CT) scans, magnetic resonance imaging, ultrasounds, and positron emission tomography-CT scans. Advanced imaging could include 3D and/or holographic radiology images. Radiological images are represented using the DICOM (Digital Imaging and Communications in Medicine) standard. The images can be quite large and are usually stored on a picture archiving and communication system (PACS). Once the imaging is complete, the next step is that a radiologist reviews the image and reports the findings. The viewing station that the radiologist uses is important and is often a high-resolution workstation. Radiologists sometimes use dictation systems to capture their findings. Sometimes, images are reviewed remotely (teleradiology). The text reports are sent to the EHR via an HL7 interface, and the ability to see the image is provided in some way to the EHR. For example, a link to the PACS could be provided. It is now possible for clinicians to access images from mobile devices, as well.

Health IT in Other Departments. The number of health IT systems is as diverse as the number of departments and functions in a hospital. In cardiology, there are systems for EKGs, cardiac catheterization, echocardiology, nuclear medicine, general cardiology, etc. Numerous technologies support the surgery suite, including anesthesiology systems, perfusion systems, automated dispensing cabinets, and RFID technology for surgical supplies and implantable devices, as well as the surgery information system. Transplant information systems manage the receipt and supply of organs for transplant purposes.

There are also systems to support local registries—examples include immunization, cancer, and bio-bank (genetic samples).

And there are departmental systems for the dietary department, patient transport, bed tracking and cleaning, patient entertainment (television), the emergency department, endoscopy, pulmonology, employee health, epidemiology, radiation oncology, credentialing, etc.

Health IT Middleware and Edgeware

Interface Engines. For hospitals that have numerous interconnected systems, an interface engine is an essential tool. Imagine the following scenario:

A patient is admitted and the admission is recorded on the patient administration system. This triggers the generation of a message containing demographic information about the patient, as well as information about his or her visit to be generated and sent to downstream systems that are interested in the information. Imagine that the hospital also has a pharmacy information system. If the pharmacy system is able to receive this patient administration message, then it can automatically create a record of the patient visit so that any subsequent orders for medications for the patient can be attached to the visit. In a similar way, if the message is sent to the EHR, this message will automatically create the encounter on the EHR, which alleviates the need for a clinician to create the visit and enter in the information.

This has two benefits:

1. Convenience and efficiency for the user of the downstream system
2. Safety for the patient, because when data are hand entered a second time, errors or discrepancies might be introduced

However, as the needs for interfacing increase (imagine interfaces between 50 systems), two problems occur:

1. Each time another system wants an interface, it has to be built on both the sending and receiving system. Eventually an unwieldy number of point-to-point interfaces exist that need to be maintained.
2. Each time an interface is needed, design, negotiation, and detailed mapping is needed to translate from the sender's interface logic to the receiver's interface logic.

To solve these problems, the following was done:

1. An interface engine sits in the middle of all interfacing—taking in all inbound feeds and then filtering, translating, and routing to the destination system.
2. The HL7 standard is a standard for messaging related to healthcare interoperability.

Both interface engines and HL7 serve a key role in healthcare organizations because, today, all of the systems in a hospital primarily communicate via an interface engine using HL7 messaging. Most systems require the following interfaces:

1. **Patient Administration Interface:** This interface receives messages from the patient administration system about all patient admissions, updates, transfers, and discharges. This information flow is often referred to as the ADT feed. ADT stands for admission, transfer, and discharge.
2. **Billing Interface:** This interface sends out charge information for services provided.
3. **Orders Interface:** The EHR and other clinician-oriented systems that include CPOE would include an outbound interface to send orders to the ancillaries that

could fulfill them. In turn, ancillary systems that fulfill clinician orders would have an inbound orders interface.

4. **Results/Documents Interface:** Systems that generate clinical results or documents will send these out to other systems. In turn, the EHR as well as other interested systems (clinical data warehouse, epidemiology, etc.) would receive clinical results and documentation via an inbound interface.

Enterprise Master Patient Index. Complex organizations that involve multiple sites and affiliations often have several assigning authorities of identifiers for patients. For example, a hospital could potentially have two medical records departments, each independently assigning medical record numbers. An Enterprise Master Patient Index (EMPI) is a best-of-breed system that owns and manages patient identification across an enterprise with multiple assigning authorities.[13] The EMPI number can become the index or linkage in shared systems and is useful in in cross-network query. The EMPI system manages demographics for the patient across the enterprise, provides an enterprise-unique patient identity (EMPI), and maintains linkages to local identifiers (e.g., MRNs) for the patient. An EMPI also often provides support for quality improvement of the index, suggesting potential duplicates and ID errors. Patient administration systems interface with the EMPI during patient search and new patient creation, making sure that the EMPI has the master copy of demographics and is able to link the enterprise identifier with local identifiers. The interface engine can add the EMPI into interfaces to systems that use the EMPI as an identifier. Enterprise systems use the EMPI to link patient records across the enterprise.

Terminology Services. As hospitals store more and more structured information on computers, the need for terminology management becomes critical. A terminology server manages concepts and their relationships to each other; it also provides mappings between current and historical local terminologies and mappings to standard terminologies. For example, the terminology server might keep track of the concept of a glucose laboratory test as represented in two different laboratory systems managed by the hospital. It might also keep a mapping to the code used to represent glucose in a system no longer used by the hospital. It could also map the local lab codes to the standard terminology LOINC© (Logical Observation Identifiers Names and Codes). Finally, it might map related concepts together—diabetes and A1C tests might both be related to the glucose test. A terminology server is able to provide a multitude of translational services and provides an intelligent repository of hospital metadata. New York-Presbyterian Hospital uses the Medical Entities Dictionary, which maintains over 100,000 interconnected concepts.[14]

Edge Servers and Health Information Exchanges (HIEs). Communication with outside organizations has become more common as we work toward inter-organizational healthcare interoperability. Hospitals may be a part of regional HIEs. If the HIE uses a federated model,[15] it will need to access patient data at the hospital site. In that case, the hospital would have an *edge server*. An edge server contains patient information accessible to other organizations. It provides a secure window into the hospital's patient data for the purposes of HIE. Hospitals will sometimes have their own internal HIEs between affiliated hospitals or sites and their own HIE software. HIE software includes interface management, patient identification services, and patient resource locator services.

Workstation Integration Technology. It is not uncommon for a desktop in the hospital to have multiple applications—for example, access to the inpatient and outpatient EHR and access to the RIS. Workstation integration software allows the user to switch between applications without losing context—for example, the new application would remember the user, the selected patient, and the selected encounter. This technology commonly uses the HL7 clinical context object workgroup (CCOW) standard.

Analytics

One of the fastest growing areas in health IT is in the area of analytics. In order to manage patients' care better and to improve efficiency, it is extremely important to study datasets collected from the EHR and other systems at the hospital. These data are also useful for research, quality, regulatory reporting, and population health management. Both clinical and business data can be collected and studied and sometimes combined for additional insight. Based on the data, one can determine trends and nuances and begin to support decisions by making predictions using the data. There could be numerous systems involved in the collection of data from many sources, preprocessing ("cleaning") of the data, and storage in specialized database systems optimized for queries that are more population based. The systems supporting analytics include clinical and business data warehouses, business intelligence tools that are able to prepare the data in formats ready for analytics, and analytics tools that allow for patterns to be discovered and displayed. Visualization tools include report writers, portals, dashboards, and others. The insights determined using analytics can sometimes automatically feed back into the operations of care provision systems to improve care.

IT Infrastructure

Finally, there are systems that support the IT service. Security and privacy is important, and there are systems to manage, control, and track access to systems. A fast and reliable network is assumed, and there are monitoring tools to keep track of performance and reliability. There are systems to manage planned changes to the production IT environment, as well as manage unplanned incidents (service desk calls). Computer applications could exist across one or more servers that could be housed in local data centers or off-site service centers/the cloud. Applications might have backup strategies in the event of failure.

CONCLUSION

Hospitals stays are intensive and expensive. Patients in hospitals are very sick and many individuals are involved in their care. Statistics have been reported on the dangers of hospitals to patients due to preventable errors. It is imperative that hospitals serve as safe places of healing, not risky adventures fraught with medical error. Computers hold the promise of organizing data and presenting critical information to users and improving communication between individuals. With continued rising costs of healthcare and the advent of healthcare reform, health IT in hospitals is more important than ever. ACOs will rely on substantial technology to ensure that information flows seamlessly across the ACO and that information is available to analyze and inform strategy to ensure ACO success.

Health IT is critical for the success of the modern-day hospital. Larger organizations could have well over 100 systems and many more intelligent devices with integration between many of the systems and the devices. Both administrative workflow and clinical workflow are supported by this technology. At the HIMSS14 conference in Orlando, Florida, attendees witnessed the power of the health IT role in hospitals at the Intelligent Hospital Pavilion.[16] At this pavilion, various areas of the hospital—maternity, emergency department, and the surgical suite—demonstrated the benefits of supporting technology. As dependent as hospitals are on cleaning staff and electricity is how essential health IT has become as part of healthcare delivery.

REFERENCES

1. *Biomedical Informatics: Computer Applications in Health Care and Biomedicine,* 3rd ed. In: Shortliffe EH, Cimino JJ, eds. Springer Science and Business Media; 2006.
2. Spronk R. The early history of HL7, Part 1. *HL7 News.* January 2014.
3. *Aspects of the Computer-based Patient Record.* Ball MJ, Collen MF, eds. Springer-Verlag; 1992.
4. Mayes R. The origins, development, and passage of Medicare's revolutionary prospective payment system. *J Hist Med Allied Sci.* 2007;62(1):21-55. Epub 2006 Feb.
5. Goodridge E, Arnquist S. A history of overhauling health care - nearly 100 years of legislative milestones and defeats. *The New York Times.* March 2010.
6. Welton JM. Mandatory hospital nurse to patient staffing ratios: time to take a different approach. *The Online Journal of Issues in Nursing.* Accessed September 30, 2007.
7. Institute of Medicine. To Err is Human: Building a Safer Healthcare System. 1999.
8. Roizen MF, Oz MC. *You, The Smart Patient - An Insider's Handbook for Getting the Best Treatment.* The Joint Commission, Free Press; 2006.
9. Adoption of Electronic Health Record Systems Among U.S. Non-federal Acute Care Hospitals: 2008-2013. *ONC Data Brief,* no. 16. Washington, DC: Office of the National Coordinator for Health Information Technology. May 2014.
10. Hirshon JM, Risko N, Calvello EJB, et al. Health systems and services: The role of acute care. *Bulletin of the World Health Organization.* 2013;91:386-388. http://dx.doi.org/10.2471/BLT.12.112664.
11. Enabling Medication Management Through Health Information Technology; Contract HHSA 290-2007-10060-I). AHRQ Publication No. 11-E008-EF. Rockville MD: Agency for Healthcare Research and Quality. April 2011.
12. HIMSS Analytics. EMR Adoption Model. www.himss.org. Accessed January 2015.
13. Lorenzi V, DaSilva G, Saini S, et al. Who Are You? The New York-Presbyterian EMPI Experience. Knowledge. www.amia.org. Accessed January 2015.
14. The Medical Entities Dictionary. http://med.dmi.columbia.edu/. Accessed January 2015.
15. Lorenzi V, DaSilva G, Saini S, et al. Technical Architecture of ONC-approved plans for statewide health information exchange. *AMIA Annu Symp Proc.* 2011.
16. intelligenthospital.org. Accessed January 2015.

CHAPTER 10

Improving Usability through the User-Centered Design Process

Janey Barnes, PhD, and Robert Schumacher, PhD

INTRODUCTION

User-centered design (UCD) is a continuous improvement process that provides a framework for iterative and continuous improvement of EHR usability. Teams with well-developed UCD processes in place include the application of human factors that takes into account human capabilities and human limitations in the context of the environment where the EHR is used. ONC's Meaningful Use Stage 2 (MU2) Safety-Enhanced Design requirements seem to have addressed the need for widespread application of UCD; however, improvements must take place to ensure the appropriate discipline with which UCD processes are applied.

BACKGROUND

Usability of electronic health records (EHRs) remains a high priority in the healthcare industry. Important steps have been taken. Education and training have been provided. Tools and resources have been made available. Policies have been put in place. Despite this, providers continue to report that poor usability of EHRs contributes to provider dissatisfaction and disruption in clinical productivity.[1,2] With all these measures, there was hope that usability and user satisfaction with these tools would increase. However, this is not just about user satisfaction; poor software user interfaces can negatively impact quality of care and result in serious patient harm, if not death.

Usability is defined as "the extent to which a product can be used by *specified users* to achieve *specified goals* with *effectiveness, efficiency* and *satisfaction* in a *specified context of use*."[3] Thus, usability is a measurable characteristic of a product or process.

Usable user interfaces result from a process aimed at optimizing effectiveness, efficiency, and user satisfaction. For many, effectiveness includes safety. ONC addresses usability through MU2 certification's Safety-Enhanced Design requirements. Safety-enhanced design is the focus on improved usability in conjunction with improved safety and risk management. MU2 Safety-Enhanced Design requires EHR development teams (i.e., vendors) to carry out a UCD process.[4,5]

Vendors are free to choose a recognized, standard UCD process that best fits the organization or to describe their own UCD process. Such processes provide a framework for iterative and continuous improvement of the usability of the EHR during design, development, deployment, and post-deployment. Examples of UCD processes that were provided in the MU2 regulation include ISO 9241-11, ISO 13407, ISO 16982, and NISTIR 7741.[4,5]

Characteristics that might result in one UCD process being selected over another UCD process include requirements defining the rigor with which UCD activities must be carried out, the specificity required for tracing findings from UCD activities throughout the product life cycle, or matching organizational continuous improvement processes currently in place.

UCD PROCESSES

The ISO 9241-210[6] (Human-Centered Design for Interactive Systems) UCD process was one example of UCD processes provided by ONC[4,5] that vendors might use to meet Safety-Enhanced Design requirements. The ISO document describes four primary activities that are carried out in an iterative fashion until defined usability objectives are obtained. Figure 10-1 illustrates the ISO 9241-210 activities:

- Understand and specify the context of use
- Specify the user and organizational requirements
- Produce design solutions
- Evaluate designs against requirements

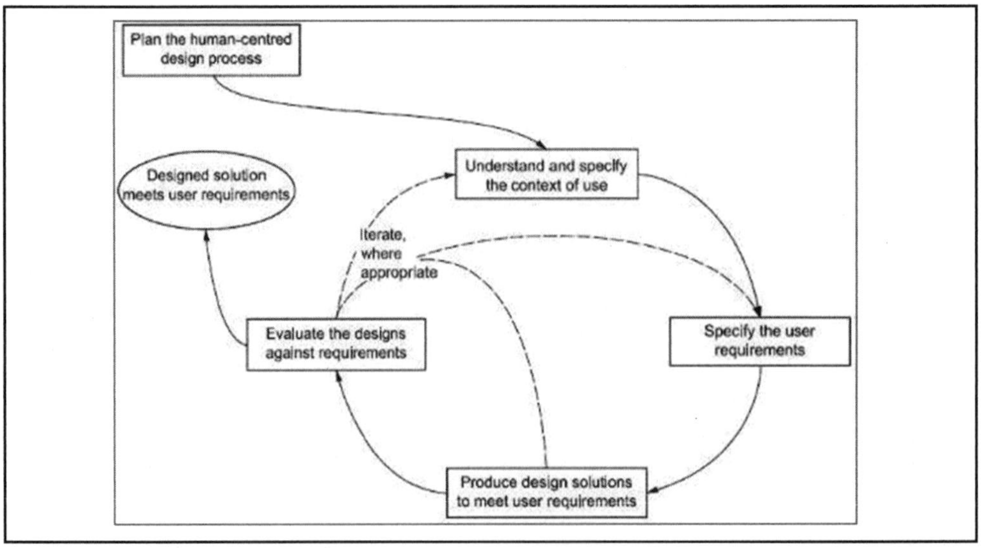

Figure 10-1: ISO 9241-210 (Human-Centered Design for Interactive Systems) Process.

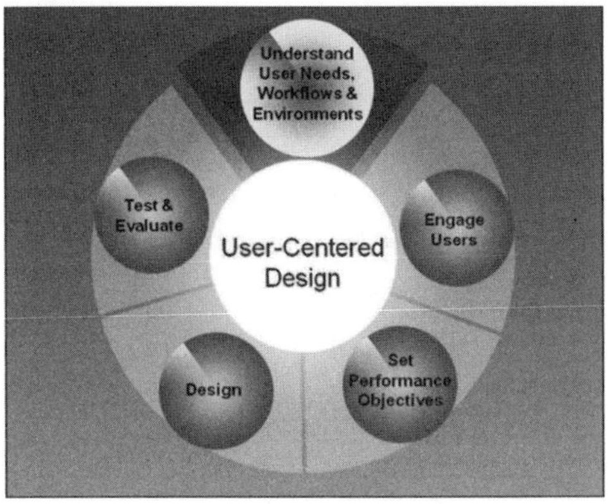

Figure 10-2: NISTIR 7741 (NIST Guide to the Processes Approach for Improving the Usability of Electronic Health Records)

The NISTIR 7741[7] document is another example UCD process that vendors might use to meet MU2 requirements.[4,5] The document describes a UCD process with the following activities (see Figure 10-2):

- Understand user needs, workflows, and work environments
- Engage users early and often
- Set user performance objectives
- Design the user interface applying known human behavior principles and familiar user interface models
- Conduct usability tests to measure how well the interface meets user needs
- Adapt the design and iteratively test with users until performance objectives are met

The similarities of ISO 9241-210 and ISO 9241-210 UCD processes are the foundation of an iterative process that is based on understanding the user, the user needs, and the user environment and the requirement to conduct user-based evaluations against performance objectives, user requirements, and/or organization requirements. The primary difference is that the ISO 9241-210 UCD process is directed toward the life cycle of computer-based interactive systems, while the ISO 9241-210 UCD process is specifically directed toward improving the usability of EHRs.

To meet MU2 certification[4,5] UCD activities must take place during the design and development of eight prioritized certification criteria and their associated capabilities:

- Computerized provider order entry (CPOE)
- Drug-drug, drug-allergy interaction checks
- Medication list
- Medication allergy list
- Clinical decision support
- Electronic medication administration record (eMAR)
- Electronic prescribing
- Clinical information reconciliation

To be considered for certification, teams must attest to applying formative UCD activities to each prioritized capability and submit a summative usability test report.

Formative activities include methods aimed at understanding the user, the user's tasks, and the user's environment, as well as evaluating alternative design solutions via analytic and task-based usability evaluations. Formative activities are performed while the product is being *formed.* Summative usability testing is a task-based method aimed at gathering objective data to evaluate the effectiveness, efficiency, and satisfaction of a product. Summative activities are performed at the end of product development to sum up whether the targeted user objectives were met. The Safety-Enhanced Design summative usability report is used for consideration of certification and is made public via the ONC Certified Health IT Product List (CHPL) website.[4,5,8] Products listed on the website have been successfully tested and certified as meeting the requirements for MU2 certification. The CHPL website includes information regarding the Safety-Enhanced Design for each product.

USER-CENTERED DESIGN AND VENDOR PRACTICES

Researchers[9,10,11,12] have explored vendors' UCD practices and perspectives. In May 2010, the Agency for Healthcare Research and Quality (AHRQ)[9] reported findings and recommendations based on interviews with seven vendor organizations and an expert panel regarding the existence and use of usability standards, best practices, and evaluation of EHR usability. Findings from the AHRQ report were available to the ONC at the time the ONC was formalizing MU2 Safety-Enhanced Design requirements. As reported, vendors included in the study were committed to assuring usable EHR products and the vendors identified that usability was a market differentiator. Vendors described a range of usability processes throughout the product life cycle. However, the AHRQ report noted some deficiencies in application of the process: the use of end users throughout the product life cycle, the use of formal task-based usability testing, the use of user-centered design processes, and the employment of personnel with expertise in usability engineering were not common.

Key recommendations from the vendors and the project's expert panel were as follows:

1. Establish usability/information design of EHRs as an essential part of certification requirements that focus on objective and important aspects of system usability.
2. Require vendors to establish and document their programs for testing usability of their systems, including an evaluation of potential impacts on quality and safety, e.g., lack of adherence to formal user design processes; dependence on post-deployment usability assessments; and the inclusion of under-sampled populations of end users.
3. Create an independent National EHR Usability Laboratory to support public-private efforts for collaboration; develop best practices; and harmonize standards including EHR usability, information design, and customization.
4. Develop tools and processes to support evaluation of the usability and information design of EHR products and their implementation.

Fairbanks and Ratwani[10] reported the findings of an ONC Strategic Health Information Technology Advanced Research – Patient-Centered Cognitive Support (SHARP-C) program aimed at understating vendor UCD processes and challenges. Ratwani's team visited nine vendor organizations and spoke with usability experts, business analysts, and product managers. In-person visits took place after the release of the MU2 Final Rule when some organizations were in the process of or had completed MU2 Certification. Vendor organizations varied in the following characteristics:

- Estimated revenue ($300,000 – $1 billion)
- Employees (10–5,000+)
- Usability staff (0–31+)

Vendors varied in their use of UCD processes and had different challenges dependent on the level of applied UCD process. One group of vendors had no true application of UCD processes. Vendors in this group noted that responding to customer requests was a UCD process, but had no formalized method for incorporating and testing user needs throughout design and development. The challenges faced by this group of vendors were lack of context and exposure to end users, no general UCD process, and lack of support to carry out the UCD process.[10]

The second group of vendors applied basic UCD practices. This group had an understanding of UCD and its importance. Vendors in this group were striving to implement UCD processes, but UCD was not fully integrated in product design and development. The challenges faced by this group of vendors included lack of usability or human factors resources, difficulty accessing usability test participants, and weak use-case development.[10]

The third group of vendors had well-developed UCD processes. These vendors had rigorous UCD processes in place, had efficient testing methods, and had an extensive infrastructure to support UCD activities. These vendors described that their UCD challenges were related to detailed workflow analysis and safety data.[10]

All three groups reported challenges related to time lines and summative testing; UCD process applied to legacy systems and patient-facing systems; challenges with customizations of the EHRs; and challenges with the development of training, which is often offered as an added cost and cannot make up for usability shortcomings.[10]

Furlough et al.[11] reviewed reports from nine EHRs (338 participants) on the CHPL website. The authors reported an error analysis on use errors from the summative tests. The error analysis took into account the severity and frequency of errors. Electronic medication reconciliation, configuration of drug-drug interaction alerts, and medication reconciliation tasks were rank ordered relatively higher in percent task fails x error score compared to electronic prescribing CDS, and medication allergy tasks. The authors concluded that continued education and improvements can be made regarding the application of UCD processes to EHRs by all stakeholders (e.g., regulatory bodies, EHR buyers, EHR end users, the vendor community).

Buchanan et al.[12] also reviewed Safety-Enhanced Design summative usability reports available on the CHPL website. Based on the summative test reports reviewed, the authors reported deviations from user-centered design best practices including the use of nonrepresentative participants, varying sample sizes, instructions that led participant performance, and variation in required reporting. The authors point out that those who might want to compare the publicly available summative usability test findings may not find the information useful.

One of the greatest values in the requirement for Safety-Enhanced Design as part of MU2 EHR certification may be increased awareness in usability as an objective measured outcome of the user-centered design process. That is, more vendor and provider organizations have become aware that usability can be objectively measured, that usability is an outcome of a continuous improvement process, and that goals for EHR effectiveness, efficiency, and user satisfaction can be set and can be achieved. However, each of the teams that reported on vendor organizations' use of the UCD processes concluded that although UCD processes exist and are followed, industry guidance is needed to ensure teams are integrating UCD into the design and development of their products.[9,10,11,12] In addition, Kannry, Kushniruk, and Koppel[13] also identified the need for healthcare organizations (practices and hospitals) to take a shared responsibility for improving usability via local usability testing units.

Fairbanks and Ratwani[10] described two areas of usability: user interface design and cognitive task support. User interface design concerns displays, controls, screen design, clicks and drags, etc. Cognitive task support concerns workflow, thought flow design, data visualization, etc. Application of a UCD process touches both areas of usability. Eric Bergman, director of human factors engineering at Fresenius Medical Care North America, was quoted in a member profile of *AAMI News*. The quote captures the essence of focus to both the user interface design and the cognitive task support during product design.

> One of the many misconceptions is that the field of human factors is only focused on making user interfaces intuitive. This view seems to hold that if we use the "right" words and icons at the surface level and follow up with enough usability testing, the problem is solved. It fails to recognize the critical role of identifying users, user requirements, tasks, mental models, and the many other factors in the process of designing and evaluating the user experience.[14]

LEARNING FROM OTHER INDUSTRIES

U.S. Food and Drug Administration

The U.S. Food and Drug Administration (FDA) requires medical device manufacturers to establish and follow Quality Systems known as current good manufacturing practices (CGMPs). CGMPs include the application of human factors engineering into the design and risk management of certain new medical devices and include post-market surveillance of these devices. The goal is to ensure that medical devices are designed to be reasonably safe and effective when used by the intended user and that medical devices remain safe and effective once the device is in use in the field.[15]

Human factors practices are to be applied during design input, verification, and validation. As part of design input, teams must come to understand user needs related to safe and effective use of the device. Potential use errors that result from interaction with the user interface are to be identified and eliminated through application of human factors methods. As part of design verification, teams are to evaluate that they are making the "right" product to address the user needs. During validation, teams must provide objective evidence that intended users are able to operate the device in a safe and effective manner under actual or simulated use conditions. The intent of the premarket human factors process[16,17] is to demonstrate and document that the team:

- Understands the *users, use environments*, and *user interfaces.*
  - Documents the user groups and their characteristics (capabilities and limitations associated with product use)
  - Documents *intended environments* where the device will be used, as well as *unsuitable environments.*
  - Documents the *intended use* and foreseen *unintended uses* of the device.
- Conducts formative analysis aimed at discovering use-related hazards.
- Conducts formative usability evaluations aimed at discovering and understanding use-related hazards and evaluating mitigation via iterative user-based testing.
- Conducts validation (summative) usability testing aimed at collecting objective evidence that the device can be used in a safe and effective manner as currently designed.

If the process appears familiar, it is because the FDA's process is to apply and document a user-centered design process to the design and development of medical devices with the focus on identifying and mitigating hazards associated with use errors. Use errors are those that result from interactions with the user interface. Through resources like HE75[18] and Do it By Design,[19] specific guidance is provided regarding:

- User interface (e.g., best practices for screen layout including consideration of alignment, content hierarchy, content distribution, and screen margins)
- User's performance (e.g., recommended character height and font sizes for various reading limits).
- Standards and standardization (e.g., alarm systems, IEC 60601)
- Usability evaluation (e.g., recommended sample size for usability testing)
- Application of a UCD process (e.g., human factors activities that can be carried out at each stage of a UCD process)

The intent of the FDA's post-market surveillance program is to ensure that devices that remain on the market are safe and effective. The FDA encourages device users and manufacturers to report serious adverse incidents involving medical devices through the Medical Device Reporting (MDR) system. Serious adverse events are analyzed from a number of perspectives, including identification of incidents where use error is involved; *use errors* are those that result from interactions with the user interface. Findings from post-market surveillance are used to improve a device's safety profile and increase patient safety.[20]

Aviation

Aviation is another safety-critical industry that has integrated human factors into their products and processes. In the technical report describing the history of human factors in aviation, Dekker describes[21] incidents in which the industry learned that design influences human performance. Bad design can lead to predictable kinds of human performance, and good design can enhance performance and prevent error. The application of human factors to cockpit design started with a focus on the user interface. Over time, the application of human factors included cognitive and cultural aspects of flight. As the industry matured, the element of human factors found its way into processes outside of the cockpit, resulting in human factors influence in aviation's operational practice.

Human factors specialists understand that people have expectations about what a control will do based on interaction with the control. For example, humans expect that moving a light switch to the *up* position turns the light on and turning a volume dial clockwise increases the volume. Early human factors activities were used to identify root causes of crashes that traced back to the mismatch of the pilot's expectations and interaction with the control. The F-111 (also known as the Aardvark) had a variable-sweep wing design. This meant the pilot could control the position of the wings based on the desired speed. When flying at slower speeds, the pilot could select for the wings to be positioned out (more perpendicular to the fuselage). When flying at faster speeds, the pilot could select for the wings to be positioned in a swept position (angled back toward the tail of the airplane). Initially, engineers designed the sweep wing control to match the airplane's throttle interaction. The result was that pilots often misused the control. That is, pilots associated the movement of the control with the movement of the wing; as the control goes, so goes the wing. The engineers changed the design of the control to match the pilot's expectation—to have movement of the wing match the movement of the control.[21]

Human factors expertise also contributed to the standardization of control placement. The industry learned that pilots who spent time flying one aircraft brought knowledge, habits, and experience to flying another aircraft. Early on, the location of the airplane's throttle, propeller pitch, and the mixture controls were varied. After incidents caused by pilots' confusion, standardization occurred and the throttle, propeller pitch, and mixture controls are now arranged from left to right in airplanes.[21]

As the aviation industry matured in usability and human factors, human factors influence become more widespread. Human factors regulatory guidance and best practices are provided for error management, prevention, detection, and recovery; workload; and automation. Recommendations include testing scenarios and procedures for evaluating human factors considerations. The application of human factors also informs training, aircraft maintenance, and air traffic control products and processes. Over the years, application of human factors has become a part of aviation's operational practice. As such, aviation has become a model for other safety-critical industries—recognizing that behavior once called human error was systematically related to the tools, tasks, and operational environment.[22,23]

ASSESSING INDUSTRY PROGRESS TOWARD IMPROVING USABILITY AND SAFETY OF HEALTH IT

Kannry, Kushniruk, and Koppel[13] identified steps toward improving usability and safety of health IT. These steps continue to be the benchmark by which to assess industry progress; they are as follows:

1. Rigorous usability engineering methods that are more widely used in the design and customization of health IT
2. The need for evidence-based heuristics and guidelines for both design and evaluation of health IT

3. Development of certification processes that provide strong evidence that systems will be safe to use and will effectively support user work activities in healthcare in a meaningful way

Kannry, Kushniruk, and Koppel identified that rigorous usability engineering methods need to be used more widely in the design and customization of health IT. While some progress was made as a result of ONC's MU2 Safety-Enhanced Design requirements, reports of variable practices and certified products that did not follow usability or human factors best practices indicate that continued improvements must be made. MU2 Safety-Enhanced Design requirements seem to have addressed the widespread application of usability methods. However, based on the variability seen in the information provided on ONC's CHPL website, the rigor with which these methods were applied is questionable at best. More specific guidance is needed regarding appropriate application of usability engineering methods so as to improve the discipline with which UCD processes are applied.

Kannry et al. also described the need for shared responsibility when designing, customizing, and implementing health IT.[13] Greater efforts can be made in this area. One step in shared responsibility is for vendors and provider organizations to work with each other both in design of the system and in customizations of the system. EHRs are highly configurable systems. At one extreme, vendors might design the EHR so that unsafe and inefficient configurations are not possible. A more pragmatic approach is for provider organizations to apply rigorous usability engineering methods to the customization of EHRs. In addition, vendors should team with their own customers to maintain and share usability best practices both for customizations and for implementations, as happens today at customer conferences.

Kannry, Kushniruk, and Koppel[13] identified the need for evidence-based heuristics and guidelines for the design and evaluation of health IT. During the time frame when vendors were seeking MU2 certification, resources were available to vendors regarding heuristics and guidelines for both design and evaluation of health IT. As part of the MU2 Final Rule, ONC provided example UCD processes that could be executed (e.g., ISO 9241-11, ISO 13407, ISO 16982, and NISTIR 7741).[4,5] In addition, the National Institute of Standards and Technology (NIST) had released NISTIR 7804 (Technical Evaluation Testing, and Validation of the Usability of Electronic Health Records) to provide guidance for evaluating the usability of EHRs,[24] and SHARP-C had made the TURF (Task, User, Representation, and Function) software available as a toolkit for usability evaluation of EHRs.[25]

Evidence-based guidelines to inform the design of EHR features have also been available to teams. During the time frame when vendors were seeking MU2 certification, design guidelines were available, including Microsoft Health Common User Interface,[26] textbooks such as Shneiderman et al.[27] and Wickens and Lee,[28] and heuristic guidelines such as Nielson's Heuristics for User Interface Design,[29] and Gerhardt-Powals' cognitive engineering principles.[30] Given these resources were available at the time vendors were carrying out UCD activities as part of MU2 Safety-Enhanced Design requirements and given the variability seen in the information provided on the ONC CHPL website, some vendors still remained unaware of UCD best practices, applied them incorrectly, or worse, deliberately chose to ignore them. Continued awareness education is needed to assure vendors are aware of resources, to assure vendors are able to find the resources, and to assure teams are able to generalize the guidelines to their own systems. The human factors community also owns a responsibility to deliver the information in a way that is approachable and consumable by health IT vendors.

In response to calls for guidelines developed for the health IT industry, more design guidelines are now available:

- Twinlist and Manylist provides evidence-based inspirational prototypes for medication reconciliation[31]
- EventFlow provides evidence-based inspirational prototypes for visualization of healthcare data[32]
- Safety-Enhanced Design Briefs provide guidelines for design of EHR functionality included in ONC's eight prioritized criteria[33]
- Inspiredehrs.org is an interactive book with clinical scenarios and example interactive designs guided by basic design principles[34]
- SAFER Guides aid organizations in addressing EHR safety in a variety of areas.[35]

Kannry, Kushniruk, and Koppel[13] identified that the concept of certification was an important step for increasing the usability of EHRs. Since then, the concept of certification has become a reality with Safety-Enhanced Design requirements. Improvements must be made in the requirements, implementation of the requirements, and the certification review. The CHPL site is meant to provide transparency regarding usability of certified products. ONC is aware of and working to fix these issues:

- Reports are difficult to find on the site.
- Some reports associated with certified products are not available on the CHPL site.
- Some reports available on the site include both the UCD method that was applied to each prioritized criteria and the summative usability test report, while other reports include only the summative usability test report.
- As described earlier in this chapter, reports associated with certified products vary greatly in terms of the rigor with which usability activities were carried out. This variability suggests that certifying bodies did not require strict adherence to the identified UCD process. Thus, some products were certified based on a higher standard (e.g., best usability practices such as representative end user, sample size, representative user tasks, non-leading instructions), whereas other products were certified based on a lower standard (e.g., not following best usability practices).
- ONC required the use of NISTIR 7742 (Customized Common Industry Format Template for Electronic Health Record Usability Testing) for reporting summative usability findings. However, certifying bodies did not require strict adherence to NISTIR 7742 for certification.

Review of the certification process is needed so as to identify how it is that so much variability is seen in reports associated with certified products. One of the characteristics of a strong certification program is reliability of the certification process. That is, the process should be repeatable and should result in the same outcome.

STEPS FOR CONTINUED IMPROVEMENT OF USABILITY AND SAFETY OF EHRS AND HEALTH IT

Looking forward there is a need to be constructive and advance the ways in which usability can be better injected into the development process. As the industry continues to focus on the (lack of) usability, the following steps should help draw attention away from the current start and move toward a plan for continued improvement of the usability and safety of EHRs and health IT:

1. Apply rigorous usability engineering and human factors methods to improve the user interface and cognitive support in the design and customization of health IT.
2. Develop and disseminate evidence-based heuristics and guidelines for both design and evaluation of health IT.
3. Identify opportunities to improve the current Safety-Enhanced Design (usability) certification requirements to the goal of decreasing the variability in how activities are reported as they relate to safety.
4. Continue development and implementation of a post-market surveillance system.
5. Create a national center for health IT safety.
6. Focus on purchasers as an important stakeholder group; educate them on the cost, productivity, and safety impacts of usability.

Continued application of usability engineering and human factors methods is critical. Usability engineering activities should be appropriately applied to user interface design; human factors methods must be applied to ensure that the EHR supports the cognitive aspects of the users' tasks. As described earlier, Safety-Enhanced Design requirements seem to have impacted the widespread application of UCD processes. Increasing the discipline in applying usability engineering and human factors and holding teams accountable for improving safety are important steps for continued improvement. Teams without usability engineering and human factors expertise should add this competency.

Good progress has been made in the development and dissemination of evidence-based heuristics and guidelines for both design and evaluation of EHRs and health IT is needed. Lack of awareness and "I didn't know" are no longer acceptable regarding application of the UCD process and application of best design practices to improve usability. As additional resources are created, they must be written for and distributed to specific identified audiences—the human factors community bears this responsibility. Resources and tools for designers and developers are different than resources and tools for product managers and other stakeholders. To increase the probability that stakeholders use these resources, the resources should be written in the language of the end user (e.g., in plain language) and made available to the audiences in easily accessible formats. As described earlier, continued education is needed to assure vendors are able to find and are able generalize the guidelines to their own systems.

As the industry evaluates the successes and opportunities for improvement to the current Safety-Enhanced Design certification process, areas for improvement are highlighted by Buchanan et al. The authors point out ONC's Safety-Enhanced Design requirement is an important first step toward improving the safety and usability of EHRs. They believe, as do others,[10,11] that this is only a first step. By intention or not, greater focus was placed on the summative usability test and less focus on the attestation to applying UCD process. Whereas the FDA requires teams to appropriately mitigate use-related safety hazards prior to market release, ONC only requires that teams report use-related safety hazards. Also, whereas the FDA requires teams to provide auditable evidence of adherence to a UCD process (e.g., understand the user, user needs, use environment, and iterative identification and mitigation of user related errors), ONC only requires that the team attest to applying UCD processes but requires no supporting evidence.[12] Human factors leaders have suggested ONC consider changing the focus of Safety-Enhanced Design certification away from usability as an outcome and stronger focus on the UCD process. By allowing vendors the choice to attest to a UCD process and provide summative results or to attach to a UCD process and provide auditable evidence of the UCD process being employed, greater gains might be made in improving usability. The choice allows vendors new to the UCD process the opportunity to start and fine-tune UCD methods in conjunction with development, while vendors with well-developed UCD processes in place may choose to expend their usability resources as desired based on need.[10-12, 36]

ONC's post-market surveillance approach calls for certifying bodies (ONC–authorized certification bodies) to assess whether certified EHRs continue to function as intended after implementation. Surveillance activities include surveillance initiated by complaints received from users of the certified EHRs, by issuance of repeated number of status requests, and calls for systematically obtaining and synthesizing feedback from users of certified products to determine if evaluation is needed with the vendor or with the user in the field—or both.[37]

ONC's Health Information Technology Patient Safety Action and Surveillance Plan[38] provides strategic and tactical steps to strengthen patient safety efforts. ONC is receiving input regarding methods to collect and analyze data regarding healthcare IT–related adverse events that will inform future policy.[39, 40]

Industry leaders[2, 9] have called for a national health IT safety center. The introduction of technology and changes in technology to a safety critical environment introduces new risks and new hazards. A national health IT safety center is another potential resource for a gathering data associated with safety incidents. ONC recently awarded a contract to RTI International to create a roadmap for the development of a center. The roadmap will define the focus, functions, and governance of a national health IT safety center.[41]

Over the past several years reports related to usability have mentioned purchasers as an important stakeholder in the discussions regarding EHR usability. Up to this point in the chapter, the missing stakeholder has been purchasers of EHRs. Kannry, Kushniruk, and Koppel argued that usability testing be required as part of the EHR selection process. Kannry et al. reported a few examples where usability data were included as part of the EHR procurement process, but the practice is not widespread.[13] Tools have been available for EHR purchasers for years,[42,43,44] but usability requirements are rarely included in RFPs for EHR purchases. One barrier to improving EHR usability is that purchasers of EHRs are typically not the users of the EHR and that the user does not always have input in the purchase decision. When deciding on criteria for purchasing an EHR, those involved in the process need to put usability considerations high on the list of concerns. As previously noted, there is a disassociation between the importance users put on usability and the usability delivered by many EHRs. Ultimately, the highest cost of most enterprise software applications is the cost of the user sitting in front of the application.

CONCLUSION

Usability can sometimes be a difficult concept to define, and that is what makes improvement a challenge. Fundamentally, human behavior can be measured and usability can be improved as a result. From a regulatory perspective, some attempts to certify improvements in usability have been unevenly implemented or poorly understood. This may be more a failure in execution than in theory. In other industries, applying user-centered design processes and good human factors have been shown to improve usability. The usability/human factors community does bear some of the responsibility to meet its users in ways that motivate and inspire software producers to collective improvement. However, there continues to be a need to overcome larger organizational difficulties for the benefit of users and patients.

REFERENCES

1. Brown D. Hospital nurses forced to develop creative workarounds to deal with EHR system flaws; outdated technologies and lack of interoperability, Reveals Black Book. *PRWeb*. October 17, 2014. http://blackbookmarketresearch.com/hospital-nurses-forced-to-develop-creative-workarounds-to-deal-with-ehr/. Accessed November 28, 2014.

2. Friedberg MW, Chen PG, Van Busum KR, et al. Factors affecting physician professional satisfaction and their implications for patient care, health systems, and health policy. Document No. RR-439-AMA; RAND Corporation; 2013. http://www.rand.org/content/dam/rand/pubs/research_reports/RR400/RR439/RAND_RR439.pdf. Accessed November 28, 2014.

3. Schoeffel R. The concept of product usability. *ISO Bulletin*. 2003;34:6-7.

4. Office of National Coordinator. Meaningful Use Stage 2 Final Rule: Health Information Technology: Standards, Implementation Specifications, and Certification Criteria for Electronic Health Record Technology. 2014 ed.; Revisions to the Permanent Certification Program for Health Information Technology. http://www.gpo.gov/fdsys/pkg/FR-2012-09-04/pdf/2012-20982.pdf. Accessed November 28, 2014.

5. Test Procedure for §170.314(g)(3) Safety-enhanced design. http://www.healthit.gov/sites/default/files/170.314g3safetyenhanceddesign_2014_tp_approved_v1.3_0.pdf. 2015 ed. Accessed November 28, 2014.

6. ISO. 9241:210 (2010). Ergonomics of human-system interaction – Part 210: Human-centred design for interactive systems. Accessed December 6, 2014.

7. NIST. 7741 (2010). Guide to the Processes Approach for Improving the Usability of Electronic Health Records. Accessed December 6, 2014.

8. Certified Health IT Product List. The Office of the National Coordinator for Health Information Technology. http://oncchpl.force.com/ehrcert. Accessed November 28, 2014.

9. McDonnell C, Werner K, Wendel L. *Electronic Health Record Usability: Vendor Practices and Perspectives*. AHRQ Publication No. 09(10)-0091-3-EF. Rockville, MD: Agency for Healthcare Research and Quality. May 2010.

10. Fairbanks R, Ratwani R. Human factors perspective on advancing EHR usability and safety. Presented to the ONC HIT Implementation, Usability, & Safety Workgroup. October 10, 2014. Slides avail-

able at http://www.healthit.gov/facas/calendar/2014/10/10/policy-hit-implementation-usability-safety-workgroup. Accessed November 28, 2014.

11. Furlough C, Barnes, J, Mauney J, et al. Observed usage errors during Meaningful Use Stage 2 safety-enhanced design summative testing. Presented at the International Symposium of Human Factors and Ergonomics in Healthcare. June 2014;3:81-86.
12. Buchanan C, Threatt A, Weinger MB, et al. High variability in summative usability test methods and reporting among clinical informatics vendors complying with federal certification requirements. Presented at Human Factors and Ergonomics Society Annual Meeting. October 30, 2014; Chicago, IL.
13. Kannry J, Kushniruk A, Koppel R. Meaningful usability: Health information for the rest of us. In: Ong K, ed. *Medical Informatics: An Executive Primer.* 2nd ed. Chicago: Healthcare Information and Management Systems Society (HIMSS); 2011.
14. Bergman E. Member News. Profile: Human factors expert casts wide net. *AAMI News.* Advancing Association for the Advancement of Medical Instrumentation. 2014;49,11:22. Accessed November 2014.
15. U.S. Food and Drug Administration. Quality system regulation/medical device good manufacturing practices. http://www.fda.gov/MedicalDevices/DeviceRegulationandGuidance/PostmarketRequirements/QualitySystemsRegulations/default.htm. Accessed November 28, 2014.
16. Kaye R, Crowley J. Medical Device Use-Safety: Incorporating human factors engineering into risk management. U.S. Food and Drug Administration. http://www.fda.gov/MedicalDevices/DeviceRegulationandGuidance/GuidanceDocuments/ucm094460.htm. Accessed November 28, 2014.
17. Draft Guidance for Industry and Food and Drug Administration Staff: Applying Human Factors and Usability Engineering to Optimize Medical Device Design. Document number 1757. June 22, 2011. http://www.fda.gov/MedicalDevices/DeviceRegulationandGuidance/GuidanceDocuments/ucm259748.htm. Accessed November 28, 2014.
18. ANSI/AAMI. HE75:2009. Human factors engineering- Design of medical devices. Association for the Advancement of Medical Instrumentation. Arlington, VA; 2009.
19. Sawyer D. (1996). Do it by design: An introduction to human factors in medical devices. http://www.fda.gov/downloads/medicaldevices/deviceregulationandguidance/guidancedocuments/ucm095061.pdf. Accessed November 28, 2014.
20. Postmarket information – Device surveillance and reporting processes. http://www.fda.gov/MedicalDevices/DeviceRegulationandGuidance/HumanFactors/ucm124851.htm. Accessed November 28, 2014.
21. Dekker S. (2003). Human factors in aviation – A natural history. Technical Report 20013-02. Lund University School of Aviation.
22. Yeh M, Young J, Donovan C, et al. (2013). Human factors considerations in the design and evaluation of flight deck displays and controls. Federal Aviation Administration. http://ntl.bts.gov/lib/50000/50700/50760/General_Guidance_Document_Nov_2013_v1.pdf. Accessed November 28, 2014.
23. Operational Use of Flight Path Management Systems: Final report of the Performance-based Operations Aviation Rulemaking Committee/Commercial Aviation Safety Team and the Flight Deck Automation Working Group. September 5, 2013.
24. Lowry SZ, Quinn MT, Ramaiah M, et, al. NISTIR 7804. Technical evaluation, testing, and validation of the usability of electronic health records. National Institute of Standards and Technology. February 2012.
25. Turf - EHR Usability Toolkit. https://sbmi.uth.edu/nccd/turf/. Accessed November 28, 2014.
26. Microsoft Health Common User Interface. http://www.mscui.net/. Accessed November 28, 2014.

27. Shneiderman B, Plaisant C, Cohen M, et al. *Designing the User Interface: Strategies for Effective Human-Computer Interaction.* 5th ed. Reading, MA: Addison Wesley Longman; 2009.

28. Wickens CD, Lee JD, Liu Y, et al. *Introduction to Human Factors Engineering.* 2nd ed. Upper Saddle River, NJ: Prentice-Hall; 2003.

29. Nielsen J. *Usability Engineering.* San Diego: Academic Press; 1994.

30. Gerhardt-Powals J. Cognitive engineering principles for enhancing human - computer performance. *Int J Hum Comput Interact.* 1996;8(2):189–211.

31. Plaisant C, Chao T, Wu J, et al. Twinlist: Novel user interface design for medication reconciliation. http://www.cs.umd.edu/hcil/sharp/twinlist/. Accessed November 28, 2014.

32. EventFlow: Visual analysis of temporal event sequences and advanced strategies for healthcare discovery. http://www.cs.umd.edu/hcil/eventflow/. Accessed November 28, 2014.

33. Safety enhanced design briefs. https://sbmi.uth.edu/nccd/SED/Briefs/. Accessed November 28, 2014.

34. Belden J, et al. Inspired EHRs: Designing for clinicians. http://inspiredehrs.org/. Accessed November 28, 2014.

35. SAFER Guides. http://www.healthit.gov/safer/safer-guides. Accessed November 28, 2014.

36. Schumacher R. Safety enhanced design in electronic health records: Evolution and current status. Presented at the Human Factors and Ergonomics in Healthcare: Chicago, IL; March 2014.

37. ONC HIT Certification Program: Program Policy Guidance #14-01. http://www.healthit.gov/sites/default/files/onc-acb_cy15annualsurveillanceguidance.pdf. Accessed November 28, 2014.

38. Health IT and safety. http://www.healthit.gov/policy-researchers-implementers/health-it-and-safety. Accessed November 28, 2014.

39. Solomon R. Partnership for health IT patient safety. Presented to the ONC HIT Implementation, Usability, & Safety Workgroup. October 24, 2014. Slides available at http://www.healthit.gov/facas/calendar/2014/10/24/policy-hit-implementation-usability-safety-workgroup. Accessed November 28, 2014.

40. Castro G. Investigations of health IT-related deaths, serious injuries, or unsafe conditions. Presented to the ONC HIT Implementation, Usability and Safety Workgroup. October 24, 2014. Slides available at http://www.healthit.gov/facas/calendar/2014/10/24/policy-hit-implementation-usability-safety-workgroup. Accessed November 28, 2014.

41. ONC Awards Health IT Safety Center Contract. http://www.govhealthit.com/news/onc-awards-health-it-safety-center-contract. Accessed November 28, 2014.

42. Schumacher RM, Webb JM, Johnson KR. How to select an electronic health record system that healthcare professionals can use. http://www.gfk.com/documents/whitepaper/ehr-selection-ux-white-paper.pdf. Accessed November 28, 2014.

43. Selecting an EMR for your practice: Evaluating usability. August 2010. http://www.himss.org/files/HIMSSorg/content/files/selecting_emr_eval_usability.pdf. Accessed November 28, 2014.

44. Selecting the right EMR vendor. http://www.himss.org/files/HIMSSorg/content/files/selectingemr_flyer2.pdf. Accessed November 28, 2014.

CHAPTER 11

Clinical Decision Support

By Ken Ong, MD, MPH, FACP, FIDSA, CPHIMS, FHIMSS

WHAT IS DECISION SUPPORT?

In our everyday lives, we are all immersed in a diversity of decision support.

The alarm clock alerts us when it is time to wake up. If you travel on the subway to work, the turnstile card reader may tell you how much you have left on your transit fare card before you have to refill it. If you drive, a speedometer, odometer, gas gauge, tachometer, and other decision support features populate your dashboard. Traffic lights tell us when to stop and go.

Decision support in health and healthcare is clinical decision support (CDS). This chapter will discuss why CDS is invaluable, what it is, and how to implement it.

THE VALUE OF CDS

The amount of information that exists in modern healthcare can be dizzying.

The National Center for Health Statistics lists and updates more than 68,000 diagnoses and complications in the newest version of the International Classification of Diseases (ICD-10-CM).[1] The U.S. Food and Drug Administration (FDA) has approved more than 6,000 drugs, which does not include the many food supplements or herbal medications that are clinically relevant.[2]

Keeping up is a challenge. The number of medical journal articles catapulted from 200,000 in 1970 to more than 800,000 in 2010, as shown in Figure 11-1.[3]

With the current number of articles published annually in medical literature, a recent medical school graduate who reads two articles every day would be 1,225 years behind at the end of the first year.[4]

The sheer growth of medical knowledge prolongs the time it takes for clinical research to effect clinical practice. One study calculated that the average time from discoveries made at the bench to reach the bedside is 17 years.[5]

Yet there is little time in the day to browse the recent literature. The old saw that there just aren't enough hours in the day applies doubly to the average physician. A study of Medicare patients revealed that physicians in private practice may interact

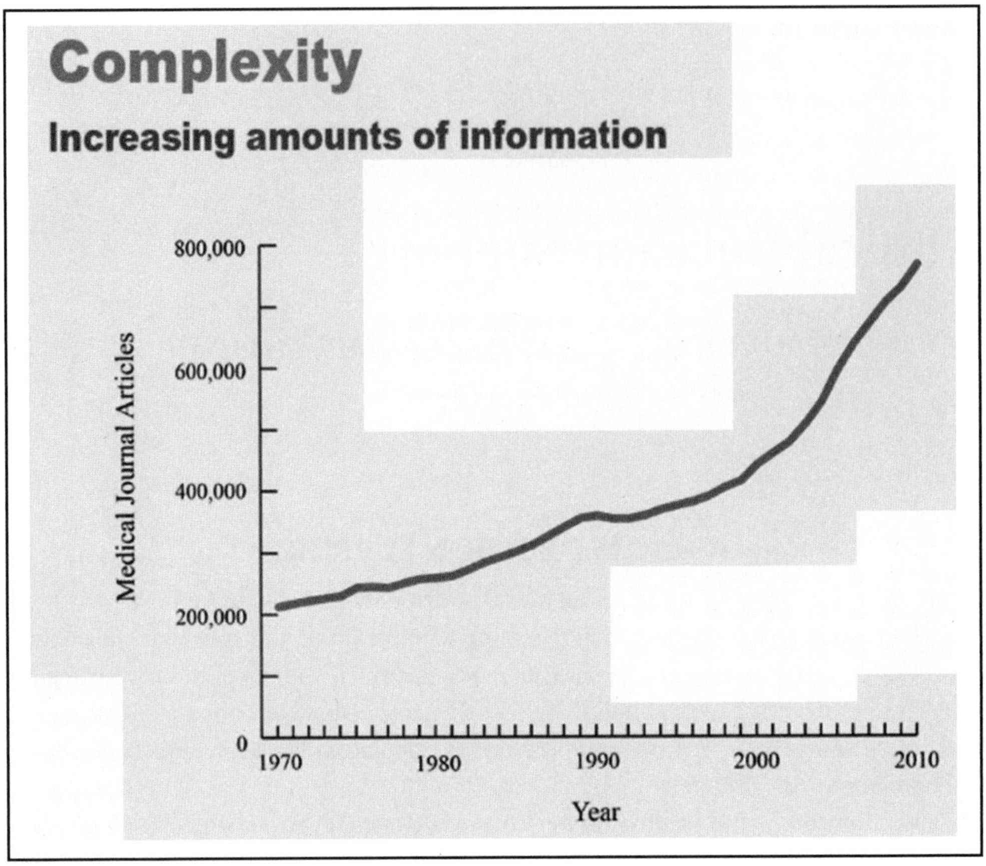

Figure 11-1: Growth in Number of Medical Journal Articles

with as many as 229 other physicians in 117 different practices. In intensive care units, clinicians may engage in 180 activities per patient per day.[3]

If a physician followed all the recommendations from national clinical care guidelines for preventive services and chronic disease management and added the time needed to answer phone calls, write prescriptions, read laboratory and radiology results, and perform other tasks for a typical patient panel of 2,500, he or she would need 21.7 hours per day.[6] Add to that the reality that only 55 percent of Americans receive recommended care;[7] information overload coupled with a paucity of time suggest the value of CDS and greater team-based care.

A systematic review of the literature concluded that CDS systems can improve healthcare process measures across various healthcare settings.[8]

WHAT IS CDS?

> Clinical decision support is a process for enhancing health-related decisions and actions with pertinent, organized clinical knowledge and patient information to improve health and healthcare delivery. Information recipients can include patients, clinicians and others involved in patient care delivery; information delivered can include general clinical knowledge and guidance, intelligently processed patient data, or a mix-

ture of both; and information delivery formats can be drawn from a rich palette of options that includes data and order entry facilitators, filtered data displays, reference information, alerts, and others.[9]

The most frequently cited example of CDS is a drug-allergy interaction alert to a physician at time of order entry. Drug-drug, drug-allergy, and drug-food interaction alerts are indeed prototypical examples of CDS, but there are other tools in the CDS toolbox.

Each CDS intervention can have a different use case, target audience, and fit in a particular point in the clinical workflow (see Table 11-1). For example, a reminder for colorectal cancer screening could be sent to a physician, practice office staff, and the patient via his or her personal health record (PHR).

The order set is one of the more powerful and adaptable CDS tools. The modern electronic order set has a proud lineage whose progenitor is the paper checklist.

The checklist was a product of the analysis of the fatal crash of an experimental aircraft during a test flight in 1935. The test pilots made this first checklist, a step-by-step list for takeoff, flight, landing, and taxiing, short enough to fit on an index card. After this modest, paper-based innovation was implemented, the aircraft that inspired it flew another 1.8 million miles without another accident.[2]

This checklist technology has crossed over into healthcare. Peter Pronovost, MD, an intensivist from Johns Hopkins University School of Medicine, partnered with the World Health Organization (WHO) to promote the Surgical Safety Checklist to prevent surgical complications and deaths. The 19-item checklist improves team commu-

Table 11-1: Clinical Decision Support Tools[9,10,11,12]

• Alerts and reminders
• Clinical guidelines
• Clinician patient assessment forms
• Data displays
• Data flow sheets
• Diagnostic support and suggestions
• Documentation templates
• Infobutton
• Smart documentation forms or documentation templates
• Extended-time guideline and protocol followers
• Order facilitators (order sets, order consequents, order modifiers)
• Patient data reports and dashboards
• Patient self-assessment forms
• Patient summaries for hand-offs between clinicians
• Performance dashboards with prompts for areas needing attention
• Procedure refreshers, training, and reminders
• Protocol/pathway support
• Reference information delivered
• Relevant data displays
• Targeted reference, including contextually relevant medical references or info buttons
• Task assistants for tasks such as drug dosing and acknowledging laboratory results
• Tracking and management systems that facilitate task prioritization and whole-service management

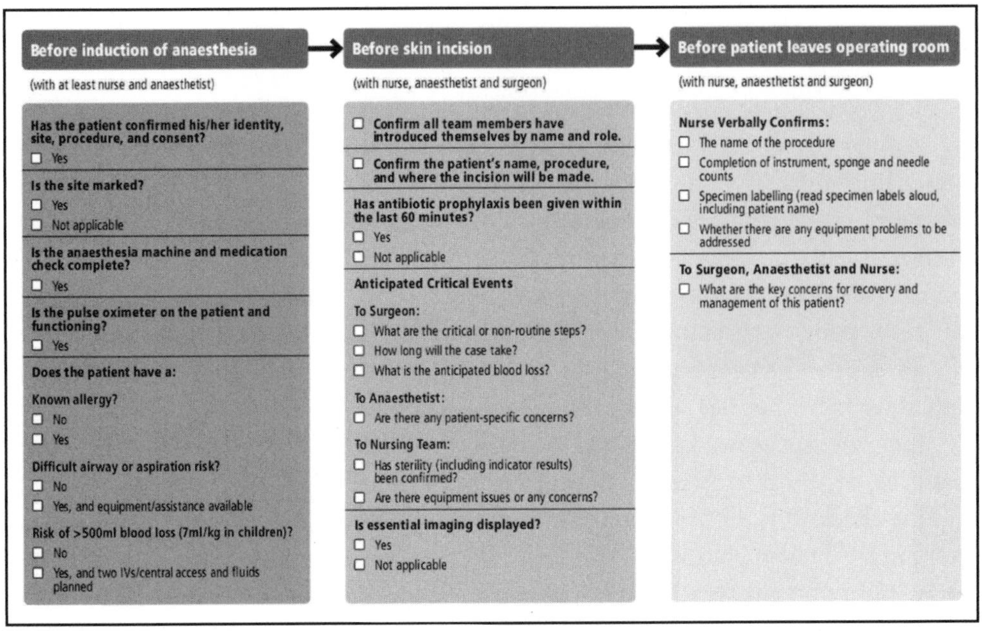

Before induction of anaesthesia

(with at least nurse and anaesthetist)

Has the patient confirmed his/her identity, site, procedure, and consent?
☐ Yes

Is the site marked?
☐ Yes
☐ Not applicable

Is the anaesthesia machine and medication check complete?
☐ Yes

Is the pulse oximeter on the patient and functioning?
☐ Yes

Does the patient have a:

Known allergy?
☐ No
☐ Yes

Difficult airway or aspiration risk?
☐ No
☐ Yes, and equipment/assistance available

Risk of >500ml blood loss (7ml/kg in children)?
☐ No
☐ Yes, and two IVs/central access and fluids planned

Before skin incision

(with nurse, anaesthetist and surgeon)

☐ **Confirm all team members have introduced themselves by name and role.**

☐ **Confirm the patient's name, procedure, and where the incision will be made.**

Has antibiotic prophylaxis been given within the last 60 minutes?
☐ Yes
☐ Not applicable

Anticipated Critical Events

To Surgeon:
☐ What are the critical or non-routine steps?
☐ How long will the case take?
☐ What is the anticipated blood loss?

To Anaesthetist:
☐ Are there any patient-specific concerns?

To Nursing Team:
☐ Has sterility (including indicator results) been confirmed?
☐ Are there equipment issues or any concerns?

Is essential imaging displayed?
☐ Yes
☐ Not applicable

Before patient leaves operating room

(with nurse, anaesthetist and surgeon)

Nurse Verbally Confirms:
☐ The name of the procedure
☐ Completion of instrument, sponge and needle counts
☐ Specimen labelling (read specimen labels aloud, including patient name)
☐ Whether there are any equipment problems to be addressed

To Surgeon, Anaesthetist and Nurse:
☐ What are the key concerns for recovery and management of this patient?

Figure 11-2: WHO Surgical Safety Checklist - 2009 Edition

nication and consistency of care (see Figure 11-2).[13,14] Eight hospitals around the globe participated in a study with an outcome of a nearly halved death rate and a significantly reduced complication rate post-surgery.[15]

A Sampler of CDS Tools

If a checklist on paper can generate so much value, imagine what can be done with an electronic checklist. The enhanced EHR order set is such a checklist but with bells and whistles. An order set can offer functionality that would either be difficult or impossible with paper.

An example of an admission order set for congestive heart failure (CHF) enables the following features:

- Links to evidence, e.g., Infobutton
- Reminders for preferred diagnostic or therapeutic interventions
- Icons to indicate order items recommended by government or quality organizations, e.g., CMS, The Joint Commission, Institute for Healthcare Improvement (IHI), or the American College of Obstetrics and Gynecology
- Preferred medications with recommended dosing, frequency, and route
- Relevant laboratory results or other patient information, e.g., serum creatinine for aminoglycosides, patient weight for pediatric dosing, patient height and weight for cancer chemotherapy

Zynx (Los Angeles, CA) is a leading provider of order sets. It offers order sets that cover the most common diagnoses and procedures for both inpatient and ambulatory care. A panel of clinical subject matter experts (SMEs) updates the order sets as needed. Order items recommended by a national professional or quality organization are indicated with a blue ribbon icon. A bell icon precedes reminders. A blue 'Z' icon links to evidence compiled by the Zynx expert panel. A prescription slip icon links to drug

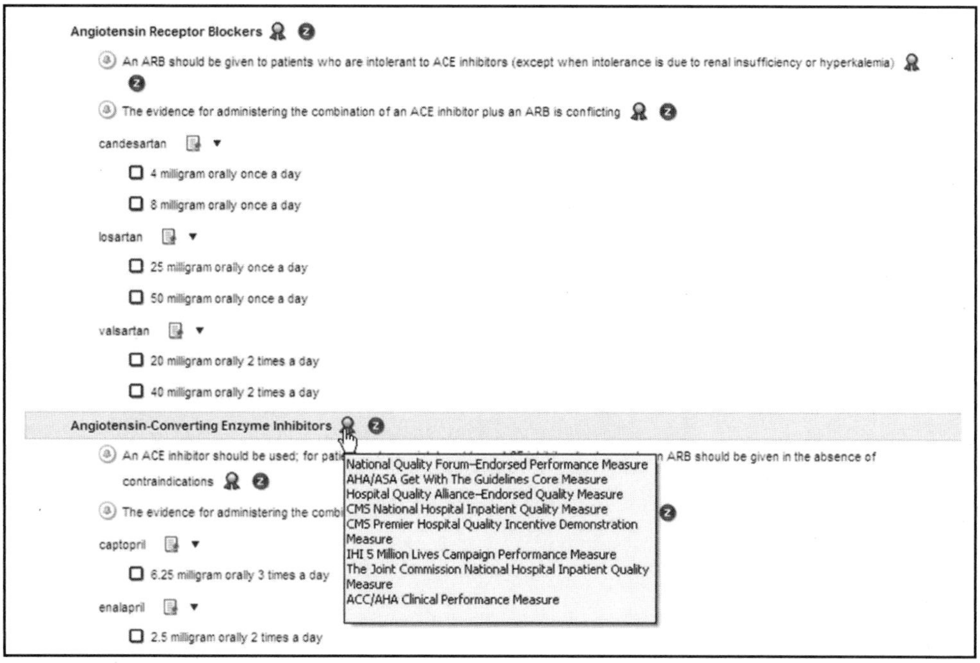

Figure 11-3: Sample of Zynx CHF Order Set

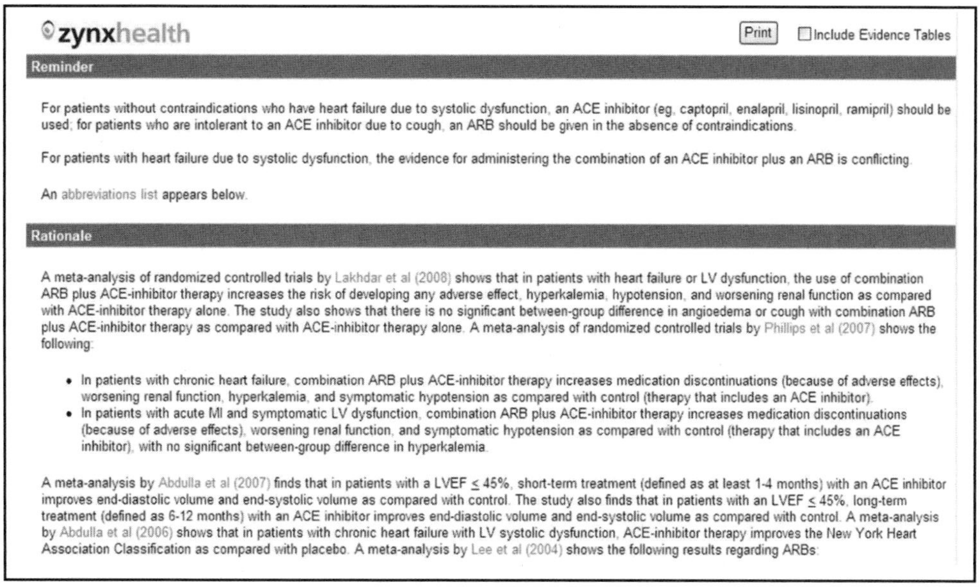

Figure 11-4: Sample of Zynx Evidence for ACE Inhibitors for CHF

information details. See Figure 11-3 for a sample Zynx order set and Figure 11-4 for a sample of Zynx evidence for ACE inhibitors for CHF.

The Zynx product provides a ready starting point for customization and ongoing updates as evidence evolves. The final order set can then be built with or without links to evidence into an EHR for computerized provider order entry (CPOE).

Order sets do work. Santolin et al. reported that a higher percentage of patients whose physicians initiated hospital therapy with standardized order sheets, which follow American Heart Association/American College of Cardiology Guidelines for acute coronary syndrome, received appropriate medications in a timely fashion.[16]

Other CDS technologies have proven beneficial.

Infobuttons are context-specific links that provide connection to resources relevant to particular diagnoses or conditions.[17] The evidence links in the order set example previously shown are Infobuttons.

Risk assessment tools can target patients at risk for given conditions and recommend focused treatment. An Agency for Healthcare Research and Quality (AHRQ)–funded study at the Children's Hospital of Philadelphia demonstrated that a pediatric asthma-control tool in the ambulatory EHR improved compliance with National Asthma Education Prevention Program guidelines.[18]

The Jesse Brown Veterans Affairs Medical Center created and implemented a standardized deep vein thrombosis (DVT) risk assessment program in its electronic medical record (see Figures 11-5 and 11-6).[19] With implementation of the DVT risk assessment program, the number of patients receiving the recommended pharmacologic prophylaxis preoperatively more than doubled and use of sequential compression devices (SCD) increased 40 percent. The percentage of at-risk patients receiving the recommended combined DVT prophylaxis of SCD and pharmacologic prophylaxis increased nearly seven-fold.

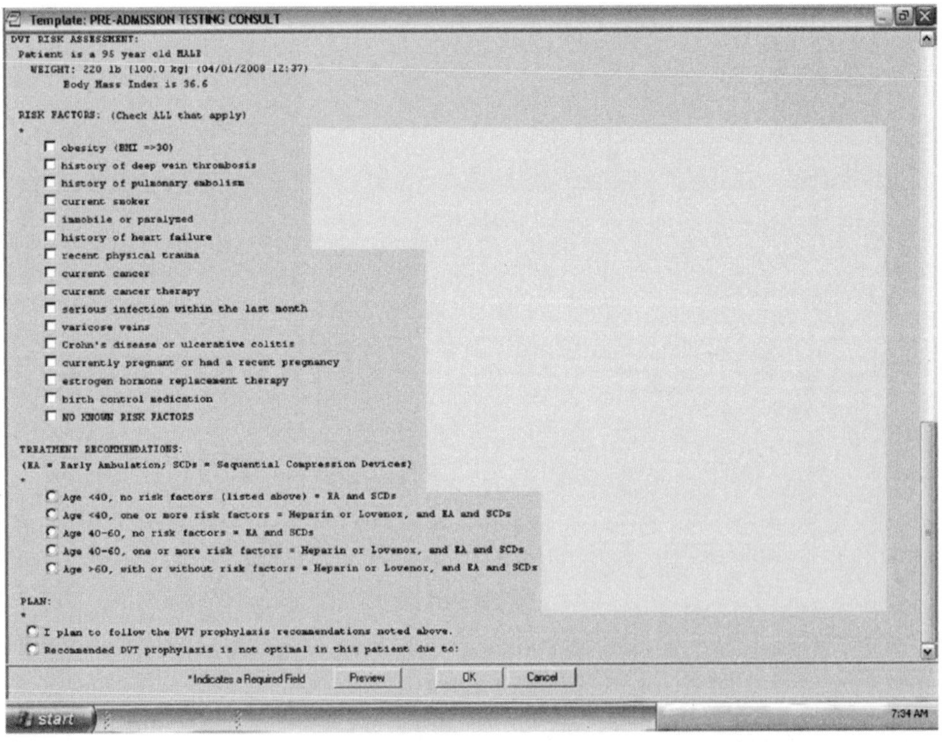

Figure 11-5: Screenshot of the Electronic DVT Risk Assessment (part of the mandatory preadmission testing that must be completed for all patients undergoing surgery)

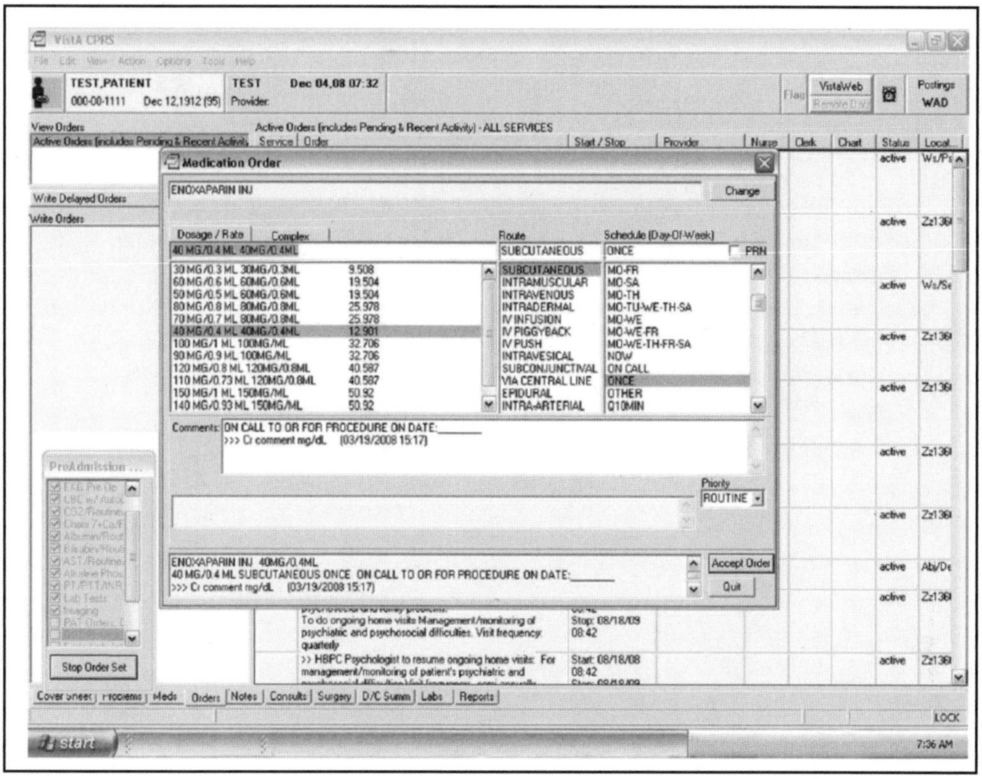

Figure 11-6: Screenshot of Automatic Orders Generated by the DVT Risk Assessment Program Based on the Different Risk Categories

An active problem list records the diagnoses and conditions necessary to treat a patient in the hospital, physician's office, and elsewhere. An active problem list for patients is also a measure for MU of the EHR. However, problem list maintenance is often difficult because updating the list falls outside the clinician's workflow. Galanter et al at the University of Illinois Medical Center developed a CDS tool that suggests adding the appropriate diagnosis to a patient's problem list based on the medications ordered.[20] An example of a levothyroxine order that prompts the addition of goiter or hypothyroidism to the problem list is shown in Figure 11-7. Other medication-diagnosis associations created are shown in Table 11-2.

CDS is not for healthcare providers alone. CDS can inform consumers and patients, as well. Mount Sinai Hospital (New York, NY) observed significant improvement in medication adherence and a reduction in rejection episodes with text messaging reminders for pediatric recipients of liver transplants.[21]

iTriage is another example of a patient-centered CDS technology. Patient self-management is a key component of the PCMH and MU, as well. iTriage is a free iPhone application developed by Healthagen. The app assists with patient self-diagnosis prior to a physician visit. In addition to medical information, iTriage has a 911 function for iPhone users.[22]

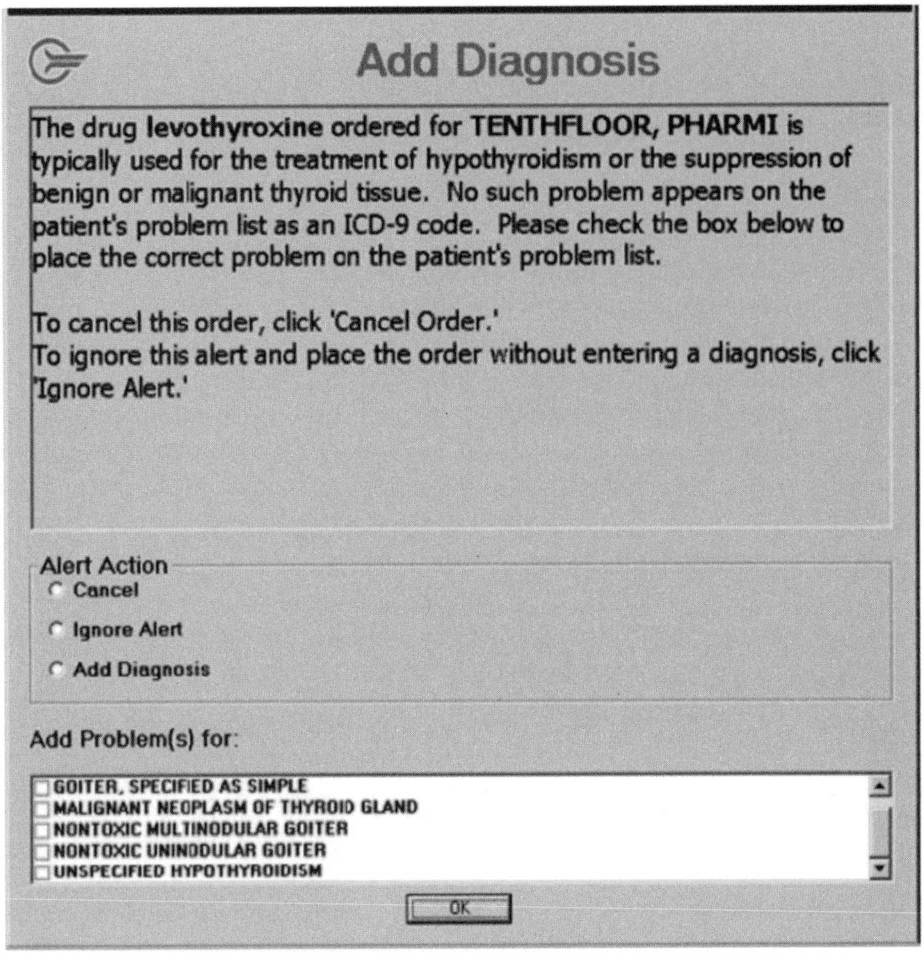

Figure 11-7: Example of a Medication-Diagnosis Link Alert. The alert is for an order of levothyroxine in a test patient.

For examples of CDS interventions that can improve asthma, coronary artery disease, diabetes, heart failure, preventive care, and medication safety, visit the website of the Office of the National Coordinator for Health Information Technology (http://www.healthit.gov/providers-professionals/clinical-decision-support-cds).

Implementing CDS

Some remarkable research has explored why CDS works or does not work. Investigators from the Veterans Health Administration, Regenstrief Institute, and Partners HealthCare System examined provider perceptions of colorectal cancer screening CDS (CRC CDS) at their facilities. They conducted interviews, focus groups, and used direct observation to better understand barriers to adoption of CRC CDS. Six common barriers were described from the primary care providers from all institutions: receiving and documenting exam results from outside the facility, inaccuracy of the CDS, compliance issues, poor usability, lack of coordination between primary care and gastroenterology, and the need to attend to more urgent patient issues.[23]

Target diagnosis group name	All ICD-9 diagnoses in group	Medication triggers
Diabetes mellitus (DM)	Diabetes mellitus (250.00) polycystic ovarian syndrome (256.4)	Exenatide, meglitinides, metformin, pioglitazone, rosiglitazone, *sulfonyluria*
Hypothyroidism	Goiter (240.0) Hypothyroidism (244.9) Multinodular goiter (241.1) Solitary thyroid nodule (241) thyroid cancer (193)	Levothyroxine
Hyperlipidemia, Coronary atherosclerosis	Unspecified hyperlipidemia (272.4) coronary atherosclerosis (414.00)	Niacin, cholestyramine, colesevelam, colestipol, ezetimibe, fenofibrate, gemfibrozil, HMG-CoA reductase inhibitors
Human immunodeficiency virus (HIV)	Human immunodeficiency virus [HIV] disease (042)	Combination medications, fusion inhibitors, nucleoside reverse transcriptase inhibitor, non-nucleoside reverse transcriptase inhibitor, protease inhibitors.
Asthma, chronic obstructive pulmonary disease	Asthma unspecified (493.90) asthma unspecified with exacerbation (493.92) obstructive chronic bronchitis without exacerbation unspecified (491.20) obstructive chronic bronchitis with exacerbation unspecified (491.21)	Fluticasone inhaled, fluticasone/salmeterol inhaled, tiotroprium inhaled
Ischemic stroke, transient ischemic attack (TIA)	Cerebral thrombosis with cerebral infarction (434.01) cerebral embolism with cerebral infarction (434.11) cerebral thrombosis without mention of cerebral infarction (434.00)	Dipyridamole/aspirin (*aggrenox*)

More then one diagnosis could be proposed for each medication and a diagnosis could be associated with more than one medication.

Table 11-2: Target Diagnosis Groups and Medication Triggers Used in the CDS Intervention

A physician reported: "One patient was sent to GI three times for a colonoscopy. Each time they told him he wasn't due. But the reminder keeps coming up. He had a colonoscopy recently, so I don't know why the reminder doesn't turn off."[23]

Kawamoto et al. from Duke University systematically reviewed the literature to determine why some CDS systems succeed while others fail. They identified 22 technical and nontechnical factors in the literature as important determinants of a system's ability to improve clinical practice. Of that number, they found four of the features were significantly correlated with system success, and one feature just over the 0.05 significance level. The four features strongly associated with a CDS's ability to improve clinical practice were decision support provided automatically as part of clinician workflow, decision support delivered at the time and location of decision making, actionable recommendations provided, and computer based.[24]

Bates and Kuperman are two of the nation's thought leaders in CDS and have done some of the seminal and groundbreaking work in CPOE and CDS. See their Ten Commandments for Effective CDS (Table 11-3).[25]

The Institute for Safe Medication Practices (ISMP) has released its Guidelines for Standard Order Sets.[26] While its focus is on medications, many of the guidelines apply to other order items.

The guidelines encompass:

- Format
  - Layout and directions for use
  - Font style and type
  - Prompts for patient information
  - Use of symbols, abbreviations, dose designations, punctuation, and Tall Man Letters[26,27]

Table 11-3: Ten Commandments for Effective Clinical Decision Support[25]

1.	Speed is everything—this is what information system users value most.
2.	Anticipate needs and deliver in real time—deliver information when needed.
3.	Fit into the user's workflow—integrate suggestions with clinical practice.
4.	Little things can make a big difference—improve usability to "do the right thing."
5.	Recognize that physicians will strongly resist stopping— offer alternatives rather than insist on stopping an action.
6.	Changing direction is easier than stopping—changing defaults for dose, route, or frequency of a medication can change behavior.
7.	Simple interventions work best—simplify guidelines by reducing to a single computer screen.
8.	Ask for additional information only when you really need it—the more data elements requested, the less likely a guideline will be implemented.
9.	Monitor impact, get feedback, and respond—if certain reminders are not followed, readjust or eliminate the reminder.
10.	Manage and maintain your knowledge-based systems—both use of information and currency of information should be carefully monitored.

- Content
  - Content development
  - Content of medication orders
- Approval and Maintenance
- Specific Criteria
  - For IV/epidural solutions/medications
  - For electrolytes and compounded products
  - For doses that include fractional amounts
  - For chemotherapy orders
  - For analgesics
  - For pediatric medications dosed according to weight
  - For all medications dosed according to weight
  - For medications intended for patients older than 65 years
  - For paper-based preprinted order sets

On a given project level, an AHRQ-funded study by Das and Eichner found challenges and barriers on the nontechnical, project level:[27]

- The management of the design of clinical decision support interventions takes considerable time and effort.
- Lack of alignment with an organization's overall goals and incentives can affect CDS projects.
- Clinicians do not agree on how prescriptive the CDS application should be.
- Local institutions and providers choose to "customize knowledge."
- Written guidelines are ambiguous and unclear, making it difficult to translate them to computable code.
- Terminology and data exchange standards are still maturing and lack constrained implementation specifications (e.g., the mapping of diagnosis codes used locally at a particular healthcare organization to SNOMED).
- Suboptimal EMR usage by clinicians diminishes the impact of CDS interventions.

For an in-depth guide on how to address very real problems like these in implementing medication CDS, see *Improving Outcomes with Clinical Decision Support: An Implementer's Guide, Second Edition*, published by HIMSS.[9] The guide is the product of a unique collaboration of quality organizations, providers, government agencies, and EHR vendors: Scottsdale Institute, Epic Systems Corporation, Advocate Health Care, Eclipsys Corporation, Memorial Hermann Health System, CPSI, and AHRQ.

The guide includes chapters on optimizing governance structures and management processes, defining outcome improvement opportunities and baselines; setting up interventions in key clinical information systems and for specific targets; deploying CDS interventions to optimize acceptance and value; measuring results and refining the program; and approaching CDS knowledge management systematically.

The guide shares practical pearls such as the CDS Five Rights model. The model espouses five critical success factors for CDS improvement:

1. The right information: evidence-based, suitable to guide action, pertinent to the circumstance.
2. To the right person: considering all members of the care team, including clinicians, patients, and their caretakers.
3. In the right CDS intervention format: such as an alert, order set, or reference information to answer a clinical question.
4. Through the right channel: for example, a clinical information system (CIS) such as an EMR, PHR, or a more general channel such as the Internet or a mobile device.
5. At the right time in workflow: for example, at time of decision/action/need.

ALERT FATIGUE

> When an oil worker told investigators on July 23, 2010 that an alarm to warn of explosive gas on the Transocean rig in the Gulf of Mexico had been intentionally disabled months before, it struck many people as reckless. Reckless, maybe, but not unusual. More recently, the National Transportation Safety Board said that a crash last year on the Washington subway system that killed nine people had happened partly because train dispatchers had been ignoring 9,000 alarms per week. Air traffic controllers, nuclear plant operators, nurses in intensive-care units and others do the same. Mark R. Rosekind, a psychologist who is a member of the National Transportation Safety Board, said the cases have something in common. "The volume of alarms desensitizes people," he said. "They learn to ignore them."[28]

We have all done it. An alert or alarm (read "decision support") goes off and we ignore it. Maybe it is jaywalking against a red walk signal on New Year's Day with no cars in sight. Maybe it is driving your car with the empty fuel icon lit trying to see how far you can drive before stopping at the next gas station.[29] We have all succumbed at one time or other to alert fatigue.

Alert fatigue is a loathsome barrier to CDS adoption and success. When the noise-to-signal ratio becomes unbearable and turns into TMI (too much information), we ignore that annoying alert. Unfortunately, with too many false alarms the one true alarm can be too easily overlooked.

Van der Sijs et al. reviewed the literature on physician response to drug safety alerts. In the seventeen studies they reviewed, drug safety alerts were overridden by clinicians in 49 to 96 percent of cases. The authors recommended that a distinction between appropriate and useful alerts should be made. The alerting system may contain error-producing conditions, such as low specificity, low sensitivity, unclear information content, unnecessary workflow disruptions, and unsafe and inefficient handling. These may result in active failures of the physician, such as ignoring alerts, misinterpretation, and incorrect handling.[30]

At Partners HealthCare, Paterno et al. analyzed 71,350 drug-drug interaction (DDI) alerts, 39,474 of which occurred at a site with non-tiered alerts and 31,876 at a site with tiered alerts. There were three grades of tiered alerts: least serious (Figure 11-8), more serious (Figure 11-9), and most serious (Figure 11-10). Compliance with DDI alerts was higher at the site with tiered DDI alerts compared with the non-tiered site (29 vs. 10 percent, $p = 0.001$). At the tiered site, 100 percent of the most severe alerts were accepted, versus only 34 percent at the non-tiered site; moderately severe alerts were also more likely to be accepted at the tiered site (29 vs. 10 percent). Tiered alerting by severity was associated with higher compliance rates of DDI alerts in the inpatient setting, and lack of tiering was associated with a high override rate of more severe alerts.[31]

In a survey of 5,001 primary care physicians, nearly a third reported missing patient results that led to care delays, which may have been due to information overload from alert notifications, electronic handoffs in care, and poor EHR usability.[32]

George Reynolds, MD, a pediatric intensivist and chief medical informatics officer at Children's Hospital Medical Center in Omaha, Nebraska, remarks, "I don't want alerts to fire at all. I want the order sets to be written well enough that they steer doctors to the right choices." Using a business intelligence application and 300 order sets, he has driven down the rate that CPOE triggers an alert to 6.6 percent of orders. Even with that alert rate, only 22 percent of the alerts result in a physician changing his or her behavior.[33]

CDS technology is not (yet) standardized. What has been coded at one hospital may not work at another hospital even if they have the same EHR vendor. If they have different EHR vendors, the CDS tool will have to be re-created (if the hospital has the staff to help develop it and the EHR vendor is willing).

As an expert panel from the American Medical Informatics Association opined, "Such multiple reinventing-the-wheel processes limit the availability of good CDS tools, as each manufacturer and implementer of such systems struggles to develop the same interventions, or, for lack of time and ability to do so, simply leaves out CDS interventions that could deliver important benefits."[34]

Sittig et al. advocate a national repository for CDS interventions would mitigate the following problems:[35]

- Difficulty translating medical knowledge and guidelines into a form usable by EHRs.
- Technical challenges in developing a standard representation for CDS content that could be shared across sites.

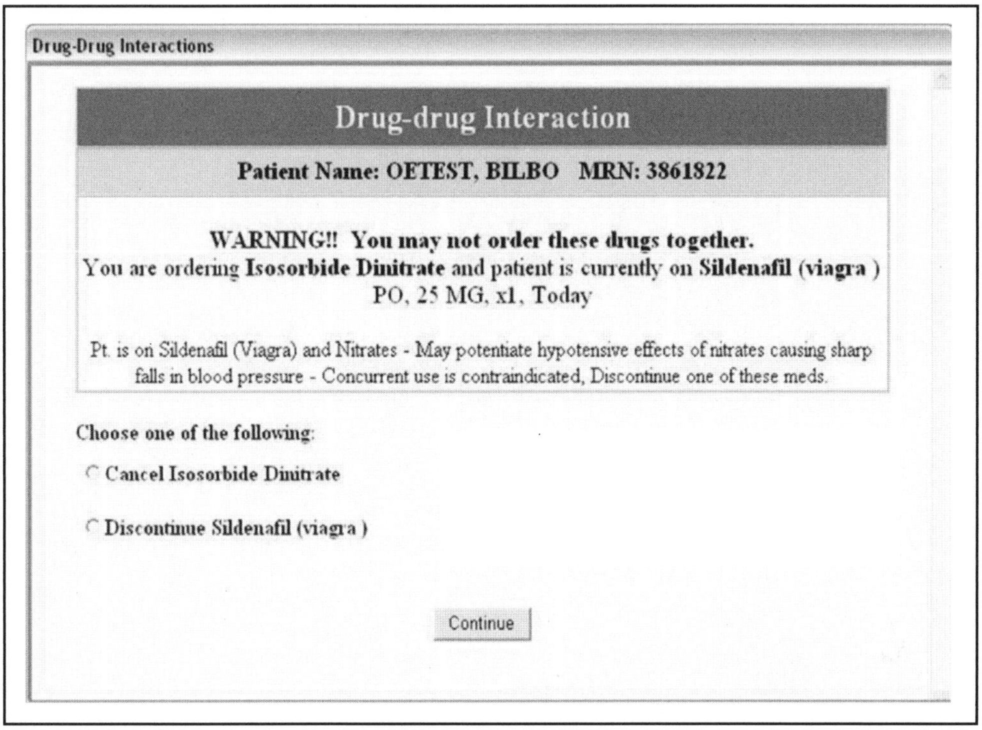

Figure 11-8: Level 1 Alert

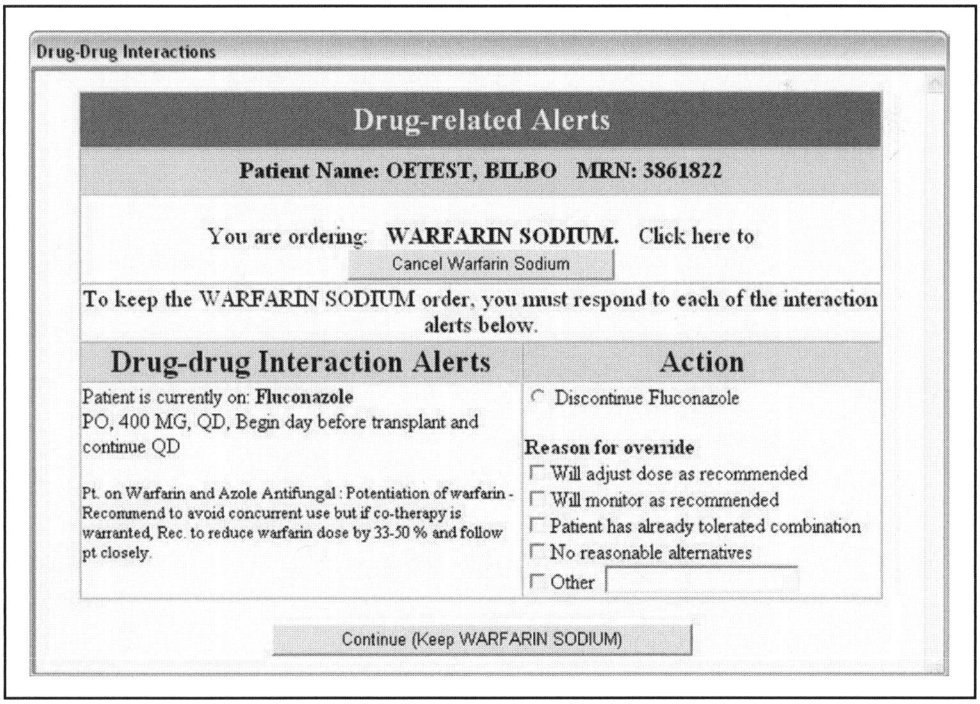

Figure 11-9: Level 2 Alert

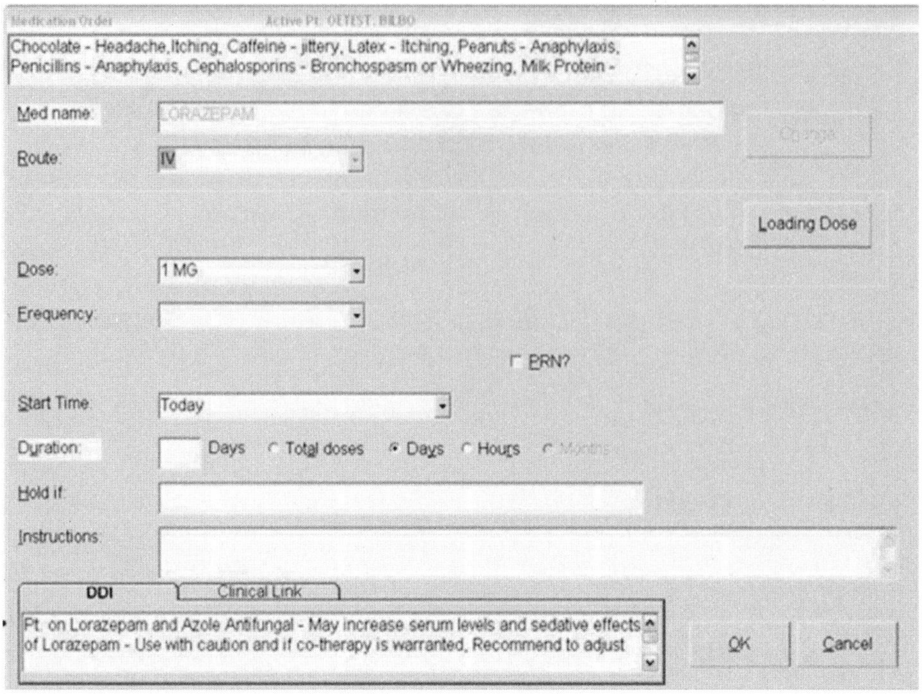

Figure 11-10: Level 3 Alert

- Absence of a central knowledge repository where human readable and executable guideline knowledge can be shared and stored.
- Challenges integrating decision support into clinical workflow and other barriers to IT adoption.
- Limited capabilities for CDS in commercially available EHRs.

They recommend the following preliminary standards for creating such a national repository:

- **Step 1:** Access to high-quality, standardized, syntactically and semantically encoded patient data.
- **Step 2:** A standard for encoded clinical knowledge that is both human and machine readable.
- **Step 3:** A set of standard CDS intervention types (DDI alerts or condition-specific order sets).
- **Step 4:** A set of standard locations within clinicians' electronically enabled clinical workflow at which CDS interventions can be presented to clinicians, and the requisite EMR functionality for the CDS intervention. For example, when selecting a medication from a list, the clinician is told that the current patient has an allergy to a particular medication.
- **Step 5:** A standard method for either requesting patient data in a standard format or having these data automatically sent to an application that is separate from the EMR (perhaps as a service on the Internet, for example).

- **Step 6:** A validated, open-access, CDS knowledge base that contains at least a starter set of standard, high-quality, clinically evaluated CDS interventions that can be downloaded and utilized, or perhaps accessed over the Internet as a service, by any CCHIT–approved EMR system.
- **Step 7:** Agreement on and development of a set of clinical quality measures that can be used to measure and monitor the effectiveness of the CDS interventions previously described.

CMS–certified EHRs and the MU measures provide an opportunity to standardize and require CDS that works. Public comments from an ONC workshop on CDS illustrate how the current national discussion on CDS can guide its future development.[11]

- CDS should support team-based care: New audiences for CDS over time may well be expected to include patients, case managers, and others as new models of team-based, information-driven care emerge to achieve high-value, accessible, affordable care for all Americans.
- A culture of quality improvement is important to effective use of CDS.
- Clinician engagement in CDS planning and implementation is critical to success.
- User adoption depends on implementation of highly usable systems.
- Greater CDS specificity can reduce alert fatigue: Multiple participants noted that the knowledge base for DDIs is such that if you turn on "all" alerts, so many alerts fire that it grinds clinical workflow to a halt. Discussions noted that there is not yet an easy or clear way to identify a subset of highest-value, highest-priority rules that will improve patient safety without impeding workflow. If a provider office or hospital chooses not to turn on all DDI alerts in order to decrease the number of alerts that do not need to be acted on, there is concern that this may lead to increased liability exposure. Discussions noted that it would be helpful to specify the top drug-drug and drug-allergy interactions, as well as the top drug dosing guidelines, for use within CDS in the meaningful use matrix.
- Other fields offer computer interaction principles that can be leveraged, e.g., nuclear power, space aviation.
- Promote collaborations among stakeholders that can support effective use of CDS.
- Including CDS in the definition of meaningful use of EHRs is important.
- MU should allow for variations in CDS techniques, objectives, and localization of goals.
- Specialties and different practice types must not be overlooked.
- Provide effective guidance and best practice examples.
- Incentives and drivers can promote CDS adoption.
- Providing liability protection or advantage may speed CDS adoption.
- Patients have a role to play in CDS.
- Translating guidelines into CDS is complex, so we should be able to leverage collective efforts.
- Opportunities for data standardization.

- Translation of knowledge into codified structures and mechanisms for dissemination of codified knowledge are key to sharing and reuse of CDS interventions.
- CDS and quality need to quickly incorporate evolving evidence.
- Outline specific ideas that stakeholder groups may consider for focused development/action.
- Identify a "short list" of the most important drug-drug, and drug-allergy interactions to support with CDS. This will necessitate the development of a model for rule creation/review/editing.
- Develop a reference of best CDS practices and exemplary implementation sites:
  - Build a library of CDS reference implementations by practice type as a starting point that others could emulate.
  - Develop a "usability checklist" that identifies standard wait times of no longer than X seconds, etc.
  - Collect good practices and exemplars associated with incorporating a computer into the exam room during ambulatory patient visits.
  - Build a national health IT simulation lab, similar to the national driving simulator, to help providers assess the functionality and usability of EHR and CDS systems. Products could be configured to address specific patient scenarios, and users could "test drive" them to assist vendors in improving their products while giving providers information on which systems are the most functional and usable.
  - Develop a vendor-independent certification for "expert implementers of health IT systems"—similar to a Good Housekeeping Seal or Angie's List.
  - Develop an accreditation for guideline developers to ensure that they follow required principles in translating guidelines into codified knowledge and CDS interventions.
  - Develop a robust set of use cases to test the hypothesis that a common data set could service both CDS and quality measurement.
  - Develop a list of CDS intervention types with key parameters as a first step in standardization and sharing of CDS across disparate EHR systems.

Clearly, we have much work to do developing and standardizing CDS to optimize meaningful use of the EHR. Nevertheless, one day effective CDS in health IT will be as ubiquitous as the dashboard in our cars.

SUGGESTED ONLINE RESOURCES

HealthIT.gov. http://www.healthit.gov/providers-professionals/clinical-decision-support-CDS Accessed June 6, 2014.

REFERENCES

1. Barta A, McNeill G, Meli P, et al. ICD-10-CM Primer. *J AHIMA*. 2008;79,5: 64-66. http://library.ahima.org/xpedio/groups/public/documents/ahima/bok1_038084.hcsp?dDocName=bok1_038084. Accessed July 17, 2014.
2. Gawande A. *The Checklist Manifesto: How to Get Things Right*. New York City: Metropolitan Books; 2011.

3. Smith MD. Best care at lower cost: The path to continuously learning health care in America. Institute of Medicine. 2012. http://www.iom.edu/Reports/2012/Best-Care-at-Lower-Cost-The-Path-to-Continuously-Learning-Health-Care-in-America.aspx. Accessed January 26, 2015.

4. Stead WW, Kelly BJ, Kolodner RM. Achievable steps toward building a national health information infrastructure in the United States. *J Am Med Inform Assoc.* 2005;12(2):113–120.

5. Balas EA. Information systems can prevent errors and improve quality. *J Am Med Inform Assoc.* 2001;8(4):398-399.

6. Yarnall KSH, Ostbye T, Krause KM, et al. Family physicians as team leaders: "Time" to share the care. *Preventing Chronic Disease.* 2009;6(2):1-6. www.cdc.gov/pcd/issues/2009/apr/08_0023.htm. Accessed August 2010.

7. McGlynn EA, Asch SM, Adams J, et al. The quality of health care delivered to adults in the United States. *N Engl J Med.* 2003;348:2635-2645.

8. Bright TJ, Wong A, Dhurjati R, et al. Effect of clinical decision-support systems: A systematic review. Bright Et Al. *Ann Int Med.* 2012;3,157:29-43.

9. Osheroff JA, Teich JM, Levick D, et al. *Improving Outcomes with Clinical Decision Support: An Implementer's Guide*, 2nd ed. Chicago: HIMSS; 2012.

10. Types and examples of CDS interventions. HIMSS Resource Library. http://www.himss.org/library/clinical-decision-support/issues?navItemNumber=13240. Accessed July 17, 2014.

11. Office of the National Coordinator for Health Information Technology. Clinical Decision Support Workshop Meeting Summary. August 25-26, 2009. www.hhs.gov/healthit/documents/m20080422/6.2_CDS_recs.html. Accessed August 2010.

12. Mercincavage L, Sherry D, Pan E. Clinical Decision Support Starter Kit. https://www.google.com/url?sa=t&rct=j&q=&esrc=s&source=web&cd=1&cad=rja&uact=8&ved=0CCAQFjAA&url=http%3A%2F%2Fwww.healthit.gov%2Fsites%2Fdefault%2Ffiles%2Fdel-3-7-starter-kit-intro_0.pdf&ei=V9eRU_n6D-HEsAS044CoBQ&usg=AFQjCNHT2jki-x52ef-tHSgAipr9maV47Q&sig2=ntW5x26YuGgyLZpSOp92lA&bvm=bv.68445247,d.cWc. Accessed June 6, 2014.

13. http://whqlibdoc.who.int/publications/2009/9789241598590_eng_Checklist.pdf. Accessed July 17, 2014.

14. Haynes AB, Weiser TG, Berry WR, et al. A surgical safety checklist to reduce morbidity and mortality in a global population. *N Engl J Med.* 2009;360:491-499.

15. Gawande A. *The Checklist Manifesto: How to Get Things Right.* If something so simple can transform intensive care, what else can it do? *The New Yorker*, December 10, 2007. www.newyorker.com/reporting/2007/12/10/071210fa_fact_gawande. Accessed July 17, 2014.

16. Santolin CJ, Boyer LS. Change of care for patients with acute myocardial infarctions through algorithm and standardized physician order sets. *Crit Pathw Cardiol.* 2004;3:79–82.

17. Cimino JJ. Use, usability, usefulness, and impact of an infobutton manager. American Medical Informatics Association Annual Symp Proceedings. *J Am Med Inform Assoc.* 2006:151-155.

18. Bell LM, Grundmeier R, Localio R, et al. Electronic health record based decision support to improve asthma care: A cluster-randomized trial. *Pediatrics.* 2010;125;e770-777. www.pediatrics.org/cgi/content/full/125/4/e770. Accessed August 2010.

19. Novis SJ, Havelka GE, Ostrowski D, et al. Prevention of thromboembolic events in surgical patients through the creation and implementation of a computerized risk assessment program. *J Vasc Surg.* 2010;51:648-654.

20. Galanter WL, Hier DB, Jao C, et al. Computerized physician order entry of medications and clinical decision support can improve problem list documentation compliance. *Int J Med Inform.* 2010;79(5):332-338.

21. Miloh T, Annunziato R, Arnon R, et al. Improved adherence and outcomes for pediatric liver transplant recipients by using text messaging. *Pediatrics.* 2009;124;e844-850.

22. www.itriagehealth.com/. Accessed July 18, 2014.

23. Saleem JJ, Militelo LG, Arbuckle N, et al. Provider perceptions of colorectal cancer screening clinical decision support at three benchmark institutions. AMIA 2009 Symposium Proceedings. AMIA. 2009;558-562.

24. Kawamoto K, Houlihan CS, Balas A, et al. Improving clinical practice using clinical decision support systems: a systematic review of trials to identify features critical to success. *BMJ.* 2005;doi:10.1136/bmj.38398.500764.8F.

25. Bates DW, Kuperman GJ, Wang S, et al. Ten commandments for effective clinical decision support: making the practice of evidence- based medicine a reality. *J Am Med Inform Assoc.* 2003;10:523–530.

26. Institute for Safe Medication Practices Guidelines for Standard Order Sets. http://www.ismp.org/Tools/guidelines/StandardOrderSets.pdf. Accessed July 18, 2014.

27. Das M, Eichner J. Challenges and Barriers to Clinical Decision Support (CDS) Design and Implementation Experienced in the Agency for Healthcare Research and Quality CDS Demonstrations (Prepared for the AHRQ National Resource Center for Health Information Technology under Contract No. 290-04-0016.) AHRQ Publication No. 10-0064-EF. Rockville, MD: Agency for Healthcare Research and Quality. March 2010.

28. Wald ML. For no signs of trouble, Kill the alarm. *New York Times.* July 31, 2010.

29. The Dealership, Seinfeld episode January 8, 1998. www.seinfeldscripts.com/TheDealership.htm. Accessed July 18, 2014.

30. Van der Sijs H, Aarts J, Berg M, et al. Overriding of drug safety alerts in computerized physician order entry. *J Am Med Inform Assoc.* 2006;13:138–147. DOI 10.1197/. M1809.

31. Paterno M, Maviglia S, Gorman P, et al. Tiering drug–drug interaction alerts by severity increases compliance rates. *J Am Med Inform Assoc.* 2009;16:40-46. DOI 10.1197/jamia.M2808.

32. Singh H, Spitzmueller C, Petersen NJ, et al. Information overload and missed test results in electronic health record–based settings. *JAMA Intern Med.* 2013;173:702-704. www.jamainternalmed.com.

33. Avoiding alert fatigue. *Health Data Management Magazine.* October 1, 2009. http://www.healthdatamanagement.com/issues/2009_71/-39039-1.html. Accessed July 18, 2014.

34. Osheroff JA, Teich JM, Middleton BF, et al. A roadmap for national action on clinical support *J Am Med Inform Assoc.* 2007;14(2):141-145. Epub 2007 Jan 9.

35. Sittig DF, Wright A, Ash JS, et al. A set of preliminary standards recommended for achieving a national repository of clinical decision support interventions. *J Am Med Inform Assoc.* 2009 Symposium Proceedings. 2009;614-618.

CHAPTER 12

E-Measures

Erika Abramson, MD, MS, and Rainu Kaushal, MD, MPH

INTRODUCTION

Performance measurement is a critical strategy for improving the quality of healthcare in the United States. Performance measurement is the process of systematically collecting, analyzing, and reporting information about the performance of a person, organization, or system. It allows baseline performance to be assessed, the response to policies and initiatives monitored, and information around performance to be disseminated to key stakeholders. While the concept may seem simple, performance measurement in healthcare is quite challenging. In this chapter, we will explore the key concepts behind performance measurement in healthcare, including the purpose of measurement, the role of health IT in facilitating measurement, national priorities for measurement, challenges, and future directions.

WHY DO WE NEED PERFORMANCE MEASUREMENT IN HEALTHCARE?

Over the past few decades, several landmark reports issued by the Institute of Medicine (IOM) have highlighted significant gaps in the safety and quality of healthcare delivered in the United States. The 1999 IOM report, "To Err is Human," estimated that 44,000 to 98,000 patients are harmed each year as a result of medical errors.[1] Recent estimates around patient harm are much higher.[2] A follow-up IOM report, "Crossing the Quality Chasm: A New Health System for the 21st Century," called for a sweeping reform of our health system due to the lack of consistent, high-quality care being delivered.[3]

The rising costs of healthcare are also of great concern. Although the pace at which costs are rising has slowed over the past few years, as of 2012, health expenditures accounted for 17.9 percent of the U.S. gross domestic product—well above that of any other nation.[4] Despite these costs, the United States generally performs lower than other developed nations on most indicators of quality.[5]

Performance measurement provides standards against which the quality of healthcare can be evaluated and thus plays a key role in efforts to improve healthcare delivery.

It is an essential tool in the Shewhart cycle, which is a model of continuous quality improvement widely used in healthcare.[6] The model consists of four distinct stages:

1. **Plan:** identify opportunities for improvement
2. **Do:** implement a change
3. **Study:** measure the outcome
4. **Act:** follow up with another action

This process gets repeated to achieve the prioritized outcomes.

Information generated by performance measurement can be used by a variety of stakeholders. For providers and organizations, it provides a way of comparing the quality of care actually being delivered to recognized standards or organizational goals. In this way, successes can be continued and opportunities for improvement identified. It can provide information to help guide consumers in their choice of where to receive care. It can also help payers monitor the quality of care provided and drive reimbursement models. Lastly, it can be used to shape public policy by identifying areas on which to focus efforts, such as care for patients with certain conditions receiving suboptimal care, or for accreditation and credentialing purposes.

TYPES OF PERFORMANCE MEASURES

There are multiple types of performance measures. One framework for classifying performance measures, developed by the National Quality Measures Clearinghouse, broadly separates *healthcare delivery measures*, used to measure the performance of individual providers, organizations, or health plans, from *population health measures*, which are applied across a specified geographic distribution of patients.[7] Healthcare delivery measures and population health measures can in turn be divided into three subgroups:

1. Quality measures
2. Related measures (such as utilization and cost)
3. Efficiency measures

This chapter will focus on clinical quality measures, which are the type performance measurement most commonly utilized in healthcare.

There are five types of clinical quality performance measures:

1. Process measures
2. Outcome measures
3. Access measures
4. Patient experience measures
5. Structural measures

Each of these will be discussed in turn.

Process measures assess whether a given activity was performed and are often structured around evidence-based guidelines. Examples include "percentage of eligible patients who received a mammogram" or "percentage of adolescents who received human papilloma virus vaccination according to the recommended immunization schedule." Process measures do not directly measure patient outcomes. Rather, they measure processes believed to be associated with positive patient outcomes. Thus, the best process measures are those with the strongest link to patient outcomes.

Outcome measures, in contrast, measure actual results of care. As a result, there has been an increasing push to focus on these types of performance measures. Examples of outcome measures include "percentage of patients with a surgical site infection within 30 days of surgery" or "percentage of patients readmitted within 30 days following hospital discharge."

Access measures assess accurate and timely attainment of care by patients. An example of an access measure is "the percentage of patients ages 5 to 18 years within a health plan that had a well-child visit with their primary care provider within the past 12 months." These types of performance measures are particularly helpful in identifying areas of unmet needs and disparities in the ability to receive care.

Patient experience measures aim to evaluate the patient's perspective on his or her own care. An example of a patient experience measure is "the percentage of adult inpatients that report their doctor talked to them with sensitivity." One common source of patient experience measurement data is the Consumer Assessment of Providers and Healthcare Systems (CAPHS) surveys. These surveys ask patients to report on multiple aspects of their experiences and are available for a wide range of settings, including the ambulatory setting, hospitals, nursing homes, home health, and in-center hemodialysis. The CAPHS program is funded by AHRQ. Of note, there is controversy over how patient reports of healthcare experience correlate with quality of care received.[8] Nonetheless, they remain an important type of performance measurement.

Lastly, structural measures focus on the conditions in which patients receive care from providers. They are useful sources of information on staffing, volumes, or procedures, and the capabilities of practices or healthcare organizations. An example includes "the percentage of providers in a given health plan that have adopted an electronic prescribing system" for ordering of medications.

HOW IS PERFORMANCE MEASUREMENT DONE?

Performance measurement has traditionally relied on analysis of administrative data, particularly claims data, or analysis of data obtained from manual chart review. Each of these methods is problematic. Administrative claims data are widely available and generally standardized. However, claims data lack the detail of clinical data and can lag behind clinical data by as much as one year.[9] Manual chart reviews allow clinical data to drive measurement performance. This results in more timely and clinically relevant information underlying performance measures. However, manual chart reviews are exceedingly labor intensive and time consuming.

Electronic measures (e-measures) are performance measures captured electronically. E-measures have tremendous potential for reducing the work needed to generate performance data. At the same time, it is hoped that use of e-measures will increase the accuracy, timeliness, and precision of performance measurement, as well as the use of performance measurement on a wide scale.

POLICY INITIATIVES IMPACTING PERFORMANCE MEASUREMENT

Unprecedented federal and state policies are incentivizing the adoption and use of health IT in the United States. Through the Health Information Technology for Economic and Clinical Health (HITECH) Act, $20 billion was invested to advance this nation's health IT infrastructure, largely by promoting the adoption and MU of EHRs by hospitals and providers. The result has been a tremendous increase in EHR adoption. As of 2013, nearly 80 percent of physicians had adopted an EHR and 87 percent of all hospitals had received at least one incentive payment for MU of an EHR.[10,11]

To receive incentive payments for EHR adoption and use, hospitals and providers must fulfill a series of requirements demonstrating that they are meaningful users of the EHR system. An important focus in the second set of requirements, known as Stage 2 MU, has been reporting on clinical quality measures.[12] In this way, widespread adoption and use of EHRs has created tremendous opportunity to advance use of e-measures on a large scale.

SETTING THE NATIONAL MEASUREMENT AGENDA

A key organization in setting the national measurement agenda is the National Quality Forum (NQF). More than 500 performance measures have been endorsed by NQF. While many of these have been paper based, the U.S. Department of Health and Human Services (DHHS) requested that the NQF convene stakeholders to develop e-measures for many of these traditionally paper-based measures. Their recommendations helped inform the clinical quality measures chosen as part of the EHR Incentive Program.[13]

NQF uses six criteria to assess whether a measure should be endorsed. For a measure to be endorsed, it must focus on a priority area, be useable and relevant, be valid and reliable, and be feasible to collect without undue burden.[14] Priority areas identified by NQF are:

1. Patient and family engagement
2. Care coordination
3. Safety
4. Population health
5. Overuse
6. Palliative and end-of-life care

Of note, NQF has increasingly focused on endorsing outcome measures. As of 2005, NQF had endorsed 90 outcome measures. By 2010, 192 outcome measures were endorsed.[9]

CHALLENGES TO MEASUREMENT IN HEALTHCARE

Although many performance measures have been proposed by NQF, very few are being widely utilized.[15] Reports generated from performance measurement are often slow to reach providers and organizations, limiting their usefulness in guiding improvement efforts. Moreover, even when publically available and read by patients, patients are generally not using them to inform their decision making about healthcare.[16]

Why does performance measurement remain so challenging, in spite of the surge in health IT adoption and use? First, there are many potential uses for performance measurement, including quality improvement, payment reform, accreditation, certification, and credentialing. As a result, there is a lack of consensus among stakeholders as to what should be measured and prioritized.

Additionally, given the potential of performance measurement to benefit a variety of different stakeholders, it is unclear who should fund performance measurement efforts.

Furthermore, specifications for reporting measures often vary between quality improvement organizations, even for the same condition. For example, Get With The Guidelines is a hospital-based quality improvement program launched by the American Heart Association designed to improve care for stroke patients by promoting standardized care based on current evidence-based guidelines. The measures for Get With The Guidelines, however, do not precisely match measures collected as part of The Joint Commission's Comprehensive Stroke Certification Program or clinical quality measures related to stroke that are part of the EHR Incentive Program, even though the common goal of all three programs is to standardize and improve care for hospitalized stroke patients. Interestingly, a research study found that Get With The Guidelines recognition was a more robust identifier of hospitals with better performance in caring for stroke patients.[17] Thus, differing measures may very well lead to differing levels of care provided to patients.

Technology limitations are also an important challenge. Complicated algorithms are required to extract performance measures. Many EHRs were not designed with this capability; rather their design was focused on optimizing documentation of episodic healthcare encounters.[9] Today, providers and organizations often use workarounds to generate performance reports to fulfill MU requirements. Without incentives, it remains unclear whether improving the performance measurement capabilities of EHRs will be prioritized by EHR vendors.

There is also concern about the validity and reliability of data captured electronically from EHRs for the purposes of performance measurement. A recent review of quality measure data captured from EHRs found a wide range of variability in the reliability and validity of data captured.[18] Particularly problematic was data derived from problem lists and medication lists.

How providers document data strongly influences the ultimate quality and completeness of data captured for performance measurement. Data capture is easiest from structured fields. Many EHRs have extensive "check box" templates that providers can use for documentation purposes. These structured data are extracted and aggregated for the purposes of performance measurement. Many providers, however, still place a large amount of clinical data in unstructured fields. These data are typically not recognized by standard EHR software used for generating performance measurement information, leading to undercounting of patients eligible for a particular service or for care actually provided during a healthcare encounter.[19] It is also possible that providers may receive credit for doing tasks that were not performed by simply clicking through required boxes to complete a template or meet regulatory requirements. This would lead to overestimation of performance.

FUTURE DIRECTIONS FOR E-MEASUREMENT

There are many ways in which the field of e-measurement can be advanced to help achieve the ultimate goal of improving the quality, safety, and delivery of healthcare.

First, many of the technology and data capture issues previously discussed must be better addressed. This includes making data extraction from EHRs easier and incorporating capture of both unstructured and structured data for the purposes of performance measurement.

Second, it is critical that there is alignment across quality improvement organizations related to performance measures so that quality measures reflect care delivery, result in improved patient outcomes, fit in with natural provider workflow, and minimize reporting burden. Organizations such as the Healthcare Information and Management Systems Society (HIMSS), which is a powerful global, not-for profit organization whose mission is to improve health through use of IT, have advocated for such.[20] Requiring that clinical quality measures for all payers and for programs such as the EHR Incentive Program be endorsed by an organization such as the NQF may help in this regard.

Third, performance measurement generally fails to address the fact that patient care is often fragmented across providers and organizations. Quality measures based on episodes of care, rather than performance measurement focused at the individual provider level, would be more patient-centric but are only in the very early stages of development.[9] To utilize episode-based quality measures, local, regional, and national health information exchange (HIE) capabilities will have to be better developed to facilitate electronic sharing of health information. Strengthening HIE is a national priority, as evidenced through requirements under the EHR Incentive Program, as well as the millions of dollars awarded through the State Health Information Exchange Cooperative Agreement Program to help states build their HIE infrastructure.[12,21]

Fourth, information dissemination must be improved. Rather than providing quarterly or annual reports about performance to providers and organizations, real-time dashboards would enable performance measurement to impact care delivery in a much more timely way. In addition, performance measurement information that gets disseminated to patients must be easily understandable and useful in informing healthcare decisions. A 2012 survey found that of nearly 2,000 adults in the United States, only 10 percent viewed available electronic health information at least once a month.[22] In addition, there must be an ongoing focus on endorsing outcome measures rather than process measures, which may not accurately reflect the changes we are trying to achieve.

Lastly, there needs to be additional research in this field. This includes research on the type of information that will be valuable to consumers to help drive their healthcare decisions, ongoing research on use of e-measures and the impact these measures have on healthcare outcomes, and better understanding of variations in data validity and reliability derived from EHRs.

USEFUL RESOURCES

- AHRQ Quality Indicators. http://www.qualityindicators.ahrq.gov/. Accessed November 17, 2014.

- EHR Incentive Programs. http://www.cms.gov/Regulations-and-Guidance/Legislation/EHRIncentivePrograms/index.html?redirect=/ehrincentiveprograms/. Accessed November 17, 2014.
- National Quality Forum. http://www.qualityforum.org/Home.aspx. Accessed November 17, 2014.
- National Quality Measures Clearinghouse. http://www.qualitymeasures.ahrq.gov/. Accessed November 17, 2014.

REFERENCES

1. Kohn LT, Corrigan J, Donaldson MS, Institute of Medicine. Committee on Quality of Health Care in America. To err is human: Building a safer health system. Washington, DC: The National Academies Press; 2000. xxi, 287.
2. James JT. A new, evidence-based estimate of patient harms associated with hospital care. *J Patient Saf.* 2013;9(3):122-8. Epub 2013/07/19.
3. Committee on Quality of Health Care in America. Institute of Medicine. Crossing the quality chasm: A new health system for the 21st century. Washington, DC: National Academy of Sciences, 2001.
4. Health expenditure, total (% of GDP). The World Bank. May 28, 2014. http://data.worldbank.org/indicator/SH.XPD.TOTL.ZS. Accessed November 16, 2014.
5. Davis K, Stremikis K. The Commonwealth Fund. Mirror Mirror on the wall: How the performance of the U.S. health care system compares internationally. 2010 Update.
6. Best M, Neuhauser D, Shewhart WA. 1924, and the Hawthorne factory. *Qual Saf Health Care.* 2006;15(2):142-143. Epub 2006.
7. National Quality Measures Clearingouse. Domain Framework and Inclusions Criteria. Rockville, MD: Agency for Healthcare Research and Quality; May 30, 2014. http://www.qualitymeasures.ahrq.gov/about/domain-framework.aspx. Accessed November 16, 2014.
8. Manary MP, Boulding W, Staelin R, et al. The patient experience and health outcomes. *New Engl J Med.* 2013;368(3):201-203. Epub 2012/12/28.
9. Anderson KM, Marsh CA, Flemming AC, et al. Quality Measurement Enabled by Health IT: Overview, Possibilities, and Challenges. Rockville, MD: Agency for Healthcare Research and Quality; July 2012. Report No.: 12-0061-EF Contract No.: Prepared by Booz Allen Hamilton, under Contract No. HHSA290200900024I.
10. Hsiao C-J. Use and characteristics of electronic health record systems among office-based physician practices: United States, 2001–2013. Hyattsville, MD: National Center for Health Statistics, 2014 Contract No.: NCHS data brief 143.
11. Mathematica Policy Research, Harvard School of Public Health, and Robert Wood Johnson Foundation. Health information technology in the United States - 2013: Better Information Systems for Better Care; 2013.
12. Health Information Technology. Standards, Implementation Specifications, and Certification Criteria for Electronic Health Record Technology. 2014 Ed. Revisions to the Permanent Certification Program for Health Information Technology. 2012.
13. National Quality Forum. Measuring performance: Electronic Quality Measures (eMeasures). Washington D.C.: National Quality Forum; 2012. http://www.qualityforum.org/Projects/e-g/eMeasures/Electronic_Quality_Measures.aspx? Accessed November 2014.
14. National Quality Forum. ABCs of Measurement. National Quality Forum. May 30 2014. http://www.qualityforum.org/measuring_performance/abcs_of_measurement.aspx. Accessed November 16, 2014.

15. Roski J, McClellan M. Measuring health care performance now, not tomorrow: Essential steps to support effective health reform. *Health Aff* (Millwood). 2011;30(4):682-689. Epub 2011/04/08.

16. Bardach HJ, Dudley RA. Users of public reports of hospital quality: Who, what, why and how? Rockville, MD: Agency for Healthcare Research and Quality. December 2011.

17. Fonarow GC, Liang L, Smith EE, et al. Comparison of performance achievement award recognition with primary stroke center certification for acute ischemic stroke care. *J Am Heart Assoc.* 2013;2(5):e000451. Epub 2013/10/16.

18. Chan KS, Fowles JB, Weiner JP. Review: electronic health records and the reliability and validity of quality measures: a review of the literature. *Med Care Res Rev.* 2010;67(5):503-527. Epub 2010/02/13.

19. Parsons A, McCullough C, Wang J, et al. Validity of electronic health record-derived quality measurement for performance monitoring. *J Am Med Inform Assoc.* 2012;19(4):604-609. Epub 2012/01/18.

20. Fields W. Response, Request for Information on the Use of Clinical Quality Measures Reported Under the Physician Quality Reporting System, the Electronic Health Record Incentive Program, and Other Reporting Programs. Chicago: Healthcare Information and Management Systems Society, 2013.

21. State Health Information Exchange. Office of the National Coordinator for Health Information Technology. 2014. http://www.healthit.gov/policy-researchers-implementers/state-health-information-exchange. Accessed November 16, 2014.

22. Bechtel C. Making IT meaningful: How consumers value and trust health IT. June 5, 2014. http://www.nationalpartnership.org/research-library/health-care/HIT/making-it-meaningful-audio-slides.pdf. Accessed November 16, 2014.

CHAPTER 13

Clinical and Business Intelligence

Ray Hess, MSA, RRT, FHIMSS

WHAT IS BUSINESS INTELLIGENCE?

Business intelligence (BI) is a term that is used regularly in the healthcare industry. Most pundits assert that it is vital for effectively managing today's complex healthcare environment. However, many people have a hard time defining what BI is and certainly cannot recall its key elements. This chapter will present a simple overview of BI, starting with defining the term and moving on to reviewing key elements and a simple strategy for using BI. Once the reader has a basic framework for understanding this key element, the chapter will delve into the merging of clinical data into BI. Finally, we discuss some advanced topics on BI. Know that this chapter only skims the surface of the topic; there are multiple referenced resources the reader should review if a deeper understanding is desired.

Here are several definitions of BI:

Business intelligence is a set of theories, methodologies, architectures, and technologies that transform raw data into meaningful and useful information for business purposes. BI can handle enormous amounts of unstructured data to help identify, develop, and otherwise create new opportunities. BI, in simple words, makes interpreting voluminous data friendly. Making use of new opportunities and implementing an effective strategy can provide a competitive market advantage and long-term stability.[1]

Business intelligence is an umbrella term that includes the applications, infrastructure and tools, and best practices that enable access to and analysis of information to improve and optimize decisions and performance.[2]

Business intelligence software (BI software) is software that turns raw data into information that businesses can use to create growth. BI software helps users to understand the strengths and weaknesses in their organizations by showing them the implications and meanings in their data. This information can be used to improve every aspect of a businsess.[3]

At first glance these definitions might not appear to answer the question, what is business intelligence? However, there are several key concepts to be found in these definitions.

- BI is a set of processes, software, or techniques
- BI takes data and seeks to turn it into information that results in intelligence
- BI seeks to give understanding to the user
- BI exists to help manage and improve the functioning of the business
- BI can show the user opportunities that otherwise may have been missed

Healthcare BI is the tool that allows the user to know about the operations of the healthcare system. It is analogous to a patient's vital signs and test results. They tell the doctor about the patient and provide direction toward the proper treatment. BI tells the administrator about the healthcare system and provides direction for how to manage the organization.

WHY IS BUSINESS INTELLIGENCE IMPORTANT?

This book is filled with chapters showing the complexity of today's healthcare environment. Each chapter presents another in an ongoing list of challenges that faces the current day administrator. BI is the tool that allows leaders to know as accurately as possible how things are going, the performance of their system, the issues that need to be addressed, and opportunities that exist. Without BI, the executive is literally flying blind.

BI provides key and timely information needed to make wise decisions. Because BI is clearly so important, why is there confusion and at times a lack of consistency in implementing BI in the healthcare environment? The answer lies in the complexity of creating a solid and effective BI infrastructure. BI has many components, each of which must be understood, implemented, and managed. Getting good BI takes work, time, and resources. There is a commitment that needs to be made to achieve successful results.

KEY ELEMENTS OF BUSINESS INTELLIGENCE

Here is a list of elements that make up BI. The reader will see that these elements often build or depend on one another. This list is not exhaustive, but it will present some of the core items needed to understand BI and to create a strong BI system.

Data Collection

Data collection is at the foundation of any and every BI process. It is the most basic element of BI and the effectiveness of any BI program rests on the quality of the data involved. Data represent each element saved in the computer systems from every activity that occurs. It can be data about the patient, such as test result values. It can represent demographics about the patient or the clinicians providing care to the patient, such as address or age. It can be charges, costs, or time values. Data can be anything and data are everything that is captured by the systems.

Many important pieces of data historically were not captured in systems. A key to BI is understanding what data exist electronically and what data need to be captured and put into systems for future use. Without data, there can be no knowledge of what is going on in a health system. Without the data first being collected into a system, there cannot be any meaningful evaluation or reporting. The first challenge in any BI effort is discovering the state of the healthcare institution's data. BI professionals cannot stop with knowing what data exists but must discover what data are needed to effectively monitor and report on the healthcare system. Over time, BI success depends on collecting key data into a system where it can be used.

Data Governance

Because data are the foundation for producing information, there must be a structure in place to evaluate and manage data. That structure is called data governance. The Data Governance Institute defines data governance this way:

> "Data Governance is a system of decision rights and accountabilities for information-related processes, executed according to agreed-upon models which describe who can take what actions with what information, and when, under what circumstances, using what methods."[4]

Data governance represents the rules and definitions that let everyone know how to interact with data. There are many aspects of data governance that are beyond the scope of this chapter. These include data definitions, data quality, data integrity, data completeness, how the data can be used and by whom. Readers are encouraged to go to the Data Governance Institute website to obtain further information on data governance.

For the purposes of this discussion, key data governance issues revolve around making sure that vital pieces of data are consistently captured using the same definition or process. A simple example is the collection of a patient's pain level. Free text inputs like "moderate" or "slight" are much harder to work with and evaluate than a set numeric pain scale of "1" to "10" with definitions of when to use each number. Having a number over the free text entry allows for a greater ability to collate and track the effectiveness of pain interventions. This is just one simple example of how data governance sets the rules and patterns for capturing usable data. Data governance is an important function that must receive regular attention for BI output to be trustworthy.

Creating a Data Warehouse

Data are created and stored in operational systems throughout the healthcare environment. Most of these systems are designed to optimize the function for which they were designed (an EMR or a cardiology system) and are not designed to provide data for analysis and reporting. A data warehouse is a database system that is designed specifically to hold and manage data for use in BI activities. The data are harvested from the source systems using a process called ETL: extract, transform, and load. Once in the data warehouse, the data can be validated, standardized, and collated for use. There are many resources on data warehousing on the web. The Data Warehouse Institute[5] is one such resource that can provide more information on data warehousing.

Reporting

The creation of reports is one of the oldest and most common BI activities. Data need to be consolidated, filtered, and placed into an easily readable format before they can be used. Reports do just that. The report writer creates a query to pull the appropriate data and then places those data in a report shell to make it easy for people to read and

American Hospital
Inpatient Volume by DRG
For the Month of: May 2014

DRG	Description	Volume	Days	Length	Mortality
795	Normal newborn	144	291	2.0	0
775	Vaginal delivery w/o complicating diagnoses	119	238	2.0	0
871	Septicemia or severe sepsis w/o MV 96+ hours w MCC	83	450	5.4	4
872	Septicemia or severe sepsis w/o MV 96+ hours w/o MCC	39	185	4.7	2
392	Esophagitis, gastroent & misc digest disorders w/o MCC	32	132	4.1	1
603	Cellulitis w/o MCC	31	103	3.3	0
794	Neonate w other significant problems	31	304	9.8	0
774	Vaginal delivery w complicating diagnoses	31	75	2.4	0
470	Major joint replacement or reattachment of lower extremity w/o	26	75	2.9	0
765	Cesarean section w CC/MCC	25	73	2.9	0
766	Cesarean section w/o CC/MCC	24	58	2.4	0
793	Full term neonate w major problems	17	67	3.9	0
291	Heart failure & shock w MCC	15	72	4.8	2
683	Renal failure w CC	15	68	4.5	1
189	Pulmonary edema & respiratory failure	13	47	3.6	1
292	Heart failure & shock w CC	12	55	4.6	1
308	Cardiac arrhythmia & conduction disorders w MCC	12	41	3.4	1
310	Cardiac arrhythmia & conduction disorders w/o CC/MCC	12	32	2.7	0
309	Cardiac arrhythmia & conduction disorders w CC	11	37	3.4	0
690	Kidney & urinary tract infections w/o MCC	11	35	3.2	0
287	Circulatory disorders except AMI, w card cath w/o MCC	10	43	4.3	0
682	Renal failure w MCC	10	42	4.2	1
419	Laparoscopic cholecystectomy w/o c.d.e. w/o CC/MCC	9	13	1.4	0
331	Major small & large bowel procedures w/o CC/MCC	9	39	4.3	0
343	Appendectomy w/o complicated principal diag w/o CC/MCC	9	21	2.3	0
247	Perc cardiovasc proc w drug-eluting stent w/o MCC	9	22	2.4	0
792	Prematurity w/o major problems	9	78	8.7	0
176	Pulmonary embolism w/o MCC	9	37	4.1	0
378	G.I. hemorrhage w CC	8	35	4.4	1

Figure 13-1: Basic DRG Report

understand. There are many types of reports, but the most basic ones show tabular or graphic representations of summarized data (see Figure 13-1).

Figure 13-1 shows a basic report of inpatient activity for a given month. The report shows the patients summarized by the diagnosis-related group (DRG)–based diagnosis and gives details like volume of patients, length of stay, and mortality. Depending on the reason for the report, it can be enhanced by adding charges, cost, and reimbursement. If DRGs are too granular, the report (see Figure 13-2) can be changed to show DRG groupings by services such as cardiology, surgery, etc. These data are displayed in a summary report that explodes into DRG detail for each service line. If more detail is needed, a report can be created (Figure 13-3) showing detail at a patient level.

Reports are powerful tools if they are created properly and if the underlying data are solid. They are the basis for most BI activity. Reports are used in all aspects of management. In some places, BI is only reporting. While reporting always needs to be a part of any functional BI structure, it should not be the only tool available to the executive.

Dashboards

Many busy leaders do not have time to wade through complex reports trying to understand what is happening in their institution. They want something that quickly provides

American Hospital
Inpatient Volume by Service Line
For the Month of: May 2014

Service Line	DRG	Description	Volume	Days	Length of Stay	Mortality
CARDIAC SURGERY	[redacted]	[redacted]	15	67	4.5	1
DERMATOLOGY	[redacted]	[redacted]	36	81	2.3	0
ENDOCRINOLOGY	[redacted]	[redacted]	23	89	3.9	1
GASTROENTEROLOGY	[redacted]	[redacted]	91	372	4.1	2
GENERAL MEDICINE	[redacted]	[redacted]	145	599	4.1	4
GENERAL SURGERY	[redacted]	[redacted]	24	68	2.8	0
GI SURGERY	[redacted]	[redacted]	59	183	3.1	0
GYNECOLOGY	[redacted]	[redacted]	6	23	3.8	0
HEMATOLOGY	[redacted]	[redacted]	10	48	4.8	1
INTERVENTIONAL CARDIOLOGY	[redacted]	[redacted]	32	79	2.5	1
MEDICAL CARDIOLOGY	[redacted]	[redacted]	103	483	4.7	3
NEONATOLOGY	[redacted]	[redacted]	67	532	7.9	2
NEPHROLOGY/UROLOGY	[redacted]	[redacted]	63	244	3.9	1
NEUROLOGY	[redacted]	[redacted]	46	135	2.9	0
NEUROSURGERY	[redacted]	[redacted]	7	45	6.4	0
NORMAL NEWBORN	[redacted]	[redacted]	144	293	2.0	0
OBSTETRICS-DEL	[redacted]	[redacted]	204	408	2.0	0
OBSTETRICS-NO DEL	[redacted]	[redacted]	13	39	3.0	0
ONCOLOGY MEDICAL	[redacted]	[redacted]	12	68	5.7	2
ONCOLOGY SURGICAL	[redacted]	[redacted]	4	21	5.3	0
OPHTHALMOLOGY	[redacted]	[redacted]	0	0	0.0	0
ORTHO MEDICAL	[redacted]	[redacted]	13	38	2.9	0
ORTHO SURGICAL	[redacted]	[redacted]	63	234	3.7	0
OTHER	[redacted]	[redacted]	9	39	4.3	0
OTOLARYNGOLOGY	[redacted]	[redacted]	13	38	2.9	0
PLASTIC SURGERY	[redacted]	[redacted]	7	16	2.3	0
PSYCHIATRY	[redacted]	[redacted]	2	8	4.0	0
PULMONARY MEDICINE	[redacted]	[redacted]	71	352	5.0	4
SPINE	[redacted]	[redacted]	5	29	5.8	0
SUBSTANCE ABUSE	[redacted]	[redacted]	1	8	8.0	0
THORACIC SURGERY	[redacted]	[redacted]	7	37	5.3	1
TRACHEOSTOMY	[redacted]	[redacted]	3	15	5.0	1
TRAUMA/INJURIES	[redacted]	[redacted]	2	34	17.0	1
Unclassified	[redacted]	[redacted]	3	14	4.7	0
VASCULAR SURGERY	[redacted]	[redacted]	6	28	4.7	0

Figure 13-2: Service Line Report

them with the information they need to know. They desire information that tells them where to focus their attention. Dashboards are the tool that provides this requirement. A dashboard should be just like the dashboard on a car. It needs to be something that the viewer can glance at quickly to see the status of things. Dashboards are graphic in nature and usually only provide very high-level information. Some advanced dashboards link into drilldown reports and or have alerts that can be set to notify the user if a certain set of conditions occur.

Figure 13-4 shows a basic dashboard for operational activity. It presents the activity by various departments for a given month and year to date. The dashboard, if seen in color, has various items highlighted as red, yellow, or green. This lets the observer know instantly how the metric is doing. The reader should note that the dashboard also contains budget numbers. Budgets are necessary to provide a context for how a function or metric is doing. Without them, a number has no reference and does not provide necessary information needed to determine if everything is okay or not. The role of the dashboard is to give the leader quick understandable information at a glance. The dashboard tells the executive the status of things: either the indicators are okay or there

American Hospital
Inpatient Discharge Detail
For the Month of: May 2014

Name	Gender	Age	MsDrg	MsDrg Desc	Admit Date	Dsch Date	Length of Stay	Adm Src Desc	Dsch Disp	Dsch Disp Desc
Jane Doe	F	44	603	Cellulitis w/o MCC	4/27/2014	5/1/2014	4	EMERGENCY FROM HOME	AHR	Routine discharge
Mary Smith	F	76	470	Major joint replacement or reattachment of lower extremity w/o MCC	4/28/2014	5/1/2014	3	FAMILY PHYSICIAN REFERRAL	ATE	Trans/disch to extended skilled nursing
John Doe	M	0	795	Normal newborn	4/29/2014	5/1/2014	2	Born inside this hospital	AHR	Routine discharge
Nancy Jones	F	34	775	Vaginal delivery w/o complicating diagnoses	4/29/2014	5/1/2014	2	FAMILY PHYSICIAN REFERRAL	AHR	Routine discharge
Tom Jones	M	61	863	Postoperative & post-traumatic infections w/o MCC	4/28/2014	5/1/2014	3	FAMILY PHYSICIAN REFERRAL	AHR	Routine discharge
Baby Boy Warren	M	0	795	Normal newborn	4/29/2014	5/1/2014	2	Born inside this hospital	AHR	Routine discharge
Tammy Warren	F	37	775	Vaginal delivery w/o complicating diagnoses	4/29/2014	5/1/2014	2	FAMILY PHYSICIAN REFERRAL	AHR	Routine discharge
Roy Dupont	M	78	853	Infectious & parasitic diseases w O.R. procedure w MCC	4/21/2014	5/1/2014	10	EMERGENCY FROM HOME	ATW	TRANS. HHA CARE RELATED TO ADM
Cheryl Hart	F	22	951	Other factors influencing health status	4/29/2014	5/1/2014	2	FAMILY PHYSICIAN REFERRAL	AHR	Routine discharge
Baby Girl Walker	F	0	795	Normal newborn	4/29/2014	5/1/2014	2	Born inside this hospital	AHR	Routine discharge
Grandma Wise	F	72	220	Cardiac valve & oth maj cardiothoracic proc w/o card cath w CC	4/23/2014	5/1/2014	8	FAMILY PHYSICIAN REFERRAL	ATW	TRANS. HHA CARE RELATED TO ADM
Peter Parker	M	56	101	Seizures w/o MCC	4/27/2014	5/1/2014	4	EMERGENCY FROM HOME	AHR	Routine discharge

Figure 13-3: Patient Detail Report

American Hospital
Operational Dashboard: Overall Hospital Indicators For May 2014

	Results for the Month							Fiscal Year To Date					
Indicators	**May 2014**	**Budget**	**Variance #**	**Variance %**	**Prior Year**	**Change #**	**Change %**	**May 2014**	**Budget**	**Variance #**	**Variance %**	**Prior Year**	**Change #**
Total IP Discharges, Observation and Extended Stay	1,581	1,501	80	5.4%	1,522	59	3.9%	17,432	16,663	769	4.6%	16,596	836
Inpatient Discharges	1,309	1,276	33	2.6%	1,273	36	2.8%	13,668	14,224	-556	-3.9%	14,153	-485
Observation Patients	202	225	-23	-10.1%	249	-47	-18.9%	2,674	2,439	235	9.6%	2,443	231
Medical Observation Patients	186	144	42	29.2%	154	32	20.8%	1,837	1,564	273	17.5%	1,555	282
Surgical Observation Patients	16	81	-65	-80.1%	95	-79	-83.2%	837	875	-38	-4.3%	888	-51
Extended Stay	70				0	70		230				0	230
Operational Avg LOS	3.79	3.87	-0.08	-2.0%	3.69	0.11	2.9%	3.78	3.87	0	-2.5%	3.88	-0.10
Emergency Department													
ED Total	3,902	3,569	333	9.3%	3,583	319	8.9%	39,504	38,771	733	1.9%	38,365	1,139
Total ED Admissions and Observation	950	920	30	3.3%	885	65	7.3%	9,718	9,994	-276	-2.8%	9,939	-221
ED Admissions	754	776	-22	-2.8%	734	20	2.7%	7,814	8,426	-612	-7.3%	8,396	-582
ED Observation	196	144	52	35.8%	151	45	29.8%	1,904	1,568	336	21.4%	1,543	361
ED Discharges	2,952	2,649	303	11.4%	2,698	254	9.4%	29,786	28,777	1,009	3.5%	28,426	1,360
Outpatient Registrations	21,072	21,072	0	0.0%	21,575	-503	-2.3%	222,702	228,908	-6,206	-2.7%	227,056	-4,354

Figure 13-4: Hospital Dashboard

is an issue. Reports and analytics will be used to identify the causes of an issue, not a dashboard. The dashboard only raises the flag that something is off target.

Analytics

Analytics is a term that can mean many things. For this discussion, it represents the process that an analyst uses to understand what the data are showing. Using the previous examples, suppose the dashboard shows that admissions are down; specifically, the report shows that it is cardiology admissions that are lower than expected. In this scenario, analytics would be used to determine what is causing the cardiology patient volumes to have fallen. The analyst would run various reports and use tools to look for the reason for the decrease. Analytics represent the processes that glean information from the data. The information is then used to determine why something is not as expected. Analytics can also be used to look for positive trends and opportunities for growth and development. Analytics represents the process of using data to create information that can provide intelligence for intervention, action, or change.

Benchmarking

The final core element of BI that will be discussed is benchmarking. Benchmarking is the process of getting other institutions' data or external target numbers for the metrics being tracked. Is a length of stay of 5 days for a given DRG good or bad? How are other hospitals of a similar size and makeup doing with their readmission rates? How much should a knee replacement cost? These are all questions that benchmarking data can help answer.

For benchmarking to work, every participant must use the same definitions and counting methodology. This is external data governance, which represents a key requirement for benchmarking to work. The benchmark requirement must be clear for the benchmark data to be valid and valuable. A good example of this is readmissions. Different payers use different definitions for readmissions. Before one institution can compare itself with other institutions, all must agree on which readmission definition to follow. While this may sound easy, it can often be challenging. Without agreement, the comparisons are weak at best, useless or dangerous at worst. Properly applied benchmarking data give the leaders fixed external points of reference that allow them to gauge how they are doing or to set realistic targets.

A SOLID BUSINESS INTELLIGENCE STRATEGY

The seven elements previously mentioned are not an exhaustive list of BI components, but they do represent a good starting point for understanding what needs to be included in a solid BI strategy. This strategy should grow out of the organization's strategic plans. The senior team needs to define the priorities for the institution. Once these are set, the BI team can start to formulate its strategy to support these strategic initiatives. BI support starts with assuring that the data needed to track and evaluate the strategic initiatives are captured in a consistent and appropriate manner in the data warehouse. The team then creates reports and dashboards to track the metrics around the strategic initiatives. The key priorities for the institution should always drive the BI work plan.

In addition to the strategic plan, the BI strategy must include methods to support regulatory requirements and key clinical and business functions. The BI strategy should never be created in a vacuum, rather it should be a collaborative and inclusive effort in which all the stakeholders have an opportunity to provide input and express their needs. The BI team will take this information and create a framework for delivering the required information. The plan should be considered the guide for BI development activity, but this cannot be too rigid. Healthcare requirements are constantly evolving, and the BI plan needs to be able to flex as changes occur or new needs arise.

The strategy, once developed, should be presented to the senior team and approved. A strategy will only be effective if it has the support of administration and only if it is known and understood by the management team generally. Therefore, the strategy should be presented to the entire management team once it is approved. Many of the managers in the institution will be involved in data governance activities and/or are consumers of the output of the BI efforts. Over time, the BI team will develop a comprehensive set of reports, dashboards, and other tools that give managers the information they need to effectively run their part of the business.

Clinical and Business Intelligence

The title of this chapter is "Clinical and Business Intelligence," but up to this point only BI has been discussed. Until recently, clinical intelligence referred only to data that was used in treating the patient. This book includes a full chapter on clinical decision support (CDS). CDS targets clinicians and helps assure they are alerted to key elements regarding a patient's care. Over the last several years, there has been a rapidly increasing adoption of EMR technology, resulting in rich databases of clinical data. This clinical data, once used only for patient care and CDS, is now being incorporated into reporting data warehouses and used to provide richer information and intelligence.

In the healthcare environment, clinical data is often a key requirement to making good business decisions. After all, the business of healthcare and clinical care is what healthcare is about. This merger of the two data sets is important if an institution hopes to survive and thrive in the changing healthcare environment. VTE (venous thromboembolism) is a good example of this concept. VTE is a high-risk condition that is often preventable with proper intervention. It is also the focus of many quality measures and a subject of pay-for-performance payer contracts. CDS will evaluate a patient, recognize the need for prophylactic anticoagulant therapy or other VTE measures, and alert the clinician. The alert is focused on an individual and the care that he or she needs to receive. Clinical and business intelligence (C&BI) aggregates the individual data and tracks trends and compliance. If the VTE prophylaxis rate is unacceptable, C&BI will provide drilldowns to look at the compliance of doctors to the CDS alerts or other factors that may be affecting the success of the VTE measure. By merging the clinical data into the BI warehouse, the system is now able to track a key performance metric that has direct reimbursement implications.

EMR systems are not designed to report data in a grouped fashion. They are optimized for transactional activity focused around one patient. Therefore, the EMR data need to be pulled into a data warehouse where it can be combined with business data in a relational format. This makes it much easier to look at the profitability of patient care, the effectiveness of various treatment regimes, and the performance of clinical programs from an efficiency or outcomes perspective. Understanding data makes the merger of clinical and business data sets a natural extension of historic BI activities. Clinical and business data combined into one large data warehouse is a very powerful source of intelligence for today's leaders. It is a necessary step forward that must be taken in today's healthcare environment.

ADVANCED BUSINESS INTELLIGENCE

A discussion of BI would not be complete without reviewing some the new and exciting tools that are currently being developed and used by BI professionals. This section will review four areas that are being integrated into healthcare BI. Many of these tools have been used for years in other industries but only recently in healthcare. These tools allow the BI profession to provide even greater value to the healthcare management team.

Data Mining

Data mining uses artificial intelligence techniques, neural networks, and advanced statistical tools (such as cluster analysis) to reveal trends, patterns, and relationships that might otherwise have remained undetected.[6] There is so much clinical and business data and so many variables to be examined that a computer program is often needed to effectively find patterns in the data. Data mining is the software process that performs these automated searches. The technique has been used for many years in other industries, but it could not handle the complexity of healthcare data until recently. Part of the challenge is that healthcare data is frequently inconsistent from patient to patient. An even bigger problem has been the large volume of unstructured data that exists in healthcare. As data mining software has advanced, it can now start to be applied to healthcare to handle these inherent challenges.

In data mining, the analyst asks a question, creates a profile for the mining tool based on that question, and then the software digs through the data looking for patterns that might provide clues to answer the question. Here is an example of how data mining might be applied in a healthcare setting. Consider a scenario in which there is a certain disease condition with divergent outcomes. One group of patients responds to treatment and recovers while another group seems to languish and not improve. Data mining could be used to profile the two sets of patients and find commonalities in the treatment regime, test results, patient history, or other elements that may represent hidden factors causing the difference in outcomes. If the sampling size is big enough, this technology can look at treatment sequencing and when interventions during the patient's course of care are most effective.

Data mining is becoming a necessary tool for the BI professional as data sets grow and become more complex. There is too much data to manually process, evaluate, and review. The key to effective data mining is knowing when and where data mining can be applied safely and appropriately to answer complex questions. As healthcare database sizes continue to grow, the use of data mining will become more prominent. It will become a foundational component of a solid BI toolkit.

Modeling and Simulation

Another area of advanced BI is the use of modeling and simulation software. This software allows the user to create a model of a working process or function. The model can be of a clinical unit such as the emergency department or operating suite. It can also be of a process such as registration or the flow for a testing procedure.

Developing the model can be challenging. The user follows strict parameters and often uses statistical representations of actual observed activity that is collected via time and motion studies. Models of physical locations may use a computer-aided design

(CAD) drawing to set up a realistic scale rendering of the unit. Models use probability and statistics to randomly determine how the modeled item will function on a given day. The model is then run hundreds or thousands of times, each representing a day, and the output is compared with the actual recorded activity of the unit or function. The model is tweaked until it provides a statistically accurate simulation of the observed values of the targeted unit or process.

Once the baseline model is completed and the iterations have shown it to be statistically sound, the analyst is then able to change one or more factors in the model. Each change represents a potential process change. The model is rerun several hundred or thousand times and the new results are captured. If done correctly, the model will produce a statistically valid representation of how a possible change will alter the overall process being studied. Changes to a working process often have a big impact on time, cost, and cause functional disruption. Simulation software is used to help assure that the actions that are being considered will have the desired outcome and that they ultimately will be successful. A model can statistically predict how an alteration will impact the process. It can protect the process from ineffective and costly failures.

In one non-healthcare setting, the weather service uses and presents models regularly. Anytime there is a hurricane, the various models build on the accumulated data and science of meteorology to project the path of the storm. There are often multiple models and the average drawn from the models is shown by the weather station. The same type of science is being applied in healthcare modeling. Obviously the storm tracker is not 100 percent accurate; however, it is usually good at determining the general area and time frame for a storm to make land. Healthcare modeling software is evolving just like meteorologic storm models did over the years. One difference between the weather service and healthcare modeling, however, is that in healthcare, the model is set to mimic actual processes and then altered to see the effect. As experience is gained, healthcare modeling is becoming stronger and more reliable in predicting the effects of process changes. Figure 13-5 shows an example of a model of an endoscopy suite.[7] This example was taken from the website of a company that performs healthcare modeling services. With many of these advanced concepts, it is often prudent to get expert support when first starting to use these tools.

Forecasting and Predictive Analytics

Forecasting and predictive analytics are similar to modeling and simulation. Using the previous weather analogy, the forecast is not a model of a storm but a scientifically based prediction of rain, the daily temperature, etc. Forecasting is similar in healthcare. The BI analyst uses scientific processes to predict the future. This is seen regularly in healthcare today. There are forecasts of decreased inpatient admissions due to increasing use of observation status or the "two midnight" rule established by the Centers for Medicare & Medicaid Services (CMS). Other forecasts include the actuarial projections of increases in healthcare utilization as the baby boomers move into their senior years. These techniques have been used for population health analysis for many years.

At an individual healthcare institution level, there are also many types of forecasting that can be done. Properly performed, this process can alert the management team to future trends or direct them to the most appropriate choices. Forecasting software can

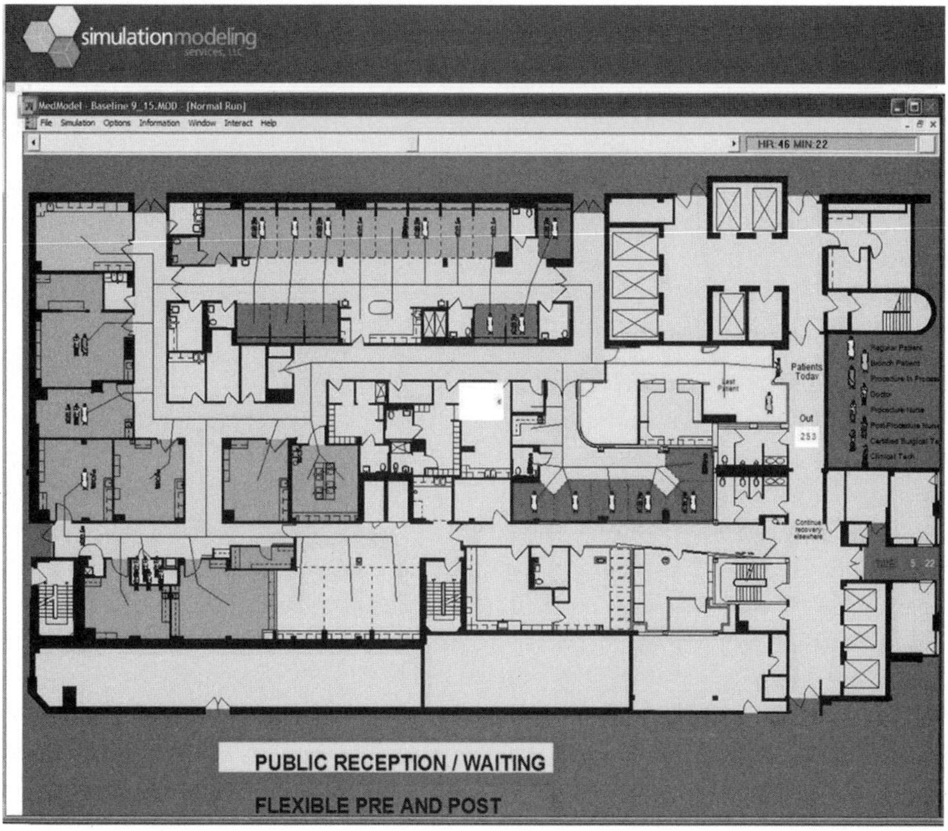

Figure 13-5: Simulation Model of an Endoscopy Suite

predict how bringing an additional orthopedic surgeon on staff might increase operating room volumes. It can project bed utilization, staffing requirements, or changes in profitability based on proposed alterations in an insurer contract. Forecasting can be a powerful tool but it must be completely understood and used wisely. Otherwise the predictions lose their credibility and following them could be dangerous.

Big Data

There are many aspects to big data and many complex definitions. Here is a simple one: data sets, typically consisting of billions or trillions of records that are so vast and complex that they require new and powerful computational resources to process.[8] *Big data* is a term being used to describe the incredible amounts of data being stored in computers today and refers to the tools and/or techniques needed to manage and work with those data. Big data in healthcare often refers to vast amounts of clinical data from across the continuum of care, genomics data, and other types of input such as data from devices that continually monitor the patient. All these data are too much for many traditional data warehouse products. New big-data methodologies and systems are being created to work with this vast ocean of data.

As healthcare moves toward population health management and personalized healthcare, the management of these massive data sets will be a key to success. Big data has come to encompass efforts to harness and manage these data, using it to discover and direct care. The sheer volume is causing the industry to develop and use new tools and techniques. However, at the core of this new and exciting element of BI is still the same foundational reality. Data governance, a solid warehouse structure, good querying and reporting tools, and solid analytics are the pillars of big data just as they are for all BI. Layered on top of these pillars are the new tools that take this massive amount of data and turn it into useful information, which then provides intelligence to the manager.

SUMMARY

Business intelligence is a vital part of healthcare management today. It is used to transform data into information and information into intelligence. It is a key factor in assuring the success of a healthcare institution. Good clinical care requires a functioning and financially stable business framework to operate within. BI provides today's leaders with the knowledge they need to manage effectively. Without it, they would be managing blind. The addition of clinical data into the data warehouse is allowing leaders to gain deeper insight into how their clinical processes are functioning. The merger of clinical and BI allows managers to have a complete view of how the healthcare operation is performing.

This chapter only skimmed the surface of C&BI. Hopefully it has provided the reader with a functional understanding of the basic tenents of the subject. If the reader is interested in additional information on the topic, here is a reference to a more in-depth review of BI.[9]

REFERENCES

1. Rud O. *Business Intelligence Success Factors: Tools for Aligning Your Business in the Global Economy.* Hoboken, N.J: Wiley & Sons; 2009. ISBN 978-0-470-39240-9.
2. http://www.gartner.com/it-glossary/business-intelligence-bi/. Accessed November 17, 2014.
3. http://businessintelligence.com/dictionary/business-intelligence-software/. Accessed November 17, 2014.
4. http://datagovernance.com/adg_data_governance_definition/. Accessed November 17, 2014.
5. http://tdwi.org/Home.aspx. Accessed November 17, 2014.
6. http://www.businessdictionary.com/definition/data-mining.html. Accessed November 17, 2014.
7. http://www.simulation-modeling.com/project_detail.asp?pcid=1&pid=16. Accessed November 17, 2014.
8. http://dictionary.reference.com/browse/big+data. Accessed November 17, 2014.
9. McKinney C, Hess R, Whitecar M, eds. *Implementing Business Intelligence in your Healthcare Organization.* Chicago, IL: HIMSS; 2012. ISBN 978-0-9844577-5-5.

CHAPTER 14

Nursing Informatics Today and Future Perspectives for Healthcare

Dana Alexander, RN, MSN, MBA, and Sarah Collins, RN, PhD

INTRODUCTION

Since the passage of ARRA and HITECH, the use of technology in healthcare has consistently advanced across all care settings to include patient and consumer engagement. Healthcare payment reform and new care delivery models have created increasing demands for information and access to information. Subsequently, this transformation has also created new demands for both the types of technology and the way technology is used and emerging roles to support the changing environment. The need to bridge between clinical workflow and care settings with technology continues to create opportunities for clinical informatics and, specifically, nursing informatics. Nurse informaticists are necessary to bridge settings of care to support healthier individuals, communities, and population health including engaging the patient and families. This chapter outlines the demonstrated need, collaboration, opportunities, and a call to action for nursing informatics.

NURSING INFORMATICS DEFINED

Nursing informatics (NI) is defined by the American Nurses Association[1] as an applied science that:

> …integrates nursing science, computer science, and information science to manage and communicate data, information and knowledge in nursing practice. Nursing informatics facilitates the integration of data, information, knowledge, and wisdom to support patients, nurses, and other providers in their decision making in all roles, and setting. This support is accomplished through the use of information structures, information processes, and information technology.

The consistent growth of NI can be attributed to the applied skills and expertise that NI brings to technology, as well as data initiatives that are so vital in healthcare transformation.

PROFESSIONAL ORGANIZATIONS

As NI and NI roles have continued to evolve, so have the professional organizations that support NI initiatives and efforts. The following is an overview of NI–related professional organizations that are integral in supporting the specialty of NI.

HIMSS continues to be a leading professional organization for NI. As a cause-based organization, HIMSS has the bench strength and expertise to drive and influence national efforts for healthcare reform related to health IT. The HIMSS NI community of more than 6,500 nurses continues to expand as a cohesive and collaborative voice providing domain expertise, leadership, and guidance for health IT initiatives, both domestically and internationally.

One of the key attributes of the HIMSS nursing community is the ability to collaborate with other nursing and NI–related organizations in aligning efforts to advance nursing practice and informatics. One example of these collaborations is the Alliance for Nursing Informatics (ANI), sponsored by HIMSS, and the American Medical Informatics Association (AMIA), representing over thirty nursing organizations. ANI enables a unified voice for the NI community to engage in issues in the public healthcare policy process; information technology standards; information systems design, implementation, and evaluation; and shared communication and networking opportunities.[2] In addition, ANI sponsors an Emerging Leaders program which identifies and develops emerging leaders in NI and involves them in a two-year program to learn about their leadership potential, opportunities for professional growth, and knowledge and experience necessary to serve NI practice and/or policy.

Other professional organizational alignments include the American Nurses Association (ANA), the American Academy of Nursing, the American Nursing Informatics Association, and the TIGER Initiative. Through these alignments, the NI profession continues to demonstrate a powerful influential force in healthcare policy, health IT standards, practice, and overall healthcare reform.

INFLUENCERS SHAPING THE INDUSTRY

The Institute of Medicine (IOM) has published several landmark reports that continue to provide a glide path for NI.

The Future of Nursing

The IOM "Future of Nursing" report is not only about nursing but the future of healthcare in the United States. The report outlines nursing practice and nursing leadership as key factors to successfully achieving improved outcomes, optimal wellness, and overall population health management.[3] Because of the breadth and depth of nursing engagement in all aspects of healthcare, nurses are in a key position to influence healthcare reform and the multidimensional needs across all care settings. This report's findings and recommendations created a call to action and ignited a series of activities and initiatives across the profession of nursing to include the HIMSS NI Position Statement discussed later in this chapter.

The IOM's report challenged the nursing profession to address a number of barriers that prevent nurses from being able to respond effectively to rapidly changing healthcare settings and an evolving healthcare system. These barriers must be overcome to ensure that nurses are well positioned to lead change and advance health. The United States has the opportunity to transform its healthcare system, and nurses can and should play a fundamental role in this transformation.[3]

Health IT and Patient Safety

The IOM "Health IT and Patient Safety" report summarizes existing knowledge of the effects of health IT on patient safety and makes recommendations to maximize and promote safety of health IT–assisted care. Findings include the following: health IT can improve patient safety even though the gaps in potential risks of health IT are not fully understood; health IT needs to be viewed as part of the larger socio-technical system; and all stakeholders need to work together for a coordinated effort to identify and understand patient safety risks associated with health IT.[4] This report sets the stage for NI engagement and leadership to identify and understand patient safety risks associated with health IT.

Best Care at Lower Cost...The Path to Continuous Learning Healthcare

The IOM "Best Care at Lower Cost" report identifies three major imperatives for change: the rising complexity of modern healthcare, unsustainable cost increases, and the outcomes below the system's potential. The report defines the foundational characteristics of a healthcare system that is efficient, delivers increased value, and is continuously innovating and improving in its ability to deliver high value to patients. The report also addresses that emerging tools like computing power, connectivity, team-based care, and systems engineering techniques—tools that were previously unavailable—make the envisioned transition possible and are already being put to successful use in pioneering healthcare organizations. The report outlines several recommendations including (a) the need for a digital infrastructure that supports the capacity to capture clinical, delivery process, and financial data for better care, system improvement, and creating new knowledge; and (b) the need to improve data utility by streamlining and revising research regulations to improve care, promote the capture of clinical data, and generate knowledge. Applying these new strategies can support transition to a continuously learning health system—one that aligns science and informatics, patient-clinician partnerships, incentives, and a culture of continuous improvement to produce the best care at lower cost.[5] This report sets the stage for NI engagement to participate in developing the right infrastructure to capture clinical and financial data for new knowledge and decision support. Nurses, one of the largest groups of clinical technology users, are well-positioned to identify salient clinical outcomes and process questions for clinically significant knowledge development in a learning health system.

HIMSS Position Statement: Transforming Nursing Practice Through Technology and Informatics

The IOM "Future of Nursing" report stimulated accelerated efforts among nursing organizations to collaborate and unite on behalf of nursing and future care delivery in the United States. In response to the call for action from the IOM report, HIMSS released the position statement, "Transforming Nursing Practice Through Technology and Informatics," providing background on key related issues and identifying specific recommendations for eliminating barriers, as well as addressing nursing's role in transforming healthcare through the use of IT, particularly in regard to the role of NI. This statement was developed by the HIMSS Nursing Informatics Committee, now representing more than 6,500 nurse informaticists, and is supported by the HIMSS Board of Directors. Together, nurses and NI must lead and be visible, vocal, and present at the table to achieve healthcare delivery transformation. This recommendation is intended to promote interprofessional collaboration and unified messaging among all stakeholders as keys to success. "We (HIMSS) believe that nurses and nursing informatics specialists are vital to accomplishing the goals described in this position paper and advancing healthcare transformation through the use of health IT."[6]

In summary, these IOM reports, as well as the HIMSS Position Statement, continue to shape and influence the healthcare landscape and provide opportunities for NI to influence, engage, and impact healthcare and the health of communities as part of interprofessional leadership activities. The focus on technical and practice standards as well as analytics strategy will ultimately support organizations' drive toward accountable care and achievement of the goals and priorities of the National Quality Strategy to achieve better health and affordable care. These report findings and recommendations also suggest opportunities that specifically require NI expertise, engagement, and leadership to influence health IT policy. To this aim, NI leaders must be knowledgeable in public policy and regulatory initiatives to successfully influence and create change. Finally, knowledge of nursing practice will drive research aspects to create the right infrastructures such as capturing clinical and financial data that align with the delivery process to provide better care and system improvement and create new knowledge that can inform innovations.

POPULATION HEALTH AND ANALYTICS

New healthcare delivery and payment models, such as PCMH and ACOs, driven by healthcare reform will require an innovative look at how patient and consumer information is captured, exchanged, analyzed, and acted on.

The movement toward accountable care emphasizes the drive toward population health management and also provides opportunity for expanded nursing roles, including nurse informaticists. NI leaders are necessary to engage in ACO strategy development, implementation, and execution. Care management is not only about improving quality, patient safety, and outcomes, but also about managing costs. Analytics beyond retrospective reporting to include near–real-time and predictive analytics are necessary components to manage care, manage cost, and achieve outcomes. Technologies must integrate both clinical and financial solutions to monitor and inform care delivery processes and clinical decision making. Nurse informaticists are essential stakeholders to

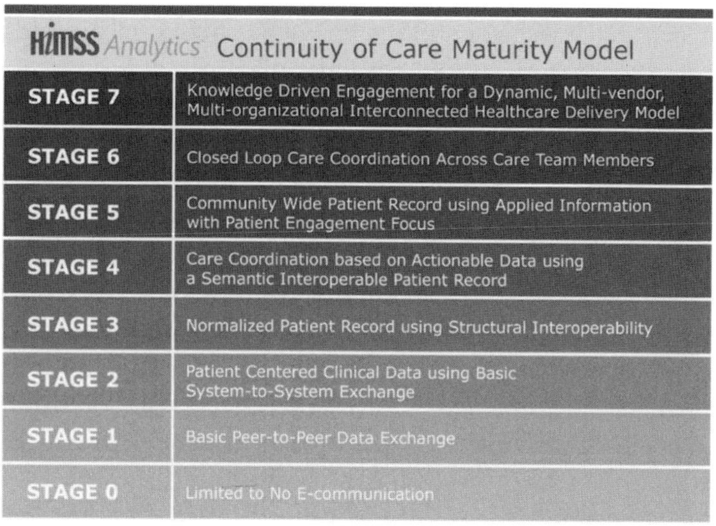

Figure 14-1: HIMSS Analytics Continuity of Care Maturity Model

orchestrate the information that must be provided, captured, and documented to support patient care as well as the associated financial and business indicators to monitor and report on outcomes management. Technology and informatics will continue to be a fundamental enabler to future care delivery models, and NI leaders will be essential to lead the way and to innovate nursing practice through technology.

Another aspect to consider is patient and family engagement. Nurses are on the front lines engaging with patients and their families and coordinating the care they receive across care settings. Nurses continue to take a leadership role in bridging information across settings of care for patients. Engaging and activating patients and their families in their care and health information management is a critical role for NI.

In 2014, HIMSS Analytics launched the Continuity of Care Maturity Model to extend beyond Stage 7 of the Electronic Medical Record Adoption Model (EMRAM)[SM] with the goal to optimize outcomes for health systems toward population health and accountable care.[7] This model addresses the convergence of interoperability, information exchange, care coordination, patient engagement, and analytics with the ultimate goal of holistic individual and population health management. Nurse informaticists are key stakeholders in their organizations for achieving the various stages of EMRAM, and it can be expected that nursing engagement in achieving the stages of the Continuity of Care Maturity Model (see Figure 14-1) will be of equal importance.

NI ROLES AND STRUCTURES

Many healthcare organizations are in the process of implementing and optimizing EHRs and other informatics innovations as a core strategy to align with the initiatives and policies discussed in the prior sections. In many organizations, nurses perform much of the EHR system configuration work, such as workflow analyses and content design, which require clinical knowledge and expertise. NI competencies are a critical component of successful interprofessional clinical informatics practice within healthcare delivery organizations. Established leadership roles include chief nursing officer (CNO), chief nursing information officer (CNIO), director of nursing informatics, and nurse informaticist. Expectations for these roles include advanced education at the masters or doctorate level. Collins et al. defined the CNO's clinical informatics role as an executive strategic leader who values, invests in, and supports interprofessional informatics practice approached from the perspective of nursing strategy and nursing practice needs.[8] The CNIO functions as a centralized and strategic leader with decision-making authority and operational oversight.[8] The CNIO and chief medical information officer (CMIO) are independent yet collaborative and partnered roles with established practice in organizations that have served as pioneers in health IT implementations and applied clinical informatics efforts.[8] Not all healthcare organizations have implemented the CNIO role, despite increasing acknowledgement of its importance. In some organizations, the director of nursing informatics functions as the central strategic leadership for NI. For organizations that have yet to adopt the CNIO position, the nature of the position of the central strategic leader for NI includes effective partnerships with executive level counterparts, such as the CMIO and chief information officer (CIO).

NI roles and titles are evolving, and while roles often lack defined and standardized titles, it is clear there is a need for strategic and decision-making NI leaders with common roles and activities.[8]

Education and Competencies, Leadership Roles, American Organization of Nurse Executives' Guiding Principles

Several sets of NI competencies exist for nursing students, nursing faculty, and nurses who practice within the clinical setting. NI competency development began in the late 1980s through a series of expert studies and publications of competencies by the International Medical Informatics Association (IMIA), the National League for Nursing, AACN, NACNEP, and later AMIA.[9,10,11] In 2002, 281 competencies were validated, based on prior work, that were categorized by four levels of practice (beginning nurse, experienced nurse, informatics nurse specialist, and informatics innovator) and three broad categories with subcategories: computer skills, informatics knowledge, and informatics skills.[12] Today, the ANA publishes *Scope and Standards of Practice for Nursing Informatics*, and the American Nurses Credentialing Center (ANCC) offers informatics certification. The TIGER Initiative published *Informatics Competencies for Every Practicing Nurse: Recommendations from the TIGER Collaborative*.[13] TIGER, an acronym for Technology Informatics Guiding Education Reform, is a HIMSS–sponsored initiative that engages nursing stakeholders to develop a shared vision, strategy, and approach for leveraging health IT to improve nursing practice, education, and patient care delivery. The TIGER Competencies are focused on (1) Basic Computer Competencies, (2) Information Literacy, and (3) Information Management (data-information-knowledge).

There have been several publications in recent years focused on describing, refining, and validating NI competencies and scales.[14,15,16,17,18] Additionally, work is increasingly focused on role-based competencies, specifically chief nurse executives and expanding the American Organization of Nurse Executives (AONE) IT competencies to consider a more strategic, broader level of knowledge aligned with innovative nursing practice.[19]

Current efforts are focused on defining role-based competencies for nurses at all levels of practice, from students to managers and leaders.

Resources for clinical informatics competencies, education, and certification can be found through the Office of the National Coordinator for Health Information Technology (ONC), AMIA, and the American Health Informatics Management Association (AHIMA), including the publicly available ONC HIT Curriculum Development Centers Program.[20]

Of note, interprofessional competencies have been published and social media competencies are emerging.[21,22] While these do not pertain specifically to NI, they are considered increasingly relevant to nursing and clinical informatics practice.

FOUNDATIONAL AND EMERGING TECHNOLOGY

Barcode medication administration (BCMA) is a technology that reduces the risk of medication errors when well integrated into nursing medication administration workflow as part of a closed-loop medication system.[23,24] Due to this evidence base, BCMA is incorporated into MU Stage 2 requirements and is a factor in the HIMSS Analytics EMRAM.[SM] A PubMed search for BCMA retrieves over 300 publications dating back to the 1990s that discuss the potential benefits of, and critical workflow and usability considerations for, the implementation of BCMA. Other common topics within the NI literature include the following: Terminology and Standards, Information Seeking, Information Needs, and Information Appraisal, Transitions and Handoff, Nursing Protocols, and Infobuttons to meet information needs and drive evidence-based practice.[25] While much work remains in each of these areas, the foundational literature is sufficiently robust to inform the development, implementation, and comparative evaluation of related technologies.

Areas of research within the nursing and clinical informatics literature that appear to be increasing include patient engagement with innovative patient-centered applications, comparative effectiveness trials of informatics interventions, data mining and clinical analytics studies that leverage nursing and clinical practice knowledge, and coordination of services in post-acute care settings.

2014 HIMSS NURSING INFORMATICS WORKFORCE SURVEY

The results of the 2014 HIMSS Nursing Informatics Workforce survey, aligned with past surveys, continue to indicate that NI has evolved into a critical and influential stakeholder in health IT.[26,27] While the 2011 survey highlighted the emergence of the CNIO role, the 2014 survey noted the shift in focus of NI roles from implementation to optimization. Twenty-four percent more respondents had completed a post-graduate degree in NI or informatics training in the 2014 survey than in 2011. In addition, more than half indicated plans to pursue an informatics certification within the next year and 43 percent of respondents indicated plans to pursue additional informatics education and training. Respondents indicated that the top barriers to success in their role were a lack of administrative support and a lack of staffing resources.[27]

TIGER AND EXEMPLARS, ONLINE TOOLKIT

The TIGER Initiative was founded in 2004. TIGER's vision is "To enable nurses and interprofessional colleagues to use informatics and emerging technologies to make healthcare safer, more effective, efficient, patient-centered, timely and equitable by interweaving evidence and technology seamlessly into practice, education and research fostering a learning healthcare system." In 2014, TIGER released a new leadership collaborative report, "The Leadership Imperative: TIGER's Recommendations for Integrating Technology to Transform Practice and Education" (2014) as a follow-up to the 2009 TIGER Leadership Development Collaborative Report.[28] The report highlights that nurse leaders must possess knowledge about the relationship between IT and practice redesign that increases standardized, evidence-based, and clinically relevant results aligned with the Triple Aim of (1) improving the experience of care, (2) improving the health of populations, and (3) reducing per capita costs of healthcare.[29,30] The report discusses a variety of significant topics such as standards, clinical analytics, faculty development, workflow integration and usability, and consumer empowerment. The report outlines characteristics, skills, and competencies of an innovative nurse leader to influence quality, patient engagement, population health, and decrease costs through the integration and adoption of innovative information technology.[28]

To further TIGER's mission to transform practice, education, and consumer engagement through the integration of health informatics, TIGER has published six exemplars of outstanding innovative nursing leadership aligned with areas identified by Judy Murphy in "The Future of Nursing: How HIT Fits in the IOM/RWJF Initiative."[31] The exemplars can be accessed through the TIGER Virtual Learning Environment (VLE).[32] The TIGER VLE is aimed at enhancing learning through access to health IT tools and other health IT–related technologies, tutorials, and scenario-based learning modules.

GLIDE PATH TOWARD THE FUTURE: CONSUMER ENGAGEMENT, MOBILE, FUTURE TECHNOLOGIES, CDS FOR NURSES

Value realization for health IT and practice redesign combined with greater adoption of communication technologies that increase efficiency and collaboration will pave the path to the future. The value proposition for consumer engagement technologies is increasing with public reporting of hospital scores on the HCAHPS (Hospital Consumer Assessment of Healthcare Providers and Systems) survey and with implications for reimbursement from CMS. A series of transformations in reimbursement structures, such as accountable care, value-based purchasing, and penalties for hospital-acquired conditions and 30-day readmissions will increase the value proposition for effective and relevant CDS and clinical analytics dashboards to drive nursing decision making at the point of care. Such tools will require mobile-enabled technologies to fit within existing hospital-based workflows for actionable and real-time data when and where it is needed. Emerging trends will also shift focus to the ambulatory and long-term care post acute care (LTPAC) settings where nurses function in critical roles as care coordinators, educators, and advanced practice nurses for population health management and preventive care. In these community and clinic settings, innovative mobile-enabled consumer and clinician-facing communication technologies will converge with CDS technologies requiring efficient and reliable interoperability and health information exchange networks.[33]

CONCLUSION

NI roles continue to evolve, expand, and emerge and are critical to achieve the necessary transformation activities that will bridge the new care delivery models into clinical practice with the right technology solutions. Collaboration among interprofessional clinical informatics leaders is critical to engage and refine informatics approaches to achieve the triple aim of improved experience, improved health, and reduced costs. As leaders in clinical informatics, nurse informaticists must be able to translate the impact of healthcare reform into nursing practice and patient care delivery while also having a voice in the planning, implementation and execution of health IT solutions and informatics innovations to achieve the requirements of the healthcare transformation that is underway.

REFERENCES

1. Collins S, Alexander D, Moss J. Nursing Domain of CI Governance: Recommendations for Health IT adoption and Optimization. *J Am Med Inf Assoc.* 10 February 2015 (online first).
2. McCormick KA, Sensmeier J, Delaney C.W, et al. Introduction to informatics and nursing. In: Bronzino JD, ed. *Biomedical Engineering Handbook.* 4th ed. Med. Devices Syst., Boca Raton, FL: CRC Press; 2013.
3. IOM. The Future of Nursing: Leading Change, Advancing Health. 2010.
4. IOM. Committee on Patient Safety and Health Information Technology. Health IT and Patient Safety: Building Safer Systems for Better Care. Washington, DC: National Academies Press; 2011.
5. IOM. Best Care at Lower Cost: The Path to Continuously Learning Health Care in America. 2012.
6. HIMSS Nursing Informatics. Position Paper on Transforming Nursing Practice through Technology & Informatics. 2011.
7. HIMSS Analytics. Continuity of Care Maturity Model. 2014.
8. Collins S, Alexander D, Moss J. Nursing Domain of clinical informatics governance: Recommendations for health IT adoption and optimization. *J Am Med Inf Assoc.* 2014; in press.
9. Grobe SJ. Nursing informatics competencies. *Methods Inf Med.* 1989;28:267–169.
10. Peterson HE, Gerdin-Jelger U, eds. *Preparing Nurses for Using Information Systems: Recommended Informatics Competencies.* National Center for Biotechnology Information; 1988.
11. Staggers N, Gassert CA, Skiba DJ. Health professionals' views of informatics education: findings from the AMIA 1999 spring conference. *J Am Med Inform Assoc.* 2000;7:550–558.
12. Staggers N, Gassert CA, Curran C. A Delphi study to determine informatics competencies for nurses at four levels of practice. *Nurs Res.* 2002;51:383–390.
13. TIGER Collaborative. Overview Informatics Competencies for Every Practicing Nurse: Recommendations from the TIGER Collaborative. 2008.
14. Hart MD. Informatics competency and development within the US nursing population workforce: A systematic literature review. *Comput Inform Nurs.* 2008;26:320–329; quiz 330–331.
15. Westra BL, Delaney CW. Informatics competencies for nursing and healthcare leaders. AMIA Annual Symposium Proceedings. 2008:804–808.

16. Yoon S, Yen P, Bakken S. Psychometric properties of the self-assessment of nursing informatics competencies scale. *Stud Health Technol Inf.* 2009;146:546–550.

17. Schnall R, Stone P, Currie L, et al. Development of a self-report instrument to measure patient safety attitudes, skills, and knowledge. *J Nurs Scholarsh.* 2008;40:391–394.

18. Kennedy M. Introducing nursing informatics and innovation into a professional practice model. *Stud Health Technol Inf.* 2009;146: 705.

19. Simpson RL. Chief nurse executives need contemporary informatics competencies. *Nurs Econ.* 2013;31:277–287; quiz 288.

20. AMIA. ONC HIT Curriculum Overview. AMIA Knowledge Center. 2014.

21. Interprofessional Education Collaborative Expert Panel. Core competencies for interprofessional collaborative practice: Report of an expert panel. Washington, DC: 2011.

22. HLWIKI Canada. Top Ten (10) Social Media Competencies for Librarians. 2012.

23. DeYoung JL, Vanderkooi ME, Barletta JF. Effect of bar-code-assisted medication administration on medication error rates in an adult medical intensive care unit. *Am J Health-Syst Pharm.* 2009;66:1110–1115.

24. Helmons PJ, Wargel LN, Daniels CE. Effect of bar-code-assisted medication administration on medication administration errors and accuracy in multiple patient care areas. *Am J Health-Syst Pharm.* 2009;66:1202–1210.

25. Collins S, Dykes P. A to Z: A Year in Review 2013. HIMSS. Nursing Informatics Symposium Proceedings. 2014.

26. HIMSS. HIMSS Nursing Informatics Workforce Survey. 2011.

27. HIMSS. Nursing Informatics. 2014 Nursing Informatics Workforce Survey. 2014.

28. The TIGER Initiative Foundation. The Leadership Imperative: TIGER's Recommendations for Integrating Technology to Transform Practice and Education. 2014.

29. Berwick DM, Nolan TW, Whittington J. The triple aim: care, health, and cost. *Health Aff.* (Millwood) 2008;27:759–769.

30. Institute for Healthcare Improvement. The IHI Triple Aim. IHI Triple Aim Initiative. 2014.

31. Murphy J. The future of nursing. How HIT fits in IOM/RWJF initiative. *J Healthc Inf Manag.* 2010;24:8-12.

32. The TIGER Initiative Foundation. The TIGER Initiative Virtual Learning Environment. 2014.

33. Hyun S, Hodorowski JK, Nirenberg A, et al. Mobile health-based approaches for smoking cessation resources. *Oncol Nurs Forum.* 2013;40:E312–319.

Chapter 15

Health Information Exchange

Gilad J. Kuperman, MD, PhD, and Jason Shapiro, MD, MA

INTRODUCTION

Clinicians and other health professionals use clinical data to make decisions about care. Clinical data are also used to support healthcare research and to inform health policy. Because patients receive care in a variety of locations, clinical data are often needed in a location other than where the data were initially generated.[1] For example, a patient may move to a new city and, to provide optimal care, the new clinical team may need access to the patient's previous records. Or the patient is transferred to a new care setting as part of his or her care continuum; for example, the patient may be transferred from an acute care setting to a nursing home, or the patient may be referred from a primary care provider to a specialist for a consultation. Or, an emergency department physician caring for a patient who is unable to provide a history may wonder whether the patient has received care elsewhere that is relevant to the current situation.[2]

There are known problems caused because of the lack of data availability at the point of care. A study by Smith et al.[3] found that clinical data relevant to care existed elsewhere in 13 percent of primary care visits. The data were present in electronic information systems 52 percent of the time. The missing data were deemed at least somewhat likely to affect care 44 percent of the time. A study by Stiell et al.[4] found that information gaps were present in 32 percent of emergency department visits. The gaps occurred more frequently in patients with a higher severity of illness, and the gaps were felt to be essential to care 48 percent of the time.

HIE makes the most sense when the patient has been to multiple providers in a community. In a 23-month study of activity in a community in New York, Campion[5] found that 41 percent of patients had visits at multiple facilities, which accounted for 68 percent of total encounters. In addition, 28 percent of encounters in the study were "transitions" of care, where the patient moved from one facility to another. In a study of emergency department care, Tamblyn et al.[6] noted that prescription data from insurance sources included 41 percent more medications than those that had been noted in the patients' charts and that providing easy access to prescription data could improve the accuracy of medication lists.

In addition to direct care scenarios, there are other scenarios that beg access to data from remote locations. For example, identification of public health trends requires the aggregation of clinical data from multiple locations.[7] The ability to robustly assess the quality of care that is delivered may require data about a patient from multiple locations, and a complete immunization record about the patient may require aggregation of data from multiple locations. Innovative models of healthcare delivery that seek to better coordinate the patient's care presume that the various participants in the patient's care will have timely access to data about the patient.[8]

Traditionally, low-technology approaches have been used to move clinical data from the place where it is generated to the place where it is needed. Even currently, the patient frequently carries paper copies of health records from one provider to another. Or paper copies of health records may be sent between providers by U.S. mail or by courier. Fax machines are frequently used to transmit clinical data between settings. A patient may arrive at a clinician's office with a CD containing images from a previous radiology study. Until recently, patients carried x-ray films between provider offices. Although these low-technology approaches helped address the problem, the healthcare system needs a robust approach to electronic health information exchange so that clinical data can be accessible where and when they are needed.

BARRIERS TO THE REALIZATION OF HEALTH INFORMATION EXCHANGE

There are several hurdles to realizing the vision of robust electronic HIE.

First, for data to be exchanged they must be in electronic form. Although some clinical data—such as laboratory results, radiology reports, and pharmacy claims data—have been in electronic form for decades, medical records data such as clinical notes written by doctors, nurses, and other members of the patient's care team were, until recently, largely in paper form. A study by Des Roches et al.[9] found that only 13 percent of ambulatory providers in the United States in 2008 were using a basic electronic health record (EHR) and 4 percent were using an advanced system. In 2009, Jha et al.[10] found that 7.6 percent of hospitals had a basic EHR and 1.5 percent had a comprehensive EHR. The Centers for Medicare & Medicaid Services' (CMS) Incentive Program for EHRs, also known as the MU program[11,12] has radically increased the prevalence of EHRs both in ambulatory settings and hospital settings. A Centers for Disease Control and Prevention (CDC) brief[13] reported that in 2013, 78 percent of office-based physicians used any type of EHR system, which was up from 18 percent in 2001. So, even though EHR adoption is increasing, until recently the prevalence of paper-based medical records had been a hurdle to HIE.

A second hurdle to HIE is competitive concerns. A healthcare provider organization may be concerned that patient loyalty could be more easily disrupted if competing organizations have access to the patient's clinical data. Also, a provider organization may be concerned that its patient flows, market shares, etc., could be relatively easily discerned and targeted by competitors if there is free flow of clinical data. Such concerns may cause provider organizations to hesitate before participating in HIE initiatives.

A third hurdle, up until very recently, had been the absence of leadership models for the advancement of HIE. Currently, all fifty states have some form of HIE services,[14] but many of these services only began emerging in 2010. In 2009, the HITECH Act led to the creation of the $540 million federally funded State Health Information Exchange Cooperative Agreement, which supported the development of state-level entities to advance HIE. State-level entities are helping to create various approaches to HIE at the regional and state level, but many of these efforts are early and many are in pilot or are active only at a regional level. Prior to the federally funded State Cooperative Agreement program, it was not clear which stakeholder in a region should be responsible for leading the development of HIE efforts.

A fourth hurdle to the establishment of HIE is the concern over how to handle patient privacy. Just because technology is available to make data accessible across institutional boundaries, the patient's wishes—and privacy laws—must be taken into account when enabling such capabilities. Federal privacy law (HIPAA) allows clinical data to be communicated from one provider to another—without the patient's consent—to support clinical care. However, state laws can supersede HIPAA and can vary among states. For example, in New York state, privacy law includes special procedures for the transfer of mental health and sexually transmitted disease data. Privacy laws related to minors vary across states, too. In addition, many state privacy laws did not foresee the advent of widespread HIE, so laws and other policies are being modified in response to the emerging capabilities. HIE initiatives have spent significant time and energy developing adequate policies, and this work is ongoing. The net result is that the need to address privacy concerns has been a significant barrier to widespread and swift adoption of HIE.

A fifth hurdle is the technology that needs to be developed to support HIE. There are technical approaches that can be used to implement HIE. Two of the important approaches—query-based HIE and direct HIE—will be discussed later in this chapter. When compared with some of the other hurdles to HIE, the technical challenges can seem quite minor; however, complex technology (servers, data interfaces, networks, etc.) still must be successfully implemented to achieve interoperability goals.

A sixth hurdle is the need to match patients across different settings of care. There is no unique patient identifier in the United States, so to link patient records across settings of care requires a matching of demographic data—for example, patient name, address, date of birth, etc. There are statistical approaches to patient matching, several of which have been in use for decades. These approaches have known limitations; for example, false positive rates and false negative rates. The goal of most patient matching algorithms is to minimize false positive rates (which would incorrectly link different patients) while tolerating false negative rates (which would fail to link records that should be linked).

A seventh hurdle to the realization of HIE is the lack of robust standards for the representation of key medical concepts in structured electronic form, as well as the lack of broad adoption of these standards when they do exist. For many purposes, electronic clinical data do not need to be represented in structured coded form. For example, a textual representation of an encounter note or a radiology report can be read by a clinician and interpreted to support clinical care. However, for other purposes such as integrating laboratory results from disparate sources to identify trends; analyzing medication data for the presence of duplicate medication therapy, drug-drug interactions, or drug allergy interactions; or integrating data to support analyses for management reporting, data must be represented in standardized structures and represented with standard terminologies. Two classes of standards are important for representing health data: (1) standards for representing data structures, and (2) standards for representing the content contained in the structures. Examples of standards for medical records structures include Health Level 7, Version 2.51[15] (used to represent laboratory results and other clinical observations), the Consolidated Clinical Document Architecture[16] (C-CDA, used to represent encounter documents, discharge summaries, and patient summaries) and the National Council for Prescription Drug Programs standard[17] (NCPDP, used to represent prescription information). Examples of content representation standards include Logical Observations, Identifiers, Names and Codes[18] (LOINC©, for laboratory test names), RxNorm[19] (for medication names), Systematic Nomenclature of Medicine[20] (SNOMED, for problem lists), International Classification of Diseases[21] (ICD, for discharge diagnoses), and Codes for Vaccines Administered[22] (CVX, for immunization data). The certification process for electronic health records[23] that is part of the Meaningful Use program[24] is helping to advance adoption of medical concept and record structure standards.

Finally, an important hurdle for the broad adoption of HIE is addressing how payment for the technology and operations will occur. Ostensibly, HIE is a technology that improves the effectiveness and efficiency of healthcare delivery. If that is the case, then value should be generated. However, it can be complex to ascertain which stakeholder in the healthcare system (e.g., provider, patient, health plan, employer, government, etc.) realizes value from the technology and how to get the beneficiary to contribute his fair share. As will be discussed in detail later, organizations that have tried to promote HIE have found it challenging to establish a financial viability model.[25]

The net impact of all the hurdles previously listed is that, currently, electronic HIE in the United States is occurring infrequently.

EFFORTS TO INCREASE HEALTH INFORMATION EXCHANGE

Beginning in the mid-2000s, to address the leadership void previously mentioned, federal and state governments took an increasing role in the advancement of HIE. At that time, the federal government advanced the concept of a regional health information organization, or RHIO.[26] The concept of an RHIO was that because most of the benefit from the successful implementation of HIE would accrue at a local or regional level, regionally oriented organizations should be formed to tackle the relevant hurdles (i.e., providing leadership, addressing privacy challenges, solving financial sustainability issues, implementing technology, etc.). AHRQ provided funding for RHIO demonstration projects. State and local governments also provided funding for RHIOs. By 2009, there were over 119 operational RHIOs nationwide.[25]

New York State in particular aggressively supported the RHIO model. In 2004, New York State passed the Health Efficiency and Affordability Law for New York (HEAL-NY). HEAL-NY was a 4-year, $1 billion bond act designed to restructure healthcare in New York State. The bulk of the funds went to "brick and mortar" restructuring of healthcare facilities; however, approximately 20 percent of the funding, as well as funding from federal and other sources, was dedicated to creating a modern IT infrastructure

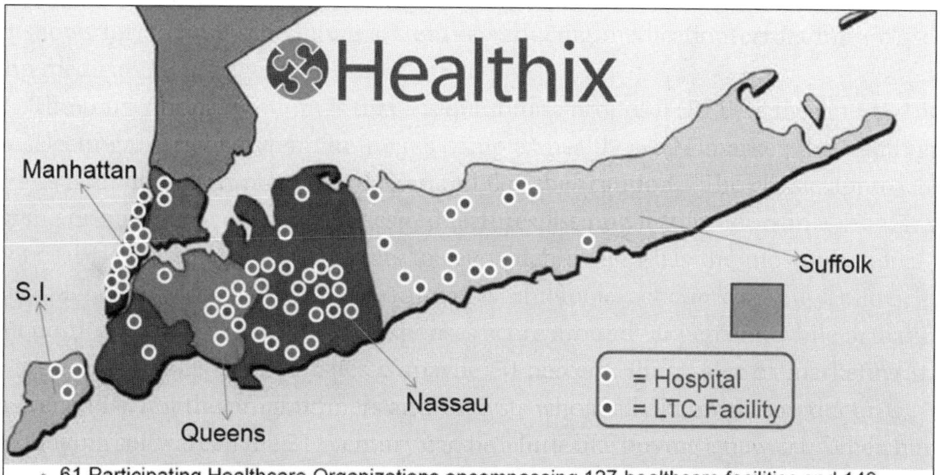

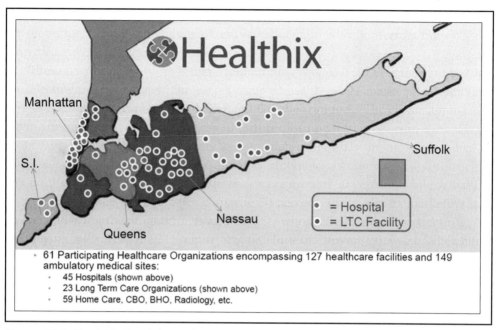

Figure 15-1: Healthix Participant Organizations, as of January, 2014

for New York State. The IT portion of HEAL-NY was divided into multiple phases: (1) 2006 – $50 million for establishment of RHIOs, (2) 2008 – $100 million for establishment of a statewide architecture, (3) 2010 – $100 million for use of health IT to support PCMHs, and (4) 2011 – $100 million for use of health IT to support chronic diseases with mental health comorbidity. No other state dedicated the extent of resources to the advancement of HIE as did New York State.

Example of an RHIO

One of the RHIOs that was established in New York State under the HEAL program is Healthix, Inc.[27] Healthix provides HIE services to healthcare providers in the metropolitan New York area (see Figure 15-1). Currently, Healthix includes over 60 healthcare organizations, which deliver care at over 120 healthcare facilities and over 140 ambulatory locations.

Technology. The technology that Healthix uses is outlined in Figure 15-2. There are several key components in the Healthix technology. Each Healthix participant takes a subset of the data from its core information systems and stores it on an edge server. As shown in Figure 15-2, an edge server is controlled by the health information participant organization and contains data from the participant that can be accessed by the HIE. Examples of the kinds of data that the participants place on the edge server are registration data, encounter data, laboratory results, radiology reports, medication data, allergy data, etc. In addition, patient demographic data are sent from each participant to the Healthix hub and those demographic data are available to the Healthix master patient index that uses statistical algorithms to match patients across sites. The master patient index enables Healthix to know the locations at which any particular patient has records. Physicians and other clinicians can use a browser-based portal application to

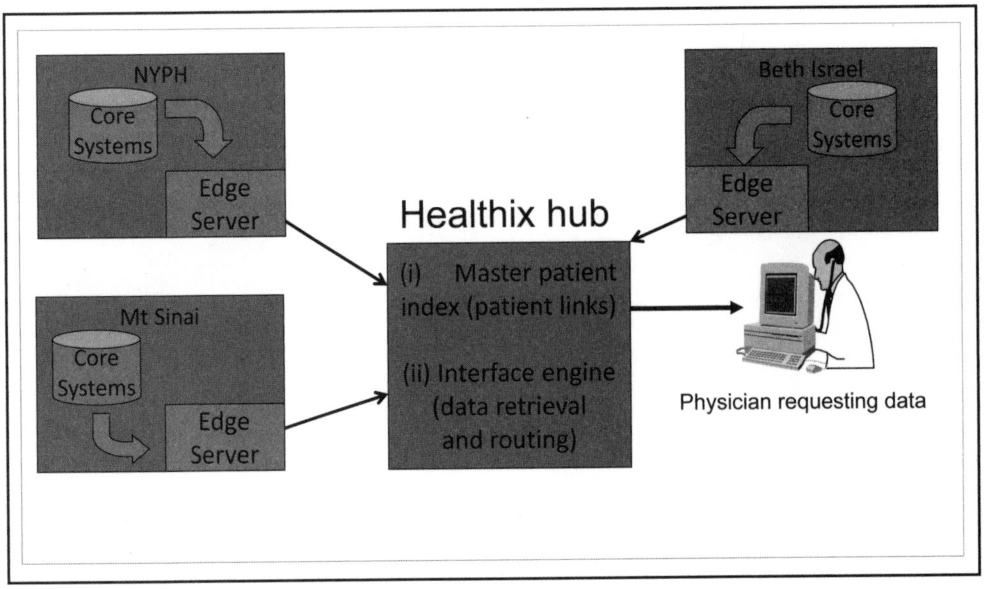

Figure 15-2: Flow Diagram of Healthix Technology.

Note: Master patient index links patients using statistical matching techniques applied to patient demographics. Interface engine retrieves data from participant sites when needed.

retrieve data from Healthix. When a clinician requests data from Healthix, the master patient index identifies the locations at which the patient has data and the Healthix interface engine retrieves the data from the various edge servers, aggregates it, and renders it in the Healthix clinician portal. Example screen shots from the Healthix clinician portal are shown in Figures 15-3 and 15-4. The Healthix portal is a results review application that shows data from multiple organizations.

Privacy policy. The New York State Department of Health has created policies that require RHIO participants to obtain the patient's written consent before the participant can access the patient's data from the RHIO. This model of consent is known as *opt-in*. The requirement to obtain the patient's consent creates operational complexities for RHIO participants, but these complexities are felt to be necessary to create public trust and comfort with HIE. In addition to implementing New York State's consent policies, Healthix also must manage an auditing process to assure that other specified privacy and security policies—for example, appropriate user authorization and appropriate access—are receiving full compliance.

Clinical event notification. Because Healthix receives encounter data from each of its participants, Healthix has the ability to detect events about patients across its network. This capability has become of increasing interest as healthcare delivery system reforms are creating incentives for more effective and efficient care, and Healthix members are beginning to participate in such innovative care programs as the Medicaid Health Home program.[28] Under these innovative programs, healthcare providers have financial responsibility for a population of patients, regardless of where these patients receive care. When a Healthix participant organization is caring for a cohort of patients, Healthix can detect events (e.g., admissions, emergency department visits) that occur in cohort members at other locations and notify the participant organization. Such

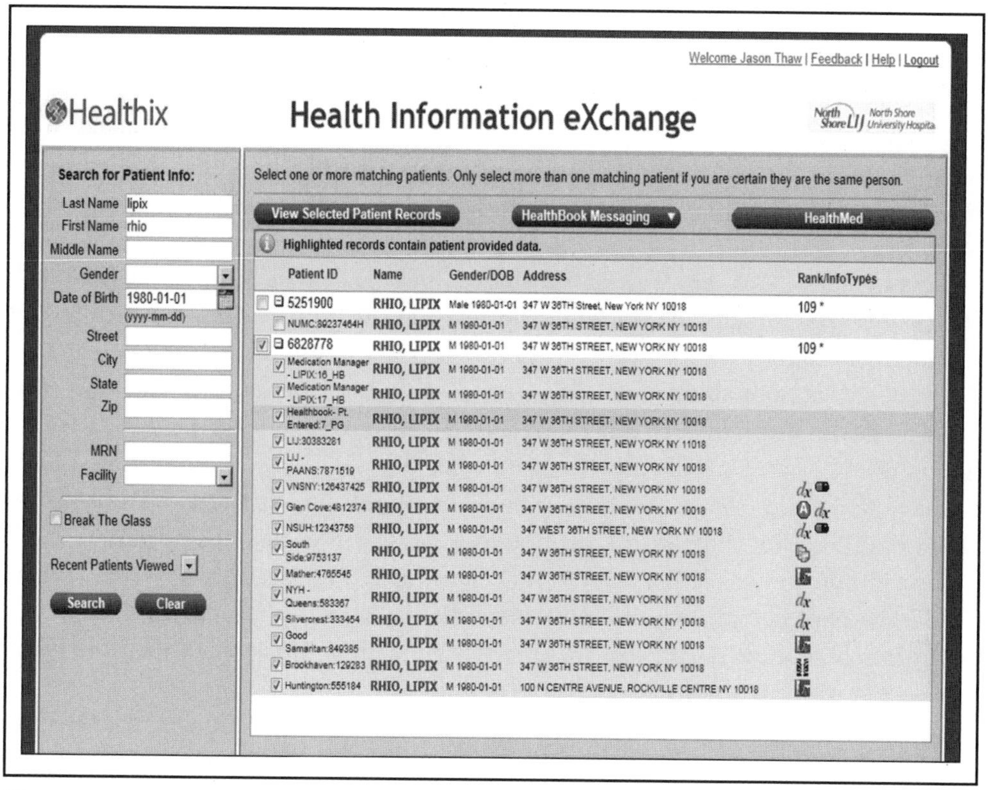

Figure 15-3: Example Screen Shot from Healthix Showing List of Facilities Visited (test patient).

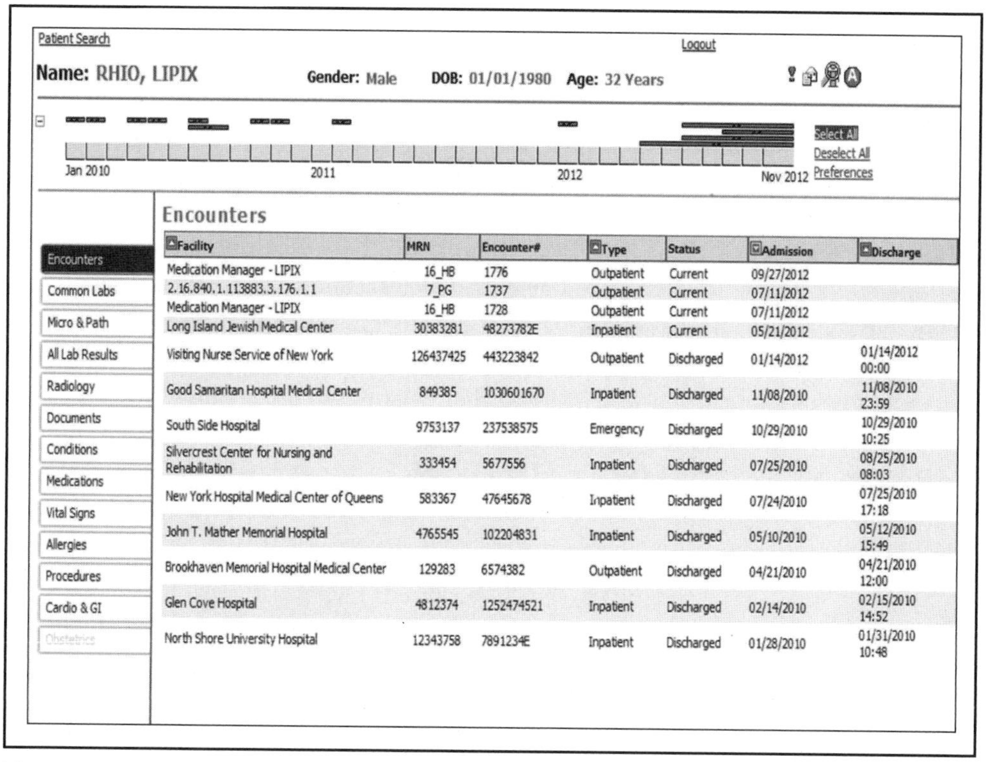

Figure 15-4: Example Screen Shot from Healthix Showing List of Encounters

clinical event detection and notification is a key service that an RHIO can provide. Innovative care delivery models that require such capabilities will expand under New York State's Delivery System Reform Incentive Program.[29]

Usage. In early 2014, Healthix clinicians were using the Healthix portal over 7,000 times per month to look up patient data, and 2,000 clinical event notification messages were being sent per month. Several testimonials have been received from clinicians about how Healthix assisted with clinical decision making and improved the effectiveness and efficiency of care. No formal studies have been published about Healthix's ability to improve quality or efficiency; however, evaluations of the impact of HIE at similar organizations are starting to appear (as will be discussed later in this chapter).

Financial sustainability and the State Health Information Network for New York. Since its inception, Healthix has received funds from the New York State HEAL programs, other granting agencies, and member dues. In early 2014, New York State included $55 million in its 2014–2015 budget to fund the State Health Information Network of New York (SHIN-NY, pronounced *shiny*).[30] A substantial portion of these funds will flow to the RHIOs in New York State, including Healthix, to support their technical, policy compliance, and outreach activities. Although budgets are approved on an annual basis, it is expected that the funding will be available to the RHIOs for three years.

SHIN-NY is an interconnected network of networks in New York State that enables the sharing of patient records.[31] SHIN-NY is under development and when completed will enable exchange of clinical data among EHRs, notification alerts, and other services statewide. There are nine independent RHIOs in New York State that mediate the statewide services. The New York eHealth Collaborative (NYeC) works with the RHIOs and the New York State Department of Health to coordinate the implementation of statewide services. The New York State Department of Health exercises overall authority of SHIN-NY through regulation and funding. The Department of Health also supports the usage of SHIN-NY for public health purposes and emergency preparedness. NYeC advances statewide interoperability, facilitates the development of privacy policies and technical standards for SHIN-NY. NYeC also operates technology and provides technical services to some of the RHIOs. The RHIOs provide basic interoperability services to their members, assure adherence to statewide policies, conduct outreach activities, and assure that the interoperability services meet the business goals of their participants.

Contact information for HIE organizations is available for each of the fifty states.[32]

Exchange of data among RHIOs and other organizations. While a RHIO enables exchange of data among participants in a particular community, there may be a need to exchange data across communities. The eHealth Exchange is a technical and policy framework that allows the exchange of patient data across HIE organizations.[33] The eHealth Exchange, which was formerly known as the Nationwide Health Information Network initiative, includes federal agencies, state-level HIEs, and other HIE organizations, and is an active test bed for addressing cross-RHIO data exchange challenges.

"Direct" Model for Health Information Exchange

Late in the first decade of the 2000s, national policymakers realized that the RHIO model was far more complex than initially recognized and that a different approach might be necessary to realize HIE at a national level. Some of the complexities with the RHIO model that were realized included:

- The data interfaces between participants' core systems and the edge servers were expensive to develop and required careful crafting to assure that the data were represented consistently across the RHIO.
- The edge servers, data centers, and networks were expensive to establish and maintain.
- New privacy policies were needed to support data retrieval across a broad network of providers. These policies were time consuming to develop.
- RHIOs required the development of new governance models.

The complexities of RHIOs were reflected in the fact that on a nationwide basis only a minority of RHIOs was projected to be able to support themselves.[25] Even in New York State, where hundreds of millions of dollars were committed to advancement of the RHIO model, progress proceeded only at a modest pace.

Also, with the advent of HITECH in 2009, the MU program had dedicated $14 billion to $27 billion in incentive payments to increase the adoption of EHRs nationally. Federal policymakers wondered whether there was a way to leverage the federal investment in EHRs to promote HIE.

In early 2010, ONC sponsored a project known as "Direct."[34] The vision of Direct was that a healthcare provider using an EHR that is certified by ONC would be able to transmit a packet of clinical information—for example, a patient summary, a procedure note, a discharge summary, etc.—to another provider who is using a certified EHR. Direct is intended to mimic electronically what already often happens with paper-based processes, i.e., one provider transmitting information to another provider about a patient to support a particular care process. Such provider-provider communication already takes place in several scenarios; an acute care hospital sends a copy of a patient's discharge summary to the nursing home at the time of discharge, a primary care provider sends key information to a specialist at the time a consultation is requested, a hospital sends relevant data to a public health agency, etc.

The technical approach to Direct is that a lightweight gateway could be incorporated into certified EHRs that could send a packet of data to another healthcare provider (Figure 15-5). The sender would need an address for the recipient (analogous to an e-mail address). A gateway on the recipient's EHR could receive the incoming data and place it into the clinician's inbox. The model for Direct includes the concept of a health information service provider, or HISP, that manages the routing of messages between healthcare providers (similar to the way that e-mail messages are routed using the Internet). A provider who wishes to use Direct will need to belong to a HISP and also will need the recipient's direct address.

The Direct model has several appealing characteristics:

- The gateway protocols needed to support Direct can be developed in a small number of months and can be added into certified systems relatively easily and inexpensively.
- No patient-matching algorithms are needed. The data recipient is responsible for assuring that the transmitted data are linked to the correct patient's record.
- No edge server or interface engine is needed.

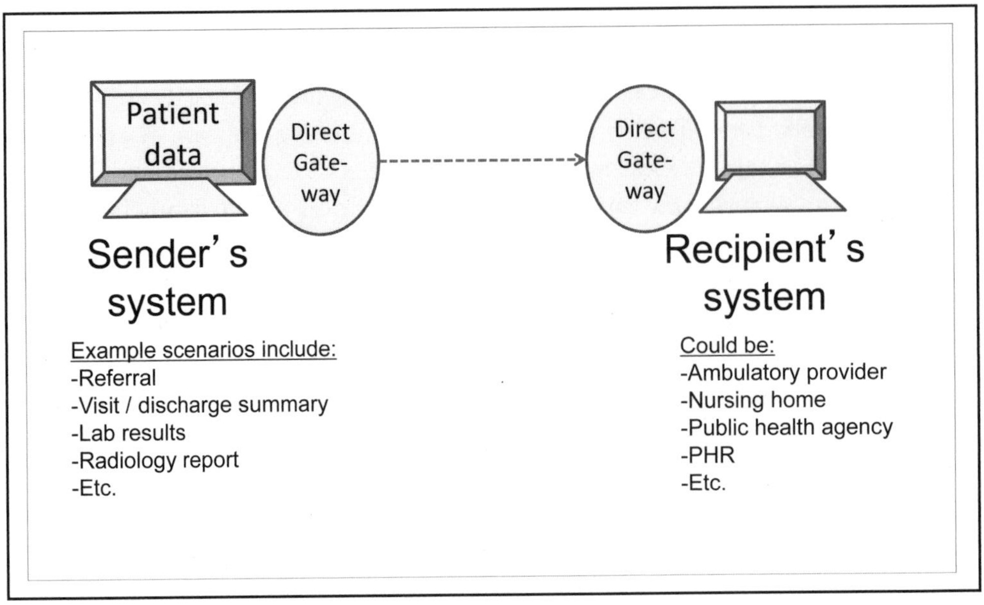

Figure 15-5: Data Flow Diagram for "Directed" Exchange

- No new complex governance structures are needed.
- No new privacy policies or laws are needed because existing privacy frameworks govern the communication of clinical data between two providers (in contrast, the RHIO model needed a privacy model to govern access to a broad network of data, which is different than what Direct enables).

To be implemented, the Direct model requires the following:

- Directories of addresses of individual providers and provider organizations
- Robust authorization processes and identity assurance, so that a recipient can be confident in the source of data
- Integration of Direct messages with providers' existing messaging workflow
- Solutions to technical concerns (robustness, timeliness of message delivery)

The RHIO model of HIE sometimes is called *query-based exchange* or a *pull* model, and the Direct model sometimes is called *directed exchange* or a *push* model. Direct is felt to be useful for a number of healthcare scenarios, such as the transfer of the patient from one care location to another, the delivery of clinical data to a personal health record, and the delivery of data to public health agencies. Direct would not be useful when a patient with no known history presents to the emergency department; for this scenario, query-based exchange would be preferable. Direct also does not support the aggregation of data for such analytic purposes as research, pharma co-surveillance, or public health. It is important to note that Direct is not intended to replace query-based exchange—the two methods are complementary. Direct is felt to be an easier, less-expensive approach to HIE, which can support important processes of care while the complexities of query-based exchange are solved.

Integration of Direct into MU. Policymakers felt that the Direct model of HIE was more scalable and more easily implementable than the RHIO-based model. For these reasons, as the federal government was looking to advance interoperability through the

MU program, it included objectives that require the use of Direct-based messaging to transmit clinical data between providers. Specifically, in Stage 2 of MU, eligible providers and eligible hospitals must provide summary of care documents electronically for 10 percent of patients being transferred to another setting of care. The electronic transmission must be done using Direct. Certified EHRs must support the Direct protocols. Compliance with the transition of care objectives for MU will be a substantial step forward for HIE for several provider organizations.

EVALUATION OF HEALTH INFORMATION EXCHANGE EFFORTS

HIE has the potential to improve the quality and efficiency of care; however, like any technology, it needs to be evaluated to understand the extent to which potential benefits are realized. IT in healthcare exists in a complex socio-technical framework[35] that includes hardware, software, human-computer interfaces, implementation and support staff, workflow considerations, policies, regulations, and monitoring and improvement of the system. Given all the challenges, there is much to be learned from implementation of HIE.

One challenge in making the best use of HIE capabilities is to assure that access to the data are easily accessible to the clinician. Many implementations of query-based HIE require the clinician to log-in to an application other than the electronic medical record system to access the data from remote facilities. Emerging models of query-based exchange will deliver data from the HIE directly to the clinician's EHRs. Similarly, Direct-based models of HIE will deliver data from a remote facility directly to a clinician's inbox.

In an analysis of use of a query-based HIE at emergency departments in Memphis, Tennessee, the system was accessed in 6.8 percent of visits.[36] This may seem like a low number, but in many emergency department visits, e.g., for a minor self-limited complaint, it may not make sense to access an HIE. Use of the system was higher in patients with comorbidities, patients known to have data in the exchange, and in repeat visits. Test results and discharge summaries were the most frequently accessed data elements. A separate analysis of interviews with fifteen physicians at four separate hospitals in Memphis[37] revealed inter-physician variation in (1) the use of the system, (2) the extent to which they believed it could influence clinical decisions, (3) their attitudes to access challenges and design flaws, and (4) their sense of value of the HIE and justification for not using it more frequently. The study highlighted various ways that the system could be improved to increase adoption by the emergency physicians.

An HIE in coastal South Carolina was accessed in 5.4 percent of emergency department encounters.[38] Through a survey, physicians estimated that when accessed, the exchange could decrease the use of laboratory studies by 30 percent, radiology studies by 47 percent, consultations by 19 percent, and admissions by 11 percent. Physicians also said that the exchange improved quality and saved time. Although encouraging, the subjective impressions were not objectively verified.

In the Memphis exchange, an analysis[39] found that emergency department encounters where the system was accessed had fewer hospital admissions (odds ratio, 0.27) when compared with matched cases when the system was not accessed. In a community in New York State, an HIE was accessed in 2.4 percent of emergency department encounters. The odds of an admission were 30 percent lower when the system was accessed.[40] The Memphis and New York experiences are early and need to be replicated, but if HIEs have even a modest impact on admissions, this would have a large financial impact because admissions are a major driver of cost.

Some studies are beginning to show an impact of HIE on the use of imaging studies. In Memphis, repeat imaging of any kind in the emergency department for back pain decreased by 36 percent when the HIE was accessed, although costs did not change because the use of computerized tomography increased.[41] Similarly, also in Memphis, use of the exchange decreased the use of neuroimaging in the emergency department for patients presenting multiple times complaining of headache.[42] Both these studies highlighted the complexity of creating the appropriate experimental design and controlling for confounders. An analysis of data from state emergency department databases in California and Florida from 2007 to 2010 found that organizations that reported involvement in HIE had an 8 percent to 13 percent decrease of repeat computerized tomography, ultrasound, and chest x-ray.[43] As with the impact of HIE with admissions, these early studies of the impact on ancillary use are encouraging and need further corroboration.

Some studies are beginning to show the impact of HIE on the quality of care. In a community in New York State, use of an HIE portal was associated with an increase in performance at or above benchmark from 57 percent to 64 percent for a set of 15 quality measures that were being used for a pay-for-performance program.[44] Measures that were expected to be affected by the portal were impacted to a greater extent than those that one would not expect to be impacted by the portal. Doebbeling et al.[45] demonstrated that multihospital infection collaboratives that included but were not limited to the use of HIE could be effective in reducing methicillin-resistant staphylococcus aureus (MRSA) infections by over 80 percent. HIE also can be used to measure quality from a community-wide, rather than an institution-specific, perspective. In one analysis, an HIE could identify 20 percent more patients who visited an emergency department more than four times in a 30-day-period, compared with data from only one institution.[46]

Some HIE implementations include the capability to notify providers when such events as admissions and emergency department visits take place. At an HIE organization in New York City, such a notification service was implemented and used to notify a federally qualified health center and a home health agency when their patients had encounters at the inpatient facilities participating in the exchange.[47] The total number of events detected in this pilot project was relatively small. One of the key lessons learned was that the organization receiving the notifications needed to have a workflow designed to manage the incoming messages.[48] A similar capability has been implemented at an HIE in Indiana.[49] Inpatient events are detected by the HIE and are communicated to health plans and Medicare-chartered ACOs. Such capabilities are in their infancy but increasingly will be a critical component of innovative care delivery models.

Some studies are beginning to analyze the ability of HIE to support public health use cases.[7] HIE organizations can serve as effective brokers between provider organizations and public health organizations; however, several challenges need to be addressed. For example, key use case and technical design decisions still need to be negotiated across all participants in the exchange. This decision-making process can be complex.[50] Data needed to support public health may be inconsistent across participants in the exchange.[51] Finally, the information systems capabilities of public health departments may limit the value that HIE can bring to public health processes.[52]

In summary, the number of evaluations of the impact of HIE on the quality and efficiency of care is increasing. Many of the studies are at their early stages and need replication and verification. It is likely that HIE will have its greatest impact when it is integrated with such programs as ACOs, PCMHs, bundling, etc., that are designed to improve the coordination of care and are intended to integrate HIE with workflow and other capabilities. Assessment of the impact of these programs—with HIE as an underlying enabling capability—will be important.

TRENDS IN HEALTH INFORMATION EXCHANGE

As mentioned previously, the RHIO model was promoted in the mid-2000s as an approach to advance interoperability of clinical data but by the late 2000s, challenges to the RHIO model, such as cost, technical complexity, governance complexity, policy complexity, and financial sustainability were beginning to be appreciated. Starting at the end of the 2000s, policy researchers began to document the challenges to the RHIO model and the impact on pioneering organizations. Adler-Milstein et al. in a survey-based analysis in 2009 found that only 41 percent of 55 operational RHIOs were self-sustaining and that only 28 percent of the remainder expected ever to be able to cover costs.[53] A subsequent analysis on the same set of organizations[54] found that involving hospitals and ambulatory providers and obtaining funding directly from participants were predictors of success while early grant funding was a negative predictor of success. In 2011, in a follow-up survey, Adler-Milstein et al.[55] found that only 25 of 75 operational RHIOs were financially viable. This called into question whether RHIOs could reasonably support HIE at a national level. In another study, using the American Hospital Association Information Technology (AHA IT) survey, Adler-Milstein et al. found that 10.7 percent of hospitals engaged in HIE with unaffiliated providers (not necessarily through a RHIO).[56] In 2013, again using an administered survey, Adler-Milstein et al.[25] found that 30 percent of U.S. hospitals and 10 percent of ambulatory providers were participating in HIE organizations; however, 74 percent of the HIE organizations did not have a robust sustainable business model. This article highlighted concern about the dependence of exchange organizations on public funding. As mentioned previously, the bulk of funding for RHIOs in New York State continues to be provided by the state through the Department of Health.

ONC,[57,58] using data from the annual AHA IT survey, noted that U.S. hospitals increased exchange with external providers from 41 percent to 62 percent in 2013 and the proportion of hospitals exchanging data with external ambulatory providers increased from 36 percent to 57 percent. These results are encouraging but they do not reflect the extent of the exchange activities, for example, to what extent some or all of the ambulatory providers affiliated with a hospital are participating in exchange activities with a hospital.

In an evaluation of the State Information Exchange Cooperative Program mentioned previously, Dullabh et al.[59] interviewed participants in 5 states and found varying factors affecting statewide HIE activity including strategy and planning, implementation experiences, technical approaches, leadership and governance approaches, approaches to patient consent, sustainability, enablers, and challenges. The researchers recommended focusing on governance, harnessing emerging innovative models of care such as ACOs and PCMHs as vehicles for the promotion of HIE, and that states can support the expansion of HIE by communicating its value as well as the need for participant involvement in funding.

In 2012, ONC laid out a strategy for the promotion of HIE.[60] They noted that HIE is critical to patient care, that little information sharing was occurring, that HIE could be expensive, and that diverse models were emerging. They said that the role of ONC was to set goals, to lead the development of standards, and to keep the focus on patient care. They recognized three forms of exchange – directed exchange, query-based exchange, and consumer-mediated exchange, for example, through the use of PHRs. Appropriate roles for states included building and maintaining infrastructure, engaging stakeholders, setting privacy and security policies, encouraging the use of standards, and increasing motivation for HIE though payment policies, e.g., Medicaid-based care delivery programs that reward quality and efficiency.

In June 2014, ONC released a "10-Year Vision to Achieve an Interoperable Health IT Infrastructure."[61] The report acknowledges progress in HIE and "renews focus on a nationwide interoperable health IT infrastructure." By 2024, stakeholders in the United States should have an array of products and services that improve care. Building on progress that has been made to date, the report lays out guiding principles including building on the existing health IT infrastructure, acknowledging that a variety of approaches will be needed to realize interoperability, involving the public, leveraging the market, taking simple steps first and more complex steps subsequently, maintaining modularity, focusing on value, and protecting privacy and security. The report lays out 3-year, 6-year and 10-year agendas that, respectively, accelerate health information exchange, use information to improve care and lower cost, and establish a full-fledged learning healthcare system. ONC says that the building blocks of the plan include core technical standards and functions; certification to support adoption of products; privacy and security protections; a supportive business, clinical, cultural, and regulatory environment; and governance for a nationwide health information network. Clearly, ONC has laid out an ambitious vision and agenda; the appropriate support of government will be critical if the vision of interoperable health IT is to be realized.

CHALLENGES TO THE FURTHER DEPLOYMENT OF HEALTH INFORMATION EXCHANGE

The HITECH Act set out to advance the nationwide dissemination of interoperable health IT in the United States. There has been great progress in the adoption of EHRs; however, the lack of robust interoperability has created questions about the value that can be derived.

A report[62] from six U.S. Senators in 2013 gave their impressions of key deficiencies in the MU program. In addition to concerns about greater costs than had been envisioned, a lack of oversight of the program, concerns about patient privacy, and concerns about the program's sustainability, the senators identified a "lack of a clear path toward interoperability" as a hurdle to realizing the program's potential benefits.

As has been noted previously, hurdles to HIE include but are not limited to technical challenges. JASON, a group of well-respected scientists, noted the challenges to HIE and recommended an overall architecture to accelerate interoperability.[63] Key characteristics of this proposed architecture include a platform-agnostic strategy; use of public application program interfaces (APIs) and open standards, interfaces, and protocols; data encryption; inclusion of metadata with the data; representation of data at an atomic level; and a migration path from current legacy EHRs.

Because patient matching is a key success factor in HIE and no unique individual identifier for healthcare data exists in the United States, statistical matching algorithms currently are used to link records across institutions. These algorithms are imperfect, which is a current limitation to HIE capabilities nationwide. To address the situation, in September 2013, ONC launched the Patient Matching Initiative.[64] The key findings of the initiative are standardized attributes should be required in exchange transactions; certification criteria should be used to assure that EHRs capture the attributes relevant to patient matching; use of additional attributes to improve matching should be studied; to support innovation, flexibility should be allowed in the algorithms; processes should be created to identify potential duplicates in large patient indexes; and government and industry should work together to advance new approaches to patient matching.

An expert panel identified seven aspects of HIE that, if not handled well, could lead to unintended consequences.[65] These aspects are as follows: the risk of missing data due to poor patient matching or technical factors that interfere with obtaining complete data about the patient, the risk of data overload, assuring that the HIE fits well into the clinician's workflow, assuring that patients understand the nature of HIE and that their privacy is assured, assuring that healthcare provider organizations are comfortable that the data in an HIE will not be used competitively and that they are not taking on legal risks by participating in the exchange, assuring that the technology functions well, and assuring that governance and other administrative aspects of participating in an HIE are not overwhelming to healthcare providers. In its strategy analysis, ONC also recognized these challenges, as well as the need to use data for secondary purposes such as research and analyses of the delivery of care.[60]

SUMMARY

HIE is a critical underpinning of a modern healthcare system. The ability to access data where it is needed, not just where it is generated, can improve clinical care, public health, research, and the discovery of new knowledge. However, the realization of this capability has proven difficult to attain. Investments by the federal government, state governments, and the private sector are laying out directions for improvement, but progress is slow. Emerging payment models, which for the first time in history require efficiencies in the delivery of care, are creating new motivations for advancement in HIE capabilities. As these capabilities are integrated into healthcare providers' workflow, the long hoped-for benefits should be realized.

REFERENCES

1. A Strategy for Building the National Health Information Infrastructure. National Center for Vital and Health Statistics. 2001. http://www.ncvhs.hhs.gov/nhiilayo.pdf. Accessed November 17, 2014.
2. Shapiro JS, Kannry J, Lipton M, Goldberg E, Conocenti P, Stuard S, Wyatt BM, Kuperman G. Approaches to patient health information exchange and their impact on emergency medicine. Ann Emerg Med. 2006 Oct;48(4):426-32.
3. Smith PC, Araya-Guerra R, Bublitz C, et al. Missing clinical information during primary care visits. JAMA. 2005;2;293(5):565-571.
4. Stiell A, Forster AJ, Stiell IG, et al. Prevalence of information gaps in the emergency department and the effect on patient outcomes. *CMAJ*. 2003;169(10):1023-1028.
5. Campion TR Jr, Vest JR, Ancker JS, et al. HITEC Investigators. AMIA Annual Symposium Proceedings. Nov 16, 2013:175-84. Patient encounters and care transitions in one community supported by automated query-based health information exchange.
6. Tamblyn R, Poissant L, Huang A, et al. Estimating the information gap between emergency department records of community medication compared to on-line access to the community-based pharmacy records. *J Am Med Inform Assoc*. 2014;21(3):391-398.
7. Shapiro JS, Mostashari F, Hripcsak G, et al. Using health information exchange to improve public health. *Am J Public Health*. 2011 Apr;101(4):616-623.
8. AHRQ – Care Coordination. http://www.ahrq.gov/professionals/prevention-chronic-care/improve/coordination/index.html. Accessed November 19, 2014.
9. DesRoches CM, Campbell EG, Rao SR, et al. Electronic health records in ambulatory care—a national survey of physicians. *N Engl J Med*. 2008;3;359(1):50-60.
10. Jha AK, DesRoches CM, Campbell EG, et al. Use of electronic health records in U.S. hospitals. *N Engl J Med*. 2009;16;360(16):1628-1638.
11. CMS. EHR Incentive Programs. https://www.cms.gov/ehrincentiveprograms/. Accessed November 19, 2014.
12. Blumenthal D, Tavenner M. The "meaningful use" regulation for electronic health records. *N Engl J Med*. 2010;5;363(6):501-504.
13. Use and Characteristics of EHRs Among Office-Based Physician Practices. NCHS Data Brief. Number 143, January 2014. http://www.cdc.gov/nchs/data/databriefs/db143.htm. Accessed November 19, 2014.
14. ONC State HIE Implementation Status. http://www.healthit.gov/policy-researchers-implementers/state-hie-implementation-status. Accessed November 19, 2014.
15. HL7 Messaging Standard Version 2.5.1. http://www.hl7.org/implement/standards/product_brief.cfm?product_id=144. Accessed November 19, 2014.
16. Consolidated CDA Overview. http://www.healthit.gov/policy-researchers-implementers/consolidated-cda-overview. Accessed November 19, 2014.
17. NCPDP Standards Information. http://www.ncpdp.org/Standards/Standards-Info. Accessed November 19, 2014.
18. Get LOINC. http://loinc.org/downloads. Accessed November 19, 2014.
19. RxNorm Overview. http://www.nlm.nih.gov/research/umls/rxnorm/overview.html. Accessed November 19, 2014.
20. SNOMED Clinical Terms. http://www.nlm.nih.gov/research/umls/Snomed/snomed_main.html. Accessed November 19, 2014.

21. International Classification of Diseases, Ninth Revision, Clinical Modification (ICD-9-CM). http://www.cdc.gov/nchs/icd/icd9cm.htm. Accessed November 19, 2014.

22. HL7 Standard Code Set CVX — Vaccines Administered. http://www2a.cdc.gov/vaccines/iis/iisstandards/vaccines.asp?rpt=cvx. Accessed November 19, 2014.

23. ONC Certification processes for EHR technologies. http://www.healthit.gov/providers-professionals/certification-process-ehr-technologies. Accessed November 19, 2014.

24. ONC Meaningful Use definition and objectives. http://www.healthit.gov/providers-professionals/meaningful-use-definition-objectives. Accessed November 19, 2014.

25. Adler-Milstein J, Bates DW, Jha AK. Operational health information exchanges show substantial growth, but long-term funding remains a concern. *Health Aff (Millwood).* 2013;32(8):1486-1492.

26. Brailer DJ. Interoperability: the key to the future health care system. *Health Aff (Millwood).* 2005 Jan-Jun;Suppl Web Exclusives:W5-19-W5-21.

27. Healthix website. http://www.healthix.org. Accessed November 19, 2014.

28. New York State Department of Health. Health homes for Medicaid Enrollees With Chronic Conditions. http://www.health.ny.gov/health_care/medicaid/program/medicaid_health_homes/. Accessed November 19, 2014.

29. New York State Delivery System Reform Incentive Program (DSRIP). http://www.health.ny.gov/health_care/medicaid/redesign/delivery_system_reform_incentive_payment_program.htm. Accessed November 19, 2014.

30. Final state budget funds New York's EHR system. Press Release, March 31, 2014. http://nyehealth.org/wp-content/uploads/2014/03/Final-State-Budget-Funds-New-York%E2%80%99s-Electronic-Health-Records-System-Press-Release_FINAL_03-31-14.pdf. Accessed November 19, 2014.

31. New York eHealth Collaborative. Statewide network (SHIN-NY). http://nyehealth.org/what-we-do/statewide-network/. Accessed November 19, 2014.

32. ONC State HIE coordinators. http://healthit.gov/sites/default/files/state-hie-contacts-april-2013.xlsx. Accessed November 19, 2014.

33. What is the eHealth exchange? http://www.healthit.gov/providers-professionals/faqs/what-ehealth-exchange. Accessed November 19, 2014.

34. ONC Direct Project. http://www.healthit.gov/policy-researchers-implementers/direct-project. Accessed November 19, 2014.

35. Sittig DF, Singh H. A new sociotechnical model for studying health information technology in complex adaptive healthcare systems. *Qual Saf Healthj Care.* 2010;19 Suppl 3:i68-74.

36. Johnson KB, Unertl KM, Chen Q, et al. Health information exchange usage in emergency departments and clinics: the who, what, and why. *J Am Med Inform Assoc.* 2011;18(5):690-697.

37. Thorn SA, Carter MA, Bailey JE. Emergency physicians' perspectives on their use of health information exchange. *Ann Emerg Med.* 2014;63(3):329-337.

38. Carr CM, Gilman CS, Krywko DM, et al. Observational study and estimate of cost savings from use of a health information exchange in an academic emergency department. *J Emerg Med.* 2014;46(2):250-256.

39. Frisse ME, Johnson KB, Nian H, et al. The financial impact of health information exchange on emergency department care. *J Am Med Inform Assoc.* 2012;19(3):328-333.

40. Vest JR, Kern LM, Campion TR Jr, et al. Association between use of a health information exchange system and hospital admissions. *Appl Clin Inform.* 2014;12;5(1):219-231.

41. Bailey JE, Pope RA, Elliott EC, et al. Health information exchange reduces repeated diagnostic imaging for back pain. *Ann Emerg Med.* 2013;62(1):16-24.

42. Bailey JE, Wan JY, Mabry LM, et al. Does health information exchange reduce unnecessary neuroimaging and improve quality of headache care in the emergency department? *J Gen Intern Med.* 2013;28(2):176-183.

43. Lammers EJ, Adler-Milstein J, Kocher KE. Does health information exchange reduce redundant imaging? Evidence from emergency departments. *Med Care.* 2014;52(3):227-234.

44. Kern LM, Barrón Y, Dhopeshwarkar RV, et al. Health information exchange and ambulatory quality of care. *Appl Clin Inform.* 2012;30;3(2):197-209.

45. Doebbeling BN, Flanagan ME, Nall G, et al. Multihospital infection prevention collaborative: informatics challenges and strategies to prevent MRSA. AMIA Annual Symposium Proceedings. 2013 Nov 16; 2013:317-325.

46. Shapiro JS, Johnson SA, Angiollilo J, et al. Health information exchange improves identification of frequent emergency department users. *Health Aff (Millwood).* 2013;32(12):2193-2198.

47. Moore T, Shapiro JS, Doles L, et al. Event detection: a clinical notification service on a health information exchange platform. AMIA Annual Symposium Proceedings. 2012;2012:635-642.

48. Altman R, Shapiro JS, Moore T, et al. Notifications of hospital events to outpatient clinicians using health information exchange: a post-implementation survey. *Inform Prim Care.* 2012;20(4):249-255.

49. AHRQ report. Statewide Health Information Exchange Provides Daily Alerts About Emergency Department and Inpatient Visits, Helping Health Plans and Accountable Care Organizations Reduce Utilization and Costs. http://innovations.ahrq.gov/content.aspx?id=3988. Accessed November 19, 2014.

50. Phillips AB, Wilson RV, Kaushal R, et al. HITEC investigators. Implementing health information exchange for public health reporting: A comparison of decision and risk management of three regional health information organizations in New York state. *J Am Med Inform Assoc.* 2014;21(e1):e173-177.

51. Dixon BE, McGowan JJ, Grannis SJ. Electronic laboratory data quality and the value of a health information exchange to support public health reporting processes. AMIA Annual Symposium Proceedings. 2011;2011:322-330.

52. Vest JR, Issel LM. Factors related to public health data sharing between local and state health departments. Health Serv Res. 2014;49(1 Pt 2):373-391.

53. Adler-Milstein J, Bates DW, Jha AK. U.S. Regional health information organizations: progress and challenges. *Health Aff (Millwood).* 200928(2):483-492.

54. Adler-Milstein J, Landefeld J, Jha AK. Characteristics associated with regional health information organization viability. *J Am Med Inform Assoc.* 2010;17(1):61-65.

55. Adler-Milstein J, Bates DW, Jha AK. A survey of health information exchange organizations in the United States: Implications for meaningful use. *Ann Intern Med.* 2011;154(10):666-71.

56. Adler-Milstein J, DesRoches CM, Jha AK. Health information exchange among US hospitals. *Am J Manag Care.* 2011;17(11):761-768.

57. Furukawa MF, Patel V, Charles D, et al. Hospital electronic health information exchange grew substantially in 2008-12. *Health Aff (Millwood).* 2013;32(8):1346-1354.

58. ONC Data Brief No. 17, May 2014. Health Information Exchange Among U.S. Non-federal Acute Care Hospitals: 2008-2013. http://www.healthit.gov/sites/default/files/oncdatabrief17_hieamonghospitals.pdf. Accessed November 19, 2014.

59. Dullabh P, Hovey L. Large-scale health information exchange: implementation experiences from five states. *Stud Health Technol Inform.* 2013;192:613-617.

60. Williams C, Mostashari F, Mertz K, et al. From the Office of the National Coordinator: the strategy for advancing the exchange of health information. *Health Aff (Millwood).* 2012;31(3):527-536.

61. ONC 10 -Year Vision to Achieve an Interoperable Health IT Infrastructure. http://www.healthit.gov/sites/default/files/ONC10yearInteroperabilityConceptPaper.pdf. Accessed November 19, 2014.

62. Senators Thune, Alexander, Roberts, Burr, Coburn, Enzi. Re-examining the strategies to successfully adopt health IT. April 16 2013. http://www.amia.org/sites/amia.org/files/EHR-White-Paper.pdf. Accessed November 19, 2014.

63. A robust health data infrastructure. http://healthit.gov/sites/default/files/ptp13-700hhs_white.pdf. Accessed November 19, 2014.

64. ONC Patient Identification and Matching Final Report. http://www.healthit.gov/sites/default/files/patient_identification_matching_final_report.pdf. Accessed November 19, 2014.

65. Kuperman GJ, McGowan JJ. Potential unintended consequences of health information exchange. *J Gen Intern Med*. 2013;28(12):1663-1666.

CHAPTER 16

Privacy and Security

Keith Weiner, RN, MSc

"Feeling guilty feeling scared, hidden cameras everywhere. Stop! Hold on. Stay in control..." (The Kinks, 1981)[1]

CYBERSECURITY – PUBLIC AWAKENING

Cybersecurity had long been little more than a science fiction, pop-culture phenomenon represented in movies such as *War Games*, *The Terminator*, and *The Matrix*. Legendary hackers possessed magical powers to break into government systems and banks with a few keystrokes. They even managed to thwart an alien invasion to save humanity in the film *Independence Day*.

Aside from cybersecurity professionals and corporate asset stakeholders, very few people have had to give data protection more than a passing thought. The occasional virus, pop-up advertisement, or email from a Nigerian Prince promising a secret fortune would present as an annoyance rather than as a genuine threat to the average computer user.

More recently, data security has at times been front and center in the news and on the minds of the general public. Headline after headline, we are reminded of the potential pitfalls of living in a connected world.

National Security Agency (NSA) contractor-turned-whistleblower Edward Snowden exposed some of the NSA's massive surveillance activities. These disclosures have shaken the foundations of international relations and informed a fearful American public that their own government may be spying on them. Even this author's 90-year-old grandmother speaks of how true privacy is rapidly being eroded.

In 2013, Target and its customers suffered the largest retail data breach in history. A heating, ventilation, and air conditioning contractor inadvertently introduced a virus into Target's network. As a result, 40 million credit card numbers and information on about 70 million customers made its way to crafty hackers in Russia and onto headlines in virtually every major news outlet.

Identity theft protection companies promote their services in light of this fresh menace. A television advertisement shows a physician accidentally leaving a patient data-rich laptop in a cab while rushing to a meeting. Of course, the identity theft protection service thwarts the efforts of the thief who just happens to take the same cab immediately after. The potential consequences of a health data breach are being highlighted to the populace.

According to Dell SecurityWorks, the price of a full United States identity dropped from $40 to a mere $25 between 2011 and 2013. Additional medical data may marginally elevate the market value. The inventory is just so overly abundant. Let that sink in for a minute. Your identity is likely worth $25 on the underground market.[2]

In this connected age of well-publicized data breaches, the general public has become more aware of the threat to their privacy, sacred health information, and finances.

WHY HEALTHCARE AND CYBERSECURITY?

What Does Cybersecurity Have to Do with Healthcare?

Stemming from the Health Insurance Portability and Accountability Act of 1996, (HIPAA), the Security Standards Final Rule was released in 2003, providing guidance on physical, administrative, and technologic measures to safeguard protected health information (PHI)—electronic or otherwise. Protecting healthcare information is more than an honorable endeavor. It is a legal responsibility.[3,4,5]

PHI is defined as individually identifiable protected health information. The term ePHI refers to PHI in an electronic format.

Traditional paper-based charting system data have always carried a breach risk. However, the pervasive introduction of the EHR to near-omnipresent levels in the United States has increased the risk likelihood and impact. Healthcare entities have experienced a challenging HIPAA game-changing scenario.

Government programs and grant opportunities as outlined in other chapters have incentivized healthcare entities and providers to adopt and implement EHRs. These technologic advancements come bundled with a significantly increased risk for data breaches. The burden is ultimately on the healthcare entities to take on the additional responsibility of safeguarding PHI.

This chapter will provide a very basic overview of healthcare cybersecurity. Information contained herein is by no means a complete how-to guide. Healthcare IT and cybersecurity are such dynamic topics that one must pursue the most contemporary material to stay current. Always consult with the text of the current legislation itself for the latest directives. Avoid putting too much stock in sources without referencing the legal text. Furthermore, blogs (Geek Doctor), news amalgamators (Google News, Slashdot), mailing lists (US-CERT, SANS), groups (interdisciplinary committees), organizations (HIMSS, GNYHA, NYCREACH), and other professional contacts offer the means by which to keep tabs on the latest information. Peers within IT and other disciplines can provide excellent insight and wisdom. Operating a security program in a vacuum would be otherwise most challenging.

Following is a small sample of links useful to commence exploration.

- HealthIT Government Website – http://healthit.gov/
- American Hospital Association - http://www.aha.org/
- Life As A Healthcare CIO - http://geekdoctor.blogspot.com/
- Google News – http://news.google.com (Can set email alerts by search topic.)

- Slashdot – http://www.slashdot.org (Staple source for computer nerds.)
- US-CERT - http://www.us-cert.gov (Sign up for mailing list.)
- SANS - http://www.sans.org (Sign up for mailing list.)
- HIMSS - http://www.himss.org (State and national membership available.)
- GNYHA - http://www.gnyha.org (New York State – see your own state and local organizations for resources.)
- NYCREACH – http://www.nycreach.org (New York City Regional Electronic Adoption Center For Health – see your own specific regional center for EHR adoption.)

For legislative resources, always go directly to the source. A few primary examples are listed next. Specific information may also be found through a search engine query and then by selecting the official government source from the results.

- **U.S. Department of Health and Human Services** – http://www.HHS.gov
- **Centers for Medicare & Medicaid Services** – http://www.CMS.gov
- **U.S. Government Printing Office** - http://www.gpo.gov (Federal Register)

PRIVACY: LEGAL AND MORAL OBLIGATION

> *"And remember every nurse should be one who is to be depended upon, in other words, capable of being a 'confidential' nurse...she must be no gossip, vain talker; she should never answer questions about her sick except to those who have a right to ask them."*[6]

The tenant of healthcare providers safeguarding the health information of patients is not a concept introduced by HIPAA, HHS's Omnibus Rule, or the HITECH Act. In Florence Nightingale's *Notes on Nursing*, published in 1859, she speaks of how nurses should only disclose confidential information on a need-to-know basis.[6]

己所不欲，勿施於人

"What you do not wish for yourself, do not do to others." – *Confucius*[7]

In all likelihood, your healthcare information and that of people you care about will end up in an electronic format if it is not already there. A reasonable assumption is that typically one would not want such information to be disclosed outside of a need-to-know basis. Safeguard with extreme care others' sensitive information as if it was your own. This "do unto others" adage is found in various forms in both testaments of the Bible, Confucius texts, ancient Greek philosophy, and India's Sanskrit tradition among many other works. Again, this universal ancient wisdom predates HIPAA.

Moral obligation notwithstanding, legislation exists to mandate the implementation and use of safeguards to minimize the risk of unauthorized disclosures.

HHS summarizes the HIPAA Privacy Rule as follows:

> *"The HIPAA Privacy Rule establishes national standards to protect individuals' medical records and other personal health information and applies to health plans, health care clearinghouses, and those health care providers that conduct certain health care transactions electronically. The Rule requires*

appropriate safeguards to protect the privacy of personal health information, and sets limits and conditions on the uses and disclosures that may be made of such information without patient authorization. The Rule also gives patients rights over their health information, including rights to examine and obtain a copy of their health records, and to request corrections."[5]

Paper-based systems could be easily tucked away from prying eyes with little chance of exposure en masse. Traditionally, charts could be copied, faxed, tampered with, or viewed without the likelihood of access being tracked. While this modality seems safe contrasted against a backdrop of sensational cybersecurity headlines, large and small paper-based breaches have occurred and continue to remain a risk.

With the EHR, data are available via multiple sources, people, and systems. Along with this liberalization of information and massive accessibility come the mechanisms by which to track, restrict access, and monitor for inappropriate access. It's a brave new world with an increase in both benefits and risks.

The policy section further along in this chapter will outline the physical, administrative, and technical safeguard components required by the HIPAA Security Rule to protect patient information. The implementation of a comprehensive information security program is beyond the scope of this chapter. However, reflect on the following points in consideration of access to ePHI:

- How is ePHI access logged? Is there remote access by healthcare personnel, vendors, and other business associates? Does anyone review or become alerted to potentially inappropriate access? Remember that even trusted employees have been known to inappropriately disclose information. Countless examples exist of information sold for a variety of reasons. People have been jailed even after making only a scant profit.
- Is information segmented in a fashion that limits access based on job role or even physical location? Maybe one hospital unit should not have access to another's information. Maybe a physician appropriately sees a different set of information than a clerk.
- Is there an education program for the workforce to help in the understanding of legislation and organization policies to which they must adhere? Are there supplementary security awareness reminders? While ignorance is no excuse for the law, HIPAA does compel entities to keep its workforce informed.
- Is there a limitation on administrative access or even any access that goes unlogged? Remember, the NSA has curtailed its system administrators in the wake of Edward Snowden's disclosures. Health IT should learn from this lesson as well.
- Can tampering of information be prevented or at least be discovered?
- What mechanisms are in place to prevent leaks from nefarious sources? (i.e., viruses, hackers, scammers, etc.)
- How secure is the information against damage, physical or otherwise? Are there contingency plans in place for periods of inaccessibility?
- Is there a disaster recovery, business continuity, and backup plan? Have you tested these plans? Careers have been cut short in disaster scenarios when untested backups fail.

- What mechanisms prevent accidental disclosure? Is there a data leak prevention system – either comprehensive through a vendor or otherwise via piecemeal? Can employees send patient files over email – internally and externally – where they reside ad-infinitum in wait for a potential hacker to come along? We see in this chapter how email has been captured by nefarious actors.
- Do you encrypt all data at rest and in motion? An inadvertent disclosure could be as simple as a download to a USB thumb drive that gets lost or an unencrypted stolen laptop that is left or taken. Stolen laptops are a huge source of breaches, by the way. Proper encryption means the would-be thief has inherited a brick-made laptop for all intents and purposes.
- Are your security mechanisms reasonable to implement? If not, people will go around them. One company made everyone change his or her password every day. So, all employees would gather every morning to choose the group password. Only their username was different. In the case of extremely complicated passwords and different usernames for various systems, employees tend to place notes with that information under their keyboards or tape them to their monitors.
- Do you have an identity and access management solution in place? In the first edition of this book, Jonathan Leviss, MD, outlined several solutions. While this topic is complex, consider how you ensure that only those with authorization obtain access. Sometimes the solutions are technological in nature (single sign-on, self-service password resets) and some are administrative (activation and termination notification).

BUILDING THE SECURITY PROGRAM

"If you choose not to decide, you still have made a choice." (Rush, 1980)[8]

Building and supporting a comprehensive security program is necessary to protect both the organization and the patients. Security should be part of an organization's governing structure. A Security Official and a Privacy Official should be named as curators of their respective areas of responsibility. This can be one individual in a dual role, or the roles can be kept separate. Individuals in these roles must be capable of either carrying out or overseeing security and privacy functions for the organization.

Most of this chapter will forego the minutiae of IT security items such as antivirus, firewalls, vulnerability scans, web filtering, and intrusion detection devices. While these and other items are a necessary part of a comprehensive program in monitoring, detecting, and providing protection against threats and are tools of the trade, the scope of this chapter is that of a broad overview.

While much of this chapter is geared toward larger organizations with appropriate resources, even the solo practitioner or small office must have a security program scaled appropriately. There are organizations and services that can help manage the security program. Figure 16-1 displays some of the factors that serve as the foundation for the security program's building blocks.

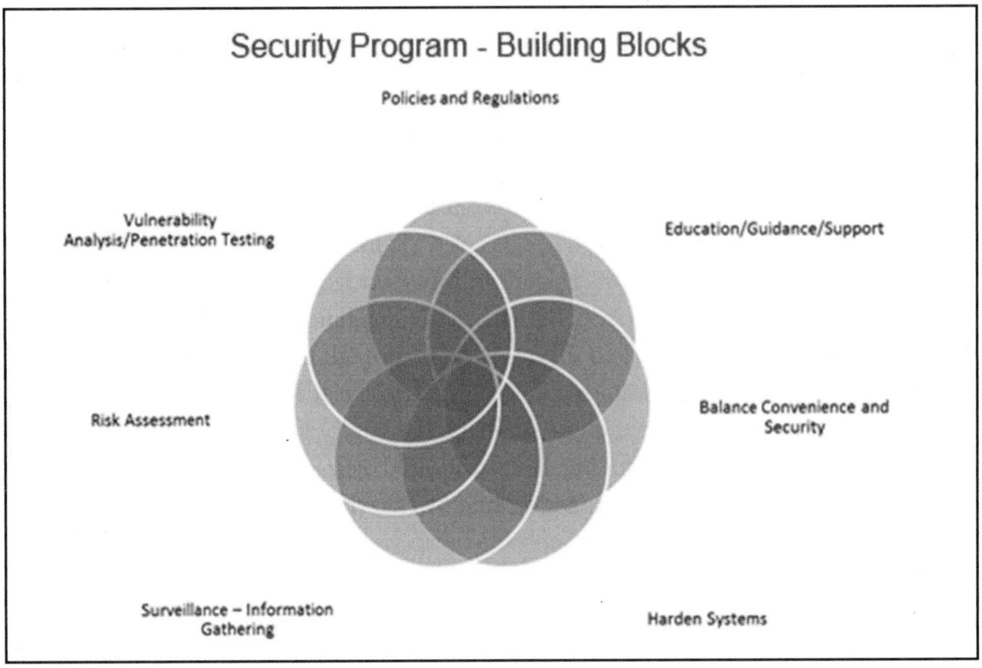

Figure 16-1: Security Program Building Blocks

HUNGRY, HUNGRY HIPAA

Some legislation to become familiar with:

- Health Insurance Portability and Accountability Act of 1996 (HIPAA): includes the protection of patient information and confidentiality.
- HIPAA Privacy Security Rules: HHS published standards to safeguard PHI.
- Health Information Technology for Economic and Clinical Health Act of 2009 (HITECH): enacted as part of the American Recovery and Reinvestment Act to promote health information technology.
- Omnibus Rule (2013) – HHS final rule: implements components of HITECH and strengthens HIPAA privacy and security protections.

Health and Human Services' Omnibus Rule
http://www.gpo.gov/fdsys/pkg/FR-2013-01-25/pdf/2013-01073.pdf

Security Rule Education Paper Series ***highly recommended***
http://www.hhs.gov/ocr/privacy/hipaa/administrative/securityrule/securityruleguidance.html

American Recovery and Reinvestment Act (including HITECH)
http://www.gpo.gov/fdsys/pkg/BILLS-111hr1enr/pdf/BILLS-111hr1enr.pdf

HITECH Enforcement Interim Final Rule
http://www.hhs.gov/ocr/privacy/hipaa/administrative/enforcementrule/hitechenforcementifr.html

Health and Human Services' Security Rule
http://www.hhs.gov/ocr/privacy/hipaa/administrative/securityrule/securityrulepdf.pdf

Health and Human Services' Privacy Rule
http://www.hhs.gov/ocr/privacy/hipaa/administrative/privacyrule/

POLICY

Policies provide the fundamental groundwork for a security program. Each organization may develop its own policies using its own methodologies and governing structure. Policies should be periodically reviewed and updated. Avoid allowing policies to sit unattended ad infinitum with technology-specific references such as Palm Pilot and Windows NT; policies require regular updates. Some organizations and services may provide guidelines, a framework, or samples for policy.

At a bare minimum, policies should follow regulations that govern the organization. These policies do not have to be all inclusive of every law in existence but should provide a framework by which a security program will operate. Policies should be flexible, relevant, and enforceable. Workforce members should be made aware of these policies and understand them.

In Figure 16-2, the Sample Hospital Policy Matrix diagram shows policies that are closely aligned with each element of the HIPAA Security Rule. As per the rule, some policies are quite prescriptive in nature while others require organization to address certain factors. The policies are divided into administrative, physical, and technical safeguards.[4] Other policies should probably exist but should not be overly complex. After all, the purpose of producing policies is that they can be adhered to. Make compliance easy to achieve and people will be compliant. In addition to regulations, policy content may be influenced or required by the organization's needs or those of outside entities such as an insurance company. Generally speaking, an acceptable use policy is a commonplace rules-of-the-road user guide, which may also reference these other policies. As part of workforce education, these policies should be readily available and known by those to whom the policy applies.

INCIDENT REPORTING

All suspected breach incidents must be logged and tracked. There are potential legal considerations and, therefore, every instance should be handled meticulously.

The 2013 HHS Omnibus Rule replaces the "harm" standard with a risk assessment, as previous determinations were more subjective and speculatively underreported. The covered entity or business associate has the burden of proof to determine that any unauthorized disclosure is not considered a breach. Under these new guidelines, business associates are also subject to these HIPAA regulations.

Exemptions to the breach notification requirement exist, such as unintentional use in good faith used within the scope of their authority and without any further impermissible disclosure. There may be an inadvertent disclosure to an authorized person or that unauthorized person could not have easily retained such PHI. In other words, HHS offers reasonable exemptions where applicable.

If PHI is disclosed in a manner not exempt by the Omnibus Rule, then a breach may be considered presumed unless the healthcare entity can determine that a low probably of breach exists based on a risk assessment containing the following elements:

Sample Hospital Policy Matrix - Addressing Each Safeguard Standard					
ADMINISTRATIVE SAFEGUARDS					
Standards	**Sections**	**Implementation Specifications R=Required, A=Addressable**		**Policy Number**	**Policy Name**
Security Management Process	164.308(1)	Risk Analysis	R	9100-204	Risk Analysis
		Risk Management	R	9100-032	Security Management Process
		Sanction Policy	R	9100-032	Security Management Process
		Activity Review	R	9100-032	Security Management Process
Assigned Security Responsibility	164.308(2)		R	9100-033	Assigned Security Responsibility
Workforce Security	164.308(3)	Authorization and/or Supervision	A	9237(100-131 and 700-702)	See: Human Resources Policies On Intranet
		Workforce Clearance Procedure	A	9237(100-131 and 700-702)	See: Human Resources Policies On Intranet
		Termination Procedures	A	9237(100-131 and 700-702)	See: Human Resources Policies On Intranet
Information Access Management	164.308(a)(4)	Isolating Health Care Clearinghouse Functions	R	9100-034	Isolating Health Care Clearinghouse Functions
		Access Authorization	A	9100-035	Access Authorization
		Access Establishment and Modification	A	9100-036	Access Establishment and Modification
Security Awareness and Training	164.308(a)(5)	Security Reminders	A	9100-037	Security Reminders
		Protection From Malicious Software	A	9100-004	Protection From Malicious Software
		Log-in Monitoring	A	9100-038	Log-in Monitoring
		Password Management	A	9100-205	Password Management
Security Incident Procedures	164.308(a)(6)	Response and Reporting	R	9100-039	Response and Reporting
Contingency Plan	164.308(a)(7)	Data Backup Plan	R	9100-040	Contingency Plan
		Disaster Recovery Plan	R	9100-040	Contingency Plan
		Emergency Mode Operation Plan	R	9100-040	Contingency Plan
		Testing and Revision Procedures	A	9100-040	Contingency Plan
		Applications and Data Criticality Analysis	A	9100-040	Contingency Plan
Evaluation	164.308(a)(8)		R	9100-042	Evaluation
Business Associate Contracts and Other Arrangements	164.308(b)(1)	Written Contract or Other Arrangement	R	9200-331	Business Associate Agreements
PHYSICAL SAFEGUARDS					
Standards	**Sections**	**Implementation Specifications R=Required, A=Addressable**		**Policy Number**	**Policy Name**
Facility Access Controls	164.310(a)(1)	Contingency Operations	A	9100-044	Contingency Operations
		Facility Security Plan	A	9100-015	Facility Security Plan
		Access Control and Validation Procedures	A	9100-030	Access Control and Validation Procedures
		Maintenance Records	A	9100-045	Maintenance Records
Workstation Use	164.310(b)	Acceptable Use Policy	R	9200-385	Acceptable Use Policy
Workstation Security	164.310(c)			9100-041	Workstation Security
Device and Media Controls	164.310(d)(1)	Disposal	R	9100-031	Device and Media Controls
		Media Re-use	R	9100-031	Device and Media Controls
		Accountability	A	9100-031	Device and Media Controls
		Data Backup and Storage	A	9100-031	Device and Media Controls
TECHNICAL SAFEGUARDS					
Standards	**Sections**	**Implementation Specifications R=Required, A=Addressable**		**Policy Number**	**Policy Name**
Access Control	164.312(a)(1)	Unique User Identification	R	9100-043	Unique User Identification
		Emergency Access Procedure	R	9100-047	Emergency Access Procedure
		Automatic Logoff	A	9100-219	Automatic Logoff
		Encryption and Decryption	A	9100-029	Encryption
Audit Controls	164.312(b)		R	9100-048	Audit Controls
Integrity	164.312(c)(1)	Mechanism to Authenticate Electronic Protected Health Information	A	9100-046	Mechanism to Authenticate Electronic Protected Health Information
Person or Entity Authentication	164.312(d)		R	9100-049	Person or Entity Authentication
Transmission Security	164.312(e)(1)	Integrity Controls	A	9100-050	Integrity Controls
		Encryption	A	9100-029	Encryption

Figure 16-2: Sample Hospital Policy Matrix

- **Nature/extent.** Determine how much information was involved, how it could be used adverse to the individuals affected, and how it could possibly be used by the person or people it was disclosed to. Was the patient information identifiable or contain particularly sensitive data?
- **Determine who accessed or received the data.** Are the individuals obligated to protect and secure this PHI? Was this information disclosed inappropriately to an employer?
- **Actually used or acquired.** Can you determine whether the information was viewed, or if there was just an opportunity for viewing? Was information sent

to the wrong address? Could information on a stolen laptop or lost hard drive actually be acquired?

- **Mitigation.** Has a confidential or other agreement provided assurances that the information will no longer be used or disclosed?

Where notification of a breach is required, all affected individuals must be notified by the covered entity within 60 calendar days since discovery of the breach. Please note the word "discovery" as one cannot be expected to start the countdown for a breach for which one is unaware.

Notice to the HHS Secretary must occur via a web form within 60 days from the end of the calendar year for breaches of fewer than 500 individuals. For breaches of 500 or more individuals, notification to the Secretary occurs within 60 days, along with a notification to the media. If 10 or more individuals cannot be contacted, a post to a website or local media is required. See current regulations for details.

The HHS website, featuring details of breaches of 500 or more individuals, is commonly referred to in the health IT industry as the "Wall of Shame." This author implores readers to view this website and study common pitfalls and how they can be avoided. Go to the HHS website or do a search for the exact website URL. Spoiler alert: encrypt everything.

BREACH STATS

To demonstrate the pervasiveness of EHR data breaches, this author has compiled statistics from various sources including HHS, Office for Civil Rights (OCR), Greater New York Hospital Association, and The Ponemon Institute.[9,10] Figure 16-3 is a snapshot in time of breaches reported to HHS with noteworthy statistics following.

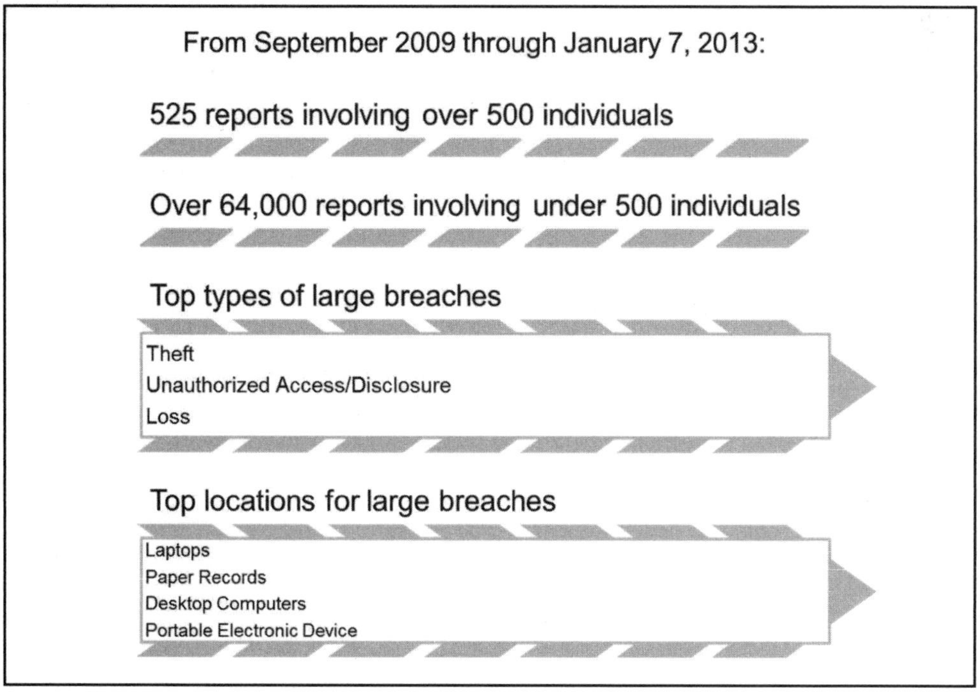

Figure 16-3: HHS Breach Statistics 9/1/2009 to 1/7/2013

- The PHI of more than 21 million individuals has reportedly been breached in United States since September 2009—more than the entire population of Florida (according to 2012 OCR statistics).[11]
- In the two prior years, 94 percent of healthcare organizations had at least one data breach, with 45 percent experiencing five or more incidents.
- $2.4 million is the average economic impact per breach, with the average per record cost of $194.
- 54 percent of organizations state they cannot detect all loss and theft of patient data.
- 51 percent of CEOs are aware that their organization received cyberattacks daily or hourly. (The other 49 percent are seemingly unaware.)
- In the U.K., 77 percent of system developers used real production data during application development. (Warning: Do not test or develop using real patient data.)
- 68 percent of U.S. companies allow BYOD (bring your own device) while 60 percent of those employees bypass their devices' security features. (Hence the need for a mobile device management software solution.)
- Top three causes: Lost or stolen computing devices (hint: not encrypted), employee mistakes, and third-party mistakes.

SPECIFIC BREACH EXAMPLES

"A billion here, a billion there, and pretty soon you're talking real money."
- attributed to Senator Everett McKinley Dirksen[12]

Following are examples of breach incidents and fines. Even the best organizations can make mistakes and learn from them. The one silver lining is that we, too, can learn from these incidents and avoid similar pitfalls.[13]

- **Cignet Health (MD)**
  - Denied patients the right of access to medical records.
  - Failed to respond to OCR's investigation.
  - Fined $4.3 million in a Civil Monetary Penalty.
- **Massachusetts General Hospital**
  - Employee lost paper health records on public transit. NOTE: PAPER INCIDENT
  - Fined $1 million.
- **UCLA Health System**
  - Repeated incidents of unauthorized access to ePHI by workforce members. (Hence the need to limit access, monitor, and let staff know of monitoring capability.)
  - Staff members were fired.
  - Fined $865,500.
- **Phoenix Cardiac Surgery**
  - ePHI was disclosed through the Internet when provider used third-party application hosted in the cloud.

  - Business associate agreements are required when sharing data with cloud computing service providers.
  - Fined $100,000.
- **BCBS Tennessee**
  - ePHI was stored on servers stolen from a deactivated data center after construction and relocation to new facility.
  - Unencrypted hard drives from 57 computers were involved.
  - Data of more than 1 million patients were breached.
  - Fined $1.5 million.
- **Alaska DHSS**
  - Portable storage device stolen from personal vehicle, symptomatic of widespread failure to implement program-wide information security safeguards.
  - The main issue: data were not encrypted.
  - Fined $1.7 million.
- **Massachusetts Eye and Ear Institute**
  - Stolen personal laptop of physician using device as desktop substitute (unencrypted)
  - Had not implemented a program to mitigate identified risks to ePHI.
  - Fined $1.5 million.
- **Hospice of Northern Idaho**
  - Breach affecting 400 individuals when laptop stolen.
  - Provider had not conducted a risk assessment or taken other measures to safeguard ePHI, as required by the HIPAA Security Rule.
  - This incident was the first settlement involving a breach of fewer than 500 individuals, therefore lowering the threshold for fines.
  - Fined $50,000.
- **New York–Presbyterian and Columbia University**
  - An "errantly reconfigured" computer server resulted in the disclosure of 6,800 patients' ePHI to Google and other search engines.
  - The fine between institutions totaled $4.8 million—the largest fine ever levied (so far) for an incident when combining each entity's financial obligation.
- **Athena Health**
  - Photocopier machines returned to the leasing agent contained ePHI of up to 344,579 individuals.
  - Copy/fax/printer machines contain hard drives that could/should be encrypted and wiped per the Department of Defense Degaussing standard before leaving the premises.
  - Fined $1,215,780.

In addition to healthcare organization penalties, individuals may also put themselves at risk. An Oregon nursing assistant was jailed for 8 days for posting photos on a social media website. A UCLA researcher was jailed for 4 months for accessing coworkers' records upon learning of his separation of employment.

BIOMED

Biomedical devices can often become infected with malicious software, which typically causes minor, unnoticed system impairment and little else. Reports indicate that malicious code is to emerge which will target these systems that are potentially rich in patient data. Even factors from the U.S. Food and Drug Administration (FDA) and biomedical vendors can restrict free reign over maintenance, potentially leaving healthcare entities with devices increasingly susceptible to malicious software. In light of this challenging paradigm, measures must be taken to ensure the safeguarding of PHI. As with other systems, biomedical devices can have inherent flaws waiting to be discovered. In other words, do not assume a closed system device with an established brand name is risk free.

Philips Example

The Philips Xper system was exploited by researchers within two hours and remote access was obtained. Patient data were revealed in this medical device hack. Not only was administrative access to the host system obtained, but so was access to patient data stored in connected databases. So severe was this vulnerability that the Department of Homeland Security and FDA took action to oversee the remedy of this severe flaw.

Pacemaker and Insulin Pump Hack Example

Barnaby Jack was a computer security expert famed with, among other things, the ability to hack into ATMs and dispense bills as if he won the jackpot at a slot machine.

He was influenced by an episode of the television program "Homeland" in which a terrorist could remotely hack the pacemaker of a U.S. vice president. In 2012, he demonstrated the means by which to send a high-voltage shock to a pacemaker from 50 feet away with lethal results. He also found a way to send the entire batch of insulin available through an insulin pump, which could have been fatal.

Barnaby Jack died in 2013, one week before presenting his findings on medical device vulnerabilities at the Black Hat Conference in Las Vegas.

RISK ASSESSMENT

A comprehensive risk assessment should be performed at least annually or where required by regulations and programs in which the organization takes part (such as meaningful use). Please note that in numerous breach incidents, the lack of a risk assessment is noted in the incident settlement statements.

According to the HIPAA Security Rule:

- **Risk Analysis § 164.308(a)(1)(ii)(A)**
  "Conduct an accurate and thorough assessment of the potential risks and vulnerabilities to the confidentiality, integrity, and availability of electronic protected health information held by the covered entity."
- **Risk Management § 164.308(a)(1)(ii)(B)**
  "Implement security measures sufficient to reduce risks and vulnerabilities to a reasonable and appropriate level to comply with § 164.306(a) [(the General Requirements of the Security Rule)]."

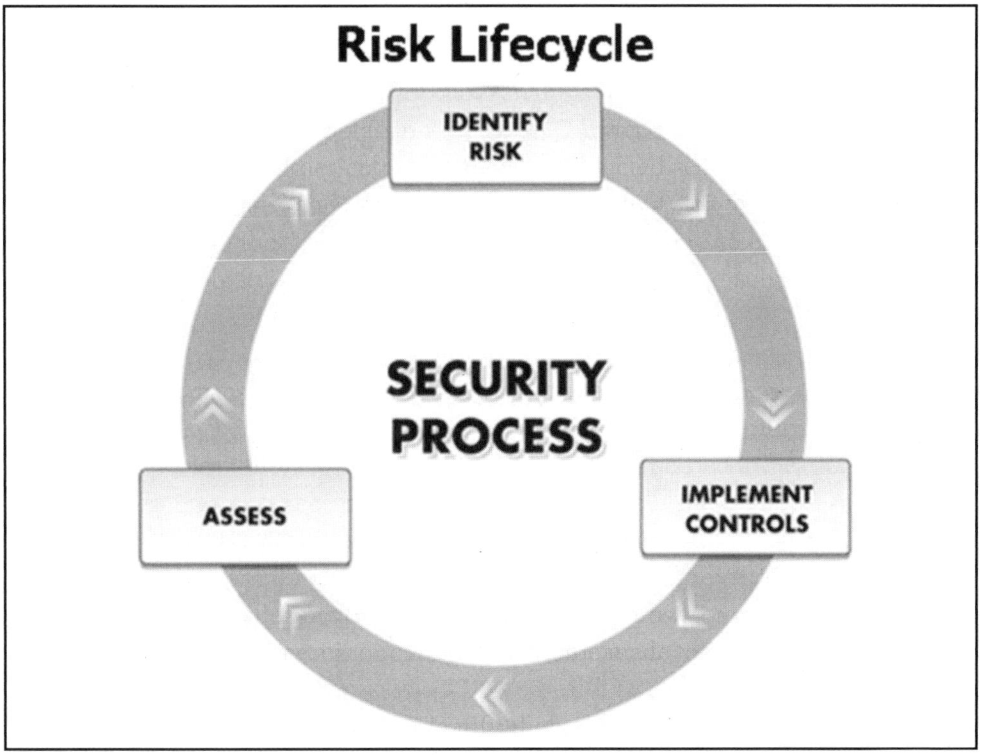

Figure 16-4: Risk Life Cycle

A security professional or vendor may lead a risk assessment if sufficient resources are not available in-house or if an independent surveyor is preferred. Commonly, variants of the NIST-800 standard of risk assessment are used as a framework. There could be separate assessments: one for the organization and one for the IT department. Every clinical, financial, and other application housing, transmitting, or processing sensitive information should be assessed in detail. The assessment is not simply a one-time event, but rather a cycle of assessment, identifying risks, and implementing controls. As illustrated in Figure 16-4, the process continues to carry on ad infinitum. This process may require multidisciplinary input and action depending on the makeup of the organization. Be vigilant in selecting or hiring your security professionals or services. Get past the smoke and mirrors of marketing. A risk assessment is more than marks in a spreadsheet or attestations from staff members—although these may be part of the process.

Think of the organization as a patient with the purpose being to diagnose, treat, prevent illness, and maintain health. Come clean with the doctor and be willing to take the good and the bad news. Objective lab tests such as vulnerability scanning and penetration testing can be most telling. How is the patient's immune system when it comes to viruses and other nefarious agents? Depending on the skill of the assessors and the condition of the patient, you may need to sit down for the results. Bad news can be constructive as an organization learns something of its risk. Once the diagnosis has been accepted and the bitter pill swallowed, the healing begins.

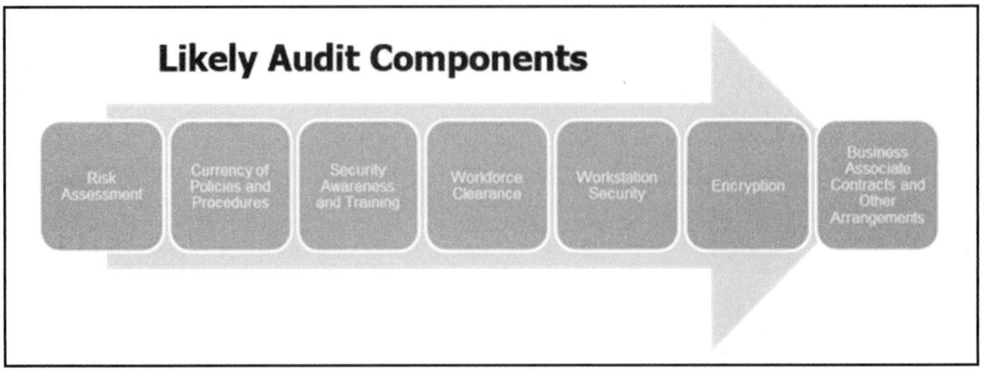

Figure 16-5: Likely Audit Components

SURVIVING AN AUDIT

The HITECH Act requires HHS to provide for periodic audits. These are conducted by the OCR, whose authority has increased under the Omnibus Rule. The audit pilot program assessed the privacy and security of 115 organizations and concluded in December 2012. We know that among other factors, the risk assessment is considered an essential component.

Meaningful Use program participants can also expect the possibility of an audit. Make certain to know the requirements of the program and what is expected of the organization to meet the measurements.

Figure 16-5 outlines some factors to be mindful of when preparing for the organization's eventual audit. Think of an audit as an inevitable when-not-if scenario. Prepare accordingly. Figure 16-6 shows how OCR facilities covered entities in safeguarding PHI above and beyond the higher profile enforcement activities.

ENCRYPTION

If there is only one thing to be learned from this chapter, it is that you must encrypt everything wherever possible. The 2013 Omnibus Rule summarizes encryption as a potential get-out-of-jail-free card.

> *"We encourage covered entities and business associates to take advantage of the safe harbor provision of the breach notification rule by encrypting limited data sets and other protected health information pursuant to the Guidance Specifying the Technologies and Methodologies that Render Protected Health Information Unusable, Unreadable, or Indecipherable to Unauthorized Individuals (74 FR 42740, 42742). If protected health information is encrypted pursuant to this guidance, then no breach notification is required following an impermissible use or disclosure of the information." - HHS Omnibus Rule (Modifications to the Breach Notification Rule Under the HITECH Act)*

Encryption is the process of scrambling data, making it completely incomprehensible to anyone other than intended parties. The National Institute of Standards and Technology guidelines call for an AES (Advanced Encryption Standard) algorithm to

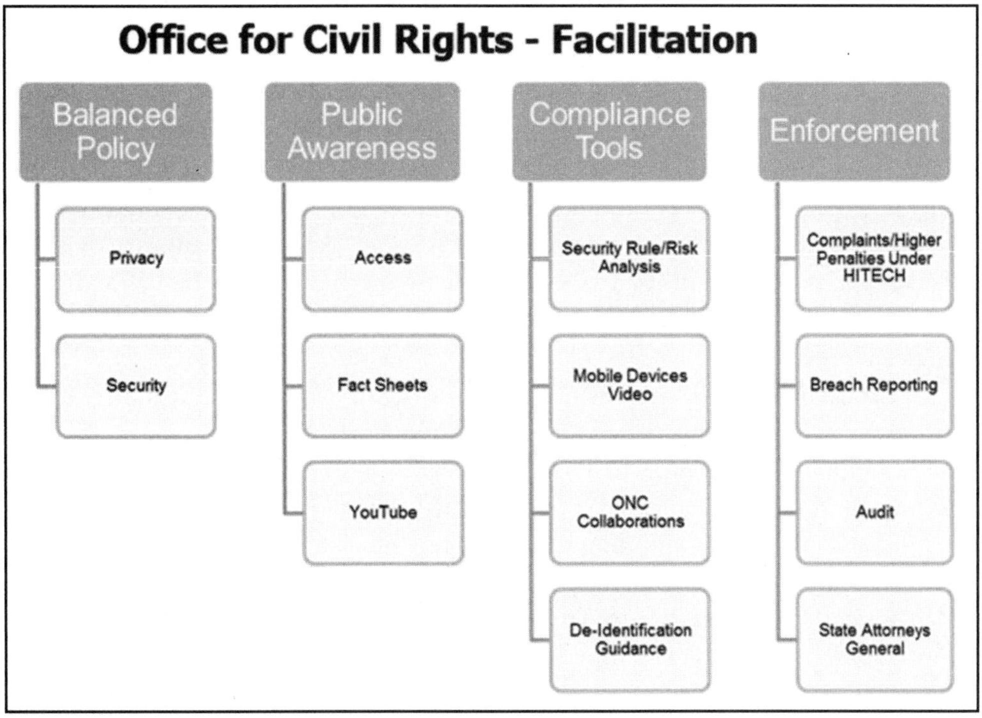

Figure 16-6: Office for Civil Rights - Facilitation

be used wherever possible. Generally speaking, 128-bit and 256-bit encryption implementations are used by the NSA for secret and top-secret information. The 256-bit encryption would take longer to hack with present day technology than the time the universe has existed—including the recently discovered extra 100 million years. On the other hand, 128-bit encryption only requires 31,536,000 years—so get cracking. Brute-force hacking is an automated system of password attempts as a last ditch effort to bust through password security. As outlined in prior examples, simply asking for a password can thwart all this technology. Of course, encryption must be properly implemented to be effective. Encryption is a part of the security program, not the whole picture.[14]

Many data breaches could have been avoided if encryption was used. The stolen laptop, the lost USB thumb drive, the errant email, the missing smartphone—all considered nonissues if protected with properly implemented encryption. Basically, unencrypted data are not safe. Encrypted data are considered safe and protected under the safe harbor provision previously quoted. Having unencrypted data is an accident waiting to happen.

Encryption is needed for data at rest such as on a laptop, desktop (yes, those too), smartphone, backup tape (commonly overlooked), and USB thumb drive. Encryption must also exist for data in motion. Data travels through the network to reach healthcare workers, but also other systems as well. This information might also be transmitted to a vendor facility or government organization. Whether the data reside on a piece of equipment or are moving through transit, encryption must be used.

A common misconception is that ePHI does not exist on the local computer. Nothing could be further for the truth. Even once a file is erased and removed from the trash container, someone with freely available tools can recover the file—and recreate the ePHI. If a file was accessed remotely, a cached copy could reside on the hard drive in one form or another. Assume that every computer can contain sensitive information and protect the organization accordingly.

Part of a comprehensive data leak protection program includes minimizing the ability to store data on a local computer, transmit data to a USB thumb drive, or even email sensitive information inappropriately or without secure mechanisms. There are products that make certain that USB drives are either not used or are at least safeguarded. Email may be filtered and encryption may occur either through manual or automated processes.

The concept of bring your own device is a rapidly emerging phenomenon that is pervasive in the healthcare industry. With these devices comes a new set of risks. Healthcare practitioners expect to use such devices without necessarily securing the information. Having a mobile device management software solution in place will mitigate the risks while still affording convenience. One can impose access restrictions and enforce security protocols such as device encryption and strong passwords. As an added bonus, lost devices may sometimes be traced and recovered. In other cases, the information can be completely wiped clean.

VIRUSES, MALWARE, AND OTHER MALICIOUS CODE

"Bad guys are evil. They put viruses in computers and turn them into bad computers." (Beth Weiner, 2014 - age 6)

The HIPAA Security Rule states covered entities must have "Procedures for guarding against, detecting, and reporting malicious software." We are to take all reasonable precautions to prevent damage from malicious software.

Many organizations have virus protection in one form or another. Hopefully, this system is centrally managed and well maintained. Servers and workstations should have configurations that consider their operating systems to be hardened. Security updates are done in a timely fashion with a patch management system.

Viruses will almost certainly exist on a network, no matter what. Having appropriate mechanisms in place to detect malicious activity is essential. Persistent intrusion detection mechanisms can tell that a computer is communicating inappropriately when traditional virus mechanisms fail. Patch management and operating system hardening guidelines should be followed to minimize the risk of infection.

Viruses exist in all four corners of the globe—and beyond. The International Space Station has been attacked by virus epidemics. Malware spread from infected devices while in orbit, proving not even computers in space are safe from viruses. One infection came from a Russian USB drive. Another came from a laptop infected with a virus used to steal gaming passwords. In other words, expect to get a virus somewhere, sometime.

A virus is more than just an annoyance that slows down a computer and causes pop-up advertisements. As demonstrated by the Target breach, viruses can also be used to steal sensitive information. They can "zombify" many computers hooked up to command and control centers just waiting for instruction to collectively commit a crime—such as knocking a government website offline. In other cases, an infected computer's web traffic is rented by the day, week, or month on the underground market. Internet traffic now connects and passes through the renter agent. Directing hospital Internet traffic to a criminal organization is a particularly dangerous scenario.

The takeaway is that viruses are often undetected, thereby presenting a serious risk to the operation and the safeguarding of sensitive data. Protocols previously outlined in addition to best practices by a security professional are warranted.

SOCIAL ENGINEERING

> *"A company can spend hundreds of thousands of dollars on firewalls, intrusion detection systems and encryption and other security technologies, but if an attacker can call one trusted person within the company, and that person complies, and if the attacker gets in, then all that money spent on technology is essentially wasted. It's essentially meaningless." – Kevin Mitnick, security expert and ex-convict*[15]

Help Desk Example

In a lecture on cybercrime, this author mentioned how one can simply call an employee and say, "This is Johnny calling from the help desk and I'm going to need your password." An exasperated participant slammed her hand on the table in self-disappointment and exclaimed that she would have just given up her password. Many people would—and there are those waiting in the wings to exploit our trust. It's just that easy.

Phone Call Example

Several hospitals have been impersonated by overseas organizations preying on the vulnerable. These groups can spoof the hospitals' phone numbers, cold-call victims, and attempt to extract details to steal identities and much more. As with many social engineering campaigns, perpetrators cast a wide net to gather whatever they can find. This is a numbers game. The more they play, the greater the odds of a significant cash-out.

Email Campaign Example

Email campaigns can be quite crafty and appear to be legitimate. Gone are the days when one could spot poor English or the unlikely scenario of a Nigerian Prince seeking to stash away a million as telltale signs of fraud. An email may appear from the help desk asking all recipients to review the new policies. The website may be hosted elsewhere but appear to be exactly like something from your organization. You log in and get to the policy page. The only problem is that you never had to log in before. Now your email credentials have fallen into the wrong hand, and many have done the same without realizing what has transpired. Now the perpetrators have access to contents of people's emails along with whatever systems share this same password (i.e., the electronic health record)!

Gone Phishing

The aforementioned scenarios are examples of phishing—or the act of tricking individuals into disclosing information. They may go after passwords, identification, credit

Figure 16-7: Tweet - Hacked Associated Press Twitter Account

cards, and banking information. Health information is also targeted for its rich financial data.

Emails may mimic the FBI, IRS, auctions, banks, charity organizations, IT administrators and more. They use baits to get bites. The wide nets tend to work a lot better than a single phishing pole. With spear phishing, a single target such as a hospital is besieged as in the fake policy example previously described. Whaling is the act of going after a big phish such as the CFO or CEO. The conventional wisdom is that those in higher ranking positions hold the keys to the castle.[16]

High Profile Phishing Example

The Associated Press' Twitter account was hacked on April 23, 2012 and tweeted the shocking bulletin seen in Figure 16-7. With news of the President Obama's injuries resulting from two explosions, the stock market crashed before quickly recovering. How could this possibly happen to such a well-established organization? A clever email with a link that looks legitimate is all that it took. Even more news agencies fell for an old hacker trick deceiving people into giving up their password. Other high-profile victims include the U.S. Marines, Facebook, Twitter, CNN, Forbes, *The New York Times*, eBay, PayPal, and Microsoft.

EDUCATION

The common thread in these examples is that human intervention can inadvertently cause breaches. Solid security mechanisms can be completely undone by human error. Part of a comprehensive security program is to have an educated workforce. They need to understand regulations, policies, and have an awareness of security. Annual training should be provided and reminders should be distributed periodically. Education may come from qualified staff or from a service.

VULNERABILITY AND PENETRATION

Part of risk management and mitigation is identifying vulnerable points on the network and being able to actively exploit them. A vulnerability detection and mitigation program can be performed either through specialized products, a security professional, or combination thereof.

A vulnerability assessment finds weak points and may provide recommendations for remediation. These procedures should be performed on a regular basis. Be prepared, as the initial results may be shocking and overwhelming. However, these should diminish over time.

The penetration testing is where trophies are sought. This is important in demonstrating that the keys to the castle may be obtained. Some methodologies involve exploiting computer systems directly, while other means can be rather deceptive. A security professional may try to dupe employees or use some reconnaissance to piece together a break-in method. A phishing email may be used to steal passwords. Please remember that this process is best done by the good guys before the bad guys get their chance.

Government Penetration Example

Security experts were sanctioned to test the defenses of a government agency that deals with cybersecurity. Using social media and a photo of an attractive female, they were able to build an identity and ultimately online friendships. The "woman" provided a virtual Christmas card with malicious code duping employees and antivirus contractors. Having carte blanche, the security experts discovered the birthday of the agency's head of security who was given a virtual birthday card. On opening, these experts had the keys to the castle—including information about foreign leaders, as well as state-sponsored attacks. This is an excellent, albeit extreme example of why security awareness training is so important. Even highly intelligent, knowledgeable individuals should not be exempt from the education program.

CONCLUSION

This chapter has served as a general overview of privacy and security considerations for a healthcare organization. The material contained herein is not meant to be a how-to or "For Dummies" all-inclusive model from which an individual could run a healthcare IT security program in lieu of prior knowledge and expertise. Rather, this is a synopsis serving as a foundation of knowledge to provide familiarity with an essential component of medical informatics. The fundamentals of running a security program and examples of breaches should provide one with an appreciation for the new challenges organizations face in safeguarding their patients' ePHI.

The maintenance of privacy and security in healthcare is a fluid concept. Events and legislation are in constant flux. Various programs and legislation are being enacted, and new innovations are constantly emerging. Having a good barometer reading of the industry is essential. Even while finalizing the draft of this chapter, 4.5 million patient records were reportedly stolen from Community Health Services by hackers—arguably creating our industry's version of the Target fiasco. In other words, the saga continues.

Here are some key takeaways from this chapter to guide you through your journey:

- Risk assessment and remediation is a continuous process.
- Think of an OCR audit as a matter of if, not when.

- Healthcare security is a specialized field requiring the hiring of appropriate specialized expertise.
- A solid program will protect both the business and the patients who put their trust of confidentiality in our hands.
- Safeguard data as if it is your own.
- Business associate agreements must be current and constructed to protect the organization's interests, which also include their clients' interests.
- Encrypt everything—period.
- Policies should reflect legislation and sensible safeguards. Inform those governed by these guidelines.
- Breaches happen. Act responsibly and respond appropriately.
- Train the workforce on matters of security and privacy. Provide periodic updates.
- Keep up to date with current events, legislation, programs, and technology.
- Definitely learn from the mistakes of others and take appropriate action.
- Accept the assessment diagnosis. That sometimes bitter pill can improve the overall health of an organization.

"Last but not least" is often the method of integrating privacy and security into informatics in lieu of a concurrent integration with business processes. Security and functionality do not have to be mutually exclusive notions. So, last but not least, bake the aforementioned concepts into the mix very early and very often as the recipe's prime ingredients. It's an acquired taste to some, but the organization should find the results of this effort to be palatable.

REFERENCES

1. Davies R. (1981). *Destroyer* [Recorded by The Kinks]. London, England.
2. Clarke E. The underground hacking economy is alive and well. SecureWorks. November 18, 2013. http://www.secureworks.com/resources/blog/the-underground-hacking-economy-is-alive-and-well/.
3. U.S. Department of Health and Human Services. Health insurance reform: Security Standards; Final Rule. *Fed Regi*. February 20, 2003. http://www.hhs.gov/ocr/privacy/hipaa/administrative/securityrule/securityrulepdf.pdf.
4. U.S. Department of Health and Human Services. Health information privacy. HHS.gov. http://www.hhs.gov/ocr/privacy/hipaa/administrative/securityrule/securityruleguidance.html. Accessed November 26, 2014.
5. U.S. Department of Health and Human Services. Health information privacy. HHS.gov. http://www.hhs.gov/ocr/privacy/hipaa/administrative/privacyrule/. Accessed November 26, 2014.
6. Nightingale F. *Notes on Nursing: What It Is and What It Is Not*. London: Harrison and Sons, 1860.
7. Waley A. *The Analects of Confucius*.
8. Peart NL. (1980). *Freewill*. [Recorded by Rush]. Morin Heights, Quebec, Canada.
9. Greater New York Hospital Association. 2014. http://gnyha.org. Accessed November 26, 2014.
10. Ponemon Institute. Ponemon Institute. http://www.ponemon.org. Accessed November 26, 2014.
11. Mearian L. Wall of shame exposes 21M medical record breaches. ComputerWorld. August 7, 2012. http://www.computerworld.com/s/article/9230028/_Wall_of_Shame_exposes_21M_medical_record_breaches.

12. United States Senate. United States Senate. Senator Everett McKinley Dirksen dies. https://www.senate.gov/artandhistory/history/minute/Senator_Everett_Mckinley_Dirksen_Dies.htm. Accessed November 26, 2014.

13. U.S. Department of Health and Human Services. HHS.gov. Breaches affecting 500 or more individuals. http://www.hhs.gov/ocr/privacy/hipaa/administrative/breachnotificationrule/breachtool.html. Accessed November 26, 2014.

14. Scarfone KS. Guide to storage encryption technologies for end user devices. Computer Security Resource Center. http://csrc.nist.gov/publications/nistpubs/800-111/SP800-111.pdf. Accessed November 26, 2014.

15. CNN. CNN.com. October 13, 2005. A convicted hacker debunks some myths. http://www.cnn.com/2005/TECH/internet/10/07/kevin.mitnick.cnna/.

16. Constantin L. Fake social media ID duped security-aware IT guys. CIO.com. October 31, 2013. http://www.cio.com/article/2381282/security0/fake-social-media-id-duped-security-aware-it-guys.html.

CHAPTER 17

Software Selection

Ken Ong, MD, MPH

INTRODUCTION

If an eligible professional or hospital wants to either qualify for MU incentives or avoid penalties, it will want an EHR that is certified by the Office of the National Coordinator for Health Information Technology. As of this writing, the Certified Health IT Product List (CHPL; http://oncchpl.force.com/ehrcert?q=chpl) has listed 3,434 ambulatory and 1,843 inpatient products with 2014 CMS certification. Clearly, ONC certification is but a first step in selecting an EHR.

SELECTING AN AMBULATORY EHR

Even if a physician practice has chosen to forego the incentives and suffer the penalties, they will probably get a better value for their dollar if they purchase an EHR certified by CMS rather than one that is not.

Here is why a CMS–certified EHR is better. Providers and patients want to be sure that the EHRs can (a) share patient information securely and confidentially with other IT systems; and (b) provide the functionality required to generate safety, quality, and efficiency. Through a rigorous review process, CMS has defined standards to ensure both.[1]

Selecting, implementing, and maintaining an EHR is expensive and difficult. Help is available at your local health IT regional extension centers (RECs). The American Recovery and Reinvestment Act of 2009/Health Information Technology for Economic and Clinical Health Act of 2009 (ARRA/HITECH) has appropriated $720 million and, as a result, some sixty RECs have been created across the nation. The latest statistics as of this writing reveal 151,322 providers have enrolled in the MU program and 136,459 are now live on an EHR.[2]

To find an REC near you, visit the CMS Health IT Extension Program website: (http://www.healthit.gov/providers-professionals/listing-regional-extension-centers#listing).

Other helpful resources:

- Center for Health IT at the American Academy of Family Practice (http://www.centerforhit.org/online/chit/home.html)

- Center for Practice Improvement and Innovation at the American College of Physicians (http://www.acponline.org/running_practice/technology/ehr/)
- Council on Clinical Information Technology of the American Academy of Pediatrics (http://www2.aap.org/informatics/COCIT.html)
- American Congress of Obstetricians and Gynecologists (http://www.acog.org/About-ACOG/ACOG-Departments/Health-Information-Technology)

For a detailed look at the work of one REC, see the chapter in this book written by Paul Kleeberg, MD (Chapter 7 – Regional Extension Centers). For more on the ambulatory EHR, see the chapter by Drs. Cole, Cheriff, Gossey, et al. (Chapter 8 – Ambulatory Systems).

Software Strategies: Best-of-Breed vs Single Source vs Best-of-Suite

One of the central debates in software selection is the choice between the best-of-breed (BoB) and single source (see Table 17-1).

Conventional wisdom argues that buying software products from a single vendor will deliver more integration; integration means greater efficiency and cost savings in purchasing and maintaining software. Some vendors repeat what has become the mantra of single source proponents. With a single vendor, there is but "one throat to choke" (see Figure 17-1). If there are problems with any software, the CIO has but one vendor to manage.

One of my favorite CIOs, Pete Garrison, gave a poignant rejoinder to a sales representative who made that pitch. Garrison countered, "We don't want to choke anyone's throat. We want a partner who will get us where we need to go."

Another painful reality is that the promise of integration may be either in development or illusory. No single vendor has a module for every department in a hospital. One vendor may buy a compendium of different software products but fail to integrate them. Changing a menagerie of different programs into a common database with integrated logic is an expensive and time-consuming challenge. Another vendor may be expanding its current product offerings but the newest modules may be immature.

The conventional wisdom argues that buying BoB means buying the best software. Business units or departments tend to prefer selecting the BoB software for their particular workflow, but there are at least three trade-offs. First, creating and maintaining interfaces costs money. Second, interfaces are complicated and may not function as desired, e.g., one-way only but not two-way (bidirectional). Finally, multiple vendor relationships have to be managed. Rather than one throat to choke, there are many. When an interface has issues, multiple vendors may engage in finger-pointing. Bewildering delays or downtime may occur.

Table 17-1: Best-of-Breed vs Single Source

Software Strategy	Pro	Con
Best-of-Breed	Best unit or departmental functionality	• Work and cost of interfacing • Many vendors to manage
Single Source	• Integrated • "One throat to choke"	• Often poor departmental functionality • Diminished negotiating cache

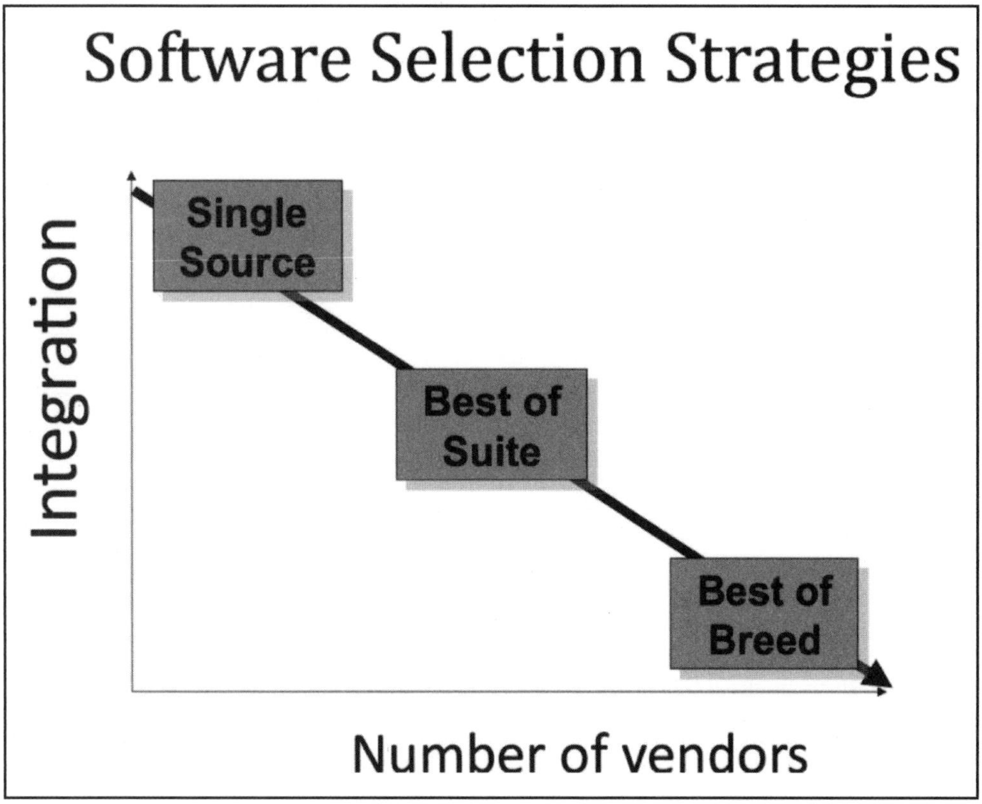

Figure 17-1: Software Selection Strategies

A third option to BoB and single source is best-of-suite (BoS), also known as best-of-cluster. The rationale of the BoS approach is that only a core group of software applications must be closely integrated. Applications that fall outside of the cluster need a lesser degree of integration. At the bare minimum, the cluster would include CPOE, CDSS, and the pharmacy system.

The more expansive definition might include all the elements of the electronic medical record (EMR). Garets and Davis suggest the EMR environment is comprised of:[3]

- Clinical Data Repository (CDR)
- Controlled Medical Vocabulary (CMV)
- CDSS
- Clinical Documentation
- CPOE
- Pharmacy Management
- eMAR
- Workflow

CURRENT STATE: HOSPITAL SOFTWARE STRATEGIES

To better understand which of the software strategies may be more closely associated with a full EHR implementation, Ford et al. analyzed the 2007 survey of the American Hospital Association (AHA), as shown in Table 17-2. A total of 1,814 hospitals

Table 17-2: EHR Strategy by Self-Reported Implementation Status

Implementation Status	Best of Breed	Best of Suite	Single Vendor	Total
In Progress				
Count	166	461	793	1,420
Expected	163.6	494.7	761.7	—
Fully Implemented				
Count	43	171	180	394
Expected	45.4	137.3	211.3	—
Total[2]	209 (11.5%)	632 (34.8%)	973 (53.6%)	1,814 (100%)

[1] Pearson chi-square = 16.684; $p < .001$.
[2] Percentages are calculated using the cell count divided by the row total.

responded to the health IT subset of questions. A multivariate analysis controlling for profit/tax status, system affiliation, Joint Commission accreditation, and teaching status found that hospitals pursuing a BoS were 34.1 percent more likely than those pursuing a single-vendor health IT strategy to have fully implemented an EHR system. Moreover, hospitals pursuing a BoS strategy were 44.2 percent more likely than hospitals pursuing a BoB strategy to have fully implemented an EHR system, but this trend was only significant at the $p < 0.10$ level.[4]

Why does a hospital have one software strategy rather than another? Another study using AHA data suggests an answer.

Using data from the 2007 AHA survey and the 2008 HIMSS Analytics Database, Burke et al. analyzed the software strategy of 3,343 hospitals.[5] The study found that 61 percent of the hospitals indicated a single vendor, 29 percent indicated a BoS, and 10 percent suggested a BoB strategy (see Table 17-3).

Single-vendor strategies were most common among hospitals that were small, standalone, for-profit, non-teaching and/or not accredited by The Joint Commission. Smaller hospitals may have fewer IT staff and, in that case, managing a single vendor contract may be easier (see Tables 17-4 and 17-5).

BoB strategies were most common among system-affiliated and Joint Commission–accredited hospitals. BoS IT strategies were most common among very large, system-affiliated, teaching and Joint Commission–accredited hospitals. Both the BoB and BoS strategies require more and better experienced IT resources and the capacity to manage multiple vendor contracts.

The study's authors conclude, "The decision to pursue a specific health IT management strategy is very complex and often involves the interplay and valuation of hard and soft factors, which ultimately results in a migration path that is unique for a given organization."

No doubt, every hospital wants to deploy the best technology to give the best patient care and excel beyond MU. Yet the resources are limited, and HITECH's funding comes after the hospital has made its investment, not before. As one industry watcher comments, "In that world, it's not about ripping and replacing, but patching, leveraging and surviving."[6]

Table 17-3: Organizational Characteristics of Hospitals (n = 3,343)

Hospital Characteristic	Frequency (%)
Hospital bed size: Small (<99 beds) Medium (100-299 beds) Large (300+ beds)	1,251 (37.4%) 1,401 (41.9%) 691 (20.7%)
System Affiliation vs. Stand Alone	1,966 (58.8%) 1,377 (41.2%)
For-profit status vs. Not-for-profit	507 (15.2%) 2,835 (84.8%)
Teaching hospital vs. Non-teaching facility	244 (7.3%) 3,099 (92.7%)
JCAHO Accreditation vs. Non-accredited hospital	2,449 (73.3%) 894 (26.7%)
HIT Management Strategy Best of Breed Single Vendor Best of Suite	343 (10.3%) 2,023 (60.5%) 977 (29.2%)
Total	3,343 (100%)

Note: Number may not add up to 100% due to rounding.

Table 17-4: Hospital Characteristics and Health IT Management Strategies

	HIT Management Strategy			
	Single Vendor Strategy	Best of Breed Strategy	Best of Suite Strategy	P-value
Bed size				
Small (1-99 beds)	921 (74%)	103 (8%)	227 (18%)	
Medium (100-299 beds)	817 (58%)	140 (10%)	444 (32%)	<0.01
Large (300+ beds)	285 (41%)	100 (15%)	306 (44%)	
System				
System-affiliate	977 (71%)	109 (8%)	291 (21%)	<0.01
Stand-alone	1,046 (53%)	234 (12%)	686 (35%)	
Tax status				
Not for profit	1,711 (60%)	306 (11%)	818 (29%)	0.05
For profit	311 (61%)	37 (7%)	156 (31%)	
Teaching Hospital				
Yes	71 (29%)	45 (18%)	128 (53%)	<0.01
No	1,952 (63%)	298 (10%)	849 (24%)	
JCAHO Accredited				
Yes	1,317 (54%)	279 (11%)	853 (35%)	<0.01
No	706 (79%)	64 (7%)	124 (14%)	

Note: Number may not add up to 100% due to rounding.
P-values calculated using the Chi-square statistic

Table 17-5: The Multivariate Relationship Between Hospital Characteristics and IT Strategy Pursued

	Dependent Variables: Type of IT Management Strategy Pursued		
	Single Vendor Strategy	Best of Breed Strategy	Best of Suite Strategy
	Odds Ratio (95% C.I.)	Odds Ratio (95% C.I.)	Odds Ratio (95% C.I.)
Independent variables			
Bed size1	0.99 (0.98 – 0.99)	1.00 (1.00 – 1.00)	1.001** (1.001 – 1.002)
System			
Stand Alone	2.00** (1.72 – 2.33)	1.00	1.00
System affiliated	1.00	1.61** (1.25 – 2.06)	1.77** (1.49 – 2.09)
Tax-status			
Not for profit	1.00	1.82** (1.25 – 2.63)	1.00
For-profit status	1.41** (1.14 – 1.74)	1.00	0.87 (0.70 – 1.09)
Teaching hospital			
No	2.08** (1.49 – 2.94)	1.00	1.00
Yes	1.00	1.52 (0.99 – 2.33)	1.62** (1.18 – 2.22)
JCAHO Accreditation			
No	2.22** (1.85 – 2.78)	1.00	1.00
Yes	1.00	1.42* (1.04 – 1.93)	2.41** (1.93 – 3.03)

1Bed size was measured continuously in multivariate analyses

Note: Each odds ratio is adjusted for all independent variables included in that table. Only positive relationships are highlighted for significance.

*p<0.05 **p<0.01

THE EMERGENCY DEPARTMENT: LET'S TALK…

> The niche systems are designed specifically for (and often by) ED physicians, and their intended users sometimes advocate passionately for them. But more and more hospitals have their eye on an enterprise electronic health record, complete with clinical decision support, where a piece of data entered in any department is immediately and automatically available to all others. An interface to a separate ED system rarely behaves with equal seamlessness, and may not be enough to achieve the benefits promised by an EHR.
>
> — *Elizabeth Gardner*[7]

Warning: This is an issue that makes for many passionate conversations among clinicians and managers inside and outside of hospital emergency departments (EDs).

MU has ratcheted up the need to share patient information between ED and inpatient. Whether the core measure is CPOE, demographics, problem list, active medication list, active allergy list, vital signs, smoking status, or providing patients an electronic copy of their health information or discharge instructions, the measure pertains to the eligible hospital (EH) or critical access hospital's workflow between the ED and inpatient services.[7]

A KLAS Research survey showed that of the 32 respondents replacing their Emergency Department Information System (EDIS), 72 percent were leaving a BoB EDIS solution in favor of an enterprise offering (see Figure 17-2).[8]

A couple of physician quotes provide the clinical rationale for integrated inpatient and ED systems:

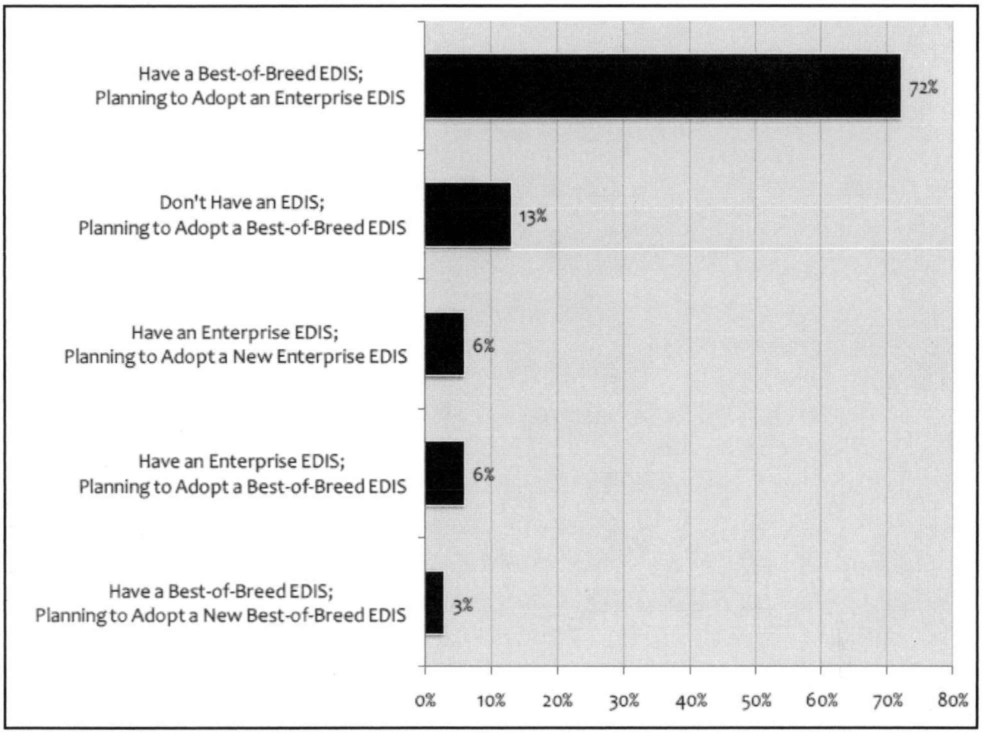

Figure 17-2: EDIS Replacement Approach (n = 32) Planned EDIS Strategy (among respondents in this study who are actively purchasing or replacing their EDIS)

> If I'm ordering a contrast agent for a CT [computed tomography] scan, I need to know whether the patient has any kidney damage. An isolated system cannot grab that creatinine measurement from three months ago and tell me as I put in the order.
> *—Reid Conant, MD, chief medical information officer at Tri-City Medical Center in Oceanside, Calif.*[9]

> Everybody liked it [BoB system], but when we began doing CPOE and moved off paper, we found we could not make it completely safe to ensure that a patient never missed a dose or never got two doses because the medication records were on different systems. You might say, 'Oh, just interface them,' but engineers can spend four years trying to make that happen. Keeping formularies and supplier lists in parallel becomes almost impossible.
> *—Michael Shabot, MD, CMO of Memorial Hermann Health System*[10]

Respondents to the above-referenced KLAS survey on ED systems faced interface challenges (see Figure 17-3). Some respondents who switched from niche ED systems to integrated ED systems complained that their new system was less user friendly and less adapted to the ED workflow.

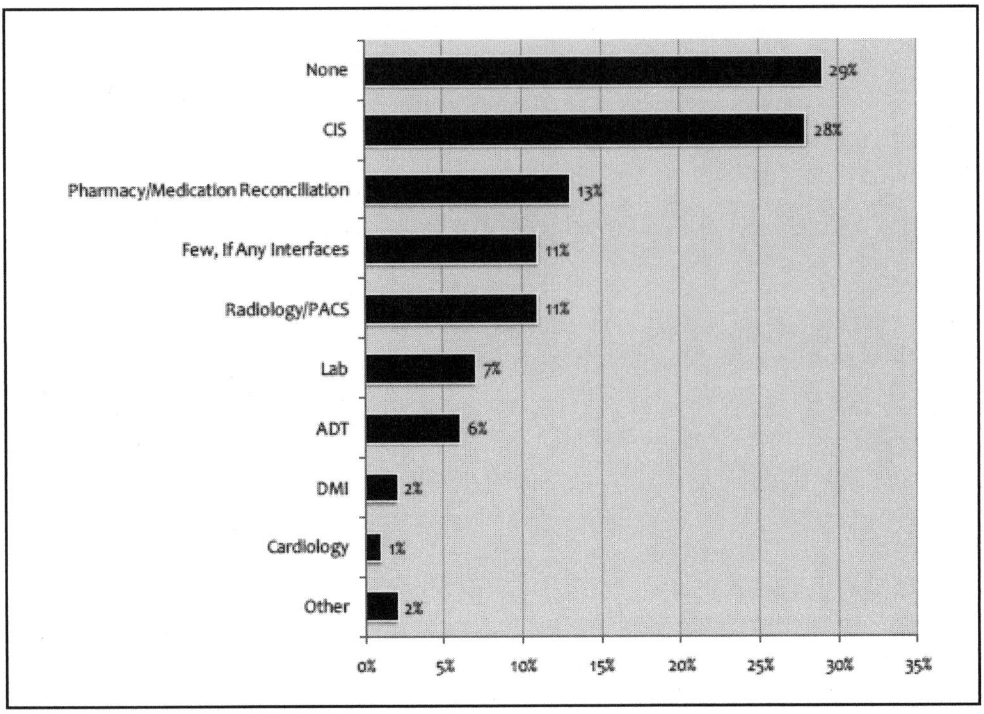

Figure 17-3: With Which Hospital Systems Are You Having Difficulty Sharing Information? (n = 211)

Note: the "Other" category includes ambulatory, niche systems, and medication cabinets.

For those already committed to an ED system, different challenges pertain to both the integrated and niche ED systems:

- Integrated ED system: Improves both the usability and workflow of their ED module.
- Niche ED system: All EHR modules must be CMS–certified. Select an ED system that is CMS–certified and create functional interfaces between the inpatient and ED system to achieve MU.

BUYING SOFTWARE IS A JOURNEY

Other than buying CMS–certified EHR software to achieve MU, why does anyone ever have to buy new software? What's wrong with the old software? Why do we need new software at all? These are common questions that all of us have heard before. No doubt these are questions we may have asked ourselves on occasion.

Why, indeed? A new project may require a purchase of software. The current version of a particular software product may sunset. A vendor sells a new software product and refuses to support the older version. Generations of software have changed from mainframe to client server or from character to Windows-driven platforms. A similar shift was seen for some products that evolved from a client server owned and maintained by the client to software-as-a-service (SaaS) owned and maintained by a software vendor.

Every new step in health reform nurtures innovation in health IT.

For physician practices complying with MU, selecting to upgrade from an uncertified to certified EHR includes considerations like start-up pricing, implementation support, migration strategy, server options, interoperability, vendor stability, and cost to connect to HIE.[11]

ACOs have their own necessary core IT software that enables coordination and collaboration.[12] Although these technologies have value outside of ACOs, they can be critical to an ACO's success. They include HIE, enterprise master patient index, mobile health, care/disease management, patient portal, telehealth, social media, and clinical/business intelligence.

ICD-10 has generated new mobile applications to facilitate appropriate coding.[13]

Changes in the health IT industry foster change as well. If a software vendor is purchased or goes out of business, their software is orphaned and left bereft of support. Even very expensive health IT may go the way of the eight-track tape player or VHS tape. Hospital or clinic mergers or other enterprise-wide initiatives may drive standardization. Standardizing software across a multihospital system can facilitate adopting best practices and lower purchase and maintenance costs for IT. Paying multiple vendors for the same software translates into multiple contracts to manage, training associated with each software product, and a Gordian knot of interfaces. Each interface can generate its own costs for maintenance and episodes of downtime.

Sidebar: The Five Rights of Purchasing

1. The right reasons
2. The right process
3. The right people
4. The right system
5. The right price

(adapted from Laker and Groeber)

Just as medication administration has its five rights,[14] purchasing IT does as well: the right reasons and the right process with the right people to find the right system at the right price.[15]

The right reasons should be the alpha and omega of every project. More in healthcare than elsewhere, IT must often serve both margin and mission. Should a clinical software system promote both patient safety and appropriate charge capture? The obvious answer is *yes* and *yes*. The right reasons should be translated into quantifiable and achievable goals. The right reason will have a measureable outcome. One metric that has become standard for many capital purchases is the payback period, better known as ROI.[16]

The right process gathers the input of all major stakeholders and ensures that an evidence-based, outcomes-focused selection proceeds and that the project is aligned with the strategic plan of the organization.[17] The process often includes a software selection team comprising both managers of the business unit or organization and the relevant executive officer(s). The software selection team may be formally charged to present its project for the approval of an executive information systems or capital expenditure approval committee. The latter committee may be responsible for approving expenses that run over the projected costs, or, in that most unhappy of circumstances, terminating a project if it fails to meet its milestones, projected costs, or post-go-live goals. The right selection process creates the foundations for a successful installation and maintenance.

> **Sidebar: The Right People for a Selection Process**
>
> - Executive sponsor
> - Project champion
> - Project manager
> - Representatives from other disciplines or business units relevant to the software application

The right people in the selection committee include an executive sponsor, a project champion, a project manager, and representatives from other disciplines or business units relevant to the software application. In addition to the formal process within the organization, the executive sponsor ensures through both formal and informal channels that the project has the buy-in of the organization's executive leadership. This buy-in includes not only the project budget but cooperation from other departments and business units to participate in the selection, the installation, and successful continuation of the project. The larger the scope of the project, the more important that buy-in becomes.

The project manager may be from either the business unit or information systems. The project manager should be involved in both the selection and installation phases of the project. His or her role is to enumerate and assign each task, coordinate disparate and limited resources, identify potential or actual problems, and deliver the project on time and within budget. Project management is a body of knowledge for which formal education and certification exist.[18] Nonetheless project management certification is often not the most important asset a project manager brings to the table.

Heerkens suggests that the four most desired traits of a project manager are (1) thinking that is like that of a generalist, (2) a high tolerance for ambiguity, (3) a high tolerance for uncertainty, and (4) honesty and integrity.[19] Certification marks a level of competence, but experience in selecting and installing projects of similar complexity is often more reassuring.

The project champion is the person from the business unit or department who can promote and advocate others to adopt the software application, the workflow changes, or the clinical transformation needed to achieve the expected project outcomes. Gladwell refers to such individuals as *connectors*.[20]

Rogers would categorize the ideal project champion as an early adopter: "Potential adopters look to early adopters for advice and information about an innovation. The early adopter is considered by many to be the individual to check with before adopting a new idea. This adopter category is generally sought by change agents as a local missionary for speeding the diffusion process. Because early adopters are not too far ahead of the average individual in innovativeness, they serve as a role model for many other members of a social system. Early adopters help trigger the mass when they adopt an innovation… In one sense, early adopters put their stamp of approval on a new idea by adopting it."[21]

Representatives of other relevant business units or departments should sit at the table; if their participation is important for a successful install, then they should be part of the selection process. As healthcare strives to improve quality and efficiency, collaboration and teamwork become increasingly vital. A chain is only as strong as its weakest link. Sometimes leaving just one person, one office, or one department out of the selection process can compromise a successful implementation.

The right system is the one that best enables the project's goals—be it reducing no-shows for a clinic scheduling system or reducing medication errors for a closed-loop medication management system.

The conventional wisdom is that a request for a proposal (RFP) is the sine qua non for selecting the right system. In today's complex healthcare IT market, the traditional RFP is not without its problems. Laker and Groeber caution, "The classic approach is buying or building a checklist of desired features, issuing it to vendors in a request for proposal (RFP), then scoring results to see which system has the most functionality. But with today's system architectures and powerful tools, vendors can say 'yes' to nearly all questions. Most vendors' RFP responses score around 90 percent, while actual use of system functions at client sites is maybe 50 percent. Plus, sales or marketing staff answer RFPs, not the programmers and analysts who really know the product."[15]

Buying software in the 21st century can be a little like buying a new car. When hunting for a new car today, we search the Web and newsstands for rating surveys, such as *Consumer Reports*. We check the car manufacturer's website for a marketing brochure. We Google online forums and blogs for opinions from consumers themselves. Whether or not they own the vehicle in question, we ask everyone we know for their opinion. We go to the car dealer to listen to that MP3–enabled nine-speaker sound system or see firsthand if the olive green looks that much cooler than the lime. During the entire journey, we share our findings with our significant other, parents, and next-door neighbor. In the end, a contract is signed and we have a new car.

Online services like KLAS[22] and MDBuyline[23] offer consumer satisfaction rankings, product-specific reports, vendor-specific client commentary, and more. Aunt Minnie[24] is a site devoted to imaging products and their evaluation. The number one ranking in a KLAS survey or most improved ranking are coveted. Consumer ratings are an invaluable reality check for that occasional end-user who has used the existing product forever and is convinced there is nothing better.

Critics, who are more often than not vendors, lament that customer satisfaction rating services are subject to gaming. They say that vendors with the highest rankings are only better at convincing their customers to participate in the satisfaction surveys. Yet that very same tactic is open to all vendors and fails to explain why some garner better rankings than others. The vendor's website should include the number of employees, annual revenues, location of the corporate headquarters, product brochures, and contact information for sales. The product information from each vendor can be the starting point for developing the selection criteria rating tool for the selection team.

A vendor assessment or selection criteria rating tool has several tangible benefits. It represents a consensus within the selection team about what it expects the software to do. The "right reasons" should permeate the selection and implementation processes. Weighting the selection criteria can define what functionality has greater priority. The rating scale should be no more complicated than 1–3 or 1–5. Even numbered rating scales (e.g., 1–4 or 1–6) force evaluations that are more clearly positive or negative. Rating scales whose highest rating exceeds 5 or 6 do not necessarily add value. Categories of specifications should be rated rather than rating each specification itself. Selection team members find rating 10 or fewer categories practical, but 100 individual specifications impossible.

Functionality is but one section in the vendor assessment tool. Other critical sections include regulatory compliance, IT requirements, usability, and vendor characteristics. A software product with all the latest bells and whistles is useless if its vendor's future looks dubious or if its security does not meet HITECH's heightened requirements for protecting health information.

Searching the Web for the latest news on vendors can uncover useful information. If one vendor purchases another with a competing product, one of the products will not fare well in the future. Learning of a company's reorganization, one should ask the vendor how that will affect their future and product support. Even a friendly acquisition may lead to a hiccup or temporary reduction in support services.

Demonstrations should be arranged and vendors rated with the vendor assessment tool. The tool can be used to ensure each vendor is asked to show the same specifications. The tool becomes indispensable if the products are complex in scope or if the number of demos includes three or more vendors over a span of days. A postmortem or debriefing after each vendor's demo can help solidify areas of consensus and disagreement. If a product offers better support for one subset of stakeholders than another (e.g., physicians or nurses), then the team will have to decide if that trade-off is worthwhile or if another product better serves all stakeholders. This advice is given full well knowing it is easier said than done.

After the scores from the vendor assessment tool are tallied, the finalists should be selected. Preliminary proposals and a list of current clients can be requested. Due diligence generally requires site visits and reference calls to existing clients. Both should be made without the vendor present. Be aware that it makes perfect sense for a vendor to refer the prospective customer to those current clients who are most happy with their product. Finding clients that have recently switched from one vendor to another is even more useful.

Sidebar: Due Diligence—Peer-to-Peer Reference Calls

- Call current clients
- Ask about satisfaction with version of the software you're considering
- What did they like about the product? This vendor?
- What didn't they like?
- What were their "lessons learned"?
- Would they buy this product again?
- Check client commentary in rating services, e.g., KLAS reports

The right price requires a thorough review of line items in the project plan. The project plan should be part of the contract. Training is always a key issue. The train-the-trainer option lowers travel expenses, decreases time lost to training, and minimizes costs required to back-fill the staff absence during training. A selected group of the customer's managers or superusers can be trained by the vendor on-site or at the vendor's corporate training facilities. The selected group of trainers can then train the remaining staff in the business unit or organization.

Subscribing to SaaS is an option many vendors now offer. Back in the day of large mainframe-based applications, the subscription model was common. The vendor would own and host the "heavy iron," the mainframe computers. The customer would pay a monthly or quarterly fee for access. Once again, courtesy of the Internet, SaaS mirrors that model and offers subscription rates. In the capital-poor environment of healthcare today, stretching the total cost of ownership over a 3- to 7-year period lowers upfront capital costs.

Finally, the day arrives in a selection process when a vendor is selected. The executive sponsor and selection team present the project to the executive leadership for approval.

A successful selection process is a prelude to a successful implementation. A hasty selection can lead to missteps in implementation. The consensus required for workflow and clinical transformation is the staging platform for implementing the software and achieving the desired patient safety and business goals. Selection and planning for implementation are very much intertwined.

Sidebar: Caveat Emptor

- Vaporware
- Visionware
- Betaware
- PPOS (PowerPoint Operating System)
- Technology on the bleeding edge (newer and riskier than the cutting edge)

If you're the type who'd hesitate to buy the first model of a new car line, you should be just as risk averse with the very latest information technology. Unless your organization classifies itself in the innovator category of the adopter distribution and has the resources to devote to developing new technology, take on "the latest and the greatest" with extreme caution.

REFERENCES

1. Certified EHR technology. http://www.cms.gov/Regulations-and-Guidance/Legislation/EHRIncentivePrograms/Certification.html. Accessed July 31, 2014.

2. HealthIT Dashboard: Regional Extension Center Cooperative Agreement Program. http://dashboard.healthit.gov/rec/. Accessed July 31, 2014.

3. Garets D, Davis M. White Paper: Electronic medical records vs. electronic health records: yes, there is a difference. HIMSS Analytics. 2006. http://www.himssanalytics.org/docs/WP_EMR_EHR.pdf. Accessed July 31, 2014.

4. Ford EW, Menachemi N, Huerta TR, et al. Hospital IT adoption strategies associated with implementation success: Implications for achieving meaningful use. *J Healthc Manag.* 2010;55,3;ABI/INFORM Global.

5. Burke D, Yu F, Au D, et al. Best of breed strategies: Hospital characteristics associated with organizational HIT strategy. *J Heathc Inf Manag.* 2009;23:2.

6. Guerra A. Guerra On Healthcare: Application rip And replace realities. InformationWeek. July 29, 2010. http://www.informationweek.com/story/showArticle.jhtml?articleID=226300107. Accessed July 31, 2014.

7. Gardner E. Emergency situation: Best of breed, or enterprise integration? *Health Data Management.* March 1, 2010.

8. Emergency department information systems: Is best of breed still the best approach? KLAS Research. December 2009. http://www.klasresearch.com/.

9. Gardner E. Emergency situation. *Health Data Manag.* 2010;18(3):68-70. http://www.healthdatamanagement.com/issues/18_3/emergency-situation-39831-1.html. Accessed July 31, 2014.

10. Intensive care, intensive information. *Health Data Manag.* May 1, 2010.

11. How to implement EHRs – Step 3: Select upgrade to a certified EHR. http://www.healthit.gov/providers-professionals/ehr-implementation-steps/step-3-select-or-upgrade-certified-her. Accessed June 7, 2014.

12. Accountable care organizations: Core IT capabilities defined. August 1, 2013. http://www.himss.org/ResourceLibrary/genResourceDetailPDF.aspx?ItemNumber=29381. Accessed June 21, 2014.

13. Schwartz E, contrib ed. Buyers guide to mobile ICD-10 apps. *mHealthNews*. http://www.mhealthnews.com/news/buyers-guide-mobile-icd-10-apps-smartphone-AppleAndroid. Accessed June 7, 2014.

14. Neuenschwander M, Cohen MR, Vaida AJ, et al. Practical guide to bar coding for patient medication safety. *Am J Health Syst Pharm*. 2003;15;60(8):768–779.

15. Laker B, Groeber V. IT purchasing strategies: Make good decisions by approaching them right. *Healthc Inform*. 2005;22(9):48.

16. Return on investment explained: Definition, meaning, and example calculations. http://www.business-case-analysis.com/return-on-investment.html#compare. Accessed July 31, 2014.

17. McDowell SW. Herding cats: The challenges of EMR vendor selection. *J Healthc Inform Manag*. 2005;17(3):63-71.

18. Project Management Institute. *A Guide to the Project Management Body of Knowledge*. (PMBOK® Guide). 3rd ed. New Town Square, Penn: Project Management Institute; 2006.

19. Heerkens G. *Project Management*. New York: McGraw-Hill; 2002.

20. Gladwell M. *The Tipping Point: How Little Things Can Make a Big Difference*. New York: Little Brown & Co.; 2000.

21. Rogers EM. *Diffusion of Innovations*. 4th ed. New York: Free Press; 2003.

22. KLAS Research. http://www.klasresearch.com/. Accessed July 31, 2014.

23. MD Buyline. http://www.mdbuyline.com/. Accessed July 31, 2014.

24. AuntMinne.com. http://www.auntminnie.com/index.aspx?sec=def. Accessed July 31, 2014.

CHAPTER 18

Project Management and Health IT

Pete Shelkin, MSHA, CISSP, PMP, FHIMSS

INTRODUCTION

The field of medical informatics relies heavily on our ability to successfully build, install, and use robust tools and systems to electronically collect, store, and manage information. These tools and systems tend to be quite complex and require much forethought and planning in order to be built and installed properly. And, because these tools will literally touch the lives of those whom we serve, there is great risk that goes along with their great potential. Therefore, effective project management practices are essential if an organization is to succeed in installing and using an EHR in a way that maximizes its overall value.

This chapter will provide an overview of the formal project management discipline as defined by the Project Management Institute (PMI) and will discuss the major project management concepts within the context of an EHR project.

OVERVIEW OF FORMAL PROJECT MANAGEMENT DISCIPLINE

Project Definition

"A project is a temporary endeavor undertaken to create a unique product, service, or result. The temporary nature of projects indicates that a project has a definite beginning and end."[1] Note that the term *temporary* refers only to the fact that the project itself will begin and end. The results of the project, that is, the deliverables, will be expected to last for quite some time. The term temporary should also not be interpreted to mean short in duration. EHR projects at large organizations can take many years to complete.

In addition to projects, the project management discipline also defines programs and portfolios.[2] PMI defines a program as "a group of related projects, subprograms, and program activities managed in a coordinated way to obtain benefits not available from managing them individually." For example, a health system may have separate projects for an EHR, MU attestation, and Quality Management. These projects share many of the same objectives, have many of the same stakeholders, rely on many of the same resources, and are fairly interdependent on each other. It would make sense in this case to manage the three projects as part of a program.

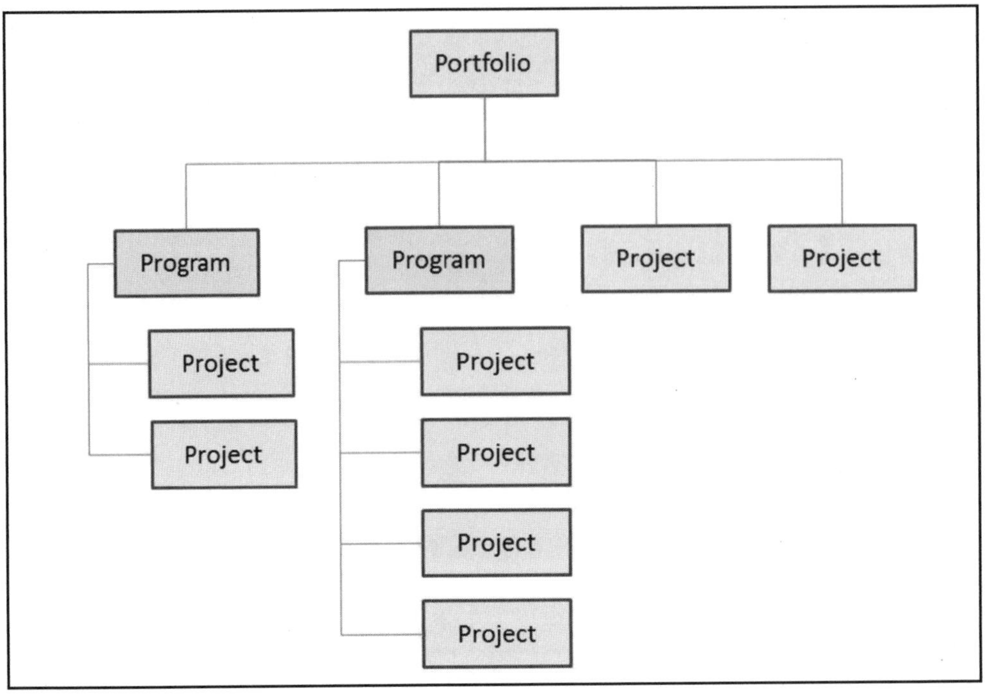

Figure 18-1: The Relationships Between Projects, Programs, and Portfolios

A portfolio is the set of projects and programs that an organization has undertaken to meet its overall strategic objectives. The projects and programs may not be directly related to each other, but they all support the organization's strategy. For example, a health system may have within its portfolio a program such as the one previously described, a project for building a new wing on the hospital and a project for reducing supply expenses. While these projects are directly related to each other, they were chosen because in combination, they maximize the ROI to the organization.

Figure 18-1 provides an overview of the relationship between projects, programs, and portfolios.

PMI Process Groups

The PMI Project Management Body of Knowledge (PMBOK) defines forty-seven distinct processes as part of the formal project management discipline. These processes are each classified as being part of a Process Group*. The five PMI Process Groups are Initiating, Planning, Executing, Monitoring and Controlling, and Closing. Figure 18-2 illustrates the relationship of Process Groups during a typical project.

Initiating: Define the business need and authorize the project. A project is formally created in the Initiating process group. It will likely have started out as an idea, or a need, or a proposal that competed for funding with other proposals, or even all of the above, but it does not become a project until it has been formally authorized. Organiza-

* We may think of things like planning and execution as "phases" of a project, but PMI uses the term *Phase* to describe "a collection of logically related activities that culminate in the completion of one or more deliverables." An example would be the conversion of an aging medical office building to a parking garage where the separate activities related to office relocation, facility demolition, and garage construction would be treated as separate phases that each required their own unique planning, execution, and management activities, yet were all part of the same overall project.

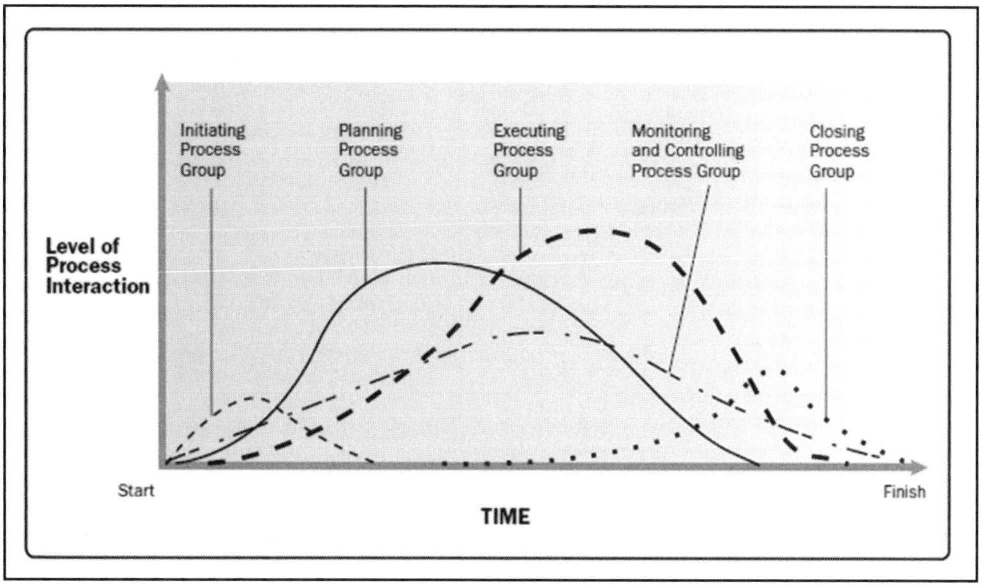

Figure 18-2: Process Groups Interact in a Phase or Project

Reprinted with permission from A Guide to the Project Management Body of Knowledge (PMBOK© Guide)–*Fifth Edition. ©2013 Project Management Institute, Inc. All rights reserved.*

tions will differ in their approach, but the basics are that a business case is developed to support the project, internal and external stakeholders are identified, a project charter is created, authorization is granted, and financial resources are committed. It is during the Initiating processes that the project manager is typically selected as well.

A key output of the Initiating processes is a project charter. Among other things, the charter will articulate the business case, define the statement of work, document any key constraints, provide a budget estimate, and define the scope of the project at a high level. The charter must name the project sponsor, and the sponsor must be someone in the organization who has the authority to commit funding and resources required to complete the project. The value in having a well-crafted charter is that it aligns stakeholder expectations in terms of goals, roles, commitments, and outcomes.[3]

It is important to note that the charter will not contain the actual schedule or budget because these are developed as part of the Planning processes. This does not necessarily mean that factors influencing the schedule and budget are not mentioned, but they are included in the form of constraints at this stage. For example, regulatory agencies may dictate that a new set of requirements must be met by a certain date. Projects that are chartered allow the organization to meet those requirements and must therefore recognize those dates as schedule constraints. Remember, though, that while a constraint may influence a schedule, it is not the schedule itself. The same reasoning applies to budgetary constraints and a project budget. A budget constraint may appear in the charter, but it is really a goal and the project budget must be built during the Planning process based on reality and not goals. If the true project budget cannot realistically meet the goal, then the project should be terminated before funds and effort are wasted.

Some constraints may be significant enough that they warrant investigation before the project can be fully committed. Such a situation would suggest that the project is a good candidate for a phased approach, as described in the earlier footnote. For example, an organization may want to conduct a feasibility study or a market analysis before committing to a project. In this case, the project could be broken into two phases. The first phase would determine if the schedule and budget constraints could be met. If so, then the project would proceed, and if not, then the project would either be terminated or the organization could try to adjust its constraints. Either way, only the resources and effort needed to get to the "go/no-go" decision point would be committed in the charter for the first phase.

Planning: Finalize the project scope and the plan for how to accomplish the objectives to meet the defined need. While most of the actual work effort and money is usually spent on the Executing processes, the Planning processes are considered by many to be the most important. In fact, twenty-four of the forty-seven processes that make up the Project Management Body of Knowledge (PMBOK) fall within the Planning process group—*more than half*! Shortcutting the Planning process is the surest way to set a project up for failure, or at the very least, assure that it runs into serious trouble in terms of quality, schedule, budget, or all three.

When tackling high-visibility projects, there is always the temptation to show visible activity as soon as possible. Because planning activities on complex projects can take months (or longer) it is not uncommon to push some of the planning activities out until further in the project, especially for those tasks that will not occur until the later stages. Figure 18-3 helps illustrate why it would be a mistake to begin work before all relevant planning activities have been completed.

Note that at the beginning of the project, there is a high degree of risk and uncertainty because there are still a lot of unknowns. Also note that changes are easy and far less costly to make at the beginning of a project because little has been set in stone. Planning serves to remove much of the uncertainty, and therefore reduces the risks. At the same time, the deeper one gets into the project, the more committed one becomes to the path undertaken, and the cost of making changes begins to greatly increase.

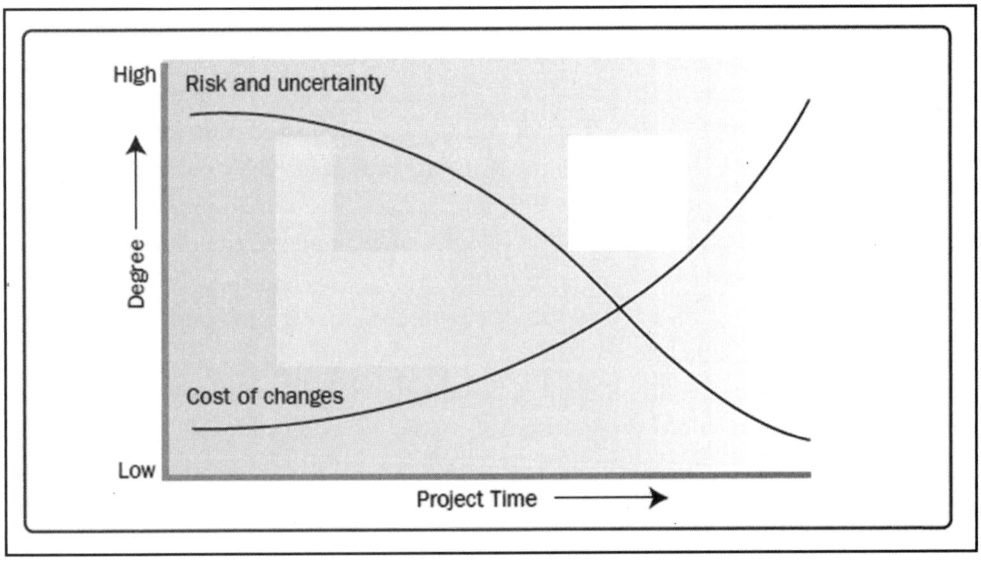

Figure 18-3: Impact of Variable Based on Project Time

Reprinted with permission from A Guide to the Project Management Body of Knowledge (PMBOK© Guide)–*Fifth Edition.*

The first set of Planning processes involve collecting all of the requirements and completing the project scope definition. This is where having a complete and well-defined list of stakeholders, as created in the Initiating processes, is essential. Without a complete set of stakeholders involved in defining requirements, one is bound to run into trouble later in the project if stakeholders refuse to accept deliverables. Recognize that not all stakeholder requirements will make it into the final requirements document, but as long as the stakeholders were involved in the discussion and the final decisions, they will be much more likely to support the outcome.

Once the requirements have been agreed on, the actual work can be defined and planned. Work activities are broken down to the task level and sequenced, after which durations and resource requirements are estimated. Finally, a schedule and budget can be created based on these estimates.

Planning processes also include quality management (how we assure we meet quality requirements), HR management (how we staff the team), communication management, and procurement management. Risk identification and analysis, as well as planning risk responses, are also carried out as Planning processes.

As important as the Planning processes are, it is also important that planning ends or the organization will suffer *analysis paralysis*, which is a common pitfall when undertaking a large, complex project with a large, diverse group of stakeholders. Executive leadership must set a clear timetable for Planning process activities just as they do for any other project task.

Executing: Using project resources to complete the approved project management plan. The Executing processes are those related to actually acquiring, developing, applying, and managing resources to produce the deliverables defined in the charter. People, whether internal staff or external staff hired specifically to execute certain tasks, will now perform the tasks laid out in the project plan, ideally within the bounds of the project schedule and budget.

Executing processes include the assignment of staff from within the organization, as well as the negotiating and signing of contracts for software, hardware, and services. Because contracts can require large capital outlays, and staff must be paid, the largest portion of the project budget will be spent during the Executing processes.

In addition to the build-related tasks, the other plans such as the communication plan, training plan, and stakeholder management plan are executed as part of the Executing processes.

During the Executing processes, the project manager spends a significant amount of time coordinating people and resources, managing stakeholder expectations, and assuring that all of the various activities are integrated in accordance with the project plan.

Monitoring and Controlling: Identify variances to the project management plan and take associated corrective actions needed to meet the project objectives. During the Monitoring and Controlling processes, the project manager monitors actual activities and compares them against baselines to control risks that could impact the project's schedule, budget, and/or quality targets. By providing continuous insight into the health of the project, the project manager can identify risks early enough to recommend corrective or preventative actions to keep the project on track.

Note that changes to schedule, budget, or the quality of the deliverables require a formal change request, which must be handled via the change management process and approved by the sponsor or the steering committee. Since such changes should be kept to a minimum, the project manager's first course of action should therefore be to take corrective action so as to avoid the need for change requests in the first place.

In cases where a change actually is required, the project manager is responsible for initiating the appropriate change process and for assuring that no stakeholders circumvent the established change control processes.

During a complex project such as an EHR project, where there are many stakeholders with differing opinions, strong egos, and power to wield, taking preventative action to avoid problems on the project can be a challenge. Project managers will find themselves relying on their *soft skills* during the Monitoring and Controlling processes, and it is during these activities that great project managers will shine and the rest can struggle.

Closing: Formally deliver the product, service, or result, gain formal acceptance of the deliverable, and close contracts. It is through the Closing processes that the deliverables are formally accepted, vendor payments are approved, the system is transitioned into an operational mode, temporary resources are released, and knowledge transfer is completed.

For an EHR project, acceptance of the deliverables should be dictated by acceptance criteria that were defined during the Planning processes. In many cases, some of these acceptance criteria are actually included in vendor contracts, so they are much more than a mere formality because they trigger final payment to the vendor, and in some cases, the approval or denial of incentive payments.

The transition of the system to an operational mode means that large teams of resources are no longer focused exclusively on the new system and are working outside of standard support processes. Once the transition has concluded, staff will need to use the traditional IT Service Processes for support. Such a transition can be difficult for those clinical staff who were part of the project team and became used to just calling someone directly to get immediate attention. It is also difficult for the IT staff to refer their former *comrades in arms* to the Service Desk when they call with an issue. Therefore, it is important that the formal transition processes be defined during the Planning processes, then formally executed during the project closure.

Project Roles

Everyone with a role on a project is a stakeholder, but not all stakeholders have a role in the project. For example, while patients are expected to benefit from the project deliverable (the EHR), they generally have no direct role in the project itself. On the other end of the scale is the project manager and other staff who are assigned full time to the project. A typical EHR project will have people identified to serve in the following roles:

Project Sponsor. The project sponsor is the person who ultimately owns and supports the business case for the project. Ownership of the business case consists of assuring that benefits expected to be derived from the project are defined and articulated in such a way as to assure alignment with the organization's goals. The business case must also assure that benefits as measured in the context of mission, vision, and values outweigh the costs. Once the business case has been defined and approved, the sponsor must acquire the necessary approval for funding and staffing the project. Once the project has been approved, the sponsor is responsible for leading the project governance process, and for assuring that the necessary decisions are identified and that they are made by the appropriate stakeholders over the project life cycle. Finally, the sponsor is the person responsible for formally accepting the deliverables during the project Closing processes.

The project sponsor should also be someone with the authority to end debate and make decisions, which on an EHR project means that they must have not only the authority but the skills needed to lead a coalition of leaders from across the organization.

Project Manager. The project manager is the person responsible for making sure that the project is successful. That can be a challenging task on a large project with many stakeholders because the project manager may have little or no direct authority over the team members and does not make any of the decisions. The project manager must therefore work closely with the project sponsor and must rely on the sponsor's authority within the organization, escalating issues in a timely manner to assure that they are addressed before problems arise.

Despite this lack of direct authority, the project manager does have responsibility for developing an accurate project plan, schedule, budget, and resource requirement list and then executing the project plan on time, within budget, and to the required level of quality. The project manager is also responsible for holding firm on issues such as scope creep and stakeholder management. A successful project manager makes good use of project measurement tools and reporting metrics to identify any potential problems and assure that they are resolved before they develop into actual problems.

As you can imagine, it takes a special set of skills to succeed in a role where one has accountability without authority! In addition to the formal skills of planning, budgeting, and measuring, a project manager must also master skills such as negotiation, team building, and conflict management. There are many project management courses ranging from day-seminars to university-level degrees where project managers can gain knowledge and access to tools. Many professional project managers also seek certification, such as the Project Management Professional (PMP) certificate from PMI to establish their level of credibility within the industry.

The PMI is a global organization with approximately 3 million members working in nearly every country in the world.[4] It sets globally recognized standards, provides project management tools, and offers certifications in the field of project management. Information on PMI and its various certifications can be found on its website (available at: www.pmi.org).

System Users. System user stakeholders are represented by department champions. A typical EHR project will have stakeholder champions from each of the departments or constituent groups that will use the system. At the very least, this list will include the direct care providers such as physicians and nurses, and depending on the breadth of the system's functionality and project scope, will typically extend to ancillary areas such as Radiology, Lab, and Pharmacy and may also extend into the OR and the ED.

Groups that may not use the system themselves still need to be included as stakeholders if upstream or downstream data or processes can have an impact on them or be impacted by them. Such groups include Registration, HIM/Coding, Revenue Cycle, etc. One can easily see how broad-reaching an EHR project is, and why it is so important to make sure that all stakeholders are identified during the Initiating processes.

IT Department. The IT department is obviously a major stakeholder, but it would be a mistake to think of it as the primary stakeholder, or as the system owner. To understand why, think of building a new home. As the buyer, you are the primary stakeholder—the owner, or in project terms, the sponsor. Just as the homeowner relies on the construction company for ideas and advice, the ideas and advice are asked for within the context of the homeowner's requirements.

With an EHR project the IT department is a major stakeholder in much the same way as the construction company is on a home project: it is a major stakeholder, but the clinical executive owns the system since it is being built to meet the clinical executive's requirements.

Vendors. Many people tend to overlook the fact that the vendors on an EHR project are stakeholders and have a huge stake in the outcome of the project as well. While their goals tend to be different from those of the providers, these for-profit technology companies are highly motivated to have satisfied customers who will serve as references and thereby drive future growth. In most projects (not just EHR projects) the vendor is the stakeholder who will often have a separate project manager. The vendor project manager will have deep reach into the vendor's organization and will work closely with the client project manager to coordinate tasks across the two organizations. Because there should only be one primary project manager on any given project, the vendor project manager will generally take direction from the client project manager. An exception to this rule is the case in which the client contracts with the vendor specifically to provide primary project management services.

Patients. Even though the ultimate beneficiaries of an EHR project are the patients, they traditionally tended to have only a very minor role as stakeholders. They are not involved in any of the Planning processes, testing processes, or decision-making processes. They do not contribute resources or direct funding. However, with MU requirements pushing EHR system vendors to include features such as patient portals and secure patient/provider messaging, patients are assuming more important stakeholder roles. In fact, in addition to the portal and messaging features of EHR systems, patients are also the key stakeholders in projects that focus on such things as home-based care management or mobile applications for managing obesity, diabetes, asthma and other chronic diseases and conditions.

Project Documentation

A formal process will generate a lot of documentation, and the more formal and more complex the process, the more the documentation. (I once knew a project manager who worked at Boeing who was fond of saying, "The project isn't over until the weight of the paper equals the weight of the aircraft.") While documentation is created in all of the process groups, the first official project document is the project charter, which is developed as part of the Initiating processes. The only other document that is generated during the Initiating processes is the stakeholder register, which is a crucial document to have to assure that the right stakeholders are involved in creating the remaining project documents.

Once the project has been approved and stakeholders are identified and on board, the Planning processes will generate the scope document, and the requirements documentation will follow based on the agreed-upon scope. The project resource requirements, budget, schedule, risk register, and other related documents will be created based on the approved requirements. In large, complex projects that impact workflows, dataflow and workflow diagrams are also generated during the Planning processes. Other planning documents include various management plans for crucial items such as procurements, communication, training, etc. It is important to understand that documents such as communication and training materials, while technically documents, are not considered project documentation because they are actually deliverables that are created during the Executing processes as tasks with specific deliverables managed under the scope of their respective plans.

Some Executing processes do create project documentation, however. Examples include procurement documentation (contracts, work orders, etc.), documentation pertaining to the actual execution of tasks, and project change requests.

Monitoring and Controlling processes tend to generate documentation around work performance, quality, and decisions pertaining to remediating risks that actually occur, or threaten to occur to the extent that they require documented decisions or action.

Closing processes will generate documentation related to accepting deliverables, lessons learned, and performance evaluations. While some organizations are tempted to relax the rigor around documenting things toward the end of a long, complex, and at times difficult project, these project documents can prove vital when the vendor is insisting on getting a formal acceptance document signed.

Of all of the documents generated as part of the project, the most important one is arguably the scope document. The reason for this is that all other documents, even those vitally important ones such as the requirements document, are created specifically to support the project scope. Various stakeholders on an EHR project will insist on requirements or functionality that conflict with the requirements of other stakeholders. It is also common for stakeholders to come up with new requirements once the project is well underway and they have a better perspective on how the new system will impact their areas. In all these cases, it is essential for the project manager to match all new or conflicting requests against the approved scope. Those that are not within the scope are not included—period—unless the scope is formally changed via the approved change management plan and change management process.

Project Tools

There are many tools that can aid in the managing of a complex project. Many people are already familiar with tools such as Microsoft Project, but it is important to understand that Microsoft Project is primarily a project scheduling and tracking tool. Other important tools include change management tools, workflow management tools, product analysis/selection tools, organizational charts, Responsible Accountable Consulted Informed (RACI) charts, and communication technology. Focus groups and facilitated workshops, while more commonly thought of as techniques, are also useful tools that can assist the project manager in gathering requirements and reaching agreements.

Practical Application of Formal PM Discipline within Healthcare

An EHR can be one of the largest capital investments a healthcare organization will make. It can rival, and even exceed, the cost of building a new facility. As such, it is imperative that the project is a success, yet a surprisingly high number of EHR projects run into serious trouble.

While there is little in the formal academic literature to indicate why there are high rates of failure for EHR projects, there is quite a bit published in healthcare trade media. Several "Top 5" and "Top 10" lists can be found online. One such list was compiled by summarizing the items listed in a long-running discussion within the HIMSS discussion group on the LinkedIn website. The two items that received the most discussion time were unclear stakeholder requirements and immature change management processes.[5]

Clearly, stakeholder engagement and requirements gathering, along with a clear definition of scope and a solid change management process, are essential if one is to avoid the pitfalls that plague many EHR projects. To improve its chances of success, an organization that is initiating an EHR project must establish a governance process that assures goal alignment and stakeholder buy-in and must properly manage changes to the project scope as the time line progresses.

Governance. Having the proper governance structure can significantly improve an EHR project's chances of success. Governance of a project occurs via a project steering committee that is made up of representatives from the various stakeholder groups. To be effective, the steering committee members must be in a position of authority within the organization such that they can make, and agree to, decisions on behalf of their departments. While there is no strict rule defining who should be on an EHR steering committee, membership will generally include the CIO, CFO, CMIO, CNO, as well as (for hospitals) senior leaders from the ED, OR, Lab, Radiology/Imaging, and Pharmacy. Senior leaders from HIM should be included because they work "downstream" and their workflows can be impacted, as should the vice president of Revenue Cycle because billing processes can be impacted as well.

A large project like an EHR selection and implementation will likely have several subcommittees and workgroups reporting up to the steering committee. Typically, the project sponsor or the project manager will chair the steering committee, and the various steering committee members will chair the subcommittees and workgroups.

Early in the project, while the Initiation and Planning processes are occurring, the focus will be on making decisions in terms of scope, resources, timing, etc. Once the Execution and Monitoring/Controlling processes begin, stakeholders who are leading workgroups will typically report on progress and discuss any issues or barriers that have arisen. Scope issues are often hot topics of discussion as the project progresses.

Stakeholder Buy-in. As mentioned earlier, an EHR project (or any project for that matter) will have an extremely difficult time being successful without buy-in from all stakeholders. No matter how well the technology works, the workflows were designed, the team executed their tasks, or the budget was met, if staff refuse to use the system, the project will fail and the goals will not be met.

To assure success, an EHR project must not only get all stakeholders to the table via the project steering committee, but the stakeholders must explicitly buy-in and support the project. This is best accomplished by having the steering committee members actually sign the project charter and the project scope document. Some organizations will have the stakeholders also sign the project schedule, the resource plan, and various other plans such as the training plan.

Clinician Engagement. Possibly the most famous healthcare-related example of a project failure is the case of Cedars-Sinai being forced to uninstall its CPOE system in fall 2002 when physicians revolted and refused to use it three months after it went live.[6] Perhaps because of this case, there have been numerous studies into the issues that clinicians, physicians in particular, consider to be important factors in successful EHR implementation projects.

One systematic review of the literature identified six critical factors for EHR success as perceived by physicians: "user attitude towards information systems, workflow impact, interoperability, technical support, communication among users, and expert support."[7] Enlisting clinical leaders as stakeholders is the only reliable way to assure that each of these factors are adequately addressed during the project.

Change Management. An EHR project is by nature complex and will cover a long span of time. Therefore, it is a certainty that there will be many change requests during an EHR project. Some will be unavoidable, such as new federal regulations that require a change in data collection, and these will generate only the discussion needed to plan for the change. Others will be discretionary, such as those that come about as the team moves deeper into the project and learns that some of its initial assumptions are no longer valid. These will generate much more discussion and will need to be dealt with on a case-by-case basis.

Regardless of whether a change request is discretionary or not, *all* change requests must be handled via a formal change management process. Typically, a large project will have established a change review board that considers proposed changes to the project requirements, scope, or deliverables. Proposed changes that warrant serious consideration or approval are then escalated to the project steering committee for discussion and determination as to whether the request should be approved or not. Changes to the project requirements, scope, or deliverables can only be approved by the steering committee because steering committee members have signed off on the requirements, scope, and deliverables during the Initiation and Planning processes. Is it clear now why all stakeholders must be represented on the project steering committee?

Change management is also important when considering the *project management triangle*, sometimes referred to as the iron triangle.[8] The three elements of the triangle are scope, time, and cost, and within the bounds of the triangle is the notion of project quality. The concept behind the triangle is that if quality is to remain unchanged, then any change in one of the sides of the triangle requires changes to at least one of the remaining sides. For example, if the steering committee decides to expand the scope of an EHR project, then the budget and time line must increase as well. Or, if there is a need to reduce the time line then there must be either a corresponding reduction in scope or an increase in cost to hire more resources. Failure to adhere to the iron triangle in each of these cases will result in an undesirable decrease in quality.

Workflow and Process Standardization. EHR projects typically include goals pertaining to workflows and processes (if they don't, then they are in big trouble before they even start!). In fact, the most active workgroups reporting up to the project steering committee will be focused on workflows and processes.

There are two important things to keep in mind when considering workflows and processes during an EHR project. The first is to use the existing quality management, physician governance, nursing council, medical informatics, and other operational governance structures that are in place. If some of these operational governance structures are not in place, then creating them should be part of the project scope. This is because once the project ends, there will still be ongoing activity in all of these disciplines, and they will occasionally dictate workflow and process changes as a means to improve quality and outcomes. The best approach, therefore, is to have the operational governance teams who will own processes going forward be the ones who define the new workflows and processes that are part of the project deliverables.

The second thing to keep in mind is that it is a mistake to install a new system with the idea that the organization will force it to support existing processes. In fact, many EHR systems were designed around specific workflows, and trying to use them to support workflows other than what they were built around is only asking for frustration at best, or costly workarounds and even failure at worst. Workflow and process issues and questions should therefore be top-of-mind during any planning and system selection activities.

Communication. Communication is essential not only among members of the project team, but it is vital outside of the project team as well. That may seem obvious and it would be hard to imagine anyone disagreeing with that statement, but it is surprising how often poor communication is cited as the cause of problems on EHR projects. A good project communication plan is crafted in the early part of an EHR project during the Planning processes, and it takes into account content, timing, frequency, delivery method, and most importantly, audiences.

The various items within an EHR communication plan will include:

- Regular project status reports for the steering committee including progress against schedule and budget, any issues that need resolving, and status of change requests.
- End-user communications, broken down by target audience (physician, nurse, ancillary, etc.) along with a communication schedule and means of delivery. Content should include not only the project schedule as it pertains to the audience, but information on when and where to expect training, how workflows will change, and so forth.
- Public communications—some organizations send mailings to patient homes, some put posters up in the facility, and some have an article published in the local newspaper.

A good communication plan also makes the distinction between planning communications and then actually delivering the communication, thereby avoiding the pitfall of deciding how to communicate to physicians the week before communications are to go out. Remember, things will be hectic as the system go-live date approaches, and it is best to have a plan already in place so that when it comes time to communicate you are ready to simply deliver the message.

Training and Education. Health IT professionals, clinical staff, and others involved with EHR projects agree that the proper level of training and go-live support plays a large role in EHR system implementations.[9] Inadequate training not only makes for a much more difficult go-live, but it can also increase the risk of harm to patients. According to one nurse who had recently been through an EHR go-live, "I am really afraid that I am going to make a mistake. I've been a nurse for 43 years, and I have had a stellar career. I've never been in trouble for anything, but I fear being in trouble with this system."[10]

As with communications, a training plan and training schedule should be created early in the project Planning processes. Organizations that wait until close to go-live to prepare to train the entire population of caregivers and other system users tend to find out the hard way that it is difficult to locate the space it will take to train so many people and to adjust everyone's schedule to allow for training.

There is also the balancing act between trying not to take too many caregivers off the floor at once and stretching the training schedule out too long. Having a short schedule means that a lot of people must be trained at once, and a long schedule means that those trained first may find that they have forgotten their training by the time the system is live.

Infrastructure. Infrastructure makes an appearance on many lists of the top risks to successful implementation of EHR projects. Even if the system implementation is a success, an unreliable infrastructure can bring the system down without warning. The most classic example of such an outage is the case of Beth Israel Deaconess, which experienced a four-day network outage that has been called "one of the worst health-care IT disasters ever."[11] During the outage, the hospital had to revert to a paper record system that had not been used in years, and lab reports that doctors were used to receiving in 45 minutes suddenly took up to 5 hours to be delivered.

Ideally, an infrastructure assessment would be conducted before the project proposal is submitted so that any shortcomings can be identified and remediation activities (and costs) will thus be included within the scope of the proposal. If it is not practical to conduct the assessment before the proposal is written, then the proposal should at the very least assure that providing the infrastructure to support the EHR is included as one of the project goals. Then, when the scope document is being created, the infrastructure components should be clearly identified as being within the scope.

Activation Strategy. There are several activation strategies to consider when planning an EHR go-live. Table 18-1 lists the most common strategies, along with pros and cons of each.

The strategy that an organization chooses will depend on a number of factors, and as with any strategic decisions, the strategy decision should involve all stakeholders and should be made at the steering committee level. The decision should also be made as early in the Planning process as practical since many other planning decisions will need to take the activation strategy into account.

Table 18-1: Pros and Cons of Activation Strategies

Strategy	Pros	Cons
The "Big Bang": The entire enterprise goes live at the same time—popular among small and mid-sized organizations.	• Quickest approach minimizes the duration—"pulling the band-aid off" • Systems are standardized across the entire organization	Resource intensive: • Compressed training schedule • Support staff will be spread thin • Any unexpected problems impact everybody—they are not isolated
Phased approach: Units and departments go live one at a time or in groups—popular among large organizations and multi-site health systems.	• More flexibility in scheduling training • Support staff can focus on smaller groups • Lessons learned in early deployments can benefit those going live later	• Systems are not standardized during the phased go-live period • Disruption is not minimized, and can cause confusion for an extended period
Use a Pilot Group, then either Big Bang or Phased for remaining areas.	Issues and problems can be identified and resolved before a broader deployment.	Pilot Group is an island that can make it difficult to coordinate care.

The Morning After

Although a project has a beginning, a middle, and an end, you will not walk away from the system once the project has ended and the champagne glasses have been washed and put back in the cupboard. An important part of project planning has to do with handing off the deliverables in such a way that the organization can seamlessly begin using those deliverables to meet its stated goals. Therefore, we will close this chapter with a few words on what should be done once the project successfully closes.

Transition to Routine Operations—the IT Department. Once the system is live, and the support structure that was put in place to manage the activation has been dismantled, the IT department must be prepared to support the new system on a day-to-day basis. Such support will generally fall into the standard categories of training issues, break/fix issues, and routine maintenance.

To prepare your front-line support team to handle the routine calls that will come in, it is a good idea to have Service Desk staff attend an abbreviated version of the training classes that system users were required to attend. This will help them understand the basics of how the system works so that they can help resolve nontechnical issues over the phone.

To prepare all of your IT staff to quickly resolve break/fix issues, the project should have defined deliverables that include knowledge-base articles for Service Desk staff, as well as process flows and decision trees for technical staff to follow when investigating issues. Vendors provide technical support for their products, and the process for contacting the vendor along with escalation paths should be documented as part of the internal IT support documentation.

Routine maintenance items must also be documented and integrated into routine IT operations as part of the project. Because many routine maintenance activities require some system downtime, these downtime windows should also be discussed during the project Planning processes and agreed on by the project steering committee.

Transition to Routine Operations—Clinical Staff. Assuming that there was adequate planning, training, and support, your routine day-to-day operations will typically settle in naturally over a short period of time once the system has gone live. However, the EHR system was almost certainly not installed with the goal of simply using it to automate tasks and recordkeeping activities. The goals that organizations set when launching an EHR project will generally be focused on quality, outcomes, practice standardization, reducing errors, eliminating duplication, and minimizing costs. Many of the measures that help track progress against these goals appear within the MU criteria of the HITECH Act. Therefore, the EHR project must include tasks designed to create the organizational oversight needed to monitor progress against the appropriate goals. Metrics must be identified, data must be generated to track using those metrics, and action plans must be created when the data indicate that improvements are necessary.

While project management principles and the PMBOK are intended to be applied to a set of activities that have a definite beginning and end, that does not mean that some of them cannot be applied to operational activities, particularly those focused on continuous improvement. In terms of an EHR project, physician and nursing workgroups that were formed during the Planning processes can easily transition to operational councils focusing on quality, workflows, and decision support. For example, an integrated health system may decide to transform the clinical governance group formed during the ER project to a permanent governance structure overseeing its new Care Process Automation activities.

CONCLUSION

Implementing a large project that impacts nearly every department, and every workflow, in a complex environment managed by very smart people who have very strong opinions is not for the faint of heart. However, there are established processes and readily available tools that can greatly increase an organization's chance of success. Key takeaways from this chapter are:

- EHR projects are big and complex, and size and complexity are both exponentially related to the difficulty of successfully completing a project.
- Established project management principles help manage the complexity and therefore maximize the chance of successfully completing a project.
- The five process groups defined within the PMI PMBOK are: Initiating, Planning, Executing, Monitoring and Controlling, and Closing. These process groups are made up of forty-seven distinct processes that embody the formal project management discipline.
- It is far less costly to make changes in the early stages of a project. Therefore, the Planning activities should never be shortchanged, despite the pressure to show visible work on a high-visibility project.
- Effective project governance creates a forum to assure that key stakeholder representatives are visibly engaged and assures that changes to the project are not made unless required to assure success.
- Key stakeholders on an EHR project include the system users (physician, nursing, ancillary, HIM, etc.), the project manager, the IT department, vendors, and

patients. The project sponsor should be an executive with responsibility for one or more of the major processes.

By following established project management processes, and by focusing on the key principles of stakeholder engagement, change management, and governance, a healthcare organization can successfully complete even the most challenging EHR project to the satisfaction of everyone involved.

REFERENCES

1. Project Management Institute. (2013). *A Guide to the Project Management Body of Knowledge (PMBOK guide).* Newtown Square, PA: Project Management Institute. (p. 3).
2. Project Management Institute. (2013). *A Guide to the Project Management Body of Knowledge (PMBOK guide).* Newtown Square, PA: Project Management Institute. (p. 4).
3. Project Management Institute. (2013). *A Guide to the Project Management Body of Knowledge (PMBOK guide).* Newtown Square, PA: Project Management Institute. (p. 66-72).
4. Project Management Institute (2014). Learn more about who PMI is and what we do. http:// http://www.pmi.org/About-Us.aspx. Accessed November 19, 2014.
5. Pietraszkiewicz T. EMR/EHR implementation failure: A summary, *The Big O Blog presented by Juran,* http://www.juran.com/blog/?p=129. Accessed August 11, 2010.
6. Connolly C. Cedars-Sinai doctors cling to pen and paper, *The Washington Post.* March 21, 2005:A01. http://www.washingtonpost.com/wp-dyn/articles/A52384-2005Mar20.html. Accessed November 19, 2014.
7. Castillo VH, Martínez-García AI, Pulido J. A knowledge-based taxonomy of critical factors for adopting electronic health record systems by physicians: a systematic literature review. *BMC Medical Informatics & Decision Making.* 2010;10(1),60-76. doi:10.1186/1472-6947-10-60.
8. Project Management. (2014, May 30). In: *Wikipedia, The Free Encyclopedia.* June 2, 2014, http://en.wikipedia.org/w/index.php?title=Project_management&oldid=610806318. Accessed June 2, 2014.
9. Daigrepont J, McGrath D. *Complete Guide and Toolkit to Successful EHR Adoption.* Chapter 2. Chicago, IL: HIMSS; 2011. ISBN: 978-0-9821070-9-6.
10. Fields W. Transitioning from a "best of breed" to a single vendor EHR with CPOE. Presented at NI8 at HIMSS-12 Nursing Symposium, Las Vegas, NV; February 2012.
11. Berinato S. (2003, February 15). Halamka on Beth Israel's health-care IT disaster. *CIO Magazine.* http://www.cio.com/article/31701/Halamka_on_Beth_Israel_s_Health_Care_IT_Disaster. Accessed November 19, 2014.

Chapter 19

Why Do Projects Fail?

Ken Ong, MD, MPH, FACP, FIDSA, CPHIMS, FHIMSS

"CEO Resigns Amid Troubled EHR Rollout"
Healthcare IT News, May 30, 2014[1]

"Hospital Takes EHR Heavyweight To Court"
Healthcare IT News, Jan 06, 2014[2]

"Setback For Sutter After $1B EHR Crashes"
Healthcare IT News, Aug 28, 2013[3]

"Go-live Gone Wrong"
Healthcare IT News, July 2013[4]

"Hospital Shuts Down CPOE System"
Health Data Management, September 29, 2005[5]

INTRODUCTION

Evidence from the United States and around the world has proven the value of the EHR and its related technology. It can improve community and patient care and reduce cost.

The Centers for Medicaid & Medicare Services (CMS) EHR Incentive Programs for Meaningful Use (MU) are national initiatives for health IT adoption. As of this writing, 255,336 Eligible Professionals and 3,877 hospitals have attested to MU.[6]

Nevertheless, like complex projects inside and outside healthcare, health IT projects can fail.

The EHR go-live at Maine Medical Center in Portland, Maine, a 600-bed hospital, cost $160 million. Four months after go-live, the EHR rollout to the rest of the Maine Health network was stopped. According to Maine Medical Center President and CEO Richard W. Petersen, "The launch of the shared electronic health record has had some unintended financial consequences. While there have been many advantages in the implementation of EHR, in some cases, we've been unable to accurately charge for the services we provide. This lack of charge capture is hurting our financial picture."[4]

In 2014, two hospitals in Montana sued another major EHR vendor for failing to meet their go-live deadline and for deploying a product that did not meet 2014 MU certification. In February 2012, a hospital in Kansas sued a major EHR vendor for "continually providing inaccurate price quotes," and also failing to implement the system to meet meaningful use requirements.[2]

Arguably, one of the most outstanding health IT failures was the suspension of CPOE at Cedars-Sinai Hospital, a highly regarded, 952-bed hospital located in Beverly Hills, California. It is one of the top 100 "Most Wired" Hospitals.[7] The suspension sent digital shock waves across the nation through the e-mail threads, list services, and blogs of health IT professionals.[7,8]

The $34 million, three-year CPOE project included billing and registration. CPOE was made mandatory for all physicians, and nonparticipating physicians risked losing staff privileges.

The list of possible reasons for the CPOE project failure is long. According to reports in the media, some physicians complained before go-live that the mandatory two-hour instructor-led and online training were too long. Yet, after go-live, others reported that training was too short. Of the 2,000 physicians, 85 percent were voluntary, which may have posed a greater challenge than would have occurred with salaried residents. Medications misspelled in free text were not recognized. Common orders were excluded, such as "Clear liquids and advance diet as tolerated." There were complaints of too many questions, alerts, and reminders. Reportedly, rank and file physicians were not involved in design and implementation. Order entry involved too many screens with 6 to 8 seconds between each screen.[9]

The temporary setback to CPOE at Cedars-Sinai was not the first for this complex technology. Fifteen years earlier, the University of Virginia Medical Center was a pioneer when it began implementation of mandatory CPOE in 1988.[2] In 1992, more than 550 terminals were deployed in three locations. Over 3,600 nurses, 1,200 residents, 800 medical students, and 200 attending physicians had been trained to use the new system. The program took three times longer and cost three times more than expected to install. Interestingly, the technology ("the strict, literal interpretation of rules by the computer") itself was only one of four factors that led to the system's temporary suspension. The other three factors that contributed to the "widespread organizational stress" associated with the implementation were dramatic changes in established workflow, unclear governance policies, and lack of physician understanding of the long-term strategic value of the system. Only after an executive committee with leaders from the major clinical departments was established was the initiative successfully implemented. The case study's author concludes: "[W]e may have gained a strategic and competitive advantage for the future by being forced to deal with issues of institutional change."[10]

Failed health information system projects are not unique to the United States. The lead story on the British Broadcasting Company's evening news of October 27, 1992, was the failure of a new computer system at the London Ambulance Service.[11] The deaths of 20 to 30 people were ascribed to the failure. Areas dead to radio transmission and incorrectly pressed buttons sent incorrect ambulance locations to the system. As a consequence, too many ambulances were sent to some calls and none to others. The growing error log compromised the system further. An official inquiry found that the project was underfinanced with an inadequate time line. The causes were several. It was unclear which of the contractors was primary, and the management of the project was inadequate. The software was judged to be unfinished and unstable. The emergency backup system was untested. Training was inadequate.

In 2007, *The Guardian* newspaper surveyed more than 1,000 physicians and found that 59 percent of respondents were unwilling to upload any patient records to the national system without specific patient consent. Another 30 percent were unsure about doing so, and only 11 percent indicated they would likely comply. Seventy percent of respondent physicians did not believe the electronic records program was a good use of National Health Service (NHS) resources, and only 1 percent rated its progress as good or excellent.[12]

The departing head of the NHS IT program, Richard Granger, has said he is "ashamed" of the quality of some of the systems put into the NHS by Connecting for Health suppliers. Likewise, Milton Keynes, the Connecting for Health lead has said "Sometimes we put in stuff that I'm just ashamed of." He said a key reason for the failings of systems was that contractors had not listened to end-users.[13]

On the other end of the world, in 1996, a major health IT failure occurred in the New South Wales public health system in Australia.[14] An information systems steering committee commissioned a consulting firm to devise their IT strategy. The consultants recommended a best-of-breed (BoB) approach to purchase three core systems: financial, pathology, and patient administration/clinicals. Scenarios with predetermined scripts were given to each vendor. Ultimately, a vendor was selected who had installed software in 100 sites in the United States. Five pilot sites were selected, none of which had taken part in developing the strategy or selecting the system. The sites pressed for more software customization than the vendor was willing to deliver. Nurses had difficulty arranging time for training, and not all adopted the new system, while physicians had limited time for training. Managers found the report generator inadequate. Clinicians found logging into the system cumbersome with four levels of login. Navigation was complicated, with up to eleven screens and forty-three key strokes to order one test. Orders were not linked with results reporting. The character-based system appeared archaic to end-users accustomed to Windows-driven systems. The IS staff was highly dependent on vendor support. After just 6 weeks in one institution and 15 months in another, with problems continuing without resolution, the $110 million project was terminated.

The ambulatory EHR has faced challenges, too. According to a study by the Medical Records Institute, nearly 19 percent of respondents to the survey indicated they either have in the past experienced the de-installation of an EMR system (12%) or are now going through a de-installation (7%). Slightly more than 8 percent of those surveyed indicated they had ripped out their EMRs and gone back to paper.[14]

ARE HEALTHCARE IT PROJECTS THE ONLY PROJECTS THAT FAIL?

Indeed, we should not be too surprised to hear of speed bumps on the path to EHR adoption.

The Standish Group collected data on business IT projects and software development projects internationally since 1985 in their "Chaos" database.[15]

Standish Group used the following definitions of project resolution:

- **Successful:** Delivered on time, within budget estimate, with required features and functions
- **Failed:** Cancelled prior to completion or delivered and never used
- **Challenged:** Late, over budget, and/or with less than the required features and functions

The proportion of failed or challenged IT projects declined between 2004 and 2012 but still exceeded the 39 percent of successful IT projects (see Table 19-1).

Standish Group reported that large projects (more than $10 million in labor content) were twice as likely to be late, over budget, and missing critical features than small projects (less than $1 million in labor content). Large projects were ten times more likely to be cancelled than small projects. They conclude that large IT projects should be deconstructed into a series of small projects.

Standish Group cited ten success factors for small projects. The five that offer the most value are executive management support, user involvement, optimization, skilled resources, and project management expertise (see Table 19-2).

Another factor in the success or failure of a software installation is the quality of the software itself. KLAS, a provider of customer satisfaction reports for health IT, conducted a study of vendor and provider perspectives on software quality. Sixty-one acute care providers and seven vendor executives representing twelve firms were interviewed. The providers represented 211 acute care hospitals, each with more than 200 beds.

The participating vendors were among the top twenty in customer satisfaction in 2004. They included many of the more established in health IT: Cerner, Epic, GE, McKesson, Mediware, Misys, PeopleSoft, Per-Se, Picis, SCI Scheduling.com, Siemens, and Unibased Systems Architecture.[16]

Vendors and providers ranked the characteristics of quality similarly. Stability and uptime were ranked first. Response time, ease of use, release management, maintenance cost, and certification and benchmarking followed. Though the scoring was most different for maintenance cost, providers scored each of the characteristics higher in importance than the vendors (see Figure 19-1).

Table 19-1: Results in IT Projects Between 2004 and 2012

	2004	2006	2008	2010	2012
Successful	29%	35%	32%	37%	39%
Failed	18%	19%	24%	21%	18%
Challenged	53%	46%	44%	42%	43%

Table 19-2: Success Factors for Small Projects

	Points
Executive management support	20
User involvement	15
Optimization	15
Skilled resources	13
Project management expertise	12
Agile process	10
Clear business objectives	6
Emotional maturity	5
Execution	3
Tools and infrastructure	1
	100

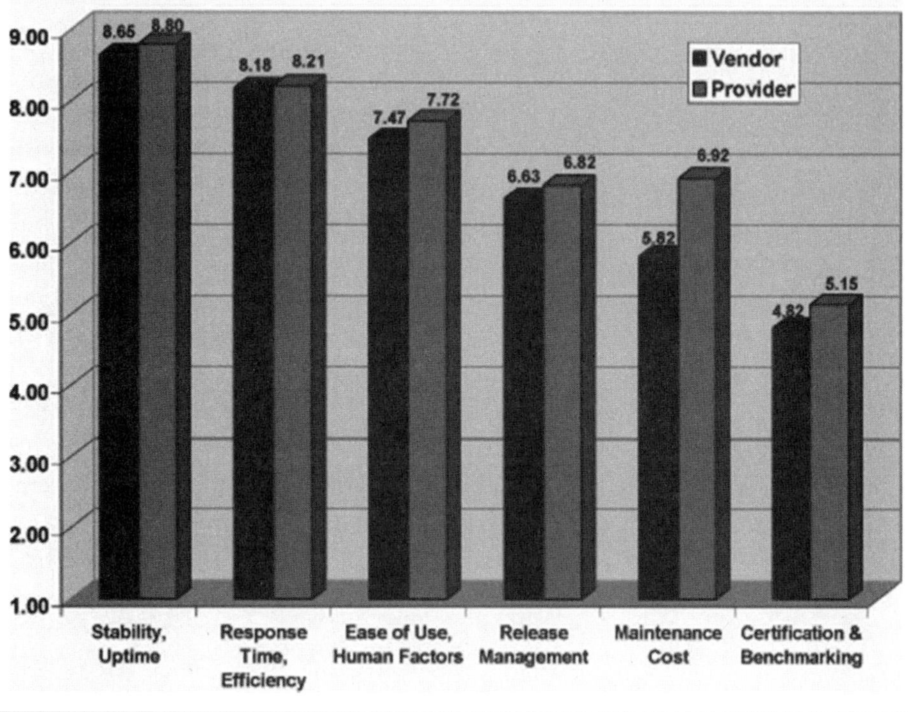

Figure 19-1: Characteristics of Software Quality

When queried how poor software quality may impact an organization, 18 to 56 percent of the providers acknowledged severe to intolerable negative effects on outcomes such as end-user disruptions, downtime of software systems, time spent recovering and fixing, testing releases, and IT effort on other quality issues (see Figure 19-2).

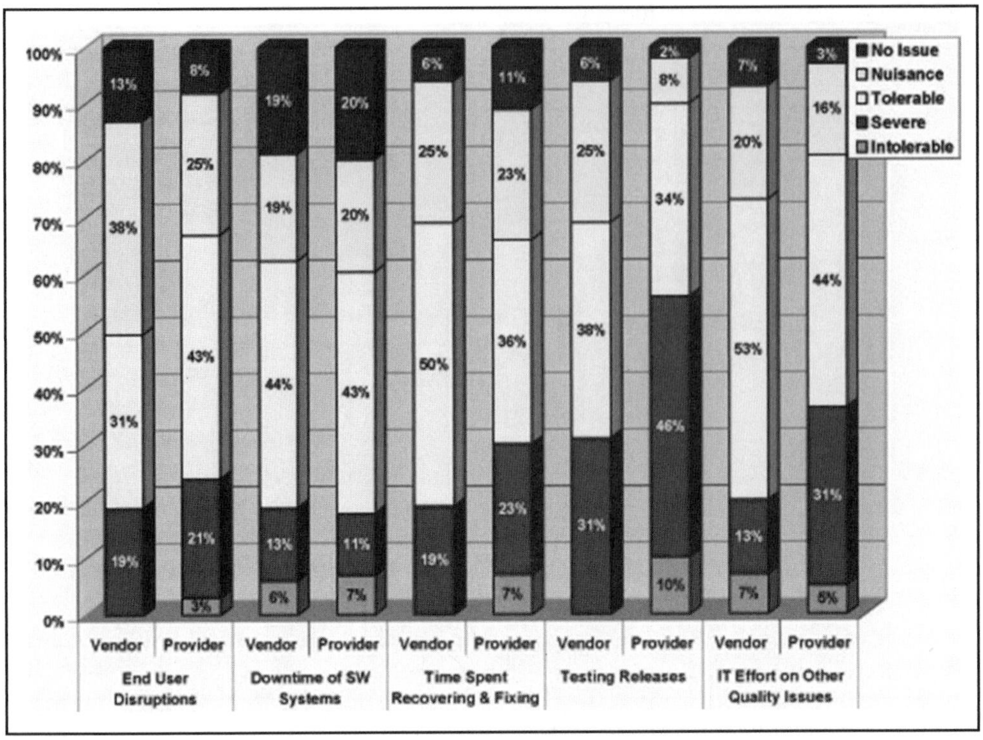

Figure 19-2: Effects of Software Quality on Provider Organizations

Not all software is created equal, and different vendors will have different on-time delivery rates. The more difficult the technology and the greater the clinical transformation required, the longer an application may take to install. The 2005 On-Time Delivery Report from KLAS gathered delivery times for CDRs, CPOE, nurse charting, pharmacy, and physician notes.[16] Physician notes projects were the most likely to be reported on time (67%). The other project types were reported to be on schedule 45 to 54 percent of the time.

Providers reported that late projects could be ascribed to vendors half the time, to providers 13 percent of the time, and both to vendors and providers 37 percent of the time. CPOE projects were the most challenging, while pharmacy projects were the least. CPOE implementations were an average of 12 months late. Physician notes implementations were 10 months late; nurse charting, 9 months late; CDR, 7 months late; and pharmacy, 5 months late (see Table 19-3).

Implementing on time and on budget is hard.

Our cursory review of the literature shows that the Cedars-Sinai CPOE project suspension was neither an isolated nor an unexpected event, given the prevalence of IT project failure both inside and outside healthcare. The KLAS and Standish Group reports established project failure as common.

KEYS TO SUCCESS

The industry press is replete with advice to those implementing health IT. One observer warns of six deadly mistakes to avoid: (1) raising expectations too high, (2) providing

Table 19-3: On-Time Delivery of Software Projects

Overall Averages	Percent On-Time*	Percent Live On-Time	Percent On-Schedule	Average Months Late
CDR	45%	29%	16%	7 Months
CPOE	54%	8%	46%	12 Months
Nurse Charting	54%	20%	34%	9 Months
Pharmacy	50%	29%	21%	5 Months
Physician Notes	67%	9%	58%	10 Months

skimpy training, (3) doing the "Big Bang" implementation, (4) leaving physicians to their own devices, (5) disregarding dissidents, and (6) giving physicians a choice.[17]

John Glaser, former vice president and CIO of Partners HealthCare, Boston, prescribed six success factors for clinical information system implementation: (1) strong organizational vision and strategy; (2) talented and committed leadership; (3) a part-

Sidebar: Ten Steps for Success Recommended by Physicians Who Implemented CPOE Successfully at University of Pennsylvania Health System, NorthShore University HealthSystem, and Cincinnati Children's Hospital[18]

1. All hands on deck: Make CPOE a top organizational priority with full support from the executive leadership to unit staff.
2. Pay physician champions: Value and protect time for a physician to design, plan, and lead CPOE implementation.
3. Analyze your workflow: New, more efficient workflows should be designed to replace inefficient extant workflows.
4. Build adequate order sets: Order sets can help standardize care and speed adoption. The number of needed order sets can number in the hundreds.
5. Recognize politics: The chief medical information officer or director of medical informatics must get buy-in from the clinical department chairs.
6. Set a deadline and mean it: Delays and postponed deadlines dampen physician and organizational enthusiasm.
7. Train, train, train: Train before, during, and after implementation. Train in formal sessions, online and on the patient care units.
8. Exploit physician resistance: Go one-on-one and find out why physicians resist and use the knowledge to improve training, create more order sets, or improve usability.
9. Sell the benefits: It is about quality care and patient safety. This is not just an IT project.
10. Crack the whip: If CPOE is mandatory, enforce it.

Sidebar: Lessons Premier Hospitals Learned About Implementing EHRs[19]

1. Challenge of Culture Changes
2 Value of Clinical Champions
3. Need for Medical Staff Training
4 Integration of Alerts and Reporting of Measures
5. Rigorous Security
6. Clear Policies To Document Communication
7. Flexible Budgets

nership between the clinical, administrative, and IT staffs; (4) thoughtful redesign of clinical processes; (5) excellent implementation skills, especially in project management and support; and, (6) good-to-excellent IT.[20]

Other principles provide guidance that applies to all IT projects. A roundtable on IT failures at the University of Houston struck a common chord with advice given elsewhere:[21]

- Shrink the development cycle time by breaking projects into smaller bites and making sure that value is delivered at each bite.
- Don't get caught in the "throwing good money after bad" trap. If value isn't being delivered, ignore the sunk costs and look only at future dollars versus benefits.
- Focus attention on the opinion leaders and the change agents.
- Vendors and business partners can help in diffusing technologies.
- Customers may sometimes serve as change agents.
- Be sure you understand the current state completely before attempting to introduce change.
- Demonstrate the value of the systems by using the worst critics as the earliest adopters.
- Know to whom you are selling.
- Have proper incentives for adoption.
- Take advantage of beta testing opportunities.
- Make sure you understand company culture and the degree that you will be affecting it.
- Make your systems as reliable as is possible within the given constraints.
- Develop measurement/reporting processes to monitor the success of diffusion.

CMS and the National Learning Consortium offer EHR implementation guidance online, which covers the following topics:[22]

- **Step 1:** Assess Your Practice Readiness
- **Step 2:** Plan Your Approach
- **Step 3:** Select or Upgrade to a Certified EHR
- **Step 4:** Conduct Training & Implement an EHR System
- **Step 5:** Achieve Meaningful Use
- **Step 6:** Continue Quality Improvement

During any software selection process, the site visits and reference calls can serve as an introduction to clients of the selected vendor who installed the product successfully. The users group can serve as a community with a depth of experience and knowledge of the product that is otherwise unavailable.

WHEN THINGS GO WRONG

Though good planning and rigorous implementation can mitigate potential problems, problems will arise. IT is complicated and expensive. The nature of healthcare in the 21st century is in and of itself complex. Any successful IT project is the result of paying meticulous attention to workflows and people.

The tools of performance improvement can be well applied to the challenges of health IT projects. Root cause analysis, workflow diagrams, the Shewhart cycle, Failure

Modes and Effects Analysis, and cause-and-effect diagrams can reveal the nuances of the human–computer interface and clinical transformation.

Horsky et al. applied a novel workflow analysis to study a dosing error related to computer-based ordering of potassium chloride. They reconstructed events chronologically from practitioner order entry usage logs, conducted semi-structured interviews with involved clinicians, and examined interface usability of the ordering system.[23] They found errors in the drug ordering process, confusing on-screen laboratory results review, system usability difficulties, user training problems, and suboptimal display of intravenous (IV) bolus injection and medicated fluid drip orders.

In response to their findings, they determined that the screens for ordering continuous IV fluid drips and drips of limited volume needed to be clearly distinct, so that the ordering of each is unambiguous; screens that list active medication orders needed to list IV drip orders; the laboratory results review screen needed to clearly and visually indicate when the most recent results are not from the current day; an alert should be added that would inform users of existing potassium administration; another alert should be added informing users ordering potassium when there has not been a serum potassium value recorded in the past 12 hours or the most recent potassium value is greater than 4.0; and other minor changes should be made to increase the consistency of ordering screen behavior.

Cause-and-effect diagrams can identify the policies, procedures, people, or technology issues that need intervention.[24] Caudill-Slosberg and Weeks report a case study of inadequate Coumadin therapy related to clinical documentation in an electronic medical record.[25] They employed a fishbone diagram to pinpoint opportunities for improvement (see Figure 19-3).

Their analysis discovered that the ambiguity of the warfarin (Coumadin) dosing on the medication order list resulted in inaccurate interpretation of warfarin dose and administration, the use of templates created visual barriers to identifying important information because of extraneous details, and the availability of both readable documentation and a copy-and-paste function gave false assurances that the available information was correct and facilitated its promulgation.

CONCLUSION

Knowing why projects fail can help projects succeed. No matter what the technology, getting the people, policies, and workflow right are always critical. No matter how grand the plan, without scrupulous attention to execution, no innovation can succeed.

From a policy perspective, the American Medical Informatics Association (AMIA) sponsored a workshop on IT project failure and made the following recommendations:

- **Research and Publication:** Support and publish qualitative and longitudinal studies of all project phases in addition to outcomes for a variety of applications, including for failed projects.
- **Best Practices:** Create databases and an AMIA White Paper translating general principles into practice.
- **Advocacy:** Advocate for regulatory changes to facilitate using best practices of health IT.

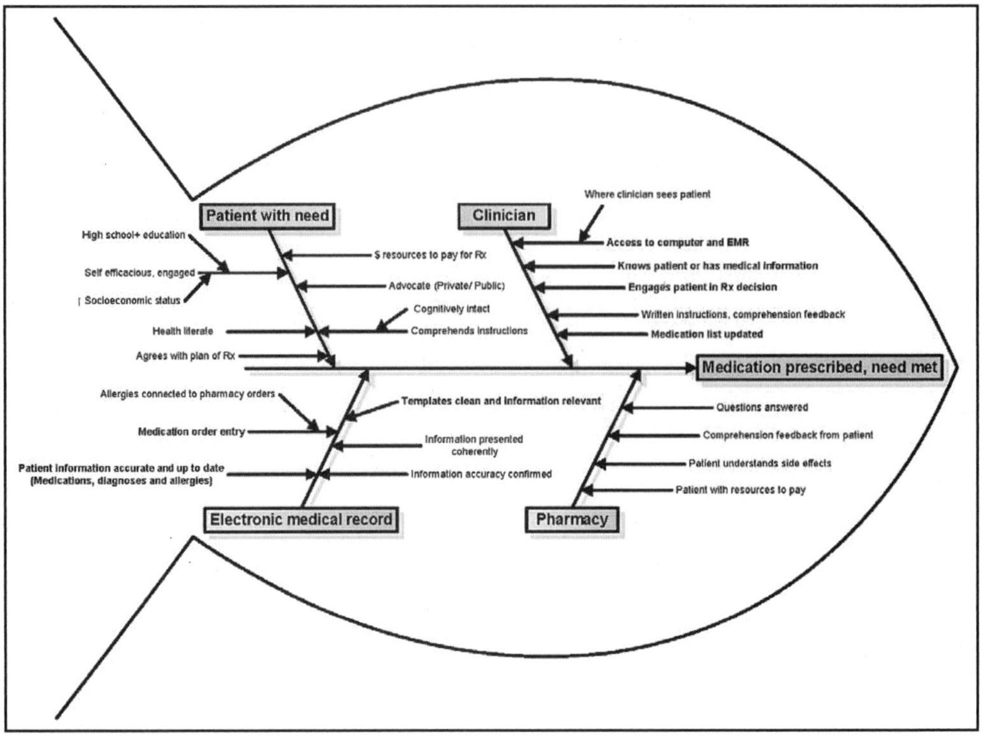

Figure 19-3: Cause-and-Effect Diagram of Coumadin Error

- **Education:** Develop curriculum on project management and organizational issues to maximize success.
- **Certification:** Partner with certifying bodies to include guidelines for better health IT development and use.
- **Databases and Knowledge Integration**: Develop repositories (database, blog) for project histories and outcomes and for best practices.

ARRA/HITECH allocated funds that adopt many of these recommendations to improve the likelihood of successful health IT implementations:[26]

- CMS certifies EHR products for defined functionality. Providers who purchase a CMS-certified EHR should be assured that the product meets basic standards and can achieve meaningful uses of the EHR.
- RECs situated across the nation have assisted priority physician practices in selecting, implementing, and maintaining their EHRs.
- The Health Information Technology Research Center (HITRC) has collected and disseminated knowledge about best practices for EHR adoption and use.
- Grants supporting workforce development have trained thousands of health IT professionals to deploy and maintain this technology.
- Beacon communities have demonstrated meaningful users of health IT among patients, hospitals, and EPs.

The CMS EHR incentives are not really about paying for technology as much as using technology to get to better patient outcomes:

> "The focus on meaningful use is a recognition that better healthcare does not come solely from the adoption of technology itself, but through the exchange and use of health information to best inform clinical decisions at the point of care." – *Health and Human Services*[27]

Health IT is still maturing. Ongoing research into optimizing workflow and human factors will enable smarter implementations of this essential technology in the future.

REFERENCES

1. McCann E, ed. CEO resigns amid troubled EHR rollout. May 30, 2014. *HealthcareIT News*. http://www.healthcarei tnews.com. Accessed November 20, 2014.
2. McCann E, ed. Hospital takes EHR heavyweight to court. *Healthcare IT News*. Jan 06, 2014. http://www.healthcareitnews.com. Accessed November 20, 2014.
3. McCann E, ed. Setback for Sutter after $1B EHR crashes. *Healthcare IT News*. Aug 28, 2013 http://www.healthcareitnews.com/news/setback-sutter-after-1b-ehrsystem%20crashes. Accessed November 20, 2014.
4. Monegain B, ed. Go-live gone wrong. *HealthcareITNews*. July 2013. www.HealthcareITNews.com. Accessed June 7, 2014.
5. Hospital Shuts Down CPOE System. Health Data Management, January 23, 2003. http://www.healthdatamanagement.com/news/7919-1.html. Accessed January 23, 2003.
6. Health Information Technology Policy Committee Meeting. June 10, 2014. http://www.cms.gov/Regulations-and-Guidance/Legislation/EHRIncentivePrograms/Downloads/HITPC_June2014_Full_Deck.pdf. Accessed July 9, 2014.
7. Cedars-Sinai Medical Center nNamed oOne of nNation's mMost wWired hHospitals. (http://www.cedars-sinai.edu/About-Us/News/News-Releases-2005/Cedars-Sinai-Medical-Center-Named-One-of-Nations-Most-Wired-Hospitals.aspx.; Accessed July 31, 2014.)
8. Connolly C. Cedars-Sinai doctors cling to pen and paper. *Washington Post*. March 21, 2005. Sec A:1. http://www.washingtonpost.com/wp-dyn/articles/A52384-2005Mar20.html. Accessed July 31, 2014.
9. Massaro TA. Introducing physician order entry at a major academic medical center: Impact on organizational culture and behavior. *Acad Med*. 1993;68(1):20-25.
10. Beynon-Davies P, Lloyd-Williams M. When health information systems fail. *Top Health Inf Manag*. 1999;20(1):66–79.
11. English IT. Effort losing support. *HDM Breaking News*. November 26, 2007.
12. Granger says he is 'ashamed' of some systems provided. *eHealth Insider*. July 10, 2007.
13. Souton G, Sauer C, Dampney K. Information technology in complex health services: Organizational impediments to successful technology transfer and diffusion. J Am Med Inform Assoc. 1997;4:112–124.
14. Conn J. Failure, de-installation of EHRs abound. *Modern Healthcare*. October 30, 2007. http://www.modernhealthcare.com/article/20071030/FREE/310300002. Accessed July 31, 2014.
15. CHAOS Manifesto 2013: Think big, act small. The Standish Group. http://athena.ecs.csus.edu/~buckley/CSc231_files/Standish_2013_Report.pdf. Accessed July 6, 2014.
16. KLAS Enterprises. Software Quality Study: Vendor and provider perspectives. January 2005.
17. Baldwin G. Avoid six deadly mistakes. *HealthLeaders Magazine*. January 2005;51–54.
18. Baldwin G. Bring order to CPOE with 10 make or break steps (and 5 myths). HealthLeaders. Magazine. November 14, 2005. http://www.methodisthealth.org/static/files/1184770136997/baldwin_cpoe_steps.pdf. Accessed August 3, 2014.

19. DeVore SD, Figlioli K. Lessons premier hospitals learned about implementing electronic health records. *Health Aff.* 29,4(2010):664-667.

20. Glaser J. Success factors for clinical information system implementation. *Hospital and Health Network's Most Wired Magazine.* June 2005.

21. Information Systems Research Center, College of Business Administration, University of Houston. Project implementation, technology diffusion, adoption and acceptance: An ISRC roundtable discussion lead by Peter A. Todd and Wynne W. Chin. *ISRC Notes.* January 2001.

22. How to implement EHRs. Step 1: Assess your practice readiness. *HealthIT.gov.* http://www.healthit.gov/providers-professionals/ehr-implementation-steps/step-1-assess-your-practice-readiness. Accessed July 9, 2014.

23. Horsky J, Kuperman GJ, Patel VL. Comprehensive analysis of a medication dosing error related to CPOE. *J Am Med Inform Assoc.* 2005;12:377–382.

24. Ishikawa (or Fishbone) diagrams. The cause and effect diagram. http://www.isixsigma.com/index.php?option=com_k2&view=item&id=1416:the-cause-and-effect-aka-fishbone-diagram&Itemid=200. Accessed August 3, 2014.

25. Caudill-Slosberg M, Weeks WB. Case study: Identifying potential problems at the human/technical interface in complex clinical systems. *Am J of Med Qual.* 2005;200(6):353ff.

26. http://healthit.hhs.gov/portal/server.pt/community/healthit_hhs_gov__hitech_programs/1487. Accessed August 3, 2014.

27. Ashish JHA. The EHR "Final Rule" (finally). http://thehealthcareblog.com/blog/tag/regional-extension-centers/. Accessed August 3, 2014.

CHAPTER 20

Case Study: Reaching Out With Technology— Telehealth in Rural America

Mary Ann Zelazny, MBA

A BACKGROUND IN RURAL HEALTH DISPARITIES

In many rural communities of the United States, health disparities are more prevalent than in urban areas, leading to higher rates of chronic diseases, more people living in poverty, and a lack of adequate resources. Rural areas experience more gaps in services, especially in the areas of chronic disease management, dental, and mental health conditions, and they have higher rates of uninsured and fewer physicians. A study done by UnitedHealth Group states that, "Rural Americans already are more likely to suffer from chronic health conditions and face greater difficulty accessing quality healthcare than urban counterparts."[1] Information from another source adds that almost "20% of the population of the United States lives in rural designated areas, but only 10% of the nation's physicians practice in those communities."[2] Poverty is a common theme in these rural areas. According to the U.S. Department of Agriculture, in 2012, "15% of the nation's population lived in poverty with rural areas having a 17.7% poverty level."[3]

Referring to the lack of health professionals, in fact, this is one of the most difficult obstacles rural communities face in accessing timely and appropriate healthcare services in primary medical care, as well as dental and mental health services and specialty care. Rural communities tend to have fewer healthcare facilities and professionals in all categories, including primary care providers and specialists such as cardiologists; endocrinologists; and ear, nose, and throat providers (ENT). Often, patients from a rural community are referred to a specialist whose office may be located quite a distance from them. The distribution of health professionals, as well as recruitment and retention issues is an ongoing problem for rural areas that must compete with urban areas to try to maintain an adequate healthcare workforce. This issue is further complicated when, based on the demographics of the patient, there is a lack of appropriate information in terms of what services are available and the basic shortages of all services that rural communities experience. Howard Rabinowitz, MD, Professor of Family and Community Medicine at Thomas Jefferson University's Medical College wrote that "The shortage of rural physicians is a huge problem…insufficient insurance payments, administrative hassles tied to insurance claims, and rising business and malpractice insurance expenses are among the most commonly cited reasons for why rural medicine is losing appeal among doctors."[4] The lack of timely clinical intervention due to poor access to routine primary, dental, and mental healthcare results in a population without needed care and patients who defer medical treatment, often making them even sicker. Geographic barriers are also an issue for rural communities. The distance between most rural areas and urban centers is considerable, with many of the necessary health and social agencies offering services in locations quite distant from the rural communities.

In addition, many rural families, due to their economic status, have limited access to a reliable source of transportation. Many times the only vehicle accessible to a patient is being used to get family members to their jobs and not available for other uses, such as medical appointments. Culture also plays a factor in readily accessing health services and can create difficulties for rural residents. There is a "rural culture" described in Rural Mental Health, published by the University of Montana: "The stereotypical country dweller is more resilient and stoic, fortified by strong family and community ties. Rural residents are more likely to downplay their symptoms and attempt to cope on their own …anonymity is not characteristic of rural life, which makes people uncomfortable with seeking help and disclosing their personal health histories."[5] Also, rural communities typically have larger numbers of older Americans. The younger generations often leave rural homes to move to urban settings due to the lack of jobs and poor economies in their home communities. Obesity is more widespread in rural areas. A study conducted by the University of Florida for the National Center for Health Statistics found that "People living in cities and those living in rural areas got about the same amount of physical activity. The researchers noted, however, that the rural residents consumed a much higher percentage of their daily calories from fat."[6] These findings demonstrate that rural communities not only need more access to healthcare, but also adequate education and preventive services to give residents an understanding of their health conditions to make more informed decisions.

A COMMUNITY HEALTH CENTER APPROACH

Finger Lakes Community Health (FLCH), a federally qualified health center program (FQHC), provides comprehensive healthcare services in several counties of the Finger Lakes region of New York State. FLCH participates in the federal Community Health Center program that consists of "community-based and patient-directed organizations that serve populations with limited access to health care."[7] This program, funded through HHS, consists of over 1,200 Community Health Center programs that served more than 21 million patients in 2013.[7] FLCH has established ten community health center sites throughout the region to provide as many services as possible to the communities served. The programs and services available to patients include medical, dental, behavioral health, nutrition, and patient advocacy services. As a Level 3 PCMH organization, FLCH uses a team-based approach to care that includes a multitude of staff including clinicians and lay health workers, as well as the patient and their families, to collaboratively provide the care that will achieve better health outcomes. In 2013, FLCH provided healthcare services to more than 21,000 patients, with many of those patients requiring additional assistance to overcome barriers due to the lack of access to care. This very rural area is named for the long narrow lakes that run north and south in the region. The lakes essentially dissect the area into strips of fertile farmland. The only way to access points on the opposite side of the lake is to travel the entire distance to the northern or southernmost point and head up or down the other side. In many cases, residents can find themselves a few miles from a village, pharmacy, or clinic, but one hour or more away by car. The area's remarkable geographical characteristics create tremendous transportation and access issues.

Farming in the Finger Lakes region is not just a business, but also a way of life. This region of New York State depends heavily on agriculture, which is its largest business sector. According to NYS Ag & Markets remarking on the region, "The value of agricultural production was over $5.70 billion in 2012."[8] Obviously farms are typically located a great distance from larger towns and cities that offer a wider range of healthcare choices and specialty care providers. When a patient is referred to a specialist for further care, again, the challenge to complete that referral hinges on ensuring that transportation is available for that visit. There are no mass transit systems in the area with the exception of very limited service in some counties. Several private taxi companies help transport people, but they don't pass through the outermost town limits, doing little good for those residing 30 and 40 miles away. Most agricultural employers do not offer any kind of health insurance, and few are eligible for those insurance products. Safety net programs such as those offered by FLCH are essential to patients and their families. For many community health center programs serving rural areas, specially tailored programs are required to reduce the tendency for patients to seek treatment only for acute problems rather than chronic conditions or for preventive services, a tendency which is a result of the frustrations patients can feel attempting to navigate their way through our often perplexing medical system.

Telehealth technologies offer FLCH important tools that provide connectivity between its rural health centers and the more urban healthcare so that patients are able to receive healthcare services regardless of their geographical location. As a tool, telehealth is a very viable option for FLCH, offering the capability to change health outcomes for patients by providing access to highly trained specialists that otherwise would not be available in the rural communities. Telehealth technologies reduced some of the barriers to care and offered solutions that included the availability of many clinical services offered remotely. There is growing evidence that telehealth has the potential to increase patient compliance and improve health outcomes, bridging the gap for rural communities by providing a link to the more urban centers. "Telehealth is an umbrella term for delivering health services and information using electronic methods. It can include physicians discussing a patient's illness by telephone, video conferencing between health facilities, and even remote surgical procedures."[2] With the new emphasis on the integration of behavioral health services into primary care, this technology can link mental health providers such as counselors, psychiatrists and substance use specialists with patients who otherwise might not have the ability to access the appropriate care due to stigma or access issues.

To fully understand the evolution of terminology used when discussing the technology used to connect two or more sites via video, there are two major definitions to consider. The Center for Connected Health Policy states that:

> Telehealth encompasses a broad definition of technology-enabled health care services. This definition includes telemedicine, which is the diagnosis and treatment of illness or injury. Telehealth services consist of diagnosis, treatment, assessment, monitoring, communications, and education. It includes a broad range of telecommunications, health information, videoconferencing, and digital image technologies.[9]

Although telehealth has been in existence for many years, improved access to more broadband across the United States, as well as many new types of diagnostic equipment have given the healthcare community tools that can make long-lasting changes in population health. Roeen Roashan, a healthcare analyst, observed that "Telehealth is about increasing the quality of healthcare in an efficient way: it is proven to decrease readmission rates significantly, while increasing the patient's experience of quality by keeping the patient at home."[10] These technologies allow the provider the ability to have more access to patients and to receive clinical data quickly to meet with patients "face to face" who are located in very remote communities. A study by the University of Texas Medical Branch found that "Real/near-time monitoring and interacting could enable a healthcare team to address patient problems before they require major interventions, creating a potentially patient-centered approach that could undoubtedly change our expectations of our healthcare system."[11] Telehealth offers tools that can help the healthcare system meet the Triple Aim. The Commonwealth Fund describes the purpose of the Triple Aim as "Designed to help health care organizations improve a populations' health and patients' experience of care (including quality, access, and reliability) while lowering—or at least reducing the rate of increase in—the per capita cost of care."[12] Telehealth can virtually increase the number of primary care and specialty providers for rural communities, provide the capability for a sharing of expertise among urban and rural providers, and reduce unnecessary usage of the emergency department of hospitals.

WHY TELEHEALTH?

The healthcare system in the United States has developed over time into a system of silos where costs are high and patient outcomes are not where they could be. Hospitals, clinics, specialists, and other healthcare professionals have traditionally not collaborated well together, thus creating this silo structure in healthcare. The ACA of 2010 has challenged that status quo and has included a series of mandates within its language that seek to address the inefficiencies and inherent problems within the current system. The legislation allows for financial incentives to providers to adopt EHRs technology to facilitate sharing patient information between acute care settings, specialists, and primary care providers. Other incentives are meant to transform provider practices into more patient-centered practices, with a more team-based approach that focuses on improved quality of care. To address many of these challenges, there has been a growing body of data that supports the use of telehealth in meeting the goals of the Triple Aim, providing better quality and performance, focusing on improving health outcomes, and lowering the costs of delivering healthcare.

MEETING THE TRIPLE AIM WITH TELEHEALTH

Telehealth technology demands a more collaborative way of providing healthcare. Video consults between rural and urban providers allows for images and live visits to be viewed, potentially recorded, and sent to all practitioners involved in the patient's care. Remote monitoring is one aspect of telehealth technology that has demonstrated a strong ROI in terms of receiving patient data such as blood pressure readings, weight, blood sugar levels, and activity levels. The primary care provider can receive continuous clinical information on a daily basis directly from the patient at home using diagnostic tools that use mobile connectivity to transmit the data. This technology has demonstrated that its use can lower the utilization of acute care settings for care by those patients, thus lowering costs for the system. The quality of the care patients are receiving is improved as healthcare professionals have quicker access to data, enabling them the ability to rapidly make changes to medication lists and treatment plans, instead of the usual means of giving the patient a medication and asking them to return in six weeks for a follow-up appointment. This type of innovation addresses the goals of the Triple Aim and has the ability to improve patient health outcomes, as well as providing a better patient experience.

PROVIDING ACCESS TO PRIMARY CARE

One of the greatest threats to the healthcare system in the United States is the lack of adequate primary care providers to see the increased number of patients needing services. ACA of 2010 was designed to "put in place comprehensive reforms that improve access to affordable health coverage for everyone and protect consumers from abusive insurance company practices."[13] This legislation has allowed for an increased number of Americans having access to health insurance, which in turn has created a greater demand on the existing pool of primary care providers. The Association of American Medical Colleges projects "...by 2015, in just three years, we'll be 63,000 doctors short of the number we need. And that number could double by 2025."[14] Telehealth can mitigate many of the barriers to care that are more prevalent in many rural communities across the United States. *Healthcare IT News* reports that "Telemedicine helps correct that imbalance by 'bringing' physicians into the rural communities in which they are needed via electronic media. Before telemedicine, a patient may have had to wait two or more days for a physician to travel to his town, or had to travel long distances to the doctor. Now, the same patient can set see his doctor via Skype when it's most convenient or most needed."[15] The technology allows for connectivity that can give a patient with hypertension access to a primary care provider that previously may not have been possible, thus placing that patient at more risk for greater complications. The patient can be tele-presented to the provider remotely using video as well as a host of digital peripheral pieces of equipment such as otoscopes, stethoscopes, and general exam cameras. These digital tools can transmit images in real time that relay the necessary information between providers. Regardless of the provider's location, rural patients can be seen in their home community using video conferencing and diagnostic equipment.

EDUCATIONAL OPPORTUNITIES AND EXPERTISE SHARING

One of the benefits of using telehealth technology is that by conducting visits using video conferencing, the providers at both ends have an opportunity to discuss a particular case together. This allows for sharing of clinical information and provides educational opportunities for rural providers who are able to ask questions directly to the specialist at the other end of the camera. One well-respected telehealth learning program is called Project Echo. This program is a telehealth program through the University of New Mexico that creates collaborative peer-to-peer learning events using telehealth technology. Project Echo was described in *The New York Times* as "a model that combined video conferencing technology to facilitate weekly case-based training (similar to the teaching approach in medical schools) with collaborative care and careful patient tracking."[16] The structure of the learning sessions is designed so that primary care providers can meet on a routine basis via video conferencing with a clinical expert in a particular field. In these sessions, providers can present their patient's case and discuss alternative treatments, new medications, or other concerns. This type of learning is vital to a rural provider, as they are able to benefit from the knowledge of their urban counterparts, as well as from clinical experts. Kim Lamb of the Oregon Health Network discussed the benefits of telemedicine stating that, "It's about connecting across the distance to build collegial relationships that allow providers to trust one another and upgrade the acuity of care in a remote community so patients are appropriately triaged and transferred to an emergency department."[17] In the end, the rural provider will benefit from these ongoing educational learning sessions, and in turn, the patient will benefit.

BEHAVIORAL HEALTH NEEDS AND TELEHEALTH

Data show that the number of Americans in need of access to behavioral health services is of serious concern. Research conducted by the Substance Abuse and Mental Health Services Administration (SAMHSA) in 2012 showed that "...nationally, 42.5 million adults aged 18 or older experienced any mental illness (AMI) in the past year, corresponding to a rate of 18.2 percent of the adult population."[18] In rural communities, this disparity is even greater due to the lack of providers. Data also show that there are higher rates of suicide in rural communities. Dr. Julie Goldstein Grumet, PhD, of the Suicide Prevention Resource Center in Washington, DC, wrote, "Suicide rates tend to be high in rural areas in part because there is greater access to firearms, high rates of drug and alcohol use, and few health-care providers and emergency medical facilities."[19] Further research by the Agency for Healthcare Research and Quality (AHRQ) shows that "Barriers to accessing high-quality care in rural settings include shortages of mental health professionals, limited or lack of inpatient and emergency psychiatric services, and the need to travel long distances to receive care."[20] The need for more integration of behavioral health services into primary care are critical for rural communities, as the stigma associated with accessing behavioral health services prevents many rural residents from going to their local mental health clinic. Often, the employees of those clinics are friends or relations of the patient, which becomes a barrier to using those services. The use of telehealth technology can be a means of delivering behavioral health services to a rural community by having the patient present at the local primary care provider and accessing a counselor or psychiatrist via video. The anonymity of the visit is based on the patient going into an exam room at the primary care office and connecting remotely. *Healthcare IT News* reported that "Although primary care and specialty care is difficult to get in lesser-populated communities, Shah continued, behavioral and mental health is even harder to access…telemedical assistance through online chat and Skype-like video conversations, and secure online messaging, though, can easily solve the problem."[15] The innovative use of telehealth technology connecting counselors, psychiatrists and other behavioral health professionals to patients in rural settings has proven to be a successful model of care that provides better health outcomes.

STAKEHOLDERS IN TELEHEALTH

There are several stakeholders that must be considered when evaluating the value of telehealth technology in a primary care setting. Any new program or project will affect the various players in some ways, either positively or negatively. With the use of telehealth, the research must include an in-depth analysis of the pros and cons of the implementation and use of the technology by providers on both ends of the connection, the patient, and also the administrative end. The financial implications of procuring the initial pieces of equipment are an important part of the equation, as well as the impact of telehealth on the public good. From the provider's perspective, there is the opportunity for more interaction with highly educated specialty care providers in particular clinical fields. This cannot be understated, as the interaction between a specialist and a primary care provider ultimately has the potential for raising the level of education and knowledge of the remote providers in rural communities. Telehealth allows the opportunity for primary care providers to become much more knowledgeable in those diagnoses that are more complicated to treat successfully. Additionally, telehealth can provide the availability of additional practitioners to primary care practices because providers from urban areas can video in and see patients. The increase in the number of available providers will enhance access to care for patients. Some of the negative implications for the implementation of telehealth for the practitioner are that there usually is an initial disruption of flow within the practice, as there is with the introduction of any new program. There is a learning curve involved with the use of telehealth technology that includes learning to operate the diagnostic peripherals competently and understanding the limitations of conducting an exam on a patient whom the provider cannot physically examine. There is also a loss of intimacy that an in-person encounter offers that is a strong negative for many older practitioners. Finally, the provider needs to ensure that the patient's confidentiality is fully protected. When seeing a patient using video, it is imperative that patient privacy and confidentiality are fully adhered to—that people aren't walking behind the provider when a clinical exam is occurring.

Table 20-1: Stakeholders' Priorites

Stakeholder	Areas of Priority
Healthcare Providers	Access to clinical experts, better patient outcomes, HIPAA adherence
Patients	Access to primary and specialty care, acceptance of technology use, HIPAA protection
Administrative	Organizational readiness, telehealth policies and procedures, administrative champions, credentialing of providers
Financial	Implementation/start-up costs, reimbursement considerations, potential to lower cost of care for patients.
Public Good	Reduction of health disparities, lower costs of healthcare, better access to care

Stakeholder Considerations

From the patient perspective, telehealth can offer critical access to care for those living in areas where provider shortages are common and acute care facilities are many miles away. Also, the ability for a patient to see a provider on a routine basis, regardless of the format, offers the potential for better health outcomes. When a patient has more access to their healthcare provider, there is more knowledge on both the patient's and the provider's end, as there is more time to investigate each clinical problem in greater depth (see Table 20-1).

However, although technology can be very powerful, many people who are unfamiliar with its use can be fearful of it. Patients must be aware prior to any telehealth visit of what to expect and must allow written consent to that type of visit. Adherence to HIPAA rules, including policies and procedures, must demonstrate that the patient's confidentiality has been protected at all times.

As healthcare entities look to adopt telehealth technologies into their practices, they will need to understand some of the ramifications of start-up costs, credentialing of providers, and any legal issues that might impede a smooth beginning. In the initial implementation of telehealth, the equipment costs can be very high, as all of the necessary video and diagnostic peripherals need to be purchased up front. Once the equipment is purchased and set up, entities must consider the time needed for involved staff to be trained on its use and care. Finally, there is the latency that will initially occur due to the introduction of telehealth visits into the normal patient flow. Staff buy-in is critical at this stage to make this transition as smooth as possible. In addition, the credentialing of any outside providers or specialists will need to be completed before any telehealth visits can occur. This process is time consuming and tedious, adding work for the HR department. Financially, there are start-up costs to be considered, as well as the lack of consistent reimbursement policies for many states in terms of telehealth visits.

The ability for telehealth technology to improve health outcomes in population health, as well as increased quality of care will help reduce the continual rise in the cost per patient for healthcare in the United States. Ultimately, the shift and possible reduction in healthcare costs may allow for reinvestment of revenues into other important areas that could also further reduce health disparities.

BARRIERS TO IMPLEMENTATION OF TELEHEALTH

The lack of adequate broadband capacity in rural communities has been a longstanding issue in that there has not been an adequate amount of bandwidth with which to transmit video and images. In addition, the high cost of the initial capital investment in broadband capacity and technology components has also deterred the adoption of telehealth for most health facilities and has seen most of its use in larger hospital settings. Other common barriers to the implementation of telehealth programs are the lack of consistent telehealth reimbursement policies across the United States and credentialing and licensure concerns that impede adoption. To reduce health disparities in rural communities, there have to be solutions that address barriers to healthcare, creating a means for change in health outcomes for these communities. The adoption, implementation, and sustainability of telehealth technology is a very challenging task as it requires a comfort level with technology that can be difficult to achieve due to a fear of the equipment used as well as the introduction of additional tasks in an already overburdened healthcare system. An entity who chooses to introduce telehealth into a primary care practice will need to develop a provider champion who will assist in rallying the staff to accept this new technology and build it into their daily workflow. It also needs to be a seamless process that doesn't use too much additional staff resources or the program will not succeed.

A COMMUNITY HEALTH CENTER'S APPROACH

Francisco, a 46-year-old migrant farmworker, was nearly blind. His uncontrolled diabetes had caused several health problems, including his rapidly deteriorating eyesight which now jeopardized his ability to work. Francisco came into one of our health centers hoping that the doctor would be able to help. Once the provider evaluated Francisco, he immediately ordered a diabetic retinopathy image to determine the extent of the damage to Francisco's retina. The image was taken right at the health center and transmitted to an eye specialist to interpret. The following day, the eye specialist notified the health center provider that Francisco needed emergency laser surgery if his eyesight was to be saved. Francisco and his advocate from the health center made the trip to the ophthalmologist where emergency laser surgery was done. Francisco's sight was saved in his left eye, but he lost vision in his right eye. If he had waited even another couple of weeks, he would have lost his vision completely. The retinopathy equipment that was used on Francisco at the health center utilizes telehealth technology to connect the patient to an eye specialist that is hundreds of miles away.

To address the challenges in providing comprehensive healthcare for rural communities that include patients like Francisco, Finger Lakes Community Health has developed a robust telehealth network to address some of the many barriers to healthcare. The ability to use technology to provide access to services with the use of video conferencing equipment and diagnostic tools between a specialty care provider and a patient has shown not only cost savings in terms of travel, but also in savings due to improved health outcomes. Using telehealth, patients are able to return to the Community Health Center nearest them, where they are known and feel safe, and still be seen by the specialist who may be 50 or 500 miles away. The Finger Lakes Telehealth Network (FLTN) was begun in an effort to address the difficulties that arise when a farm-worker patient is referred to a specialist for ongoing care. Rather than driving a patient to the urban provider office, which often results in the patient losing a day of work and pay, FLTN has developed collaborative relationships with several key specialty practices to use technology to conduct the clinical visits. The model that FLTN uses is focused on three major components to build a sustainable and robust telehealth program. First, the issue of broadband or high-speed Internet is critical, as video streaming demands much higher levels of Internet capacity to transmit video images. Secondly, FLTN focuses on the necessary video equipment, diagnostic peripherals, and other technology used to do the actual transmission of each visit. The third and most important component is in the area of program development, which includes working with each specialty care provider to develop a mutual work plan that incorporates the needs of the specialist, the primary care provider, and the patient. A resource manual for each specialty area has been developed by FLTN that includes policies, procedures, and consent forms in multiple languages, patient and provider satisfaction forms, and emergency and safety policies and procedures that might be required, particularly in working with behavioral health services. To date, telehealth programs through FLTN have been implemented in psychiatry, ENT, counseling, nutrition therapy, pediatric neurology, HIV/AIDS care, pulmonology, diabetic retinopathy, pediatric dentistry, and interpretation services. The relationships between the primary care providers and the specialty care providers in urban areas result in an increase in completed referrals and high satisfaction scores by both the patients and the providers. The opportunity for primary care providers to attend the specialty care visit virtually gives them the ability to learn and interact with the specialist on potential new therapies and difficult cases. In addition to achieving better health outcomes, the savings realized are seen in terms of reduced travel for health center staff, reduced numbers of no shows for appointments, and data that show improved health outcomes due to more access to care for our patients.

Telehealth has already proven its value in the acute care setting in areas such as telestroke that provides rapid access by rural acute care settings to stroke experts at larger designated stroke center hospitals. Although the initial capital costs for equipment to conduct telehealth programming can be high in many circumstances, the expectation is that there will be a cost savings by keeping patients out of the hospital, using the technology to provide access to care, the ability to bring more care into the primary care setting, and to reduce the use of hospitals for care that can better be dealt with in other less costly healthcare settings. FLCH instituted a telehealth program in collaboration with the University of California - Berkeley using diabetic retinopathy equipment to screen a sample of ninety diabetic patients. Within 8 months of monitoring each patient's blood levels, as well as introducing diabetic retinopathy as a prevention tool, data showed a decrease in patients' HA1c levels in 87 percent of patients in the sample group. "Over 50% of those patients had a 2-point level drop or more."[21] These data demonstrate that telehealth implementation and use has the ability to improve access to care and can potentially lead to better health outcomes, and in turn, lower costs of care as patients are healthier. Another successful telehealth program involved access to a pediatric neurologist for those young patients who had attention deficit/hyperactivity disorder diagnoses. The ability to have a top pediatric neurologist conduct a thorough evaluation of the patient via video in real time gave the primary care provider the ability to attend the session as the "telepresenter." Each visit allowed for in-depth discussion on the needs of each patient with an expert in that field. Data showed the following results:

- Decreased time to treatment (38 days vs 60 days), which exceeded national averages on NCQA performance measures.
- 75 percent of patients had changes or additions to their med regimens.
- 87.5 percent were diagnosed with mental health comorbidity.
- 100 percent were referred to behavioral health.
- 63 percent showed improvement in function at school and home.[21]

The FLCH Pediatric Dentistry program was created because of the high rate of children younger than 10-years-old who were continually referred to pediatric dental specialists for care due to high rates of caries. The tele-dental program, in conjunction with Eastman Institute for Oral Health was developed to provide access to the pediatric dental team, located in the urban center about 50 miles away. The premise was to perform as many of the visits between the child and the dental specialist via live consultations as possible, thus decreasing the number of trips that the child's family had to make in person to complete the treatment plan. The successful outcomes from this program have been very impressive and have provided a much higher level of access to care for these small children who otherwise would have continued to experience severe tooth decay, as well as other health-related problems. Data for the tele-dentistry program showed the following results:

- Decreased travel to specialist (average of 54 miles each way). We were able to go from five visits to two visits needed in person. All other visits done remotely.
- Decrease in no-show rates by 76 percent
- Improved access to pediatric dental care
- 97 percent of children referred had all treatment completed.
- Increased interaction between dental providers and dental specialist
- Children's first appointment wait time improved from 8 months to current level of 3 weeks.[21]

The use of telehealth technology is a valuable tool that can assist in bridging the geographical gap for rural communities, many of which have greater health disparities and suffer from more chronic diseases while lacking an adequate number of practitioners to meet their needs. Telehealth can address some of these issues by connecting to urban primary care providers for additional healthcare services. For many providers, like FLCH, who do practice in rural or underserved areas, connecting with urban specialists virtually can bring enhanced benefits such as peer learning opportunities, the ability to receive feedback on difficult cases, and learning the newest treatment options. Telehealth works very well in providing access to psychiatry and counseling services in rural communities where there is a critical shortage of mental health providers and much stigma involved. The goal of changing the healthcare system in such a way as to meet the Triple Aim of better outcomes, better quality, and lower costs are much more achievable with the use of telehealth to reach out to establish collaborative relationships that will benefit patients and providers.

REFERENCES

1. United Health Center for Health Reform and Modernization. Modernizing rural health care. Coverage, quality and innovation. Minnetonka, MN: UnitedHealth Group.July 2011. http://www.unitedhealthgroup.com/~/media/UHG/PDF/2011/UNH-Working-Paper-6.ashx. Accessed November 21, 2012.

2. Rural Assistance Center. What are some of the health disparities found in rural America. Rural Assistance Center. 2014. http://www.raconline.org/topics/rural-health-disparities/faqs#some. Accessed November 21, 2012.

3. USDA. Rural overty in America. United States Department of Agriculture. 2014. http://www.ers.usda.gov/topics/rural-economy-population/rural-poverty-well-being/poverty-overview.aspx#.U8czovldXpU.

4. Kavilanz P. Doctor-starved: America's heartland in crisis. *CNN Online*. March 28, 2010. http://money.cnn.com/2010/03/26/news/economy/health_care_rural_care_country_doctors/. Accessed November 21, 2012.

5. Gamm L, Stone S, Pittman S. Rural healthy people: Mental health and mental disorders - A rural challenge. Texas A & M School of Public Health. 2003. http://sph.tamhsc.edu/centers/rhp2010/Volume1.pdf. Accessed November 21, 2012.

6. Dallas ME. (2012, September 13). Obesity hits rural areas harder than cities. MedicineNet. September 13, 2012. http://www.medicinenet.com/script/main/art.asp?articlekey=162980. Accessed November 21, 2014.

7. HRSA. Community health centers. HRSA.gov. 2014. http://bphc.hrsa.gov/. Accessed November 21, 2012.

8. NYS Dept. of Ag & Markets. Ag Facts. New York State Department of Agriculture and Markets. 2014. http://www.agriculture.ny.gov/agfacts.html. Accessed November 21, 2012.

9. CCHP. What is telehealth? 2014. Center for Connected Health Policy. June 11, 2014. http://cchpca.org/what-is-telehealth. Accessed November 21, 2014.

10. Bojanowski J. Telehealth puts powerful tools in the hands of providers. *mHealthNews*. May 13, 2014. http://www.mhealthnews.com/news/telehealth-puts-powerful-tools-hands-providers?page=2. Accessed November 21, 2014.

11. Vo A, Brooks B, Farr G, et al. Benefits of telemedicine in rural communities. Univ. of Texas Medical Branch. 2012. Galveston, Tx: Internetinnovation.org. Accessed November 21, 2012.

12. McCarthy D, Klein S. The Triple Aim journey: Improving population health and patients' experience of care, while reducing costs. The Commonwealth Fund. July 22, 2010. http://www.commonwealthfund.org/publications/case-studies/2010/jul/triple-aim-improving-population-health. Accessed November 21, 2012.

13. WhiteHouse.gov. Health Care that Works for Americans. 2014. http://www.whitehouse.gov/healthreform/healthcare-overview. Accessed November 21, 2012.

14. Gjelten T. Prognosis worsens for shortages in primary care. Washington, D.C. National Public Radio. August 7, 2012. http://www.npr.org/2012/08/07/158370069/the-prognosis-for-the-shortage-in-primary-care. Accessed November 21, 2012.

15. McNickle M. Five ways telemedicine can boost care in rural communities. October 13, 2011. *HealthcareIT News*. http://www.healthcareitnews.com/news/5-ways-telemedicine-can-boost-care-rural-communities. Accessed November 21, 2012.

16. Bornstein D. The power to cure, multiplied. *New York. Times*. June 11, 2014. nytimes.com/2014/06/11/the-doctor-will-stream-to-you-now. Accessed November 21, 2014.

17. Lamb K. Strategy and planning best practices. Oregon Health Network. June 2014. http://www.oregonhealthnet.org/content/12-best-practices-1-strategy-and-planning. Accessed November 21, 2012.

18. SAMHSA.gov. (2014, February 28). State estimates of adult mental illness from the 2011 and 2012 National Surveys on Drug Use and Health. SAMHSA.gov. February 28, 2014. http://www.samhsa.gov/data/2k14/NSDUH170/sr170-mental-illness-state-estimates-2014.htm. Accessed November 21, 2012.

19. Clay R. Reducing rural suicide. *Monitor on Psychology*. 2014;45,4:36. http://www.apa.org/monitor/2014/04/rural-suicide.aspx. Accessed November 21, 2014.

20. AHRQ. Mental health care in rural settings. Agency for Healthcare Research and Quality. December 4, 2013. http://www.innovations.ahrq.gov/issue.aspx?id=168. Accessed November 21, 2014.

21. Yonker T. ROI for Telehealth. 2012. Penn Yan: Finger Lakes Community Health.

CHAPTER 21

Case Study: Children's Medical Center Dallas

Patient Engagement

Children's Medical Center Dallas received the 2013 HIMSS Davies Enterprise/Organizational Award.

INTRODUCTION

Children's Medical Center Dallas (Children's) seeks to meet its customers where they are: online. Therefore, the organization leveraged technology to offer a customized online experience for clinicians, physicians, patients and families, the community, donors, and employees. On login, Childrens.com recognizes the user, presents unique content, and allows the patient to designate an English or Spanish language preference. Patients also have the ability to connect with one another through social media, communicate with clinicians via direct messaging, and provide clinically relevant data through remote care logs. Through implementation, Children's has created efficient online workflows that save costs; satisfy patients, families, and other audiences; and make Children's the preferred provider for complex care.

BACKGROUND KNOWLEDGE

Children's serves two full-service inpatient hospitals, licensed for 595 beds (418 operating, of which 100 are intensive-care beds), 54 specialty care clinics, and six pediatric PCP offices/medical homes. More than 2,100 medical staff members, as well as day-to-day staff of more than 5,000 full-time employees support the various locations.

Implementation of the EHR provided the foundation of Children's patient engagement initiative, internally named the Online Experience (or OLE). OLE was launched with the primary goal of providing patients and families with direct access to their medical information. This goal was tied to MU requirements. In addition, Children's identified secondary goals associated with EHR implementation including:

- Improving the patient experience by creating a more customer-friendly process.
- Streamlining hospital operations.

- Yielding cost savings as a result of automation.
- Developing an EHR-Enabled Text Messaging Pilot designed to engage asthma patients.

LOCAL PROBLEM BEING ADDRESSED AND INTENDED IMPROVEMENT

Children's had an online presence (internal and external) prior to the OLE initiative; however, the infrastructure was insufficient to meet the needs of a growing base of users that included clinicians, physicians, patients and families, the community, donors, and employees.

Increasingly, patients and families expressed a desire to access information about their care, along with the ability to connect with caregivers and others with similar health issues, and to share information online. Concurrently, clinicians sought innovative opportunities to educate, engage, and communicate with patients and families during the course of care.

These goals aligned with the organization's need to execute a digital strategy to attract users to www.childrens.com and to increase awareness of Children's to consumers, the community, and referring physicians. The Children's OLE solution was developed to meet the needs of patients and families, clinicians, and the organization by incorporating multiple customer-centric technologies that spotlight Children's as the preferred resource for pediatric care, to enhance communications, and to better engage internal and external audiences.

Design and Implementation

The OLE became a strategic multiyear initiative designed to:

- Upgrade the existing physician's portal to current technologies.
- Develop a multiphased plan to increase public awareness (by redesigning the external public-facing website).
- Redesign the Children's employee portal (the intranet), and later address other community-related needs.
- Develop a more user-friendly portal solution utilizing Web 2.0 technologies for patients and families to connect with their care providers.
- Encourage self-management of the patient's health condition.

Children's spent the first year interviewing stakeholders, identifying needed technologies, writing a multiyear roadmap, and establishing a strong governance structure. The organization established the OLE Steering Committee, comprising executive leadership across Marketing and Communications, Medical Affairs, Operations (Inpatient and Outpatient), and Information Services (IS) departments. There are four active subgroups: Patient Populations, Communications, Infrastructure, and Clinical Operations. Two other groups, the Employee OLE and the Physician OLE, also meet periodically to address future developments.

Phase 1 of the initiative involved redesigning www.childrens.com and implementing a new content management system, which allowed Children's to decentralize content management and allowed clinicians to own, manage, and update their own online content. This system provided a means for end users to keep content current and granted the ability to update content on the fly, ensuring only the most current and relevant information was available on Childrens.com.

Phase 2 of the OLE initiative focused on developing content and tools for patients and families behind a login screen. First, the organization implemented the Children's Social Network, and in 2011 it launched social media sites for every patient population at Children's. Participating families can create a profile and join Children's social networking communities to share experiences and struggles that they go through in their daily lives. The sites also allow participants to blog about experiences, provide information about the disease from respected medical resources, and provide a 21st-century approach to family support groups. As an example, when patients receive diagnoses that may be overwhelming or frightening to them, they are able to use the Children's Social Network to connect with other families whose children have received similar diagnoses. As a result, the families are able to encourage and support one another and rest in the knowledge that they are not alone. Additionally, the social media sites provide Children's the ability to keep track of the community patient populations and their perceptions of care.

In addition to the Children's Social Network, the expanding portal (also known as MyChart) experience allows the patient's parent or guardian to interact more regularly with physicians and other clinical staff with questions or as they schedule appointments. The portal will continue to provide an increasing level of interaction for patients, family members, physicians, and clinical staff.

In December 2011, Children's implemented the patient-family portal for endocrine patients (one of the organization's largest specialty-care populations) to include the integration of the EHR with the Children's portal technology. In addition to the features provided by the EHR, which included scheduling appointments, messaging, and lab results (to name a few), the portal allows families to register for immediate access to their child's medical record, enter clinically relevant information into remote care logs (such as a pain journal for gastrointestinal patients, symptom calendar for the asthma management program, a diet record for the food allergy clinic), access disease-specific educational materials, and complete forms online. In turn, clinicians have access to the data provided in the remote care logs, resulting in a better means to manage the patient's care.

Children's continues to engage additional patient populations with online forms, customized remote care logs, and education materials specific to each disease. The entire patient and family site behind the login is available in Spanish and English to better serve the Hispanic population.

Patient and family access to information has transformed the online experience for the family and clinical audiences and provides users with a unique experience tailored to their preferences. This approach better engages users, encouraging them to be more involved with Children's, whether it is as a physician, patient, employee, donor, volunteer, or a member of the general community.

As an extension of these services, Children's also launched an asthma management texting program. The texting program is a six-month program designed to educate, create participative patients, and send reminders about taking medication. The program includes a consent form and integrates into Epic on the back end. Patents join the program by first receiving and replying to an opt-in email. The program is available in both Spanish and English.

HOW WAS HEALTH IT UTILIZED?

Children's leveraged a combination of existing and new technologies to support the OLE initiative.

www.childrens.com Redesign

The redesign of the Children's public website used a premier content management system, which allowed for decentralized content management.

Children's Social Network

The Children's Social Network was developed using a top-tier social software solution. This technology provided all the functionality needed to configure a patient/family network with disease-specific communities, blogging, and the ability to share experiences.

Children's Patient/Family Portal

The Children's Patient/Family portal was developed with existing portal infrastructure, an enterprise-wide solution. This technology supported Single Sign On requirements, the ability to build a wrapper around the existing EHR capabilities, and interfacing using web services. The portal integrates with a forms tool to support remote care logs, as well as a web analytics product to provide metrics.

VALUE DERIVED/OUTCOMES

The Childrens.com sign-in page averages 19,000 unique visitors every month from patients, families, providers, and employees. When the Children's portal went live in late November 2011, just over 5,300 patient/family accounts were active. Since that time, participation has steadily increased due in part to the organization's efforts to educate staff, patients, and families through the use of posters, signage, table tents, targeted mailings, and a professionally- produced video. During the 12-month period between January 2012 and January 2013, the portal averaged approximately 345 new accounts per month with a January 2013 total nearing 10,000 active accounts (see Figure 21-1).

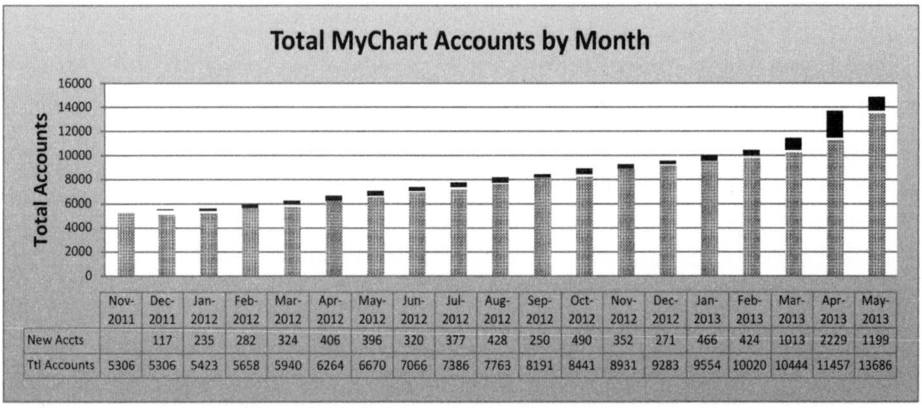

	Nov-2011	Dec-2011	Jan-2012	Feb-2012	Mar-2012	Apr-2012	May-2012	Jun-2012	Jul-2012	Aug-2012	Sep-2012	Oct-2012	Nov-2012	Dec-2012	Jan-2013	Feb-2013	Mar-2013	Apr-2013	May-2013
New Accts		117	235	282	324	406	396	320	377	428	250	490	352	271	466	424	1013	2229	1199
Ttl Accounts	5306	5306	5423	5658	5940	6264	6670	7066	7386	7763	8191	8441	8931	9283	9554	10020	10444	11457	13686

Figure 21-1: Total MyChart Accounts by Month

This adoption rate was viewed as good, but it was not good enough. So Children's reevaluated its Patient Portal adoption rate and began looking for ways to increase patient adoption. To that end, Children's worked with operational groups to build patient sign-up and portal education tools into staff workflows. This approach has proven successful—portal activation rates have significantly increased from a high of 466 in January 2013 to over 1,000 in March 2013 (1 month after the new workflow was rolled out), and to more than 2,200 in April 2013. Based on these results, Children's believes that the upward trend will continue and increase as the staff grows more comfortable with the new workflow.

Real benefits have been shown in process improvement and reduced clinical phone calls. Previously, school forms required a physician signature and, consequently, had to be completed when the family visited the office. Prescriptions and patient education materials were on paper, and questions could not be submitted online but rather through phone calls. Today instead of making a phone call, patient/families can log in to view sick day and work excuses, see lab results, refill prescriptions, ask nonurgent clinical questions, obtain patient education materials, and access online support tools. These operational efficiencies reduce the time Children's clinical staff spends on administrative tasks and improves the safety and quality of care for patients and families.

As of March 2013, patients and families had sent more than 12,000 total messages to their care providers, averaging approximately 480 messages a month for the prior 6 months. This results in 480 fewer phone calls and messages/call backs required by staff. Patient use of this messaging functionality continues to grow (see Figure 21-2).

Since the phased implementation of the patient portal began in November 2011, Children's has seen a steady increase in appointment requests for existing patients. While there was a small dip in the fourth quarter of 2012, the monthly average is trending upward toward 100+ requests per month. As a result of online appointment request capability, the number of phone calls is reduced—allowing staff to spend more time

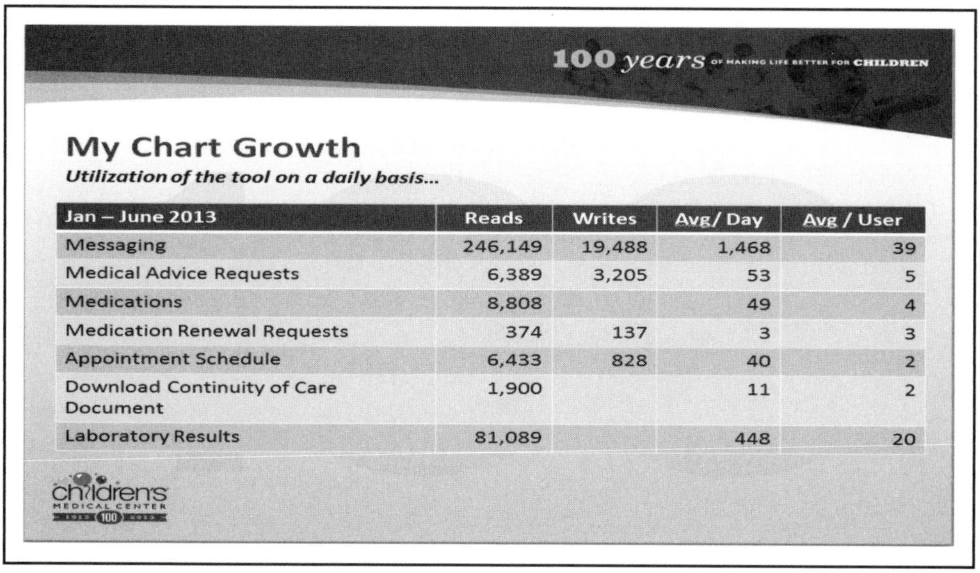

Jan – June 2013	Reads	Writes	Avg/ Day	Avg / User
Messaging	246,149	19,488	1,468	39
Medical Advice Requests	6,389	3,205	53	5
Medications	8,808		49	4
Medication Renewal Requests	374	137	3	3
Appointment Schedule	6,433	828	40	2
Download Continuity of Care Document	1,900		11	2
Laboratory Results	81,089		448	20

Figure 21-2: MyChart Growth

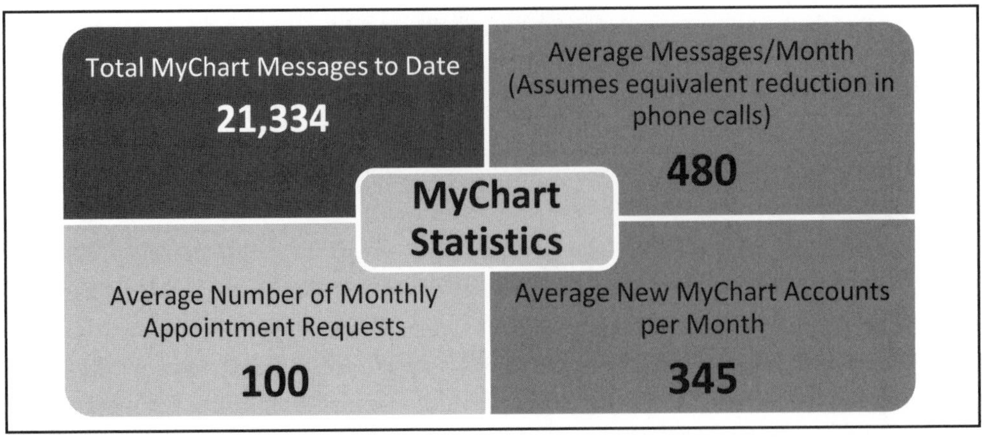

Figure 21-3: MyChart Statistics

with patients, focusing on their care, and less time on administrative matters (see Figure 21-3).

Continued marketing and promotion of the patient portal remains critical to patient and family adoption. Additionally, efforts are under way to incorporate physician referral and new patient appointment requests into the online space with a goal to process most requests digitally.

The asthma pilot has produced promising results. Well over 35 of the 50 original pilot participants have actively utilized text message prompts on appropriate follow-up care. Since launching in December 2012, those 35 active participants have engaged in text messaging at an average of 3 to 12 texts per month, which is a significantly higher percentage of engagement than the patient portal receives (see Figure 21-4).

Children's plans to expand the program to other specialties in 2014, starting with a survey of current plan participants to measure their satisfaction level and analyze any comments and suggestions.

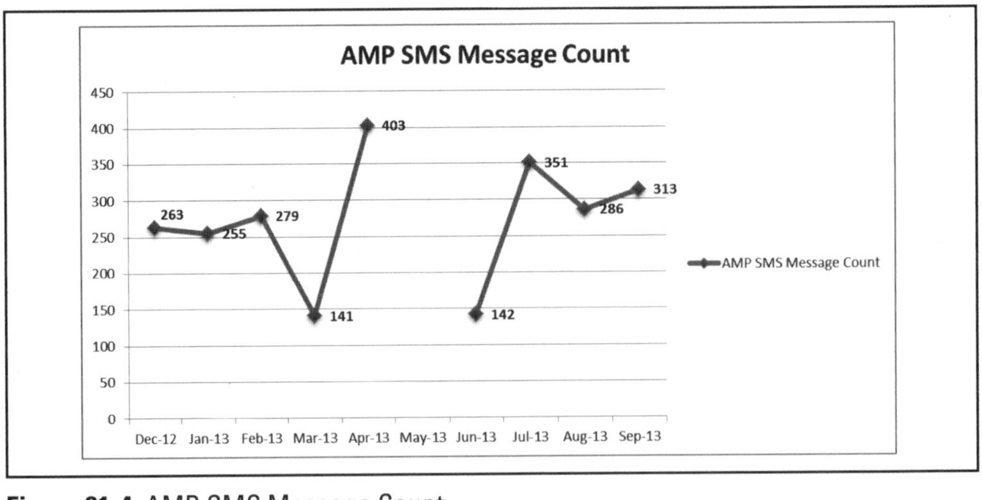

Figure 21-4: AMP SMS Message Count

LESSONS LEARNED

Comfort is Key: Implementing the patient/family portal required the involvement of front-line clinicians and staff. The portal provided by the EHR requires patients to register in the clinic, relying on clinic staff to encourage families to enroll. Despite efforts to train staff on portal functionality and features before and after implementation, clinic staff members remained uncomfortable with their understanding of the portal's features and functionality. Further, clinic staff did not have access to the portal to review and self-educate, so they did not feel they could adequately communicate the portal's benefits with families. As a result of the clinic staff members' lack of familiarity with the portal, patients and families were not encouraged to sign up for the portal, which was counterproductive to the goal.

To address this challenge, Children's developed unique login IDs and specific use cases in a test environment to allow staff to gain familiarity with the features of the portal. These specific use cases allow clinicians to log in as a family and see what the family sees, helping to bridge the understanding gap between clinicians and patient families. The benefit is that clinicians are better equipped to discuss the benefits of the portal with their patients and encourage them to enroll.

Show and Tell Doesn't Always Work: Through the process, Children's has realized that it takes more than just showing and telling staff about the tools. These concepts are part of the process, but it is also important to incorporate the education and marketing process into staff interaction with patients during the patient encounter. Adding portal education and marketing elements into the daily workflow makes sense to both the staff and the patient, and it has created significant positive impacts to the portal adoption rate.

Educational materials for both staff and families have been created and distributed, and targeted patient populations have received materials by mail detailing the benefits of the portal. Training and demonstrations for staff continue.

In addition to the measures previously outlined, Children's invested in a professionally produced video to communicate Children's vision and to highlight key functionality available through the portal. The video, *Get the Essential Tools to Manage Your Child's Care Online*, was intended for all audiences and truly captures the spirit of and reasons behind the project. This video is available on Children's YouTube channel and website, www.childrens.com.

Be On the Same Page: In the interest of transparency, Children's identified opportunities for improvement with the concept of decentralized Web content. Initially, it was thought that clinical content on the public site could be created and maintained by clinical staff. However, some of the clinical staff lacked the skill set necessary to manage content, while others felt that maintaining content took time away from their primary duties of caring for children. To address these concerns, Children's is reevaluating its tools and approach in an effort to identify more user-friendly content management technologies.

Utilize Multiple Strategies: To take advantage of the growing use of cell phone and smartphone technologies, Children's adopted an EHR-enabled solution for a pilot program that provided text updates to asthma patients with best practice guidance for follow-up care. Based on early utilization rates, it appears that getting information directly through text messaging is a possible solution to challenges with getting patients to use other log-in–based portal technologies.

FINANCIAL CONSIDERATIONS

Phase 1 of the OLE initiative was funded with a combination of capital and operating dollars. The capital dollars allocated to the project equaled $1.67M with a supporting operating budget of $.9M. Phase 2 was funded by a capital budget of $3.43M. The projected 5-year capital costs encompassing all audiences (patient family, physician, employee, and public) are expected to exceed $17M. These budgeted amounts include considerations for clinical staff training and Web development hours.

Prior to the deployment of the MyChart patient portal, approximately 25 percent of all encounters at Children's required that results be mailed out to patients and families. With MyChart, lab results are available online and do not need to be mailed to patients and families. This has resulted in a decrease in the associated staff, printing, and mailing costs. Figure 21-5 shows the resulting ROI expected through 2016.

Children's expects indirect, long-term financial benefits including:

- Reduced time, space, and expense spent on paperwork/faxing
- Better use of provider and staff time
- Increased appointment capacity
- Components of routine care managed online

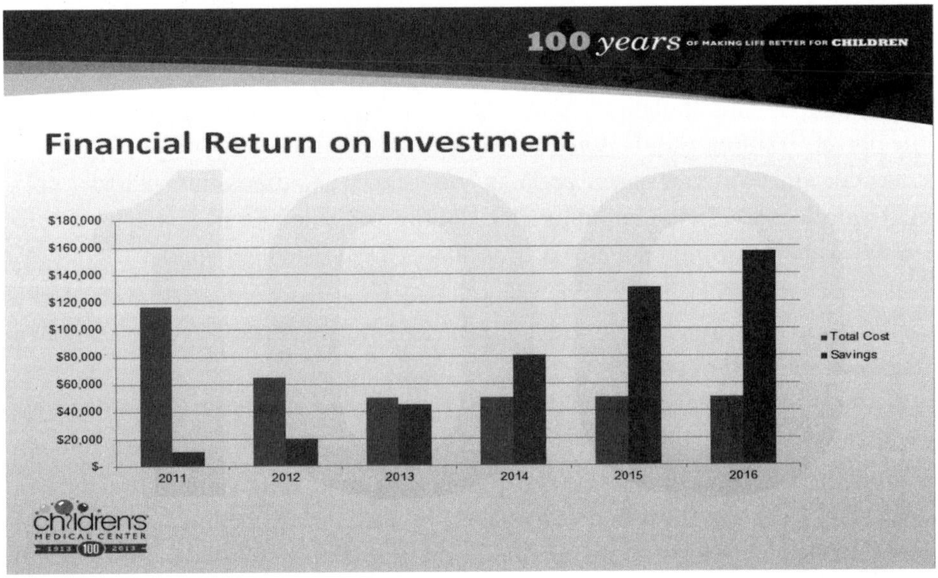

Figure 21-5: Financial Return on Investment

CHAPTER 22

Case Study: White River Family Practice

Population Management

White River Family Practice received the 2013 HIMSS Davies Ambulatory Award.

INTRODUCTION

White River Family Practice (WRFP) installed an integrated EHR system in 2010. Following initial training and system configuration, WRFP began using the EHR to systematically improve our provision of four priority primary clinical care elements as detailed in our Clinical Value core case study. Our practice then applied our EHR to improve the healthcare of defined populations of patients with chronic disease and enabled selective recall of patients who do not meet certain metrics of chronic disease management for more intensive focused care. Using a combination of alerts, clinical decision support, redesigned patient workflows, standing orders, and routine registry searches for population care surveillance, the practice has achieved measurable improvement in both processes of care and patient outcomes for those patients with diabetes mellitus and/or asthma. The following case study details the essential steps taken at WRFP to improve our management of populations of patients with these conditions.

BACKGROUND KNOWLEDGE

As an independent ambulatory care practice, WRFP provides primary care to approximately 10,000 residents of Vermont and New Hampshire along the Connecticut River in northern New England. Three major commercial insurance carriers cover approximately 57 percent of our patients with an additional 17 percent utilizing Medicare and 13 percent utilizing Medicaid. The practice is staffed with six family physicians, three family nurse practitioners (Advanced Registered Nurse Practitioners, ARNPs), and a support staff of fourteen. WRFP is a teaching site for students of the Geisel School of Medicine at Dartmouth. Our mission is to provide high-quality, state-of-the-art primary medical care to our community of patients with compassion, professionalism, and excellent communication.

LOCAL PROBLEM BEING ADDRESSED AND INTENDED IMPROVEMENT

WRFP believes that a patient's current status with respect to guideline-recommended care and chronic disease management should be readily available to that patient's PCP even if that care is ordered or provided elsewhere. This capability increases the efficiency of scheduling patient appointments, is respectful of patients' time and resources, and is more likely to result in more patients being current on recommended care.

As we focused attention on patients with either diabetes or asthma, we recognized a number of deficiencies in our pre-EHR management of these populations. In the paper-record environment, we had been unable to identify those patients who were in need of particular services such as a glycosylated hemoglobin determination (HgbA1c) in diabetic patients or an updated Asthma Action Plan (AAP) for asthmatic patients. We recognized that some patients had undergone HgbA1c determinations more frequently than recommended, while others had not received this determination in many months. In the case of patients with asthma, we could not stratify patients by severity of asthma or degree of control, and we were forwarding guidance regarding asthma management to local schools only when requested by the school nurses.

With a properly configured EHR, we could identify subsets from among populations with these chronic diseases and could electronically notify them of potential gaps in their care or the availability of special services (e.g., seasonal immunizations in high-risk populations). As a clinical microsystem (defined next), WRFP practitioners and staff could employ our EHR to develop techniques to improve the care provided to these populations and subsequently scale-up those techniques to other patient populations both in health maintenance and management of chronic disease.

A clinical microsystem has been defined as "a small group of people who work together on a regular basis to provide care to discrete subpopulations of patients" and having "clinical and business aims, linked processes, a shared information environment, and [producing] performance outcomes."[1]

DESIGN AND IMPLEMENTATION

Assisted by the Vermont Information Technology Leaders (VITL), WRFP identified and installed the integrated EHR system. As we did so, practitioners verified the diagnoses of specific chronic disease for each patient and agreed—to the extent possible—on specific language to use in patients' problem lists to enable correct identification of these populations in the EHR's registry.

Focusing on our management of diabetes, alerts were configured in the EHR to support real-time notification of indicated care elements for diabetic patients seen in WRFP such that any employee—provider or support staff—could offer or provide the recommended care, consistent with established office protocols and standing orders. The EHR's Clinical Decision Support System (CDSS) was fully configured to support standards of care for diabetic patients in accordance with the Standards of Medical Care in Diabetes - 2013.[2] Providers and support staff were taught how to use the CDSS system in the course of an office visit to update patients' care using linked orders and structured data fields. Our Medical Assistant (MA) staff was instructed that a diabetic patient who presented to the office lab for any reason and who lacked a current HgbA1c, fasting low-density lipoprotein (LDL), creatinine, or urine microalbumin determination (as defined in our standing orders) should have these analyses drawn (or ordered) without requiring a specific request by that patient's practitioner.

WRFP formalized previsit preparation, identifying specific care elements to be entered by our MAs in structured fields of the electronic record for a diabetic patient's upcoming visit (e.g., date and result of most recent diabetic foot examination or most recent HgbA1c determination, etc.).

Initially we accepted patients' assertions that certain care had been received from another provider (e.g., diabetic retinal examinations); however, we found this to be unreliable and have since instituted a requirement that our staff obtain a copy of the outside practitioner's note attesting to completion of the examination. That note is then scanned into the record with an associated structured value (e.g., named "diabetic retinal examination").

With regard to management of asthma, WRFP participated with other Vermont practices in the Vermont Asthma Learning Collaborative, leading to standardized management of all patients with asthma in our practice.

We defined information required for previsit preparation for patients with asthma. We specified that MAs obtain peak flow measurements (entered as vital signs in the EHR) when rooming the patient and specified that an Asthma Control Test (ACT) be completed and scanned into the patient's record with an associated structured name at defined intervals. We formalized the completion of an AAP for any patient with asthma, to be done when clinical management changes and at least annually.

We initially requested that our EHR vendor electronically integrate the AAP available from the National Heart, Lung, and Blood Institute into our EHR; however, because of cost and required development time we ultimately chose to complete a paper facsimile of this form during the asthmatic patient's visit. Once completed, the AAP is provided to the patient together with educational materials and a copy is scanned into the patient's record with an associated structured value (name) for later registry retrieval. In the case of asthmatic children, a copy of the completed AAP is forwarded with parental consent to the appropriate nursing staff at the child's school, day-care, or camp.

HOW WAS HEALTH IT UTILIZED?

WRFP's EHR was configured with appropriate alerts and clinical decision supports to facilitate standardized provision of guideline-recommended care for populations with either asthma or diabetes. We defined staff and provider responsibilities for the care of patients in each population in previsit planning, in-office care, patient education, laboratory analyses, and e-prescribing for medication management.

WRFP receives daily notification of hospital care provided to our patients (emergency department visits and hospital discharges). Our Medical Records staff creates a "telephone encounter" for each such patient and forwards this to the patient's primary care physician (PCP). For patients whose hospital contact was related to an exacerbation of asthma, the telephone encounter is forwarded to our Care Coordinator or Triage Nurse who then contacts the patient, assessing clinical status to facilitate a smooth transition of care to the outpatient arena with previsit planning and an office visit to assess clinical improvement and update the AAP.

The current status of a diabetic patient with respect to guideline-recommended care is continuously updated as care is ordered or provided, and a practitioner can determine the date and value of that patient's ancillary care or laboratory analyses by referring to the patient's structured data windows in the EHR.

Quality outpatient primary care has typically been assessed by measuring the fraction of patients who receive appropriate services or who are up to date with respect to the care element in question. Quality care assessment from the patients' perspective has lagged in development.[3] However, patients' sense of the quality of their healthcare is an important component to a practice's quality assessment, and patients' sense of self-confidence in disease management is essential to improving their health. Realizing this, WRFP also provides a link on our website to an Internet-based assessment and reporting tool (HowsYourHealth.org - HYH) that makes improving patients' health confidence central to its reporting functions. Patients are encouraged to use this prior to health maintenance visits and Medicare Wellness Examinations. Our EHR vendor has attempted development of analogous tools within their program, but their use depends on staff or provider input; we believe enabling patients to self-assess from their own homes is more efficient and more likely to result in honest, frank input. Patients are invited to complete the HYH survey in advance of a health maintenance visit and to securely transmit the results to WRFP. Patients' responses are then scanned into our EHR with an associated structured value (name) to be available to providers at their patients' office visits.

VALUE DERIVED/OUTCOMES

After WRFP providers and staff were trained and comfortable with EHR use in the provision of patient care, a WRFP physician began routine extraction of population management data from our EHR registry, graphing these data on plots to demonstrate change over time. In constructing these graphs, WRFP makes abundant use of statistical process control (SPC), believing that this methodology is essential to develop an understanding of the causes of any variation in our performance.[4] The graphs are produced using an SPC program (SPCXL, Sigmazone) to depict our average (green line) performance at baseline (2011) and the upper and lower bounds of statistically significant difference in our performance (red lines). Each data point on each graph represents the proportion of EPs seen that month who received the indicated care or achieved the indicated care outcome (e.g., HgbA1c). The software electronically identifies significant variation in any one period's performance from the underlying random variation in results (i.e., distinguishing "signal from noise") by calling attention to those points on the developing graph in red. We can then rapidly confirm whether any recent process change has been beneficial or not and continue our Plan, Do, Study, Act (PDSA) cycles of improvement effort.

Figures 22-1, 22-2, 22-3, and 22-4 present a mix of process and outcome measures. WRFP posts similar graphic examples of our performance on key population health measures on our practice's website at http://whiteriverfamilypractice.com/. WRFP recognizes an ultimate goal of improving outcomes in chronic disease management, but

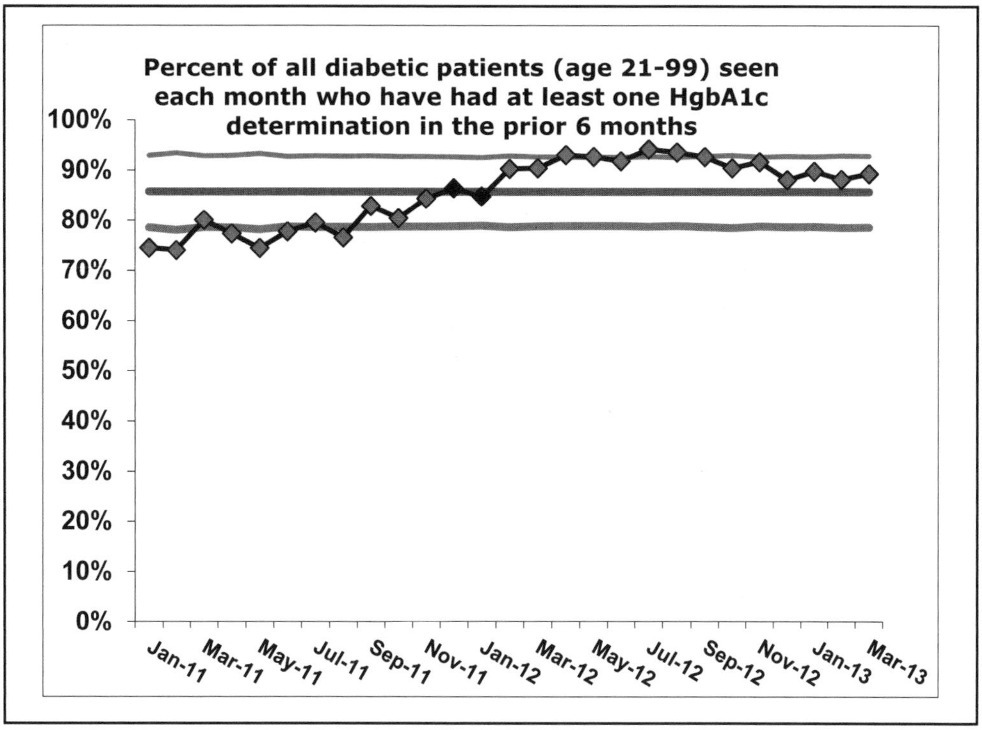

Figure 22-1: Increasing Proportion of Diabetic Patients Who Are Receiving Periodic Glycosylated Hemoglobin (HgbA1c) Determinations

Note: Percent of all diabetic patients (age 21-99) seen each month who have had at least one HgbA1c determination in the prior 6 months.

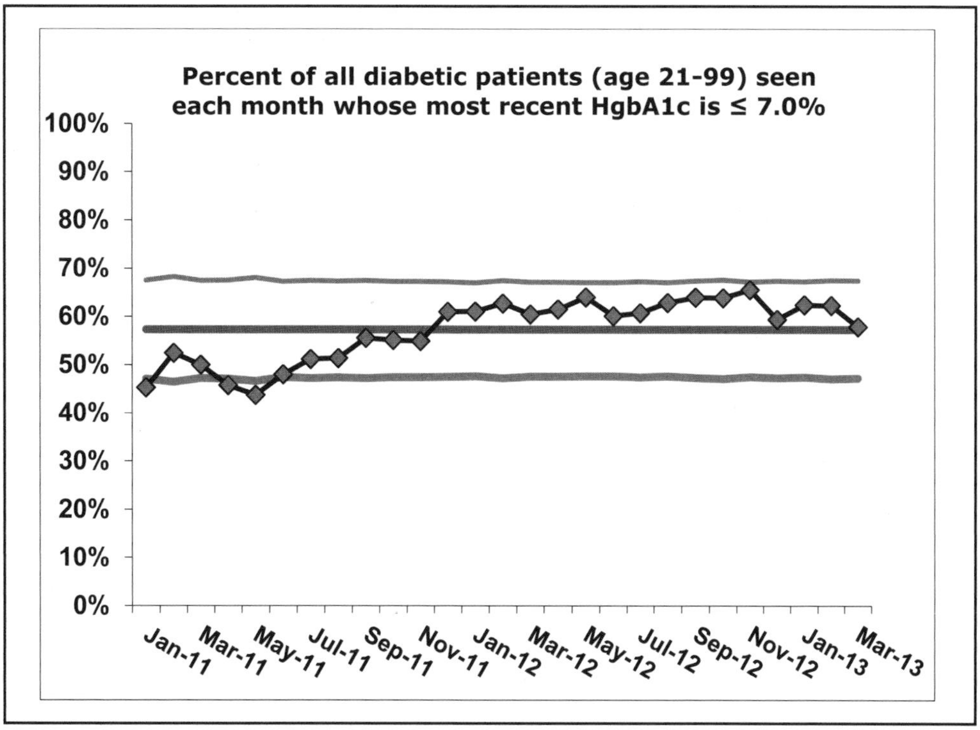

Figure 22-2: Improving HgbA1c Control among WRFP Diabetic Patients

Note: Percent of all diabetic patients (age 21-99) seen each month whose most recent HgbA1c is ≤7.0%.

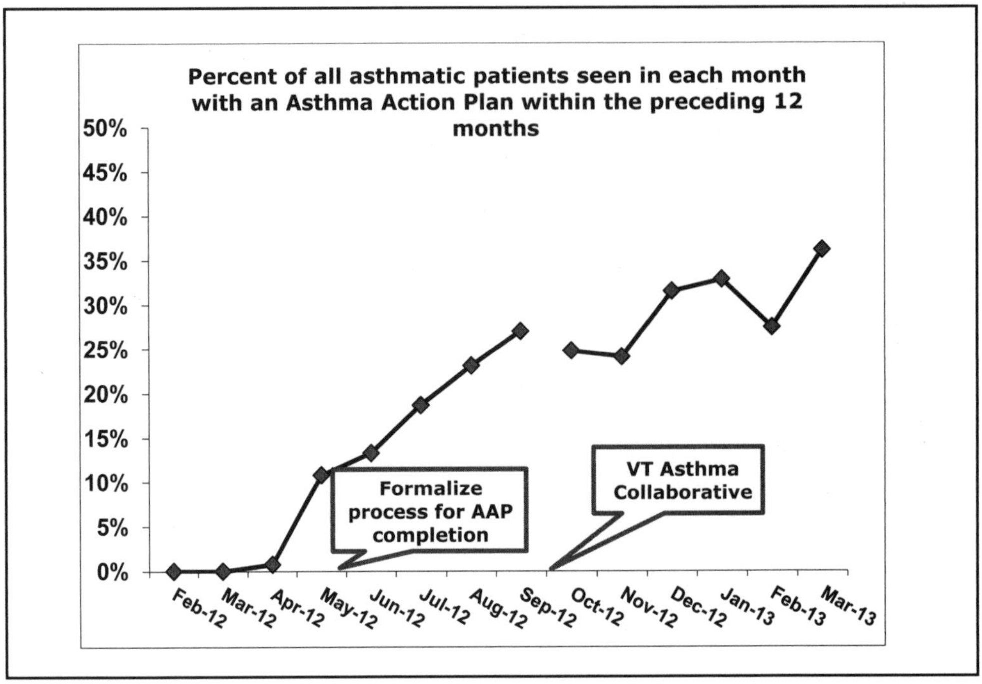

Figure 22-3: Improving Proportion of Asthmatic Patients with a Current Asthma Action Plan (AAP)

Note: Percent of all asthmatic patients seen in each month with an Asthma Action Plan within the preceding 12 months.

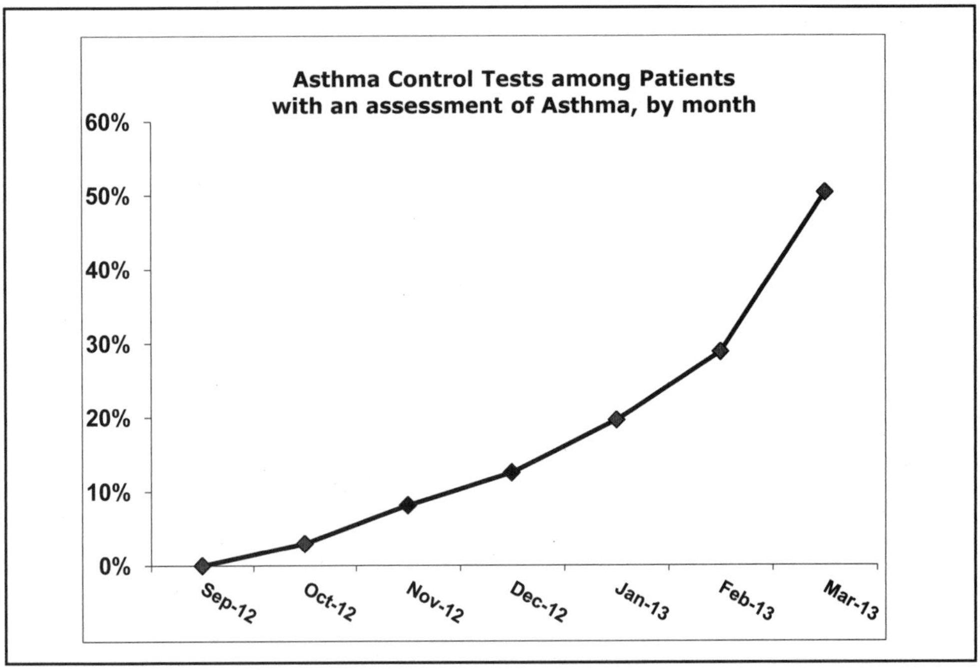

Figure 22-4: Improving Proportion of Asthmatic Patients with a Current Asthma Control Test (ACT)

Note: Asthma control tests among patients with an assessment of asthma, by month.

we also believe the most immediately effective relevant task is to measure and improve our processes of chronic disease management for those patients who are actually seeing us at each visit.

LESSONS LEARNED

- Define the periodicity of laboratory analyses and care elements for the management of your targeted populations. Develop clear standing orders empowering staff to order or obtain any tests or care that are lacking (without a new order from the practitioner). This may require periodic reinforcement to members of your clinical microsystem.
- Define the population(s) of interest. For example, WRFP found an initial challenge in agreeing on the definition of which patients to include as "asthmatic." To date, we have tolerated the exclusion of patients with rare and intermittent "reactive airways" while identifying any patient using an inhaled anti-inflammatory medication as asthmatic.
- Learn to use the registry function of the EHR. Properly configured registry queries will provide the data required for population health management. Likewise, understand the value and use of structured (and therefore searchable) data, which is critical for optimal registry use. For example, WRFP considers dilated retinal examinations (DREs) for diabetic patients to be included in the bundle of periodic health maintenance care for diabetic patients. We defined a structured data value as "diabetic retinal examination" and included it among the "Diagnostic Images" portion of our EHR. We can therefore search the EHR's registry for patients who have (or have not) had a current DRE. Defining a second structured data value to be the name of a patient's eye-care provider enables us to search for all diabetic patients who receive eye care from a particular practice. WRFP can then communicate with that particular office regarding all WRFP patients receiving care there to improve our coordination of care for our diabetic patient population.
- Sharing clinical information electronically (with appropriate patient consent) across institutions (e.g., to hospitals or among other practitioners involved in caring for the patient) is a persistent challenge as medical professionals increasingly depend on IT to deliver high-quality, safe, effective, and efficient care. In our region, VITL has established a secure electronic link ("VITLdirect"), which allows participating providers to communicate and share clinical data and records. Using this link, WRFP now receives reports of completed retinal examinations from the optometrist's office from which a substantial number of our diabetic patients receive their care. A WRFP staff position downloads, scans, and electronically forwards the retinal examination report to the patient's PCP as structured information.
- Your EHR registry should allow specific metrics of interest to be customized. In our case, the embedded quality registry identifies diabetic patients whose blood pressure is not below 130/80 whereas the current Standards of Medical Care in Diabetes - 2013 recommends accepting a systolic blood pressure of < 140 mm Hg in some patients.[2] WRFP and others using this system have provided feed-

back on this point to the vendor. Practices considering this EHR as a platform on which to optimally manage populations in accordance with evolving standards of care should consider requesting that the vendor develop the ability to customize registry parameters within the system.

FINANCIAL CONSIDERATIONS

WRFP was fortunate to receive $140,000 in grant funding from VITL toward the acquisition of our EHR. WRFP used a $70,000 line of credit (repaid within the first year of EHR operation) to finance our transition so that implementation costs above those supported by the grant would not adversely affect operations. Beyond the initial funding of our EHR, subsequent licensing and support fees, as well as workstation replacements have been funded through income from operations.

Nonreimbursed expenditures have included physician and staff time to participate in the Vermont Asthma Collaborative, meeting time to plan new patient-care work flows, and the time required to develop the databases from which our performance improvement graphs have been drawn. WRFP has found that our improvement in population management would be difficult or impossible without the after-hours work of some individuals and the willing support of the rest of the office to follow their lead.

However, our success in EHR implementation and our demonstrated improvement on population measures has enabled WRFP to successfully attest to MU in years 1 and 2, allowing WRFP to optimize incentive payments under this CMS program. In addition, the Vermont Blueprint for Health provides incentive funding proportional to the number of Vermont residents receiving care and to an office's PCMH certification score. WRFP was able to achieve a very high score (93 of a possible 100 on the 2011 NCQA Guidelines) as the practice successfully certified as a Level III PCMH with focus on these two diagnoses as examples of improving chronic disease management, thus providing additional funding from operations.

REFERENCES

1. Nelson EC, Godfrey MM. *Quality By Design: A Microsystems Approach.* San Francisco: Jossey-Bass; 2007.
2. American Diabetes Association: Standards of medical care in diabetes—2013. Position Statement. *Diabetes Care.* 2013;36 (Suppl 1):S11–S66.
3. Bishop T. Pushing the outpatient quality envelope. *JAMA.* 2013;309(13):1353-1354.
4. Carey RG. *Improving Healthcare With Control Charts: Basic and Advanced SPC Methods and Case Studies.* Milwaukee, WI: ASQ Quality Press, 2003.

CHAPTER 23

Case Study: Texas Health Resources

Clinical and Business Intelligence

Texas Health Resources received the 2013 HIMSS Davies Enterprise Award.

EXECUTIVE SUMMARY

Texas Health Resources (THR) is a large, integrated healthcare system that has grown and diversified through acquisitions. As a result, THR has multiple EHRs and patient management systems, as well as a home-grown financial system. While THR now has all 14 wholly owned hospitals on the same platform, the acquisition of a large physician network introduced a variety of different EMR installations.

THR, like most healthcare organizations, has a variety of systems that support the delivery of healthcare. To obtain a complete 360-degree view of a patient's care, data from disparate systems must be integrated, including data from physician practices, hospitals, and post-acute providers.

THR has invested $7,000,000 in capital with a budgeted $1,000,000 annual operating costs, in a clinical business intelligence (CBI) solution. Through our initial ACO dashboard, we have already seen an increase from less than threshold at 92 percent to the maximum score at 99 percent.

We expect an annual return of $5 million to $8 million from better decisions on surgical materials, reduced practice variability, more efficient processes, and higher data quality through our ability to extract complex data requirements for advanced analytics.

BACKGROUND KNOWLEDGE

THR's mission is to improve the health of the people in the communities we serve. To accomplish our strategic objectives in support of our mission, we recognized the need to integrate data into a "single source of truth" and to analyze data from across the care continuum, including pre-acute, acute and post-acute providers from various source systems. THR's data warehouse, CBI, was funded in mid-2011 and integrates data from disparate systems in support of specific use cases. This system provides clinicians and business personnel with access to analytical dashboards, which provide aggregate views of key measures at system and leadership levels. Drill-down capability to physician and patient level detail is provided for root cause analysis as authorized by security requirements.

LOCAL PROBLEM BEING ADDRESSED AND INTENDED IMPROVEMENT

THR was constrained in its ability to deliver information and analytics to the organization and there was a backlog of 100+ aging report requests. Data needed to support THR's analytic needs exists in several operational systems and may contain different patient identifiers for the same patient, different business rules, and inconsistent data definitions. THR developed manual data extraction and integration processes to create personalized point solutions to address specific analytical needs. Data extraction, integration, and analysis were redundant, personalized to the analyst doing the work, time-consuming and inconsistent. These point solutions were not extensible to the enterprise. THR was unable to keep up with the demand for analytics and reporting, which was only increasing and growing in strategic significance.

Faced with healthcare reform and the future growth of the THR system, we recognized the urgent need to integrate data, to improve quality and outcomes, to reduce readmissions, and to support new payment models. Required targets for value-based purchasing are increasing and THR stands to lose significant reimbursement for Medicare and Medicaid, should targets not be met. What once was adequate will not be strong enough to sustain THR in the future.

We embarked on a journey to develop and deploy a data warehouse, Clinical Business Intelligence (CBI). CBI brings data from disparate source systems into a single repository (see Figures 23-1 and 23-2). A unique patient identifier is assigned, enterprise data definitions and business rules are applied to the data, and consistent metrics are derived and shared across the THR enterprise. As a result, THR is empowered with self-serve reporting capabilities that included guardrails to ensure accuracy of information, resulting in minimal reliance on IT to create reports and data extracts. This allows more time to analyze information rather than gather, clean, and integrate data.

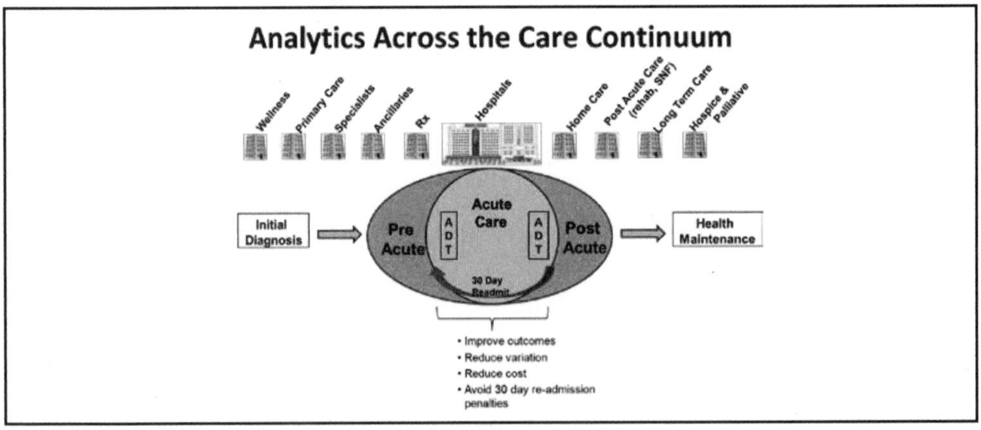

Figure 23-1: Analytics Across the Care Continuum

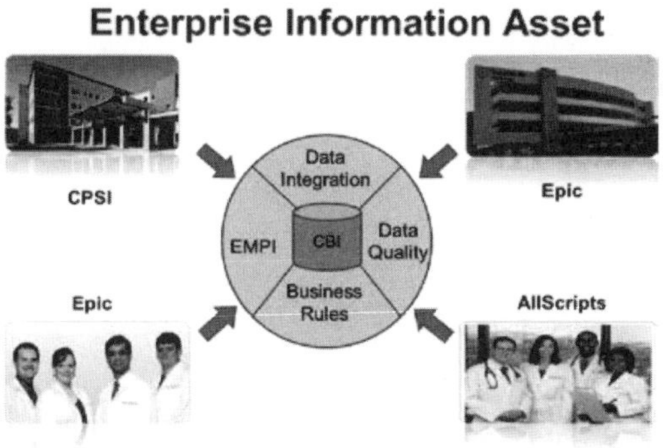

Figure 23-2: Enterprise Information Asset

DESIGN AND IMPLEMENTATION

We began our CBI journey by establishing a governance process. A CBI Steering Committee (CBI SC) was formed and consisted of senior level executives from across the THR system. The CBI SC established its charter and the guiding principles for CBI. Key guiding principles remain in place today to drive the strategic initiatives of CBI—a single data repository with a unique patient identifier, consistent business rules across all systems, and self-service reporting capabilities.

We conducted interviews with stakeholders from across THR to identify the initial use cases and requirements that CBI would support and that were aligned with THR's strategic plan. From this process, four use cases emerged:

- Population health analytics
- Heart & Vascular (H&V) procedural analytics
- H&V care redesign
- Referral management analysis

An RFP was conducted to select a technology solution. The CBI Steering Committee approved the use cases, technology solution, execution roadmap, costs, and anticipated ROI. These four use cases contained a common quality theme, and a quality dashboard was initiated as a beta project to prove out the technology and capabilities. The project replaced a manual data manipulation and delivery process with automated integration of data from the EHR and as well as our collaborative partner Premier Healthcare Alliance.

Data are now more timely, accurate, and accessible. Executives and clinicians can view results through an easy-to-use graphical dashboard interface that provides trend reporting and drill-down capabilities.

The team followed the approved roadmap. We installed the technology, and the data were acquired into CBI incrementally, beginning with CareConnect, THR's EHR, and sequencing the data into subject areas such as foundational data (encounter, patient, provider), then more clinical data, and then moving on to the physician practice EHR. The team delivered data to the business and clinicians every 90 days so that value is provided as quickly as possible. We established and delivered several dashboards to the system. These included a First View Dashboard intended to acclimate users to the tools and data, the Quality Dashboard previously described and shown in Figure 23-3, and

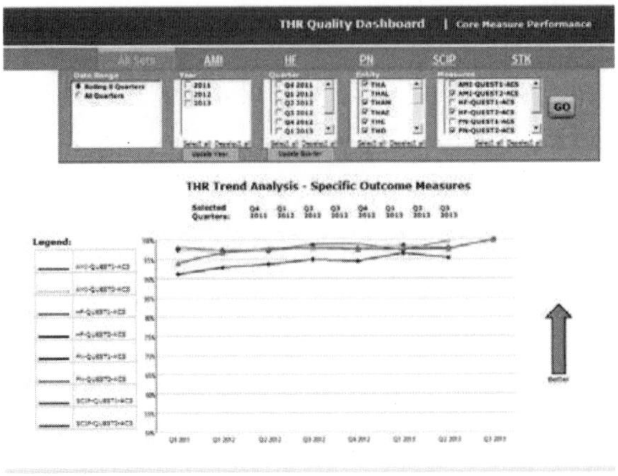

Figure 23-3: The Quality Dashboard

Table 23-1: CBI Data Content

CBI Data Content

Subject Area	Record Count
Practitioners	27 Thousand
Patients	5.9 Million
Immunizations	1.8 Million
Encounters	50 Million
Diagnoses	61 Million
Procedures	8.4 Million
Pharm Orders	64 Million
Clinical Orders	258 Million
Flowsheets, Vitals, Lab & Procedure Results	3 Billion

recently, a Population Health Dashboard that provides visibility to the ACO-33 measures for various populations. This is the first time THR can view data from multiple EMRs in the same dashboard. The dashboard is deployed systemwide and, while it is too soon to see measureable improvements, they are expected as performance is now visible and closely monitored across the enterprise. An Executive Dashboard was also delivered, containing key performance indicators (KPIs) and other measures that monitor performance of THR's transformational themes.

Through the iterative deployment methodology, CBI has grown and become a significant information asset to THR (see Table 23-1).

HOW WAS HEALTH IT UTILIZED?

THR purchased a vendor-supported data warehouse technology stack, which includes the hardware and software to integrate and analyze data, data privacy and security components, and a healthcare data model (see Figure 23-4).

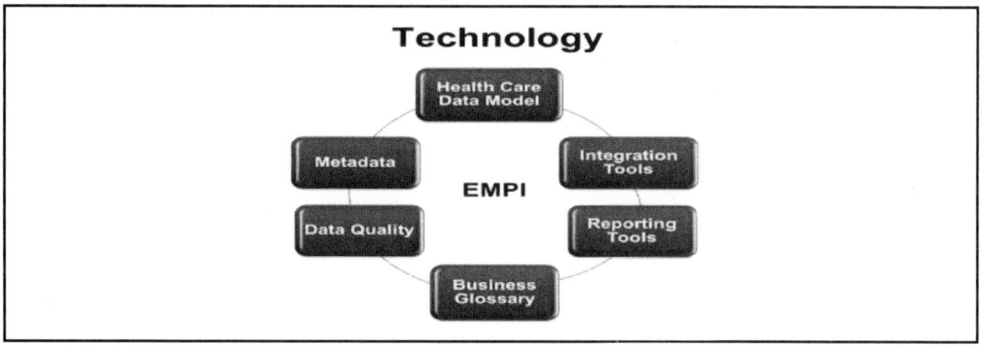

Figure 23-4: Data Warehouse Technology Stack

The data warehouse technology stack enables THR to integrate large volumes of data from disparate acute and ambulatory applications providing the information needed to identify and drive the appropriate clinical interventions. The system contains data integration capabilities, including extract, transform and load (ETL) tools to move data into a comprehensive healthcare data model. The warehouse provides an integrated glossary of business terms and full data lineage to manage information across the enterprise.

We delivered reporting and analytics to the users through our business intelligence tool and included capability to allow for self-service analysis. This health IT solution enables THR to identify opportunities for improvement in clinical or operational process areas, as well as to identify best practices to be shared across the system. This required a fully integrated solution that, at its core, has become the single source of trusted data to meet the data quality standards and information needs of THR.

We developed a strong governance process with cross-functional executive leadership to prioritize the transformation. We created an initial historical load and continued to process the data every day to ensure that information was current and relevant. We optimized the solution around a specialized analytics appliance to deliver specific insights with superior performance to the business users and clinicians.

Value Derived/Outcome

Many results in our outcomes are becoming easily viewed through CBI (as shown in Figure 23-5). Our existing dashboards have already given us advanced analytics such as:

- Within the Quality Dashboard, the Appropriate Care Scores (ACS) for all conditions have increased from less than threshold at 92 percent to the maximum score at 99 percent. Due to CBI, we can see comparative data over time and drill down into ACS-specific outcome measures over time. Because of our ability to closely monitor and analyze the data, we can now identify specific outcome measures needing attention and develop action plans, and then follow the improvement over time.
- As shown in Figure 23-6, the Accountable Care Organization Dashboard (ACO) provides information on specific clinical conditions for at-risk populations, including diabetes and congestive heart failure. Physicians can see how

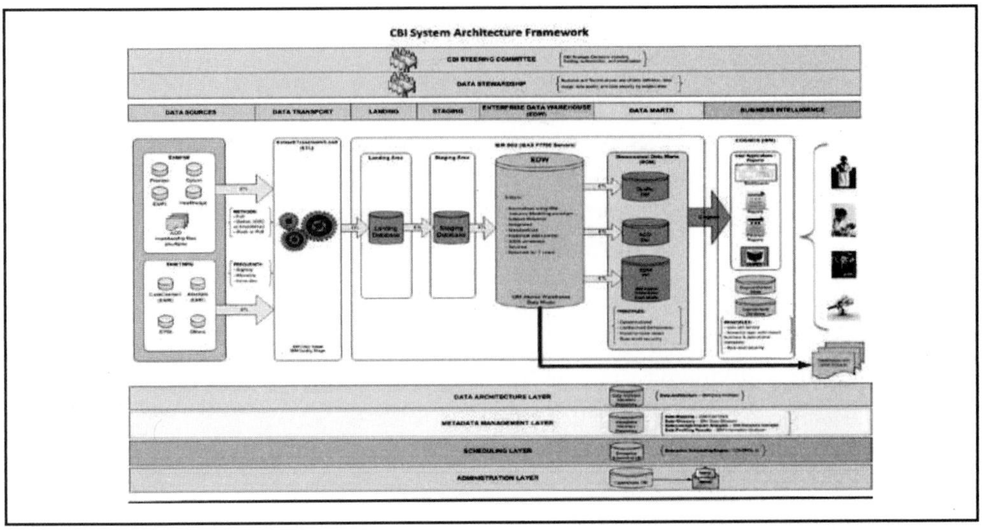

Figure 23-5: CBI System Architecture Framework

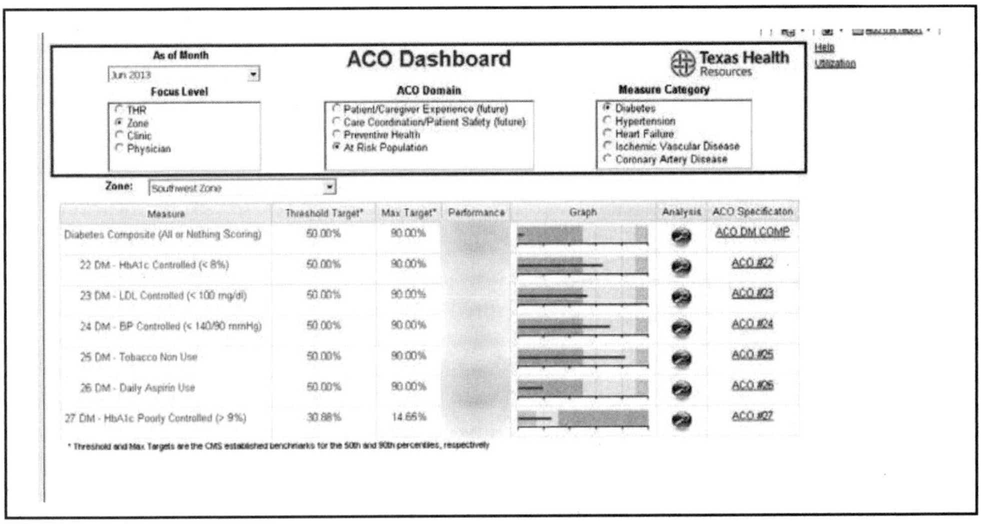

Figure 23-6: ACO Dashboard

they are trending and benchmark against established thresholds as well as their peers.

- For managing population health, clinics can be ranked as to their performance against specific patient populations and action plans developed, or best-case practices promoted across the organization.

Integrating large volumes of data from multiple source systems across a healthcare system is daunting. Key to THR's success is senior executive level and business sponsor support. Additionally, a methodically planned roadmap sequences data acquisition into manageable subject areas with iterative delivery where value can be realized quickly. The CBI Steering Committee is actively engaged in vetting and prioritizing additional needs for information and analytics.

LESSONS LEARNED

- THR's initial deployment of the Quality Dashboard to prove out the technology also provided valuable feedback on techniques to increase user adoption. THR found that early exposure of the dashboard's look and feel to a subset of the users during the design aspect of the project provides input that will help ensure user acceptance of the dashboard. In addition, web-based training is an easy and informative way to communicate across a diversely located enterprise of users.
- During the second phase of CBI, a First View Dashboard was delivered to a subset of the end-user community. While the dashboard did not provide all data for all the requested analytics, it did provide the end users with an opportunity to become acclimated to the reporting tool and to get an early look at the data.
- At the beginning of the project, THR established the technology blueprint and standards, and implemented design and code reviews to ensure the standards are adhered to for consistency in the CBI application to ease future support.
- We attempted an enterprise view for data governance. However, because of the overwhelming change and transformation taking place at THR, and the lack of resources available, we had to take a grassroots approach. Data governance consisted of THR subject matter experts (SMEs) either in ITS or the business who provided data mapping and data definitions for the enterprise application. A better approach would be a governance model that includes an additional step where stakeholders from across the enterprise validate these items to ensure a true enterprise view. As data became visible via CBI, the business users saw the direct alignment with EMR data recording, and dashboard reporting interest grew to expand our data governance model.

FINANCIAL CONSIDERATIONS

CBI is a capital project with an initial investment of $7,000,000 and a significant operation costs investment by THR. Ongoing operating costs are also in excess of $1,000,000 per year, representing a very costly investment in this project. The ROI on business intelligence solutions is driven by the actions taken on the data, not on the data itself. During the funding approval process, ROI was projected for three of the initial use cases:

H&V Procedural Analytics

- ROI was projected from a case study of a large East Coast hospital (525 beds) that had created a surgical analytics data mart from a CBI System.
- Using this case study, an estimated savings of $5 million to $8 million/year for THR is expected from better decisions on surgical materials, reduced practice variability, more efficient processes, and higher data quality.

H&V Care Redesign

- Benefits projected based on:
  - Reduced operating expense from realized efficiencies

  - Increased revenue from physician efficiency
  - Pay-for-performance from payers
  - Value of physician time saved
  - Avoidance of 30-day readmissions
- THR projected savings based on a use case analysis of a large integrated delivery network (IDN) is $6.2 million/annually.

Referral Analytics

- This use case focuses on identifying lost revenue opportunities by analyzing referral and usage patterns to identify and close gaps on reasons why THR patients leave the system.
- The estimated revenue loss is $174 million over 5 years; the estimated increased revenue is $3.4 million/year, assuming a 10 percent recovery on lost revenue opportunity.

Chapter 24

Case Study: UC Davis Health System

Health Information Exchange

University of California Davis Health System received the 2013 HIMSS Davies Enterprise Award.

EXECUTIVE SUMMARY

As a tertiary healthcare provider, many UC Davis Health System (UCDHS) patients transition through different types of care settings: tertiary referrals, telemedicine encounters, trauma admissions, emergency transfers, and other clinical partnerships with community-based care providers. Given the reality of multiple nonaffiliated providers and organizations managing patient care in the northern California area, the ability to exchange patient information is critical to ensure optimal clinical and cost-effective care. Sharing data at the community level has been complicated by multiple failed attempts to create a viable California-wide health information exchange (HIE) capability. As UCDHS deployed an electronic health record (EHR), the ability to support the exchange of patient clinical data within the health system and with community-based care providers was prioritized.

UCDHS has been able to exchange 3.7 million patient records of multiple types since October 2008. The success of HIE at UCDHS has been a key element of earning the designation in 2011, 2012, and 2013 as one of the "Most Wired" healthcare organizations by *Hospitals and Health Networks* and the "Most Connected Hospital" in 2011 and 2012 by *U.S. News & World Report*, and was the 102nd organization to qualify for Stage 7 in the HIMSS Analytics EMR Adoption Model in 2012.

BACKGROUND

UCDHS has been able to electronically exchange 3.7 million patient records of multiple types (average of 64,079 records per month) with nonaffiliated care providers in the community and the region since October 2008. Patient records have been shared with providers and hospitals who have used the EpicCare Everywhere technology, and with providers who use EHRs from other vendors. They are able to access patient records generated by UCDHS, and UCDHS is able to access their patient data for a more complete clinical record on each patient when needed. In addition, over 3,269 northern California providers have read-only access to patient records through the UCDHS EHR and radiology picture archiving and communication system (PACS). As these community providers implement modern EHRs and interfaces for two-way access in the future, they will also be able to support integration of their patient records into the patient's electronic medical record.

LOCAL PROBLEM BEING ADDRESSED AND INTENDED IMPROVEMENT

UCDHS needed an HIE capability that matched the geographic scope of care the organization delivers. This capability had to reach outside the UCDHS organization for sharing and access of patient data between and among all providers, whether affiliated with UCDHS or not, in the geographic region. But like other care providers in the area, the organization was faced with the fact that California has not been successful in creating statewide HIE.

To achieve full benefit from the EHR, UCDHS and the northern California region needed the ability to share patient data. When UCDHS assessed its ability to share patient data within the health system and with other organizations, a number of information-sharing gaps were identified as reflected in Table 24-1.

Design and Implementation

The leadership of UCDHS made deployment of the EHR and all required HIE connections an organizational priority. This priority was evidenced by clinician leadership providing strong support of EHR use, organizational leadership funding increases in IT budgets, and updating of procedures and policies. This strong support created an organization-wide commitment to the change, funding, and hard work needed to deploy an HIE.

IT partnered with physician and nursing leadership and clinical departments to identify and prioritize the clinical data that needed to be shared to support patients across transitions of care. An inventory was created of all clinical software and content

Table 24-1: UCDHS's Ability to Share Patient Data and Information-sharing Gaps

UC Davis Health System Data-Sharing Gap	Resulting In....
Many niche clinical software systems were not interfaced to the EHR and key clinical tests (cardiology, pulmonary function, others) could not be ordered from within the EHR nor were the test results available in the her	Significant delays and rework
Clinical equipment used to support care that created important clinical data about patients was not integrated with the EHR	Important clinical data not easily accessible and rework
Many patients bringing CD ROMs to visits with clinical images created by other care providers, but UCDHS clinicians unable to easily access the images on the CDs nor include them in the UCDHS patient record	Potential care delays and duplicate testing
Physicians often found patients had recent clinical tests performed by other care organizations, but this clinical data was not available to UC Davis	Duplicate tests, extra cost

in the organization. Relevant processes that impacted transitions of care were reviewed, both internal to the health system and with community care providers outside the system.

It was important to create partnerships and interfaces with other care providers, hospitals, and pharmacies in the community to share patient data. The UCDHS EHR was defined as the target location to store or link all relevant clinical information.

An evaluation was done to assess the capability and readiness of the IT division to write and maintain mission-critical clinical interfaces. An interoperability technical team was appointed. A review of interface technologies was performed, resulting in the selection and deployment of Intersystems' Ensemble interface engine, which has the ability to create both internal and community-level interfaces with other organizations. Training was provided on both interface technologies and data-sharing standards.

Using the clinical content inventory and prioritization as a guide, interface projects were started and managed through a dashboard showing all requested interfaces, interfaces in progress (with key project information and dates), and a full inventory of completed interfaces. Monthly meetings with the CIO were held to guide interface work. Regular updates on the status of internal and external interoperability projects were also shared with organizational leadership.

UCDHS has deployed a growing list of specialized health exchange technologies that securely move patient records within UC Davis and also share data with other care providers in the community. A detailed summary of the health IT used by UC Davis and the breakdown of the 3.7 million patient records shared is shown at the end of this case study; highlights include:

- **OnBase Content Management System:** Over 6 million multi-page clinical paper documents have been scanned and linked to the EHR.
- **PACSGEAR:** Specialized software loaded on UC Davis clinical workstations so clinical images taken by other providers but brought by patients to UCDHS during clinical encounters can be loaded—over 160,213 outside image studies have been shared to date using this method.
- **PACS to PACS Interfaces:** UCDHS has directly interfaced its radiology PACS to other PACS systems used by two community care providers to securely exchange clinical images.
- **Surescripts ePrescription Network:** All five federally mandated ePrescription interfaces are in place. Over 3.3 million prescription records have been shared.
- **eHealth Global Technologies:** A technology and services vendor that, in the case of UCDHS, supports new cancer patients prior to their first encounter at UCDHS by going into the community to scan any paper records, copy DICOM clinical images, and obtain pathology slides from prior care encounters. UCDHS interfaces these records directly into the EHR, the OnBase content management system, and the radiology PACS to ensure critical clinical data are available to oncologists and other clinicians.

HOW WAS HEALTH IT UTILIZED?

In addition to the data sharing done with clinicians, the tethered personal health record (PHR) from Epic called MyChart currently supports over 80,709 UCDHS patients accessing their clinical data and exchanging secure messages with their UCDHS physician and care team. Clinicians can request "outside records" from within the Epic EHR, and to date have shared over 18,268 EHR records with community physicians, leveraging interfaces with the Epic EHR, EHR products from other vendors, the U.S. Social Security Administration, community pharmacies, and nursing homes. Additionally, more than 6 million multi-page clinical paper documents have been scanned and linked to the EHR; given the digital nature of the UCDHS medical record, the majority of any paper records now scanned at UCDHS are from other care providers.

The UCDHS HIE tool links providers beyond northern California and now makes UCDHS patient information available electronically and immediately accessible to other major health systems and their physicians. A complete list (as of March 2013) appears at the end of this chapter; it includes the following:

- Sutter Health in northern California
- U.S. Social Security Administrator
- Dignity Health in Sacramento, California
- Stanford Hospital & Clinics
- University of California San Francisco
- OCHIN (49 federally qualified health center [FQHC] clinics in 7 states)
- Community pharmacies (ePrescribing records shared with a total of 5,469 community pharmacies in the United States)
- California Department of Public Health

The UC Davis HIE technical foundation is being leveraged and expanded.

- UC Davis is in the first group of thirteen care providers in the nation to become full members of Healtheway, formally referred to as the Nationwide Health Information Exchange Network (NwHIN Exchange) that began as the federal ONC national HIE in 2007. The other members of Healtheway are HIE entities or federal agencies. UCDHS has partnered with the U.S. Social Security Administration (SSA) to share patient data via standard Continuity of Care Document (CCD) formats. These interfaces are triggered when a UCDHS patient has applied for Social Security benefits. The HIE–based data-sharing process with a number of care providers has enabled SSA to reduce the time it takes to evaluate disability claims from 2 to 4 months to as little as 24–48 hours; a huge benefit to patients needing these services. In the first 7 months of use, UCDHS has shared over 1,600 patient records with the SSA.
- The UCDHS Healtheway membership will be the foundation for many other HIE connections, such as an early discussion with the Veterans Health Administration (VHA)—given both UCDHS and the VHA are full members of Healtheway.
- An interface using NwHIN Exchange standards was created between UC Davis and the five Dignity Health (Mercy) hospitals in Sacramento (that use different EHR vendors) and went into production use in fall 2012. This point-to-point interface between UCDHS and Dignity Health was converted in May 2013 to be a standard Healtheway interface using this national HIE organization and capability. This is one of the first interfaces between two care providers using the standard Healtheway HIE to share patient data.

- An interface was successfully completed in 2012 to share syndromic data with the Public Health Division of Sacramento County. The county has changed direction, and at their request UCDHS is now creating an interface with the Centers for Disease Control BioSense syndromic tracking program.

VALUE DERIVED/OUTCOMES

Improved Patient Care and Outcomes

There are ongoing efforts at UCDHS to study and measure the value that HIE is providing to the community, organizations, clinicians, and patients. Not only are data accessible to all providers within the UCDHS system, but to date 18,268 patient records have been shared with and accessed by providers who are not affiliated with UCDHS. While metrics are not yet available on the clinical and financial results of this sharing of data, the real value of HIE can be best understood by sharing several examples from UC Davis physicians regarding the ability to share EHR content created in other hospitals and clinics in the greater Sacramento and northern California region.

HIE Example #1 - Infectious Disease: *"I just saw this patient this past week in Infectious Diseases clinic. I saw her as a second opinion for persistent infections. This 34-year-old woman with a complicated orthopedic history from a motor vehicle accident with right leg amputation developed traumatic arthritis in the left knee requiring knee replacement in January 2011. She has had multiple infectious diseases and complications with three surgeries and subsequent removal of the knee. She came to me with an old set of labs and a discharge summary from her last admission.*

I sat down with the patient and using the ability in the EHR to access data from other hospitals (Epic Care Everywhere) we reviewed her history (using the EHR H&P and discharge summaries), labs (including her microbiology culture results), and radiology studies (including multiple x-rays, MRI [magnetic resonance imaging], and a nuclear medicine study). She had a very thorough evaluation from the other hospital, and it would have been a total waste of time and money to re-do that evaluation. She left very happy and confident in the treatment plan recommendations because of my ability to thoroughly review her last 6 months of evaluation and treatment."

HIE Example #2 - Sharing Blood Culture Tests Results Between Hospitals: *I saw this case when I was on medicine wards in the hospital. A 46-year-old woman was seen at the emergency room at Sutter for severe cellulitis of the face (periorbital). She was subsequently admitted to the Sutter Hospital and transferred to us after admission on hospital day #2 after initiating antibiotics at Sutter. We continued her care in the hospital and she quickly improved.*

Typically I would have switched her to oral antibiotics and sent her home. However, when I reviewed the case on hospital day #4, I decided to review her community hospital records through the EHR ability to access records from other hospitals (Epic Care Everywhere). Her blood cultures from the community hospital had turned positive overnight.

Thus, the paperwork she came with showed preliminarily no growth on the blood cultures, but my electronic review was more up-to-date and showed Staphylococcus aureus. This is an important clinical pathogen that requires intravenous antibiotics for treatment—not oral antibiotics. We were able to make the right clinical decision and arranged for home IV antibiotics at discharge. In this case, the electronic record was more accurate than the paperwork she came to us with because it is more up to date. The patient was also happy and confident with our care."

Operational Benefits Derived from the HIE

When niche clinical software was interfaced to the EHR, many improvements were immediately realized: (1) clinical orders and results were shared electronically, thereby eliminating paper-based workarounds, reducing delays when ordering and receiving test results, and eliminating the need to create and store paper order forms and clinical result reports; (2) each new type of content that was added or linked to the EHR (from internal or external sources) created internal efficiencies and an increasingly more complete clinical record for clinicians to use while caring for patients; and (3) the EHR content became more valuable, via the UCDHS HIE, to nonaffiliated community-based care providers and patients throughout the region.

LESSONS LEARNED

First and foremost, the HIE must be defined as a priority by organizational leaders. HIE must be a core goal in technology and clinical data decision making.

The ability to deliver HIE starts when choosing clinical technology (software or clinical equipment), and the ability to support modern interfaces should be required even when not immediately used. Investments in technology without interoperability create future roadblocks to share data and participate in the emerging digital healthcare industry.

Once the optimal technology is chosen, it is important to design and deploy the technology to support data sharing and support patient care transitions. To achieve the optimal community-level HIE design, it is important to keep the patient at the center of all technology decisions and deployments.

While managing different viewpoints and competencies can be challenging, clinical data sharing will not be accomplished without deep internal and external partnerships with clinical care providers. Once significant internal data sharing has been accomplished, internal experiences and lessons are reusable when working with other organizations.

HIE is not achievable without adjusting clinical processes and workflow. While these changes can be daunting at first, they often become interesting and exciting for clinicians and support staff: to finally focus on what is important to the patient and care giver, and eliminate years of inefficiencies and delays.

Financial Considerations

To achieve the HIE outlined in this case study, $432,000 in capital funds were spent for the interface engine, servers, and storage. UCDHS spends approximately $3.4 million per year in ongoing costs to extend and manage interfaces. Just over $3 million of this covers the cost of 22 FTEs who work on interfaces and HIE. The balance is used for technical support and software updates.

UC Davis found the cost of delivering interfaces and HIE are a small percentage of its IT budget (3.4%), but it creates significant value, especially to a busy tertiary care provider where patients experience many transitions of care. Studies are in progress at UC Davis to more deeply assess and measure the clinical and financial impact of HIE now in place and new types of data sharing capabilities that will soon be added.

All Types of Patient Records UCDHS has shared with other Care Providers Shared

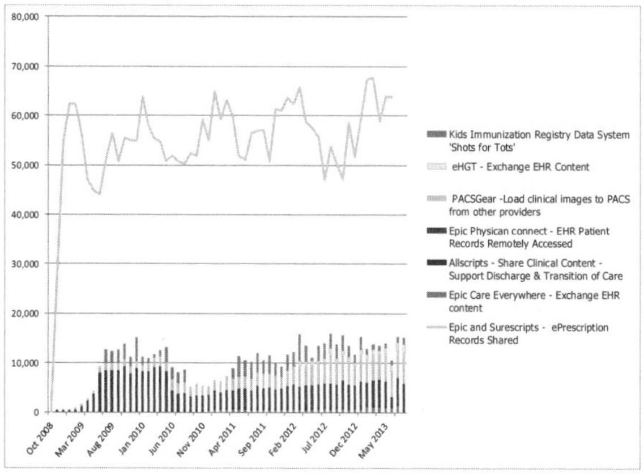

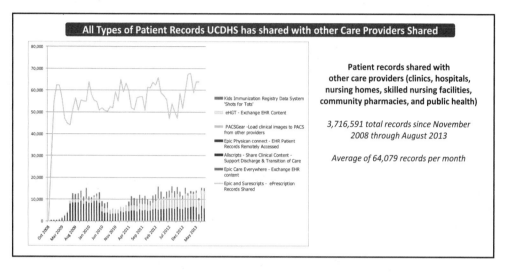

Patient records shared with other care providers (clinics, hospitals, nursing homes, skilled nursing facilities, community pharmacies, and public health)

3,716,591 total records since November 2008 through August 2013

Average of 64,079 records per month

Outside Clinical Images Loaded

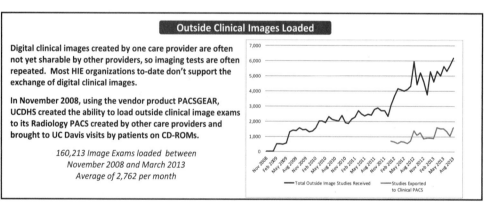

Digital clinical images created by one care provider are often not yet sharable by other providers, so imaging tests are often repeated. Most HIE organizations to-date don't support the exchange of digital clinical images.

In November 2008, using the vendor product PACSGEAR, UCDHS created the ability to load outside clinical image exams to its Radiology PACS created by other care providers and brought to UC Davis visits by patients on CD-ROMs.

160,213 Image Exams loaded between November 2008 and March 2013
Average of 2,762 per month

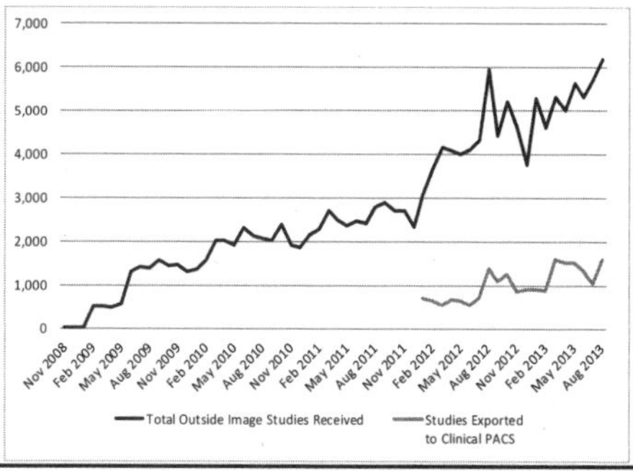

Sharing ePrescription records with community pharmacies

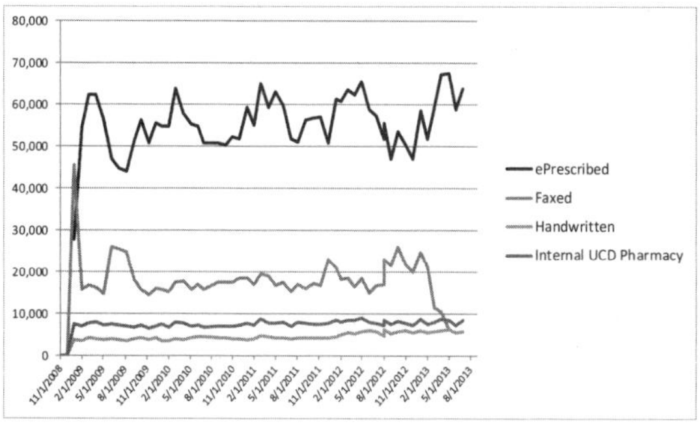

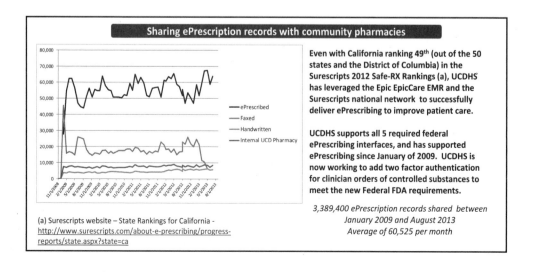

Even with California ranking 49th (out of the 50 states and the District of Columbia) in the Surescripts 2012 Safe-RX Rankings (a), UCDHS has leveraged the Epic EpicCare EMR and the Surescripts national network to successfully deliver ePrescribing to improve patient care.

UCDHS supports all 5 required federal ePrescribing interfaces, and has supported ePrescribing since January of 2009. UCDHS is now working to add two factor authentication for clinician orders of controlled substances to meet the new Federal FDA requirements.

3,389,400 ePrescription records shared between January 2009 and August 2013
Average of 60,525 per month

(a) Surescripts website – State Rankings for California - http://www.surescripts.com/about-e-prescribing/progress-reports/state.aspx?state=ca

Summary of the information exchange technology UCDHS has deployed and resulting data sharing

HIE Technology	Description of Technology	UC Davis Health System Outcome Data from 2008 – August 2013
EpicCare Electronic Health Record (EHR)	Loaded or linked patient clinical data across the continuum of care	Over 2.2 million patient records stored in the UC Davis EHR
MyChart tethered Personal Health Record (PHR)		- Over 80,709 patients use the tethered PHR at UC Davis via Web and iPhone and iPad
(Epic Systems Corporation)	Shared immunization data with 'Shots for Tots' registry	- Shared immunization records for 107,298 patients with 'public health
Epic Care Everywhere (Epic Systems Corporation)	Epic software module to connect the UC Davis EHR with EHRs used in other organizations – both Epic and other software vendor EHRs UCDHS has shared over 400 patient records via the Continuity of Care Document (CCD) standard with the Social Security Administration via the Healtheway HIE and also connects to Dignity Health via Healtheway.	18,268 patient records shared with 26 other organizations using Epic EHRs and EHRs from other software vendors
EpicCare Link – called 'Physician Connect' at UC Davis (Epic Systems Corporation)	Supports community physicians and staff to access the UC Davis EHR and Radiology PACS over a secure Internet connection Especially useful for small physician practices and hospitals without an EHR	Over 3,269 community based physicians & staff access the UC Davis EHR and radiology PACS online - over 262,218 unique patient records have been accessed
OnBase Enterprise Document Management Software (Hyland Software Inc.)	Content management system-loads scanned paper medical records and JPEG, TIFF, or WAV files taken in support of patient care – Interfaced with Epic EHR. The paper medical records UCDHS now scans into OnBase are now mostly from other care providers	Scanned all current internal and external paper medical records to OnBase – and load digital patient images taken with digital cameras (such as Dermatology). 6,012,778 multi-page clinical documents scanned to-date
PACSGEAR (PACSGEAR, Inc.)	Loaded on 4,000+ UC Davis client computers – loads DICOM clinical images created by other care providers and shared via CD ROM to UCD Phillips Radiology PACS	Over 160,213 patient digital image studies have been loaded to the UC Davis radiology PACS
Surescripts ePrescription Network (Surescripts)	Transmits ePrescription records from and to UC Davis EHR and community pharmacies and insurance companies	3,389,400 ePrescription records shared to date in support of all 5 federally mandated ePrescription interfaces
eHealth Record Retrieval Service (eHealth Global Technologies, Inc. - eHGT)	For complex referrals UCD requests eHGT to find & copy patient records and images - eHGT transmits via interfaces to UCD and loads scanned paper medical records to OnBase, and the Philips Radiology PACS	18,551 oncology patient records loaded to UCDHS clinical systems
Allscripts Care Management (Allscripts Inc.)	Supports discharge planning and placement - shares patient data electronically with post-acute care facilities	Have shared 29,045 patient records with post-acute facilities in multiple formats they can use
Ensemble interface engine and HealthShare to support community level HIE (InterSystems Corporation)	Interface engine used to create standards-based interfaces-provides audit tools and real-time monitors	Over 160 interfaces in production use, with 28.3 million transactions per month shared internally

Annual IT Direct Cost to Create and Maintain Interfaces

Cost Type	Capital Cost	Annual Operating Cost	
		Salary & Benefits	Maintenance
Staffing			
22 FTEs working on Interfaces and HIE		$ 3,190,000	
Internal - HIE			
Interface Engine Software application	$296,125		$45,000
Servers supporting interfaces	$104,000		$20,000
Storage supporting interface	$32,000		$40,000
External - HIE			
EHR HIE usage fees	$0		$67,800
HIE usage fees			$19,900
Subtotal	$432,125	$3,190,000	$192,700
Grand Total	**$432,125**	**$3,382,700**	

IT infrastructure elements that are also required to be successful with interfaces: data center, databases, EHR software and hardware, network connections, and others.

The direct cost of the IT interface function represents 3.4% of the IT annual budget...to support the monthly sharing 64,070 patient records of some type with community care providers and 28.3 million internal interface transactions. The ability to exchange data between software applications and between care providing organizations add dramatic value.

Organizations UCDHS shared CCD or CCD-equivalent Records with as of -August 2013

UCDHS has used three methods to share continuity of care (CCD) patient records:

- **Epic Care Everywhere**
- **Point to point interface**
- **Via Healtheway HIE**

The point to point data exchange was created between UCDHS and with Dignity Health to initially achieve data exchange in support of patient transitions of care, but this interface was converted to a Healtheway interface on May 12, 2013.

Epic has been a leading vendor partnering with Healtheway and they are working to utilize Healtheway for its HIE connections to ensure Epic customers exchange data via an ONC approved HIE as required by EHR meaningful use. As this transition occurs, UCDHS will likely soon have all of its HIE data exchange done via Healtheway.

Dignity Health and Sutter Health have been great partners with UCDHS to deliver HIE to support patient care transitions.

#	Organization	Location	# Records
1	Sutter Health	Northern California	15,433
2	Social Security Administration	United States	1,606
3	Dignity Health - 5 Mercy Hospitals in Sacramento	Sacramento, CA	936
4	Stanford Hospital & Clinics	Stanford, CA	85
5	University of California San Francisco	San Francisco, CA	85
6	OCHIN (49 FQHC clinics in 7 states)	Portland, OR	72
7	Contra Costa County Health Services Dept	Contra Costa County, CA	12
8	Providence Health & Services	CA, OR, WA, AK, and MT	6
9	Kaiser Permanente	CO, So CA & HI	5
10	Sansum Clinic	Santa Barbara, CA	5
11	Legacy Health	Portland, OR	3
12	Gundersen Lutheran	LaCrosse, WI	2
13	Oregon Health & Science University	Portland, OR	2
14	Salem Health	Salem, OR	2
15	The Vancouver Clinic	Vancouver, WA	2
16	University of Washington Medicine	Seattle, WA	2
17	Capital Area Shared Services Organization	Baton Rouge, LA	1
18	Fairview	Minneapolis, MN	1
19	Group Health Cooperative	Seattle, WA	1
20	Kettering Health Network	Dayton, OH	1
21	North Memorial Health Care	Robinsdale, MN	1
22	Premier Health Partners	Dayton, OH	1
23	Riverside Medical Clinic	Riverside, CA	1
24	St. Luke's Health System	Kansas City, MO	1
25	University of California San Diego Health System	San Diego, CA	1
26	Valley Medical	Santa Clara, CA	1
		Total	18,267

CHAPTER 25

Case Study: Mount Sinai Medical Center

How the Preventable Admission Care Team (PACT) Used IT to Expand Program

Mount Sinai Medical Center received the 2012 HIMSS Davies Enterprise Award.

EXECUTIVE SUMMARY

Preventing avoidable readmissions by patients with certain chronic conditions within 30 days of discharge is a primary success factor for hospitals seeking to adhere to forthcoming changes in the reimbursement model used by Medicare. The Mount Sinai Medical Center (MSMC) set out to establish an electronic health record (EHR)–based process whereby patients at risk of being readmitted to the hospital are efficiently and accurately identified and managed.

Once identified, these patients are enrolled into MSMC's Preventable Admissions Care Team (PACT) program, where psychosocial drivers of readmission are assessed and addressed through a 35-day social work–led intervention that begins upon discharge. By incorporating the identification process into the design and implementation of the Epic EHR, MSMC has effectively been able to hard wire key workflow processes required to reduce readmissions, improve care, and lower the costs of care.

The program has been very successful. A 56 percent reduction in 30-day readmission rates has been observed, and these gains have been sustained at 60 and 90 days of discharge. Ninety-one percent of patients enrolled in PACT (n = 615) made follow-up appointments within 7 to 10 days, with 84 percent of patients keeping their appointment. MSMC and its partners have received generous grant funding to continue to evolve this groundbreaking program. Further, the PACT program is expected to be a centerpiece of MSMC's emerging ACO program.

Background

MSMC encompasses both the Mount Sinai Hospital and the Mount Sinai School of Medicine. The Mount Sinai Hospital, founded in 1852, is a 1,171-bed tertiary and quaternary care teaching facility and one of the nation's oldest, largest, and most respected voluntary hospitals. In 2012, *U.S. News & World Report* ranked Mount Sinai Hospital fourteenth on its elite honor roll of the nation's top hospitals based on reputation, safety, and other patient-care factors. Nearly 60,000 people were treated at Mount Sinai as inpatients in 2011, and approximately one million outpatient visits took place. Mount Sinai's location in the Upper East Side area of New York City places it at an intersection of the wealthiest and the poorest zip codes in the United States; MSMC has the responsibility of meeting the unique medical needs both of those from affluent backgrounds and of patients requiring indigent care.

LOCAL PROBLEM BEING ADDRESSED AND INTENDED IMPROVEMENT

The PACT Program at MSMC had been using admission history data for about the past two years to identify and target for intervention patients at high risk of a 30-day readmission to the inpatient setting. Without an integrated EHR, this identification process was very labor intensive and required a concentrated review of manual paper documents. In addition, it did not allow for identification of patients who are at high risk for a 30-day readmission, but who do not have a history of admissions.

In an effort to refine the identification process and enable the PACT workers to target additional patients who might benefit from the intervention, MSMC's Department of Health Evidence and Policy developed a risk prediction model for readmission within 30 days using logistic regression that did not rely on admission data: the higher the score, the higher the risk of readmission. The analysis was performed on the 2010 Medicare Fee For Service (FFS) beneficiaries and their associated readmission rates. The score utilizes comorbidities and demographics that are readily available and can be used in real time. Integrating this risk prediction score into Epic not only makes it possible to easily and quickly identify patients at high risk for readmission, it also improves awareness of services being provided to the patients. By tailoring the electronic admissions history form in the Epic EHR to electronically capture responses to discrete questions (such as whether the patient has been seen at MSMC or anywhere else in the past 12 months and/or the past 6 months), as well as integrating the risk prediction score into Epic, the enrollment process into the PACT program would be streamlined. Once patients have been identified and enrolled into the PACT program, their profiles in the EHR are flagged and shared longitudinally, alerting other clinicians of the patients' higher risk of readmission. The alert signals the need for the PACT team to become immediately involved with the care of these patients to avoid readmissions. Figure 25-1 illustrates the overall process for the PACT program.

For those at-risk patients who are targeted for the PACT intervention, a comprehensive bedside assessment is completed. The PACT assessment covers fifteen areas of psychosocial strain that MSMC has deemed primary contributors toward the likelihood of being readmitted. The areas covered by the PACT assessment are identified in Figure 25-2.

The program also addresses those factors that place the patient at high risk for readmission. By addressing clinically relevant topics such as ethnicity, past medical history, and similar universally recognized risk factors, it is possible to assign risk scores to patients and also group them accordingly. Figures 25-3 and 25-4 show both the risk

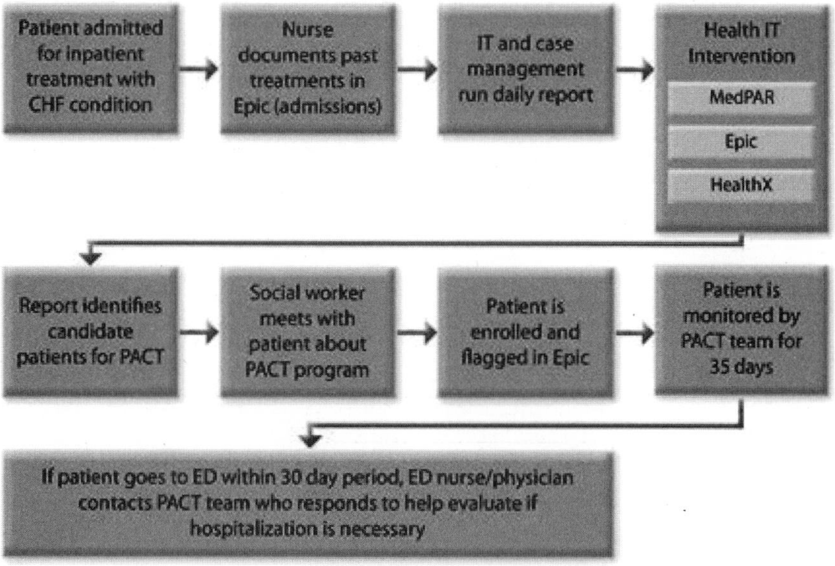

Figure 25-1: Overall Process of the PACT Program

Income	Mental Health	Informal Social/ familial support	Formal/community-based support
Language/culture	Literacy	Caregiving responsibilities	Primary care
Specialty	Health Insurance	Legal	Transportation
Housing	Nutrition	Pain	

Figure 25-2: Areas of Psychosocial Strain

Condition or Characteristic	Coefficient	Odds Ratio	95% CL for OR		Risk Score
Chronic Kidney Disease	0.3869	1.5	1.199	1.809	2
HF	0.2569	1.3	1.058	1.580	1
Osteoporosis	0.3374	1.4	1.040	1.888	1
COPD	0.6851	2.0	1.485	2.651	3
Depression	0.5553	1.7	1.277	2.377	2
Stroke	0.9292	2.5	1.590	4.035	4
AMI	0.8912	2.4	1.639	3.628	3
HIP Fracture	1.055	2.9	1.306	6.316	4
Alcohol Abuse	0.7603	2.1	1.100	4.160	3
Breast Ca	0.8597	2.4	1.124	4.967	3
Dual Eligible	0.279	1.3	1.104	1.583	1
Black	0.4201	1.5	1.228	1.887	2
Hispanic	0.2914	1.3	1.078	1.661	1
CKD & AFIB	1.1159	3.052	1.756	5.305	4
CMD (<65 yrs)	0.5437	1.722	1.220	2.431	2

Figure 25-3: Risk Factors Assessed

<table>
<tr><th>Score</th><th>Patients at Each Score</th><th>Patients/ Group</th><th>Avg Risk/Group</th><th>Blended Risk</th></tr>
<tr><td>2</td><td>1717</td><td rowspan="2">2883</td><td rowspan="2">20.6%</td><td rowspan="13">29.2%</td></tr>
<tr><td>3</td><td>1166</td></tr>
<tr><td>4</td><td>809</td><td rowspan="11">2509</td><td rowspan="11">39.0%</td></tr>
<tr><td>5</td><td>572</td></tr>
<tr><td>6</td><td>535</td></tr>
<tr><td>7</td><td>281</td></tr>
<tr><td>8</td><td>146</td></tr>
<tr><td>9</td><td>67</td></tr>
<tr><td>10</td><td>56</td></tr>
<tr><td>11</td><td>21</td></tr>
<tr><td>12</td><td>17</td></tr>
<tr><td>13</td><td>3</td></tr>
<tr><td>14</td><td>2</td></tr>
</table>

Figure 25-4: Risk Factors Scored

factors assessed and how these are scored along with historical readmission rates for these groups.

The PACT assessment is documented using Epic and then facilitates communication among providers to enhance understanding of the unique issues driving readmissions for a particular patient. The clinical staff sees a flag in the header area of the electronic chart as a visual cue to the relative readmission risk that follows the patient wherever care is provided at MSMC.

DESIGN AND IMPLEMENTATION

Development of workflow processes prior to implementation of the Epic EHR was key to the success of the PACT program being able to effectively utilize Epic's capabilities. During the design and implementation of the Epic EHR, the established preadmission assessment workflow, the high-risk questionnaire, the PACT assessment, and a rounding list were built into the Epic software. MSMC estimated upwards of 25 percent of high-risk patients were being missed by a manually intensive process that depended on history of admission data versus the more accurate scoring model now used. The need for this scoring model also recognized that while the patient might not have a documented history of admissions to MSMC, there was still a high statistical risk for a readmission to occur at some point.

The move from a paper process to one highly facilitated by an EHR was an evolutionary one, occurring from 2010 to present day with these key milestones:

- Excel spreadsheets, extracted from the legacy EHR, that included all patients with a prior MSMC hospitalization were emailed throughout the hospital to manually identify high-risk patients.

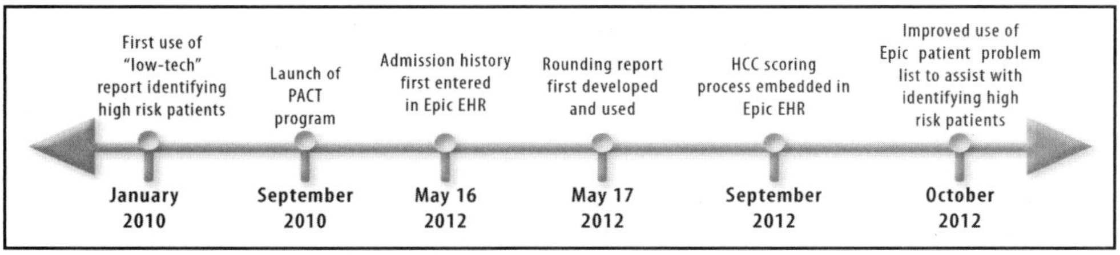

Figure 25-5: Timeline of the PACT Program Evolution

- A logistic regression model was developed by the MSMC Health Evidence and Policy Department, which used a sophisticated statistical tool and added both past medical admissions and comorbidities into the model.
  - The model still required some manual additions by the caregivers to get to the final risk score.
  - The model was validated in actual clinical practice.
- The PACT model was fully implemented in Epic
  - Medicare data were used so the model could incorporate any prior admissions in New York, not just those occurring at Mount Sinai.
  - Social workers now document psychosocial assessment and scoring using Epic automation.
  - The flag symbol is now displayed on various screens for clinicians across the continuum of care.

Specific enhancements recently made to the Epic system include:

- Building the admissions history form in Epic to ask discrete questions such as:
  - Has the patient seen his or her primary care physician in the past 12 months?
  - Has the patient been seen in an ED in the past 6 months?
- The patient profile in Epic noticeably indicates via a "red flag" that the patient is a high risk for readmissions, thereby generating a daily rounding report out of Epic (based on diagnosis) so the PACT team can conduct intervening rounding where the patient is engaged to assist with the aforementioned fifteen areas of psychosocial strain.

Figure 25-5 provides a time line of the PACT program evolution.

HOW HEALTH IT WAS UTILIZED

Without automation, it would have been impossible for the program to be scalable with rising patient volume. In the first year of the program, 488 patients were enrolled, while 4,800 were expected for 2012. The algorithms (such as the scoring model) embedded in the EHR allow more patients at high risk for readmissions both to be quickly identified and also to be more accurately identified than with manual processes. The scoring process utilizes coding data that are readily available through our EHR, while other scoring methods utilize administrative data that are not available in real time to hospitals. Finally, the EHR provides real-time communication (such as a red flag that displays with the patient information) to all care settings as soon as a high-risk patient is identified. This too would not be possible using a manual system.

The Epic EHR plays a central role in the PACT program, given its longitudinal view of the patient and the user's ability to customize the system. Enhancements include:

- A flexible assessment form that MSMC has tailored to include questions specific to identifying high-risk patients for readmission
- Production of a daily report that identifies all patients enrolled in PACT, which in turn, enables PACT associates to round to PACT patients
- The ability to aggregate information from the psychosocial assessment to trend readmission contributors and facilitate the development of community-based resources
- A far-reaching electronic patient profile that is central to the patient electronic record, regardless of the area in which the patient presents in the medical center. This central record provides an automatic signal, alerting caregivers of a high-risk patient.

Without automation, it would have been impossible for the program to grow in patient volume.

VALUE-DERIVED OUTCOMES

In summer 2011, the predictive model was applied to patients enrolled in the PACT program to determine how many were at high risk for 30-day readmission. "Ninety-five percent of PACT enrollees had a risk score greater than 3, meaning their readmission rate was between 20 percent and 39 percent," said Jill Kalman, MD, Director of the Cardiomyopathy Program, Associate Professor of Medicine (Mount Sinai's Cardiovascular Institute), and Medical Director of PACT. Dr. Kalman further states, "If these results can be substantiated through further study, we believe this could have national implications for identifying high-risk patients in real time."[1]

MSMC reported a 56 percent reduction in 30-day readmission rates (baseline 39 to 17 percent) in 2011. While MSMC is only held to reducing 30-day readmissions, these gains were sustained at both the 60- and 90-day mark. MSMC also measured overall utilization. On a subset of 111 patients, using each patient as his or her own control, MSMC measured hospitalization and ED visits for 6 months prior to the PACT intervention and for 6 months after the PACT intervention. MSMC had a 43 percent reduction in hospitalizations and a 54 percent reduction in ED visits (for the 6-month period). Ninety-one percent of patients enrolled in PACT (n = 615) had 7- to 10-day follow-up appointments made, and 84 percent of patients kept their appointment.

This reduction is directly attributed to the EHR–enabled processes of identifying high-risk patients and aggressively managing factors that contribute to readmission within 30 days post-discharge. PACT patients are provided with phone numbers for the PACT program, collaboration with MSMC's homecare partner, Visiting Nurse Service of New York (VNSNY), and open access to the PACT clinic staffed by nurse practitioners and clinical social workers.

The PACT program's value to the community was highlighted by a National Public Radio[2] segment that outlined how the program at MSMC is playing a major role in reducing readmissions. Focusing on a case study of one patient as an example, the reporter showed how the PACT program saved taxpayers $86,000 annually for the

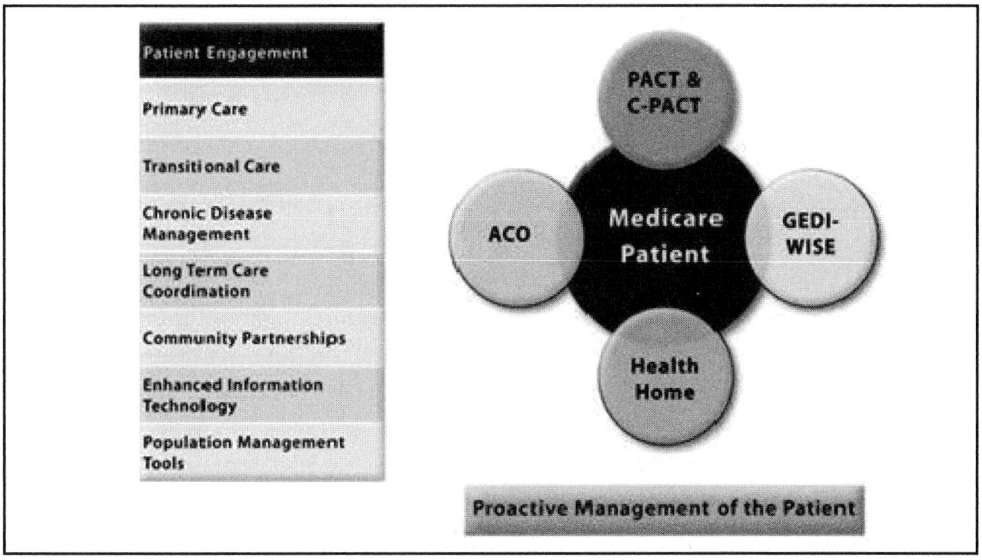

Figure 25-6: Services Related to PACT Program

patient by reducing emergency and overnight visits from twenty to only seven occurrences over the course of a year.

Other related areas of MSMC were integrated into this program so all could benefit from the PACT risk assessment. MSMC's Medicare population was the focus, as they were the largest group served by the program. Because we regard healthcare as a continuum, the synergy that would result from recognizing the PACT risk assessment would have a tangible, far-reaching impact. Figure 25-6 summarizes both the services and scope of services related to the program.

LESSONS LEARNED

From a patient-identification perspective, there are challenges with identifying patients at moderate risk to be readmitted. Industry-standard assessment forms typically identify the high-risk patients based on diagnosis, family history, functional deficits, and comorbidities. To be more precise in identifying patients with a moderate risk of being readmitted, the assessment process needed to be refined to include questions specific to the past medical encounter history.

Members of PACT believe that during the Epic go-live, the value of fine-tuning the risk assessment tools would have been facilitated if they had the ability to gather patient data sooner. Specifically, the team believes IT professionals should have been brought into the process sooner. Not only would there be a better understanding of population needs, but also the ability to plan for and address future needs such as clinical and community partnerships.

A key lesson learned was the importance of effectively and consistently utilizing the EHR's patient problem list. A more regimented use of the electronic problem list keeps chronic disease registries accurately updated and allows further tightening of the patient identification process.

Other lessons learned include the following:

- Point-of-care (POC) integration was desired and proved to be one of the keys to the success of PACT. Without a visual cue for providers in various care settings at the POC, providers would not be able to intervene in real time as needed for patients at risk.
- Integration went beyond simply identifying high-risk patients and required links and IT development for external calculations, reporting, modifier settings, and flagging.
- Flagging high-risk patients was important for reporting (rounding, etc.), but more importantly it turned out to be a key visual identifier on the patient's electronic record, so all providers accessing the record are apprised of the patient's condition.
- The integration required for the PACT program has had many positive effects on care coordination beyond the original intent of the program. The increased care coordination has advanced MSMC's ACO, the Geriatric Emergency Department Innovations in Care Program (GEDI WISE), and the Home Health program, to name a few as seen in Figure 25-6.
- The process and IT developments created for PACT have been, and continue to be, incremental. The PACT team anticipates continual improvement within the PACT toolset for the foreseeable future.

FINANCIAL CONSIDERATIONS

The PACT program has been funded through the hospital and was recently awarded a multimillion dollar five-year award from the CMS Center for Medicare and Medicaid Innovation for Community-based Care Transitions Program (CCTP) in partnership with the Institute for Family Health. If the award money is taken into account, the program is breaking even financially. It is believed that hard ROI will quickly become apparent as MSMC moves from an FFS to an ACO model of reimbursement.

From a cost perspective, in the pilot phase, the cost per year was \$627 per patient for an annualized cost of \$376,000. IT costs were modest at \$14,500 per year. PACT was also able to draw from the wide talents of MSMC staff with participation from the health policy team and physicians who provided their skills, talents, and knowledge at no charge to the program.

The ability to facilitate shared savings in MSMC's emerging ACO is expected to be significant. The combined reductions in hospitalizations and ED visits over a 6-month period post PACT saved an estimated \$1.6 million in Medicare spending. Using individual patients as their own controls, the number of hospitalizations and ED visits were compared for pre- and post-PACT enrollment for a 6-month period. An average reimbursement of \$9,000 was used for each hospitalization and \$450 per ED visit was used to estimate overall savings to Medicare.

REFERENCES

1. Minich-Pourshadi K. How predictive modeling cuts hospital readmissions. *HealthLeaders Media*. April 27, 2012. http://www.healthleadersmedia.com/page-1/FIN-279439/How-Predictive-Modeling-Cuts-Hospital-Readmissions##. Accessed July 3, 2012.

2. Mogul F. Hospitals' challenge: Slow down revolving door. *WNYC News*. December 13, 2011. http://www.wnyc.org/articles/wnyc-news/2011/dec/13/hospitals-challenge-slow-down-revolving-door. Accessed December 5, 2014.

APPENDIX

Acronyms Used In This Book

AAFP	American Academy of Family Physicians
AAP	American Academy of Pediatrics
AAP	asthma action plan
ABN	advanced beneficiary notice
ACE	angiotensin-converting enzyme
ACO	accountable care organization
ACS	appropriate care score
ACT	asthma control test
ADT	admit discharge transfer
AEHR	ambulatory electronic health record
AHA IT	American Hospital Association Information Technology
AHEC	Area Health Education Council
AHIMA	American Health Information Management Association
AHRQ	Agency for Healthcare Research and Quality
AMDIS	Association of Medical Directors of Information Systems
AMI	any mental illness
AMIA	American Medical Informatics Association
ANA	American Nurses Association
ANCC	American Nurses Credentialing Center
ANI	Alliance for Nursing Informatics
ANSI	American National Standards Institute
AONE	American Organization of Nurse Executives
API	application programming interface
ARNP	Advanced Registered Nurse Practitioner
ARRA	American Recovery and Reinvestment Act of 2009
ASC	Accredited Standards Committee
ASP	application service provider
B2B	business-to-business
BCMA	barcode medication administration
BI	business intelligence
BMI	body mass index
BoB	best-of-breed
BoS	best-of-suite
C&BI	clinical and business intelligence
CAH	critical access hospital

CAPHS	consumer assessment of providers and healthcare systems
CAUTI	catheter-associated urinary tract infection
CBI	clinical business intelligence
CBI-SC	CBI Steering Committee
CBSA	core based statistical area
CCD	continuity of care document
C-CDA	Consolidated-Clinical Document Architecture
CCHIT	Certification Commission for Health Information Technology
CCOW	clinical context object workgroup
CCR	continuity of care record
CCTP	community-based care transitions program
CDA	clinical document architecture
CDC	Centers for Disease Control and Prevention
CDR	clinical data repository
CDS	clinical decision support
CDSS	clinical decision support system
CEHRT	certified EHR technology
CEO	chief executive officer
CFAH	Center for Advancing Health
CGMP	current good manufacturing practice
CHC	community health center
CHF	congestive heart failure
CHPL	Certified Health IT Product List
CIO	chief information officer
CIS	clinical information system
CLIA	Clinical Laboratory Improvement Amendments of 1988
CMIO	chief medical information officer
CMMI	CMS Center for Medicare and Medicaid Innovation
CMO	chief medical officer
CMS	Centers for Medicare & Medicaid Services
CMV	controlled medical vocabulary
CNIO	chief nursing informatics officer
CNO	chief nursing officer
COO	chief operating officer
COPP	Council of Pediatric Practice
CPHIMS	Certified Professional in Healthcare Information and Management Systems
CPOE	computerized provider order entry
CPT	current procedural terminology
CQM	clinical quality measure
CRC	colorectal cancer
CSHCN	children with special healthcare needs
CT	computed tomography
CTO	chief technology officer
CUI	common user interface
CVX	Codes for Vaccines Administered

DICOM	Digital Imaging and Communications in Medicine
DIY	do-it-yourself
DOH	Department of Health
DOQ-IT	Doctors Office Quality Information Technology
DRE	dilated retinal examination
DRG	diagnosis-related group
DVT	deep vein thrombosis
ECG	electrocardiography
ED	emergency department
EDI	electronic data interchange
EDIS	emergency department information system
EFT	electronic funds transfer
EH	eligible hospital
EHR	electronic health record
eMAR	electronic medication administration record
EMPI	electronic master patient index
EMR	electronic medical record
EMRAM℠	HIMSS Analytics EMR Adoption Model℠
ENT	ear, nose and throat
EOB	explanation of benefits
EP	eligible provider
EP	eligible professional
ePHI	electronic protected health information
ERA	electronic remittance advice
ETL	extract, transform and load
FAQ	frequently asked question
FDA	U.S. Food and Drug Administration
FFS	fee for service
FFY	federal fiscal year
FLCH	Finger Lakes Community Health
FLTN	Finger Lakes Telehealth Network
FQHC	federally qualified health center
FTE	full-time employee
FYI	for your information
GEDI	Geriatric Emergency Department Innovations
GUI	graphical user interface
HAI	hospital-acquired infection
HCAHPS	Hospital Consumer Assessment of Healthcare Providers and Systems
HCPCS	Healthcare Common Procedure Coding System
HEAL NY	Health Efficiency and Affordability Law for New York
Health IT	health information technology
HEDIS	healthcare effectiveness data and information set
HHS	U.S. Department of Health and Human Services
HIE	health information exchange
HIM	health information management

HIMSS	Healthcare Information and Management Systems Society
HIPAA	Health Insurance Portability and Accountability Act of 1996
HIS	hospital information system
HITECH	Health Information Technology for Economic and Clinical Health Act of 2009
HITPC	Health IT Policy Committee
HITRC	Health Information Technology Research Center
HIV/AIDS	human immunodeficiency virus/acquired immune deficiency syndrome
HL7	Health Level 7
HPH	Hawaii Pacific Health
HR	human resources
HRSA	Health Resources and Services Administration
HYH	HowsYourHealth.org
ICD	International Classification of Diseases
ICU	intensive care unit
IHI	Institute for Healthcare Improvement
IMIA	International Medical Informatics Association
IOM	Institute of Medicine
IPPS	inpatient prospective payment system
IQR	inpatient quality reporting
ISMP	Institute for Safe Medication Practices
IT	information technology
KBM	KBM Group
KeyHIE	Keystone Health Information Exchange
KPI	key performance indicator
LAN	local area network
LDL-C	low-density lipoprotein-cholesterol
LDL	low density lipoprotein
LIS	laboratory information system
LMRP	local medical review policy
LOINC®	Logical Observation Identifiers Names and Codes
LTPAC	long-term post-acute care
MA	medical assistant
MAR	medication administration record
MCH	Miami Children's Hospital
MRI	magnetic resonance imaging
MSMC	Mount Sinai Medical Center
MU	meaningful use
MU2	Meaningful Use Stage 2
NCD/LCD	national and local coverage determination
NCPDP	National Council for Prescription Drug Programs
NCQA	National Committee for Quality Assurance
NI	nursing informatics
NLC	National Learning Consortium
NSA	National Security Agency
NQF	National Quality Forum

NwHIN	Nationwide Health Information Network
NYC	New York City
NYCREACH	New York City Regional Electronic Adoption Center for Health
NYDHA	New York Digital Health Accelerator
NYeC	New York eHealth Collaborative
NYHQ	New York Hospital Queens
NYP	New York Presbyterian
NYS	New York State
OCR	Office for Civil Rights
OLE	online experience
OM	office manager
ONC	Office of the National Coordinator for Health Information Technology
PA	physician assistant
PACS	picture archiving and communication system
PACT	preventable admissions care team
PAM	patient activation measure
PC	personal computer
PCMH	patient-centered medical home
PCP	primary care physician
PDSA	Plan-Do-Study-Act
PHI	protected health information
PHIS	pharmacy information system
PHR	personal health record
PMBOK	Project Management Book of Knowledge
PMI	Project Management Institute
PMO	project management office
PMS	practice management system
POC	point-of-care
PPACA	Patient Protection and Affordable Care Act
PPC®	Physician Practice Connections
PPC®-PCMH™	Physician Practice Connections Patient Centered Medical Home
PQRS	Physician Quality Reporting System
PwC	Pricewaterhouse Coopers
QI	quality improvement
QIO	quality improvement organization
RACI	responsible, accountable, consulted, informed
REACH	Regional Extension Assistance Center for HIT
REC	regional extension center
REMM	Radiation Emergency Medical Management
RFID	radio-frequency identification
RFI	request for information
RFP	request for proposal
RHIO	regional health information organization
RIS	radiology information system
ROI	return on investment

RTLS	real-time locating system
SaaS	software as a service
SAMHSA	Substance Abuse and Mental Health Services Administration
SBIR	Small Business Innovation Research
SCD	sequential compression device
SHARP-C	Strategic Health IT Advanced Research – Patient-Centered Cognitive Support
SHIN-NY	Statewide Health Information Network of New York
SME	subject matter expert
SNOMED-CT	Systematized Nomenclature of Medicine—Clinical Terms
SPC	statistical process control
SSN	Social Security number
THR	Texas Health Resources
TIGER	Technology Informatics Guiding Education Reform
TMI	too much information
tPA	tissue plasminogen activator
TURF	task, user, representation, and function
UC Davis	University of California Davis
UCD	user-centered design
UCDHS	University of California Davis Health System
UCSF	University of California San Francisco
UDS	uniform data system
UHG	UnitedHealth Group
UTHSCSA	University of Texas Health Science Center, San Antonio
UTSW	University of Texas Southwestern Medical Center
VA	Veterans Administration
VC	venture capitalist
VDT	view, download, and transmit
VITL	Vermont Information Technology Leader
VLE	virtual learning environment
VNSNY	Visiting Nurse Service of New York
VTE	venous thromboembolism
WHO	World Health Organization
WOW	workstation on wheels
WRFP	White River Family Practice
wRVU	work relative value unit
YC	Y Combinator

Index

f =figure entry
t = table entry

C

D

E

F

H

N

P

R

S

T

U